Not June Cleaver

In the series
Critical Perspectives on the Past,
edited by Susan Porter Benson,
Stephen Brier, and
Roy Rosenzweig

NOT JUNE CLEAVER

Women and Gender in
Postwar America,
1945–1960

Edited by
Joanne Meyerowitz

Temple University Press
Philadelphia

Temple University Press,
Philadelphia 19122
Copyright © 1994
by Temple University
All rights reserved
Published 1994
Printed in the United States of America

The paper used in this publication
meets the minimum requirements of
American National Standard for
Information Sciences—Permanence of
Paper for Printed Library Materials,
ANSI Z39.48-1984 ∞

Library of Congress
Cataloging-in-Publication Data
Not June Cleaver : women and gender
in postwar America, 1945–1960 /
edited by Joanne Meyerowitz.
    p.   cm. —
    (Critical perspectives on the past)
    Includes bibliographical
    references.
    ISBN 1-56639-170-9. —
    ISBN 1-56639-171-7 (pbk.)
    1. Women—United States—
History—20th century.
2. Women—Employment—United
States—History—20th century.
I. Meyerowitz, Joanne J. (Joanne Jay)
II. Series.
HQ1420.N68   1994
305.42'0973'09045—dc20

                    93-26987

Contents

Not June Cleaver

CHAPTER 1

Joanne Meyerowitz

INTRODUCTION

Women and Gender in

Postwar America,

1945–1960

$\mathbf{M}$ost of us are familiar with a well-entrenched stereotype of American women in the post–World War II years. Domestic and quiescent, they moved to the suburbs, created the baby boom, and forged family togetherness. Popular since the 1950s, this tenacious stereotype conjures mythic images of cultural icons—June Cleaver, Donna Reed, Harriet Nelson—the quintessential white middle-class housewives who stayed at home to rear children, clean house, and bake cookies.[1] The stereotype persists today in television reruns of situation comedies, in popular movies, and sometimes in scholarly historical accounts of the postwar years. My students come to class with this image of womanhood set squarely in their vision. And college textbooks often reinforce it by placing postwar women, if they include them at all, under such subheadings as "The Suburban Family," "Life in the Suburbs," "Domesticity," and "Back to the Kitchen."[2] For some, this postwar story is a romance steeped in nostalgic longing for an allegedly simpler, happier, and more prosperous time. For others, it is an ironic story of declension, in which the housewife finds herself trapped in a domestic cage after spreading her wings during World War II. In either case, it flattens the history of women, reducing the multidimensional complexity of the past to a snapshot of middle-class women in suburban homes.

While some women fit the stereotype, many others did not. To state the obvious, in the years following World War II, many women were not white, middle-class, married, and suburban; and many white, middle-class, married, suburban women were neither wholly domestic nor quiescent. In recent scholarship, these other women have begun to take center stage. A revisionist approach places the domestic stereotype in historical context and questions both its novelty and pervasiveness in the postwar years. It attempts to complicate our stories of the past; it reminds us that during this era, most American women lived, in one way or more, outside the boundaries of the middle-class suburban home.

This volume is part of this ongoing revisionist endeavor. Each of the fifteen essays explores a different piece of postwar U.S. women's history. Several of the essays focus on women in the labor force and in activist organizations. Others examine cultural constructions of gender and subcultural challenges to them. Taken together, the essays point first to the diversity among women and the multifarious activities in which they engaged. The essays demonstrate that women's sense of themselves included not only gender identity—their sense of themselves as women—but also their interrelated class, racial, ethnic, sexual, religious, occupational, and political identities. The essays also suggest that the postwar public discourse on women was more complex than often portrayed. They address the postwar domestic stereotype and its meanings, how and where it was produced, and the manifold ways that women appropriated, transformed, and challenged it. They investigate the competing voices within the public discourse on women and the internal contradictions that undermined and destabilized the domestic stereotype even as it was constructed.

Historians and Women of the Postwar Era

Until recently, U.S. women's historians paid less attention to the years from 1945 to 1960 than they did to the years before and after them. For historians, women of the postwar era, it seems, were less captivating than women workers during World War II or political activists of the 1960s. Postwar women provided a coda to the saga of Rosie the Riveter or a prelude to the story of 1960s feminists. But as the subjects of serious study in their own right, they were, until recently, relatively neglected.

If any historical approach has prevailed thus far, it is one that focuses on the conservatism of the postwar era and the formidable ideological and institutional

New, Brand 10, previously mythological "Super Housewife"
Martha Stewart has glamorized this ideal x10.
Cross breed of "Celebrity Homemaker"
hyped domestic

constraints faced by women. Historical accounts stress the postwar domestic ideal, the reassertion of a traditional sexual division of labor, and the formal and informal barriers that prevented women from fully participating in the public realm. In this historical narrative, postwar conservatism shaped women's identities, weakened their limited protests, and contained their activities within traditional bounds.

An early and influential formulation of this position appeared in journalist Betty Friedan's bestselling liberal feminist polemic, *The Feminine Mystique,* published in 1963. In the postwar era, Friedan argued, social scientists, educators, advertisers, and magazine editors promoted a conservative ideal, "the feminine mystique," that portrayed women as happy housewives whose fulfillment derived solely from marriage, motherhood, and family. This ideal, Friedan claimed, damaged American women and trapped them in the suburban home.[3] With *The Feminine Mystique,* Friedan gave a name and a voice to housewives' discontent, but she also homogenized American women and simplified postwar ideology; she reinforced the stereotype that portrayed all postwar women as middle-class, domestic, and suburban, and she caricatured the popular ideology that she said had suppressed them.[4]

In the mid-1970s and after, more sophisticated variants of this approach appeared in numerous accounts of World War II and the immediate postwar years. These works often focused on wage-earning women, but they joined Friedan in emphasizing the conservatism and constraints of the postwar era. Studies of postwar culture found that government propaganda, popular magazines, and films reinforced traditional concepts of femininity and instructed women to subordinate their interests to those of returning male veterans. Studies of war industries explored the sexist and racist discriminatory practices that resulted in postwar layoffs of women, women's unsuccessful efforts to resist the loss of their wartime positions, and the processes by which employers reestablished the prewar sexual division of labor. As the last chapter of World War II, the late 1940s looked bleak indeed.[5]

return to our place

The conservatism-and-constraints approach reached its apex in works on the 1950s. To give the most prominent example, Elaine Tyler May's *Homeward Bound,* a study of families in the 1950s, found that white middle-class Americans, in search of security, turned to an idealized vision of home and family that domesticated and subordinated women. May linked the containment of communism in Cold War politics with the containment of women in the postwar domestic ideal. In the midst of Cold War anxiety, "the family seemed to offer a psychological fortress," a buffer against both internal and foreign threats. In this ideological climate, independent women threatened the social order. Under cultural pressure and with limited options for work outside the home, women, contained and constrained, "donned their domestic harnesses."[6]

a safe place

Women as stabilizers of society in flux. Not unlike women as icons of spiritual ideals in the unstable conservative Iranian society. (Vessels of spirituality)

1950's woman as victim! false

a strong case made

While no serious historian can deny the conservatism of the postwar era or the myriad constraints that women encountered, an unrelenting focus on women's subordination erases much of the history of the postwar years. It tends to downplay women's agency and to portray women primarily as victims.[7] It obscures the complexity of postwar culture and the significant social and economic changes of the postwar era. Sometimes it also inadvertently bolsters the domestic stereotype. Especially in works on the 1950s, the sustained focus on a white middle-class domestic ideal and on suburban middle-class housewives sometimes renders other ideals and other women invisible.

a gain of self-confidence

From early on, some historians have challenged the conservatism-and-constraints approach. Historians have long acknowledged that increasing numbers of women sought and found wage work, albeit in traditionally female jobs, in the postwar era. As early as 1972, William Chafe argued that "the most striking feature of the 1950's was the degree to which women continued to enter the job market and expand their sphere."[8] In other accounts of World War II and its aftermath, postwar social and cultural changes received at least some recognition. Various studies noted women war workers' enhanced self-confidence in the postwar era, a "nascent feminist consciousness" in Hollywood films of the late 1940s, more egalitarian relations between postwar husbands and wives, and new state laws that strengthened women's rights. These social and cultural transformations suggested that the immediate postwar years should not be dismissed simply as years of retrenchment.[9] Eugenia Kaledin's *Mothers and More,* published in 1984, brought a variant of this approach to the 1950s. Through the sheer number of prominent women authors, activists, and artists she listed, Kaledin made a case against "the dominant myth of [women's] victimization" in the 1950s. As a compendium of women's public accomplishments, the book slighted the vast majority of women who did not achieve fame or fortune, but it gave readers a fresh view of the variegated ways in which some women moved beyond the domestic ideal.[10]

unsung valor

Most influential, though, were case studies that by the mid-1980s began to transform the history of postwar women. Recent works have explored the public campaigns and private networks of postwar feminists, women in politics, and women labor, peace, and civil rights activists.[11] Others have investigated the varied subcultural challenges posed by lesbians, communist women, and white rebellious teens.[12] Taken together, these works point to pockets of resistance, to significant groups of women who questioned and loosened postwar constraints. At the same time, studies of books, films, and television shows, reading against the grain, discovered subtle expressions of ambivalence, contradiction, and self-parody in postwar gender ideals.[13] And cultural histories investigated how deeply postwar concepts of gender were informed by issues of race, ethnicity, and class.[14] Bit by bit, the historical evidence mounted until our image of the postwar era was irrevocably fractured; the quiescent housewives were joined by a wide array of women workers, community activists, politicians, and rebels, and the domestic ideal, with internal contradictions, was conjoined with other cultural constructions of women. Despite the conservatism and constraints, the postwar era now seems a time of notable social change and cultural complexity.[15]

A Collective Reinterpretation

This anthology is a sampler of current work on postwar U.S. women's history, a first attempt to bring new pieces of scholarship into one volume. Rather than posit one overarching history of women or one gender ideology, it relates multiple histories of women and multiple constructions of gender. The authors of the essays do not speak with one voice, and readers will notice differences in interpretation and method. Some authors emphasize the conservatism of the postwar era, while others stress the undercurrents of change. Some point to the impact of the domestic ideal, while others question its strength. Two essays fuse personal narrative with historical analysis in what Wini Breines labels "sociological memoir." Others engage in the thick description of social history or the discourse analysis of cultural studies.

Nonetheless, despite such differences, several themes emerge from these essays, suggesting the contours of a new and multifaceted history of women and gender in the postwar United States. First and foremost, these essays displace the domestic stereotype, the June Cleavers and Donna Reeds, from the center of historical study. To give just one example, Xiaolan Bao's essay on Chinese women garment workers in New York City reminds us that postwar women included immigrants fresh off the boat, newcomers to the city. As federal immigration policy changed, a massive influx of Chinese women transformed a predominantly male Chinese American community. Despite the postwar growth of suburbs and the service sector, the new immigrants moved into and revitalized an urban ethnic neighborhood and an urban industry. Along with other essays in this volume, Bao's study demonstrates what should be obvious: that American women were culturally and ethnically diverse during the postwar years, just as they were during other historical eras.

The essays on wage workers move us beyond the decline of war industry, away from aggregate statistics on labor force participation, and toward close historical case studies of economic change in specific communities and female-dominated occupations. The shift in focus invites us to ask questions about the postwar years that historians have long asked about earlier eras in American history. How, for example, did the increase in married women workers affect family relations? In one community, Xiaolan Bao finds that wives' economic contribution challenged the patriarchal prerogatives of their husbands and shifted the balance of power within Chinese American working-class families.

Women who entered the labor force in the postwar era did not simply comply with the invisible hand of supply and demand; at least some of them engaged in conscious debates and struggles that altered the workplace. Susan Rimby Leighow's study of registered nurses shows how, in a period of labor shortage, the expressed needs of married nurses reshaped the occupation. Married nurses demanded and won part-time work, better pay, maternity leaves, and employer-sponsored child care. As Dorothy Sue Cobble illustrates, women union leaders in other occupations fought for some of the same benefits. Women workers of the postwar era have a history of union activism, not only in industrial workplaces, but also in the more rapidly growing service sector. Women labor leaders negotiated for better contracts and lobbied for new state and federal policies on behalf of women workers. They did not offer any serious challenge to the entrenched sexual division of labor, but they sustained the activism of the war years in vocal campaigns for workplace equity and reform.

In fact, the activism of postwar women was wide-ranging. The essays in this volume alone portray women of varied backgrounds participating in trade unions, the peace movement, the civil rights movement, and civic reform. Despite the conservatism of the era, women in voluntary associations carried on the tradition of female association work from the nineteenth and early twentieth centuries. In the postwar era, women worked at both national and local levels in all-female associations and increasingly in mixed-sex groups. As in earlier eras, though, as several essays testify, women rarely achieved the highest positions of leadership in organizations in which they worked alongside men.

Central to women's postwar voluntarism was a revitalized conception of maternalist politics. The postwar domestic ideal not only offered justifications for women to stay at home; as in the early twentieth century, it also authorized maternal activities in the public realm.[16] In their essays on women pacifists, Harriet Hyman Alonso and Dee Garrison trace the maternalist language of postwar women reformers. Garrison, in particular, explores how housewives in New York City used their role as maternal protectors to join with veteran radicals, such as Dorothy Day, in a little-known late-1950s mass-protest antinuclear movement.[17] But maternalist politics also appeared in other unlikely places. Women in the Communist Party, as Deborah Gerson's essay shows, adopted postwar familial rhetoric when they organized to defend their husbands and protect their children from the ravages of the Red Scare. Likewise, in Ruth Feldstein's analysis of the Emmett Till case, Mamie Till Bradley emerged as a spokesperson for the National Association for the Advancement of Colored People (NAACP) because she spoke with a mother's voice. In each of these instances, women used their culturally sanctioned authority as mothers, as caretakers for children, to legitimate their public demands for social justice. But as Feldstein demonstrates, the maternalist argument, by portraying women primarily as mothers, also restricted them: A mother's authority was limited in scope, and women portrayed as "bad mothers" had no authority at all.[18]

Postwar women reformers, Susan Lynn explains, showed a concerted interest in issues of race. As the civil rights movement blossomed, black and white women worked together, not without difficulty, to battle racism. They employed the traditional pressure-group tactics of earlier women's organizations, but they also emphasized the transformative power of interpersonal relations. In this way, they foreshadowed the "personal politics" and consciousness raising of the 1960s. To some extent, the rising interest of white women reformers in issues of racial justice replaced their earlier interest in white working-class women and children. For these postwar reformers, race relations replaced class relations as the primary form of social injustice. On the national level, for example, the Young Women's Christian Association (YWCA) gradually shifted its work from efforts with women industrial workers to campaigns for racial desegregation. For white women reformers, race became a new and compelling terrain for social reconciliation.

The fight for racial equality extended across the nation. In the South, Septima Clark, Rosa Parks, Jo Ann Gibson Robinson, Daisy Bates, and Ella Baker joined hundreds of lesser-known women in launching the massive protests of the civil rights movement.[19] Just as black women engaged in community organizing and protest in the African American South, so Chicanas engaged in community organizing and protest in the Mexican American West. In the Community Service Organization (CSO), Margaret Rose reports, women and men, predominantly Mexican American and working class, forged a coalition of local organizations in which "women's issues"—neighborhood safety, education, health care—moved to the center of civic activism. While a few of these women rose to positions of prominence in the CSO and the labor movement, many others worked anonymously, hosting fund-raising parties, teaching citizenship classes, and organizing their neighbors. Thus, women brought their traditionally female issues and traditionally female skills to a mixed-sex voluntary association. Here, as in the workplace, they rarely questioned the sexual division of labor. But they laid the organizational groundwork, and in some cases trained the leaders, for the better-known national activism of the 1960s and 1970s, including Chicana feminist protest.[20]

This is not to imply that feminism as such vanished during the postwar era. The small band of self-avowed feminists in the National Woman's Party (NWP) survived the postwar era despite the marked hostility to their efforts.[21] Other activists expanded the spectrum of feminist activity, broadly defined, even as they distanced themselves from the NWP, which monopolized the feminist label. Numerous women's organizations lobbied for "women in policy-making positions," and some women's organizations, such as the YWCA, pushed for gender equity on other fronts as well.[22] Some prominent black women, including novelist Ann Petry and lawyer Pauli Murray, made their concerns for gender justice abundantly clear in the postwar African American press, and through the 1950s, women unionists and their allies pressed for equal-pay legislation and "sex-blind" treatment in male-dominated industry.[23] In Dorothy Sue Cobble's formulation, working-class trade union women also put forth a distinctive feminist defense of women workers in female-dominated jobs. This was not the liberal individualist feminism of the National Woman's Party; it embraced a version of working-class feminism that recognized gender difference, acknowledged the existing sexual division of labor, and devised collective demands for workplace equity, including equal pay for comparable work, maternity leaves, and revised minimum-wage laws. This form of feminism, Cobble finds, did not simply survive the postwar years; it grew and flourished.

If some women activists flourished during the postwar era, others did not. The Cold War and the attendant Red Scare severely damaged women's organizations, especially those associated in any way with the left. "Left feminists" founded the short-lived Congress of American Women (CAW), but, as Harriet Hyman Alonso shows, they could not sustain an openly leftist organization in the repressive climate of the postwar era.[24] After the Justice Department ordered the CAW's board to register as "foreign agents," the CAW disbanded, and a later attempt to reorganize it foundered. Other women's organizations endured cutthroat internal strife and self-censorship. The Women's International League for Peace and Freedom, for example, suffered from dissension as members red-baited each other. In the meantime, women in the Communist Party were forced to devote their energies to fending off harassment.[25]

Beyond its direct and repressive impact on individual women, their organizations, and political expression, the Cold War had other meanings. In some instances, Cold War rhetoric bolstered the domestic ideal.[26] But in other cases, women (and men) used Cold War rhetoric to promote women's public participation. Some mainstream women's organizations adopted the language of the Cold War to strengthen their public mission in the postwar era.[27] Quasi-official policy groups, as Susan Hartmann shows, supported women's wage work and education by depicting women as crucial and underused national resources in the Cold War competition.[28] And popular magazines, my own essay suggests, used Cold War rhetoric to encourage women to enter politics. As a political ideology adopted by a broad range of liberals and conservatives, the Cold War had no fixed association with the domestic ideal.

More generally, it seems, postwar culture was not as inextricably tied to the domestic ideal as Betty Friedan and some historians have implied. Susan Hartmann's essay reveals how policy planners promoted women's employment and attempted to sway public opinion toward support for women's wage work. My essay contends that postwar magazines contradicted the domestic ideal with numerous articles that validated women's public participation and celebrated the public accomplishments of "successful" women. And Susan Rimby Leighow's essay finds that married women nurses repeatedly defended their labor force participation, not only as a source of family income, but also as a needed public service. In short, despite the domestic ideal, women were recognized, and recognized themselves, as legitimate public actors.

Postwar concepts of womanhood were deeply imbued with racist assumptions. In the mainstream popular culture, to give the most blatant example, women were almost always pictured as white. The burgeoning African American press, in particular, countered this racially biased imagery with an insistent focus on black women as mothers, workers, activists, entertainers, and beauties.[29] But, in the postwar era as earlier, black women encountered racist stereotypes that portrayed them as servile mammies, as sexually loose women, and increasingly as damaging matriarchs.[30] Ruth Feldstein's essay on Mamie Till Bradley reconstructs the cultural tightrope that African American women walked. A woman who sought public authority had to dispel racist stereotypes and assert her respectability, which others might easily contest. Regina Kunzel's essay on unwed mothers outlines the origins of the postwar racial bifurcation that depicted white unwed mothers as individual "neurotics" and black unwed mothers as symbols of "cultural pathology." [31] Just as some postwar white women reformers turned their attention from issues of class to issues of race, so some social workers and sociologists gradually shifted the etiology of unwed pregnancy from an emphasis on class (working-class "sex delinquency") to an emphasis on racial difference (white "neurosis" and black "pathology"). Here, too, concepts of race, portrayed as black and white, were increasingly salient in middle-class constructions of gender, with issues of class decidedly muted. But in this instance, the focus on race had a different meaning: Concepts of racial difference prevented black women from receiving the social services available to whites.

In the postwar prescriptive literature, women who defied sexual convention were vilified as deviants.[32] Not only unwed mothers, but also women who performed abortions, women who sought abortions, prostitutes, and lesbians challenged the dominant sexual order. As Rickie Solinger and Donna Penn attest, both women abortionists and lesbians encountered new and hostile public exposure in the postwar era. Popular and expert observers defined "normal" heterosexual marital relations through surveillance, regulation, and sometimes conflation of various forms of deviant behavior. Patrolling the borders of sexual propriety, they studied, recorded, and broadcast their own peculiar renditions of the increasingly visible enclaves where abortionists met their clients and where lesbians met each other. Marked as dangerous sexual outcasts, as uncontained women in need of control, as social threats, and even as demons, abortionists and lesbians, like prostitutes, faced public derogation and criminal prosecution. Still, despite the attacks, the various sexual subcultures survived. In different ways, abortionists and lesbians reworked the public discourse, redefined the sexual order, and defended themselves against the cultural onslaught.[33] Their sustained public presence reveals a thriving sexual underworld that included more than the demimonde of prostitution.

Self-conscious defiance of middle-class culture also appeared among the Beat generation bohemians discussed by Wini Breines. While the stereotypic Beat was a young male poet, young women too were attracted to this cultural rebellion.[34] Women who joined the Beats and women who admired them from afar often shared a sense of alienation from bourgeois conventions. White middle-class women bohemians protested the restrictions of the domestic ideal and pursued "authenticity" in the Beat subculture, even though they did not openly attack its sexism. Their attraction to working-class men, African American men, and male rebels, Breines claims, revealed their search for a new identity for themselves, a subdued precursor to the overtly feminist quest of the 1960s.

The other women in this volume also engaged in active construction of their own identities. They drew their sense of themselves not simply from their familial roles or from the domestic ideal. In the pages that follow, various women portray themselves as garment workers, nurses, unionists, public servants, citizens, political activists, community organizers, pacifists, communists, victims of harassment, immigrants, Chinese Americans, African Americans, Mexican Americans, white women, unwed mothers, abortionists, lesbians, butches, femmes, and Beat bohemians. The ways they portray themselves demonstrate that women in the postwar era saw themselves as more than women or wives or mothers. These essays begin to explore how women forged these identities, mediated among competing and contradictory ideals, and grappled with the conservatism of the era and the constraints they encountered.

Most of the essays in this collection question historical accounts that portray the postwar era as somehow anomalous; instead, they draw historical links between the wartime and postwar eras and between the postwar era and the 1960s. As various essays illustrate, the postwar employment of married women, women's activism, maternalist politics, domestic ideals, and racialized constructions of gender all had distinct roots in the prewar and wartime eras. Similarly, social change in the 1960s and 1970s—women's employment,

racial justice movements, antiwar activism, feminism, gay and lesbian liberation movements, youth rebellion, personal and confrontational politics—all
have clear ties to the postwar years. The postwar era can no longer serve as
a foil, as either the good old days, set in contrast to an allegedly turbulent,
violent, and amoral present, or as the bad old days, set in contrast to the triumphant rebirth of social change in the 1960s. It provides a not-so-hidden missing
link, what Susan Lynn calls a "bridge," that connects the transformations of
the 1960s with transformations earlier in the twentieth century.[35]

This anthology is only a beginning. It marks the rise of new approaches
to postwar U.S. women's history, but it presents only fragments of the larger
history yet to be written. The postwar history of working-class women, ethnic
women, and women of color, including housewives, has only begun to emerge,
and the postwar history of women on the right, sexual violence, and women,
consumerism, and glamour, to name just a few topics, are not addressed at
all. This volume makes no attempt to provide a comprehensive history. It aims
instead to showcase new directions in postwar women's history, to subvert the
persistent stereotype of domestic, quiescent, suburban womanhood, and to
generate new histories of a complicated era.

NOTES

Acknowledgments: I thank Susan Porter Benson, Susan Hartmann, Bruce
Levine, Susan Lynn, and Pat Swope for comments on an earlier version of
this essay. I thank Roger Daniels, Susan Lynn, Leslie Reagan, and especially Susan Porter Benson, Janet Francendese, and Irene Glynn for advice
on editing this volume.

1. June Cleaver was the fictional mother and wife, played by actress Barbara
Billingsly, in television's "Leave It to Beaver." Actresses Donna Reed and Harriet
Nelson played housewives in the television comedies "The Donna Reed Show" and
"The Adventures of Ozzie and Harriet."
2. Alan Brinkley et al., *American History: A Survey,* 8th ed. (New York: Knopf,
1991), 862; Robert A. Divine et al., *America: Past and Present,* 3rd ed. (New York:
HarperCollins, 1991), 859; Paul Boyer et al., *The Enduring Vision: A History of the
American People* (Lexington, Mass.: D.C. Heath, 1990), 1025; Gary B. Nash et al.,
The American People: Creating a Nation and a Society, 2nd ed. (New York: Harper
& Row, 1990), 935. For texts that do not include discussions of postwar women, see
John M. Blum et al., *The National Experience: A History of the United States,* 7th ed.
(San Diego: Harcourt Brace Jovanovich, 1989); Winthrop D. Jordan et al., *The United
States,* 6th ed. (Englewood Cliffs, N.J.: Prentice Hall, 1987).
3. Betty Friedan, *The Feminine Mystique* (New York: Norton, 1963).
4. For other critiques of Friedan, see Ruth Schwartz Cowan, "Two Washes in the

Morning and a Bridge Party at Night: The American Housewife between the Wars," *Women's Studies,* no. 2 (1976); Rachel Bowlby, "The Problem with No Name: Rereading Friedan's *The Feminine Mystique,*" *Feminist Review,* September 1987.

5. For studies that focus on postwar culture, see Leila J. Rupp, *Mobilizing Women for War: German and American Propaganda, 1939–1945* (Princeton: Princeton University Press, 1978); Susan M. Hartmann, "Prescriptions for Penelope: Literature on Women's Obligations to Returning World War II Veterans," *Women's Studies,* no. 3 (1978): 223–239; Maureen Honey, *Creating Rosie the Riveter: Class, Gender, and Propaganda during World War II* (Amherst: University of Massachusetts Press, 1984); Sonya Michel, "Danger on the Home Front: Motherhood, Sexuality, and Disabled Veterans in American Postwar Films," *Journal of the History of Sexuality,* July 1992, 109–128. For studies of war industry, see Joan Ellen Trey, "Women in the War Economy: World War II," *Review of Radical Political Economics,* July 1972, 50–53; Lisa Anderson and Sheila Tobias, "What Really Happened to Rosie the Riveter? Demobilization and the Female Labor Force, 1944–47," Module 9 (New York: MSS Module Publications, 1974); Lynn Goldfarb, with Julie Boddy and Nancy Wiegersma, *Separated and Unequal: Discrimination Against Women Workers After World War II (The U.A.W., 1944–1954)* (Silver Spring, Md.: Women's Work Project, Union for Radical Political Economics, 1976); Alan Clive, "Women Workers in World War II: Michigan as a Test Case," *Labor History,* Winter 1979, 46–71; Karen Beck Skold, "The Job He Left Behind: American Women in the Shipyards during World War II," in *Women, War, and Revolution,* ed. Carol Berkin and Clara Lovett (New York: Holmes and Meier, 1980), 55–72; Karen Tucker Anderson, "Last Hired and First Fired: Black Women Workers during World War II," *Journal of American History,* June 1982, 82–97; Ruth Milkman, *Gender at Work: The Dynamics of Job Segregation by Sex during World War II* (Urbana: University of Illinois Press, 1987); Amy Kesselman, *Fleeting Opportunities: Women Shipyard Workers in Portland and Vancouver during World War II and Reconversion* (Albany: SUNY Press, 1990). The more general works on women and World War II are less monolithically focused on conservatism and constraints, but they too tend to emphasize postwar conservatism. See Karen Anderson, *Wartime Women: Sex Roles, Family Relations, and the Status of Women during World War II* (Westport, Conn.: Greenwood Press, 1981); Susan M. Hartmann, *The Home Front and Beyond: American Women in the 1940s* (Boston: Twayne, 1982); D'Ann Campbell, *Women at War with America: Private Lives in a Patriotic Era* (Cambridge, Mass.: Harvard University Press, 1984). Within this voluminous literature, there are a number of areas of disagreement, including whether women chose to leave war jobs, reluctantly acquiesced, or actively resisted; to what extent unions were to blame for postwar labor practices; and whether African American women's position in the labor market improved or deteriorated in the postwar era.

6. Elaine Tyler May, *Homeward Bound: American Families in the Cold War Era* (New York: Basic Books, 1988), 11, 113. For other works on the 1950s that emphasize conservatism and constraints, see Benita Eisler, *Private Lives: Men and Women of the Fifties* (New York: Franklin Watts, 1986); Carol A. B. Warren, *Madwives: Schizophrenic Women in the 1950s* (New Brunswick, N.J.: Rutgers University Press, 1987); Myra Dinnerstein, *Women between Two Worlds: Midlife Reflections on Work and Family* (Philadelphia: Temple University Press, 1992); Brett Harvey, *The Fifties: A Women's Oral History* (New York: HarperCollins, 1993).

7. From the mid-1960s on, various historians have made forceful arguments against

histories that portray African Americans, workers, and women solely as victims. While these arguments were highly influential in U.S. women's history generally, they had less impact on the history of women of the postwar era.

8. William H. Chafe, *The American Woman: Her Changing Social, Economic, and Political Roles, 1920–1970* (New York: Oxford University Press, 1972), 218; for an updated version of this work, see William H. Chafe, *The Paradox of Change: American Women in the Twentieth Century* (New York: Oxford University Press, 1991). For other accounts that emphasize postwar labor force participation, see Paddy Quick, "Rosie the Riveter: Myths and Realities," *Radical America*, July–August 1975, 115–131; Alice Kessler-Harris, *Out to Work: A History of Wage-Earning Women in the United States* (New York: Oxford University Press, 1982), 300.

9. Sherna Berger Gluck, *Rosie the Riveter Revisited: Women, the War, and Social Change* (Boston: Twayne, 1987); Andrea S. Walsh, *Women's Film and Female Experience, 1940–1950* (New York: Praeger, 1984), 197; Campbell, *Women at War with America;* Hartmann, *The Home Front and Beyond.* Hartmann, in particular, offers a carefully balanced account that addresses both continuity and change in the late 1940s.

10. Eugenia Kaledin, *Mothers and More: American Women in the 1950s* (Boston: Twayne, 1984), xiii.

11. Leila J. Rupp and Verta Taylor, *Survival in the Doldrums: The American Women's Rights Movement, 1945 to the 1960s* (New York: Oxford University Press, 1987); Cynthia Harrison, *On Account of Sex: The Politics of Women's Issues, 1945–1968* (Berkeley: University of California Press, 1988); Susan Ware, "American Women in the 1950s: Nonpartisan Politics and Women's Politicization," in *Women, Politics, and Change,* eds. Louise A. Tilly and Patricia Gurin (New York: Russell Sage Foundation, 1990), 281–299; Nancy F. Gabin, *Feminism in the Labor Movement: Women and the United Auto Workers, 1935–1975* (Ithaca: Cornell University Press, 1990); David J. Garrow, ed., *The Montgomery Bus Boycott and the Women Who Started It: The Memoir of Jo Ann Gibson Robinson* (Knoxville: University of Tennessee Press, 1987); Vicki L. Crawford, Jacqueline Anne Rouse, and Barbara Woods, eds., *Women in the Civil Rights Movement: Trailblazers and Torchbearers, 1941–1965* (Brooklyn: Carlson Publishing, 1990); Susan Lynn, *Progressive Women in Conservative Times: Racial Justice, Peace, and Feminism, 1945 to the 1960s* (New Brunswick, N.J.: Rutgers University Press, 1992).

12. John D'Emilio, *Sexual Politics, Sexual Communities: The Making of a Homosexual Minority in the United States, 1940–1970* (Chicago: University of Chicago Press, 1983); Elizabeth Lapovsky Kennedy and Madeline D. Davis, *Boots of Leather, Slippers of Gold: The History of a Lesbian Community* (New York: Routledge, 1993); Donna Penn, "The Meanings of Lesbianism in Post-War America," *Gender and History,* Summer 1991, 190–203; Lillian Faderman, *Odd Girls and Twilight Lovers: A History of Lesbian Life in Twentieth-Century America* (New York: Columbia University Press, 1991), 130–187; Kate Weigand, "The Red Menace, the Feminine Mystique, and the Ohio Un-American Activities Commission: Gender and Anti-Communism in Ohio, 1951–1954," *Journal of Women's History,* Winter 1992, 70–94; Wini Breines, *Young, White, and Miserable: Growing Up Female in the Fifties* (Boston: Beacon Press, 1992).

13. For early examples, see Paul Boyer, "Minister's Wife, Widow, Reluctant Feminist: Catherine Marshall in the 1950s," *American Quarterly,* Winter 1978, 703–721; Brandon French, *On the Verge of Revolt: Women in American Films of the Fifties* (New York: Frederick Ungar, 1978); Janey Place, "Women in Film Noir," in *Women in Film*

Noir, ed. E. Ann Kaplan (London: British Film Institute, 1980), 35–54. For more recent examples, see Nancy Walker, "Humor and Gender Roles: The 'Funny' Feminism of the Post-World War II Suburbs," *American Quarterly,* Spring 1985, 98–113; Janet Walker, "Hollywood, Freud and the Representation of Women: Regulation and Contradictions, 1945-Early 60s," in *Home Is Where the Heart Is: Studies in Melodrama and the Woman's Film,* ed. Christine Gledhill (London: British Film Institute, 1987), 197–214; James West Davidson and Mark Hamilton Lytle, *After the Fact: The Art of Historical Detection,* 2nd ed. (New York: Knopf, 1986), 2:364–92; George Lipsitz, *Time Passages: Collective Memory and American Popular Culture* (Minneapolis: University of Minnesota Press, 1990), 77–96; Jackie Byars, *All That Hollywood Allows: Re-Reading Gender in 1950s Melodrama* (Chapel Hill: University of North Carolina Press, 1991).

14. Jacqueline Jones, *Labor of Love, Labor of Sorrow: Black Women, Work, and the Family from Slavery to the Present* (New York: Basic Books, 1985), 268–274; Judith E. Smith, "The Marrying Kind: Working Class Courtship and Marriage in Postwar Popular Culture," paper, 1990; Byars, *All That Hollywood Allows,* 210–258; Rickie Solinger, *Wake Up Little Susie: Single Pregnancy and Race Before Roe v. Wade* (New York: Routledge, 1992).

15. For a brief overview of the postwar era that includes some of this revisionist literature, see Sara M. Evans, *Born for Liberty: A History of Women in America* (New York: Free Press, 1989), 243–262.

16. On maternalist politics in the late nineteenth and early twentieth centuries, see Sonya Michel and Seth Koven, "Womanly Duties: Maternalist Politics and the Origins of Welfare States in France, Germany, Great Britain, and the United States, 1880–1920," *American Historical Review,* October 1990. On maternalist politics in the early 1960s, see Amy Swerdlow, "Ladies' Day at the Capitol: Women Strike for Peace versus HUAC," *Feminist Studies,* Fall 1982.

17. On women pacifists, see also Lynn, *Progressive Women in Conservative Times.* Lynn acknowledges the maternalist arguments of some postwar women pacifists, but she sees these arguments as weaker and less prevalent than in the post–World War I pacifist movement; see p. 97.

18. In fact, the postwar outcry over domineering "moms" and "matriarchs" may well have been part of a cultural challenge to resurgent maternal power.

19. See Garrow ed., *The Montgomery Bus Boycott;* Crawford et al., eds., *Women in the Civil Rights Movement;* Paula Giddings, *When and Where I Enter: The Impact of Black Women on Race and Sex in America* (New York: Bantam Books, 1985), 261–275; Daisy Bates, *The Long Shadow of Little Rock: A Memoir* (New York: McKay, 1962); Cynthia Stokes Brown, ed., *Ready from Within: Septima Clark and the Civil Rights Movement* (Navarro, Calif.: Wild Trees Press, 1986).

20. On postwar protest among working-class Mexican American women, see also Michael Wilson and Deborah Silverton Rosenfelt, *Salt of the Earth* (Old Westbury, N.Y.: Feminist Press, 1978).

21. See Rupp and Taylor, *Survival in the Doldrums.*

22. Harrison, *On Account of Sex,* 53; Lynn, *Progressive Women in Conservative Times,* 111–140.

23. See Ann Petry, "What's Wrong with Negro Men?," *Negro Digest,* March 1947, 4–7; Pauli Murray, "Why Negro Girls Stay Single," *Negro Digest,* July 1947, 4–8; Alice Kessler-Harris, *A Woman's Wage: Historical Manings and Social Consequences*

(Lexington: University Press of Kentucky, 1990), 101–109; Gabin, *Feminism in the Labor Movement*, 144.

24. In her essay on historian Eleanor Flexner, Ellen DuBois writes of a postwar "left feminist" perspective that "fused a sense of women's systematic oppression with a larger understanding of social inequality." Ellen DuBois, "Eleanor Flexner and the History of American Feminism," *Gender and History*, Spring 1991, 84–85.

25. On the impact of the Cold War on women's organizations, see also Rupp and Taylor, *Survival in the Doldrums*, 136–144.

26. See May, *Homeward Bound.*

27. Twelve national organizations of women formed the Assembly of Women's Organizations for National Security in 1951. By 1954, five more organizations had joined. The assembly favored "maximum participation and use of womanpower in national security." The member organizations included the American Association of University Women, General Federation of Women's Clubs, National Federation of Business and Professional Women's Clubs, National Association of Negro Business and Professional Women's Clubs, National Federation of Republican Women, and Women's Division of the Democratic National Committee. See Dorothy G. Stackhouse, "Assembly of Women's Organizations for National Security," *General Federation Clubwoman*, January 1954, 10–11, 26–29. On anticommunist feminists in the National Woman's Party, see Rupp and Taylor, *Survival in the Doldrums*, 136–137.

28. See also Kessler-Harris, *Out to Work*, 304.

29. Jones, *Labor of Love*, 268–274. The postwar publications of other racial and ethnic groups also included images of women. Further study is needed to determine how these subcultural presses corroborated, reworked, or challenged dominant gender ideals. Further study is also needed to investigate the meanings of the middle-class domestic ideal to women who were not white and middle class; see Lynn, *Progressive Women in Conservative Times*, 12.

30. Patricia Morton, *Disfigured Images: The Historical Assault on Afro-American Women* (New York: Praeger, 1991).

31. See also Solinger, *Wake Up Little Susie.*

32. See May, *Homeward Bound.*

33. On abortionists, see also Carol Joffee, "Portraits of Three 'Physicians of Conscience': Abortion before Legalization in the United States," *Journal of the History of Sexuality*, July 1991; on lesbians, see also D'Emilio, *Sexual Politics;* Kennedy and Davis, *Boots of Leather, Slippers of Gold;* Audre Lorde, *Zami: A New Spelling of My Name* (Trumansburg, N.Y.: Crossing Press, 1982); Joan Nestle, *A Restricted Country* (Ithaca: Firebrand Books, 1987).

34. See Diane Di Prima, *Memoirs of a Beatnik* (San Francisco: Last Gasp Press, 1988); Joyce Johnson, *Minor Characters* (Boston: Houghton Mifflin, 1983); Hettie Jones, *How I Became Hettie Jones* (New York: Dutton, 1990).

35. In her study of the League of Women Voters, Susan Ware makes a similar point when she writes of "previously overlooked continuities in women's postwar political behavior. It is too simplistic to contrast the doldrums of the 1950s with the explosions of the 1960s and 1970s." Ware, "American Women in the 1950s," 294. Other recent works that point to neglected continuities between the postwar era and the 1960s include Barbara Ehrenreich, *The Hearts of Men: American Dreams and the Flight from Commitment* (Garden City, N.Y.: Anchor/Doubleday, 1983); Maurice Isserman, *If I*

Had a Hammer . . . The Death of the Old Left and the Birth of the New Left (New York: Basic Books, 1987); Todd Gitlin, *The Sixties: Years of Hope, Days of Rage* (New York: Bantam, 1987); W. T. Lhamon, Jr., *Deliberate Speed: The Origins of a Cultural Style in the American 1950s* (Washington, D.C.: Smithsonian Institution Press, 1990); Ellen Herman, "Being and Doing: Humanistic Psychology and the Spirit of the 1960s," in *Sights on the Sixties,* ed. Barbara Tischler (New Brunswick, N.J.: Rutgers University Press, 1992), 87–101, 250–252.

PART I

Women and
Wage Labor

CHAPTER 2

Xiaolan Bao

WHEN WOMEN
ARRIVED

The Transformation

of New York's

Chinatown

W orld War II affected the lives of all Americans, but it had a particularly profound impact on Asian Americans. The end of the war marked an especially important turning point in the history of New York's Chinatown. From a relatively homogeneous, highly segregated, and small, service-oriented bachelor society, New York's Chinatown was transformed into a relatively diverse and family-oriented community with manufacturing industries. Although the extent of change was evident only after the passage of the amendment of the U.S. immigration law in 1965, the changes originated in the immediate postwar era.

The entry of Chinese women immigrants into the United States, a key factor in this transformation, resulted from changes in federal law during and after World War II. The 1943 repeal of the Chinese Exclusion Acts made Chinese, but not other Asians, eligible for naturalization and provided Chinese with an immigration quota. Among the new laws that lifted restrictions on Chinese, some specifically fostered the entry of Chinese women: The 1945 War Brides Act allowed men who had served in the U.S. military to bring spouses to the United States as nonquota immigrants, and the 1946 Alien Fiancees and Fiances Act allowed the Chinese wives of U.S. citizens, both native-born and naturalized, to immigrate on a nonquota basis. The 1953 Refugee Relief Act further provided women with opportunities for immigration by reserving a number of visas for Chinese refugees and their families, including those already "stranded" in the United States, to "escape" from the communist government in China. As a result, Chinese women began to enter the United States in significant numbers,[1] initiating profound changes in family pattern, economic structure, and culture of major Chinese settlements in the United States. Focusing on New York's Chinatown, this essay examines the impact of these changes and traces the important role of women, working-class women in particular, in bringing about the transformation.

New York's Chinatown before 1945

As John Kuo Wei Tchen states, New York's Chinatown was not simply "an extension of San Francisco's and [the] Pacific Coast's," its foundation having "been laid long before the surge of the anti-Chinese sentiment on the West Coast."[2] The regional particularities of the early Chinese population were shaped by the more cosmopolitan nature of New York City as an important national and international port.

With respect to the scarcity of Chinese women, New York was exceptional. Although the sex-ratio imbalance was a common phenomenon among Chinese settlements in this country for most of the nineteenth century, by 1870 the Chinese female population had reached 3,873 in California, but "no Chinese women seemed to have actually settled in New York."[3] The small number of Chinese women who entered the city in the following years were predominantly the wives of Chinese merchants, women who were kept strictly indoors and hardly ventured beyond. The sight of Chinese women was such a rarity that they were said to be treasured as "pearls" in the bachelors' eyes. For a mere glance of a female compatriot, a Chinese man was said to have waited in vain on a corner of Mott Street from morning till night for two days in a row.[4] Even at the end of World War II, when the national sex-ratio imbalance of the Chinese population had dropped significantly, New York City's remained at almost six males to one female.[5]

One obvious consequence of this imbalance was intercultural marriage in New York, which was clearly recorded in state census records of the second half of the nineteenth century. In 1855, of the thirty-eight Chinese men found by the census takers in the third, fourth, and fifth wards of old Lower Manhattan, eleven were married to Irish women.[6] In 1870, the census taken in the fourth and sixth wards of the same area showed that eighteen of the sixty-four

Chinese male residents were married to European American women, with a total of twenty-one bicultural children.[7] The rate of Chinese-Irish intercultural marriage began to decline only when anti-Chinese sentiment began to sweep through the city in the late nineteenth century.

The rate of Chinese intercultural marriage in New York in this era never surpassed one-third of the entire population,[8] largely for financial reasons. Census records show that the Chinese who married Irish women were financially secure; Chinese men without means had little opportunity for intercultural marriage.[9] The ethnocentric nature of traditional Chinese culture probably discouraged many other Chinese men from out-marriage. If the early settlers had few opportunities, forced bachelorhood became nearly universal for Chinese by the end of the nineteenth century, with the passage of the Chinese Exclusion Act of 1882, which strictly prohibited the immigration of the wives of Chinese laborers, and the mounting anti-Chinese sentiment. Many men were members of what sociologist Evelyn Nakano Glenn terms the "split household," characterized by the separation of the breadwinner from his family; this family pattern was common in the first seventy years of Chinese settlements in the United States.[10] Family life did not become a dominant living arrangement in New York's Chinatown until the postwar period.

This pattern of "split households" and forced bachelorhood tended to undermine the patriarchal nature of traditional Chinese culture and its family system. Traditional Chinese culture emphasized the importance of family-line continuity, with its ideal of extended multigenerational family. Centering on the male's role as *wai zi,* the only breadwinner of the family and the sole dealer with the outside world,[11] Chinese tradition invested the male patriarch with absolute authority over women and the younger generation in the family.

The immigration experience deprived Chinese male laborers of their male prerogatives in several spheres. From the beginning of their experience in this country, most Chinese laborers were forced to resign themselves to a life of bachelorhood. Although it was the common assumption that married and single Chinese men would go back to China, to visit their families or to marry, few could afford to do so. Consequently, most married men were severed from their families, the traditional domain of their power, and bachelors with no options for marriage were unable to carry on their family lines.

In this period, married Chinese men did try to maintain their traditional position in the family by sending remittances to their male kin and relying on them to oversee their wives; but they had little control over their families. Their absence particularly affected their roles as fathers. In traditional Chinese families, children tended to have a formal and distant relationship with their fathers, which was, for the most part, due to the culturally constructed *yan fu,* or stern image of the father.[12] It was from this awesome image as discipliners that men derived their authority over their children. In the Chinese American "split household," the *yan fu* image was undermined by the father's lack of daily contact with his children because of his prolonged absence from the family. Children's strong sense of alienation from their father was so intense that a family reunion in later years could hardly heal the wound and bridge the gap.[13]

A strengthened mother–child relationship filled the vacuum in the Chinese American "split household." As the anthropologist Margery Wolf aptly pointed out, an informal mother-centered, or "uterine" family operates in the formally male-dominated Chinese extended family. Since the mothers conducted the sons' early socialization in the traditional Chinese family, close emotional ties could be formed between them; this bond was reinforced by filial piety, a central value of Confucianism, and in many cases led the son to act as the mother's spokesman in domestic and public affairs. Thus married women were able to wield a degree of power in the male-dominated world,[14] and women whose husbands were in America had fewer obstacles to acquiring such power.

Moreover, the prolonged absence undermined the Chinese fathers' dominant position in the family, and their traditional masculine roles were further reduced by the feminization of their occupations in this country after anti-Chinese agitation began to grow. By the 1870s, Chinese men in New York City no longer engaged in the wide range of occupations they had previously held.[15] The Chinese laborers who had come to this country in search of gold found jobs on railroads, mines, and farms; when anti-Chinese sentiment mounted across the nation, they were relegated to the service sector, especially in small ethnic enterprises. The hand laundry business, along with restaurants, grocery stores, and gift shops, became major occupations in New York's Chinatown.[16] Unlike trades that required a large amount of capital, a familiarity with tradesmen elsewhere, and a degree of English-language skill, the laundry business originally required only soap, scrubbing boards, and physical labor.[17] Limited by their capital, many former laborers went into this trade in partnership. One- or two-man Chinese hand laundries proliferated; by the 1930s, an estimated seven to eight thousand Chinese hand laundry shops involved almost half of the adult population in New York's Chinese community.[18] Commonly working from twelve to sixteen (and some reported twenty) hours a day, wielding an eight-pound iron in a hot, cramped environment, the Chinese men called their work "the blood and tears eight-pound livelihood."[19]

In China, as in other parts of the world, women traditionally did laundry.[20] "The Chinese laundryman [did not] learn his trade in China, . . . they were taught in the first place by American women."[21] Driven into a labor sector that they would have shunned in China "for fear of losing their social standing," the Chinese laundry men probably experienced profound psychological injury as a result of this restriction to what they regarded as women's work.[22] Holding on to their dream of returning to China (which had already changed in their absence), some men in New York's Chinese enclave sought emotional escapes in gambling, opium, tong wars, and prostitution, outlets common to many male-dominated societies. What made the vice-plagued bachelor society of New York's Chinatown unique among the major Chinese settlements in the United States was the presence of prostitutes from many ethnic groups, another consequence of the scarcity of Chinese women in the community.[23]

If the wives left behind in China were (as we have said) able to gain some additional influence, they paid a high price.[24] Toiling day and night for the families left behind by their husbands, taking care not only of their children but also members of their husbands' families, they shouldered tasks that were culturally allocated both to themselves and to their husbands.[25] Aunt Yueng, a Chinese woman who was married to a young Chinese man from the United States in the mid-1940s and was left behind, recalled her life after marriage: "The Yueng's family was not rich enough to buy a slave, but they got the labor of a slave by letting their son marry me. . . . Who cared about me at that time? No one. Really, no one."[26]

Their drudgery was not appreciated. While they labored for their husbands' families, their conduct and chastity were constantly under the strict surveillance of their husbands' kin. The suffering of Chinese women during this period was enormous. The loneliness, frustration, and unfairness could hardly be compensated for by the possible strengthening of their relations with their children as a result of their husbands' prolonged absence. Their anger and resentment are conveyed in the following lines:

> Right after we were wed, Husband, you set out on a journey.
> How was I to tell you how I felt?
> Wandering around a foreign country, when will you
> ever come home?
> You are wasting many joyous years of our precious youth.
> My spring heart has turned to ashes.
> Poverty does not allow me the luxury of a choice.
> But let it be known to all my sisters:
> Don't ever marry a young man going overseas![27]

The Postwar Transformation

Not until the end of World War II did family life become the norm in New York's Chinatown. As immigration restrictions were lifted, Chinese women came to the United States in large numbers. In fact, women constituted almost 90 percent of the Chinese immigrants between 1947 and 1952. The national sex ratio of the Chinese population nearly balanced in forty years, dropping from 285:100 in 1940 to 110:100 in 1979.[28]

This influx of women in the postwar era significantly changed the Chinese community in New York City. Of the 7,956 Chinese women who entered the United States between 1945 and the end of 1950, it is estimated that half settled in New York's Chinatown.[29] The sex-ratio imbalance in the city dropped from almost 6:1 in 1940 to 3:1 in 1950.[30] As many families entered small-capital and labor-intensive trades—grocery and restaurant and, mainly, the laundry business—a new form of family economy emerged, the "small producer household." Glenn has asserted that this pattern had become dominant in other major Chinese settlements by the 1920s,[31] but it appeared in New York City almost three decades later.

In New York City and elsewhere in the country, the Chinese "small producer household" blurred the demarcation between family and work life. This was especially true in the Chinese laundry enterprise.[32] The family living quarters, situated behind or above the shop for reasons of "thrift, convenience, or lack of options," [33] were where women and children worked, providing housekeeping and other kinds of assistance to the family business. Men worked in the shop, taking care of customers and dealing with the outside world. By pooling together the labor of all members of the family, Chinese working-class families in New York City managed to survive. As families entered the laundry business, most laundry shops were transformed from male partnerships to family ownership.

During this period of family reunion or formation, traditional Chinese family values seemed to be reasserted in the Chinese American family in New York City. The former Chinese laborers had their family business entirely under their control and the free labor of their wives and children at their disposal. They resumed their traditional status and regained their power in the family. Yet, a careful analysis shows that this was not exactly the case. While women's and children's labor became indispensable to the family business, few Chinese men could confidently deal with the outside world because they lacked facility in the English language and knowledge of the larger American society. They could no longer independently play their traditional role of the family's sole provider and public representative.

Compared with their status in the extended family in China, women fared better in the "small producer family." Constrained by the family's economic situation, the Chinese American "small producer household" in New York City, as elsewhere, tended to be nuclear. Younger women in extended families in China had to operate under the stern supervision of their mothers-in-law, a

Mrs. Fong Lai came to the United States under the terms of the War Bride's Act. In 1951 she lived in a one-room apartment in New York's Chinatown with her husband and five children. *Leonard McCombe,* Life *magazine* © *Time Warner*

form of power and control exerted by older women who dominated the operation of the informal uterine family. Chinese women in the United States could enjoy a greater degree of autonomy in their lives, but at high cost. Freed from the control and pressure of the extended family, Chinese immigrant women were also deprived of the companionship and possible assistance of their female kin at home. Shouldering the entire child-care and household responsibilities while providing indispensable assistance to the family business, many women were strictly confined to their living quarters and barred from any opportunity to learn about the outside world. The consequence for such women was deplorable; Aunt Chen of Brooklyn is one such case.

In the early 1950s, Aunt Chen came to join her ex-GI husband, who was twelve years her senior. From the moment of her arrival in New York City, she worked in the family laundry business. For more than thirty years, she barely ventured outside her family's apartment. She had never even visited Chinatown without the company of her husband or her children. "I am, indeed, blind with a pair of seeing eyes," as she put it. Her mission in life, taking care of the family, giving birth to one child after another, raising them and providing all services to the family business from the back, not only had consumed all her time and energy but also had denied her access to the outside world. By the time I interviewed her in the summer of 1987, her husband had recently died and her married sons and daughters had moved away. Left entirely on her own, she was forced to rely on her Chinese friends in the neighborhood for every detail in her life. Frustrated by her hopeless situation, she lamented that if she had known what her life would be like at the time of her husband's death, she "would have followed him to death." [34]

Some Chinese immigrant women who arrived in the postwar era from urban China and with some formal education found it easier to adapt to their new environment. They learned English, dressed themselves in Western apparel, and tried to make friends with their American neighbors. But even they often experienced discrimination. Mrs. Yu, for instance, whose experience was reported in 1951 in the *China Daily News,* came in 1948 with English-language skills and a previous experience of serving in a Red Cross organization in Kunming City, China. She wholeheartedly embraced the values of democracy, which she believed could be found only in the United States. After her husband retired from the army, however, the couple had a difficult time finding a home to rent because of the racial bias of white homeowners. Dismayed, she knew she had been unfairly treated by people who did not acknowledge her predicament. "I knew people had different feelings, but I did not expect I would be discriminated just because of the color of my skin. People said we did not want to move out. In fact, it is not that we do not want to move out, but that we are restricted by our conditions." [35]

The majority of Chinese immigrant women of this period were from rural China and had little education. The language barrier and difficulties in adapting to an entirely alien culture were aggravated by the hostility to the Chinese in New York City. Coverage of their difficult lives appeared frequently in Chinese community newspapers. A Chinese woman immigrant, whose husband worked long hours in a restaurant, found her life in the new land like "being detained in jail." [36] Another woman, a very young wife of a restaurant worker, was constantly panicked by her inexperience and lack of assistance in taking care of her newborn baby. She regretted immigrating and said that she would rather toil in the fields of China than live as she did in New York. [37]

Many more suffered not only from household chores and loneliness but also from tensions with their husbands. Strained marital relations were commonplace among the newly formed or recently reunited families in this period, with couples citing the lack of sufficient understanding and affection as a major cause. Most Chinese women who came to the United States in the immediate postwar period were wives who had long been separated from their husbands or new war brides who had recently married ex-servicemen of Chinese origin. These two groups differed in terms of age, level of education, cultural adaptability, and life experience. The reunited wives tended to be much older and had suffered long periods of separation from their husbands. The younger war brides were slightly better educated but were under more pressure for cultural adaptation as the young men they married were more Americanized than their fathers. Despite the differences between them, both groups had entered into marriages without a foundation of adequate understanding and affection.[38]

These already strained marital relations were commonly aggravated by economic problems. Unable to shoulder their family responsibilities, men tended to vent their frustrations and anger on their wives. As many articles in the Chinese newspapers of the period show, women were frequently battered, abused, and even forced to divorce their husbands.[39] Zhonghai Chen, president of the pro-Taiwan Chinese Consolidated Benevolent Association (CCBA), the most influential political organization in the community at that time, was revealed to have battered, abused and abandoned his wife. Interestingly, this case was covered by the pro-Beijing *China Daily News* (or *Huagiao Ribao*) to attack his political loyalty,[40] but the coverage ignored the widespread problem of wife abuse in the community. The fact that Zhonghai Chen, a public figure, had recklessly abused his wife in a community where one's reputation was treasured most suggests that wife battering transcended any political interpretation.

The difficulties in their lives drove some immigrant women to commit suicide. According to one estimate, up to the late 1970s the suicide rate among Chinese women in New York remained twice that of women of other groups in the city.[41] Many other Chinese women were reportedly on the verge of nervous breakdown.[42] High suicide rates and high divorce rates among newly reunited or married couples were recognized as major problems in the community at a time when family life had significantly mitigated old vices in the community.[43]

The rise of the garment factories in Chinatown in the late 1940s and early 1950s offered a solution to some of these problems. The help-wanted advertisements of the garment shops first appeared in the *China Daily News* on June 27, 1952. After that, a slowly increasing number of Chinese American women began to enter the garment industry. Work in these shops carried different meanings for women of different social status. For the very small number of women who were from relatively well-off families, garment factories provided important channels to socialize and make use of their talents. Jenny Wong, a seventy-three-year-old respondent, told me such a story.

Wong came to the United States with a high school education, a little knowledge of English, and some high school teaching experience in China. She first worked in a small American shop, making artificial flowers, and then in a garment factory. After sewing for two years, she decided to help a relative start a garment shop and later became a partner in the shop. When asked her reason for entering the industry, she shrugged away any economic considerations. Well supported by her husband, who was an engineer, she insisted that killing time and ending loneliness were her only reasons for working in the shop.[44]

For the majority of women, however, the garment factories offered an important supplement to their family income. Their employment helped ease the anxiety and tension in their lives. For some, the need for wage-earning labor was only temporary. This was true for many of the wives of the "stranded" Chinese students who chose to stay in the United States when the communists took over China in 1949. To help finance the education of their husbands, who were no longer supported by funds from China, some women chose to work in garment shops. Their numbers were small, and they often were isolated from the rest of the workers because of their dialect and cultural and class differences.[45] Many of these workers moved out of the industry to become "uptown" Chinese after their husbands completed their education and obtained professional jobs.[46]

For many garment workers, however, their incomes remained crucial to their families. A dialogue recorded in a local newspaper of the time vividly illustrated this aspect of wage work.

> "Old Aunt Mark, where are you going, why are you in such a hurry and out in such an early hour?"
> "I am rushing to work."
> "Then what about the kids? Who takes care of them?"
> "Well, to tell you the truth, with two kids needing to be taken care of, I do wish I could stay home. But things are not always as good as you wish. You know that, in the past, Old Mark could get three to four days' work a week. The thirty something dollars he earned each week was barely enough to pay our rent and board. Now, as our luck would have it, Old Mark has been sick for months and we could only live on money borrowed from friends and relatives. . . . How could we live on like this? I cannot but come out to work."
> "Isn't it too hard on you?"
> "Well, I ask a woman to take care of the kids and pay her fifteen dollars a week. I myself work in the shop and earn more than thirty dollars a week. After paying the babysitter, I still have some money left for family expenses. I feel much better now." [47]

The employment opportunities provided by the garment industry were so crucial to some families that, as one older woman put it, "without the garment industry, I really can't imagine how my family could survive to this day." [48]

Garment shops first appeared in the Chinese community around 1948.[49] By 1952, there were three Chinese-owned garment shops in the Chinatown area, hiring approximately fifty workers. Women workers were relatively young; even the finishers, who now tend to be much older, were only in their thirties. This was mainly because the laundry business continued to remain the major source of income for the community. Older women tended to help their husbands with the laundry business at home. Furthermore, garment shop owners did not hire older women because they believed they could not work as rapidly as younger women. Also, husbands of the younger women were not yet able to have businesses of their own, and their wives worked in the shops.[50]

The number of Chinese-owned garment shops grew slowly from three in 1952 to eight in 1960 and thirty-five in 1965.[51] By 1965, they hired approximately 10 percent of the Chinese female adult population of the city.[52] Although the impact of the garment industry was limited, it brought tangible changes to the community and foreshadowed the future transformation of New York's Chinatown. First, it gave rise to the "double wage-earner family" in New York's Chinatown. This family pattern, characterized by the labor force participation and economic contribution of both husband and wife, challenged traditional Chinese family values. The story of Mary Yan is a case in point.

Like many Chinese women who came to the United States after the passage of the War Brides Act, Yan had a rosy dream of life in the "Golden Mountain." The dream was crushed after she arrived. Her husband was in poor health and could not guarantee a regular income. After giving birth to two children, Yan started a career as a seamstress. Her husband worked out of town, where there was less competition than in the city. Yan, who was now the main breadwinner and sole parent at home, saw her children as her only hope. Like many working mothers in Chinatown, she devoted most attention to her children's education; she was stern when they did not do well at school and a most loving mother when they performed excellently.[53]

Her struggles paid off in the following years. One of her children became an accountant with a big Manhattan firm and the other a lawyer. As Yan related, both her son and daughter appreciated what she had done for them: "Without Mom," they said, "we would not have had our lives today." Yan considered her children's respect the greatest reward for her hard life.[54] The parent–child relationship in her family suggests the mother–centered nature of many "double wage-earner" Chinese American families. Although women garment workers were not common at that time, the new pattern of family life was to become increasingly evident among Chinese American working-class families in New York City.

Second, the growth of Chinatown's garment industry and its unionization integrated Chinese workers into the larger American society. The International Ladies' Garment Workers' Union (ILGWU) began to unionize Chinatown garment shops in 1957, the year in which information about union benefits first appeared in the *China Daily News*. Since then, the garment industry has become the only unionized industry in the community. Although the white, male-dominated leadership of the ILGWU was indifferent to the particular interests of its Chinese members, especially before the 1982 Chinese garment workers' strike, unionization carried tremendous meaning for Chinese women workers. It provided them with benefits and services and exposed them to the world outside Chinatown.[55]

Third, the low prices in Chinatown's garment shops were also noted in this period. Despite the insignificant position of Chinatown's garment industry in the city in the immediate postwar era, there existed an area in the midtown garment center that was called "Chinatown" by clothing manufacturers. Located on 35th Street between Lexington and Eighth avenues, this area was well known for its low-priced products.[56] Staffed with Jews, Italians, blacks, and Puerto Ricans, it had nothing to do with the Chinese. Nevertheless, the derogatory connotation of its name regrettably mirrored the nature of Chinatown garment production in the following years.

Chinatown from the 1960s to 1980

The modern dual wage-earner family did not become the dominant family pattern in New York's Chinatown until the late 1960s, when the garment industry began to grow dramatically and the laundry business was almost entirely wiped out by modern washing machines, dryers, and laundromats. The number of Chinese-owned laundry shops in the New York metropolitan area dropped from about five thousand in 1946 to one thousand in 1970.[57] With the decline of the laundry business, men looked for employment in the larger community, many of them working in restaurants. Because of the men's limited incomes and the unstable nature of their employment, working-class Chinese American families badly needed a second income. It was at this juncture that the garment industry stepped into the economic center of the community.

Three major factors contributed to the growth of the Chinatown garment industry: the availability of inexpensive loft space and housing in the area; the entry of a group of Chinese entrepreneurs eager to make a fortune in their new land and ready to take advantage of changing market opportunities; and, most important, the 1965 amendment to the Immigration and Nationality Act, which phased out the discriminatory national-origins quotas and allowed Chinese immigrant women to enter in large numbers and supply the labor force needed by the garment industry.[58]

From 1966 to 1970, more than 19,500 Chinese immigrants came to the United States annually. The number soared to almost 23,000 in the 1970s and reached over 42,000 in the 1980s.[59] From 1966 to 1989, a total of 734,521 Chinese immigrants came to the United States, making the Chinese the largest Asian group and the second-largest immigrant group in the United States.[60] New York City became a mecca for Chinese immigrants. From 1965 to 1977, 22 percent of all Chinese selected New York City as their destination before their arrival; seven out of twelve Chinese who landed in San Francisco ended up in New York City; and few Chinese left New York once they had settled there.[61] Between 1960 and 1980, the Chinese population in New York City increased fourfold. By 1970, New York had replaced San Francisco as the city with the largest concentration of Chinese residents in the United States.[62]

The jobs available in New York City, easily learned and requiring little English, influenced the type of immigrant. Many of the best-educated and highly skilled Chinese settled in California; many of the relatively poor, less-educated, and low-skilled Chinese settled in New York City.[63] Although an increasing proportion of Chinese Americans were middle-class professionals, Chinese immigrants in New York City were predominantly working class.

Like other newcomers after 1965, more than half of the Chinese immigrants were women, effectively lowering the sex-ratio imbalance of the Chinese population in the city.[64] Most of the new Chinese immigrant women did not speak English and had lower-level skills; most were married, and their families were in straitened economic circumstances.[65] Fortunately, most were also in the prime of their working years.[66] Under the pressure of economic need, they were eager to work at any wages and at any time. One-third to one-half of the Chinese women who immigrated to the city with their families changed their occupation from full-time housewife to garment worker.[67]

The Chinese women workers were in many ways similar to the women who came to the Lower East Side from Europe in the late nineteenth and early twentieth centuries. Clustering in the same area as the earlier immigrants, these Chinese workers had few alternatives to poorly paid work in the garment industry, which at the time was threatened by a shortage of labor. Confined to the highly competitive low-priced lines, the garment industry in Chinatown managed to grow by hiring these women at low pay.

The number of Chinese-owned shops grew from 34 to 247 between 1965 and 1975 and reached a peak of 430 in 1980.[68] As the number of jobs in the traditional midtown garment center dropped from 40,000 to 22,000, the number of jobs in Chinatown's garment industry grew from 8,000 to 13,400, and the number of union-affiliated shops more than tripled.[69] By 1980, Chinatown held 40 percent of the recorded production jobs in the women's outerwear industry in the city.[70] It became the largest center for garment production in the United States.

The rise of the Chinatown garment industry had a tremendous impact on the Chinese community. Garment shops employed one-third of Chinatown's labor force in 1969.[71] By 1983, it provided incomes for 60 percent of Chinatown families and 40 percent of the Chinese American families in the city.[72] The garment industry rejuvenated the restaurant business in the area, which had begun to decline in the 1960s. Catering to the needs of workers whose long hours forced them to eat two meals in the shop, small restaurants, offering fast and reasonably priced food, grew quickly in the area.[73] The garment industry also offered many Chinese immigrants a path to proprietorship. Many restaurant owners, heads of import–export companies, and realtors originally made their money in the garment shops.[74]

The garment industry also transformed the family life of working-class Chinese Americans in the city. By 1980, almost 60 percent of the Chinese female working population was employed in the industry, which significantly challenged the male-dominated nature of the Chinese American family.[75] The mother-centered Chinese working-class family, which emerged in the postwar era, became more evident, for several reasons. First, women's labor participation was indispensable to their families' well-being. The garment industry was the only one to offer family health insurance to its members, which was a benefit badly needed by the immigrant families. Also, because of the increased competition and declining wages for men's employment, women's economic contribution was no longer secondary to men's. Second, many men spent long hours away from home. Chinese restaurant workers had irregular work hours; most male employees worked from ten or eleven in the morning to eleven or later in the evening if business was good. For most of the week, home for them was merely a place to sleep, a "hotel," as one interviewee put it. Chinese male restaurant workers who worked outside the city visited their families only two days every other week. Exhausted by their long workdays, they played no significant role when they were home. This failure to play a substantial role in the life of their families, coupled with their decreased economic role, made them virtually invisible in their families. The entire household responsibilities fell on the shoulders of the women garment workers, whose work hours were more regular and flexible.

Christine Lin, a daughter of a garment worker and a waiter in New York's Chinatown, spoke for her counterparts in the community: "We can hardly see our Dad during the week. Every night he comes home, we are in bed; when we are up, he is in bed. On his day off, he is so tired that he has no patience to talk to us. . . . I don't know what to talk to him about either. . . . I love my Mom. She is always there. . . . Whenever we are hungry, we have problems, we go to Mom. . . . We can do without Dad, but we can't do without Mom."[76]

Although this mother-centered, dual wage-earner family imposed a heavy burden on women workers, it also provided them self-confidence. This confidence in turn stimulated their political awakening. In 1982, a large-scale garment workers' strike took place in New York's Chinatown. Facing the Chinese shop owners' resistance to signing a new labor contract, twenty thousand women workers turned out to join the union rally, which remains the largest one in the history of New York's Chinatown.

How far will this new family pattern develop among the Chinese working class of New York City? Time will tell. Meanwhile, we know that its origin can be traced to the immediate postwar era, when the Chinese community was transformed.

NOTES

1. The best accounts of these new laws can be found in Roger Daniels, *Asian Americans: Chinese and Japanese in the United States Since 1850* (Seattle: University of Washington Press, 1988), 186–98, 299–316; and David M. Reimers, *Still the Golden Door: The Third World Comes to America* (New York: Columbia University Press, 1985), 11–29.

2. Both quotes are from John Kuo Wei Tchen, "New York Chinese: The Nineteenth-Century Pre-Chinatown Settlement," in *Chinese America: History and Perspectives 1990,* (San Francisco: Chinese Historical Society of America/Asian American Studies, San Francisco State University Press, 1990), 183–184.

3. Ibid., 173; see also Judy Yung, *Chinese Women of America: A Pictorial History* (Seattle: University of Washington Press, 1986), 119.

4. Zhengzhi Guo, *Huafu Cangsang: Niuyue Tangrenjie Shihua* (The Vicissitude of a Chinatown: The History of New York's Chinatown) (Hong Kong: Buoyi Press, 1985), 56.

5. Bernard P. Wong, *Chinatown: Economic Adaptation and Ethnic Identity of the Chinese* (New York: Holt, Rinehart and Winston, 1982), 59.

6. Tchen, "New York Chinese," 161–162.

7. Ibid., 173.

8. Ibid., 162, 173.

9. As pointed out by Tchen, eleven Chinese men who married Irish women in 1855 included boardinghouse operators and merchant mariners. None of the peddlers, who constituted one-third of the Chinese population found by the census takers in the area, was among them. Ibid., 161–162.

10. Evelyn Nakano Glenn, "Split Household, Small Producer and Dual Earner: An Analysis of Chinese-American Family Strategies," *Journal of Marriage and the Family,* February 1983, 35–46.

11. *Wai zi,* the culturally constructed name for the husband, means the person who deals with the outside world (external affairs). It was used versus *nei zi,* the wife, meaning the person who deals with the inside world (internal, or domestic, affairs).

12. "Stern father." It was derived from the phrase *ci mu yan fu,* meaning "loving mother and stern father." This phrase defines the different ideal roles played by the father and the mother in the Chinese family.

13. This aspect of life not only has been captured in scholarship on Chinese Americans; it has also been vividly represented in Chinese American literature. The discussion of the strained father–son relationship can be found in Wong, *Chinatown,* 62, and Rose Hum Lee, *Chinese in the United States of America,* (Hong Kong: Hong Kong University Press, 1960), 204. The representation of it can also be found in Louis Chu, *Eat a Bowl of Tea* (Seattle: University of Washington Press, 1961). In the novella, Ben Loy, the young central character, like most of his counterparts, never felt comfortable with his

father, whom he had not met until the age of seventeen, when he came to join him in the United States. Even though they lived in the same apartment, the father remained a perfect stranger to the son. In conscious defiance of his father's wishes, Ben Loy chose to assuage his loneliness through relationships with older white prostitutes. Ben Loy's covertly defiant attitude was, indeed, not uncommon among youths during that time, as confirmed by many of my informants who had grown up with the same experience.

14. For a detailed discussion of this particular feature of the traditional Chinese family, see the discussion of the informal mother–centered uterine family in Margery Wolf, *Chinese Families in Rural Taiwan* (Stanford: Stanford University Press, 1975); and Kay Ann Johnson, *Women, Family and Peasant Revolution in China* (Chicago: University of Chicago Press, 1983) 10, 18–20.

15. Tchen, "New York Chinese," 161.

16. Wong, *Chinatown,* 37.

17. For a detailed discussion of the early trades in New York's Chinatown, see ibid., 41–42.

18. Renqiu Yu, *To Save China, to Save Ourselves: A History of the Chinese Hand Laundry Alliance of New York* (Pennsylvania: Temple University Press, 1992), 9.

19. Chen Hsiang-shui and John Kuo Wei Tchen, "Towards a History of Chinese in Queens," working paper, Asian American Center/CUNY Queens College, 4.

20. Wong, *Chinatown,* 37.

21. As pointed out by an early 1860s Chinese immigrant in Lee Chew, "The Life Story of a Chinaman," in *The Life Stories of Undistinguished Americans as Told by Themselves,* ed. Hamilton Holt (New York, 1906), 289–290, quoted from Ronald Takaki, *Strangers from a Different Shore: A History of Asian Americans* (New York: Penguin, 1989), 92. For a more detailed account of the experience of the Chinese men who came to work at their relatives' laundry businesses, see Paul Sui, *The Chinese Laundryman: A Study of Social Isolation* (New York: New York University Press, 1987), 113–121.

22. Wong Chin Foo, "The Chinese in New York," *The Cosmopolitan,* June 1888, 298; also quoted from Takaki, *Strangers from a Different Shore,* 93.

23. Guo, *Huafu Cangsang,* 214.

24. See also Glenn, "Split Household," 39.

25. Due to the patrilocal nature of the traditional Chinese family, once married, women had to move into their husbands' families. They were expected to take care not only of their own family but also of all members of their husbands' families.

26. The following is based on an interview with Aunt Yueng, conducted by the author in Taishan dialect, December 2, 1987. To protect the identity and privacy of those interviewed for this project, most names that appear in the text or notes have been changed or only the last name is given.

27. Marion K. Hom, *Songs of Gold Mountain: Cantonese Rhymes from San Francisco Chinatown* (Berkeley: University of California Press, 1987), 146.

28. Daniels, *Asian Americans,* table 6.3, p. 199; and Yung, *Chinese Women of America,* 118.

29. The number 7,956 was arrived at from Daniels, *Asian Americans,* table 6.3, p. 199. The estimate that half the Chinese women who came to the United States settled in New York's Chinatown was suggested by Xia Zhu (Chu, Y. K.), *Meiguo Huaquiao Gaishi* (A General History of the Chinese in America) (New York: China Times, 1973), 135. This is a very rough estimate, subject to dispute.

30. Abeles, Schwartz, Hacckel, and Silverblatt, Inc., *The Chinatown Garment Industry Study* (hereafter cited as *Study*), a study commissioned by Local 23–25, International Ladies' Garment Workers Union, and the New York Skirt and Sportswear Association, 1983, 95; and Wong, *Chinatown,* 59.

31. Glenn, "Split Household," 39.

32. Wong, *Chinatown,* 60; Chen, "Towards a History," 4; and Glenn, "Split Household," 40.

33. Glenn, "Split Household," 40. Similar interpretations are also given in Chen, "Towards a History," 4.

34. Interview with Aunt Chen, conducted by the author in Taishan dialect, April 7, 1986.

35. *China Daily News* (hereafter cited as *CDN*), November 26, 1948.

36. *CDN,* December 6, 1951. The name stands as it was in the newspaper.

37. Ibid., April 5, 1952.

38. As testified by the separated wives, their husbands' departure usually took place after the first or no longer than the sixth month of their marriage. For the war brides' marriages, courtship and wedding usually had to be accomplished all within the month of their men's leave of absence from work. Lee, *Chinese in the United States of America,* 203–230.

39. *CDN,* May 27, June 22, and November 24, 1950.

40. Ibid., May 5, 1950.

41. Ibid., September 22 and 24, 1979.

42. Ibid.

43. Ibid., November 24, 1950; Lee, *Chinese in the United States of America,* 200–201, Guo, *Huafu Cangsang,* 62–64, Xia Zhu, *Meiguo Huaqiao Gaishi,* 179–182.

44. Interview with Jenny Wong, conducted by the author in Cantonese, March 4, 1986.

45. These workers spoke Mandarin, and most of them came from urban sections of northern China, while the majority of workers spoke Taishan dialect and were from rural Guangdong Province.

46. A discussion of the "uptown" Chinese in this period can be found in Peter Kwong, *The New Chinatown* (New York: Hill and Wang, 1987), 59–60.

47. *CDN,* May 29, 1952, translated by the author. A good discussion of the Chinese immigrant families in this period can be found in ibid., May 14, 1952.

48. Interview with Aunt Yeung, conducted by the author in Taishan dialect, December 5, 1987.

49. The exact date of the first appearance of garment shops in New York's Chinatown remains in dispute. The year 1948 is based on Peter Kwong's assessment in *The New Chinatown,* 32, and the transcripts of the workshops on the garment industry organized by the New York Chinatown History Project in 1984. The transcripts are located at the New York Chinatown History Museum (formerly New York Chinatown History Project) at 70 Mulberry Street, New York City.

50. This discussion is based on Guo, *Huafu Cangshang,* 88–89.

51. *Study,* 42.

52. Ibid., 94.

53. As she recalled regretfully, once she was so angry with her son because of his poor schoolwork that she ordered him to kneel on the floor with his book on his head for more than half a day.

54. Interview with Mary Yan, conducted by the author in Cantonese, April 30, 1989.

55. The most important union benefit was family health insurance, which I discuss later in this paper.

56. To be more exact, according to the way the Chinese described it in the 1960s, it covered an area with West 40th Street as its northern end, West 34th Street as its southern end; the No. 7 train ran through its middle, the No. 9 line on its west end, and the No. 6 on its east end. The prices of its products ranged from only 16 cents a piece before World War II to $2.75 a piece in the postwar era. *CDN*, December 31, 1962.

57. The 1946 figure is from Ruzhou Chen, ed., *Meiguo Huajiao Nianjian* (Handbook of Chinese in America) (New York: Office of China People's Foreign Affairs Association in New York, 1946), 381; the 1970 figure is from Wong, *Chinatown*, 40; and Kwong, *The New Chinatown*, 28.

58. These three major factors are discussed in *Study*, 44–72.

59. U.S. Immigration and Naturalization Service, *Annual Reports*, 1966–1989.

60. *Study*, 45; and Kwong, *The New Chinatown*, 4, 22.

61. Kwong, *The New Chinatown*, 25. The net immigration of 45,846 Chinese to New York between 1970 and 1980 is the number remaining from the 48,364 overseas Chinese immigrants who came to the city during that period. *Study*, 94.

62. Ibid., 45.

63. The 1979 data show that 70 percent of the New York arrivals with prior occupational experience had worked in blue-collar or service occupations. Only 3.2 percent of the Chinese professional and technical immigrants intended to stay in New York. *Study*, 45, 98.

64. Ibid., 95; and Wong, *Chinatown*, 11.

65. Many of the women workers were originally agricultural workers in China or urban women engaged in homework in Hong Kong. The preponderance of low-skilled workers was so pronounced that in 1979 only 20 percent of the adult female newcomers reported any previous work experience; of these, only 5 percent had been employed in white-collar positions, and only 30 percent had engaged in factory production. *Study*, 45, 97–98. In addition, most of them were married. The 1979 data show that 71 percent of the Chinese women arrivals over nineteen were married. Ibid., 95.

66. Almost 75 percent were between the ages of sixteen and sixty-four, and 37 percent were twenty to forty years old. Ibid.

67. Betty Lee Sung, *Survey of Chinese American Manpower and Employment* (New York: Praeger, 1976), 91.

68. *Study*, 44.

69. They grew from 73 to 247. Ibid., 41.

70. Ibid., 84.

71. Chinatown Study Group, "Chinatown Report: 1969," Columbia University East Asian Studies Center, 1969.

72. *Study*, 64.

73. Kwong, *The New Chinatown*, 32–33.

74. Ibid., 32.

75. Zhou Min, *Chinatown: The Socioeconomic Potential of an Urban Enclave* (Philadelphia: Temple University Press, 1992), 170.

76. Interview with Christine Lin, conducted by the author in English, August 9, 1989.

CHAPTER 3

Susan Rimby Leighow

AN "OBLIGATION TO PARTICIPATE"

Married Nurses' Labor Force Participation in the 1950s

In 1955, as part of a series on married registered nurses, Louise Alcott wrote an article for the *American Journal of Nursing (AJN)* describing her experiences as a wife, mother, and private-duty nurse. Portraying her job enthusiastically, Alcott also took great pains to prove that her house was clean, her meals were nutritionally balanced, and her son was properly supervised. Unwilling to admit that she worked for financial reasons or personal satisfaction, she emphasized the severe shortage of nurses and her family's support of her choice: "I am sure there are times when I would not feel justified in leaving my home for a big portion of the day if I were doing so solely to satisfy my desire to continue with my career. But my family feels that I am making a worthwhile contribution."[1] One month later, Elinor Quandt, the mother of eight- and six-year-old children, echoed Alcott, downplaying financial need and emphasizing self-sacrifice: "My husband and children fully understand the need for nurses."[2]

Louise Alcott and Elinor Quandt were not alone in juggling family and work in the post–World War II era. After nearly two decades of social turmoil caused by economic depression and war, some women expressed a desire to return to traditional gender roles. Females' median age at first marriage dropped from 22, a figure that had remained constant since 1890, to 20.1 by 1956. Fertility rates rose from 2.3 in 1937 to a peak of 3.7 twenty years later.[3] Yet women's employment outside the home also increased. Married American women's labor force participation grew by 15.8 percent during the 1940s, 1950s, and 1960s, compared with a growth rate of 6.9 percent between 1890 and 1940. Among white married women, those over the age of thirty-five, who were most likely to have school-age or adult children, had the highest employment rates. By 1960, 35.4 percent of white married women aged 35–44 and 38.6 percent of white married women aged 45–54 worked for wages. Over 60 percent worked in the traditionally female occupations of teaching, nursing, clerical work, and retail sales.[4]

Social scientists have attributed this significant shift in behavior to several postwar demographic, social, and economic trends. Compressed spacing of offspring and a longer school year freed some women from decades of full-time childrearing.[5] Economic changes also contributed. After two decades of depression and war, families that wanted consumer goods often found that they needed two wage earners to reach or maintain a comfortable standard of living. Employers, faced with a shortage of young and single female workers in the clerical and service sector, dropped prohibitions against hiring married women, raised wages, and permitted mothers to work part-time.[6]

The trends in nursing matched the trends in the larger society. Because of a critical nursing shortage, employers dropped the unspoken "marriage bar." Eager to practice their hard-earned skills, R.N.s pressured employers into offering incentives such as part-time work and on-site day care. Health-care institutions responded by changing employment conditions to attract married females; nursing, traditionally a single woman's job, became an occupation dominated by wives and mothers. Married women, only 20 percent of employed nurses during the 1920s, represented 42 percent by 1949 and 66 percent of the total by 1966.[7]

R.N.s' public statements about employment reflected the social tension created by married women's participation in the labor force. Most nurses who wrote in the professional press explained their employment in terms of public service, noting that the urgent need to care for the sick took precedence over family demands. Their argument was partially rooted in traditional female roles; American women had performed the bulk of nursing work since the colonial period. Nevertheless, the suggestion that married R.N.s had an obligation to work outside the home undermined family claims on wives and mothers. This justification, unique to public-service jobs, allowed nurses to combine career and family in the midst of the 1950s, an era usually characterized by domesticity. This essay explores how nurses shaped their occupation to meet the needs of working mothers. It also examines why married R.N.s seemed eager to engage in professional work, despite societal pressure to stay home.

Like most female wage earners in the late nineteenth and early twentieth centuries, nurses were young and single. In her study of nursing from 1850 to 1945 Susan Reverby found that in both 1890 and 1900 only 13 percent of employed nurses were married. By the 1920s, this proportion had increased to 20 percent, but most married nurses still left the profession in their twenties and thirties to tend to their families.[8] In 1928 nursing school superintendents, responding to a national survey, estimated that only 9 percent of actively employed R.N.s were married. Twenty percent of the nurses who participated in this study signed their questionnaires with "Mrs.," but this figure included widowed, divorced, and separated women, as well as those living with their husbands.[9]

Although no explicit marriage bar existed, working conditions virtually dictated that nurses be unmarried. Until the mid-1930s most R.N.s worked as private-duty caregivers in patients' homes. The private-duty nurse worked long hours, often for weeks at a time. When called to take a case, she knew she would be at the patient's bedside literally twenty-four hours a day. Furthermore, women who practiced private-duty nursing had to be ready to accept cases on a moment's notice.[10]

R.N.s working in other fields also found paid work and family life incompatible. Head nurses in hospital wards or superintendents in training schools and hospitals came from the ranks of single women. Hospitals commonly staffed their wards with student apprentices and hired graduates only to fill available administrative and instructional positions. Generally, these teachers and supervisors came from the institutions' own graduating classes. Since nurses' training schools admitted only single women and did not permit students to marry while in training, wives and mothers simply were not part of the administrative applicant pool. Furthermore, the selection process routinely passed over single women with romantic interests or family aspirations. The message to ambitious young nurses was clear: Nursing was an "either–or" proposition. Women who wanted to practice in the more lucrative and prestigious fields of administration or education would have to give up goals of marriage and family.[11]

During the 1930s and 1940s, as hospital use became more common and graduate nurses more often worked on hospital staffs, a married nurse was still exceptional. Hospital administration maintained paternalistic work environments, requiring nursing staff members to live on-site and maintaining curfews and other social restrictions. Supervisors complained that married workers had

Table 3.1.

Percentage of Nurses in Labor Force by Marital Status, 1949–1962

	Single	Married	WDS[a]
1949	89	41	81
1951	90	45	81
1956	92	60	83
1962	57	57	80

Sources: ANA, *Facts about Nursing, 1949* (New York: ANA, 1949), 14; ibid., *1952,* 18; ibid., *1961,* 16, 18; ibid., *1964,* 18, 25.
[a]WDS refers to widowed, divorced, and separated women

high rates of absenteeism and lacked loyalty to the institution.[12] In a society in which most women fully expected to leave the workforce after marriage, and in which the majority of women did marry, nursing conformed with dominant values about women's roles.

These notions about a woman's proper place broke down somewhat during the years of World War II, when married nurses worked in both civilian and military agencies. In 1943 the Army Nurse Corps (ANC) reversed an earlier policy barring married women. A U.S. Public Health Service survey conducted in 1943 revealed that 40 percent of women working as civilian nurses were married.[13] Even as these "retired" nurses mobilized to meet the wartime emergency, attitudes about married women's employment remained virtually unchanged. Both the profession's leaders and the reemployed nurses stressed that married women worked only "to meet a defense need." [14] Despite intense recruitment campaigns, many homemakers refused to undertake employment. A sampling of nurses in nine states during 1941 found that 93 percent of inactive R.N.s considered themselves unable to work because of family obligations.[15] Retired New York nurses, responding to surveys conducted in Nassau and Oneida counties, gave similar reasons for their inactivity.[16]

After demobilization, married nurses behaved as expected. The *American Journal of Nursing* in 1946 found that one-third of ex-ANC personnel who did not resume nursing cited marriage as their reason.[17] Similarly, 47 percent of the civilian nurses under age forty planned to leave the profession at war's end, presumably because of family responsibilities.[18] The American Nurses Association's (ANA) first Inventory of Registered Professional Nurses, conducted in 1949, found that 60 percent of inactive R.N.s left the profession after 1945. Seventy-one percent of these inactive nurses were under forty years of age, and many were probably married.[19]

Table 3.2.
Percentage of All Employed Nurses in Each Age Cohort, 1951–1966

	20–29	30–39	40–49	50–59	60+	Unknown	Total
1951	34	30	19	9	4	4	100
1956	30	25	21	13	7	4	100
1962	25	25	23	18	7	2	100
1966	25	22	24	17	8	4	100

Sources: ANA, *Facts about Nursing, 1952* (New York: ANA, 1952), 17; ibid., *1962–63,* 15; ibid., *1964,* 15; ibid., *1968,* 16.

Despite the exodus from paid labor at the close of World War II, wives and mothers were still more likely to practice nursing in the late 1940s than they had been earlier in the century. The 1949 inventory found that 41 percent of active nurses were married and that one-third of the married and employed R.N.s had children under eighteen years of age.[20] Throughout the 1950s, the proportion of married women engaged in professional practice grew steadily, with the largest increases occurring between 1951 and 1956 (see Table 3.1). Older married women accounted for most of the increase (see Tables 3.2 and 3.3). Between 1951 and 1962, the proportion of women aged forty to fifty-nine in the nursing labor force grew significantly, while the proportion of R.N.s in their twenties and thirties declined (see Table 3.2). The median age of employed nurses, which had been 33.9 in 1949, rose to 39.6 by 1962.[21]

This influx of married women and mothers occurred because new trends in health care and the subsequent need for personnel created a crisis in a profession unprepared to deal with shortages. Nursing had experienced both an oversupply of practitioners in the 1910s and 1920s and serious unemployment during the Great Depression.[22] World War II changed this situation dramatically as the military absorbed large numbers of nurses and civilian agencies replaced those who had enlisted.[23] After V-E Day, the professional literature began to speculate about a peacetime civilian and military nursing shortage.[24]

These predictions were correct. Throughout the late 1940s and 1950s, health-care professional and the federal government both stated that the nation needed more nurses. In 1946, R.N.s attending the ANA convention in Atlantic City heard the association president, Katharine J. Densford, call for 220,000 more nurses.[25] One year later, the editor of the *American Journal of Nursing,* comparing this situation to the challenges Florence Nightingale faced a century earlier in the Crimea, called the postwar shortage "the most critical period in the history of nursing since Scutari."[26] The president-elect of the American

Table 3.3.

Percentage of Married Nurses in Labor Force in Each Age Cohort, 1956–1966

	20–29	30–39	40–49	50–59	60+
1956	61	49	59	62	51
1962	59	51	62	65	49
1966	64	52	63	67	51

Sources: ANA, *Facts about Nursing, 1962–1963* (New York: ANA, 1963), 26; ibid., *1965*, 14; ibid., *1968*, 16.

Medical Association (AMA), writing in 1947, agreed that "a serious crisis had developed in the field of nursing," since the United States had only 60 percent of the R.N.s it needed to meet the nation's health needs.[27] In 1948, nursing leaders were predicting that the shortage would continue into the 1960s.[28] In 1956, a shortfall of seventy thousand R.N.s remained.[29]

This shortage developed despite an increase in nurse–patient ratios throughout the postwar period, from 200 per 100,000 people in 1945 to 249 in 1955, 306 in 1965, and 356 in 1970. During these years, both the total number of R.N.s in the United States and the percentage who practiced professionally also grew (see Table 3.4). The nation's supply of R.N.s never seemed adequate in these postwar years because both demographic trends and changes in American health-care practices led to a greater demand for nursing services and consequently caused a strain on existing resources. Population growth, particularly among the very young and the elderly, created a tremendous demand for health-care facilities and personnel.[30] At the same time, increases in group medical insurance and advances in areas such as pharmacology, psychiatry, and cardiac care expanded the number of people under treatment, increased the demand for facilities and health-care providers, and multiplied the number of procedures performed on patients.[31] The Hill-Burton Act of 1946, which allotted federal funding for nonprofit hospital construction, and the growth of the nursing home industry led to a mushrooming of facilities that needed personnel.[32] Thus, even though the number of practicing nurses rose during these years, the increase did not equal existing need. In 1958, for example, 11 percent of full-time hospital positions remained vacant.[33]

Other sectors of the health-care industry suffered as well. Because of the growing elderly population requiring home care and the burgeoning number of school-age children, the ratio of public health nurses to the general population dropped at the same time agencies expanded services. In 1959, according to a National League for Nursing survey, a 4 percent vacancy rate existed in the field.[34] Meanwhile, professional leaders estimated that the number of nurs-

Table 3.4.
Registered Nurse Supply, 1949–1966

	1949	1951	1956	1962	1966
Total RNs	506,050	556,617	650,014	847,531	909,131
Percentage in labor force	59.4	60.1	66.7	65.3	67.5

Source: "Inventory Shows 75 Percent of Nation's Nurses Work," *American Journal of Nursing* 80 (November 1980): 1948.

ing faculty members produced annually was only half what was needed. The armed forces, suffering from an "acute" R.N. shortage, called for several hundred more recruits annually.[35] The Korean war and fears about nuclear attack during the Cold War put additional strains on the nation's nurse supply.[36]

Mindful of the demands on their profession, nursing leaders in the 1950s sought to increase the number of practicing R.N.s even further. Leaders proposed improving nurses' employment conditions, recruiting more female high school graduates, providing scholarships for needy nursing students, and utilizing health-care staff more efficiently.[37] These tactics alone, however, did not produce the required workers. While nurses' salaries traditionally had been low, even for a female-dominated occupation, only 10 percent of women who left the field took nonnursing jobs.[38] Even though the absolute number of student nurse enrollments rose, the percentage of female high school graduates entering the profession dropped from 7 to 5 percent during the mid-1950s.[39] Furthermore, given the rate of population growth, nursing leaders realized that increasing the nurse supply merely through educating high school graduates would simply not fill the need.[40] Where, then, were the nurses to come from? The answer: from the ranks of the inactive. Women who had retired from active duty to raise children could alleviate the shortage. Nursing leaders argued that older R.N.s, who no longer had pressing family responsibilities, could effectively rejoin nursing. Older workers, they stated, constituted a more stable labor force than new graduates, who would likely marry, get pregnant, and leave the profession at least temporarily.[41] Furthermore, since hospitals had eliminated the practice of "living in" during the 1940s, married women and mothers could return to work without sacrificing family life.[42]

Utilizing inactive nurses, as the leadership well knew, was problematic. World War II experiences had proven that homemakers faced obstacles that made paid labor extremely difficult. Furthermore, both tradition and employer preference for single women discouraged inactive nurses from returning to the labor force.

Because of the beliefs about married nurses expressed during World War II, professional associations launched a campaign in which they sought to allay fears about older nurses' job performance and impress on the women themselves the desperate need for their services. As early as 1949, the editor of the *American Journal of Nursing,* the ANA's official organ, asked, "Are we overlooking an important supply when we pass by the group of inactive professional registered nurses?" Decrying this waste of untapped workers, she reminded her readers that "the education of the nurse . . . is an expense not only to the school but to society as well." Advising her married readers to work at least on a part-time basis, she admonished them: "A married woman does not completely escape her obligation to participate." [43] Another nurse, writing in *Nursing Outlook* in 1953, pointed out that inactive nurses made excellent potential employees. Citing studies that commented favorably on older women's health, intelligence, and emotional stability, she advised employers to remember that these women "were not so likely to leave the profession for a few years," as were new graduates.[44]

This campaign to get married women back into nursing, however, could not convince employers and nurses to change existing behavior. Mothers expressed an unwillingness to leave their children for full-time nursing positions. As one homemaker observed, "All good mothers want to be home when their children return from school. . . . Few [mothers] can leave the house at 6:00 a.m., leaving the children to fend for themselves and a husband to prepare breakfast and get the children off to school." [45] In a similar vein, Ruth Roswal, mother of a two-year-old child, wrote to the *American Journal of Nursing* that she wanted to work but hesitated to leave her son with "local babysitters." [46] Other married nurses noted that salaries were inadequate. As one New York R.N. complained in 1953, "I am a retired registered nurse and had thought of going back to work, since I am only 39 years old. However, I have changed my mind. If I want to work, I can earn $100 a week as a waitress, so why should I work for the ridiculous salary hospitals are offering nurses today?" [47] Ten months later, a Washington nurse, Marian Austin, similarly observed, "A truck driver I know earns $3.50 an hour. I earn $1.50 an hour." [48] Furthermore, retired nurses, who had often been out of the labor force for decades, felt inadequate in the face of modern health-care technology and practice. Returning R.N.s, interviewed by the *American Journal of Nursing* in 1952, reported feeling "apprehensive," "fearful," and "unqualified" during their first few weeks on the hospital floor.[49]

The severity of the postwar nursing shortage forced employers and nursing leaders to consider possible solutions. As their letters made clear, married R.N.s would accept jobs only if employers addressed their concerns about family obligations, salaries, and new technologies. As the shortage worsened, hospitals in particular found themselves forced to make changes to provide at least a minimum of professional nursing care for their patients.

Faced with high vacancy rates, institutions resurrected a World War II solution.[50] During the 1950s, administrators reported increased use of part-time scheduling. Minneapolis General Hospital was one of the first to write of its experiences with part-time workers. The director of nursing realized that R.N.s who lived in the city would work if they had some control over their schedules. The hospital organized a system whereby nurses with family responsibilities or who were attending college could work part-time, for as few or as many hours as they chose. Mothers who wanted to work only on weekends, when their husbands could provide child care, were encouraged to do so. The director of nursing declared this experiment a success and found the new employees to be "capable," despite the "irregular" schedules they kept.[51] Other administrators also found married nurses "eager to work" partial shifts and weekends. Four directors of nursing, for example, writing for the *American Journal of Nursing* in 1953 from Texas, Minnesota, and Illinois, reported that anywhere from 34 to 80 percent of their R.N.s had husbands and children. All four expressed complete satisfaction with the women's work performances, observing that married workers exhibited lower absenteeism and turnover than single women.[52]

Nurses also liked the opportunities that part-time hospital work afforded them. One woman, who wrote that "home responsibilities did not permit her to work full-time," received "great psychic satisfaction" from her part-time employment.[53] Another woman, who said, "I cannot afford to work full-time and pay child care," worked two weekends a month. This enabled her to continue nursing while her husband cared for the children.[54]

In the face of these successful experiences the number of nurses working part-time climbed steadily upward. Between 1956, when the ANA first published statistics on part-time workers, and 1962, the number of nurses employed on this basis increased from 10 to 21 percent. By 1962, part-timers worked in 80 percent of nonfederal U.S. hospitals and delivered one-fifth of the nursing care received there. Ninety percent of these workers were married women, and 80 percent had children. Seventy-one percent stated in a U.S. Public Health Service survey that family obligations did not permit them to take full-time jobs.[55]

Increasing opportunities for nurses outside the hospital setting also enabled many more women to obtain employment that did not interfere with home responsibilities. In response to the trends discussed earlier, public health agencies and schools of nursing hired greater numbers of R.N.s after World War II. Industrial plants also employed more occupational health nurses during these years in response to the nation's expanding economy. Since nurses who worked in these settings did not take rotating shifts, and many did not work weekends or holidays, these jobs were very appealing to married women, particularly those with school-age children. The experiences of a Georgia nurse who wrote to the *American Journal of Nursing* in 1970 suggest that nurses eagerly sought these opportunities. Discussing her own successful return to nursing years earlier, she warned other women in her position to steer clear of hospitals where administrators expected employees to work rotating shifts. She advised R.N.s to consider "work in settings where nobody takes shifts—birth control clinics, baby clinics, psychiatric day care clinics, visiting nurse associations, public health agencies, the American Red Cross." [56]

These agencies made a conscious effort to attract married women. One of the first groups to do so were civil defense organizations. In 1956 the ANA's Committee on Nursing Resources to Meet Civil and Military Nursing Needs recommended that married women be hired to teach special classes in disaster nursing to both R.N.s and the general public. [57] Later, other agencies effectively utilized inactive nurses. In New York City, for example, the director of the Bureau of Public Health Nursing recruited at-home mothers. Reasoning that women who had children in school might "welcome a chance to return to nursing at a time and place convenient to them," he hired inactive R.N.s for the city's public and parochial schools. Two years after initiating this program, New York had hired 136 additional nurses who worked in 325 schools. [58] Tulsa, Oklahoma, public health agencies likewise solved their "acute nursing manpower shortage" by employing inactive R.N.s to teach Red Cross home nursing classes, immunize schoolchildren, and screen senior citizens for glaucoma. [59]

Improvement in nursing salaries and benefits also encouraged inactive nurses to return to practice. The 1950 census noted that female nurses earned several hundred dollars a year less than women teachers, librarians, and social workers, who had comparable levels of education and job responsibility. Additionally, nurses were among the lowest-paid professional and technical hospital employees. In 1950, only X-ray and medical technicians earned less than registered nurses. [60] Under the circumstances, many mothers were reluctant to take jobs that barely covered work-related expenses. One young nurse, writing from New York in 1952, expressed this concern to the *American Journal of Nursing* three months after the journal had run a recruitment article. "I read continuously about the urgent need for nurses, and besides, I would like to do some work to keep up with the current trends in nursing. . . . With the hospitals paying nurses $10 a day, it would hardly be worth while. Can the salary now offered nurses ever entice a married nurse to go back to work?" [61]

Wages did increase in the 1950s as health-care agencies tried to recruit and retain nurses and as the growth of medical insurance plans allowed institutions to pass along salary costs to third-party payers. [62] ANA hospital surveys, conducted in 1954 and 1959, found that staff nurses' wages increased 24.5 percent, head nurses' salaries rose 18.5 percent, and supervisors and directors experienced gains of 20 and 21.4 percent, respectively. During these years, researchers found that public health nurses' salaries increased 10.8 to 27.1 percent and that occupational health nurses received raises of 35 to 61 percent depending on educational level and position. Nursing faculty also benefited from rising wages, receiving increases of 13 percent between 1956 and 1958 alone.[63] While nursing leaders maintained that these increases were "not in keeping with their [nurses'] educational requirements and professional responsibilities," they acknowledged that salaries "have come a long way since 1946."[64]

Part-time employment opportunities, increasing numbers of jobs outside hospitals, and rising salaries proved instrumental in getting inactive R.N.s back into the workforce. For many nurses, however, favorable hours and wages were not sufficient inducements. Given the rapid technological changes occurring in American health care, women who had left the profession felt unable to resume employment, particularly on busy hospital wards. Inactive nurses often wrote to the professional press stating their desire to work and their fears about rusty and out-of-date skills. One nurse, interviewed by an *AJN* staff writer in 1952, recalled that after accepting a hospital position, she worried for months about giving patients the wrong drugs.[65] Another, a homemaker for twenty years, remembered bursting into tears during her first day on the ward because of fear and tension.[66]

Recognizing the older nurses' fears and unfamiliarity with recent advances in nursing, professional associations began implementing refresher courses designed to acquaint retired women with the newest procedures and bolster their self-confidence. These programs, usually lasting several weeks, combined formal class work with supervised clinical practice.[67] Initially the ANA's state affiliates organized the programs. Hospitals and state employment services, eager to recruit nurses, also established courses.[68]

Communities that implemented refresher classes reported that large numbers of women completed the course requirements and returned to paid employment. A 1962 study of Chicago nurses who had taken classes between 1957 and 1961 found that 75 percent of these formerly inactive women resumed the practice of nursing, with 44 percent working full-time.[69] Those who enrolled in classes testified to the benefits of "easing back" into practice via this route. One returning nurse reported: "One of the greatest benefits derived from the refresher course was the renewal of our self-confidence."[70] Another declared: "It would have been foolish for me to have gone on duty without some review."[71]

Although refresher courses removed obstacles for older nurses, they did not solve the problems of younger inactive R.N.s, who hesitated to leave their children even on a part-time basis. While acknowledging the shortage and their own desires to resume nursing, mothers worried about leaving their children without proper supervision. As one R.N. noted: "No conscientious nurse is going to let her children run wild while she works." [72] The 23 percent of women in the Chicago study who did not return to work after taking refresher courses cited lack of day care as a major problem.[73] Retired nurses, responding to a U.S. Public Health Service questionnaire, listed the inability to make suitable child-care arrangements as their second-most-important reason for being inactive.[74] In response to the shortage and their critical staffing needs, employers had to come up with solutions to the child-care problem.

In the 1950s a few health-care agencies included maternity leave in nurses' fringe-benefit packages. While nursing directors publicly stated that pregnant women should not work and new mothers should be home with their babies, they also argued that the shortage made such policies necessary. Throughout the 1950s, nursing associations set minimum maternity-leave standards and requested employers to implement them. These generally allowed the nurse a six- to eight-month leave, beginning in the second or third trimester of pregnancy and continuing until the new infant was several months old. While nurses on leave did not receive any pay, their jobs were guaranteed, and some agencies allowed the mother to return to work on a part-time rather than a full-time basis.[75] Employers who utilized maternity leave found it beneficial. A hospital nursing director noted that while pregnant nurses caused "headaches," she "couldn't run the hospital without them." [76] Public health directors, reporting to the *American Journal of Nursing,* believed their willingness to grant time off for childbirth was "a great convenience" and resulted in mothers who returned to work "well and happy." [77]

In addition to providing maternity leave, some employers helped mothers develop solutions to the riddle of reliable child care. One nursing director of a small Kansas hospital found she could solve staffing problems by securing babysitters for R.N.s' children. Advising other administrators to do the same, she explained that any inconvenience to herself had been offset by the loyalty of the married nurses, who greatly appreciated this service.[78]

Many agencies found that providing on-site child care resolved staffing and turnover problems nicely. Driven by the nursing shortage, institutions experimented with day-care centers. Many had experienced dilemmas similar to those of a New Jersey hospital that never had enough nurses and sometimes found it "impossible" to meet staffing demands. The enterprising administrator reasoned that married nurses in the community might return to work if they could find reliable child care at a minimal cost. He established the Nurses' Day Nursery, which, two and a half years after opening, cared for the children of twenty-seven women. Housed in a former nursing school classroom, the center cared for children aged five months to five years, whose mothers worked the day shift. Since mothers paid only a minimal fee, the nursery operated on a deficit. The director found the added expense "negligible," however, amounting yearly to the equivalent of one beginning nurse's salary. From his point of view, providing this service was clearly worth the expense. The day nursery relieved staffing pressures, allowed the hospital to fill more beds, and assured patients of quality nursing care.[79]

Other institutions, seeking to recruit inactive nurses, used similar day-care programs. Some offered the service without charge, others provided care during evening and night shifts, but in all facilities the basic features remained the same. Nurses left their children in safe, attractive quarters on the hospital premises, where the youngsters played, ate, and napped under the supervision of reliable caretakers. The employing agencies reported in all cases that their nursing labor forces stabilized and turnover declined once the facilities were in operation.[80] One Tennessee director of nursing estimated that two-thirds of her employees would not have been available if the nursery had not been in operation.[81] Nurses also supported on-site child care. Pauline Stack Cooper, for example, warmly endorsed her Ohio hospital's day nursery in 1959. The mother of four children under eight years of age, Cooper felt relieved to know that her youngsters were "just a step away from the wards" and that she could "look in on them" during her lunch hour.[82]

Married nurses, then, benefited from the chronic shortage of personnel during the 1950s. Health-care institutions desperately needed staff and subsequently met the needs of mothers. These accommodations—part-time scheduling, refresher courses, day care, and better economic rewards—enabled postwar R.N.s, even those with young children, to carve out dual roles as professionals and mothers. Women in other occupations did not have the same opportunity. Both private-sector employers and school districts dropped the marriage bar after World War II. Part-time work in the retail sales and clerical sectors increased 26 percent during the 1950s. Most firms and schools, however, still refused to hire or retain mothers of preschool children, and day-care centers never flourished in corporate America. In many companies, a pregnancy bar replaced the marriage bar.[83] Young married nurses did not encounter this level of discrimination.

As the professional literature shows, nurses eagerly embraced the opportunities created by the shortage. Women who had undergone the rigors of professional training had a solid commitment to nursing. They identified strongly with the profession even when they did not work in the field. During interviews with several retired R.N.s, historian Barbara Melosh observed that women who had been long-time homemakers still saw themselves as nurses. Most hoped to return to work someday.[84] Sociologist Everett Hughes, who studied nurses in the mid-1950s, found that 80 percent of his sample had both career and family aspirations.[85] In 1962 a *Nursing Outlook* survey indicated that 53 percent of retired nurses hoped to reenter the workforce. A majority kept up to date by performing volunteer nursing. The editor remarked:

> Something in nursing is uniquely appealing to those who enter this profession, and such women never really leave it.
>
> We suspect that such persons may find that other activities, particularly those of maintaining a home and family, can never fully use up the store of caring and wanting to help with which they are endowed.[86]

Rank-and-file women agreed with this assessment. As a returning nurse remarked in 1952: "I think it is the feeling we all have about our work, once we have been in active nursing—the idea of service to others—that draws us back into it."[87] Another R.N., writing in 1957, asserted that inactive nurses "wasted their nursing educations."[88] Furthermore, women enjoyed the intellectual stimulation of working and the sense of satisfaction that came from earning their own money. In 1947 a married nurse explained that her decision to return to work had been based on her boredom with full-time homemaking. She disliked spending her days "puttering around in a little two- or three-room apartment, wishing I had more to do."[89] In 1953 a Washington R.N. listed as reasons for her working "because I like to keep up with the times [nursing technology], because I like working, and because the money I earn raises our standard of living."[90]

In public statements, however, nurses sometimes adopted a defensive posture about their nondomestic behaviors. Women like Louise Alcott and Elinor Quandt publicly justified their outside employment by citing the nursing shortage and characterizing their work as a sacrifice. Even Pauline Stack Cooper, who had combined nursing and motherhood for seven years, felt compelled to defend her mothering skills. In a 1959 article she hastened to assure *AJN* readers that day care had not harmed her youngsters or weakened the maternal–child bond: "There is no question about being relieved from duty when a mother finds that she must care for a sick child at home. Their father and I believe that the nursery care has helped them to develop independence. However, they greet me with eager arms and kisses when going-home time comes. They know my off-duty time is all theirs."[91]

Even R.N.s with teenage or adult children described their employment in terms that did not challenge conventional notions about women's roles. One woman, for example, called her part-time nursing job "good therapy" for coping with empty-nest syndrome.[92] Others referred to their employment as "a pleasant addition to our lives" or as a "way of helping children through college." [93] Publicly at least, returning women placed their work as nurses in a secondary role after family and household responsibilities.

The entry of married women and mothers into the nursing labor force constituted a significant development for the profession. Married nurses consciously used the personnel shortage to their advantage. Aware that employers were desperate, they pressured health-care agencies to meet the needs of working mothers. Postwar R.N.s were highly successful in this regard. By the 1950s they had won not only part-time scheduling and higher pay rates but also concessions such as maternity leave and on-site child care, accommodations not yet available to teachers, secretaries, and retail clerks. Using the call to public service as their justification, employed nurse-mothers received tangible and moral support from their professional associations and health-care administrators. Despite a public discourse that showed some conflict over female roles, married R.N.s were able to function as both family members and professionals during the 1950s.

The entry of married women and mothers into the nursing labor force did not in itself change attitudes about woman's place in society. Nevertheless, it constituted a significant development for the profession. This transformation of the nursing labor force during the 1950s represents a "critical period" for the profession, as important as Nightingale's radical experiment at Scutari.

NOTES

1. Louise Alcott, "Combining Marriage and Nursing," *American Journal of Nursing,* November 1955, 1344.

2. Elinor Quandt, "Letters—Pro and Con," *American Journal of Nursing,* October 1955, 1160.

3. Eugenia Kaledin, *Mothers and More: American Women in the 1950s* (Boston: Twayne, 1984), 17–18; Alice Kessler-Harris, *Out to Work: A History of Wage-Earning Women in the United States* (New York: Oxford University Press, 1982), 301–302; Steven D. McLaughlin et al., *The Changing Lives of American Women* (Chapel Hill: University of North Carolina Press, 1988), 56–57, 126–127, 196–197.

4. I have focused on white women because more than 97 percent of R.N.s in the 1940s and 1950s were white. For statistics on white women's labor force participation in the post–World War II era, see Claudia Goldin, *Understanding the Gender Gap: An Economic History of American Women* (New York: Oxford University Press, 1990), 17–19, 138–154, 174–184; McLaughlin et al., *Changing Lives,* 113–114. For information on nurses' racial characteristics, see Darlene Clark Hine, *Black Women in White: Racial Conflict and Cooperation in the Nursing Profession, 1890–1950* (Bloomington, Ind.: Indiana University Press, 1989), x–xi; Barbara Melosh *"The Physician's Hand": Work Culture and Conflict in American Nursing* (Philadelphia: Temple University Press, 1984), 123–124.

5. Ethel Klein, *Gender Politics: From Consciousness to Mass Politics* (Cambridge,

Mass.: Harvard University Press, 1984), 54–55, 60–61; McLaughlin et al., *Changing Lives*, 56–58.

6. Goldin, *Understanding the Gender Gap*, 174–184; Kessler-Harris, *Out to Work*, 302.

7. American Nurses Association, *Facts about Nursing, 1950* (New York: ANA, 1950), 14; Evelyn Moses and Aleda Roth, "Nursepower: What Do Statistics Reveal about the Nation's Nurses?" *American Journal of Nursing*, October 1979, 1746; Susan M. Reverby, *Ordered to Care: The Dilemma of American Nursing, 1850–1945* (New York: Cambridge University Press, 1987), 112–113.

8. Reverby, *Ordered to Care*, 15–19, 112–113.

9. May Ayres Burgess, *Nurses, Patients, and Pocketbooks* (New York: Committee on the Grading of Nursing Schools, 1928), 243–244.

10. For a discussion of private-duty nurses' personal characteristics and working conditions, see Melosh, *"Physician's Hand,"* 85–91; Susan Reverby, " 'Neither for the Drawing Room nor for the Kitchen': Private Duty Nursing in Boston, 1873–1920" in *Women and Health in America*, ed. Judith Walzer Leavitt (Madison: University of Wisconsin Press, 1984), 454–457.

11. Melosh, *"Physician's Hand,"* 40–41, 53; Nancy Tomes, " 'Little World of Our Own': The Pennsylvania Hospital Training School for Nurses, 1895–1907" in Leavitt, *Women and Health in America*, 473, 477.

12. Melosh, *"Physician's Hand,"* 171–176; A Superintendent of Nurses, "Graduates versus Students," *American Journal of Nursing*, May 1933, 479–480.

13. "Wartime Nursing Is Different," *American Journal of Nursing*, September 1943, 836–837; "With Army and Navy Nurses," *American Journal of Nursing*, March 1943, 306.

14. Jean S. Alexander, "Letters—Pro and Con," *American Journal of Nursing*, January 1946, 57; Katharine J. Densford, "Letters from Readers," *American Journal of Nursing*, October 1941, 1203; "Married Student Nurses?" *American Journal of Nursing*, August 1942, 857; "Part-time Nurses in Civilian Hospitals," *American Journal of Nursing*, March 1945, 181; Eloise Partridge and Martha B. Teter, "Soldiers' Wives," *American Journal of Nursing*, June 1943, 567.

15. Pearl McIver, "The National Survey," *American Journal of Nursing*, January 1942, 23–26.

16. "News Here and There," *American Journal of Nursing*, September 1945, 761–762; ibid., October 1945, 861–862.

17. Edna E. Sharritt, "Where Are the Ex-Service Nurses?" *American Journal of Nursing*, December 1946, 850.

18. "5,000 Civilian Nurses," *American Journal of Nursing*, December 1945, 1020.

19. American Nurses Association, "Age, Marital Status, and Employment of Professional Registered Nurses," *American Journal of Nursing*, February 1950, 68.

20. Ibid.

21. American Nurses Association, *Facts about Nursing, 1965* (New York: ANA, 1965), 9.

22. Burgess, *Nurses, Patients, and Pocketbooks*, 20, 37, 80; Philip A. Kalisch and Beatrice J. Kalisch, *The Advance of American Nursing*, 2nd ed. (Boston: Little, Brown, 1986), 456–459, 497; Melosh, *Physician's Hand*, 41, 87.

23. Colonel Florence A. Blanchfield, AUS, Superintendent, ANC, "Letters—Pro and Con," *American Journal of Nursing*, February 1946, 134; Kalisch and Kalisch,

Advance of American Nursing, 527; "Nursing—on V-E Day and Beyond," *American Journal of Nursing,* June 1945, 424; "With Army and Navy Nurses," *American Journal of Nursing,* April 1946, 261–262.

24. Kalisch and Kalisch, *Advance of American Nursing,* 504; "News about Nursing," *American Journal of Nursing,* November 1944, 1084; ibid., December 1944, 1178; ibid., June 1945, 486; "Urgent Need for Nurses," *American Journal of Nursing,* November 1944, 1017.

25. Katharine J. Densford, "Address of the President," *American Nurses' Association Proceedings, Volume I—House of Delegates, Thirty-fifth Biennial Convention, September 22–27, 1946, Atlantic City, New Jersey,* Mugar Library, Boston University, 11.

26. Mary N. Roberts, "The Rich Report and the Crisis in Nursing," *American Journal of Nursing,* April 1947, 208.

27. E. L. Bortz, "The Nursing Crisis," *American Journal of Nursing,* August 1947, 527.

28. Mary N. Roberts, "Nursing in 1947 and Beyond," *American Journal of Nursing,* January 1948, 1.

29. Clara A. Hardin, "Supply of Professional Nurses in 1956," *American Journal of Nursing,* December 1956, 1545–1546.

30. American Nurses Association, *Facts about Nursing, 1955–56* (New York: ANA, 1956), 190; American Nurses Association, *Facts about Nursing, 1964,* (New York: ANA, 1964), 244, 247; American Nurses Association, *Facts about Nursing, 1968,* (New York: ANA, 1968), 222, 224, 227.

31. "Challenges for Nurses Require Determined Action—Mrs. Porter," *Convention Journal,* April 27, 1954, Mugar Library; Clara A. Hardin, "Supply of Professional Nurses in 1956," *American Journal of Nursing,* December 1956, 1546; Kalisch and Kalisch, *Advance of Nursing,* 575–578, 586–587, 591–592; "Need for Coordinated Planning," *American Journal of Nursing,* August 1948, 481; "Nursing in 1947 and Beyond," 1; Roberta R. Spohn "Some Facts about the Nursing Shortage," *American Journal of Nursing,* July 1954, 865–867.

32. American Nurses Association, *Facts about Nursing, 1952,* (New York: ANA, 1952), 88; American Nurses Association, *Facts about Nursing, 1959* (New York: ANA, 1959), 203; American Nurses Association, *Facts, 1964,* 218; American Nurses Association, *Facts, 1968,* 194–195.

33. American Nurses Association, *Facts, 1959,* 16.

34. Zella Bryant and Helen H. Hudson, "The Census of Nurses in Public Health," *American Journal of Nursing,* December 1962, 104; Vera Freeman, "Staff Nurse Vacancies in Selected Public Health Nursing Agencies—1961," *Nursing Outlook,* February 1962, 112; Mildred Gaynor, "Public Health Nursing for the Future," *Nursing Outlook,* July 1957, 399; "News Highlights," *American Journal of Nursing,* April 1958, 494.

35. Martha Z. Belote, "Nurses and the Army Build-Up," *American Journal of Nursing,* February 1962, 84–85; Lucile Petry Leone, "Where Will We Find Teachers?" *American Journal of Nursing,* December 1955, 1461; "News," *American Journal of Nursing,* September 1964, 44.

36. Joint Committee on Nursing in National Security, "Mobilization of Nursing in National Security," December 7, 1950, Dorothy J. Novello Memorial Library, Pennsylvania Nurses Association, 1; "News from All Quarters," *American Journal of Nursing,* January 1952, 90; ibid., September 1952, 1126, 1128; ibid., October 1952, 1262.

37. "Four-Point Plan Proposed in New York," *American Journal of Nursing,* June

1955, 732; "Rich Report," 208; "To Meet Our Nursing Needs," *American Journal of Nursing,* September 1958, 1266.

38. Lily Mary David, "The Economic Status of the Nursing Profession," *American Journal of Nursing,* July 1947, 456.

39. American Nurses Association, *Facts about Nursing, 1961* (New York: ANA, 1961), 80; "Professional Nursing School Admissions Decline in 1956," *American Journal of Nursing,* August 1957, 1006.

40. American Nurses Association, "Calling American Nurses to Action," *Convention Journal,* April 26, 1954, Mugar Library; Leone, "People, Nurses, and Students," 933; "Nurses for a Growing Nation," *American Journal of Nursing,* June 1957, 771.

41. American Nurses Association, "Nurse Supply Vital Issue," *Convention Journal,* June 12, 1958, Mugar Library; Nell V. Beeby, "It's June Again," *American Journal of Nursing,* June 1953, 673; Mary Roberts, "Married Nurses," *American Journal of Nursing,* November 1949, 680; Margaret Ranck, "Our Readers Say," *Nursing Outlook,* February 1953, 68.

42. David, "Economic Status," 458; Alice K. Leopold and Ewan Clague, "The BLS Survey," *American Journal of Nursing,* September 1958, 1261; Mary M. Richardson, "This Pay Cafeteria Works," *American Journal of Nursing,* August 1948, 496–497.

43. Roberts, "Married Nurses," 680.

44. Ranck, "Our Readers Say," 68.

45. C. B., "Letters—Pro and Con," *American Journal of Nursing,* April 1947, 255.

46. Ruth Roswal, "Letters—Pro and Con," *American Journal of Nursing,* July 1952, 792.

47. R.N., "Letters—Pro and Con," *American Journal of Nursing,* February 1953, 134.

48. Marian D. Austin, "Letters—Pro and Con," *American Journal of Nursing,* December 1953, 1414.

49. "They Donned Their Caps Again," *American Journal of Nursing,* July 1952, 842.

50. "Finding Nurses to Work Part Time," *American Journal of Nursing,* October 1943, 903–904; Partridge and Teter, "Soldiers' Wives," 567; "Part-time Nurses Are Helpful," *American Journal of Nursing,* November 1943, 1000–1001; "Part-time Nurses in Civilian Hospitals," *American Journal of Nursing,* March 1945, 178–181.

51. Hannah Burggren, "Part-time Nurses Can Be An Asset," *American Journal of Nursing,* November 1949, 681.

52. "Married Nurses and Hospital Staffing," *American Journal of Nursing,* April 1953, 438–439.

53. Jane Wood, "Letters," *American Journal of Nursing,* October 1966, 2176.

54. Helen L. McCarty, "Letters," *American Journal of Nursing,* March 1964, 66.

55. American Nurses Association, *Facts, 1961,* 7; American Nurses Association, *Facts, 1965,* 7; Arthur Testoff, Eugene Levine, Stanley E. Siegal, "The Part-Time Nurse," *American Journal of Nursing,* January 1964, 88–89.

56. Jeanne R. Shaw, "Letters," *American Journal of Nursing,* March 1970, 490.

57. Annabelle Peterson, "Report from the Committee on Nursing in National Defense," *American Journal of Nursing,* May 1957, 605.

58. Grace M. McFadden, "The Part-Time Nurse in the School," *Nursing Outlook,* October 1964, 62.

59. Mary Ann Staab, "Reclaim Those Lost Nurses!" *Nursing Outlook,* June 1970, 52–53.

60. American Nurses Association, *Facts, 1954,* 110; American Nurses Association, *Facts, 1957,* 116.

61. Roswal, "Letters," 792.

62. Marian Martin Pettengill, "Multilateral Collective Bargaining and the Health Care Industry: Implications for Nursing," *Journal of Professional Nursing,* September–October 1985, 277.

63. American Nurses Association, *Facts about Nursing, 1960,* (New York: ANA, 1960), 120, 132, 144, 151.

64. Evelyn Moses, "How Much Nurses Are Paid," *American Journal of Nursing,* May 1961, 92.

65. "They Donned Their Caps Again," 841–842.

66. Marion Pearce, "Something Really Refreshing," *American Journal of Nursing,* February 1962, 98.

67. Ibid., 98–99; Madeline Tabler, "Welcome Back to Nursing," *Nursing Outlook,* September 1966, 67–68; Elizabeth Worley, "Monsters, Monitors, and the Merry Mouseketeers," *American Journal of Nursing,* July 1969, 1444–1445.

68. Helen C. Anderson, "Refreshed Will Work Part-Time," *American Journal of Nursing,* October 1968, 2188–2189.

69. Dorothy E. Reese, D. Ann Sparmacher, Arthur Testoff, "How Many Caps Went On Again?" *Nursing Outlook,* August 1962, 519.

70. Tabler, "Welcome Back to Nursing," 68.

71. Pearce, "Something Really Refreshing," 98.

72. Isabel Jolley, "Letters—Pro and Con," *American Journal of Nursing,* October 1950, 6.

73. Reese, Sparmacher, and Testoff, "How Many Caps," 519.

74. Dorothy E. Reese, Stanley E. Siegel, Arthur Testoff, "The Inactive Nurse," *American Journal of Nursing,* November 1964, 125.

75. American Nurses Association, *Facts, 1954,* 91; "If You Ask Me," *American Journal of Nursing,* June 1959, 810–811.

76. Helen F. Callon and Margaret Farrell, "The Pregnant Hospital Employee," *American Journal of Nursing,* May 1963, 111.

77. "If You Ask Me," 810–811.

78. Lois Bookman, "Letters—Pro and Con," *American Journal of Nursing,* August 1950, 4.

79. George C. Schicks, "Hospital Turns Baby Sitter," *Nursing Outlook,* November 1954, 574–575.

80. "Day Care Services Help Recruit Nurses," *American Journal of Nursing,* September 1963, 97–100.

81. Luella Samuelson, "Our Summer Day Nursery," *American Journal of Nursing,* July 1952, 871.

82. Pauline Stack Cooper, "A Successful Venture in Day Nursery Care," *American Journal of Nursing,* March 1959, 364–365.

83. Goldin, *Understanding the Gender Gap,* 175–176, 181.

84. Melosh, *"Physician's Hand,"* 66.

85. Everett C. Hughes, Helen MacGill Hughes, and Irwin Deutscher, *Twenty Thousand Nurses Tell Their Story* (Philadelphia: Lippincott, 1958), 49–60.

86. "Did We Say 'Inactive?' " *Nursing Outlook*, November 1962, 721.

87. "They Donned Their Caps Again," 842.

88. Gladys Washington, "Letters—Pro and Con," *American Journal of Nursing*, October 1957, 1238.

89. S.M., "Letters—Pro and Con," *American Journal of Nursing*, April 1947, 255.

90. Austin, "Letters—Pro and Con," 1414.

91. Cooper, "Day Nursery Care," 365.

92. Jean Gaylord, "Letters," *American Journal of Nursing*, October 1968, 2118.

93. Anderson, "Refreshed Will Work Part Time," 2189; Jane Chips, "Letters," *American Journal of Nursing*, February 1968, 263.

CHAPTER 4

Dorothy Sue Cobble

RECAPTURING WORKING-CLASS FEMINISM

Union Women in the Postwar Era

Recent scholarship has created a new appreciation of the influence of wage-earning women on social movements formerly seen as shaped almost wholly by the middle class. But for a full account of female activism to take shape, the gender-conscious activities of working women must be examined within their working-class institutions as well as in the cross-class feminist organizations and movements in which they participated.[1] If feminism is taken to be a recognition that women as a sex suffer inequalities and a commitment to the elimination of these sex-based hierarchies, then the struggles of union women for pay equity and for mechanisms to lessen the double burden of home and work should be as central to the history of twentieth-century feminism as the battle for the enactment of the Equal Rights Amendment (ERA).[2]

In the decades between the suffrage movement and the 1960s, few women outside the National Woman's Party (NWP) described themselves as feminists. Yet many devoted their lives to the achievement of gender equality, and many considered the eradication of the problems faced by women to be their principal concern.[3] In particular, in the aftermath of the labor upheavals of the 1930s and undergirded by the continuing feminization of the workforce in the 1940s and 1950s, a sizable group of union women activists emerged whose politics were informed both by class and gender. They built the first sustained and widespread labor organizations in such female-dominated sectors as food service, sales, and telecommunications. And in conjunction with women activists in manufacturing industries, they used their unions as vehicles for the collective advancement of women. This essay details the activism and gender ideology of these union women activists.[4]

Recovering the activism of working-class women forces a reassessment of the conventional contours and definition of twentieth-century feminism. In the postwar years, the character of feminism changed—its goals and tactics shifted under the influence of working-class women—yet the vitality of the movement endured. Far from being an era of retreat for women's activism, working-class feminism flowered in the postwar decades, due in part to the steady increase of wage-earning women and the rise of union power.

The Rise and Feminization of the Labor Movement

The historian Nancy Gabin has suggested that once the experience of working-class women is incorporated into the history of American feminism, unions will emerge as crucial organizational vehicles for gender-based protest. My research confirms this notion. Indeed, in the 1940s and 1950s, labor organizations may have spurred feminism among wage-earning women much as civil rights and New Left organizations did for a very different group of women in the 1960s and 1970s.[5]

This emerging portrait of unionism as a vehicle for feminist aspirations stands in marked contrast to earlier scholarship on World War II and the immediate postwar era that viewed the relation between working women and unions as problematic. The first research monographs, for example, documented the poor treatment wartime "Rosies" received at the hands of the craft union brotherhoods and held the newer industrial unions responsible for the wholesale layoffs of women after the war and their subsequent rehire into lower grade classifications.[6] Writers depicted the powerful union institutions of the 1940s and 1950s as bureaucratic, male-dominated organizations with little sensitivity or interest in their now-diminished female constituency.[7] In part, scholars reached such negative assessments because they focused almost exclusively on male-dominated craft unions and unions in mass production. In part, the dismissal flowed from the widespread assumption that unions historically have been bastions of male power and unwavering agents of patriarchal impulses.[8]

Along with the new institutional labor history, more recent scholarship has begun to reassess the relation between female activism and unions.[9] Ruth Milkman's 1987 study of the auto and electrical industries in the 1940s, for example, argued that management must shoulder a major share of the blame for the job discrimination women suffered; critical management decisions involving layoff and rehiring of workers were not yet subject to union control.[10] In her 1991 book, *Feminism in the Labor Movement,* Nancy Gabin carried this reassessment into the 1950s and 1960s, contending that the new prominence given to women's issues during World War II by such progressive CIO unions as the United Auto Workers (UAW) was institutionalized after the war.[11] Recent theses on women unionists within the United Electrical Workers (UE) and the United Packinghouse Workers of America support Gabin's work.[12] The UAW women were not atypical: Working-class female activism survived and even flourished in the 1950s. This essay offers a framework within which to place the many excellent case studies of female activism in manufacturing unions that have emerged; it also extends and complicates the revisionist scholarship by analyzing the experience of women in service-sector unions.

Unions representing female-dominated industries not only experienced a surge of membership during wartime, but in contrast to the UAW, for example, their ranks continued to expand once the war ended. As women were laid off from jobs in auto plants and shipyards, they returned to the "pink collar" ghetto, swelling the membership of unions such as the AFL-affiliated Hotel Employees and Restaurant Employees (HERE), the National Federation of Telephone Workers (NFTW), and others.[13] By 1950, more than two hundred thousand female food-service workers were organized, for example, and they constituted 45 percent of the union's membership, almost double the prewar figure. Women also constituted 40 percent or more of organized telephone workers, department store employees, and bakery and confectionary workers, and they composed the majority of union members in such older female-dominated industries as garment and textile.[14]

Even within manufacturing, certain industries and shops maintained their wartime female majorities. Between 1946 and 1958, approximately 40 percent of all UE workers were female, slightly below their wartime peak of 49 percent, but certainly above their prewar numbers. Depending on the electrical product being manufactured, "women constituted from 25 to 75 percent of the workforce in any given shop."[15]

Overall, then, despite the wholesale layoffs of women in manufacturing during reconversion, women emerged in a much stronger position within the labor movement than before the war. Less than a tenth of union members (some eight hundred thousand) were female before 1940. Although female membership skyrocketed to 3 million (or 22 percent of organized workers) during wartime and then fell abruptly at the war's end, the number of union women throughout the late 1940s and 1950s still vastly exceeded its prewar level. By 1954, for example, close to 3 million women belonged to unions—some 17 percent of all union members.[16] Of equal importance, with their shift out of male-dominated organizations into unions in which women made up a large if not majority constituency, women union members now wielded considerable power at local and even national levels. They used this newfound power to reshape the labor movement along more gender-conscious lines and to win significant victories for wage-earning women.

The Demand for Collective Bargaining

By the 1930s and 1940s, a large proportion of working-class women (in contrast to middle-class and professional women) sought to realize their aspirations for workplace justice through collective bargaining. During the war and afterward, they institutionalized the new bargaining relations begun in the 1930s. For example, particularly in the expanding service-sector unions, women played an integral if not dominant part in the widespread and militant strikes following World War II.

With 350,000 employees on strike, 230,000 of them women, the 1947 nationwide telephone strike was the largest walkout of women in U.S. history. Carrying signs that proclaimed *The Voice with a Smile Will Be Gone for Awhile,* around-the-clock pickets paraded throughout the South, the Midwest, and in rural towns across America. In New Jersey alone, twelve thousand women operators left their posts, defying a state law that called for jail sentences and steep fines for utility strikers. The Washington, D.C., traffic (telephone operator) local, emboldened by some two hundred successful work stoppages in the previous year and a half, effectively cut off telephone access to the White House and other government offices. Although the NFTW failed to win its economic demands, the walkout ensured that the newly emerging system of collective bargaining would be retained in the telephone industry. By 1948, the fragmented and chaotic NFTW had reconstituted itself into a strong national union, the Communications Workers of America (CWA), which affiliated with the CIO in 1949.[17]

Women retail and food-service workers also challenged the authority of employers through shopfloor actions, mass picketing, and strikes, ensuring the permanent status of their fledgling collective bargaining system. In Oakland, California, women department store clerks walked out in November 1946 over union recognition, fomenting a general strike that involved more than 120,000 workers, shut down city services, and eventually forced department store owners to bargain. In the aftermath of a strike in which "Oakland's workers took control over the city . . . [determining] which businesses would open and what prices they would charge," a combined AFL and CIO political action committee also secured the election of four prolabor representatives to the Oakland City Council and the promise of city government neutrality in future labor disputes.[18] In the hotel and restaurant industries, major strikes occurred in Detroit, New York, San Francisco, and smaller communities across the country, resulting in significant advances in wages, hours, and working conditions. By the end of the 1940s, the separate-sex waitress locals moved ahead of all other food-service crafts in terms of size and influence. San Francisco waitresses doubled their 1940 membership, claiming more than six thousand women; the Los Angeles membership rose from eight hundred on the eve of wartime to close to five thousand by the early 1950s.[19]

From this position of power and influence, women unionists began to reformulate the agenda of their mixed-sex, class-based organizations, adding a strong feminist component to the legislative and collective bargaining activities of many unions. They led national struggles to close the wage gap between men and women, and they sought legislative and contract provisions that would protect the employment rights of women. They also lobbied for family support policies such as day care, maternity leave, and limitations on mandatory overtime.

Closing the Wage Gap

Although working-class women did not always agree on tactics or on what "gender equality" meant, women from a wide variety of unions viewed the achievement of economic equity with male workers as central to their postwar agenda. Historically, equal-pay proposals within the labor movement had been promulgated by male unionists concerned with preserving men's jobs. By the 1940s, however, equal pay became a demand supported largely by women.[20] In large part, equal pay became the rallying cry of women rather than men because as the workforce feminized and "pink collar" occupations increased, equal pay more often resulted in raising women's pay rather than preserving male employment. Whether a woman worked in a male-dominated or female-dominated occupation or industry proved critical in determining the impact of equal pay. Where employers preferred men and hired women only when they were cheaper, equal pay cost women their jobs. But in heavily feminized occupations or industries, sex typing could protect women from job loss. As one union feminist explained in 1946, although equal pay may have benefited men in male-dominated industries, "in her industry, where more than half the workers were women, equal pay was forced on the men." [21]

The shifting support for equal pay in the food-service unions offers one example of how feminization, combined with other historical trends, transformed equal pay from a male to a female demand. Waitresses opposed equal-pay resolutions introduced by men during World War I and again in the early 1930s when men still constituted close to half of all food servers. Waitresses rightly feared that employers would prefer male workers over female where women were restricted to eight hours a day (and covered by various other legal protections requiring benefits not enjoyed by men) or where men appeared to enjoy customer preference, such as in the dinner trade. But by the 1940s, as food service rapidly sexualized and feminized—approaching 70 percent female— waitresses reversed their stance and adopted equal pay as one of their primary goals. The experience of receiving equal pay during World War II (as a result of National War Labor Board rulings, new state laws, and contract provisions) may have made many loath to return to inequality. But waitresses also observed the reality of a changing food-service labor market—that is, that employers increasingly preferred female service workers to men even when required to pay men and women the same. Indeed, some employers preferred women even where state law provided benefits and protections to women only. The expanding service economy in the postwar decades undercut any remaining fears of job loss. [22]

Once a consensus existed on equal pay, women unionists pressed for such provisions in union contracts. In food service, for example, a majority of culinary locals negotiated equal-pay provisions by the late 1940s in response to lobbying from female members, and in California, a State Department of Industrial Relations survey revealed that every single culinary contract had identical hourly rates for waiters and waitresses by the late 1950s. [23]

Union women secured equal-pay clauses in other sectors of the economy as well. Angela Gizzi Ward, a business agent representing male and female clerks working at the Pacific Gas and Electric Company in San Francisco, won the first equal-pay provisions in that industry in 1947. In her small-group meetings with female clerks, the women always put equal pay at the top of their agenda, Ward remembered, but the male clerks, "very dignified with their white collars, natty ties and navy blue suits," were reluctant to admit that female clerks did the same work. Eventually, the men relented, and as a result, female salaries almost doubled. Next, Ward turned to getting women "the same right to promotion." [24]

In 1944, Mary Gannon, national NFTW chairwoman for telephone operators, editorialized in favor of equal pay for equal work in the NFTW newspaper, arguing that "rates must be established on the basis of the jobs being done [and] no other factor." Outraged to find in 1945 that "the highest rate for a woman in a clerk's job was lower than the lowest rate for a man, although the jobs were practically the same," women telephone operators pressed for change. When male unionists ignored "educational materials" on equal pay, NFTW Education Director Ruth Wiencek recalled in 1946, "our female workers . . . forced equal pay for equal work upon our plant divisions. We made it pretty embarrassing for them . . . [being] 60 percent women [we] are able to do that. It depends [also] on how vocal your women's groups are." [25]

From the 1940s until the mid-1950s, UE women launched a wholesale assault to eliminate wage inequities at General Electric (GE), Westinghouse, and other major employers. In what Lisa Kannenberg has deemed "an explosion of women's activism . . . in a decade generally viewed as the dark age of American feminism," UE women organized conferences on women's wages; they picketed, struck, and filed lawsuits in pursuit of wage equity. In 1945, they won a landmark case before the War Labor Board (WLB), in which, arguing that the "equal pay for equal work" standard should be expanded, they called for "the elimination of sex differentials in wages, the abolition of so-called women's jobs, and their re-evaluation from the minimum rate paid to common labor." Siding with the union, the WLB allowed wage adjustments because "the jobs customarily performed by women are paid less, on a comparative job content basis, than the jobs customarily performed by men," but GE ignored the order after the WLB disbanded.[26]

In response, UE made wage discrimination a top priority in the 1946 strike against GE, and they narrowed the wage gap significantly. UE turned inward in the late 1940s, buffeted by internal dissension and Cold War accusations, but by the early 1950s, the fight resumed. UE issued model contracts and pamphlets detailing how locals could "tackle rate discrimination." In 1951, the seventeen-thousand-member GE-Schenectady unit instigated noonday demonstrations and other work stoppages until they won rate increases on 373 job classifications.[27]

The International Union of Electrical Workers (IUE), UE's politically conservative rival, mirrored the UE's concern over wage inequities, especially after 1955 when many of UE's larger locals shifted to the IUE. In its 1954 contract proposals with GE and Westinghouse, the IUE called for "equal pay for equal work" and the elimination of "the special category of women's rates." Individual locals struck over gender wage inequities in 1953 and 1954, and in 1957, the IUE held its first National Women's Conference. The 175 women representatives named "equal pay" and "work and job advancement opportunities" as their top priorities. They urged GE and Westinghouse to grant "equal pay," explaining that "by this we mean not only equal pay for identical work but equal pay for work of equal value no matter where it is done." [28]

This cartoon from the *IUE News* of March 1, 1954, demonstrates union support for equal pay for equal work. *Courtesy of the IUE Archives, Special Collections and Archives, Rutgers University Libraries*

As is evident in the language of the women telephone and electrical workers, in the minds of women unionists and their supporters, pay equity was not limited to demands for "equal pay for equal work." They argued for fair "rates for the job irrespective of the sex of the worker." As Mary Anderson, the immigrant shoeworker who rose to be head of the U.S. Department of Labor

Women's Bureau, explained in 1944, "equal pay for equal work is a catchy slogan," but its effect is limited to situations where women "take the place of men in the same work that men have been doing." The "rate for the job" idea, remarkably similar to the comparable-worth arguments of the 1980s, questioned the very basis by which most women's jobs were evaluated and assigned pay grades. The potential for upgrading women's pay relative to men's was thus vastly improved; not only those jobs where women did exactly the same work as men, but also female-dominated job categories could theoretically be affected. As Cornelia Anderson of the Food, Tobacco, Agricultural and Allied Workers maintained: "From the point of view of industries like canneries and tobacco plants, which is largely women employing, . . . you can very beautifully establish the principal of equal pay for equal work and yet have large numbers of women making less than the men, simply because of women working in . . . entire jobs and categories that are always women-employing. When you talk about rate for the jobs . . . there is a possibility of re-studying and re-evaluating jobs throughout the plant [and of asking] why should a woman who sits and packs be paid 20 to 25 cents less than a man who sweeps the floor?" [29]

The key role played by trade union women in developing and carrying forward this new, more encompassing definition of pay equity is apparent in the actions of union women in individual unions like the UE.[30] The records of Women's Bureau meetings with women union leaders in the 1940s provide further evidence.[31] At one 1945 conference, for example, the Women's Bureau brought together thirty-one hand-picked women labor leaders representing more than 3 million women. Female labor leaders in attendance *agreed* that equal pay was "much too limiting and that the rate for the job was the proper approach." One woman unionist suggested a study "re-evaluating jobs through the plant," analyzing what each job "means and what it takes in skill and experience." "Women's skills have been under-estimated," the new director of the Women's Bureau, Frieda Miller, stated in support of the idea. Such an evaluation "would give us some basis for upping many of the types of occupations that women have had in the past." [32]

Another Women's Bureau special conference in 1945 drew up recommended language for state and federal equal-pay laws that would "cover situations where women replace men, where men and women are employed on comparable jobs, and employment of women in so-called women's jobs or women's departments." Although activists and the general public referred to the proposed bills and the laws eventually passed as "equal pay legislation," much of the discussion and activity centered on enacting legislation that would have the widest possible application. The federal equal-pay bill submitted later that year prohibited wage differentials for "work of a comparable character" or work requiring "comparable skills." [33]

The lobbying efforts of union women and their labor organizations proved critical in the passage of equal-pay legislation. At a 1946 Women's Bureau Conference, called "to coordinate passage of equal pay laws," the primarily union delegates decided to use the already established Union Women's Advisory Committee as the vehicle for disseminating information on state legislative campaigns involving equal pay. The committee had prominent women union leaders from almost all unions with large female memberships. The Women's Bureau contacted the appropriate woman on the committee when they knew of work being done in a state for equal pay, and those women became responsible for mobilizing union locals throughout the state.[34] Breakthroughs on the state level occurred quickly. Before World War II, only two states had enacted equal-pay laws. By 1955, the number had jumped to sixteen plus Alaska, and state legislation covered more than half of all wage-earning women.[35]

Advocates for the federal bill worked primarily through the National Committee on Equal Pay, a coalition that joined union women from the CWA, IUE, ACW, UAW, and other unions with middle-class groups such as the Business and Professional Women, American Association of University Women, General Federation of Women's Clubs, and the YWCA. The CIO endorsed and lobbied for the bill from its inception in 1945; the AFL finally adopted the CIO position in 1956 when the two labor federations merged.[36] In 1961, President Kennedy appointed as Women's Bureau director Esther Peterson, a long-time labor educator and union staffer (Peterson served as a labor lobbyist for the ACW in the 1940s and for the AFL-CIO Industrial Union Department in the 1950s). With "consummate lobbyist" Peterson at the helm of the campaign, the equal-pay proponents finally overwhelmed the opposition of the business community and conservative legislators in 1963. Peterson relied on her old labor network (which included Caroline Davis of the UAW and Helen Berthelot of the CWA), on the Kennedy administration's strong ties to organized labor, and on the personal support of administrative officials such as labor secretary Arthur Goldberg, a former CIO general counsel.[37]

But the legislative campaigns for equal pay fell short of the goals of their backers. Legislators watered down many equal-pay laws before passage, and once on the statute books courts interpreted them narrowly. Moreover, despite the best efforts of equal-pay advocates, the laws often protected only a small slice of the female labor force. In the 1963 Federal Equal Pay Act, for example, all references to "equal pay for work of comparable value" were deleted.[38]

Yet despite these limitations, equal-pay statutes have provided protection for the sizable number of women who do work in jobs "substantially equal" to those held by men and have been the basis for millions of dollars in wage adjustments.[39] Moreover, recent precedent-setting court decisions indicate that at least eleven states have "equal pay" laws with broad enough language that comparable-worth claims would be warranted. In 1992, a Massachusetts court awarded $1.5 million in back pay to forty-one women HERE cafeteria workers who claimed work comparable to male custodians. According to the presiding judge: "The legislative history of the Massachusetts law, an analysis of the debate over federal equal pay legislation, and precedents under similar Maine and Oregon laws convinced him that a narrow definition of comparable was not justified." [40] And lastly, as Alice Kessler-Harris concludes in *A Woman's Wage,* although the Equal Pay Act failed to dent labor-market segregation, the struggle for its enactment "expanded notions of justice, encouraging perceptions of male/female equality that had previously been invisible." [41]

Aware of the potential limitations of equal-pay laws, union women combined equal pay with other strategies for lifting women's wages, especially the wages of those in the "women-employing fields." At the 1945 and 1946 Women's Bureau conferences for trade union women, a "broad consensus" emerged in favor of "minimum wage by law as a means of underpinning the wages of low-paid workers." Not only did the value of women's jobs need to be reassessed and public opinion revised, but the delegates insisted that minimum-wage legislation was necessary if the wages of women *as a whole* were to be raised. Like the "rate for the job" campaign, minimum-wage legislation appealed to trade union women because it potentially could affect a broad cross-section of wage-earning women.[42]

Middle-class social reformers led the early struggles to enact minimum-wage laws,[43] but by the 1940s, trade union women dominated the coalition pushing for extended coverage and better enforcement. In particular, domestic workers, store clerks, restaurant employees, switchboard operators, and others in small businesses and intrastate industries not yet protected under the wage and hour provisions of the 1938 Fair Labor Standards Act needed coverage under state laws. Although their long-term objective was coverage for men as well as women, the existing statutes (almost all of which protected only women) were to be retained in the interim.[44]

Their efforts resulted in numerous new wage orders raising the legal minimums, the passage of *new* minimum-wage legislation protecting both men and women, and the amendment of existing laws to cover men. By 1950, the Women's Bureau announced that twenty-three new wage orders had been issued, sixty-two orders revised, and the laws extended to men in New York, Rhode Island, and Massachusetts. In fact, "all but a few minimum wage jurisdictions had taken some steps to better the legal minimum-wage situation of women in drug stores, restaurants, department and clothing stores, and other businesses in which sizable numbers of women earn their living." By the

1960s, out of forty-one state minimum-wage laws, thirty-one had been extended to protect men, and new higher wage orders had upped the earnings of millions of women.[45]

Another, more limited effort was directed at ending sex-based discrimination in hiring and promotion. In the decades following the war, UAW women, for example, repeatedly objected to such practices as sex-based seniority lists and the refusal of employers to hire married and older women.[46] And although bitter divisions occurred on these issues, a considerable number of women in the UE also fought to protect the jobs of married women and "to eliminate women's jobs as such."[47] UAW and UE women were not alone in their concerns. In 1944 the union women's advisory committee to the Women's Bureau issued "suggested standards for union contracts," which in addition to "no sex differentials in wage rates" urged "no discrimination based on sex or marital status," seniority provisions granting women the same rights to promotion and transfer as men, and no "sex-labeling of jobs or of departments."[48] They reiterated this demand in 1946 when a conference recommended the adoption of contract clauses prohibiting "discrimination based on sex, color, creed, and national origin . . . in all matters pertaining to hiring, upgrading, lay-off, wages, and seniority."[49]

As Nancy Gabin concludes, then, the 1940s did witness the beginnings of a critique of the sexual division of labor among working-class feminists. Nevertheless, the majority of union women failed to challenge consistently the sex typing of jobs and the discrimination in hiring and promotion that followed from sex-based occupational segregation, preferring instead to focus on expanding and upgrading the female sphere. This view predominated among women in service- and other female-dominated industries—the majority of women workers—and held considerable sway even in such classic male-dominated labor markets as auto until the 1960s and 1970s.[50] Mary Callahan, IUE executive board member and Kennedy appointee to the Commission on the Status of Women, explained how everyone including herself took job segregation in the 1940s and 1950s as a "way of life": "We never questioned it when they posted female and male jobs . . . we didn't realize it was discrimination. I never thought of it. I figured who the heck wants a job over there; it's a male job, you know."[51]

Recognizing Difference

In addition to approaches demanding more equitable compensation and treatment in the workplace, many women unionists supported policies that required differential treatment of the sexes. In particular, the majority of working-class feminists supported sex-based protective legislation until the 1970s, and opposed the Equal Rights Amendment because they feared its impact on the "hard won. labor laws protecting women in industry." [52] Their stance did not necessarily reflect a commitment to a more traditional view of women as the "weaker sex" or a belief in restricting women's labor force participation to ensure that women fulfilled their family responsibilities in the way deemed best by a patriarchal society. Instead, attitudes toward sex-based protective legislation often were based as much on judgments about the impact of individual laws on the working conditions and job opportunities of those in a particular occupation as on an ideological conviction concerning sexual difference. As noted by previous scholars, women competing directly with men often favored repeal because the laws put them at a disadvantage in securing employment; women who were more insulated from direct competition (usually as the result of strong sex typing of jobs) saw protective laws as beneficial. [53]

But determining the impact of particular laws could be difficult. Some laws provided what could be seen as better daily working conditions—rest breaks, seats, reductions in daily hours, assignment to the day shift, restrictions on lifting and other hazardous tasks—yet these same laws might also deprive women of more lucrative or interesting jobs working at night, on longer shifts, or involving physical labor. The key question was whether the so-called benefits outweighed the so-called opportunities. Were "light" or "women's" jobs actually easier than "heavy" or "men's" jobs? Would better-paying "men's" jobs really open up to women if protective laws were revoked? Would they open up even to women without access to training and/or women with family ties— ties that in themselves restricted when and for how long women could work? Would the economic advantages of these jobs offset the loss of female community and the sometime pleasure of the "emotion work" associated with the personal interactions often required in "women's" jobs? [54]

As the economic and cultural context for wage-earning women changed over the course of the twentieth century, opening up job opportunities for women and lessening the hardships associated with entering a "man's" job, union women altered their position on particular sex-based statutes, increasingly judging them to be more debilitating than protective. But the *idea* and *acceptance* of differential treatment as a means to achieve equality was never wholly abandoned. Certain statutes were hotly contested; others less so. Union women also debated the impact of the 1947 Status Bill proposal to allow "reasonable distinctions" between the sexes, but the recognition of gender difference and the felt need to restructure the work world to accommodate women's desire for family and personal time were retained. [55]

The controversy over night work affords one example of the division among union women over protective legislation and how and why perspectives on sex-based statutes could shift. The majority of labor organizations (and the

Women's Bureau) assessed night work restrictions as beneficial as late as the 1960s. Yet by the 1940s, women food servers reached the opposite conclusion regarding this particular "protection." Previously the "ownership" by men of certain night jobs such as late-night supper and cocktail service had gone undisputed, but the economic and social changes prompted by the war caused waitresses to reconsider their stance, for several reasons. First, once women entered these jobs during the war, they quickly learned how lucrative they could be. Second, since female wait staff functioned well in this new environment and drew in additional patrons, many employers desired the continued presence of women. Waitresses and waiters were now directly competing for these jobs. Last, the conventional moral reasons for prohibition—that is, that night work was dangerous to the health and well-being of mothers (and future mothers) and their children—appeared increasingly less persuasive to female servers by the 1940s, especially when balanced against their belief that being a good mother also meant providing economically for one's family.[56]

Sex-based statutes restricting the hours of women proved equally controversial. UAW women, continually fighting to maintain their toehold in a high-wage, male-dominated industry, developed a critique of such laws in the 1940s and became increasingly vocal in their demand for repeal. UAW feminist Dorothy Haener pinpointed the loss of her wartime inspector job as the turning point in her thinking. Management claimed the nine-hour law prevented them from hiring women on jobs where ten-hour shifts might occur; Haener never forgot the adverse impact of these "protections" on her life. By the 1960s, Caroline Davis, the head of the Women's Department of the UAW, represented the consensus of UAW female sentiment in her sharp objections to sex-based hours legislation. As a member of the Kennedy Presidential Commission on the Status of Women, Davis issued the sole dissenting report objecting to blanket endorsement of protective laws.[57]

In contrast to UAW activists, most women union leaders backed hours laws until the 1970s. When the Business and Professional Women of California proposed liberalizing the eight-hour work limit for women in 1957, for example, HERE women tenaciously defended the current laws, arguing that in their industry the advantages overrode the disadvantages. Overtime pay was minimal, and few waitresses feared they would be replaced by men willing to work long hours. The responsibilities of motherhood also necessitated legislated controls over hours. Without controls, "you are setting the stage for excessive compulsory overtime," explained one HERE female official. The concept of allowing voluntary overtime appeared reasonable in principle, argued another, but for nonprofessional women, an employer "suggestion becomes an order." Former hotel maid Bertha Metro, representing the primarily black Hotel and Club Service Workers, declared that many working women with children in day care would be forced to quit their jobs if required to work overtime. "Who's going to pick up the kids, cook their dinner?" asked Elizabeth Kelley of the San Francisco Waitresses' Union. "We're happy that we have a little legislation, and we'll fight to keep it. We're not a bunch of college women, we're waitresses." [58]

In explaining the divisions among working women over night work and overtime legislation, the 1968 insights of industrial relations scholar Alice Cook still appear persuasive. Women will resist such legislation, she argued, in industries where men and women work many of the same jobs and in certain individual cases where women are primary wage earners and are available to work overtime. But where the majority of workers are "secondary," where they have preschool and school-age children, and where their "jobs are insulated to some considerable degree from competition with men," they will probably not assess the legislation as burdensome.[59]

Other laws based on difference proved less controversial than those limiting hours and night work. At the 1945 Women's Bureau conference for union women, Julia Parker of the operator's division of the International Brotherhood of Electrical Workers (IBEW) raised one of the few objections to the endorsement of paid maternity leave (with job guarantee on return) and disability payments during pregnancy. Intoning that "inequality can come in the back door as well as the front," Parker feared that seeking "to impose upon industry a special payment for women" jeopardized claims for "equal pay and equal treatment of women as citizens and workers." Pregnancy was simply "one of nature's discriminations. On what grounds do you ask for pay?" Her dissent was dealt with summarily. "We make no bones about the fact that there are certain things women need that men don't," one delegate countered. Another remarked dryly that pregnancy was not "developed by women for their entertainment"; it was a social function and as such should be borne by the community.[60]

Union women successfully transformed their consensus on this issue into concrete legislative and contract gains. Women in HERE, CWA, UE, IUE, UAW, and other unions were instrumental in amending state unemployment insurance laws to include disability payments during pregnancy and to allow for more control by the pregnant woman over the timing and length of the leave. They also secured contract clauses that offered paid maternity benefits, job protection, transfer rights, no loss of seniority, use of accrued sick leave, and health insurance during pregnancy.[61]

Lastly, during and after the war, women unionists devoted attention to family support policies such as child care and nursery schools.[62] HERE women in San Francisco and New York, for example, lobbied vigorously for local, state, and federal funding of child-care centers and income tax breaks for working mothers. Waitresses' Local 48 in San Francisco helped instigate a Central Labor Council "Committee on the Care of Children of Working Mothers" in 1942. Through this group and others, they urged the permanent state financing of child-care centers throughout the 1940s and early 1950s and created such a furor over the discontinuation of federal funding for child care after the war that San Francisco's city government became one of the few in the country to provide municipal funds for child-care centers.[63] In addition to "pushing for child care centers in their communities," the Women's Committee in New York's hotel workers local used the union's welfare department to advise members about child-care facilities, adoption of children, unemployment insurance, and divorce proceedings.[64] Seattle waitress leader Beulah Compton won reelection in her thirty-seven-hundred-member local in 1953 on a platform promising a union-sponsored nursery for children during afternoon and evening union meetings. Once elected, Compton also arranged for an older, former waitress to be on call through the union when working waitresses needed emergency child care.[65]

Conclusion

Recovering the traditions of working-class feminism broadens our understanding of the goals and strategies pursued by U.S. feminists. Working-class women articulated and acted on a distinctive feminist vision, one that did not always define equality or advancement in the same way as middle-class women did. First, class loyalties and communitarian "class" values shaped their concepts of justice and equality.[66] Union feminists sought advancement as a group, not merely as individuals. They argued that economic justice and fair treatment for the majority of women can be provided only through employee representation and collective power, not through individual upward mobility. Rather than focus primarily on moving individual women into the higher-paying jobs held by men, they opted for improvements in the jobs traditionally held by women. Upward mobility for the few did not seem as important as the economic advancement of the many. They sought security, respect, and dignity for the millions of women who were likely to remain in the "pink collar" ghetto.

As a result, at times they ended up at odds with middle-class feminists, who often were rooted in the liberal traditions of individualism and upward mobility. Mary Callahan of the IUE expressed her differences with middle-class feminists in clear class-based terms: "They're snobs . . . they're suspect. Some of them are looking at, 'How can *I* become the manager. Not, 'How can *we* get along and improve our lot in life?' It's 'How do *I* get up there.' "[67]

Second, the gender equality envisioned by working-class feminists parted ways with the more strictly "equal rights" approach epitomized by the National Woman's Party. Although some of the UAW women and others pushed for explicit, sex-blind policies, as Nancy Gabin has demonstrated, the majority of union activists advocated a different kind of feminism, one that pushed for upgrading and revaluing the jobs done by women, rather than moving women into jobs usually held by men.[68] Indeed, anticipating insights that resurfaced among feminists only in the 1980s, they argued that equality cannot always be achieved through identity in treatment and that differences must be accommodated. Justice and equality should not have to be based on "sameness." They wanted "equality" *and* special treatment, and they did not see the two as incompatible. In HERE International Vice-President Myra Wolfgang's words: "The chief conflict between those who support the ERA and those of us who oppose it, is not whether women should be discriminated against, but what constitutes a discrimination. We, who want equal opportunities, equal pay for equal work and equal status for women, know that frequently we obtain real equality through a difference in treatment, rather than through identity in treatment. . . . We do want our cake and eat it too."[69]

Third, rather than deny the tension between home and work responsibilities, they sought to design policies that accommodated and recognized women's dual commitments.[70] They wanted to ease the burden of family responsibilities by restructuring the workplace as well as by providing family support measures such as paid maternity leave and child care. Union feminists often saw the demands of family as taking precedence over expanding workplace opportunity, yet it cannot be assumed that this emphasis was necessarily a submission to the larger patriarchal culture or to corporate capitalism. As Myra Marx Ferree has pointed out, "placing career needs and goals in the central position is . . . often taken as a model of independence of women, and [thus] working-class women are seen as deficient."[71]

Union feminists might be faulted for reifying sex differences, but the problem of changing male behavior in the public and private spheres was formidable and not easily subject to rational persuasion. Many wage-earning women no longer assume, as they did in the 1940s and 1950s, "that only women could care adequately for children" and that men will never take on responsibility for domestic chores.[72] Yet despite the pursuit of equality in the private sphere as well as the public, men's share of housework and child care is still minimal; the work world remains structured on the male model of full-time, continuous commitment; low-cost, quality child care is not available for most working women; and even the most committed feminists waver in the face of child-rearing advisers who insist in the mass media that mothers should stay home with their children in their early years, maybe longer.[73] In the face of such constraints, union women's attempts to accommodate women's dual responsibilities at work and home reflected a pragmatic realism as much as a commitment to maintaining the sexual division of labor.

The record of working-class activism in the postwar decades also provides new perspectives on scholarly controversies about the era itself. For one, the wartime experience for wage-earning women may have had more lasting consequences than for elite women. To dredge up William Chafe's oft-debated thesis, the war may have actually been a "watershed" for working-class women.[74] A consensus on equal pay emerged among working-class women for the first time during the war. Moreover, many began qualifying their universal support for protective legislation. A number even came to condemn sex-based job classification systems as discriminatory. In short, the war had a dramatic and lasting impact on the gender ideology of working-class women and the strategies they pursued in attaining equality.[75]

Of equal importance, the beachhead of equality secured during the war was not totally surrendered. Wartime feminism found an institutional home in the heavily female service-sector unions as well as in such male-dominated organizations as the UAW.[76] Although the 1940s witnessed the most militant and perhaps widespread instances of gender-conscious activism among union women, the campaigns for equal pay, minimum wage, pregnancy benefits, and other rights extended into the 1950s and beyond. Not only is there greater continuity between the wartime and postwar era than has been recognized, but progress on gender issues was an important element in that continuity.[77]

For working women, the postwar era was a period of mass mobilization, intense activity, and even advancement.[78] Recent accounts of these decades that view with surprise the significant policy changes occurring in the absence of a "widespread social movement" have ignored the rise and feminization of labor organizations—one of the primary vehicles through which wage-earning women have advanced their gender interests.[79] To the extent that unionism gained power in the United States by World War II and to the extent that women gained control over parts of that movement, it should come as no surprise that the economic and social agenda of wage-earning women moved ahead in this period.

Finally, the decisive and widespread mobilization of union women and their gender-conscious activism in the postwar era prompts a remapping of the contours of twentieth-century feminism. Our understanding of the cycles of feminism in the twentieth century has been class biased, based primarily on the activities of elite women. The postwar years, judged as quiescent because the middle-class traditions of equal rights feminism were subdued, were neither doldrum years nor an era in which feminism was kept alive solely by elite women in the National Woman's Party or by middle-class reformers within a "Women's Bureau coalition." [80]

Working-class feminists bore the torch of gender equality and justice in the 1940s and 1950s, and many lived to see the realization of their ideas in the early 1960s.[81] As Cynthia Harrison points out, Women's Bureau Director Esther Peterson "did not create a new agenda—she simply sought the implementation of the program that labor women had long supported: equal pay legislation and a national commission on women." The long-awaited Commission on the Status of Women confirmed the priorities of union women: they rejected the philosophy of the Equal Rights Amendment and recommended increased minimum wages, equal pay, paid maternity leave, and equalization of employment opportunities.[82]

Yet by the late 1960s the postwar generation of working-class feminists felt the sting of rejection by the younger equal rights feminists who came to dominate the movement. But in a grand pendulum swing, in the 1990s a new gender politics has again taken hold, which, like its predecessor in the postwar decades, is rooted in the labor movement and "accepts difference as a strategic basis for making demands that will ultimately move toward equality." [83] Whether the contemporary comparable-worth movement and other present-day attempts to alter the values and structures of the workplace will move women closer to equality is difficult to predict, but one can only hope that as women's minority status in the workforce recedes into the past, so will the subordination that has accompanied it.

NOTES

1. A similar argument has been made in regard to women of color. Their activities within their community-based organizations must be taken into consideration for a full history of feminism to emerge. See Marie Laberge, " 'We Are Proud of Our Gains': Wisconsin Black Women's Organizational Work in the Post World War II Era," paper presented at the Eighth Berkshire Conference on the History of Women, June 9, 1990; and Jacqueline Jones, *Labor of Love, Labor of Sorrow: Black Women, Work and the Family, From Slavery to the Present* (New York: Vintage, 1985), 232–330.

2. Nancy Cott's definition of feminism is similarly inclusive. Feminism, in Cott's view, is "an integral tradition of protest against arbitrary male dominion." See Cott, "What's in a Name? The Limits of 'Social Feminism'; or, Expanding the Vocabulary of Women's History," *Journal of American History,* December 1989, 809. Problems arise in applying the label when the historian must evaluate whether the policies and actions of any one group preserved or challenged male power. Moreover, the consequences of certain acts may be at odds with the motivations of the adherents, may have a differential impact on different groups of women, or both. Evaluating whether protective legislation was a feminist strategy, for example, is fraught with many of these dilemmas.

3. For recent accounts of feminist activism, see Nancy Cott, *The Grounding of Modern Feminism* (New Haven: Yale University Press, 1987), for the pre–World War II era; and Cynthia Harrison, *On Account of Sex: The Politics of Women's Issues, 1945–1968* (Berkeley: University of California Press, 1988), for the postwar decades.

4. The limited scope of this essay and the preliminary nature of my research into unions other than HERE prohibit any speculations at this point concerning ethnic and racial variations. Most of the union leaders I quote in this paper are white. With additional research, I hope to incorporate the voices of minority women and more fully detail the sentiments of the rank and file.

5. Nancy Gabin, *Feminism in the Labor Movement: Women and the United Auto Workers, 1935–1975* (Ithaca: Cornell University Press, 1990), 232. See also Sara Evans, *Personal Politics* (New York: Vintage, 1979), 212–232.

6. For example, D'Ann Campbell, *Women at War with America: Private Lives in a Patriotic Era* (Cambridge: Harvard University Press, 1984), 148–154; and Lyn Goldfarb, *Separated and Unequal: Discrimination against Women Workers After World War II*, Union for Radical Political Economics pamphlet, Washington, D.C., 1976.

7. For a synthetic work illustrating this view, see James R. Green, *The World of the Worker: Labor in Twentieth-Century America* (New York: Hill and Wang, 1980), 174–248.

8. Heidi Hartmann's influential article "Capitalism, Patriarchy, and Job Segregation by Sex," *Signs*, Spring 1976, 137–169, argued that working-class men through their unions had played a central role in maintaining gender inequality.

9. See Ruth Milkman, "Gender and Trade Unionism in Historical Perspective," in *Women, Politics and Change*, ed. Patricia Gurin and Louise Tilly (New York: Russell Sage Foundation, 1990), 87–107. See also Dorothy Sue Cobble, "Rethinking Troubled Relations between Women and Unions: Craft Unionism and Female Activism," *Feminist Studies*, Fall 1990, 519–548.

10. Ruth Milkman, *Gender at Work: The Dynamics of Job Segregation by Sex During World War II* (Urbana: University of Illinois Press, 1987), chap. 7.

11. Ibid., chaps. 5, 8; Gabin, *Feminism in the Labor Movement*, 188–236; Milkman, "Gender and Trade Unionism in Historical Perspective," 87–107.

12. See Lisa Kannenberg, "From World War to Cold War: Women Electrical Workers and Their Union, 1940–1955," Master's thesis, University of North Carolina, Charlotte, 1990; and Bruce Fehn, "Striking Women: Gender, Race, and Class in the United Packinghouse Workers of America," Ph.D. dissertation, University of Wisconsin, Madison, 1991.

13. Women's share of membership in unions like the UAW dropped from a wartime peak of 25 percent in 1944 to 10 percent during reconversion. Milkman, *Gender At Work*, 13; and Nancy Gabin, "Trade Union Feminism: Advocating Women's Rights and Gender Equity in the UAW, 1935–1975," talk presented at the annual meeting of the Organization of American Historians, 27 March 1988, Reno, Nevada. The California Department of Industrial Relations studied the relation between women and unions over a seven-year span in the 1940s and found that the number of women plummeted in unions such as the Machinists, the Boilermakers, and the transport workers after the war, but in a significant number of "friendly" unions—ones representing traditionally female occupations—women maintained their numbers and continued their upward spiral in the late 1940s. Campbell, *Women at War with America*, 141–143.

14. See Dorothy Sue Cobble, *Dishing It Out: Waitresses and Their Unions in the*

Twentieth Century (Urbana: University of Illinois, 1991), tables 5A–5C, 6, 7, 8. See also Jack Barbash, *Unions and Telephones: The Story of the Communications Workers of America* (New York, 1952), chaps. 1, 9; Thomas R. Brooks, *Communications Workers of America: Story of a Union* (New York: Mason/Charter, 1977), 63, 238; John Schacht, *The Making of Telephone Unionism, 1920–1947* (New Brunswick, N.J.: Rutgers University Press, 1985), 26–27, 166; George Kirstein, *Store and Unions: A Study of the Growth of Unionism in Dry Goods and Department Stores* (New York: Fairchild Publications, 1950), 217. For national figures gathered by the Women's Bureau, see "Summary of Conference of Trade Union Women and Women's Bureau on War and Postwar Problems of Working Women," April 19–20, 1945, File "1945 Union Conference," Box 1544, Records of the Women's Bureau, National Archives and Record Service, Washington, D.C. (hereafter cited as RG-86).

15. Kannenberg, "From World War to Cold War," 12, 69, 73; Milkman, *Gender at Work,* 13.

16. Ruth Milkman, "Union Responses to Workforce Feminization in the United States," in *The Challenge of Restructuring: North American Labor Movements Respond,* ed. Jane Jenson and Rianne Mahon (Philadelphia: Temple University Press, 1993), 226–250.

17. Schacht, *The Making of Telephone Unionism,* chap. 8; Philip Foner, *Women and the American Labor Movement: From World War I to the Present* (New York, Free Press, 1980), 400–402; *Telephone Worker,* December 1945 and March 1947.

18. George Lipsitz, *Class and Culture in Cold War America: "A Rainbow at Midnight"* (South Hadley, Mass.: J. F. Bergin Publishers, 1982), 81–84; Kirstein, *Stores and Unions,* 102; Interview with Marion Sills, conducted by author, 1977, Women in California Oral History Collection, California Historical Society, San Francisco.

19. Cobble, *Dishing It Out,* chap. 4 and table 8.

20. There is no full book-length treatment of the history of pay equity. Consult Alice Cook, "Equal Pay: A Multinational History and Comparison," manuscript in possession of the author; and Alice Kessler-Harris, *A Woman's Wage: Historical Meanings and Social Consequences* (Lexington: University Press of Kentucky, 1990): 83–112.

21. "Summary of Discussion at WB Conference with Women Union Leaders, October 30–31, 1946," File "Conf. 10/46," Box 897, RG-86.

22. For documentation, consult Cobble, *Dishing It Out,* esp. chap. 1, pp. 152–156, table 1. Lisa Kannenberg, "From World War to Cold War," 4, 11–42, shows how in the electrical industry pay equity shifted from an issue motivated by the desire to protect male wage rates to an issue of gender equality.

23. Consult Dorothy Sue Cobble, "Sisters in the Craft: Waitresses and Their Unions in the Twentieth Century," Ph.D. dissertation, Stanford University, 1986, 403–408; Cobble, *Dishing It Out,* 154–155.

24. Interview with Angela Gizzi Ward, conducted by author, 1976, Women in California Oral History Collection, California Historical Society.

25. Transcript, "Women's Bureau Conference for Women Union Leaders, October 1946," 35, File "Conf. 10/46," Box 897, RG-86; *Telephone Worker,* April 1944 and September 1944.

26. See Milkman, *Gender at Work,* 79–83; Kannenberg, "From World War to Cold War," 16–19, 31–38, 101. Quote from 95 and 103.

27. Kannenberg, "From World War to Cold War," 7, 43–44, 81–90.

28. *IUE News,* April 7, 1952, December 21, 1953, January 18, 1954, June 6, 1955,

August 16, 1954, May 13, 1957, June 24, 1957, June 9, 1958; see also IUE Archives, Box 2186, 1957 Women's Conference, Special Collections, Alexander Library, Rutgers University, New Brunswick, New Jersey.

29. Alice Angus to Frieda Miller, August 21, 1944, Box 901, RG-86; Mary Anderson to Blanch Freedman, Exec-Sec, New York WTUL, June 7, 1944, File "WTUL," Box 852, RG-86; Transcript, "Conference of Trade Union Women," April 1945, 69, File "1945 Conference," Box 1544, RG-86.

30. Kannenberg, "From World War to Cold War," 11–42.

31. Summary, "Conference of Trade Union Women," April 1945, 2, File "1945 Conference," Box 1544, RG-86.

32. Transcript, "Conference of Trade Union Women," April 1945, 56, 67, 181, File "1945 Conference," Box 1544, RG-86; "Summary of Discussion at Women's Bureau Conference with Trade Union Leaders," October 1946, 2, File "Conf. 10/46," Box 897, RG-86; Transcript, "Women's Bureau Conference with Women Union Leaders, October 1946, 24–5, 66, File "Conf. 10/46," Box 897, RG-86; Summary, "Conference of Trade Union Women," April 1945, 19, File "1945 Conference," Box 1544, RG-86.

33. Sheet entitled, "March 17, 1945 Conference," File "Conf. 10/46," Box 897, RG-86; Transcript, "Women's Bureau Conference for Women Trade Union Leaders, October 1946," 13, File "Conf. 10/46," Box 897, RG-86.

34. Transcript, "Women's Bureau Conference for Women Union Leaders, October 1946," 13, File "Conf. 10/46," Box 897; "Summary of Discussion of Women's Bureau Conference with Women Union Leaders, 1946," 1, File "Conf. 10/46," Box 897, RG-86.

35. Susan M. Hartmann, *American Women in the 1940s: The Home Front and Beyond* (Boston: Twayne, 1982), 134; Leopold, "Federal Equal Pay Legislation," 21; *CWA News*, June 1955, 5; Cobble, *Dishing It Out*, 155–156. By 1963, 22 states had equal pay statutes. See Transcript, "Women's Bureau Conference for Women Union Leaders, October 1946," 40, File "Conf 10/46," Box 897, RG-86 for a discussion of the organizations active in the equal-pay campaigns.

36. Leopold, "Federal Equal Pay Legislation," 19–21; *IUE News*, March 30, 1953 and June 6, 1955; *Telephone Worker*, October 1945, 9, 11. See also *CWA News*, March 1948, 3; June 1950, 1, 5; May 1951, 7; January 1954, 5; February 1954, 6; April 1957, 2. According to Harrison, the National Committee to Defeat the UnEqual Rights Amendment set up the equal-pay committee in 1945. Mary Anderson chaired the committee, expanding and renaming it in the 1950s. Harrison, *On Account of Sex*, 39–51.

37. Harrison, *On Account of Sex*, 89–105; Gabin, *Feminism in the Labor Movement*, 189–194.

38. Cobble, *Dishing It Out*, 155–156; Harrison, *On Account of Sex*, 104–105.

39. In the first ten years of its enforcement alone, discrimination victims received $84 million in back pay. Harrison, *On Account of Sex*, 105.

40. *Jancey v. Everett School Committee*, Massachusetts Superior Court, Case No. 89–3807, August 13, 1992, as reported in Bureau of National Affairs, *Daily Labor Report*, August 20, 1992.

41. Kessler-Harris, *A Woman's Wage*, 112.

42. Summary, "Conference of Trade Union Women," 1945, 2, 5, 18, File "1945 Conference," Box 1544, RG-86; Gertrude Lane to Hugo Ernst, "11/12/46 Report on

the Meeting of the Union Women Advisory Committee," Reel 145, HERE International Archives, Washington, D.C.

43. See Susan Lehrer, *Origins of Protective Labor Legislation for Women, 1905–1925* (Albany: SUNY, 1987); Elizabeth Baker, *Protective Labor Legislation with Special Reference to Women in the State of New York* (New York: Columbia University Press, 1925); Alice Kessler-Harris, *Out to Work: A History of Wage-Earning Women in the United States* (New York: Oxford University Press, 1982); Ronnie Steinberg, *Wages and Hours: Labor and Reform in Twentieth Century America* (New Brunswick, N.J.: Rutgers University Press, 1982).

44. See *Catering Industry Employee*, July 1941; August 1941, 16; San Francisco Local Joint Executive Board (LJEB) Minutes, March 18, 1941, 6 May 1941, April 18, 1950, September 5, 1950, February 5, 1952, Hotel Employees and Restaurant Employees, Local 2 Archives, San Francisco, California; News Release, April 12 1976, Photo Files—Myra Wolfgang, HERE International Archives, Washington, D.C.; and Cobble, "Sisters in the Craft," 285–288. See also *CWA News*, June 1956, 5; *IUE News*, June 24, 1957.

45. "Summary of Discussion at Women's Bureau Conference, 1946," File "Conf, 10/46," Box 897, RG-86; Transcript, "Women's Bureau Conference with Women Union Leaders, October 1946," 205, File "Conf. 10/46," Box 897, RG-86; Summary, "Conference of Trade Union Women, 1945," File "1945 Conference," Box 1544, RG-86; Transcript, "Conference of Trade Union Women, 1945," 55, Box 898, RG-86; *Catering Industry Employee*, September 1940; USDL release, January 11, 1950, "Survey Material for Bulletin 227," Box 991, RG-86. Barbara Babcock et al., *Sex Discrimination and the Law: Causes and Remedies* (Boston and Toronto: Little, Brown, 1975).

46. Gabin, *Feminism in the Labor Movement*, chap. 4.

47. Kannenberg, "From World War to Cold War," 30, 43–67; see also *Telephone Worker*, January 1945, 7, for CWA proposed strike action on behalf of discharged married woman, and *IUE News*, February 16, 1953, for a similar example from the electrical industry.

48. "Suggested Standards for Union Contracts," File "Union Conf., February 1944," Box 901, RG-86.

49. Summary, "Conference of Trade Union Women, 1945," 12, 23, File "1945 Conference," Box 1544, RG-86. See also comments by Ruth Young of the UE and Cornelia Anderson of the Food, Tobacco, Agricultural and Allied Workers in Transcript, "Conference of Trade Union Women, 1945," 127, 138, Box 898, RG-86.

50. Kessler-Harris, *Out to Work*, chap. 11; Dorothy Sue Cobble, "'Drawing the Line': The Construction of a Gendered Work Force in the Food Service Industry," in *Work Engendered: Toward a New History of American Labor*, ed. Ava Baron (Ithaca: Cornell University Press, 1991), 216–242. Even within the UAW, Gabin notes that "not all female union leaders rejected the longer-standing emphasis on gender differences." Gabin, *Feminism in the Labor Movement*, 140.

51. Interview with Mary Callahan, conducted by Alice M. Hoffman and Karen Budd, 1976, Twentieth Century Trade Union Woman: Vehicle for Social Change, Oral History Project, Institute of Labor and Industrial Relations, University of Michigan/Wayne State University.

52. Editorial in *Hotel and Club Voice*, official newspaper of HERE Local 6 in New York City. April 19, 1947, 7. In 1945 a coalition of some 43 national organizations,

including 26 trade union groups, formed the "Committee to Defeat the Unequal Rights Amendment." The AFL-CIO and most international unions officially maintained their opposition to the ERA until 1973. Dorothy S. Brady, "Equal Pay for Working Women," *Annals of the American Academy,* May 1947, 11; James Kenneally, "Women in the U.S. and Trade Unionism," in *The World of Women's Trade Unionism: Comparative Historical Essays,* ed. Norbert C. Soldon (Westport, Conn.: Greenwood Press, 1985), 79–83. For a thorough statement of this position as late as 1972, see Bernard Rosenberg and Saul Weinman, "Young Women Who Work: An Interview with Myra Wolfgang," *Dissent,* Winter 1972, 29–36.

53. For example, see Elizabeth Baker, *Protective Labor Legislation With Special Reference to Women in the State of New York* (New York: Columbia University Press, 1925), 425; Alice Cook, "Women and American Trade Unions," *Annals of the American Academy of Political and Social Science,* January 1968, 124–132; Nancy Schrom Dye, *As Equals and as Sisters: Feminism, Unionism and the Women's Trade Union League of New York* (Columbia: University of Missouri Press, 1980), 152, 158.

54. The concept of "emotion work" is borrowed from Arlie Hochschild, *The Managed Heart: The Commercialization of Human Feeling* (Berkeley: University of California Press, 1983), 7. In Hochschild's view, many women's jobs involve the expression of emotions. When the worker controls these interpersonal encounters, "emotion work" can be rewarding. But when the employer manages these encounters, requiring the expression of certain emotions (sympathy, cheerfulness, attentive listening, etc.) and the suppression of others (anger, irritation, depression), the worker must expend considerable effort to produce the desired emotion. Hochschild labels this effort "emotional labor."

55. In the discussion over the 1947 Status Bill, a bill that proposed to set up a commission to study the status of women and the prohibition of sex discrimination but the continuation of protective legislation where "reasonable," union women evidenced considerable concern that differentiation be made on "reasonable" grounds only and that "reasonable distinctions" be defined clearly. They did not want sex-linked distinctions made that could later be used to justify discriminatory practices and female subordination. Harrison, *On Account of Sex,* 26–28.

56. See Cobble, " 'Drawing the Line,' " 216–242.

57. Interview with Dorothy Haener, conducted by Lyn Goldfarb, Lydia Kleiner, and Christine Miller, 1976, Twentieth-Century Trade Union Woman: Vehicle for Social Change, Oral History Project, Institute of Labor and Industrial Relations, University of Michigan/Wayne State University; Carol Kates, "Working-Class Feminism and Feminist Unions," *Labor Studies Journal,* Summer 1989, 28–45.

58. Unidentified newspaper clippings, Bertha Metro Collection, Box 3, File 24, San Francisco Historical Society, San Francisco; Myra Wolfgang to James Del Rio, May 31, 1968, Myra Wolfgang Collection, Box 1, File 3, Walter Reuther Archives, Wayne State University, Detroit, Michigan. For later examples, see Alice Cook, "Women and American Trade Unions," *Annals of the American Academy* 375 (January 1968): 12; *Hotel Bar Restaurant Review,* October 1969.

59. Cook, "Women and American Trade Unions," 127.

60. Transcript, "Conference of Trade Union Women, 1945," 103–106, Box 898, RG-86.

61. "Suggested Standards for Union Contracts," File "Union Conference, February 1944," Box 901, RG-86; Summary of Conference, 1945, 22, File "1945 Conference,"

Box 1544, RG-86; Report, "1945 Women's Bureau Conference on War and Postwar Problems for Trade Union Women," 6, 21, Box 1544, RG-86. *Catering Industry Employee,* December 1951, 14; *Cafeteria Call,* New York, February 1952, 6; *CWA News,* March 1951, 3, August 1958, 3, June 1969, 9; Kannenberg, "From World War to Cold War," 38; *IUE News,* April 7, 1952. For an example of the key role played by union women in amending state unemployment insurance to allow disability payments for pregnancy, see Elizabeth Kelly Correspondence, Waitresses Local 48; Local Joint Executive Board Minutes, September 5, 1950, July 17, 1952, HERE Local 2 Files, San Francisco.

62. Report, "1945 Women's Bureau Conference on War and Postwar Problems for Trade Union Women," 26–27, Box 1544, RG-86.

63. *Cafe Call,* October 1942, 5–6; *Catering Industry Employee,* July 1953, 30. *Hotel and Club Voice,* February 14, 1948, June 25, 1949, 4. *Local 240 News,* February 1954, Reel 342, HERE Files. John Shelley to San Francisco Labor Council, August 28, 1942, File "Committee on Care of Children of Working Mothers, 1942," Box 41, San Francisco Labor Council Records, Bancroft Library, University of California at Berkeley; Helen Wheeler to John O'Connell, April 2, 1943, File "Local 110, 1943," Box 46, ibid.; Minutes and letters, File "Committee on Care of Working Mothers, 1943," Box 44, ibid., File "LJEB, 1951," Box 65, ibid. Waitresses' Local 48 Minutes, August 10, 1949, July 26, 1950, September 5, 1950, January 16, 1951, HERE Local 2 Files.

64. *Hotel and Club Voice,* September 7, 1940, 8, March 23, 1946, 2, June 25, 1949, 4.

65. HERE Local 240 Records, 1951–1954, and *240 News,* February 1954, Reel 342, Local Union Records, HERE Files; interview with Beulah Compton, conducted by Elizabeth Case, 1978, Twentieth Century Trade Union Woman: Vehicle for Social Change, Oral History Project, Institute of Labor and Industrial Relations, University of Michigan/Wayne State University.

66. See Maurine Greenwald, "Working-Class Feminism and the Family Wage Ideal: The Seattle Debate on Married Women's Right to Work, 1914–1920," *Journal of American History,* June 1989, 118–149; and Dolores Janiewski, *Sisterhood Denied: Race, Gender, and Class in a New South Community* (Philadelphia: Temple University Press, 1985).

67. Interview with Mary Callahan, conducted by Alice M. Hoffman and Karen Budd, 1976, Twentieth Century Trade Union Woman: Vehicle for Social Change, Oral History Project, Institute of Labor and Industrial Relations, University of Michigan/Wayne State University.

68. It is important to clarify that I am speaking of dominant philosophical tendencies rather than reified and non-overlapping oppositional categories. Not all working-class women thought alike; neither did all supporters of the NWP nor all middle-class second-wave feminists. See Cott, "The Limits of 'Social Feminism,' " 822–825.

69. Myra Wolfgang, "Some of the Problems of Eve," talk before the AFL-CIO Conference Women at Work, March 13, 1971, 4, Myra Wolfgang Collection, Box 1, File 6, Walter Reuther Archives, Wayne State University, Detroit.

70. Harrison criticizes feminists in this period for their failure to address adequately the problem of women's dual responsibilities at home and in the labor force. She points out that the solution offered by feminist groups like the National Woman's Party amounted to a denial of the tension between home and work commitments. Harrison, *On Account of Sex,* 13–15.

71. Myra Marx Ferree, "She Works Hard for a Living: Gender and Class on the Job," in *Analyzing Gender: A Handbook of Social Science Research*, ed. Myra Marx Ferree and Beth Hess (Newbury Park, Calif.: Sage, 1987), 340. In addition, as James Henretta has argued, many working-class women may not have aspired to individual upward mobility, or if they did, may not have seen it as a real possibility given their educational and financial resources. Too often, upward mobility is assumed to be a goal across all classes and groups in society. Henretta, "The Study of Social Mobility: Ideological Assumptions and Conceptual Bias," *Labor History*, 1977, 165–178.

72. Harrison argues that the majority of feminists in both the Women's Bureau Coalition and the National Women's Party held this belief. *On Account of Sex*, 13–15.

73. Such articles as Robert Karen's "Becoming Attached," *Atlantic Monthly*, February 1990, 35–70, in which he warned mothers of the psychological harm of infant day care, have received serious and widespread credence.

74. William Chafe, *The American Woman: Her Changing Social, Economic, and Political Roles, 1920–1970* (New York: Oxford University Press, 1972); and Chafe, *The Paradox of Change: American Women in the 20th Century* (New York: Oxford University Press, 1991), 121–238. The debate over the impact of World War II is extensive, but the class-skewed nature of its impact has not been addressed. See Ruth Milkman, "Review Essay," *Contemporary Sociology*, January 1987, 21–25.

75. Sherna Gluck also makes explicit connections between the wartime experiences of the "Rosies" and their later receptivity to feminist thought. Sherna Berger Gluck, *Rosie the Riveter Revisited: Women, the War, and Social Change* (Boston: Twayne, 1987).

76. That the wartime feminism of working-class women carried over into the postwar decades might be explained in part by the different work experiences of the classes. A much greater number of working-class women continued on in the workforce and an even greater number worked in full-time jobs as primary income-earners. As Myra Marx Ferree has demonstrated for contemporary women, it is likely that women in the 1940s and 1950s who remained in the labor force, especially those for whom wage earning meant economic survival, held different, "more feminist" conceptions of sexual equality and female advancement than those who worked full-time in the home. Myra Marx Ferree, "Working-Class Feminism: A Consideration of the Consequences of Employment," *Sociological Quarterly*, Spring 1980, 173–184. Kessler-Harris also notes the importance of women's increasing participation in wage work in laying the basis for the feminist upsurge of the 1960s. See her chapter "The Radical Consequences of Incremental Change" in *Out to Work*, 300–319.

77. This interpretation questions the general consensus positing conservatism after the war. Compare Chafe, *The American Woman*, chaps. 8–9, and Campbell, *Women at War with America*, chap. 8.

78. The class militancy of these women may have been fueled in part by their wartime experiences. Working-class women who entered unionized, high-paying sectors of the economy during the war or who, like waitresses, simply moved into "nontraditional" jobs in their own industry, experienced heightened expectations about working conditions and wages and learned about the processes and protections of collective bargaining. They carried these expectations with them when they returned to typical female-dominated occupations.

79. Harrison, *On Account of Sex*, xii.

80. My work builds on Harrison's and Leila Rupp and Verta Taylor's *Survival in*

the Doldrums: The American Women's Rights Movement, 1945 to the 1960s (New York: Oxford University Press, 1987), which began the reassessment of the postwar years. My interpretations, however, differ in some respects. For example, I see feminism as a broader phenomenon than Rupp and Taylor describe. I would also take issue with Harrison's description of the Women's Bureau Coalition (a group led by shoe-worker Mary Anderson and composed largely of union women) as "primarily educated, middle-class white women" as well as her conclusions that it lacked "major labor organizations and political clubs" and that the policy advances in these years happened in the absence of a mass movement. See Harrison, *On Account of Sex,* xiii, 8–9.

81. Harrison, *On Account of Sex,* 87.

82. Kenneally, "Women in the U.S. and Trade Unionism," 79–83.

83. See Milkman, "Union Responses to Workforce Feminization in the United States," 245.

CHAPTER 5

Susan M. Hartmann

WOMEN'S EMPLOYMENT AND THE DOMESTIC IDEAL IN THE EARLY COLD WAR YEARS

In examining the history of American women in the fifteen years following World War II, scholars have stressed the incongruence between dominant values and norms and the realities of women's lives. In an era marked by the quiescence of organized feminism and the celebration of domesticity by public figures and popular culture, increasing numbers of women were seeking employment outside the home.

A closer examination of this period suggests that it was one of transition rather than paradox.[1] Along with the celebration of women's traditional roles in the dominant discourse, opinion-leading individuals and groups worked to make practices and attitudes more congruent with women's increasing labor force participation. This essay explores the work of two such bodies, the National Manpower Council (NMC) and the Commission on the Education of Women (CEW). It also examines the enactment of legislation directed at accommodating tax policy to women's employment outside the home, a provision in the Revenue Act of 1954 that for the first time established the deductibility of child-care expenses for some employed mothers.

In many ways, the Cold War operated to sustain traditional gender roles and inhibit change. McCarthyism, the most obvious domestic manifestation of the Cold War, suppressed dissent and reform impulses among women as well as men. Although McCarthyism was only one of many factors contributing to the low level of women's activism during the post–World War II era, the anti-communist crusade discredited individual women and induced caution among women leaders and organizations.

For example, Congresswoman Helen Gahagan Douglas lost her bid for the Senate in 1950 to Richard Nixon, who smeared her with charges of radicalism and association with communists. Another victim of the Red Scare was Dorothy Kenyon, a long-time feminist and leader in major women's organizations and U.S. representative to the UN Commission on the Status of Women. In 1950 Kenyon was accused by McCarthy of being a fellow-traveler. Though she was ultimately cleared by the Senate investigating committee, she received no more political appointments.[2]

The Red Scare had a chilling effect on women's organizations as well as on individual women. Esther Caukin Brunauer and Kathryn McHale, former and current executive directors of the American Association of University Women (AAUW), underwent loyalty investigations, in Brunauer's case for having associated the AAUW with "subversive" organizations. Like other black organizations, the National Council of Negro Women was particularly vulnerable to red-baiting. Following the example set by male-led black organizations such as the Urban League, the Congress on Racial Equality (CORE), and the National Association for the Advancement of Colored People (NAACP), in 1951 the National Council of Negro Women's board of directors instructed members and affiliates to "prove our patriotism" by shunning alliances with any individuals or organizations that might be considered subversive.[3]

Other forces related to the Cold War strengthened the status quo. As Elaine Tyler May has demonstrated, the insecurity and anxiety generated by the presumed Soviet threat put a premium on family stability and linked women's traditional domestic roles to the nation's security. National leaders as well as popular culture proclaimed that women's role in the international crisis was to strengthen the family and raise new citizens emotionally and mentally fit to win the Cold War.[4]

Democratic presidential candidate Adlai Stevenson envisioned a role for women in the Cold War era, but he defined woman's political responsibilities in strictly domestic terms. Speaking to the Smith College graduating class of 1955, Stevenson acknowledged that they might feel frustrated with their future roles as wives and mothers. Nevertheless, he insisted, they could "defeat totalitarian, authoritarian ideas" by inculcating in their homes "a vision of the meaning of life and freedom." [5]

Moreover, in the rhetoric of Cold War competition, American leaders stressed women's traditional roles as wives, mothers, and consumers to demonstrate the superiority of the nation's institutions and values. In the famous "kitchen debate" between Soviet Premier Nikita Khrushchev and Vice-President Richard Nixon at an exhibit of American consumer products in Moscow in 1959, Khrushchev boasted of the productive capacity of Soviet women workers. In response, Nixon pointed to a display of labor-saving home appliances and said, "What we want is to make easier the life of our housewives." [6]

Nixon was not alone in extolling American women's role in the home as ammunition in the ideological Cold War. In 1960, Undersecretary of Labor James O'Connel noted the high proportion of Soviet women in such fields as education and medicine. O'Connel remarked, "Perhaps we ought to applaud the USSR and emulate their accomplishment. I don't think so. . . . When a woman comes to be viewed first as a source of manpower, second as a mother, then I think we are losing much that supposedly separates us from the Communist world. The highest calling of a woman's sex is the home." [7]

The celebration of domesticity notwithstanding, by the mid-1950s, rates of women's employment matched the artificially high levels attained during World War II. Most striking was the rising employment of married women, which grew by 42 percent during the 1950s. By 1960, 30 percent of married women were employed, and 39 percent of all mothers with school-age children were in the labor force. Moreover, the rising numbers of married women seeking employment did not reflect dire economic need; employment rates rose fastest among middle-class women.[8]

Explanations for women's growing employment lay in a complex range of technological, demographic, economic, and social factors that reflected both growing demand and supply. What scholars have tended to overlook is the public reconsideration of women's status and the support for women's employment expressed by leading decision makers and opinion shapers. In an era dominated by the celebration of domesticity and women's traditional roles, experts and opinion leaders not only recognized and approved of women's increasing employment but also sought to adjust public opinion and public policy to accommodate women's greater participation in the public sphere.

The Cold War itself contained conflicting elements. While concerns about international instability helped sustain cultural conservatism in the United States, they also promoted gender role changes. Specifically, by focusing attention on the need for fuller utilization of the nation's resources, the Cold War helped draw attention to women's employment and education. In 1951, after the Cold War had erupted into actual fighting in Korea, two semiofficial bodies began a decade-long investigation of women's status in the United States. Representing a broad spectrum of industry, education, government, and women's organizations, both bodies tied expanding public activities for women to the national interest and recommended ways to facilitate that change.

The first group was the National Manpower Council, established in 1951 at Columbia University with funding from the Ford Foundation. Chaired by Erwin D. Canham, editor of the *Christian Science Monitor,* and managed by Henry David of Columbia's Graduate School of Business, the commission was composed of leaders from the private sector, with links to the federal government. Responding to the need "to expand our industry to new heights, to assist our allies, and to maintain a military force strong enough to deter aggression [and] to build a base for full-scale mobilization," the NMC sought "to stimulate the improved utilization of the nation's manpower resources during this period of national crises and increasing military and economic mobilization." To this end, it conducted research and sponsored conferences designed to influence both public opinion and public policy.[9]

Though not on its immediate agenda, the NMC recognized early on that it needed to study womanpower. Beginning in 1955, it held sixteen meetings throughout the country to examine issues relating to women's employment, published two books on those issues, and offered a series of recommendations to government, educational institutions, employers, and labor unions.[10]

Participants in the council's work came from businesses, labor unions, educational institutions, women's organizations, the military, and civilian agencies of the federal and state governments. While industrial corporations such as Standard Oil, General Electric, Lockheed, and R.J. Reynolds were represented, most employers came from service-sector businesses that hired large numbers of women, including retailers, insurance companies, banks, telephone companies, and hospitals. Nearly every large labor union took part, as did educational institutions and government officials. Margaret Hickey, editor of the Public Affairs Department of the *Ladies' Home Journal* and past president of the National Federation of Business and Professional Women's Clubs (BPW), played an active role as consultant to and subsequently member of the NMC. Through participation of the BPW and groups such as the League of Women Voters, the American Association of University Women, the YWCA, the National Association of Colored Women's Clubs, the American Nurses Association, and women's religious organizations, the views of women themselves informed the council's work.[11]

The Women's Bureau of the Department of Labor was also associated with the NMC. It provided statistics, sent representatives to conferences, released one of its employees to work with the director of research for the NMC, and at the council's request, scrutinized drafts of *Womanpower*, the council's report on women's employment. The Women's Bureau, however, did not always see eye to eye with the NMC. Women's Bureau staff members, for example, wanted stronger recommendations for facilitating older women's return to employment, a high priority for the bureau in the 1950s. In addition, although the bureau had shifted from support to neutrality on the issue of protective legislation, its staff objected to passages in the council's report critical of special laws for women workers. Further illustrating the tendency to be more cautious than the NMC, bureau staff objected to a description of the agency as "fostering the employment of women," which nevertheless remained in the final copy. In general, bureau staff believed that the council "has apparently made no attempt to accommodate for Women's Bureau comments." After reading the draft of the council's report, the bureau's director, Alice K. Leopold, wanted it to make clear that findings and recommendations were solely those of the NMC. And reflecting the bureau's sense of self-preservation, as well as its caution on the issue of protective legislation, Leopold asked for bureau representation in any recommendations for a commission to investigate laws regarding women's employment.[12]

The second body concerned with women's status was the Commission on the Education of Women sponsored by the American Council on Education (ACE). Responding to the "urgent questions [raised by the Korean War] about just how and in what respects women could serve the defense of the nation," in 1951 ACE organized a conference on Women in the Defense Decade. More than nine hundred men and women attended that conference, and it energized professional women to press for sustained attention to issues concerning the education of women.[13]

Concerned about discrimination faced by professional women in higher education, the National Association of Deans of Women (NADW) seized on the interest generated by the conference "to strengthen the position of women in higher education." With the support of Mrs. Ellis L. Phillips, founding president of NADW, they secured a pledge of $50,000 from the Ellis L. Phillips Foundation and then asked the American Council on Education to sponsor a Commission on the Education of Women. Having secured outside funding, it was not difficult to win endorsement for the commission from ACE. Council President Arthur S. Adams did insist, however, that the commission refrain from looking at women "as an underprivileged minority" or seeking "to advance the special purposes of one segment of the population."[14]

Starting to work in 1953, the CEW project drew together college and university administrators, researchers, government officials, and representatives of women's organizations to investigate women's current status, especially their increasing employment outside the home, and ascertain their long-range educational needs. With additional funding from the Carnegie Corporation and the Lilly Endowment, the CEW, like the National Manpower Council, promoted research, sponsored conferences, and published its findings.

Neither the NMC nor the CEW posed a substantial challenge to prevailing views about race. One African American woman, Ruth Brett Quarles, former dean at Fisk University, served on the CEW, and a handful of individuals representing the Urban League, the NAACP, and black colleges participated in the NMC conferences. But the token nature of their involvement was reflected in the general neglect of African American women—and, indeed, all minority women—in the NMC and CEW reports. Although it listed under "Negro Women" a number of studies being conducted, the CEW failed to address the particular circumstances of black women's education in either of its two major publications. The NMC paid only slightly more attention to racial differences, noting the greater propensity of black married women to work outside the home and the additional discrimination all African American women faced in the labor market.[15]

The strength of tradition was also evident in the considerable ambivalence about women's expanding roles displayed in the work of the NMC and CEW. For example, a summary of the findings of the 1951 Conference on Women in the Defense Decade, reported general agreement that "there will be women in the armed forces . . . [and that] women must work, and will work, outside their homes." But conference participants also agreed that "the primary effort of women in a defense period, after supplying from their numbers the ones needed in the armed services, *should be directed toward protection of the human relations in the home,* the family unit." This ambivalence continued to characterize the work of the NMC and CEW, representing in part their efforts to include a wide range of views and to take an evenhanded approach to controversial issues. Thus their work expressed assumptions that had much in common with the dominant domestic ideology.[16]

Both the NMC and CEW dissociated themselves from explicit feminism. Repeating the caution of its sponsor, ACE President Arthur Adams, the CEW stated explicitly that it wanted to avoid "considering women as an underprivileged minority for whom special pleading should be made." The NMC, evenhandedly recounting the pros and cons of the proposed Equal Rights Amendment, noted that most groups seeking to improve women's status "are not calling for striking innovations in public policy" and that charges of sex discrimination are "now not made with either the same regularity or intensity as in the past."[17]

Women sometimes chafed at the tendency of men associated with the two bodies to explain women's inferior position as a function of their lack of training or ambition, rather than a result of sex discrimination. For example, Althea K. Hottel, who was appointed director of the CEW, complained that while Arthur Adams agreed "there is a lag in the acceptance of well qualified -women" in higher education positions, he believed that "the main reason is that we do not have enough educated for the jobs." Reporting on a regional NMC conference, a Women's Bureau staff member recounted assertions by male employers that the only thing standing between women and managerial and technical opportunities were women's lack of qualifications, unwillingness to make sacrifices, and low level of interest or ambition. Skeptical of executives' contentions that women willing to make the effort could occupy higher-level jobs, the staff member concluded that "the effort would have to be great," given employers' tendency to "generalize [about] women's lack of interest in these positions." [18]

In their deference to women's roles as wives and mothers, both bodies reflected time-honored assumptions about women's essential purpose. The CEW's interim report of 1955, for example, maintained that its proposals for broader participation of women in employment or other areas of the public arena "must not detract from the importance of their roles as wives and mothers." [19]

Given its interest in meeting economic needs, the National Manpower Council paid more attention to facilitating women's employment than to reminding them of their domestic responsibilities. Yet it gave ample hearing to those who favored tradition, including Secretary of Labor James P. Mitchell, keynote speaker at the NMC's Conference on Work in the Lives of Married Women held in 1957. Acknowledging that his view might sound "either old-fashioned or heretical," Mitchell declared that "the most fundamental job of the American woman" was "being a good wife, a homemaker, a mother." [20]

Implicit or explicit throughout the work of the NMC and CEW was the assumption that women's childrearing role was central. The reports reconciled that assumption with their goal of facilitating women's employment by favoring a pattern that reflected current conditions for many women: work outside the home before childbearing, preoccupation with domestic responsibilities at least until children reached school age, and thereafter a return to employment or other substantial community activity.

Despite the deference to traditional roles, both bodies assumed leadership in fostering change in popular attitudes and in institutional policies and practices. As the decade progressed, the NMC and CEW paid less attention to upholding women's family roles and more attention to accommodating women's public roles. In many ways, their comments and recommendations foreshadowed elements of the feminist movement that would emerge a decade later.

Both bodies repeatedly cited a wide range of discriminatory practices against women. The NMC noted, for example, that "many employers still apply different hiring, training, and promotion policies to women workers"; reported disapprovingly that "jobs at all levels are still usually designated as belonging to either men or women"; and asserted that black women suffered "marked discrimination," having "far more limited job opportunities" than white women. The CEW did not address racial discrimination, but it challenged the "persisting prejudice against women in education," the "economic and power urges which underlie all such discrimination," and the harmful consequences of sex discrimination to women and to society in general.[21]

Recommendations of the NMC specifically addressed sex discrimination. The council called on employers to "hire, assign, train, and promote all individuals regardless of sex on the basis of their personal qualifications," and for both employers and unions to "apply the principle of equal pay for equal work." While the council took a neutral stance on federal equal-pay legislation, it asked the secretary of labor to review all federal and state laws that affected women. Although the NMC minimized the negative effects of protective legislation on women's employment opportunities, it pointed out instances where such laws disadvantaged women and reported the views of union women who believed that "differential legislation provides employers with a justification for hiring men for work which women have in fact done or could undertake."[22]

In contrast to officials such as Vice-President Nixon and Undersecretary of Labor O'Connel, who measured U.S. superiority over the Soviet Union in terms of its ability to keep women in the home, the NMC expressed concerns about America "losing out in a race [with the Soviet Union] for highly trained manpower." It contrasted the thirteen thousand female engineers graduating each year in the Soviet Union with the fewer than one hundred women obtaining engineering degrees in the United States.[23]

While the NMC sought to break down sex segregation in jobs and professions, the CEW challenged other ideas and practices that sustained distinctions between men and women. The report on Women in the Defense Decade, for example, argued for "less differentiation between the work done by the man and woman in a home." Moreover, the CEW minimized assumptions about sex differences on which discrimination was often based. After undertaking a survey of research on sex differences, the CEW reported that *"no basis exists for a general statement as to differences in variability between the sexes"* and solicited greater attention to cultural expectations as a means to understanding variations in the behavior of men and women. The assertion at one CEW conference that "men and women differ biologically, socially, psychologically and intellectually" was atypical, and such arguments tended to be politely ignored by the commentators.[24]

Both the NMC and the CEW aimed at changing popular attitudes. Through their conferences, sponsored research, press releases, and publications, these bodies sought to influence the thinking of employers, governments, labor unions, educators, and others who had the power to change policies and practices concerning women's roles in the public sphere. They hoped to make these influential groups aware of changes already taking place in women's employment and to persuade them to alter attitudes and customs to afford women greater opportunities.

Because attitudes lagged behind the actual behavior of women, the NMC and CEW also acknowledged the need for raising the consciousness of women. Noting that educational choices of young women were "attuned more to older patterns of women's employment than to its present and emerging characteristics," the NMC insisted that young women needed to be made aware of "the probability that paid employment will occupy a significant place in their adult lives." It called for government, employers, and private groups to expand fellowship and scholarship programs to enable more women to continue their education. Along with improved vocational guidance, these changes would encourage women to prepare for employment more compatible with their abilities than was currently the case.[25]

Anticipating another goal of the resurgent feminist movement, the CEW commented approvingly on the development of what would later be called women's studies courses. Both the NMC and CEW recognized the need for more research on women; in addition, the CEW was concerned with what students were taught. It recognized "the need for men and women to understand something of the cultural history of women and the changes that have occurred in their lives" and offered as models such courses as "Women's Role in Modern Society," taught at the University of Michigan, and "The Status and Responsibilities of Women in the Modern World," offered at Syracuse University.[26]

Even on the most controversial issue—the employment of mothers—the NMC and CEW promoted views that challenged tradition. To be sure, experts associated with these bodies assumed the centrality of motherhood in most women's lives. Moreover, there was general agreement with the position of the Children's Bureau that individual care was much to be preferred over group care for children under the age of three years. Participants at NMC conferences decried the inadequacy of existing arrangements for child care, but exhibited no consensus about the role of employers or the government in providing child-care facilities.[27]

NMC experts considered the employment of African American mothers more problematic than it was for white mothers. On the one hand, they recognized that black mothers were more likely to be employed and that because of racism African American children needed "even more emotional support than other children." But they also applied racist stereotypes to the black family, characterizing it as "matriarchal" and suffering "the handicap of a relatively weak father image." Asserting that care given to very young children by grandparents or other relatives was "not likely to be adequate" for white or black children, an NMC report suggested that in minority groups, "where there is a greater need for a good parent–child relationship in the early years, the chances are smaller that this will exist." [28]

Nonetheless, in discussing the overall issue of employed mothers, there was general agreement that children could be separated from their mothers "for substantial periods during the day, if adequate substitute care is provided." The National Manpower Council reported that all available research showed no evidence of "a causal relation between maternal employment and either juvenile delinquency or the maladjustment of children." Instead, the mother's employment was "only one of the very many factors bearing upon a child's development." NMC publications also pointed to benefits resulting from the employment of mothers outside the home—a higher standard of living for the family, growing participation of fathers in child care, greater partnership between the parents, and mothers who were more satisfied with their lives. Finally, NMC experts maintained that "it is not the amount of time spent with the child but what happens during that time that really matters." [29]

CEW reports paid less attention to mothers' employment and were more accommodating to a pattern that kept women home while their children were young, noting, for example, that "under present societal conditions . . . the full satisfactions of a dual career are not for every young wife, not even for all our best college graduates." Yet CEW experts joined the NMC in challenging the presumed link between juvenile delinquency and maternal employment, as well as the belief that a mother's full-time attention was essential to infant development. Rejecting the idea "that only the mother can give the infant . . . that loving care that will make it a healthy personality," one CEW consultant cited psychologists' conclusions that "the infant would be happy and would thrive mentally and physically no matter who it is that fulfills his needs." [30]

When the National Manpower Council completed its exploration of women's employment at the end of the 1950s, it concluded that the new pattern of work outside the home for married women had, "by and large, desirable social and economic consequences." The activities of the council and of the Commission on the Education of Women came largely in response to a situation created by the economy's need for labor and the individual decisions of hundreds of thousands of women. But the two semiofficial bodies explicitly approved this development and sought to change attitudes and policies in order to facilitate women's employment. [31]

The work of the NMC and CEW also strengthened ties among women interested in broadening women's opportunities and built a foundation for the President's Commission on the Status of Women (PCSW) established in 1961. In examining women's legal status, women in politics and public office, and family planning, the PCSW covered a broader range of issues than the earlier bodies. Yet in areas where the focus of the PCSW overlapped with that of the earlier groups—women's employment and women's education—its commentary and recommendations repeated much of what had appeared in the publications of the NMC and CEW.[32]

Individual women formed direct links among the three groups. A number of them participated in the activities of both the NMC and CEW, and more than a dozen were subsequently involved in the work of the President's Commission on the Status of Women. Esther Lloyd-Jones, a Columbia University professor, chaired the CEW, participated in NMC conferences, and served on the Committee on Federal Employment of the PCSW. Margaret Hickey, former president of the National Federation of Business and Professional Women's Clubs, was a consultant for the NMC project and served on the PCSW. Government lawyer and self-identified feminist Marguerite Rawalt, Caroline Davis of the United Automobile Workers, and Eleanor Guggenheimer, leader of the national day-care movement, were also involved with both the NMC conferences and the PCSW. Although Davis was unique in becoming a founder of the National Organization for Women (NOW), the work of these and other women who connected the NMC and CEW with the PCSW established groundwork for the even greater attention to sexual stratification that occurred in the 1960s and contributed to the resurgence of feminism later in the decade.[33]

Policy change, of course, lagged behind the views advanced by the NMC and CEW. Both political parties endorsed a national equal pay law, and President Eisenhower included it in his economic agenda every year from 1956 to 1960, but Congress failed to act.[34] Yet national legislators indicated that they, too, were beginning to see women's roles in a different light. Although elected officials took a more cautious approach than did individuals associated with the NMC and CEW, passage of a provision in the Revenue Act of 1954 for the deductibility of child-care expenses exhibited a growing recognition and acceptance of married women's employment outside the home.

Deductions for child care arose in a comprehensive tax reform measure proposed by President Eisenhower to stimulate economic growth and eliminate what he and other Republicans considered inequities in taxation. His bill offered hefty reductions for corporations and wealthy individuals, but it also contained some more broadly based benefits. Along with greater deductions for dependents and medical expenses, Eisenhower proposed a deduction of up to

$300 for child-care expenses for children under the age of seven years; the deduction would be available to widows, widowers, divorced or legally separated individuals, and mothers who provided most of the family's support.[35]

Legislators had been introducing bills for that purpose since 1947, and in 1953 the House Ways and Means Committee held extensive hearings on the topic. When Congress approved the child-care deduction in 1954, it went beyond the administration's proposal, applying it not only to single parents but also to any employed mother whose annual family income did not exceed $4,500, covering child-care expenses for any children under twelve, and increasing the deduction to $600. The $4,500 income cap extended the provision beyond the poor and working class, since roughly half of all families had incomes below that level in 1954. An estimated 2.1 million taxpayers would gain $130 million of tax relief from the measure.[36]

At committee hearings, a broad range of organizations and individuals supported deductions for child-care expenses. Advocates included not only such women's organizations as the General Federation of Women's Clubs, the National Federation of Business and Professional Women, and the American Nurses Association but also chambers of commerce in Georgia and West Virginia, the American Institute of Accountants, the American Bar Association, and the American Hospital Association. Among organized labor, the American Federation of Government Employees, Office Employees International Union, and the Congress of Industrial Organizations (CIO) supported tax relief for employed mothers. Less responsive to women's needs than the CIO, the American Federation of Labor (AFL) professed sympathy for the principle but believed that the bills under consideration would "permit wholesale evasion and abuse" and urged instead greater exemptions for all low-income families.[37]

Providing deductions for child-care expenses attracted support from most Democrats, in part because they saw it as a means to liberalize what they considered a "rich man's tax bill." Many of its Republican supporters, in fact, used the child-care deduction to refute charges that the tax bill as a whole favored the wealthy. A number of Democrats, southerners as well as traditional northern liberals, introduced their own, more generous, versions of the child-care deduction, as did Maine Republican Senator Margaret Chase Smith and House Republicans from New York, Jacob K. Javits and Kenneth B. Keating. Two female representatives, Edna F. Kelly (D, N.Y.) and Leonore K. Sullivan (D, Mo.), argued forcefully for the deduction at congressional hearings.[38]

Debate over the issue was inextricably linked to the propriety of married women's employment. With little outright opposition, disagreements centered on what groups of employed parents would be covered and how to prevent "abuses." Committee testimony and congressional debate contained views ranging from those concerned primarily with the relationship between female employment and national needs to those stressing equity and justice for women. Most advocates argued on grounds of both expediency and justice.

To be sure, the persistence of conventional attitudes regarding gender roles colored much of the debate, most notably in discussions of those entitled to coverage. Liberal Senator Paul Douglas (D, Ill.) was among the staunchest supporters of tax fairness for employed mothers, but he nonetheless asserted his "fervent" belief that "mothers' place is in the home caring for their children." Many legislators supported a deduction to help women who truly needed to work, but they did not want to encourage the employment of other mothers. For example, Arthur G. Klein (D, N.Y.), strongly supported tax relief for employed mothers but did not want the deduction to include "some of these women" who "decide they do not like housework and want to get a job." Agreeing "that the mother ought to be at home looking after her children where there is a wage earner in the family," Treasury Secretary George M. Humphrey opposed extending the deduction to all employed mothers, not only because of the cost, but also to prevent "child-deliquency." [39]

Representative Noah M. Mason (R, Ill.), the most outspoken opponent of a child-care deduction for anyone but widows or widowers, castigated married women whose husbands earned "a good living" and who took jobs merely to buy "a $750 fur coat" or other luxuries. Like Humphrey, seemingly oblivious to the fact that a child-care deduction could enable parents to provide for proper supervision of children, Mason disparaged the mother who "learned she could earn money during World War II and now insists upon doing it while the children are running loose and becoming a nuisance in the town." Other skeptics resisted provisions that would help parents send children to a "very fancy nursery school." To prevent such "abuses," the law restricted the amount of child-care expenses that could be deducted to $600. Families with incomes below $4,500 were eligible for the full deduction, and those earning more than $5,100 were excluded entirely. [40]

Despite expressions of concern about potential "abuses," most legislators, including those who confined their support of married women's employment to cases of economic necessity, recognized that married women workers were a fact of life. Citing Women's Bureau statistics that placed 5 million mothers at work outside the home, noting that economic need drove many others into the labor force, and recognizing that women's employment was critical to the national economy, they sought to narrow the gap between public policy and those realities. [41]

Expediency arguments also endorsed the need to protect the family, promote the welfare of children, and reduce juvenile delinquency by enabling employed mothers to secure adequate supervision of their children. Other expediency arguments advanced the measure as a means to reduce "welfare dependency." For example, Representatives Kelly and Louis B. Heller (D, N.Y.) supported the measure on grounds of justice to women, but they also argued that the child-care deduction would facilitate the employment of mothers and thus provide an alternative to "idleness" and welfare and encourage "initiative and self-respecting independence." [42]

Like the NMC, proponents of the child-care deduction stressed the contributions of female labor to national economic and security interests. Representatives of the American Nurses Association and the American Hospital Association testified that tax relief for employed mothers would encourage nurses to go back to work, thereby relieving a critical shortage. In addition to recognizing that women were "an integral part of our Nation's economic life," other supporters pointed specifically to the shortage of nurses, teachers, and other skilled workers and viewed the deduction as a means of overcoming labor shortages and promoting "rapid mobilization to meet a wartime emergency." [43]

Although expediency arguments predominated, advocates of the child-care deduction also stressed the discriminatory features of current tax laws and insisted on equal treatment for women. They repeatedly pointed out that businessmen could deduct entertainment, travel, country club memberships, and the like as legitimate expenses and insisted that child care was also a necessary cost in the production of income. Testimony from the Office Employees International Union, for example, charged that current tax laws imposed a "discriminatory hardship on working mothers," while Representative Sullivan contended that the laws intensified the "double duty and double burden" shouldered by mothers who worked outside the home. Justice and fairness, supporters argued, required that women be entitled to deductions available to businessmen. [44]

Providing deductibility for child-care expenses in lower-income families represented but an incremental accommodation of public policy to the expansion of women's work outside the home. Moreover, the debate around that issue revealed the strength of conventional values that frowned on the employment of married women. Yet the new policy also manifested congressional acknowledgement that employed mothers were a fact of life and that current tax policy discriminated against them. Inclusion of the child-care deduction in the Revenue Act of 1954 inched public policy one step away from the domestic values heralded in the popular culture.

Scholars are correct in pointing to America's obsession with family life and traditional gender roles in the postwar period, and they have demonstrated how the Cold War contributed to that obsession by linking women's traditional roles to national security. But the international crisis also encouraged leaders to look toward women's employment as an important element in the nation's readiness to meet that crisis. As the actual behavior of women increasingly deviated from the celebration of domesticity, the NMC, the CEW, and, in one instance, Congress promoted the view that the expansion of nontraditional roles for women was compatible with the national interest. Seen in this light, the first fifteen years of the Cold War represented an important transition period for American women, promoting undercurrents that would emerge as dominant trends in the 1960s and 1970s.

NOTES

1. Nancy F. Gabin has argued that this period was a transitional one for labor union women in *Feminism in the Labor Movement: Women and the United Auto Workers, 1935–1975* (Ithaca: Cornell University Press, 1990). Alice Kessler-Harris has shown how the Women's Bureau of the Department of Labor gradually shifted from "helping women who happened to hold jobs . . . to helping a nation decide how to use women better," in *Out to Work: A History of Wage-Earning Women in the United States* (New York: Oxford University Press, 1982), 300–311.

2. Susan M. Hartmann, *The Home Front and Beyond, American Women in the 1940s* (Boston: Twayne, 1982), 156–157.

3. Richard M. Fried, *Nightmare in Red: The McCarthy Era in Perspective* (New York: Oxford University Press, 1990), 164–165; Hartmann, *The Home Front and Beyond,* 157.

4. Elaine Tyler May, *Homeward Bound: American Families in the Cold War Era* (New York: Basic Books, 1988).

5. *New York Times,* June 7, 1955, 36.

6. May, *Homeward Bound,* 17–18.

7. O'Connel quoted in Judith Sealander, *As Minority Becomes Majority: Federal Reaction to the Phenomenon of Women in the Work Force, 1920–1963* (Westport, Conn.: Greenwood Press, 1983), 139–140.

8. Claudia Goldin, *Understanding the Gender Gap: An Economic History of American Women* (New York: Oxford University Press, 1990), 119–158.

9. National Manpower Council, *A Report on the National Manpower Council* (New York: Graduate School of Business, Columbia University, 1954), 7.

10. National Manpower Council, *Womanpower* (New York: Columbia University Press, 1957); National Manpower Council, *Work in the Lives of Married Women: Proceedings of a Conference on Womanpower* (New York: Columbia University Press, 1958).

11. National Manpower Council, *Womanpower,* xi–xxviii.

12. Eli Ginzberg to Alice K. Leopold, January 4, 1955; Jean Scott Campbell to Alice K. Leopold, June 17, 1955; Ethel Erickson to Alice A. Morrison, February 1, 1956; Alice A. Morrison to Alice K. Leopold, August 14, 1956; Alice A. Morrison to Alice K. Leopold, August 27, 1956; M. S. Barber to Alice K. Leopold, October 4, 1956; Alice K. Leopold to Henry David, October 17, 1956; Alice K. Leopold to Erwin D. Canham, December 5, 1956. Records of the Women's Bureau, RG-86, Gen-

eral Correspondence, Box 24, File 6-5-4-2. Mildred S. Barber to Alice K. Leopold, January 23, 1957 and February 11, 1957; Alice K. Leopold to Eli Ginzberg, February 28, 1957. Records of the Women's Bureau, RG-86, General Correspondence, Box 68, File: "Womanpower-Manpower Council Reports."

13. Opal D. David, ed., *The Education of Women: Signs for the Future* (Washington, D.C.: American Council on Education, 1959), 3–4.

14. Althea K. Hottel to Arthur S. Adams, May 1, 1952; Minutes of the Advisory Committee of the National Association of Deans of Women, May 16, 1952; Esther Lloyd-Jones to Arthur S. Adams, July 10, 1952; Arthur S. Adams to Esther Lloyd-Jones, July 16, 1952. Papers of the Commission on the Education of Women (hereafter cited as CEW), 1:2, Schlesinger Library, Radcliffe College. Minutes of the Commission on the Education of Women, March 23, 1953, CEW, 1:3; Ruth O. McCarn to Members of NADW, January 6, 1953, CEW, 7:92.

15. Althea K. Hottel, *How Fare American Women?* (Washington, D.C.: American Council on Education, 1955), 63; National Manpower Council, *Womanpower*, 77, 100. In 1954 and 1955, Jeanne L. Noble, a doctoral candidate at Columbia University, undertook a comprehensive study of African American women's higher education. Her major adviser was Esther Lloyd-Jones, chair of the CEW, who in that capacity wrote the Foreword to the published study *The Negro Woman's College Education* (New York: Teachers College, Columbia University, 1956).

16. Raymond F. Howes, ed., *Women in the Defense Decade* (Washington, D.C.: American Council on Education, 1952), 16–17.

17. Hottel, *How Fare American Women?* v; National Manpower Council, *Womanpower*, 343–344.

18. Althea K. Hottel to Esther Lloyd-Jones, February 24, 1953, CEW Papers, 1–3. Report on Womanpower Conference, Montana State College, July 25–27, 1957. Records of the Women's Bureau, Box 67, File 6.

19. Hottel, *How Fare American Women?* v.

20. National Manpower Council, *Work in the Lives of Married Women*, 15.

21. National Manpower Council, *Womanpower*, 53, 100, 102; National Manpower Council, *Work in the Lives of Married Women*, 21, 75–81; David, *The Education of Women*, 10, 135.

22. National Manpower Council, *Womanpower*, 4–6, 331–336, 345–349.

23. National Manpower Council, *Womanpower*, 260–262.

24. Margaret Culkin Banning, *A New Design for the Defense Decade* (Washington, D.C.: American Council on Education, 1951), 5; Hottel, *How Fare American Women?* 21–25; David, *The Education of Women*, 64–68, 71, 94–95, 107.

25. National Manpower Council, *Womanpower*, 4, 32; National Manpower Council, *Work in the Lives of Married Women*, 41, 45; David, *The Education of Women*, 116, 118.

26. David, *The Education of Women*, 102; Hottel, *How Fare American Women?* 31–32.

27. National Manpower Council, *Work in the Lives of Married Women*, 145, 183–184, 189–194.

28. Ibid., 186.

29. Ibid., 135, 141–145, 151, 187–189.

30. David, *The Education of Women*, 53, 58–59.

31. National Manpower Council, *Work in the Lives of Married Women*, 201.

32. *American Women: The Report of the President's Commission on the Status of Women* (New York: Scribner's, 1965).

33. National Manpower Council, *Womanpower*, vii–xxviii; *American Women*, 254–262.

34. Cynthia Harrison, *On Account of Sex: The Politics of Women's Issues, 1945–1968* (Berkeley: University of California Press, 1988), 48–51.

35. Chester J. Pach, Jr., and Elmo Richardson, *The Presidency of Dwight D. Eisenhower*, rev. ed. (Lawrence: University Press of Kansas, 1991), 54; *New York Times*, January 3, 1954, 1, 49.

36. Congress, House, Conference Report on H.R. 8300, *Internal Revenue Code of 1954*, 83rd Cong., 2nd sess., July 26, 1954, Report No. 2543, 31–32; Congress, Senate, 83rd Cong., 2nd sess., *Congressional Record*, June 28, 1954, 8994.

37. Congress, House, Committee on Ways and Means, *General Revenue Revision: Hearings on Forty Topics Pertaining to the General Revision of the Internal Revenue Code*, 83rd Cong., 1st sess., June 16–18, 23, and July 8, 9, 14–16, 21, 1953, 49–52, 55, 60–61, 68–72; Congress, Senate, *The Internal Revenue Code of 1954: Hearings on H.R. 8300*, 83rd Cong., 2nd sess., April 22, 23, 1954, 1798, 2185.

38. Congress, House, *Hearings on General Revenue Revision*, 26–29, 54–55, 64–65; Congress, Senate, *Internal Revenue Code of 1954*, pt. 4, 1798; Congress, House, 83rd Cong., 2nd sess., *Congressional Record*, March 15, 1954, 3291; Congress, Senate, 83rd Cong., 2nd sess., *Congressional Record*, June 28, 1954, 9271.

39. Congress, House, Committee on Ways and Means, *General Revenue Revision*, 35, 53; Congress, Senate, Committee on Finance, *The Internal Revenue Code of 1954*, 117; Congress, Senate, 83rd Cong., 2nd sess., *Congressional Record*, July 2, 1954, 9605.

40. Congress, House, Committee on Ways and Means, *General Revenue Revision*, 27, 28, 38, 63.

41. Ibid., 32, 37–41, 57, 64; Congress, Senate, 83rd Cong., 2nd sess., *Congressional Record*, July 2, 1954, 9605.

42. Ibid., 26, 30, 32, 38, 56–59, 68, 69; *Congressional Record*, July 2, 1954, 9605.

43. Congress, House, Committee on Ways and Means, *General Revenue Revision*, 32, 39–40, 51–52, 60–62, 64, 70; Congress, Senate, Committee on Finance, *Internal Revenue Code of 1954*, 1060.

44. Congress, House, Committee on Ways and Means, *General Revenue Revision*, 26, 29, 31–32, 34–36, 38, 40–41, 50, 55, 58; Congress, Senate, Committee on Finance, *Internal Revenue Code of 1954*, 116.

PART II

*Activist Women and
Their Organizations*

CHAPTER 6

Susan Lynn

GENDER AND
PROGRESSIVE
POLITICS

A Bridge to

Social Activism

of the 1960s

In 1951, the American Friends Service Committee hired two women—Irene Osborne, who was white, and Alma Scurlock, who was black—to staff an experimental project in Washington, D.C. Their goal was to create sufficient public pressure to convince the School Board and the Department of Parks and Recreation to integrate the city's schools and parks. Washington restaurants, theaters, hotels, and schools were all strictly segregated by race. A minor exception was the municipal system; the Department of Parks and Recreation had adopted a policy of gradual desegregation of playgrounds in 1949, but after three years only 30 of 140 areas were operated on an integrated basis.[1]

Osborne and Scurlock formed a Joint Committee on Education from representatives of private agencies and concerned individuals who supported integration. The committee blanketed the city with information by publishing a newsletter, offering speakers to church and civic groups and college and university classes, and conducting a series of mass community meetings. "It was terribly exciting,"

Osborne recalled. "Almost from the beginning we could feel that we were on the edge of a breakthrough." Before the project "you couldn't mention the word integration" in a public setting. "It was so shocking it was like using a swearword. Within a few months, we created an atmosphere where we were all talking about it." [2]

The prevalent image of American women in the years immediately following World War II was that of the suburban housewife who centered her life on marriage and children. Yet Irene Osborne and Alma Scurlock exemplify an alternative path to fulfillment selected by many middle-class women who joined the quest for social justice and a new world order based on peace and international cooperation. [3] Women's political activism in the postwar era remains relatively unexplored in part because of the prevailing assumption that most women's lives were awash in a sea of domesticity. Women did, of course, embrace the joys and frustrations of family life in record numbers following the war. Yet our understanding of the meaning of domesticity in women's lives has been distorted in three distinct ways.

First, scholars who have focused on the intense post–World War II media campaign that pushed women back into the domestic sphere often assumed, rather than demonstrated, the all-pervasiveness of that ideal. The notion that domestic ideology suffused American society, popularized by Betty Friedan's *The Feminine Mystique,* gradually made its way into standard accounts of the period. In fact, the ideology of the period was not nearly as uniform as this literature suggests; the most strident messages about a return to domesticity represented only the conservative edge of public discourse. A strikingly different view appeared in many popular magazines of the period; many experts urged women to combine domestic duties with paid work, community and political activities, or both. [4]

This literature illuminates a second misunderstanding—the assumption that marriage and family precluded women's involvement with social and political activities. For many women who came of age after World War II, early marriage and close spacing of children tended to leave more years free from childrearing responsibilities than for any previous generation. [5] A major outlet for women's energies and commitments was civic activism. Furthermore, domestic values were often employed to support women's public efforts, just as they had been at the turn of the century. For example, a dramatic confrontation occurred when members of Women Strike for Peace (WSP) were called to testify before the House Committee on Un-American Activities in 1962. The WSP women justified their opposition to the arms race and nuclear testing by portraying themselves as mothers anxious to protect their children. [6]

Finally, racial differences have not been explored. Economic necessity had driven married black women into the labor force in much higher numbers than white women throughout the twentieth century. During the immediate postwar years, black women were pursuing college degrees and professional careers at higher rates than either black men or white women. Furthermore, since the Progressive era, middle-class black women had tackled the problems of improving the social and economic conditions faced by the African American community, because they hoped to improve conditions for their own families and because they understood that their status in American society was linked to that of poor blacks. Black women viewed activism in civic and political affairs as an extension of, rather than a contradiction to, family life.[7]

For a significant minority of middle-class American women of both races, the urgency of America's social and political problems weakened the attraction of full-time domesticity. Historians studying women activists of this era have focused on the tiny group of self-avowed feminists in the National Woman's Party (NWP), a militant suffrage organization that advocated an Equal Rights Amendment (ERA) for five decades following the passage of woman suffrage. Yet women in a loose coalition of organizations committed to progressive social reform goals far outnumbered those in the NWP and represented a more significant political trend during the postwar years. Most members of this coalition opposed the NWP because they feared that the ERA would undercut hard-won protection for working-class women. Furthermore, many were repelled by the racist, anti-Semitic, and right-wing leanings of some members of the NWP.[8]

These progressives promoted a variety of causes: an expanded welfare state, a powerful labor movement, a strong tradition of civil liberties, the principle of racial equality, and a new international order in which nations would share economic resources more equitably and negotiate disputes through the United Nations. They worked along a variety of fronts within peace, civil rights, religious, and women's organizations, and in the case of working-class women, in labor unions. Some women worked in all-female associations; others in mixed-sex organizations. Among the most important of these for middle-class participants were the American Association of University Women, the American Friends Service Committee, the League of Women Voters, the National Council of Jewish Women, the National Council of Negro Women, the National Association for the Advancement of Colored People, the Women's International League for Peace and Freedom, and the Young Women's Christian Association.[9]

The postwar progressive coalition played a crucial role as a bridge that linked the prewar progressive work of women reformers with women's activism in the civil rights, antiwar, and feminist movements of the 1960s. That bridge was evident in the tactics employed and the goals pursued during the 1940s and 1950s. As their predecessors did, women in the postwar coalition continued to work through older voluntary groups to achieve change through education, publicity, and lobbying. They also employed new strategies and styles of organizing that relied on a specifically female ethic. In recent decades feminist scholars have outlined gendered patterns in such areas as psychological and moral development and styles of learning, concluding that women emphasize connectedness to others and devote more energy toward nurturing personal relationships and building networks of support, whereas men lay more emphasis on separateness.[10] Such gendered patterns influence styles of social activism as well. In the "municipal housekeeping" efforts of women in the Progressive era, for example, the settlement house movement built on networks of women reformers, though class and ethnic differences limited the boundaries of such networks.[11] Postwar women employed this female ethic specifically to build bridges *across* racial lines. Their emphasis on personal relationships foreshadowed the "personal politics" of the 1960s.[12]

Postwar women reformers encompassed both old and new goals. Efforts to achieve world peace, for instance, bridged the pre- and postwar era, but a new context reshaped the struggle. Yet what differed most markedly between the prewar and postwar generations was the shift in focus from efforts to improve conditions for working-class women and children to the struggle to end racial segregation. Women in the Progressive and interwar periods focused on the "maternalist" politics of helping the weak and the unfortunate, particularly women and children, through the provision of social welfare measures and protective legislation.[13] By the 1940s and 1950s, women activists were much more concerned with just rules of governance, particularly for racial minorities, and the defense of civil liberties in the face of McCarthyism.[14]

Racial justice began to emerge as the central paradigm of the battle for social justice during the war. The crusade for civil rights gathered momentum in the late 1940s and 1950s, providing the spark that would ignite the protest movements of the 1960s, including the feminist movement. The 1940s and 1950s, then, represented a watershed in women's social reform activism, one that would ultimately lead to more general challenges to discrimination based on race and gender in American society.

The Young Women's Christian Association (YWCA) and the American Friends Service Committee (AFSC) provide good illustrations of women's activism before and after World War II: both led efforts to achieve racial justice in the postwar years, and both offered women opportunities for leadership in social reform. Gender roles, however, played out differently in the single-sex context of the YWCA and the mixed-sex ranks of the AFSC.

Both organizations shifted emphasis from economic to racial issues. Established in 1917 by a group of prominent Quakers, the AFSC was part of a revived American peace movement born of the cataclysm of war and became a leading pacifist organization during the interwar period. During the 1930s, the AFSC responded to the crisis of the depression by collecting and distributing large quantities of clothing and by developing a self-help economic development project in the devastated Appalachian coalfields. Having devoted little attention to racial issues before the war, the AFSC responded to race riots of 1943 by initiating a Race Relations Program. By the 1950s, the organization focused on the problems of poverty primarily in racial–ethnic communities.

The YWCA showed a similar shift in priorities but emphasized the needs of women. The YWCA was among those single-sex organizations that advocated protective labor legislation and encouraged trade union organization of women during the first half of the twentieth century.[15] Organizing the Industrial Girl Clubs in the first decade of the twentieth century, the YWCA provided a forum for working-class women to discuss wages, safety and health standards, and protective legislation. Working women flocked to the Industrial Department, which sponsored worker education programs and served as a working-class women's pressure group within the larger YWCA. At its peak in 1930, the Industrial Department had almost sixty thousand members.[16]

The need for such an organization became much less compelling with the rise of the Congress of Industrial Organizations (CIO); during the late 1930s and early 1940s, CIO unions became the primary locus of working-class women's efforts toward better conditions and political change. Simultaneously, membership in the YWCA Industrial Department dropped precipitously. Over the strenuous objections of many of its Industrial Secretaries, the YWCA abolished its separate industrial women's assemblies in 1949.[17] Racial discrimination gradually replaced class oppression as the major paradigm of social inequality in the Y's program, as it did in American life.

Social activists had succeeded in obtaining significant improvements in conditions for both male and female industrial workers, and in agitating for laws to end child labor. New Deal reforms were the culmination of decades of struggle for government intervention to protect the American working class, and the incorporation of women into the trade union movement further improved the situation for many working women. Coupled with postwar prosperity, these reforms satisfied many middle-class women that the tremendous extremes of economic inequality (at least among whites) were nearly eliminated. In addition, the political repression of the McCarthy period decimated the left and forestalled any further progress in this area. For liberals, the victories seemed satisfying enough; for the more radical, the 1940s spelled the end of a dream.

Progressive women activists' new sense of urgency about the nation's troubling racial problems reflected shifts in public opinion in the United States. The contradiction of fighting against fascism abroad while endorsing racism at home, was underscored by demographic changes that accompanied World

War II, especially the movement of African Americans from the South to northern cities where they could more easily vote. Cold War competition between
the United States and the Soviet Union for allegiance of the newly emerging
nations of Africa also highlighted domestic racial issues. The decades-long insistence by black activists on ending racial segregation suddenly found favor
among liberal whites. The issue of racial equality gradually became a litmus
test for progressive activists, a core issue for those concerned with social justice.

This represented a sharp break from the indifference and outright hostility
most white suffrage leaders displayed toward potential African American allies
throughout the late nineteenth and early twentieth centuries. Excluded by white
women's organizations, African Americans abandoned hopes for an interracial
alliance for social reform and concentrated on concerns specific to their own
community. Several attempts at interracial cooperation among southern women
activists focused on formulating demands for improved conditions in the African American community, but during the interwar years white women proved
unwilling to confront racial segregation directly. In the North, the Women's
International League for Peace and Freedom welcomed a token number of
African American women into its ranks, but antiracist work was never a focus
of the organization. The Communist Party was one of the few organizations
with an explicit and detailed program that attacked racism in American society
during the 1930s, embracing (if not always equally) black and white male and
female members.[18]

In the years immediately after World War II, white women progressives
began to challenge the legitimacy of the American system of racial segregation
and discrimination. Nonetheless, even as many endorsed racial integration,
only a few organizations made concerted efforts to end racial injustice and
even fewer rooted their efforts in interracial alliances among women. One of
the most important organizations in this regard was the YWCA. Throughout
the early twentieth century, black women within the YWCA had pressured the
organization to deal with their concerns. By 1920, they forced the YWCA to
grant some degree of autonomy to black associations, as well as representation
on local boards and the national board, thus beginning a struggle to move the
YWCA from a biracial toward an interracial organization.

During the interwar years, black women in the Student Division, on the
national board, and in some community YWCAs began to demand desegregation; following the endorsement of their position by the Executive Committee
of the Student YWCA in 1923, Student Y conferences and meetings slowly
but steadily became integrated. Regional summer conferences held throughout
the country were integrated during the interwar decades, with the exception
of those in the South; in 1944 the southern Student YWCA withdrew its sup-

port from the one remaining segregated regional conference, putting it in the forefront of racial change in the South. The national board of the YWCA also took steps toward racial integration, deciding in 1934 that all national meetings would be integrated.[19]

In 1946 the persistent demands of black women and their white allies for integration culminated in the attempt to establish a policy for the YWCA as a whole. Responding to a request from the Student Division, the 1940 national convention authorized the national board to conduct a study of interracial relationships in community YWCAs. Published in 1944, the study documented an extensive pattern of racial segregation in community YWCAs and recommended racial integration of all aspects of the organization, including program activities, committees, boards, staff, and facilities. The report was disseminated to all community YWCAs and put on the agenda for the 1946 national convention.

As members of the YWCA gathered in 1946 to establish new guidelines for their organization, the top item on the agenda was the "Interracial Charter," which read:

> Wherever there is injustice on the basis of race, whether in the community, the nation or the world, our protest must be clear and our labor for its removal, vigorous and steady. And what we urge on others we are constrained to practice ourselves. We shall be alert to opportunities to demonstrate the richness of life inherent in an organization unhampered by artificial barriers, in which all members have full status and all persons equal honor and respect as the children of one Father.[20]

The proposal raised heated controversy, with resistance centered primarily in the South, where more than one hundred community YWCAs were located. White women from many of these Y's feared that the move toward integration would jeopardize their funding sources and alienate their white constituents. Their hesitancy was countered by other white women, who spoke more forcefully on behalf of racial justice than in earlier decades. Mary Shotwell Ingraham, president of the YWCA, played a critical role in the 1946 convention, arguing fervently in public addresses as well as behind-the-scenes caucuses with women from resistant southern associations that the Y had a Christian commitment to equality. After extensive discussion by the delegates, Ingraham called for a vote on the convention floor. She asked the audience whether, if adopted, the Interracial Charter would be easy to implement. A resounding "no" arose from the room. She then asked those present to raise their convention books in the air to signify aye or nay. It was an exhilarating moment for the integrationist forces when delegates realized that not a single woman had raised her book to vote no. Some southern associations had withdrawn from the convention before the final vote, but most had been persuaded of the moral imperative of the Interracial Charter. The YWCA had pledged itself to breaking down the barriers of race and creating within its ranks an "interracial fellowship."[21]

While gender differences are not easily explained, it seems clear that progressive women's increasing concern with racial justice distinguished them from their male allies. Certainly there were many men whose views were every bit as progressive as those of women in the YWCA, and both white men and women exhibited a greater concern with racial justice after the war. Furthermore, the social reform politics of men and women converged to some degree during this period, as women focused less on the needs of women and children or discrimination based on sex and more on seemingly gender-neutral concerns. But differences are nevertheless evident in the social reform politics of men and women. The clearest case for contrasting goals can be made by examining the male counterpart to the YWCA, the YMCA.

The YWCA and the YMCA had developed from Christian evangelical roots in the late nineteenth century, and both had been heavily influenced by the Social Gospel in the early twentieth century. During the 1920s and 1930s, black members challenged segregated practices in the two organizations with only modest results outside the Student Divisions; only after decades of internal struggle did the YWCA and the YMCA pledge themselves to racial integration in 1946. Despite their apparently parallel courses, throughout the postwar period the YWCA had a reputation for a forthright commitment to racial justice that the YMCA did not. A 1946 survey conducted by the YMCA of city officials, editors, ministers, and educators, black and white, from twenty-four cities across the country, concurred that in most communities the YW was far ahead of the YM in race relations. The president of a local branch of the NAACP summed it up by saying, "We're welcome at the YWCA. We know we're not wanted at the YMCA." A number of blacks in southern communities interviewed in the late 1950s for a study of YM–YW relationships reported that the YWCA often provided their only channel of communication with the white community.[22]

Women in the YWCA were quite aware of the contrast, and that awareness provided a major incentive for resisting efforts on the part of the YMCA and funding agencies to merge the two organizations in the postwar years. Dorothy Height, who was the most influential black woman on the staff of the national board of the YWCA for three decades after she was hired in 1944, argued that women's voluntary organizations, not men's, "have been in the forefront" of the struggle for social change.[23]

The explanations for the differences between the two organizations are elusive, but four factors seem critical. First, the leadership of black women within a predominantly white organization was key. Unlike most women's organizations, which were racially exclusive, the Y was a predominantly white organization that embraced a substantial number of women of other racial groups as well. African American women made up approximately 10 percent of the membership during the 1940s and 1950s, and women of Japanese, Chinese, and Mexican descent also were members. Black women on the national board and its staff, in local community associations, and in the Student YWCA, consistently applied pressure on their white sisters to endorse racial integration in the two decades preceding World War II.

The significance of religious ideals in the YWCA helps explain why white women were more receptive to this pressure from black members than their white male counterparts in the YMCA. Religious idealism had been a potent factor in the lives of American women and had drawn thousands of white women into the antislavery struggle. Women have predominated in the congregations of most American religious groups since the early nineteenth century, and today "by nearly every indicator" they continue to "manifest greater attachment to religious beliefs and practices than do men." [24] Many participants believed that the YWCA's Christian purpose served as a touchstone for their efforts to build an interracial organization. That purpose pledged all members "to build a fellowship of women and girls devoted to . . . those ideals of personal and social living to which we are committed by our faith as Christians" and to "share his (Jesus) love for all people." [25]

Third, some participants have suggested that YWCA members had better education, better training, and deeper grounding in the issues than YMCA members. Here, the power of sexism is evident. In contrast to men, women had scant opportunity for leadership in the wider society, and the more highly educated and determined might have seen such opportunity in YWCA membership. The YWCA also provided more in-service training for the development of leadership qualities, a key goal of the organization, and its characteristically democratic procedures enabled women to become experts on issues. The YWCA's national conventions featured extensive discussion of the social and political issues of the day, and so many women spent considerable time preparing for the conventions with study and discussion. The YMCA national conventions put less emphasis on discussion and democratic decision making and seem to have been more hierarchical.[26]

Class interests also shaped the differences between the two organizations. Community YMCAs were dominated by conservative business elements throughout much of the twentieth century. Wealthy women also dominated the national and local boards of the YWCA before World War II, but during the late 1940s middle-class women increasingly served on these boards. Working-class women were active, particularly during the interwar period, maintaining a steady leftward pressure on the YWCA; working-class men were less involved in the YMCA, in part because they had greater access to labor unions.[27] Usually less active in creating and defending wealth than men, women historically have had a more marginal relationship to economic power; elite women do defend the social order that secures their privilege but seem more open than men to challenging it.[28]

As progressive women became more concerned with racial justice, changes in goals did not automatically mean changes in tactics. During the first four decades of the twentieth century, women's voluntary organizations developed and pursued pressure-group politics, conducting thorough examinations of social problems and then devising educational programs and lobbying activities to promote solutions.[29] These techniques remained the favored techniques of most postwar women's organizations. Civil rights measures, for instance, became a major focus of the YWCA's Public Affairs program. Immediately after the war, the Y supported a trio of proposals that constituted the highest priority of civil rights groups: antilynching legislation, abolition of the poll tax, and the creation of a permanent Fair Employment Practices Commission. In addition, the YWCA endorsed all the major civil rights bills considered by Congress during the postwar years. Mildred Persinger, a white woman elected chair of the Public Affairs Committee in 1958, recalled that the YWCA gave her "a marvelous opportunity to see that these issues (of social justice) were given attention" by bringing the weight of a large organization to bear in Washington. At the local level, Public Affairs committees sponsored educational forums and urged their members to support national civil rights legislation and fair housing statutes at the state level. After the Supreme Court's decision in *Brown* v. *Board of Education,* which declared that racially separate schools were inherently unequal, the YWCA pushed for implementation of the decision on a number of fronts.[30]

Newer strategies emphasized a female ethic as central to creating social change, particularly through building friendships across racial lines. The YWCA's widespread effort to educate young women and girls to an antiracist consciousness after World War II emphasized the importance of promoting personal communication between women of different races as a means of breaking down racial stereotypes. The Y offered literature, speakers, educational forums, and discussion groups that hammered home the message that racial minority groups were unfairly subordinated. But the summer conferences of the Student YWCA, held in every region of the country, provided the central emotional and intellectual experience in the Y's drive to create antiracist consciousness, and here personal relationships were key.

Conferences often provided interracial experiences that transformed racial consciousness. Of a typical conference experience, one young white woman reported, "I had never eaten previously at a table with a Negro—I had never gone swimming with a Negro, I had never talked to a Negro girl about dating and marriage. Before long I realized that in hundreds of little ways we felt the same whether our skin was dark or light. For the first time in my life I was talking to and working with Negro women who had as good and in many cases a better educational background than I. I had to *admit* to myself that they knew what they were talking about—that as a beginner there was much I could learn from them, and I had to accept them on my own level." Conferences broke down racial stereotypes among young black women as well, as the words of one young adolescent suggest: "I learned to mix with white girls and discovered all whites are not prejudiced." Nor were these isolated voices. A study of girls who attended Y-Teen summer conferences in the southern region from 1958 to 1962 found that 78 percent of those attending interracial conferences responded that the most important part of their conference experience related to "race relations." Furthermore, Y records are replete with hundreds of personal testimonials from all parts of the country that speak to the power of personal contacts in breaking down racial preconceptions and promoting a sense of racial equality.[31]

Black and white women agreed on the importance of developing comfortable interpersonal relationships across racial lines. But the effort necessarily put different burdens on each group. White women might face criticism from black colleagues for racist remarks and actions, but blacks had the more difficult task of confronting the sting of racial prejudice, with its implication of inferiority. Just as they had in the interwar period, black women shouldered the burden of educating their white colleagues about racism, believing that only through persistent efforts would whites begin to change racist attitudes. It was not always a pleasant task, but it was one undertaken out of deep conviction. When an "open door" policy was adopted in white YWCAs in the immediate postwar period in an attempt to create integrated programs, black participation was often minimal. One black leader commented, "You have no idea what you have to be continually doing to keep up the morale of Negro girls so that they can take the kind of things they have to meet. . . . It is not any fun to be in a mixed group; some girls do it because they think it is important, but it takes courage."[32]

Yet black women also insisted that an examination of personal relationships and personal prejudice was only part of the struggle against racism. On the national board of the YWCA Dorothy Height continually pressed this point. Height was "brilliant, and a wonderful teacher," recalled a prominent white member of the board. She was gracious, thoughtful, and outspoken. Height had a quick response ready when some board members complained that she always brought up the issue of racial justice: "That's my job." Height sensed that many of her white colleagues who professed concern with racial equality were preoccupied with whether they were personally free of prejudice. From Height's perspective, these women were using relationships with people of color "to test themselves, rather than to be sensitive to the needs of others." She exhorted them to take a broader view, focusing on organizational aspects of racism and pointing out that in the YWCA this often took the form of white domination of leadership positions. Insisting that white women could not successfully represent the interests of black women, she stressed the need for white and black women to share leadership roles.

Jewel Graham, a black woman who was active in the late 1940s and later became president of the YWCAs of the USA (1979–1985) and president of the World YWCA (1987–1991), echoed Height's understanding of the different perspectives of black and white women in the Y. "I didn't see a tremendous difference in style [of working]," she recalled, "but I think that the black women always had race on their agenda and saw issues through that perspective and sometimes white women would forget." [33] Height and Graham understood that the issue of racial justice was not simply personal but political as well.

YWCA leaders, black and white, aimed not merely to transform attitudes but to inspire women to work against racial injustice in the larger society. Their hopes were at least partially realized. The combination of moral exhortation, information, and interracial experience in the YWCA was a potent mixture that sparked a genuine change of consciousness among many participants. Those most profoundly affected by the Y's message joined the struggle against racial injustice. For example, Mary King and Casey (Sandra) Hayden, two southern white women who would play important roles in the Student Non-Violent Coordinating Committee (SNCC) in the early 1960s, credited the YWCA with their dawning awareness of racial injustice. Casey Hayden recalled that it was at YWCA regional meetings "that I first came into contact with the personal feelings of young black people about segregation." When the sit-in movement reached Austin, Texas, where Hayden was attending the university, she immediately joined it. [34]

Thus the YWCA continued to influence the political process through the traditions of pressure-group politics developed by women's groups in the first four decades of the twentieth century. At the same time, the YWCA's emphasis on the quality of personal relationships presaged the concern with "personal politics" so evident in the social movements of the 1960s. Y leaders viewed personal interracial encounters as a means to consciousness raising. But the development of good personal relationships between people of different races was not simply a means to an end but an end in itself, one defined in terms of Christian ideals. The southern civil rights movement in the early 1960s shared a similar understanding of the centrality of love in building "the beloved community"—not simply a new politics but a new way of living with and relating to other people was necessary. The northern student movement echoed some of these themes. Ultimately, the women's liberation movement developed the slogan "the personal is political" to suggest that social inequality was reflected in personal relationships and that transforming the latter was one avenue toward transforming the former.[35]

Throughout the late nineteenth and twentieth centuries, women activists confronted a major dilemma in their pursuit of social reform goals: whether to fight for influence within male-dominated organizations or to maintain autonomy by working through separate female institutions. The incentives for allying with or working within male organizations were obvious: access to greater financial resources and more political clout. Yet the liabilities were equally telling. Women hoped that their political perspectives and personal capabilities would be respected by male colleagues, only to be disappointed as they found themselves relegated to positions of little power. Still, the decision to work in a mixed-sex organization did not have to preclude single-sex membership in another organization, and many women, black and white, participated in both types during the postwar period. For example, black women often joined one or more single-sex organizations such as the YWCA, the National Council of Negro Women, or the black sororities and at the same time worked with the NAACP or the Urban League.

Significant cracks in this pattern of marginalization of women within mixed-sex organizations first began to occur in mainstream political parties only in the 1970s, with the partial exception of Franklin Roosevelt's New Deal administration. But within mixed-sex social reform and labor organizations, women experienced a growing degree of influence in the period after World War II.[36] Women's power was rarely evident at the highest levels of such organizations; they achieved positions at the middle ranks of organizational hierarchies, and often made their presence felt by working in less publicly visible ways than did male leaders.

Women's activities in the American Friends Service Committee clearly illustrate this pattern. In the 1940s and 1950s the AFSC was a male-dominated organization: the chairman of the board of directors, the executive secretary of the National Office, and all the executive secretaries of the Regional Offices, with one exception, were male. But in the postwar era, women began to obtain significant positions as program administrators within the organization. For example, Julia Branson headed the Foreign Division from 1950 to 1955, and Barbara Moffett has headed the Community Relations Division from 1956 until today; many other women headed specific programs as well. Below the top level of administration, then, men and women worked as colleagues roughly equal in status; they led projects, administered programs, and worked as community organizers. The task at hand was creating social change, and men and women within the organization assumed that both sexes could contribute to that goal. The assumption that women were capable of exercising public influence grew directly from the Quaker tradition of women's leadership and activism in the Society of Friends. In the nineteenth and twentieth centuries, women were often among the most influential and active individuals in local Friends meetings.[37]

A brief look at several progressive labor unions and civil rights organizations suggests that the AFSC was not the only mixed-sex organization in which women achieved influence in the postwar world. The massive influx of women into auto plants during World War II changed the role and status of women in the United Auto Workers (UAW), for example. Women organized to exert their collective power, protesting layoffs of women from the auto industry and fighting to retain seniority rights. In civil rights organizations as well, women moved into increasingly influential positions in the 1940s and 1950s. Most influential of all was Ella Baker, who became national director of branches for the NAACP in 1943, coordinator of SCLC's Atlanta office in 1957, and the chief adviser to SNCC from 1960 to 1964. In Paula Giddings's words, "Ella Baker had become midwife to the two organizations that would have the most far-reaching impact on the civil rights movement: SCLC and SNCC."[38] Yet in all these instances, the pressures of sexism were such that women exerted their influence behind the scenes, never achieving the public visibility of male leaders.

One area in which women exerted considerable power was in the AFSC's Race Relations program (later Community Relations), initiated in 1943. Early efforts were focused on changing the attitudes of those who had power over racially segregated institutions. The board of directors envisioned programs that would rely on Quaker methods of friendly persuasion and be less focused on "getting results" than "expressing our measure of truth" to those in positions of power. In this spirit, the first major project undertaken was the Job Opportunities Project, where staff members visited employers in such fields as banking, insurance, and retail trades to convince them to open jobs traditionally reserved for whites to nonwhite applicants. Unlike the board, staff members, male and female, felt an urgency to achieve observable results, and during the 1950s they gradually transformed the focus of AFSC programs.[39]

That shift was most evident in the AFSC's efforts to integrate the schools. In 1950 the AFSC initiated its first project to facilitate school integration in Washington, D.C. in anticipation of the Supreme Court's *Brown* v. *Board of Education* decision. Irene Osborne and Alma Scurlock scheduled many individual conferences with school board members and other government officials to try to persuade them to desegregate the schools. At the same time, they mobilized the community's teachers, professionals, and government workers to put pressure on the school board. Scurlock brought her particular skills to bear in the process, for she had received a Master's degree in social work from Columbia University with a specialization in community organizing. The project thus coupled traditional Quaker methods of friendly persuasion with community organizing. Irene Osborne recalled that supervisory staff members in the AFSC national office in Philadelphia were "a little nervous at first," when she and Alma Scurlock insisted on reaching out to the larger community, instead of confining themselves to conferences with officials.[40] Osborne and Scurlock worked closely with the Joint Committee on Education, a group they had organized, to prepare statements directed to Congress and the commissioner of the District of Columbia, urging the adoption of a school desegregation plan. As the litigation that was to culminate in the *Brown* decision moved through the courts, the Board of Education requested advice from the AFSC staff. Osborne, who had primary responsibility for dealing with school issues, met frequently with officials of the board, offering suggestions and pressing for change. Scurlock concentrated on the Department of Parks and Recreation, which was moving more quickly toward integration.

Osborne also set up a series of seminars that brought together teachers from the racially segregated school system, providing the first opportunity that many black and white teachers had to meet and discuss their fears and concerns across racial lines and to explore methods for defusing the problems they anticipated in newly integrated classrooms. Led by people familiar with schools in transition, the seminars provided an atmosphere that fostered honest communication and proved so popular that they were repeated many times. Similar seminars were designed for high school students, PTA groups, and community leaders.

When the Supreme Court announced its historic school integration decision, change followed quickly. In part because the community had been galvanized in support of integration, the Washington School Board was ready to move. On May 25, 1954, eight days after *Brown*, the Board of Education announced a plan to integrate the school system. By September 1954 about two-thirds of the city's schoolchildren were attending integrated schools, and the Board of Education had called for full integration by 1960. AFSC staff members had been working within a context where many forces supported progressive and peaceful change. The Eisenhower administration made significant moves to encourage desegregation in Washington, D.C., and the Coordinating Committee for the Enforcement of the D.C. Anti-Discrimination Laws provided grass-roots support for desegregation of theaters and restaurants. Nevertheless, Osborne and Scurlock and the Joint Committee they created could claim considerable credit for facilitating a smooth transition to racial integration of schools in the nation's capital.[41]

Following the successful experiment in Washington, women activists in the AFSC were involved in many similar projects in other southern communities. Jean Fairfax, an African American woman with ten years experience in the AFSC, was hired in 1957 as national representative of southern programs, a new position that reflected the AFSC's increasing focus on school integration. Barbara Moffett, executive secretary of the AFSC's Community Relations Division, credited Fairfax with setting "the framework for the work we did in the south . . . for the next decade or twenty years."[42] Before the decade was out, the AFSC was involved in a number of school integration projects throughout the South that provided support to black parents attempting to enroll their children in integrated schools and simultaneously put pressure on white officials and community leaders to endorse school integration. A major testing ground of this strategy occurred in Little Rock, Arkansas.

The AFSC assigned Thelma Babbitt to promote racial integration in the violence-torn city of Little Rock, which had been catapulted to national and international attention in 1957 when Governor Orville Faubus used the National Guard to prevent the entrance of nine black students into Central High School. Incited by the governor's action, white mobs defied a court order to integrate and used violent means to prevent students from attending school. As the violence escalated, President Eisenhower federalized the Arkansas National Guard to restore order, and under armed escort, black students entered Central High. In a final stratagem to prevent integration, Governor Faubus closed all the public schools in Little Rock for the 1958–1959 school year.

During the summer of 1958, several members of the Little Rock Friends Meeting requested that the AFSC send a community worker to help reduce tensions and restore communication in the city. Daisy Bates, president of the local chapter of the NAACP, was actively involved in providing support to black students and their families, but there was virtually no communication between blacks and sympathetic whites. When Babbitt arrived to assume her new role, she quickly set to work contacting church groups and individuals in both communities, and she organized supporters of school integration into the interracial Committee of Community Unity (CCU), which sponsored a series of unprecedented interracial conferences to promote dialogue across racial lines. The first conference "was a very moving experience for everybody, so that at the end of the day people were . . . stunned and couldn't quite realize what happened," Babbitt recalled.

Out of these conferences emerged a program to support parents of black children who wanted to serve as the advance troops in integrating schools, undertaken jointly by the NAACP, the National Urban League, and the Arkansas Council on Human Relations. When illness forced Babbitt to resign in the winter of 1959–1960, the vigorous alliance she had organized continued to function, working successfully to defeat proposed state legislation that would allow local communities to close the schools. After Faubus's defeat at the polls in 1960, the schools reopened. Babbitt's most important contributions had been to encourage white liberals to speak out in the face of reprisals and to cement an alliance with the black community that would remain in place when the civil rights revolution swept through Little Rock in the early 1960s.[43]

Activists in the AFSC, male and female, had moved from quiet attempts to persuade officials and employers to endorse racial integration to bolder attempts to marshall communities to demand that racial segregation be dismantled. But by 1959 the AFSC had begun to reevaluate its Community Relations programs. The strategies of applying moral suasion, coupled with organizing supporters of racial integration to demand change through conventional channels, had brought only modest gains. For four years, AFSC staff members had encouraged black parents to initiate transfers of their children to white schools under the Pupil Placement Acts enacted by southern states. The results produced a meager handful of black students attending racially integrated schools. These strategies were clearly inadequate in the face of the massive resistance mounted by white southerners. At a Community Relations staff retreat in early 1960, Jean Fairfax questioned the effectiveness of moral suasion in the present situation, arguing that the legal framework would have to be altered before substantial change on school desegregation could be achieved. Barbara Moffett, secretary of the Community Relations Division of the AFSC, summarized the discussion in the following words: "We are now questioning whether our activities are strong enough to challenge a wrong law. . . . We need to look at our ability to confront leadership on the evasiveness of token desegregation." Given these limitations, AFSC staff looked increasingly to the techniques of nonviolent resistance that had proven so effective in the 1955–1956 Montgomery bus boycott to provide an alternate model for racial change. When the sit-in movement erupted in 1960, the AFSC was quick to rally behind this confrontational approach, offering support to high school and college students engaged in the struggle.[44]

In the context of this mixed-sex organization, there was more similarity than difference evident between men and women activists. A small and relatively cohesive group, the AFSC brought together men and women of similar political and religious perspectives who agreed about the social reform goals they wished to pursue. Furthermore, they were employed by the AFSC in parallel positions in a variety of Community Relations and other programs, particularly during the 1950s, and both men and women were viewed as successful organizers of such projects. Nevertheless, some subtle differences emerge on close examination.

Although strictly drawn gender lines did not divide programs, some division occurred. For example, men who had been conscientious objectors during World War II tended to dominate the peace efforts of the AFSC; most Peace Education secretaries were men, though women also worked in this program. In contrast, women gravitated toward the Community Relations programs, although men were active here as well.

A sharper division of labor was evident among grass-roots activists. Because many of their efforts focused on school integration or community development, AFSC staff members often found themselves working with a mostly female group of committed local activists. School integration efforts have tended to draw more heavily on the efforts of female activists, white or black. During the 1950s, for example, the Women's Division of Christian Service of the Board of Missions of the Methodist Church led a major drive to integrate the schools. The first whites to protest the closing of the schools in Little Rock, Arkansas, had been a group of women who organized the Women's Emergency Committee for Public Schools, although both men and women in the black community were active in the struggle. Jean Fairfax, who headed the AFSC's southern programs during the late 1950s, observed that "often in rural counties it was this group of very determined tough black women," many of whom were paid a small stipend by the AFSC to aid their organizing efforts, who provided the sustained efforts to obtain equal educational opportunities for their children.[45]

This emphasis on women's activities should not be taken as an attempt to minimize the efforts of men. In southern rural communities, fathers of children who pioneered in integrating the schools had to be just as strong and courageous as mothers, for they too were subject to economic and physical reprisals. And in Washington, D.C., which had a well-developed middle-class black community, men dominated among the black activists involved in school integration, while the whites involved were more evenly divided between men and women.[46] Here, leadership patterns may have varied between middle-class black communities in urban areas and poorer black communities in rural areas. But, in general, women predominated in the work on school integration. Historically, women's concern with children has led them to be particularly involved in school issues, serving on school boards and running the PTA. The issue of quality schooling for children may have been nearer to the hearts of mothers; certainly in cases where schools were closed, they bore the immediate burden of increased child-care responsibilities.[47]

Women staff organizers faced fewer social barriers than men in making connections with grass-roots activists, most of whom were women. These women staff members were particularly effective in drawing on and helping to sustain female networks of community activists, activities that called on female patterns of socialization.[48] At the same time, women did not shirk the many daily tasks that organizing entailed. Men also were involved in networking; but women seem to network more easily, as such activities fit well within their lifetime patterns of behavior.

Barbara Graves, who administered several of the AFSC's overseas programs in the postwar period, reflected on the subtle gender differences within the organization, recalling: "Certain attitudes bothered me—patterns of refusing to acknowledge that anybody needed any help or any supervision . . . this strong sense of the individual and *his* light being what guided us in this institution. I struggled a lot to develop better personnel policies and some understanding of the suffering that men and women went through overseas with loneliness, a sense of failure, and a lack of support. I attributed a lot of that to the male ethic that dominated our institutional patterns."[49] Despite that male ethic, women activists in the AFSC worked to ensure the incorporation of a female ethic in the ongoing daily work of AFSC projects.

Following in the footsteps of earlier generations, women progressive activists continued to seek social and political change in the postwar world. The efforts of women in the 1940s and 1950s provided an important bridge between earlier generations of women activists and those involved in social movements of the 1960s. During this transitional period, a consensus began to develop about the need to eliminate racial segregation and discrimination from American society, and many women activists moved far beyond the tentative attempts taken in the interwar period to create interracial dialogue. A new sense of urgency about racial injustice informed the efforts of white progressive women activists after 1945. A number of women's organizations opened their membership to equal participation of African American women, and some worked actively to transform the nation's racist attitudes and practices. Not until the 1960s did the struggle for civil rights take center stage on the nation's reform agenda, but women in the YWCA and the AFSC had consistently worked for an end to racial segregation in the preceding decades. The strategies and tactics employed by women activists to achieve that goal drew on the heritage of the past, yet transformed women's progressive politics as well. Traditional methods of pressure-group politics, developed by women's voluntary groups in earlier decades, remained a significant focus for the YWCA, which relied on its large and influential membership to apply pressure in favor of civil rights legislation. The AFSC also sought to put pressure on government and private individuals deemed sufficiently powerful to bring about change, thus working through established channels of influence even when not directly engaged in lobbying activities.

Newer techniques that presaged the "personal politics" of the civil rights and feminist movements of the 1960s were also evident during the 1940s and 1950s. Women in both the YWCA and the AFSC employed a female ethic in their organizing efforts, one that relied on building interpersonal networks to raise consciousness and sustain the daily tasks of organization. The YWCA's efforts to change the consciousness of its members about racial injustice as a means of changing underlying racist attitudes were markedly similar to the later attempt of the women's movement to transform the ideas of individual women about gender relations as a means of transforming those relations. At an institutional level, the AFSC gave less explicit attention to individual needs and relationships. Yet in the context of work that relied heavily on networks of women activists in local communities, women in the AFSC worked to maintain a female ethic in their daily organizing activities. Furthermore, as men and women together within the AFSC sought to mobilize larger groups in the community to demand change by the 1950s, they moved away from an emphasis on applying moral suasion in one-on-one encounters with influential individuals and embraced the techniques of community organizing to apply pressure on officials. The civil rights organizations took the next step, staging massive nonviolent demonstrations that became the hallmark of the movement.

Women in the post–World War II era did not abandon social activism; among others, those in the YWCA and AFSC played critical roles in sustaining a progressive critique of American society during precisely those decades when so much effort was made to mute female voices. They endorsed racial integration within women's voluntary groups, lobbied for civil rights legislation, and worked in communities to open schools, housing, and employment opportunities to all Americans. They contributed substantially to the transformation of the American racial order by building a groundswell of support for the ideal of racial equality on which the civil rights movement could build. Women made an important difference in both single-sex and mixed-sex organizations, bringing a female ethic to the work they did in communities and organizations. The story of this generation of women political activists reminds us of the importance of sustaining women's social reform efforts during conservative eras, in order to maintain and transform the traditions and ideas that younger generations of activists can build on.

NOTES

Acknowledgments: I thank Joanne Meyerowitz for her thoughtful comments, which helped me sharpen and refine my argument. I also benefited from the careful reading and thoughtful comments of Paula Giddings. Nancy Hewitt gave generously of her time as an editor; her suggestions were invaluable. Steven Lawson, Charles Payne, and an anonymous reviewer for *Gender and History* also read the manuscript; I appreciate their helpful comments. I also thank Estelle Freedman, Susan Hartmann, Sorca O'Connor, Peggy Pascoe, and Kathryn Kish Sklar, who read and commented on earlier versions of this article. I thank Elizabeth Norris, archivist and librarian of the national board of the YWCA, for information on the class composition of the YWCA board structure.

1. *Toward the Elimination of Segregation in the Nation's Capital; A Report of an AFSC Community Relations Project with Public Schools and Recreation Areas, 1951–1955* (Philadelphia: AFSC, 1955).

2. Interview with Irene Osborne, conducted by author, March 5, 1984; interview with Alma Scurlock, conducted by author, June 17, 1989.

3. Much of the literature on domesticity focuses on middle-class experience. We need further research on the relation of working-class women to domestic ideals. See Dorothy Sue Cobble, "Reassessing the 'Doldrum Years': Working Class Feminism in the 1940s," paper presented at the Eighth Annual Berkshire Conference on the History of Women, Douglass College, Rutgers University, June 1990; Joanne Meyerowitz, "Beyond 'The Feminine Mystique': The Discourse on American Women, 1945–1950," paper presented at the Eighth Berkshire Conference on the History of Women, Douglass College, Rutgers University, June 1990.

4. Betty Friedan, *The Feminine Mystique* (New York: Norton, 1963). Joanne Meyerowitz presented an important reinterpretation of this literature in "Beyond the Feminine Mystique: A Reassessment of Postwar Mass Culture, 1946–1958," *Journal of American History,* March 1993.

5. Ethel Klein, *Gender Politics: From Consciousness to Mass Politics* (Cambridge, Mass.: Harvard University Press, 1984).

6. Amy Swerdlow, "Ladies' Day at the Capitol: Women Strike for Peace versus HUAC," *Feminist Studies,* Fall 1982, 493–520.

7. Paula Giddings, *When and Where I Enter: The Impact of Black Women on Race and Sex in America* (New York: Morrow, 1984), 243–246; Rosalyn Terborg-Penn, "Discontented Black Feminists: Prelude and Postscript to the Passage of the Nineteenth Amendment," in *Decades of Discontent: The Women's Movement, 1920–1940,* ed. Lois Scharf and Joan M. Jensen (Westport, Conn.: Greenwood Press, 1983), 274; Jacqueline Ann Rouse, *Eugenia Burns Hope: Black Southern Reformer* (Athens: University of Georgia Press, 1989); Cynthia Neverdon-Morton, *Afro-American Women of the South and the Advancement of the Race, 1895–1925* (Knoxville: University of Tennessee Press, 1989); Anne Firor Scott, "Most Invisible of All: Black Women's Voluntary Organizations," *Journal of Southern History,* February 1990, 3–22; Eileen Boris, "The Power of Motherhood: Black and White Activist Women Redefine the 'Political,' " *Yale Journal of Law and Feminism,* Fall 1989, 25–49.

8. Leila J. Rupp and Verta M. Taylor, *Survival in the Doldrums: The American*

Women's Rights Movement, 1945 to the 1960s (New York: Oxford University Press, 1987); Cynthia Harrison, *On Account of Sex: The Politics of Women's Issues, 1945–1968* (Berkeley: University of California Press, 1988).

9. Other organizations in the progressive coalition included the Congress of Racial Equality, the Fellowship of Reconciliation, the War Resister's League, the Federal Council of Churches, and the Anti-Defamation League of B'nai B'rith. A strong working-class component was represented by the AFL-CIO and a number of progressive unions such as the United Auto Workers.

10. Carol Gilligan, *In a Different Voice: Psychological Theory and Women's Development* (Cambridge, Mass.: Harvard University Press, 1982); Mary Field Belenky, Blythe McVicker Clinchy, Nancy Rule Goldberger, and Jill Mattuck Tarule, *Women's Ways of Knowing: The Development of Self, Voice, and Mind* (New York: Basic Books, 1986); Nancy Chodorow, *The Reproduction of Mothering: Psychoanalysis and the Sociology of Gender* (Berkeley: University of California Press, 1978). Gilligan and Chodorow have been criticized because their studies are based on white middle-class women. Yet African American women scholars have also noted the centrality of networks of extended family and friends in the lives of black women; see Patricia Hill Collins, "The Social Construction of Black Feminist Thought," *Signs,* Summer 1989, 745–773; Elsa Barkley Brown, "Mothers of Mind," *Sage: A Scholarly Journal on Black Women,* Summer 1989, 4–11.

11. Kathryn Kish Sklar, "Hull House in the 1890s: A Community of Women Reformers," *Signs,* Summer 1985, 658–677.

12. Sara Evans, *Personal Politics: The Roots of Women's Liberation in the Civil Rights Movement and the New Left* (New York: Vintage Books, 1980).

13. Seth Koven and Sonya Michel, "Womanly Duties: Maternalist Politics and the Origins of Welfare States in France, Germany, Great Britain, and the United States, 1880–1920," *American Historical Review,* October 1990, 1076–1108.

14. The shift from maternalism toward interracialism occurred somewhat earlier among black women and a few of their white allies, for during the interwar years black women began to demand racial integration in groups like the YWCA. See Jacqueline Dowd Hall, *Revolt against Chivalry: Jessie Daniel Ames and the Women's Campaign against Lynching* (New York: Columbia University Press, 1979); Rouse, *Eugenia Burns Hope.*

15. Nancy F. Cott, *The Grounding of Modern Feminism* (New Haven: Yale University Press, 1987), 87–89; Alice Kessler-Harris, *Out to Work: A History of Wage-Earning Women in the United States* (New York: Oxford University Press, 1982), 305–306.

16. Mary Frederickson, "Citizens for Democracy: The Industrial Programs of the YWCA," in *Sisterhood and Solidarity: Workers' Education for Women, 1914–1984,* ed. Joyce L. Kornbluh and Mary Frederickson (Philadelphia: Temple University Press, 1984).

17. By 1947, membership in the YWCA's Industrial Department dropped to 11,000. See Karen Sue Mittelman, " 'A Spirit That Touches the Problems of Today': Women and Social Reform in the Philadelphia Young Women's Christian Association, 1920–1945," Ph.D. dissertation, University of Pennsylvania, 1987. On women's activism in the CIO, see Ruth Milkman, *Gender at Work: The Dynamics of Job Segregation by Sex During World War II* (Urbana, Il.: University of Illinois Press, 1987); Nancy Gabin, *Feminism in the Labor Movement: Women in the United Auto Workers, 1935–1975* (Ithaca: York: Cornell University Press, 1990).

18. Terborg-Penn, "Discontented Black Feminists"; Angela Y. Davis, *Women, Race and Class* (New York: Vintage Books, 1981). On the Communist party, see Robin D. G. Kelley, *Hammer and Hoe: Alabama Communists during the Great Depression* (Chapel Hill: University of North Carolina Press, 1990).

19. The YWCA was a multiracial organization before World War II, yet racial segregation remained the rule in most community YWCAs. In communities with large black populations, the YWCA had established black branches, administered by black staff but ultimately controlled by and dependent on funding from central white YWCA associations. Of 417 Associations, 73 had black branches in 1940. See Adrienne Lash Jones, "Struggle among Saints: Black Women in the YWCA, 1860–1920," paper presented at the Organization of American Historians, Louisville, Kentucky, April 12, 1991. On the Student YWCA, see Frances Taylor, "On the Edge of Tomorrow: Southern Women, the Student YWCA, and Race, 1920–1944," Ph.D. dissertation, Stanford University, 1984.

20. National Board of the YWCA, "The Interracial Charter and Related Policy, 1955." YWCA, National Board Archives, New York.

21. Dorothy Sabiston and Margaret Hiller, *Toward Better Race Relations* (New York: Woman's Press, 1949), 2–3; interview with Helen Grant, conducted by author, October 27, 1983.

22. Jesse Howell Atwood, *The Racial Factor in YMCAs: A Report on Negro–White Relationships in Twenty-Four Cities* (New York: Association Press, 1946), 56; Dan W. Dodson, *The Role of the YWCA in a Changing Era: The YWCA Study of YMCA–YWCA Cooperative Experiences* (New York: National Board of the YWCA of the USA, 1960), 85–86.

23. Ruth Edmonds Hill, ed., *The Black Women Oral History Project: From the Arthur and Elizabeth Schlesinger Library on the History of Women in America, Radcliffe College* (Westport, Conn.: Meckler, 1991), 5:94.

24. Robert Wuthnow and William Lehrman, "Religion: Inhibitor or Facilitator of Political Involvement among Women?" in *Women, Politics, and Change,* ed. Louise A. Tilly and Patricia Gurin, (New York: Russell Sage Foundation, 1990), 302. On black men in the YMCA, see Nina Mjagkij, "A History of the Black YMCA in America, 1853–1946," Ph.D. dissertation, University of Cincinnati, 1990.

25. Gladys Gilkey Calkins, "The Negro in the Young Women's Christian Association: A Study of the Development of YWCA Interracial Policies and Practices in this Historical Setting," Master's Thesis, George Washington University, 1960, 82. Participants and scholars concur on the importance of the YWCA's purpose in promoting racial equality. See, for example, interview with Dorothy Height, conducted by author, June 13, 1990; Sharlene Voogd Cochrane, " 'The Pressure Never Let Up': Black Women, White Women, and the Boston YWCA, 1918–1948," in *Women in the Civil Rights Movement: Trailblazers and Torchbearers, 1941–1965,* ed. Vicki L. Crawford, Jacqueline Anne Rouse, and Barbara Woods (New York: Carlson Publishing, 1990), 259–269; interview with Helen Grant, conducted by author, October 27, 1983.

26. Interview with Garnet Guild, conducted by author, July 7, 1990; interview with Charlotte Bunch, conducted by author, April 2, 1991; telephone conversation with Adrienne Lash Jones, April 15, 1991.

27. On the contrast between working-class involvement in the YW and the YM, see Kenneth Fones-Wolf, "Gender, Class Relations and the Transformation of Voluntary Organizations: Labor Reform in the Philadelphia YM and YWCAs, 1890–1930," paper

presented at the Organization of American Historians' Annual Meeting, Washington, D.C., 1990.

28. For an interesting contrast between affluent men's and women's voluntary efforts in Chicago, see Maureen A. Flanagan, "Gender and Urban Political Reform: The City Club and the Woman's City Club of Chicago in the Progressive Era," *American Historical Review*, October 1990, 1032–1050. In another example, wives and sisters of local manufacturers in Durham, North Carolina, took up the cause of white women employed in the textile mills in their state during the 1920s, much to the chagrin of their male relatives. See Dolores E. Janiewski, *Sisterhood Denied: Race, Gender, and Class in a New South Community* (Philadelphia: Temple University Press, 1985), 83.

29. Cott, *The Grounding of Modern Feminism*.

30. Interview with Mildred Persinger, conducted by author, April 3, 1984; Young Women's Christian Associations of the USA, 18th National Convention, 1949, *Proceedings*, YWCA, National Board Archives, New York; Statement of the National Board of YWCAs of USA in support of civil rights legislation, July 8, 1958, Records Files Collection, YWCA, National Board Archives, New York (hereafter cited as RFC, YWCA); Minutes of the National Board, May 6, 1959, RFC, YWCA; Black Women Oral History Project: Dorothy I. Height, 1974–1976, transcript, p. 123; "Summary of Report on Project Responsibilities, 1956–57," Grace T. Hamilton to Edith Lerrigo, August 28, 1957, RFC, YWCA; "Report of Projects Undertaken in the Area of Racial Inclusiveness during the Current Triennium, 1955–1958," RFC, YWCA.

31. "Methods of Combatting Discrimination: Descriptive Record Submitted to World YWCA by YWCA of USA, 1954," RFC, YWCA; "A Study of the Effect of the Interracial Aspect of the Program of Six Y-Teen Summer Conferences in the Southern Region on Girls Who Attended from 1958 through 1962," Reported by Lillian H. Jackson, Field Consultant, Southern Region, RFC, YWCA.

32. Sabiston and Hiller, *Toward Better Race Relations*, 21.

33. Persinger interview; Interview with Dorothy I. Height, conducted by author, April 3, 1984; Interview with Jewel Graham, conducted by author, December 12, 1990.

34. Casey Hayden, "The Women's Movement and Nonviolent Direct Action Movement against Segregation, 1960–65," in author's possession; Evans, *Personal Politics;* Mary King, *Freedom Song: A Personal Story of the 1960s Civil Rights Movement* (New York: Morrow, 1987).

35. Evans, *Personal Politics*.

36. Susan Ware, *Beyond Suffrage: Women in the New Deal* (Cambridge, Mass.: Harvard University Press, 1981); Susan Ware, *Partner and I: Molly Dewson, Feminism, and New Deal Politics* (New Haven: Yale University Press, 1987).

37. Elizabeth Potts Brown and Susan Mosher Stuard, eds., *Witnesses for Change: Quaker Women in Historical Perspective* (New Brunswick, N.J.: Rutgers University Press, 1989).

38. On women in labor unions, see Milkman, *Gender at Work;* Gabin, *Feminism in the Labor Movement.* For quote on Ella Baker, see Giddings, *When and Where I Enter*, 275; see also Crawford et al., *Women in the Civil Rights Movement: Trailblazers and Torchbearers, 1941–1965;* Charles Payne, "Ella Baker and Models of Social Change," *Signs*, Summer 1989, 885–899.

39. *In the House of Friends: A Social Science View of a Quaker Program in Race Relations* (Philadelphia: Community Relations Program, AFSC, 1955), 53.

40. Interview with Irene Osborne, conducted by author, May 23, 1989.

41. Osborne interview, March 5, 1984; "Toward the Elimination of Segregation in the Nation's Capital"; Scurlock interview; Michael S. Mayer, "The Eisenhower Administration and the Desegregation of Washington, D.C.," *Journal of Policy History,* Fall 1990, 24–41.

42. Interview with Barbara Moffett, conducted by author, March 8, 1984.

43. "A Report on Little Rock Community Relations Program," September 1959 to December 1960, by Thelma W. Babbitt, director, AFSC Archives, Philadelphia; taped material provided by Thelma Babbitt in response to author's questions, September 1984; interview with Thelma Babbitt, conducted by author, September 23, 1987; Daisy Bates, *The Long Shadow of Little Rock: A Memoir* (New York: McKay, 1962).

44. Minutes of the Community Relations Round-up, February 28 to March 4, 1960, AFSC Archives, Philadelphia; "Public Schools and Token Desegregation in North Carolina," Bill Bagwell, resource paper for 1960 Community Relations Roundup, AFSC Archives; Community Relations Round-Up, April 7–12, 1957, AFSC Archives, Philadelphia; Max Hierich, "Summary Evaluation of AFSC Workshop on Nonviolence," April 2, 1960, AFSC Archives, Philadelphia; Visit to Southeast Regional Office, August 31 to September 2, 1959, Jean Fairfax; memo to Subcommittee on Southern Programs from Jean Fairfax, November 8, 1960, AFSC Archives, Philadelphia.

45. Alice G. Knotts, "Methodist Women Integrate Schools and Housing, 1952–1959," in Crawford et al., *Women in the Civil Rights Movement,* 251–258; on the Women's Emergency Committee for Public Schools, see Julia Kirk Blackwelder, "Race, Ethnicity, and Women's Lives in the Urban South," in *Shades of the Sunbelt: Essays on Ethnicity, Race, and the Urban South,* ed. Randall M. Miller and George E. Pozetta (Westport, Conn.: Greenwood Press, 1988); interview with Jean Fairfax, conducted by author, March 4, 1984.

46. Interview with Irene Osborne, conducted by author, March 6, 1991.

47. See, for example, Marie Laberge, " 'We Are Proud of Our Gains': Wisconsin Black Women's Organizational Work in the Post World War II Era," paper presented at the Eighth Berkshire Conference on the History of Women, Douglass College, June 9, 1990.

48. In a study of union organizing efforts at Duke University Medical Center in the 1970s, Karen Sacks observed similar gender differences between men and women activists: "Women created the detail, made people feel part of it, and did the menial work upon which most things depended, while men made public pronouncements, confronted, and negotiated with management." See her *Caring by the Hour: Women, Work, and Organizing at Duke Medical Center* (Urbana: University of Illinois Press, 1988), 120.

49. Interview with Barbara Graves, conducted by author, November 11, 1983.

CHAPTER 7

Harriet Hyman Alonso

MAYHEM AND
MODERATION

Women Peace Activists

during the

McCarthy Era

World War II devastated the U.S. women's peace organizations that had formed between 1914 and 1924. The Women's Peace Society, the Women's Peace Union, and the National Committee on the Cause and Cure of War disintegrated because of depression economics and war fever. Only the Women's International League for Peace and Freedom (WILPF), founded as the Woman's Peace Party in 1915, survived the war. With just a few hundred members, the organization tried desperately to rebuild its membership. From 1945 to 1955, the peak of the McCarthy era proved extremely trying for WILPF as well as for those newly developed postwar women's peace organizations such as the Congress of American Women (CAW) and its successor, American Women for Peace (AWP).

In 1945 the U.S. section of WILPF celebrated its thirtieth anniversary. The organization had survived two world wars, the 1920s Red Scare, and the Great Depression; and in 1946, one of its founders and international leaders, Emily Greene Balch, won the Nobel Peace Prize for her work with the organization. Despite its longevity and its accomplishments, in the postwar era WILPF members felt they were under suspicion for their anti-war activities. The vulnerability reached from the national board in Philadel-phia to local branches situated throughout the United States. During these years, membership did not easily expand and overly cautious landlords de-nied local branches places to meet. Worse, WILPF members became suspi-cious of one another. The paranoia so rampant in U.S. society played itself out within specific branches, ripping the organization apart from within. The national board attempted to address the problem by condemning the govern-ment's political repression of Communists and at the same time portraying the organization as non-Communist.[1] This resulted in a paralyzing distrust among members who embraced a variety of ideologies.

More left-leaning women who formed such new organizations as the Con-gress of American Women and American Women for Peace were also ham-pered by the laws and spirit of the McCarthy era. The government openly attacked the CAW, whose members refused to cooperate in any way with McCarthyite tactics. As a result, the organization was forced to disband. American Women for Peace had little success in recapturing the support behind the CAW and languished after only three years of organizing.

The post–World War II era was characterized by the worst Red Scare in the history of the United States.[2] Just as peace was declared, the Cold War with the Soviet Union accelerated. Allies during the war became enemies immedi-ately after, and, as in the 1920s, people in the United States who had opposed war and supported societal reform became targets of a government campaign to uncover "Communist traitors." President Harry Truman, an ardent anti-Communist, encouraged this popular unrest. In 1947, his administration ini-tiated the investigations into the loyalty of well over three million U.S. gov-ernment employees. Three years later, the U.S. government dismissed alleged "security risks." Repercussions eventually reached beyond the government to labor unions, college campuses, the media, and political action organizations. By 1949, with the Soviet A-bomb test, the rise of a communist China, and the continuing development of communist governments in Eastern Europe, anticommunist sentiment in the United States had escalated.

In 1950, when Senator Joseph McCarthy claimed to have a list of more than two hundred names of State Department employees who were Communists, the hysteria entered a new stage. Now labeled "McCarthyism," the Red Scare included a series of hearings before the House Committee on Un-American Ac-tivities (HUAC), which attempted to expose Communists and their supporters. Political action organizations, in particular, suffered from the 1950 Internal Security (or McCarran) Act, which required members of government-labeled "Communist-front" organizations to register with the Subversive Activities

Control Board. The act also prohibited members of such organizations from holding defense jobs or traveling abroad. In this climate, peace organizations became particularly vulnerable because their members favored friendly relations with all nations, communist or not. Government representatives often portrayed pacifists as weak links and dupes, vulnerable to Communist trickery. Such societal and govermental paranoia made it virtually impossible for the peace groups to operate as they had earlier.

WILPF's story was one of the most dramatic. As World War II ended and the Red Scare emerged, WILPF continued to push for pacifism. Through the late 1940s, for example, the organization's national leaders supported the United Nations as *the* tool for establishing world peace. In a pamphlet on the subject, WILPF emphasized how the UN was necessary for achieving diplomatic cooperation and "the abandonment of violence in international relations." As one of seventy-one nongovernmental international organizations (or NGOs, as they are called) to have "Consultative Status," WILPF supported all UN efforts toward "the peaceful settlement of international disputes, the complete disarmament of nations, universality of membership in the U.N., respect for the worth and dignity of the individual as expressed in the Universal Declaration of Human Rights, self-determination of peoples, and the increased use of the Specialized Agencies to promote world reconstruction by peaceful means as an alternative to world destruction by war." [3]

In evaluating the U.S. government's record in achieving international accord, the national board found the Truman administration lacking. In 1948, the women pointed out various ways the United States could improve its behavior with other countries. These included cultivating better relations with Latin America; opposing apartheid in South Africa; encouraging civil, rather than military, control of Germany; ending the military occupation of Japan; welcoming more women representatives in government; and demilitarizing U.S. society physically, culturally, and psychologically.

Closely tied to this commitment to the UN was WILPF's concern over the continuing development of atomic weapons. The organization was quick to react to the A-bomb's existence. As early as 1945, it published a leaflet entitled, *The Atomic Bomb and Its Message to You,* which warned that the world needed to "Make Peace or Perish." [4] WILPF leaders paid close attention to U.S. nuclear policies. When a struggle was waged within the government over who would control nuclear energy at home, the military or a civilian-led Atomic Energy Commission, WILPF leaders stood strongly behind civilian control, which was achieved in 1946. While abhorring the new weaponry, the women conceded that peaceful use of atomic energy, if controlled through the UN, might be of some help to humankind, as long as conventional arms, chemical warfare, and atomic weapons were eliminated.

As in its past, WILPF leaders continued to relate international events to women's interests. Throughout the 1950s, the national board designed short radio spots encouraging women to speak out against the nuclear arms race. As an added reflection of the times, which once again emphasized the ideals of home and family, the spots specifically addressed traditional housewives and mothers. In one appeal, the writers played on the name of the organization, bringing the concept of "peace and freedom" from the international sphere directly into the home:

> What we want to talk about is simple. So simple that it can be summed up in two words—PEACE and FREEDOM; we don't believe that the two can be separated. World peace and freedom! World peace so that you and I—and all the mothers all over the world—can go to sleep without thinking about the terrors of the Atomic Bomb or the H-Bomb . . . or any new, nightmare way of killing people. . . . Women do not want to send their husbands and their children to another war. None of us do. As a matter of fact, we know by this time that another war would reach us all. Our cities, and our homes would be battle fields; everyday people as well as soldiers would be the victims. You know . . . a bomb doesn't care in the least whether you are wearing a soldier's uniform or a housewife's apron.[5]

A second spot emphasized the intelligence and patriotism of women, especially wives and mothers. WILPF encouraged women to exercise their political clout:

> We recognize that it takes more intelligence and harder work to achieve PEACE than to engage in War. . . . As women, as wives and mothers, and as good citizens of the United States, we believe it is important that we learn to understand peoples of various cultural and political backgrounds. That is one thing we CAN do—open our minds to new, and we hope to better, ways of living together. . . . No one has the right to withdraw from the world of action at a time when civilization faces its supreme test: The Emergency Committee of Atomic Scientists has offered this challenge, which is particularly significant to women . . . for in nearly every country, women today constitute a majority of the adult population and of the voting population. Therefore, if women were to use their influence unitedly on any issue—and especially on the issues of Peace and Freedom— they could change the direction of their own nations' policies and the world's thinking.[6]

Even though it continued its pacifist activism, WILPF suffered great set-backs during the McCarthy era. Although letters from HUAC dated 1952 and 1955 verified that the group had not been cited as "Communist-front" or "sub-versive," WILPF leaders still felt it was absolutely necessary to defend them-selves and the organization against media slurs and personal attacks.[7] WILPF, after all, took strong stands against the nuclear arms race and U.S. military ac-tivity in Korea and in favor of civil rights for African American citizens. This put the organization in the center of controversy. So did the group's stand on free speech.

As a national organization, the leaders strongly and consistently opposed both the red-baiting and the legislation intent on punishing political progres-sives. At its annual meeting in 1949, for example, the organizers issued this statement: "We vigorously oppose all forms of discrimination against individu-als on the basis of political opinions." Nevertheless, the women also seemed to feel it was necessary to issue a disclaimer. They went on to add: "Fully recognizing the danger of fascist and communist totalitarianism, the League believes that such forces can be best opposed by open discussion and by the strengthening of our own democratic procedures, rather than by attempts at di-rect control."[8] The national board attempted to distance the democratic WILPF from what it interpreted to be totalitarian communism. Since the Communist Party embraced the concepts of class warfare, a one-party system, atheism, and revolution, Communists, in the view of WILPF's leaders, could not pos-sibly fit into WILPF, an organization opposed to all forms of war, in favor of a multiparty political system, abhorrent of violent revolution, and open to people of all religious and political faiths. Reflecting on the rigid political system im-plemented by Soviet leader Joseph Stalin, Emily Greene Balch claimed, "I feel that no honest person can be at once a member of the WIL and a supporter of Communism in the current sense."[9]

Because of its bad experience during the 1920s Red Scare, when gover-ment officials and the media had characterized WILPF leaders as pro-German and pro-Russian traitors, the organizers in the 1950s tried to walk a very thin line between defending free speech and denouncing communist ideology. Ac-cording to the national leaders, one of the "difficulties" WILPF faced was that of "working for goals which the Communists and other groups *seem* to be working for also," namely peace and justice issues (emphasis added). Just because the goals might appear similar did not mean the groups had anything in common. "We must insist that because we are espousing a cause which the Communists are also working on, does not mean that we are Communists, fellow-travelers, Communist-infiltrated, etc. OUR WORK MUST BE JUDGED BY WHAT WE STAND FOR, AND THE REASONS FOR THIS STAND. *NOT* BY WHO ELSE IS ALSO WORKING FOR A SIMILAR PURPOSE."[10] Therefore, WILPF's stand on world disarmament, which dated back to 1915, was not to be perceived as a means of weakening the United States but as a way of abolishing war. In addition, the organization's opposition to the execution of Ethel and Julius Rosenberg as atomic spies was based on its historical stand against the death sentence. The leaders voiced no opinion on the couple's guilt or innocence. In regard to Russia, the U.S. section of WILPF could voice no opinion because international WILPF policy demanded that its members only comment on their own government's policies.[11]

In 1953, Mildred Scott Olmsted, the executive secretary of the U.S. section, announced her intention to control, but not expel, any Communists working within WILPF. She wrote to the national board that, as in the 1920s, WILPF most likely had some Communist or "near-Communist" members, who had joined the organization in order to have new avenues for their work, since they "dared" not organize openly. Even though WILPF could not "disavow" them because of the nature of its open membership, it could control them by insisting that branches not oppose specifically stated national board policy. As Olmsted expressed it: "The important thing, the essential thing, then as now is that our leadership always remained clearly in the hands of the genuine pacifists. Those who thought to 'infiltrate' us had either to content themselves with working within our framework and putting their energy into promoting our program or they go out. Eternal vigilance and hard work ourselves, not ejection and timidity, is the price of peace within our organization."[12]

Straddling the fence on the issue of Communism became complicated, for while the national board tried to present itself as non-Communist, it still stood strong as an "anti-anti-Communist" organization. As such, it was one of the few groups that continuously supported Communist Party members' right to free speech, even though its leaders disagreed with the party's politics. WILPF priorities for 1950 therefore included opposition to all national, state, and local acts that attempted to restrict people's freedom of speech. WILPF expressed strong antagonism to the Smith Act of 1940, the McCarran Act of 1950, and the Communist Control Act of 1954. WILPF also opposed the use of loyalty oaths, as an "infringement of the right of freedom of thought," and condemned the congressional investigating committees and "vigilance groups of 'super patriots.'" All these efforts, the women believed, would lead to a society based on "unthinking conformity, enforced silence, and to the penalizing of courageous dissent." In effect, they would "undermine the foundation of the American government."[13] In a democracy, the women stressed, dissent was a necessity.

Because of its strong stances against political repression and its denunciations of Communism, WILPF suffered during the 1950s. National membership hovered around its January 1955 level of only 4,336, rather than regaining its pre–World War II level of approximately 13,600. Local branches suffered greatly, since suspicions forced some women to resign, while prospective members stayed away in droves. As Mildred Scott Olmsted reported to the national board in 1953, unlike the 1920s, when the organization was under constant governmental scrutiny, in the 1950s, WILPF was "remarkably free from outside attack." The organization was being disrupted "from within, by our own members who have become frightened by the current hysteria and want us to start labelling members and changing our traditional tolerant attitude." Olmsted feared the repercussions of these internal suspicions. "Attacks solidify as is well known to political leaders, but *internal* suspicions and lack of confidence, secret whisperings and the growth of cliques and factionalism can break down an organization faster, can be more fatal to its spiritual life, to its health and to its usefulness than any number of outside attacks." [14] Two case studies of local WILPF branches (Denver and Chicago) illustrate how the political climate produced such internal suspicions.

In Denver, Colorado, the root of the problems lay in an incident in 1952 when the loyalty of active Denver WILPF member Eunice Dolan was called into question. In the 1940s, Dolan's husband, Graham, published the Communist newspaper *Challenge* and served as an official of the International Union of Mine, Mill and Smelter Workers, headquartered in Denver. Eunice Dolan's participation in her husband's political work and her guilt by association became a major branch issue. At the time, several members resigned, claiming that Dolan's presence represented an attempt by Communists to take over the organization. As they later reported, they felt that WILPF should "be on the alert" lest they let into their ranks persons whose methods were "counter" to their own. Being vigilant was the only way to prevent the organization from "being corrupted from within." Other members protested the accusations, reiterating many times that WILPF's "avowed policy" was "not to inquire into the politics or past activities of any prospective members" as long as they worked "WITHIN THE FRAMEWORK OF THE WIL," which Eunice Dolan apparently did. [15]

In February 1954 the issue reemerged. The instigator of the renewed interest was one William B. Fogarty, a man who claimed to be a member of the War Resisters League (WRL), the Fellowship of Reconciliation (FOR), and the Episcopal Pacifist League, and who had served time in prison during World War II as a conscientious objector. Fogarty had moved to Denver in 1952 where he worked as a freelance publisher. On February 2, 1954, he joined the Denver branch of WILPF and reopened a Pandora's box that had been somewhat successfully closed two years before.

One of Fogarty's publications, *Memo,* was a newsletter reporting on the events and activities of the various Denver peace groups. At approximately the same time as he joined the branch, Fogarty distributed three hundred copies of *Memo,* which included statements about Eunice Dolan that had appeared in the January 15, 1954, issue of the *Denver Post,* claiming that the woman was both an active member of WILPF and had "communist sympathies." [16] "Some time ago," he wrote, "the question of Communist infiltration into the local WILPF, in which Mrs. Dolan figured prominently, came up . . . and a number of members withdrew in protest, while among those who stayed there have been expressions of a determination to press for clarification of this matter, and of a determination to protect their organization from perversion from within." [17] In addition, Fogarty named Virginia Jencks as another branch member with a questionable past. Jencks's husband, an official of the same union as Dolan's, had been convicted the previous month in El Paso, Texas, of lying "when he swore he was not a Communist." Jencks had been sentenced to five years in prison. What Fogarty called for was "clarification of the issue." He also planned to emphasize it before the organization's April elections. [18]

The local board, which met on February 10, generally felt that Fogarty had "acted in bad faith" by reprinting the *Post*'s accusations against Eunice Dolan. Individual members responded in a variety of ways. One "octogenerian with all the fire and superior mental equipment of her useful life still intact" was shocked by the seriousness of the incident. She was "all for having the FBI notified of this real threat!" Another woman, a Ph.D. who had had a long career in the public schools, was "distressed" by the whole affair and resigned, taking another member with her. The second member claimed, "I can't afford to stay in . . . I have my job to consider—and my place in the community life." Only one woman, a "devout" Christian Scientist, saw a greater evil. She claimed to be so "much more worried about Catholic dangers to the U.S." that she could not find time to worry about Communist threats. [19]

By early March, on the appeal of the Denver branch, the national WILPF's Committee on the Special Problems of Branches' chair, Bertha McNeill, tried to save the branch from complete disintegration. McNeill, a resident of Washington, D.C., was one of the very few African American leaders of the organization during the 1950s. An active community leader and member of several organizations besides WILPF, McNeill was asked to be in charge of one of the most sensitive issues ever to face both the national board and the local branches.

One of the first issues to be addressed was William Fogarty himself. Who was he? What were his intentions? The branch officers, while suspicious of Fogarty, tried to handle the issue as diplomatically as possible. They advised McNeill that they believed Fogarty to be "an egoist and a publicity seeker" because, even though he might sincerely desire to rid the branch of Communists, he handled the issue without regard for the reputation of the individuals involved or for the organization. Furthermore, the officers feared that Fogarty, in his quest for notoriety, might turn his attacks on the national organization "and do greater harm" than he had done already. They claimed that the "basis" for their concern was his "peculiar actions, threat, and apparent unsympathetic disregard of the results." [20] When they had requested that Fogarty retract his statements, for example, he had blatantly refused. Even though the local women saw Fogarty as "pleasant," "young," and "nice appearing" with good pacifist credentials, they questioned his motives because he had managed to obtain the branch's mailing list without the officers' knowledge.[21] Furthermore, Fogarty's article about the branch was in very bad taste because it rehashed a sensitive, but previously resolved, issue.

In a letter to Mildred Scott Olmsted, the branch publicity chair inquired about national WILPF's policy on male members. She was most likely motivated by her own disbelief that a women's organization could be torn asunder by a male member, and one possibly working as an agent for the FBI. The woman wrote that Fogarty had just popped up one day and that no one really knew anything about him. Olmsted, obviously alarmed by the entire chain of events, asked the New York branch to inquire about Fogarty through their War Resisters League connections. The WRL responded that Fogarty had been a good member who had done some organizing for them on the West Coast. Other than that, there was not much known about him. A follow-up letter went so far as to say that if Fogarty had found a problem with the Denver branch, then there obviously had to be one.[22]

Meanwhile, at least two members of the Denver branch board had some sense that Fogarty was in cahoots with the FBI. One woman was approached by FBI agents three times before notifying the WILPF national board of the situation. Another woman actually cooperated with the agency. She had been the only local board member who had stood against Eunice Dolan after Fogarty's article had been printed. In a letter to national WILPF headquarters, she reported that in 1952, Dolan and her friends had taken over the leadership of the branch and that she had remained to try to "wrest it back into legitimate hands." Apparently, in 1954, she had been called on by members of the FBI, who had sworn her to secrecy, a pledge she stood by until she decided to write to the WILPF leaders in Philadelphia. She felt sure that Bill Fogarty had referred the agents to her as she, Fogarty, and his "charming German born wife" had become good friends. The FBI men told her that they had no intentions of "labelling" anyone but that they had "orders from headquarters" to "get the goods" on certain persons, notably Eunice Dolan. The agents asked this woman for her cooperation in pointing to "real subversive action" within the group.[23]

Believing that her actions were truly beneficial to the branch, the woman complied. She wrote that her behavior did not represent any "hysteria" on her part since she had already "lived" with the situation for two years. Nevertheless, "the weight of public opinion," already so against the continuation of the group that many of the "fine things" done in the name of "WIL" came to "naught," made her believe that she had to help purge "the disease in the body politic." Hence, she began naming names, and, literally, spying on her peers. She watched the activities of one new member who had recently arrived from Chicago and who, she was informed, had been instructed by the Communist Party to contact Eunice Dolan. She wrote of another member, recently resigned, whom the FBI also called "practically in so many words" a Communist. One of the agents even attended a branch gathering and told her that he recognized "several Communist workers" in the audience. The woman also heard from Fogarty that a Mrs. Robnett, an active African American member, was "somewhat suspect of being subversive," but she felt that Robnett and her husband were driven to work with the "extreme leftist crowd" because of their frustrations over racism. As she concluded: "All the REAL workers for peace from the churches, FOR, WRL, and other groups" stayed "well away" from WILPF, "letting this undesirable crowd take control." [24] The agents situated in Denver, it seems, were able to feed her *their* ideas and manipulate her into giving them back the information they wanted to hear. In dismay over all that was occurring, she resigned from the branch at the end of March.

As national WILPF officials became more aware of the complexities of the Denver situation, they decided to take action. The traditional WILPF policy was to allow branches complete autonomy. In this way, although some guidelines were mandated on specific issues, the local membership could be as diverse and independent as possible. Throughout the 1950s, the national board tried to retain this position, but it was not always possible or helpful. In Denver, in mid-March 1954, the Committee on the Special Problems of Branches called an emergency meeting. Overall, the national leaders still wanted the Denver women to solve their own problems; however, the committee did take three authoritative steps. First, Bertha McNeill offered recommendations regarding the upcoming branch elections. She urged the branch, on behalf of the committee, not to run any member for office who was "under suspicion" of being a Communist or any person who had joined the branch within the last year. The first suggestion followed the WILPF national board's private policy of being wary of a Communist takeover. The latter suggestion would prevent William Fogarty from running for office. As McNeill stated, the branch's situation demanded that there be a new slate of officers who would be "above question" in the community. [25] Second, the committee sent one of its most valued members, Kitty Arnett, to Denver to offer advice and hands-on help. Third, McNeill wrote a letter to Fogarty, deploring his actions as "non-pacifist and unrepresentative of the methods of the Women's International League for Peace and Freedom."

She lambasted Fogarty for not appealing to the national board first so that much of the bad publicity could have been avoided and stated that his "method" was "such a striking example" of what WILPF was "*not*" that the committee could not help but feel that the branch's complaints about him were warranted.[26]

Kitty Arnett's visit to Denver helped in the sense of showing a parent body's support for its offspring. In more concrete terms, however, the woman's short visit did not produce the results the national board desired. To the credit of the remaining members, the branch retained Mrs. Robnett and Mrs. Sorrentino, two leaders with "questionable" politics, as officers. On the one hand, Mildred Scott Olmsted thought that perhaps Kitty Arnett could have gotten other names on the ballot if she had had more time; on the other hand, she acknowledged the branch's intention not to make "any more changes than they [could] help to." This was especially true of Robnett's position. The branch informed Olmsted that they wanted to keep her because of "her color and her liberal attitudes." Kitty Arnett disagreed with Olmsted's desire to elect new branch officers in order to solve the problems. She felt that the Denver women were up against serious red-baiting and that getting people who were above suspicion to serve as officers was extremely difficult. Since Eunice Dolan had resigned, much of the publicity surrounding her membership had subsided. Nevertheless, the leftist influence in the branch was still visible. As Olmsted wrote to Bertha McNeill, those remaining Denver board members who were traditional WILPFers would be "very much subject to management by the strong-minded very leftist members of the committee, and perhaps that is the best which we can do under the circumstances."[27]

The Denver branch continued to function, although several members lamented the loss of both Eunice Dolan and Virginia Jencks. In a letter to Bertha McNeill, one local board member expressed this regret:

> With regard to infiltration of the Denver Branch, you know that none of us ever suspected either before or after the Bill Fogarty affair that Eunice and Virginia Jencks were Communists. We do not know it now, and certainly neither of them said or did anything that would make us believe or suspect it. The policy of the WIL as we interpreted it was to judge a member by whether or not she was working in the organization according to the principles and policies. Neither of the girls held an office, except that Eunice was chairman of finance, as you know, and a very hard and efficient worker for the Branch. It is difficult to replace her. Both appeared to be sincere in their loyalty to our democratic form of government, though deploring what is being done to curtail our civil liberties at this time, as don't we all?[28]

While the Denver women wrangled with each other, women in Chicago faced similar internal struggles. Chicago, the original home of the Woman's Peace party, had felt the brunt of red-baiting back in the 1910s when Jane Addams was in charge. The office had been ransacked and defiled several times. But in the 1950s, Chicago, like Denver, suffered from purging from within. During the 1950s, the Chicago branch was made up of WILPF's traditional white upper-middle-class membership and by working-class women from the city's South Side. Like the Denver branch, the local group split over the issue of perceived Communist infiltration. Unlike, Denver, in 1954 local Chicago board members immediately contacted national WILPF headquarters for advice. What they said they wanted was a clear statement of WILPF's policy on Communist members. What they apparently meant was that they wanted a way to exclude Communist members from their branch.

The national board would not comply with their wishes. Years later, Mildred Scott Olmsted recalled how the "struggle" in Chicago "came to a head" when the local branch president appeared before the national board threatening that if "a very clear anticommunist statement excluding communists per se from WIL membership" did not come forth, then she and her supporters would withdraw from both the branch and the national organization. "I am happy to say," reported Olmsted, "that our Board kept its head and we refused absolutely to make any such statement." As a result, several members did resign, and the few left in the South Side group disbanded and joined with the larger Chicago branch. Those remaining continued to struggle with the issue. Olmsted claimed that for years after, some of the "oldtime" Chicago members who had resigned continued to plague the organization. "Every time anybody came and wanted to join or a new person moved there," she added, "one or the other would quietly take them aside and tell them that we were a communist front organization." [29]

By April 1954, the Chicago branch, like Denver, was crippled by the effects of McCarthyism. Membership was down, donations were dwindling, and husbands afraid of losing their jobs pressured their wives into quitting WILPF. The remaining members were still divided over the issue of Communist membership. Some of the older women continued to be suspicious of women they believed were infiltrating the branch in order to pursue Communist goals. These experienced WILPFers worried that the newly elected local board, which consisted of younger, more liberal women, would not be able to prevail. As one woman wrote about the new board: "It leaves me with a Board who have not read enough or had experience enough to realize the danger we are in of the pro-Communists taking over." [30] Other members defended the women accused of Communism. One member wrote to Kitty Arnett that the situation had caused "*great nervous strain*" on the "accused" women. She commented that the victims were mostly "mature women, several with children" whose husbands were situated in high positions in such places as the CIO and the University of Chicago, while a few of the women were employed as social workers and teachers. According to the letter, at least four of them claimed they had joined WILPF "joyfully, on discovering a Peace Group such as they had been looking for for years, and insist, in spite of the treatment they have received that they want to continue." This woman hoped that since seven of the older members had resigned, the new board would "take a new attitude" and issue a "moral reinstatement" of the accused women so that they could once again function as full members of the local branch.[31]

The problems in Chicago lasted into the fall. Members continued to resign, several because, as one woman claimed, they had "lost confidence" in the national office for "its failure to long ago recognize the communist threat to peace and freedom, and its techniques for infiltrating and taking over organizations, and also the failure to give guidance to branches in meeting the communist threat." This woman feared that even after two years, the national board did not realize that WILPF had been, as she perceived it, infiltrated. "Sooner or later the communist group will take over." [32]

In the midst of the madness in Denver and Chicago, the national board, under pressure especially from Chicago, formed a committee that issued a "Packet on Infiltration and Attack." The eight-page, single-spaced, typed memo was designed to aid each branch in its struggles with McCarthyism. The committee indicated that it did not wish to create alarm if none existed nor to cause branches to look for problems where there were none. Nevertheless, the national board was aware that "some" branches felt very strongly that WILPF faced "two dangers:—(1) attempts by 'leftists' to use WIL for their own ends and (2) attempts by 'rightists' to accuse WIL of communism and thus discredit us and render our work ineffective." As a result, the committee reminded its members that the organization was one devoted to the concepts of "peace and freedom," not only in the international sphere, but right down to the local community level. But the national board once again took an anticommunist stand while declaring itself open and broad-minded. The opening statement concluded in a strong, yet fearful, tone: "in our effort to keep our organization free from subversion and to defend it from overt attacks, we must neither abandon our basic principles and program nor stoop to the totalitarian methods we abhor. The challenge before us is, not to ignore the realities of our situation, but to deal with them by sane and worthy means." [33]

The first section of the packet emphasized the importance of members "maintaining confidence" in WILPF's basic principles and nonviolent methods of operation. It pointed out the number of times the organization had been misunderstood by the government, the media, and the public. During

World War I, women were accused of being "German sympathizers" because they opposed the war. During World War II, they were "charged with ignoring the moral issues involved" because they did not "join in the chorus of hate" against the Germans and the Japanese. Then, in 1954, the organization was "sometimes" accused of being "sympathetic" to Communism. This latter accusation, the packet continued, was more difficult to avoid because Communists often spoke in terms of "peace and freedom" and often supported such similar goals as "peace, the rights of subject peoples, the meeting of men's basic economic needs." [34]

The danger to WILPF, the women believed, was from both communists and anticommunists. "The danger from the Communists is the more obvious, both because of their power and of their confessed totalitarian philosophy. But in many places, their opponents with different political creeds are using similar methods in an attempt to control men's minds." [35] WILPF's job was to fight Communism "and other forms of totalitarianism" by using "democratic" means. "We do not have to choose between communist infiltration and methods of witch-hunting, character assassination and demagoguery. Both are evil; both are threats to freedom and democracy. We repudiate both." [36] Free discussion, decision making by consensus, and constant open debate were ways to ensure WILPF's openness and integrity.

The national board assumed that U.S. Communists echoed the Soviet Union's doctrinaire Stalinist style. WILPF consistently used images of "class warfare" and "totalitarianism" to describe the difference between itself and a Communist group. What it could not acknowledge was that some of its members, often those from working-class and African American communities, not only accepted communist ideology but also embraced the principle of nonviolence. In addition, the leaders could not accept that many so-called Communists in the United States believed in open discussion and all the other "democratic" principles adhered to by the WILPF leaders. In a difficult era, the national WILPF leaders tried to retain the integrity of their organization by portraying all Communists as violent and dictatorial. In effect, they chose to lump all U.S. Communists under one Stalinist umbrella. The unintended effect was the all-too-easy acceptance of persecution of long-time loyal members and of some of the newer blood the leaders had so desperately wanted to attract.

The "Packet on Infiltration and Attack" accepted without question that "communist" meant any person who was literally controlled by the Communist Party, which allegedly got its orders from Moscow—in other words, a person whose primary allegiance was to the USSR. Part III of the "Packet," entitled "Dealing with Communist Infiltration," advised branches that there were several "problems" that WILPF members were "obligated to give serious attention to." One of these problems was "How we may distinguish between the liberal or non-conformist citizen who is loyal to his country and the individual who gives his allegiance to another country by adhering to a party line dictated by that country." Another "problem" stated: "How we may demonstrate to the world that democracy has more to offer than communism (*a*) by upholding at home the things for which democracy stands and (*b*) by helping the underpriviledged peoples of the world to achieve the better life which communism promises but cannot deliver." [37]

The committee advised branch leaders on how to identify "signs of possible infiltration." These included

1. Members who want the branch to select from the WILPF program only those issues in which the Communist party is interested and to neglect all other parts of the program.

2. Members who are totally uncritical of the USSR and who do not show a balanced judgement in their criticism of U.S. policies.

3. A group of members fairly new in the WILPF, who seem to be trying to use offices to control program and policy for the branch.[38]

Once these members were identified, they should be guided to recognize on their own that the WILPF principles and program were "genuinely better." Many of these women could become excellent WILPFers. The "Packet" warned that WILPF members who had joined "front" organizations, signed petitions, or had "leftist tendencies" should not be "condemned" because WILPF "welcomed diversity." [39] Where to draw the line and how to define each member's attitudes was left to the branches. If any branch needed help, it was to report the problem to the Committee on Special Problems of the Branches, which had been set up specifically to meet this crisis.

It is amazing that WILPF could be as productive as it was in the 1950s. In places such as Louisville, Kentucky, Providence, Rhode Island, and Miami, Florida, WILPF members were called before HUAC, though not as WILPFers. Yet work continued, whether it was opposition to the Korean war or the nuclear arms race or in favor of the UN or, especially, in support of the civil rights movement. The organization persisted through the 1950s and beyond. But local tensions such as those in Denver, Chicago, and other places, combined with the national office's rather confusing and compromising stance on Communism, probably kept many prospective members at bay.

Although WILPF emphasized its suffragist roots and savored its female leadership, the organization had ceased emphasizing women's rights issues back in the 1920s. Women who wanted to be more militantly feminist–pacifist, and who found no appeal in WILPF, turned to another newly formed organization in order to work for both world peace and women's rights. This group was the Congress of American Women, which grew out of the November 26, 1945, first World Congress of Women.[40] The meeting, held in Paris, was called by the Union des Femmes Francaises, a group of female leaders from the French Resistance movement of World War II. It attracted more than eight hundred women from forty-one different nations, many from Eastern Europe. Included were representatives from England, China, India, the United States, the Soviet Union, Spain, Finland, "the liberated European countries," Poland, Greece, Yugoslavia, Hungary, and Czechoslovakia. Unlike WILPF conferences before World War II, which had attracted wealthier, educated, and professional women, this congress consisted of "housewives, working women, trade unionists, farmers, doctors, lawyers, artists and women in government." The result of the meeting was the founding of the Women's International Democratic Federation (WIDF) whose platform reflected a strong feminist stance. It consisted of "(1) the eradication of all remnants of Fascism in every country in the world, and the maintenance of world peace; (2) the advance of women into full economic, political and legal status; and (3) the full protection of children in health, in education and the realization of their special talents and abilities."[41] The founders emphasized that women could not achieve their rights in an unjust society. Political, economic, and social conditions had to change in order to allow for equality. In addition, advancement depended on the "liquidation" of illiteracy. Only through open "access to all avenues of education and vocational training" could women become full participants in the "cultural life" of their communities.[42] The leaders of the WIDF noted the importance of national self-determination and the elimination of racism and apartheid as basic elements for the success of their program. Likewise, they embraced the overall concept of world peace and universal disarmament.

The WIDF placed special importance on the right of women who had struggled equally with men during the war for the fruits of peace and freedom. In a press release written on International Women's Day, March 8, 1946, the organizers of the Congress of American Women emphasized this history:

> The Congress of Women recounted in many ways the heroic role of women in the struggle against fascism and the place in the life of their countries which they have won and must sustain. The millions of women who plowed fields, sowed the grain and reaped the harvest, the thousands who worked in factories building the planes, the tanks and the ammunition for victory, the women who nursed the wounded, gave themselves to the dangerous work of the Resistance, and in an atmosphere of fear and death strove to preserve the remnants of a home for their children—these women in

the days of privation and suffering proved that they were superbly capable of sharing responsibility with men for the economic, political, social and cultural regeneration and growth of their countries. These women told of the old and the new status which women hold, of their determination to achieve complete citizenship by reason of the fact that they earned it.[43]

In February 1946, soon after the initial meeting of the World Congress of Women, U.S. representatives to the conference formed the Congress of American Women, the U.S. branch of the WIDF. Leaders offered a picture of diversity. There were several well-educated and professional women, such as Dr. Gene Weltfish, anthropologist at Columbia University; Dr. Beryl Parker, educator; Jacqueline Cochran, a director of Eastern Airlines; Florence Eldridge March, an actress married to the actor Frederick March, and Cornelia Bryce Pinchot, a former suffragist. There were also several women whose politics leaned toward the left or who had union organizing experience, including Muriel Draper, chair of the Committee of Women of the Council of American Soviet Friendship; Ann Bradford, a member of the CIO auxiliary; Elizabeth Gurley Flynn, the elderly and respected labor leader and chair of the Women's Commission of the Communist Party of America and Claudia Jones, another party member. As the CAW intended to build a racially balanced organization from the start, women of color were involved on the initial organizational level. These women included Dr. Charlotte Hawkins Brown, Thelma Dale, and Vivian Carter Mason, all active leaders in African American organizations.

The CAW got off to an active start. It was the first feminist peace organization to hold celebrations on March 8 for International Women's Day, a holiday celebrated in the communist world at that time but not in the United States. The festivities pointed up the organization's feminist and antifascist roots during one of the most reactionary times in U.S. history. In May, the group held its first Working Conference at New York's Essex House. At this meeting of nearly five hundred delegates, the important issues centered on women's postwar unemployment, health-care needs, and support for the Equal Rights Amendment. Soon after, CAW representatives appeared before a hearing in the nation's capital in favor of the Pepper-Norton Maternal and Child Welfare Act, which would have established a national health program for children and pregnant women. The CAW also placed great emphasis on women's rights and on supporting the mission of the UN to create "a true peace for the world."[44] In this effort, its members recognized the importance of building on the friendship with Soviet women that they had begun in Paris.

The Congress of American Women maintained a strong multinational, interracial, and cross-class stance that reflected its close identity with the WIDF. It

In 1947 delegates from the Congress of American Women protested President
Truman's plan to send aid to Greece and Turkey. *Courtesy of the Swarthmore College Peace Collection and the Bettmann Archive*

ambitiously recruited women of color and from the working class. The organization's pamphlets emphasized the importance of women in U.S. history,
using as examples suffragists such as Lucretia Mott, Susan B. Anthony, and
Elizabeth Cady Stanton and such African American leaders as Sojourner Truth
and Harriet Tubman. Writings also stressed the importance of the nineteenth-
century Lowell mill girls and the women garment workers of the early twentieth
century. By 1949, the organization claimed a quarter of a million members.
There were branches in New York City, Cleveland, Chicago, Pittsburgh, Los
Angeles, Detroit, Milwaukee, and Seattle. Affiliates included several labor
and social organizations. The CAW's Commission on the Status of Women
was chaired by Susan B. Anthony II, the grand-niece of the well-known suffrage leader. It emphasized the need for equal pay for equal work, job training
for women, the elimination of racial discrimination at work, the support of
child-care centers, the institution of low-cost carry-home dinners or in-plant
feeding for workers, and the benefits of communal kitchens and dining areas in
public housing projects. The commission also called for equal educational opportunities for women and the elimination of quotas for admission to medical
schools.[45]

In 1948 the full brunt of the Red Scare fell on the Congress of American Women, especially since the WIDF received substantial support from the Soviet Union. In addition, unlike the national WILPF leadership, the CAW openly included known Communists and did not try to avoid the issue during the McCarthy era. While WILPF managed to avoid direct governmental assault, the U.S. attorney general placed the CAW on its list of subversive organizations. The California Committee on Un-American Activities referred to the organization as "one of the most potentially dangerous of the many active communist-fronts." [46] The women's participation in WIDF conferences held in Eastern Europe did not help their image. The press saw them as gullible and pro-Russian and painted the organization as anti-American. HUAC started an investigation, citing the organization as subversive. In its *Report on the Congress of American Women,* published in 1949, HUAC discredited the CAW's professed connection with the women's rights movement, calling the identification "fraudulent." The report particularly criticized Susan B. Anthony II and Elizabeth Cady Stanton's granddaughter, Nora Stanton Barney, for affiliating with the group. [47] Despite these accusations, the Congress of American Women continued to sponsor activities and issue policy statements until January 1950. At that time, the Department of Justice ordered the organization's board to register as "foreign agents." To avoid further harassment, the CAW leaders voted to sever connections with the WIDF. Considering the political climate, the effort was too little and too late. Later that year, rather than register with the Justice Department or assume a costly legal battle, the organization's leaders voted to disband.

About the same time that the Congress of American Women was succumbing to federal pressure, another organization, American Women for Peace, emerged. The organization, about which little is known, appears to have been a reincarnation of the CAW. It existed from August 8, 1950, to at least the end of 1953. Several names from the CAW appear among those of American Women for Peace, including Lula Stone, treasurer of a local of the United Electrical Workers, Nora Stanton Barney, and Clementina J. Paolone, a physician and member of the American Labor party. [48] In the summer of 1951 the organizers participated in the Chicago Peace Congress, an event coordinated with the Women's International Democratic Federation.

American Women for Peace emphasized the women's peace movement's connection between motherhood and peace. In its "Declaration of Principles," the organizers stated: "Because the privilege of giving birth is uniquely the labor of women, it becomes a natural responsibility of all women to preserve life, and especially to protect it from the dangers of useless and criminal warfare." The "Declaration" supported the principles of mediation and negotiation embraced by the UN Charter. It stated: "The lives of our daughters and sons can be secure only in a world at peace—a world which will steadfastly safeguard the health, education and welfare of its future generations." To achieve peace, nuclear weapons needed to be banned, and such confrontations as the one then taking place in Korea had to be mediated and settled. The concept of "preventive" warfare had to be rejected. To reach these goals, women of all races, ethnic backgrounds, and classes needed to organize. The group was willing to function as an umbrella organization as well as an individual association. In this way, American Women for Peace could become "a source of strength for all women throughout our great country" so that the voices for peace would "never be hushed" and the fight for peace would be carried on "with greater vigor than ever before." [49]

Within two years, American Women for Peace had branches in Chicago, Salt Lake City, Boston, Los Angeles, and in five New York City neighborhoods—the East Bronx, Tremont, Harlem, Yorkville, and the Interborough. In an effort to address peace and justice issues, the organization included both domestic and international perspectives. For example, under its auspices, the African American poet Beulah Richardson, later known as Beah Richards, wrote a pamphlet entitled *A Black Woman Speaks of White Womanhood—of White Supremacy—of Peace,* a poem which emphasized the crime of lynching. In addition, the organization worked with local PTAs in the hope of stopping A-bomb civil defense drills, which "terrorized" young children. In Los Angeles, two thousand women marched under its banner on Mother's Day, 1951, to protest nuclear weapons, and in 1953, the organization sent representatives to the World Congress of Women.[50]

The Congress of American Women and American Women for Peace, short-lived as they were, represented concerted efforts by feminists to work for peace during a conservative era. Rather than abandon its openly leftist politics or be victimized by McCarthyism, the CAW disbanded. In this way, McCarthyites obstructed the efforts of left-leaning women, but at least some of them regrouped and persisted through American Women for Peace. Despite the Cold War and despite "the feminine mystique," these activists insisted that women had a right and a duty to voice their opinions. Although these two groups did not survive the McCarthy era, many of their members moved on to the civil rights and anti-Vietnam war movements. In 1975, several former members of the Congress of American Women and American Women for Peace cooperated in the founding of Women for Racial and Economic Equality (WREE), an organization that still reflects the ideology and programs of its 1950s foremothers.[51]

WILPF's attempts to appear moderate and nonthreatening were most likely key to its survival. In a time of political conservatism, the U.S. government maintained the facade that the nation supported "free speech." WILPF used its history to prove that it supported the same definition of "democracy" as the government did. This definition, however, demanded the denigration of communism and its proponents. WILPF's anti-Communist stand permitted the government to tolerate its dissenting views on McCarthyist policies. Did this survival mechanism succeed or backfire? In the short term, it seems to have backfired, damaging but not crippling the organization's ability to function. Even though WILPF remained a respected organization within the peace movement, membership remained low until the anti-Vietnam war movement emerged. In the long run, thanks to its long-time supporters, some reaching back to the suffrage era, WILPF was able to persevere until in the 1980s its membership reached its peak of fifteen thousand.

Women's peace organizations faltered in the postwar era, not only because of the renewed emphasis on domesticity but also because the anti-Communist panic had tangible, damaging effects. The openly leftist CAW was forced to disband, and its successor, American Women for Peace, was short-lived. Meanwhile, WILPF branches suffered from divisive internal accusations. Nonetheless, the women's peace movement survived. WILPF, in particular, continued its pacifist activities by adopting anti-Communist rhetoric even as it opposed the government's McCarthyist tactics. As unpleasant as it seems, WILPF's survival in the postwar "democratic" system seems to have relied on its anti-Communist stance, its moderation, and its compromises— its ability to fit into the acceptable parameters of dissent in a conservative historical era.

NOTES

Acknowledgments: I thank Dee Garrison, Lawrence Wittner, Amy Swerdlow, John Chambers, Charles Chatfield, and Joanne Meyerowitz for their helpful comments on various versions of this article.

1. For clarification, "Communist" (upper case) refers only to the Communist Party, while "communism" (lower case) refers to the ideology. This distinction may not be consistent in directly quoted material.

2. To get a picture of the effects of McCarthyism on various people and organizations, see, for example, Victor S. Navasky, *Naming Names* (New York: Viking, 1980); Walter and Miriam Schneir, *Invitation to an Inquest* (New York: Pantheon, 1965, 1983); Ellen W. Schrecker, *No Ivory Tower: McCarthyism and the Universities* (New York: Oxford University Press, 1986); and Lawrence S. Wittner, *Rebels against War: The American Peace Movement, 1933–1983* (Philadelphia: Temple University Press, 1984).

3. "The Women's International League and the United Nations," no. 1; "How the WIL Works with and for the U.N.," pamphlet, n.d., reel 37, Women's International League for Peace and Freedom/U.S. Section, 1919–1959, Swarthmore College

Peace Collection, Scholarly Resources Microfilm Edition. Hereafter cited as WILPF/ US: SCPC-mf.

4. "The Atomic Bomb and Its Message to You," 1945, Box 30, Women's International League for Peace and Freedom–U.S. Section Papers, Swarthmore College Peace Collection. Hereafter cited as WILPF/US: SCPC. I thank Lawrence Wittner for this source.

5. Radio Spot no. 1, 1950s, reel 37, WILPF/US: SCPC-mf.

6. Radio Spot no. 2, 1950s, reel 37, WILPF/US: SCPC-mf.

7. Senator Hubert Humphrey to Annalee Stewart, March 27, 1952, reel 30, WILPF/ US: SCPC; Thomas W. Beale, Sr., to Mary Ford Hann, March 25, 1955, courtesy of the Jane Addams Peace Association office, New York, hereafter cited as JAPA: N.Y.

8. "Freedom of Thought and Speech," statement at 1949 annual meeting, reel 1, WILPF/US: SCPC-mf.

9. Emily Greene Balch, 1926 and 1950, quoted in "Materials for Discussion: Not for distribution," ca. 1952, WILPF/US: SCPC.

10. Ibid., WILPF/US: SCPC.

11. This policy is sometimes problematic because WILPF had spoken out against apartheid and other issues concerning foreign nations.

12. Mildred Scott Olmsted to National Board Meeting, January 29–31, 1953, reel 4, WILPF/US: SCPC-mf.

13. "Principles and Policies, 1954–1955," reel 1, WILPF/US: SCPC-mf.

14. Olmsted to National Board Meeting, January 29–31, 1953.

15. Board Meeting Minutes, February 10, 1954, reel 87, WILPF-US: SCPC-mf.

16. *Denver Post,* January 15, 1954.

17. "Battle Seen on League Red Charge," *Denver Post,* February 21, 1954, sec. 3A.

18. Ibid.

19. Board Meeting Minutes, February 10, 1954.

20. Letter to Bertha McNeill, March 3, 1954, reel 87, WILPF/US: SCPC-mf. In this note and in others that follow, the name of the letter writer is not included so as to protect the confidentiality of the source.

21. Report from the Officers of the Denver Branch of WILPF to the Committee on Special Problems of Branches Regarding Actions of Mr. William Fogarty, March 8, 1954, reel 87, WILPF/US: SCPC-mf.

22. WRL to Denver Branch, March 19, 1954, reel 87, WILPF/US: SCPC-mf.

23. Letter to WILPF Headquarters, March 3, 1954, reel 87, WILPF/US: SCPC-mf.

24. Ibid.

25. Bertha McNeill to Denver Branch, March 22, 1954, reel 87, WILPF/US: SCPC-mf.

26. Bertha McNeill to William Fogarty, March 23, 1954, reel 87, WILPF/US: SCPC-mf.

27. Mildred Scott Olmsted to Bertha McNeill, May 7, 1954, reel 87, WILPF/US: SCPC-mf.

28. Letter to Bertha McNeill, October 13, 1954, reel 87, WILPF/US: SCPC-mf.

29. Interview with Mildred Scott Olmsted, conducted by Mercedes Randall, February, 1972, IV:9, Mildred Scott Olmsted Papers, Swarthmore College Peace Collection.

30. Letter to WILPF, April 3, 1954, reel 87, WILPF/US: SCPC-mf.

31. Letter to Kitty Arnett, May 29, 1954, reel 87, WILPF/US: SCPC-mf.

32. Letter to Bertha McNeill, October 17, 1954, reel 87, WILPF/US: SCPC-mf.

33. *Packet on Infiltration and Attack Issued by the National Board of the WIL*, received May 17, 1954, courtesy of JAPA: N.Y., 1.

34. Ibid., 1–2.

35. Ibid., 2.

36. Ibid.

37. Ibid., 4–5.

38. Ibid., 5.

39. Ibid.

40. The details on the Congress of American Women are culled from primary documents or from Amy Swerdlow, "The Politics of Motherhood: The Case of Women Strike for Peace and the Test Ban Treaty," Ph.D. dissertation, Rutgers University, 1984, 59–70.

41. "What Is the Congress of American Women?" leaflet, n.d., Rosika Schwimmer/Lola Maverick Lloyd Papers, New York Public Library, Rare Books and Manuscripts Division, Astor, Lenox and Tilden Foundations, New York. Hereafter cited as S/L: NYPL.

42. "Constitution and Programme of the WIDF, 1963 addendum," Courtesy of Women for Racial and Economic Equality National Office, New York.

43. Congress of American Women Press Release, March 8, 1946, S/L: NYPL, I:4.

44. Muriel Draper, "Report of Commission on Action for Peace and Democracy," May 25, 1946, S/L: NYPL, I:7.

45. Susan B. Anthony, "Report on the Commission on the Status of Women," May 25, 1946, cited in Swerdlow, "Politics of Motherhood," 63.

46. *California Committee on Un-American Activities Report*, 1948, 228–231, cited in Swerdlow, "Politics of Motherhood," 104, n. 42.

47. *Report on the Congress of American Women*, cited in Swerdlow, "Politics of Motherhood," 65.

48. Historians will find it of interest that Gerda Lerner was listed as a member of both the Congress of American Women and American Women for Peace.

49. "Declaration of Principles," as appeared in *The Peacemaker* 1, no. 2 (November 1950): 1, American Women for Peace Papers: Swarthmore College Peace Collection. Hereafter cited as AWP: SCPC.

50. Clementina Jaolone, "Report on Women's Activities at the Chicago Peace Congress, June 29–July 1, 1951," 1, AWP:SCPC.

51. For more on WREE and the women's peace movement after the McCarthy era, see Harriet Hyman Alonso, *Peace as a Women's Issue: A History of the U.S. Movement for World Peace and Women's Rights* (Syracuse: Syracuse University Press, 1993.)

CHAPTER 8

Deborah A. Gerson

"IS FAMILY DEVOTION NOW SUBVERSIVE?"

Familialism against McCarthyism

In the spring of 1952 I was sick with a series of childhood illnesses: mumps, chicken pox, scarlet fever. I remember the salmon-colored children's aspirin I took, the many shots of penicillin I endured, and the bundle of toys I received from the Families Committee.

The Families Committee of Smith Act Victims was an organization of women, predominantly wives of Communist Party leaders indicted under the Smith Act, organized to give financial, material, and emotional assistance to the children and spouses of Smith Act victims and the prisoners themselves. Playing a supporting role in the drama of anticommunist arrests, trials, and underground existence, the Families Committee worked to ensure the continued stability of children and families, raising money for summer camps and nursery school, fares for trips to faraway federal prisons, and holiday or birthday presents. The Families Committee was one of many organizing efforts against the Smith Act and other forms of McCarthyite repression, and its work was understood as dangerous to the purveyors of anticommunism. In 1953 the Families Committee was placed on the attorney general's list of allegedly subversive organizations.

Briefly mentioned in several histories and memoirs of the period, the Families Committee has engendered no research specifically focused on it.[1] When I began this research I contacted Helen Lima, wife of a California Communist Party leader, who sent me a letter written in 1951 by John McManus, editor of the weekly *National Guardian,* which asked for financial support for the Families Committee and referred readers to a longer article in the newspaper. Both the letter and the article, which I eventually obtained, contained a series of photographs of children, of whom I was one.

The experience of receiving that letter thrust me into an even greater intimacy with my subject than I had been aware of. Thus this work became a journey from autobiography to history, from the terrors and confusions of that five-year-old child to the drama enacted around her. But writing the drama necessitated unearthing an unwritten history. The archives of the Communist Party USA had no files or records of this committee of women. I went back to original documents in private collections around the country and to the women who had participated in the Families Committee. I was assisted in my efforts by my mother, Sophie Melvin Gerson, who was active in the Families Committee from its inception, and by my father, Simon W. Gerson, who was arrested under the Smith Act in June 1951. The experience of my family led me to an almost completely unchronicled history and allowed me access that might have been difficult for an outsider.

The harassment of women and children that engendered the formation of the Families Committee was the fruit of the repressive apparatus of the state. The FBI attacked kin and community with a doggedness born of ideological fervor; Communist Party leaders, and their spouses and children, became symbols of international communist infiltration and targets of the state's campaign to contain and silence this perceived threat. In its assessment of gender-based divisions the FBI showed a rare sophistication; it attacked women and children at their point of vulnerability: in the living, working routines of their daily lives, at home, on the job, with friends and relatives, in child-care centers and summer camps. The relentlessness of FBI surveillance was revealed in hideous and ridiculous detail in the 700 pages of documents filed on the Families Committee and released to me through the Freedom of Information Act.

While conservative politics and ideology of the 1950s shored up the alliance between motherhood, family, and anticommunism, the Families Committee resisted state repression with a strategy that made use of the valorization of family. The alliance between patriotism and familialism was challenged by women who pointed to the state as the destroyer of family freedom, security, and happiness. But in the process of undertaking the defense of their families,

John J. McManus

June 7, 1952

Dear friend:

Here is an act of neighborliness which I feel certain you will hasten to join -- guaranteeing a healthy, happy, unharrassed summer vacation for each of the 70 children of the Smith Act victims now in prisons or before the courts in Chicago, Detroit, Pittsburgh, California and Hawaii.

I need not review in this letter the torment visited on these children in their schools and neighborhoods in the backwash of the prosecution of their parents for their political opinions. The May 29 issue of National Guardian has presented many of the facts; author Albert Kahn's searching pamphlet offers damning detail.

However, the opportunity is near at hand to provide each of these youngsters with a few carefree weeks in the country. Your dollar can do it.

An addressed envelope is provided for your response. Please make it as generous as you can, and as quickly -- so that when the trains and busses depart for vacationland at the close of school, these youngsters will be there.

Most sincerely yours,

John T. McManus

John T. McManus

This letter from John T. McManus, editor of the *National Guardian,* supported the fund-raising efforts of the Families Committee. *Courtesy of Helen Lima* the women who constituted the Families Committee of Smith Act Victims also altered their own position as political actors. In a situation resonant with historical precedent, the very process of asserting their familial ties of maternity and marriage became vehicles for political action and empowerment.[2]

Feeling the Heat of the Cold War

When the FBI knocked on our door on the morning of June 20, 1951, my father, Simon W. Gerson, became one of the 126 defendants added to the ranks of Smith Act victims in the second wave of indictments. First passed in 1940 (and originally entitled the Alien Registration Act), the Smith Act enabled the federal government to prosecute individuals for conspiracy to teach or advocate the overthrow of the established government by force or violence. Eleven members of the Communist Party (CP) national leadership had been indicted under the Smith Act in 1948. The conviction of the first eleven in 1951 after the year-long Foley Square trial in New York City, the arrest of Julius and Ethel Rosenberg in 1950, the arrest of more than one hundred state leaders of the CP in 1951, and the various attempts (some of them successful) to deport foreign-born U.S. citizens suspected of being Communists gave little doubt that the long arm of the law was to be used to silence and punish political dissent.[3]

The Communist Party had emerged from World War II strong and energetic, with a membership of about eighty thousand, buoyed by the wartime alliance with the Soviet Union and the Popular Front strategy of organizing and coalition building with other progressive forces. But when Cold War ideology began to point to world communism as a threat to American security and affluence, U.S. Communists were identified as a foreign threat who would deny Americans their freedom and prosperity. The passage of the Taft-Hartley Act in 1947 legally codified what had been the practice of the previous two years: the virtual elimination of communists from any position of leadership within the trade union movement. On a political level, the CP lost an operational base; on a personal level, many individuals and families saw their lives devastated. Industries often blacklisted displaced union leaders, and the new leadership, committed to the clean face of anticommunism, refused to help them find jobs. Unemployment insurance boards, part of a social program for which the CP had struggled in the 1930s, denied them benefits on a variety of spurious and basically punitive grounds.[4]

The decision by four of those convicted at Foley Square to become "unavailable"—that is, to go underground and not appear to serve their sentences —reflected a partial victory by the faction of the party pushing for a disciplined, cadre organization equipped to defend its ranks against the threat of imminent fascism.[5] While critics of the Communist Party blame CP leadership for increasingly defensive, paranoid stances toward the judiciary and the American public, defenders see a necessary connection between the escalating repression of Communists in many arenas of activism and the CP's increasingly inward-looking and defensive stance.[6]

The harassment and persecution of Communists, suspected Communists, fellow travelers, progressives, and left sympathizers of every stripe preceded the career of Senator Joseph McCarthy; the crusade was carried out by the Justice Department, the president, Congress, the Immigration and Naturalization Service, and countless other institutions and individuals in federal, state, and local governments who concurred in thinking that communism was the single greatest threat to American society. Public opinion supported the repression of Communists and the denial of their constitutional rights.

While some scholars have painted a picture of contrasts between a foreign policy premised on the demonic threats of international communism and the benign tranquility of suburban family life, Elaine Tyler May argues for "previously unrecognized connections between political and familial values." A culture committed to containment of communism abroad developed a "domestic version of containment" in the home, where "potentially dangerous social forces of the new age might be tamed." [7]

But in a period characterized by retrenchment in women's gains and aspirations and a resurgence of neo-Freudian, essentialist thinking, the Communist Party maintained a vision of women as active agents within the working class. The CP as an organization was committed, in theory, to the full equality of women and in practice maintained a level of participation by and respect for women unparalleled in either major party or in the dominant culture. Robert Shaffer's description of women's place in the CP in the 1930s could also describe the 1950s: "Despite the sexism encountered in the CP and the fact that most of the party's leadership was male, women could find in the CP a structure that encouraged their participation in progressive collective activities, including activities that addressed their special concerns as women." [8] But the rise of the Cold War and the exigencies of intraparty politics created demands on CP women that far outstripped the woman question. Under attack on many fronts, the CP began shrinking and turning inward in defense of its ranks. The passion and struggle that had propelled young cadre in the 1930s to challenge their habits of thinking no longer conditioned their daily lives in the 1950s. Frontline political activism was difficult with young children at home. My mother's own biography is illustrative: In 1929, at the age of nineteen, Sophie Melvin (not yet Gerson) was arrested for her leadership role in the textile workers' strike in Gastonia, North Carolina. In 1951, at the time of her husband's arrest, she was working part-time, the primary caretaker of her two children and distant from the centers of struggle within the CP.

But the exigencies of the Smith Act arrests, trials, and prison time propelled women like Sophie Melvin Gerson into activism within the Families Committee of Smith Act Victims, making use of their commitments as mothers and wives as well as their experience as political activists and organizers.

Answering the Knock on the Door

During the Foley Square trial, Elizabeth Gurley Flynn, a member of the National Committee who had escaped indictment and opposed the decision to send the leadership underground, mobilized the wives of the defendants to speak out on their husbands' behalf.[9] An FBI report covering the period from May to June 23, 1949, describes a meeting in San Francisco at which five wives of defendants addressed an audience of five hundred women and quotes Flynn as saying, "Off the record, the women's commission said they were better speakers than their husbands. Now we have requests from all over for one or more of the wives to speak and we hope to fan it out as the women get more confidence and indignation."[10] While public speaking increased the women's confidence, it created ambivalence for the male leadership. Peggy Dennis, wife of (then) Communist Party General Secretary Eugene Dennis commented,

> For the Party leaders it was a very novel idea and they weren't too comfortable with it, this idea of their wives coming out as being the spokesmen on their behalf and on the behalf of the Party. . . . When we had to go to Detroit for the weekend the guys grumbled about being left alone with the kids. It was quite a novel experience for them. . . . For the first time in our Party raising the human factor, this was partly what made the guys a little uncomfortable.[11]

But after the disappearance of the "unavailables"—the leadership that went underground—harassment of their wives and children increased, and uneasiness about the human factor gave way to real anxiety about the safety and well-being of the families of those arrested. Forbidden by security precautions to maintain any contact with their families and fully aware of the harassment their wives and children were enduring, the "unavailables," along with other defendants, were supportive of a vehicle that would address their families' needs.

The new indictments of more than a hundred of the Communist Party's state leadership in 1951 considerably altered the magnitude of the problem of Smith Act defense and may have increased party willingness to engage in a variety of strategic responses. The earlier hesitancy of CP leadership about the formation of a committee that would focus on the "experience of women as women," that is, as wives and mothers rather than as workers, was overcome by pressure from within their own ranks.[12]

In the summer of 1951, on the heels of the conviction of the eleven and a protracted struggle to raise bail for the second group indicted (a struggle in which the wives played a preeminent role), Elizabeth Gurley Flynn called Peggy Dennis and a few other wives of defendants together to conceive a committee that would support the families of Smith Act defendants. This meeting resulted in the formation of the Families Committee of Smith Act Victims in the fall of 1951. Despite its initiation by Communist Party leadership, the committee was clearly a response to the needs of the families of the defendants. Following a spate of arrests during the previous summer, defendants and their families were in a state of turmoil: The need to raise bail and organize a legal and political defense for the arrested leaders vied with children's needs for security and order in their lives. Esther Cooper Jackson, a black activist and wife of Smith Act defendant James Jackson, pointed to three major reasons for the formation of the Families Committee: to organize a movement to fight back; to help the children gain support by seeing and knowing other children going through the same thing; and to offer mutual support for the women.[13] Children and parents were deeply upset by the arrests and personal harassment; a vehicle for resistance and mutual support was necessary.

After each new arrest, newspapers listed the names of those indicted, often followed by their addresses. An inflamed public was all too ready to visit the sins of the parents on the children. Albert Kahn's pamphlet *Vengeance on the Young: The Story of the Smith Act Children* documents case after case of attacks on children.[14] The FBI followed the children of fugitives, although it was obvious that no information could be gleaned from them. Esther Jackson recalls that her children were followed to school daily; Edna Winston reports that friends walking her daughter in a baby carriage were followed by agents. The misuse of power by schoolteachers exposed children to unusual forms of mental torture. While Steve Nelson was on trial for sedition in Pittsburgh, his daughter Josie's teacher "would give the child carefully selected words . . . to spell aloud before the rest of the class—words such as 'trial,' 'jury,' 'guilty,' and 'conviction.' " Bill Gerson remembers the attendance teacher sarcastically commenting on the reason for his absence the day after our father's arrest. Because of such harassment, Peggy Dennis transferred her son out of public school in the supposedly urbane Upper West Side of Manhattan.[15]

Even institutions firmly embedded in the progressive movement were forced to act in ways that were hurtful and isolating to children of Smith Act defendants. Danny Green, Josie Green, and Ellen Thompson, children of fugitive Communist Party leaders, were removed from the bus about to depart for Camp Wyandot (a progressive, interracial children's camp) after the FBI threatened to place the camp under constant surveillance if the children were allowed to attend.[16]

Even the placement of toddlers in nursery schools could prove problematic: FBI harassment of school directors led them to search for reasons to exclude children from school. Attempts to disqualify Esther Jackson's daughter Kathy were based on claims that Mrs. Jackson had unreported income; Sophie Gerson and Rose Kryzak spoke of the attempt to expel the children of Henry and Edna Winston from school. In the latter case, the Families Committee organized a counterpressure group, mobilizing social workers and teachers to visit the school director and insist that the children be retained. In a rare break from conventional Cold War politics, professionals were enlisted to lend their credibility to the group of Communist-identified women.[17]

As the burden of single mothering was thrust on Smith Act wives by their husbands' incarceration, trial, or "unavailability," FBI efforts made both child care and employment difficult. The level of harassment experienced by Lillian Green is evident in an agent's report of a conversation with her at her place of work, a job she found after months of looking, being hired, and then fired days later after the FBI contacted her employers. The agent writes that Lillian Green

> recognized the writer and approached him with inquiries as to whether or not her present employer had been contacted and to whether or not she was going to be fired from her job. Lillian Green stated that she had three children to feed. . . . Green was advised that the FBI reserves the privilege of interviewing anyone deemed advisable in its efforts to locate her husband. . . . Lillian Green then related that the FBI must be crazy if they think her husband would contact her at her place of employment.[18]

In response to such intimate and unrelenting harassment, wives and other kin of Communist Party leaders joined the Families Committee. Peggy Dennis describes the committee as bringing together "three divisions of Party leaders: the prison wives of the political prisoners, the wives of 'unavailables,' and the families of those in various stages of litigation."[19] Although several women were indicted under the Smith Act, there is no evidence of male activists in the Families Committee. Some men were left at home to parent after the arrest of their wives, but it was women who were forced to bear the brunt of hostile community response to the Smith Act indictments.[20] In New York City, where the Families Committee had its national headquarters and its largest chapter, almost the entire membership consisted of wives of defendants. A notable exception was Rose Kryzak, the sister of New York defendant Bill Norman.

While New York City's Families Committee of Smith Act Victims was the most active and well organized, social networks in other cities mobilized in support of local Smith Act defendants. An FBI report from 1954 referred to an advertisement for a children's Christmas and Chanukah party sponsored by the Families Committee of the Philadelphia Smith Act Defendants. This same report lists a series of organizations, including the Philadelphia Women's Committee to Repeal the Smith Act and Aid Its Victims, Committee of Wives of Smith Act Victims, and the South Philadelphia Committee to Aid Smith Act Victims, alleged to "have been generally under the guidance of the wives of the Philadelphia Smith Act subjects." [21]

In Chicago, friends and relatives formed a support committee for the families of Lil Green and Doris Fine, who were wives of Gil Green and Fred Fine, both "unavailable." The FBI file recognized the existence of the "Chicago Families of Smith Act Victims" while raising the question whether the local group was merely a paper organization, used to sponsor specific events (like a Christmas party) and raise funds, or one engaged in ongoing organizing. Indeed, the FBI was so unimpressed with the Chicago group that it recommended putting the investigation on inactive status: "The Chicago division is not in possession of information indicating the Chicago Families of Smith Act Victims is affiliated organizationally with the national organization known as Families of the Smith Act Victims. Informants advise that funds raised through local affairs are to their knowledge used and distributed locally." [22] But this relatively sanguine assessment should not be misinterpreted. While the FBI may have staged a strategic retreat in its surveillance of the committee, they were relentless in their harassment of Lillian Green and her three children.[23]

Although CP strategy pointed to the need for mobilizing a mass opposition to the Smith Act trials, no effort was made to make the Families Committee into a mass organization, that is, an organization that could recruit people relatively inexperienced in political organizing or less committed to a particular ideological stance. The women I interviewed were unable to explain clearly the reasons for maintaining a small organization in the face of the huge tasks they were undertaking. In retrospect, the reason seems obvious: At a time when several leaders of the Communist Party were fugitives, when FBI surveillance was unremitting and public harassment was escalating, the Families Committee could jeopardize the security of the prisoners and "unavailables" by opening its ranks to unknown recruits.

In a *Daily Worker* story celebrating the five-year anniversary of the Families Committee, Peggy Dennis attributes the beleaguered position of the Families Committee to a reluctance by other progressives to come to the aid of Communists:

> We found ourselves virtually alone since 1951, as advanced Left and
> progressive organizations retreated under the government assaults,
> and the theory spread out that to muster for an all-out defense of
> the constitutional and legal rights of the Left would turn the orga-

nizations of the advanced workers into "narrow defense organizations."[24]

Despite their enthusiasm for the Families Committee, participants remained divided about their proper political role. Struggle ensued between those who wished to limit the work of the committee to fund raising and emotional support for wives and children and those who pushed for an expanded role in the political struggle, in which the Families Committee would fill in some of the leadership vacuum resulting from the Smith Act prosecution of Communist Party leaders. Eventually, a middle ground was established in which the Families Committee addressed itself to the Smith Act indictments and the anticommunist campaign that fueled it, as well as to the particular situation of the defendants, their spouses, and children: more than a women's auxillary but less than CP leadership. By the time of the first national meeting of the Families of Smith Act Victims, June 26–27, 1952, in New York City, four areas of work had been delineated:

I.   In defense of our children
II. To meet the needs of Smith Act political prisoners
III. Families of political refugees
IV. Smith Act activities[25]

The last item reflected the Families Committee's commitment to participation in the broad political campaigns against anticommunist repression. But it was the Families Committee's emphasis on the effects of anticommunist repression on their children, necessitated by FBI harassment and community hostility, that represented the most radical departure from the Communist Party's history of worker-centered struggles.

In formulating a program to counter the attacks on the children of Smith Act defendants, the Families Committee put special emphasis on the vulnerability of children and the costs of social ostracism and community hostility. The minutes of the June 1952 meeting articulate a sophisticated program of attention to both the needs and feelings of children:

> In planning the special program concerning the welfare and security of our children, we do so with this purpose in mind:
>
> a. to demonstrate in practical and tangible forms, and at times on levels understandable to children, that they are not alone because of their parents' political beliefs.
>
> b. that they are loved, accepted and respected because they are the children of Smith Act victims.

c. that their needs and problems are the concern (or will be made the concern) of labor and the progressive movement, and that together, all these forces will fight for their fathers' and mothers' return.[26]

To support summer camp, prisoner visits, and commissary needs, and to place the experiences of the children on the agenda of progressives, the Families Committee persuaded the *National Guardian* newspaper to spearhead a fund-raising campaign begun in May–June 1952 and repeated biannually for seven years. Despite the left identification of the *National Guardian,* it took several meetings before the Families Committee convinced the *Guardian*'s editorial board to support a political campaign that would identify them with the Communist Party. On June 7, 1952, a letter signed by editor John McManus was sent to the entire *Guardian* subscription list, asking for contributions and referring readers to a longer article and to Albert Kahn's pamphlet (*Vengeance on the Young*) documenting "the torment visited on the children in their schools and neighborhoods in the backwash of the prosecution of their parents for their political opinions." [27] Rose Kryzak described the yearly pre-Christmas appeal as a mass campaign "like the one hundred neediest"; another appeal before summer vacation specifically asked for money to send children to camp.[28] The letter was short and understated, but the presence of a column of photographs of seven children brought home the point. Rose Kryzak recalls: "the response to those letters was the greatest heartwarming thing that any group could possibly want. . . . The response came in thousands of letters. It came in dollar bills, it came in twenty dollar bills, it came in small amounts. And that was the beginning of our great activity." [29] The campaign not only provided the financial backing for the committee but it put the situation of the families and the reality of FBI surveillance and harassment on the political agenda of the noncommunist left. A Families Committee newsletter underscored the importance of reaching beyond the boundaries of the Communist Party and its defenders on the left: "The political value of this campaign cannot be overestimated as we have been able to bring the Smith Act and its effect upon the American family, as represented by us, to many people throughout the country who are not reached by our press." [30]

Money raised by these campaigns funded prisoner visits, the printing of pamphlets, and tuition for summer camp for Smith Act children. These racially integrated summer camps were havens for the children. While class struggle and racial emancipation remained beyond the horizon of American politics, in summer camp we lived out the left's human values: antiracist, propeace, socialist, and internationalist.[31] In my own family, for myself and my brother, camp became the locus of our emotional relationships: Our best friends were made at camp, boys and girls who shared our values and among whom we gained respite from the burden of carrying "one enormous secret, greater by far than all the rest, [which] permeated every aspect of our lives." [32] Among the children of other "progressives," our fearful secret became a badge of honor or, better still, an irrelevance, allowing for solidarity and support without the necessity for active resistance.

But the success of the fund-raising campaign did not forge an unproblematic solidarity among the women of the Families Committee. Nor did their shared relationship to CP leadership make "fighting together" a simple undertaking for women of different class, race, ethnic, and political backgrounds, attempting to work together under conditions of incredible emotional duress, in a period in which there was little available language for articulating those differences. (Nor has the development of a language of difference made understanding or united action simpler in the contemporary period!) Esther Cooper Jackson recalled that for her family, "the harassment was worse . . . but in some ways we had it better. The Black press, the community just understood about harassment." At the same time, Jackson remembers experiencing

> a patronizing attitude, even on the part of some other women. . . .
> There were different levels of understanding; some people knew nothing about me, assumed I just didn't know anything. . . . This is something you just live with being Black. . . . You run into it in the Left movement all the time. . . . It's not surprising; it's there. You struggle; you take it up when it's important; other times you just let it go.[33]

Tension and resentments also developed around differing opinions of a wife's behavior after her husband's arrest. Some women simply went out and got jobs (if they had not been working), while others expected the party organization to take care of them or expected to be paid to work full-time as organizers. Anger was voiced to me about the amounts of money some women wanted for clothes for their children, and intimations of class elitism were made. Within the committee, these resentments remained subterranean, dividing women who had no process for dealing with them. Nonetheless, of the five women for whom I have personal accounts, four refer to long-standing relationships forged in that period and maintained to this day.[34]

The relationship between families of the "unavailables" and families with husbands in jail or on trial was often difficult politically and personally; at times, the wives of the "unavailables" were jealous of those who had husbands in prison, who at least knew where their husbands were and could write to them, visit them, and actively organize for their release.[35] Communist Party leaders' decision to make certain people unavailable was a response to an analysis that saw fascism on the horizon; it was made in the absence of discussion with families and without regard to family circumstances, constructing a situation in which party loyalty conflicted with familial bonds. Gil Green describes his wife Lillian's clear objections to the decision to send him underground: "I think it's a mistake," she said, "Do you really expect fascism? . . . But why you, why not someone without young children?" [36]

But the primary activity of the Families Committee, fund raising for defendants and their families, aroused the most conflicting feelings among the women. Peggy Dennis recalled: "Some of the women just felt degraded by that, they felt that it was undignified and insulting." [37] The women with whom I talked were divided in their explanation of why some women felt this way. Some attributed it to an elitism arising from being the wives of leaders: "They believed the Party should take care of them, because they were the wives of [leaders]." [38] Others saw it as middle-class reticence about asking for money.

Nonetheless, fund-raising activities continued to be the major vehicle for talking to people about the Smith Act and the continued FBI harassment of women and children. Sympathetic intellectuals, artists, and performers supported the Families Committee; an undated leaflet of the period shows Jack Gilford and Zero Mostel performing in a benefit musical review that boasted sketches by Melvin Brooks.[39] Rose Kryzak recalls a toy-store owner donating thousands of dollars of toys, which were sold at fund-raising bazaars.[40] Through sympathetic leadership, a segment of the trade union movement pledged money to the Families Committee and eventually formed the Trade Union Committee of One Thousand to Repeal the Smith Act. The Mine, Mill and Smelter Workers' Union in Denver pledged $10 a month for six years.[41] Peggy Dennis writes of farmers offering summer vacations to children, and Esther Jackson told of whole towns adopting children of Smith Act defendants and sending them presents on their birthdays and at Christmas.[42]

In an era in which political protest was increasingly silenced, the Families Committee maintained a voice. Peggy Dennis reflected:

> We created a channel whereby the widest spectrum of people could participate in a fight-back against McCarthyism in humanitarian terms, in protective support of the individual victims and their families. Given the political climate of the time, such simple acts were affirmations of constitutional and democratic issues and involved acts of political solidarity.[43]

Christmas and Chanukah bazaars, humanitarian appeals, and children's summer camp hardly seem the material from which subversion is wrought; nonetheless, in 1953, two years after the Families Committee began its work, it

This leaflet was distributed after the Families Committee was placed on the attorney general's list in 1953. The front of the leaflet (not shown) asks, "Is Family Devotion Now Subversive?" *Courtesy of Sophie M. Gerson*

was placed on the attorney general's list. This list, begun in the 1920s by Attorney General A. Mitchell Palmer and updated during World War II and again in 1948 following President Truman's initiation of the Federal Loyalty Program, had no legal power; it was used as a weapon of political coercion.[44] Listed organizations were denied meeting rooms and tax-exempt status; membership in a listed organization was used as a pretext to brand someone a security risk and deny employment, housing, or induction into the armed forces. Putting the Families Committee on the attorney general's list was an attempt to undermine the broad base of financial, political, and emotional support that the committee had gathered in its first two years.

Unwilling to respond to this quasi-legal attack (set forth in a sixteen-page document containing forty questions that they were instructed to answer), the Families Committee chose instead to appropriate the cultural icon of family security. They responded to the attorney general's list by issuing a pamphlet headlined *Is Family Devotion Now Subversive?*, which warned that "the menacing shadow of creeping fascism has crossed the threshold of the family circle" and asked, "Is it subversive . . . to warn (the American People) that, just as in Hitler's Germany, no home is safe, no family life secure, as long as our loved ones are persecuted and imprisoned for exercising their constitutional right to speak out for their political ideas?"[45] If motherhood and family devotion were the bulwark of patriotic, postwar America, was not the state violating its own values by attacking families? If a free and affluent America necessitated a stay-at-home mother, a working father, and safe children, could the families pictured in this pamphlet be a threat?

But placement on the attorney general's list did not destroy the Families Committee; it continued to function throughout the Smith Act repression, until the conditions that necessitated its existence no longer prevailed. In 1957, the Supreme Court, headed by Chief Justice Earl Warren, handed down the crucial *Yates* v. *United States* decision in which it ruled that prosecution for mere advocacy of ideas, without plans for future action, is unconstitutional. The Families Committee narrowed its focus in the years following the *Yates* decision, although it did not formally dissolve until 1959. Two more years passed before the last two original Smith Act defendants, Gil Green and Henry Winston, were released from jail. Junius Scales, a leader of the North Carolina Communist Party who had been retried and convicted in 1958, was not released until 1962, when President Kennedy granted him amnesty.[46]

Good Info

Wife, Mother, American, Communist: Dilemmas of Women's Activism

The Families Committee's choice of a strategy that emphasized "women as women," that is, as wives and mothers rather than workers, and their use of an explicit familialism, could appear surprising in view of the Communist Party's long history of emphasizing worker-centered, economic issues. But it is important to recognize that this focus was not developed to push forward women's special needs as a group but to exemplify and concretize the social and human costs of anticommunist repression. Moreover, in an era in which "anxiety concerning modern sexuality and females roles" was answered by the "call for a revitalization of domesticity . . . accompanied by an astounding rush into family life," the adoption of familial ideology in the defense of political prisoners was an expeditious move.[47] By framing anticommunist attacks as threats to family life, the Families Committee was able to challenge the moral high ground of anticommunism as well as the demonization of Communists, which included their reputed commitment to "free love." [48]

But to argue, as does one contemporary writer, that women in the CP were attempting "to maintain the patriarchal family" is to misconstrue adaptation as allegiance and confuse material necessity with ideological adherence.[49] Certainly, it was not simply loyalty to husbands or patriarchy that sustained these marriages through years of separation and sustained individual women in their daily lives. The women in the Families Committee were themselves Communists; many had been activists and organizers before they met their husbands and had children.[50] Peggy Dennis speaks of her "determination not to make drastic either/or choices (which) led me to adjust the forms of my activism." Esther Cooper Jackson, a black activist in her own right, had not used her husband's name until after his arrest, when she wrote the pamphlet used in his defense campaign entitled *This Is My Husband*.[51] Her description of the period of adaptation that took place after James Jackson returned home is indicative of the independence developed by many women in their husbands' absence: "Well, there were difficulties. . . . I had been making all the decisions on everything for the family, and he used to get a little irritated and say we would walk a half a block ahead of him all the time. We'd forget [he was there]." [52]

While all the women in the neighborhood performed the "mother role," their activism and political commitments distinguished them from their women neighbors. The ease with which Sophie Gerson traveled to "the city" (meaning Manhattan, a subway ride away from our Brooklyn neighborhood) and packed up her own and other children to attend museums, concerts, ballet and theater, while disdaining the weekly hairdresser appointment and Mah Jong game, set her apart from the more circumscribed life led by most women in the

This Is My Husband

Fighter for His People
Political Refugee

by ESTHER COOPER JACKSON

25c

In this 36-page pamphlet published in 1953, Esther Cooper Jackson used familial imagery to defend her husband, James. The pamphlet presented the Smith Act prosecutions as an attack on democracy and "Negro leaders." *Courtesy of Esther Cooper Jackson*

neighborhood. Although the story (repeated by my brother) about my mother going to jail for shooting the sheriff is an apocryphal reference to an accusation made during her labor organizing days, Sophie Melvin Gerson's history of militant action did clearly set her apart from most women outside the left and many within it.[53] Likewise, the ability of Esther Cooper Jackson to function as an organizer and to withstand FBI harassment was honed by years of organizing within the Southern Negro Youth Congress in Birmingham, Alabama. Indeed, the Birmingham CP had engaged in struggles about sexism (raised as the "woman question" and pushed by its strong female cadre) in ways not paralleled in New York City.[54]

The ability of Gerson, Cooper Jackson, Dennis, and other Families Committee members to travel freely on their own, attend meetings, make speeches, and confront hostile power was not a direct outcome of Families Committee participation but the expression of their own history of political activism. Although differences between men and women in activity level and position within the CP clearly developed through the course of marriage and childrearing, one cannot conclude that this was the result of a lack of ideological commitment on the part of the women or an attempt to maintain the patriarchal family. In an ethnographic study of U.S. Communist Party members, Paul Lyons describes CP marriages as "relatively egalitarian," characterized by shared interests in politics and culture and committed to a model of political activism that allowed space for a woman to pursue her own political and vocational activities.[55] The disparity in political activity between husband and wife among Smith Act families can only be explained by the gender division of labor, which left women with major child rearing responsibility, rather than an ideological glorification of domesticity.

Families Committee women were determined to make a decent life for their children, to provide some measure of economic and emotional security in a period of great duress. Mothers helped their children negotiate their encounters with anticommunist attacks, everyday racism and sexism, and the full range of bourgeois values experienced by a child growing up in the 1950s. The mothers were the purveyors of progressive social values to their children and the mediators between the often rhetorical or ideological stances of the party and the contradictory reality of everyday life. Jane Lazarre, herself a child of Communists, wrote in the *Village Voice,* that although "father made great efforts to train our minds, mold our politics," it was the mothers who

> called themselves materialists but were concerned with the human spirit. They abhorred idealism, but were in the business of finding a practical method for making dreams come true . . .[they] had to find the bottom line, as one so often does with children, in order to

explain to us who they were—so we would never mistake them for who the newspapers said they were.[56]

Concern for and commitment to family—husbands, children, and other kin—and a strategy that attempted to reach a public ready and willing to demonize Communists made familialist rhetoric the choice for outreach. To equate these women's lives with their pamphleteering misses both their complex histories and the pressing political situation that made the familialist "frame" so effective.

Although the Families Committee waged a successful financial and educational campaign, enabling it to provide concrete material support to Smith Act families, few of the women credit it with providing the daily emotional support they needed. This support was not absent; instead, it was garnered on an individual basis outside the organizational structures. In the CP there was no structural space for feelings as such; neither the New Left's prefigurative politics nor consciousness raising nor psychotherapy had yet altered the terms of "political" discourse. Peggy Dennis comments:

> Internally, we became the recipient of all the tensions and emotions which had no outlet. With husbands gone and the Party organization we had always relied on absent, living with insurmountable family problems and fears and apprehensions, we were thrown upon our own resources and upon each other. We were not equipped to help each other because we had no experience in the Party to meet each other as individuals, only in impersonal political concepts.[57]

But despite Dennis's admission of emotional stress, few of the women I interviewed verbalized disappointment with the emotional ambience of the Families Committee. It is possible that the space of thirty years has softened harsh memories. Nonetheless, unlike the women's movement, the Communist Party placed no special value on the expression of one's own feelings; focusing on personal upsets bore the stigma of "subjectivity" and was disdained. In the absence of a language or structure that valorized subjectivity, "feelings" as such were minimized, in the interest of daily survival.

In a 220-word letter written while her husband was underground and her children, relatives, and friends were under constant FBI surveillance, Lillian Green spent more time commenting on the Chicago weather than on her state of mind, which she sums up with classic understatement: "As to Doris and I personally, to say we are constantly harassed is putting it mildly. But you can be sure we don't let it get us down." [58]

Peggy Dennis recalls being questioned by Nancy Bridges (wife of Harry Bridges, a labor leader then undergoing his third deportation attempt): "You make it sound like you are all amazons of strength and paragons of objectivity," she said bitterly. "Tell me, aren't you ever afraid? Don't you ever lay in your bed at night and cry?" [59]

The distance between the private world of feeling and the political world of action is revealed in Dennis's retelling of her own emotional process, her insistence on active resistance rather than emotional expression: "How can I share what it really feels like without being maudlin, non-political. My tears at night. My nightmares. My child's dreams from which he wakes up screaming. I look at the women waiting silently. And I reply, "Yes, I'm afraid. And I cry at night. But I've got to keep fighting back. And we all need each other, fighting together." [60]

Attempts to make the CP more responsive to the needs and feelings of women and children or to use it as an arena for struggle around daily life issues between men and women were unsuccessful: "The Party is not a social [work] agency" was one response.[61] Officially, the CP stood opposed to male chauvinism, as it did to white chauvinism. But the latter engendered a four-year struggle to rout white chauvinism from its ranks, during the 1949–1953 period, while nothing of that scope was ever initiated around the issue of male chauvinism.[62]

For the women who had spent ten or twenty years in the CP, were married to leaders and had been activists themselves, the contradiction between the party line on women and its practice was apparent. Sophie Gerson noted that once children were on the scene, "the more the husband is involved, the less the wife becomes involved, unless she can really battle things." [63] But this battle was an infrequent occurrence; anger presumes a critique of what is as well as a vision of what could be; the urgencies of political repression demanded action and diminished personal animosity.

Peggy Dennis concluded that the very structure of the Communist Party hierarchy tended to exclude mothers: "The very few women who reached any leadership positions had, over the years, neither children nor a permanent personal relationship. . . . To comply with the methods governing party work, a woman had to be willing or able to relegate the children to an around-the-clock surrogate parent." [64]

But despite the failure of the CP—and most other activist political groups—to develop forms of leadership that could accommodate women's—or men's—commitments to children, women expressed little emotional or political bitterness. The problems of household division of labor that are so destabilizing to contemporary relationships were not the terrain of legitimate personal or political struggle for these women, expecially during the years of anticommunist repression.

Forced to do battle for their husband's freedom and their children's security, the women of the Families Committee were not feminists fighting for the rights of women, but neither were they merely soldiers in the army, fighting for socialism. Nonetheless, the very fact of organizing independently, in a group that focused on daily experience, was a source of validation of that experience. Speaking out in any context, including that of wife and mother, can be an empowering experience, and the response that the women received confirmed their skills as speakers and organizers. The necessity of functioning in a male-dominated world without the support of men allowed these women to develop a level of confidence in their own thinking that was often difficult in male-dominated organizations. While some members of the Families Committee had a history of activism, others showed a more typically gendered reticence about taking leadership. Monette Weinstone described the transformation of self that occurred while her husband was imprisoned:

> I was always very shy and I never wanted to step forward. I never wanted to speak publicly. . . . Friends of mine commented on what happened to me when Will was in prison. How I changed they said, how I bloomed and blossomed. I spoke up and I got up and partici-pated. . . . I didn't feel I was suppressed; but they say I arose out of suppression. I think the situation created it.[65]

By creating a political context separate from men, where women spoke out, the Families Committee furthered the challenge to female subordination begun by the Communist Party. Without an explicit critique of gender divisions in politics or the home, the actual practice of a group organized and led by women allowed for the emergence of capacities that had remained submerged in the mixed-gender context of the Communist Party.

The climate constructed by Cold War hysteria after World War II created an emotional monolith resistant to most intellectual and political attack; the Families Committee's appeals to family sentiment attempted to pierce the ideo-logical armor. If the twin pillars of anticommunism and familialism were the ideological bulwarks of the public and private worlds, an assault on both these fronts would be doomed to failure.[66] The Families Committee chose a strategy likely to win hearts and minds within the broadest stratum of American society. But the focus on family issues was more than merely tactical: The Families Committee was a survival organization responsible for the economic and emo-tional stability of families whose lives were immeasurably disrupted by the Smith Act trials, imprisonment, and FBI harassment. In contrast to the postwar "age of anxiety" brought on by prosperity, consumerism, suburbanization, and the Bomb, the families of Smith Act defendants were forced to cope with the very real problems of family dissolution, imprisonment, unemployment, and harassment.

Until we live in a world in which men and women are equally active, dedicated and vulnerable, as political activists and as parents, the work of supporting families and children will fall unequally on women, who will be faced with the dilemma of asserting their knowledge without reifying the position from which it develops. The women of the Families Committee struggled to defend, not some abstract "family" valorized by conservative ideology, but their actual children, husbands, friends, and comrades, not to defend the family as an institution, but to enable men, women, and children to have the freedom to dissent, protest, and survive.

NOTES

Acknowledgments: This essay began as a paper for a seminar on the history of the family at San Francisco State University and went on to become a Master's thesis, "Legacy of Courage, Legacy of Pain: The Families Committee's Struggle Against the Smith Act" (1983) under the thoughtful direction of Naomi Katz. An earlier version of this paper was presented at the Berkshire Conference of Women Historians, June 1987, where I received feedback and encouragement from Ros Baxandall, Marge Frantz, Ellen Schrecker, and many others in attendance. The research and writing of this paper was totally unsupported by any institutional grants.

In June 1984 I became a mother myself, making intellectual work a more difficult endeavor. My parents, Sophie Melvin Gerson and Simon W. Gerson, have provided emotional and logistical support as well as being key sources and contacts for this research. I thank Marcy Darnovsky, Mary Ryan, Joanne Meyerowitz, and Annalise Orleck for helpful feedback on subsequent revisions; Arlene Stein for comradeship, support, and editing; and Annie Popkin for just being there.

1. See Peggy Dennis, *The Autobiography of an American Communist: A Personal View of a Political Life, 1925–1975* (Westport/Berkeley: Lawrence Hill, 1977) 211–215, for the most complete written treatment. Michael R. Belknap, *Cold War Political Justice, the Smith Act, the Communist Party and American Civil Liberties* (Westport, Conn.: Greenwood Press, 1977), the most thorough study of the Smith Act trials, makes no mention of the Families Committee. David Caute's nearly 700-page work, *The Great Fear, The Anti-Communist Purge under Truman and Eisenhower* (New York: Simon and Schuster, 1978) discusses the Families Committee in one paragraph (p. 211) in which he comments: "The families themselves experienced, on the whole, rather less ostracism and hostility from their local communities than might have been expected."

2. The use of motherhood as a basis for making claims on the state has been explored by scholars in a variety of disciplines. Moral arguments based on protection of female virtue and family loyalties were used by both the abolitionist and woman suffrage movements. See Sarah Grimké, "Letters on the Equality of the Sexes, Letter VIII, On the Condition of women in the United States," and Angelina Grimké,

"An Appeal to the Women of the Nominally Free States" in *Root of Bitterness,* ed. Nancy Cott (New York: Dutton, 1972); Aileen Kraditor discusses the use of ideologies of domesticity in the struggle for female suffrage in *The Ideas of the Woman Suffrage Movement 1890–1920* (New York: Anchor Books, 1971). See also Nancy Cott, *The Grounding of Modern Feminism* (New Haven: Yale University Press, 1987); and Seth Koven and Sonya Michel "Womanly Duties: Maternalist Politics and the Origins of the Welfare States in France, Germany, Great Britain and the United States, 1880–1920" *American Historical Review,* October 1990, for discussions of the use of maternalist ideology in the passage of protective legislation and the making of the welfare state. The ambivalence—for feminists—that accompanies the use of motherhood in what she calls "motherist" movements is explored with great subtlety by Ann Snitow, "A Gender Diary," in *Conflicts in Feminism,* ed. Marianne Hirsch and Evelyn Fox Keller (New York: Routledge, 1990). I describe the rhetorical and ideological tactics of the Families Committee as "familialist," rather than motherist or maternalist, because I think that is a more accurate description of their strategy. They were not seeking specific goods or services for women and children but an end to forms of political repression that they understood as dividing their families.

3. Foley Square refers to the location of the federal court in New York City. The term probably originated with journalists covering the trial; both Belknap and Caute maintain the appellation. I use Communist (upper case) to refer to members of the Communist Party; I use communist (lower case) to refer to all adherents to the ideology.

4. Caute, *The Great Fear,* 361–375.

5. The term "unavailable" was used by the Communist Party; it served to avoid publicly stating that CP leaders were sent underground. The press and the state saw these people as fugitives from justice.

6. See Gil Green, *Cold War Fugitive* (New York: International Publishers, 1984), 59; Joseph Starobin, *American Communism in Crisis, 1943–1957* (Berkeley: University of California Press, 1972), 206ff, 219ff, for two different takes on the decision to go underground.

7. Elaine Tyler May, *Homeward Bound: American Families in the Cold War* (New York: Basic Books, 1988), 14.

8. Robert Shaffer, "Women and the Communist Party, USA, 1930–1940" *Socialist Review,* May–June 1979, 74.

9. See Joseph R. Starobin, *American Communism in Crisis, 1943–1957* (Berkeley: University of California Press, 1972), 306, n. 10. Although Starobin's account is quite partisan (he left the CP and became a bitter critic of its politics), there are good reasons to accept his assessment of Flynn's stance.

10. U.S. Department of Justice, Federal Bureau of Investigation, File re. Elizabeth Gurley Flynn, Report on May 2–June 23, 1949. (Thanks to Rosalyn F. Baxandall for sharing this file.)

11. Interview with Peggy Dennis, conducted by author, Berkeley, California, January 18, 1983.

12. Ibid.

13. Interview with Esther Cooper Jackson, conducted by author, New York City, January, 1982.

14. Albert Kahn, *Vengeance on the Young: The Story of the Smith Act Children* (New York: Hour Publishers, 1952). I was unable to locate a copy of this pamphlet, of which

20,000 copies had been published; fortunately it was preserved by the archives of the Federal Bureau of Investigation. FBI file, Families of the Smith Act Victims, SAC New York, document 100-384313-11.

15. Kahn, *Vengeance on the Young*, 2; Interview with Bill Gerson, conducted by author, January 4, 1982; Dennis, *Autobiography of an American Communist*, 187.

16. Gil Green, *Cold War Fugitive* (New York: International Publishers, 1984), 76; Kahn, *Vengeance on the Young*, 6. This incident also became a scene in an autobiographical theater piece about the life of Ellen Thompson performed by "It's All Right to Be Woman Theater" in the early 1970s.

17. Interview with Sophie Gerson, conducted by author, New York City, January 9, 1982; interview with Rose Kryzak, conducted by author, New York City, January 9, 1982.

18. Green, *Cold War Fugitive*, 82.

19. Dennis, *Autobiography*, 211.

20. The atypical experience of being deprived of a mother by the Smith Act arrests and the subsequent parenting by a father is told by Kim Chernin, *In My Mother's House: A Daughter's Story*, (New Haven and New York: Ticknor & Fields, 1983).

21. FBI file, Families of Smith Act Victims, SAC Philadelphia, Report PH 100–31535, February 5, 1954.

22. FBI file, Chicago Families of the Smith Act Victims, SAC Chicago, document 100–32829, September 9, 1956.

23. One measure of FBI surveillance is the number of reports filed on a person or group; the more reports or pages filed, the more surveillance was occurring. In his introduction to *Cold War Fugitive*, Gil Green writes: "First, the heavily censored FBI files deal nearly exclusively with the hunt for *me*. . . . Second, the FBI has not given *all* the files pertaining to me, only a select portion amounting to over 20,000 pages, out of what was—as they informed my attorney Edward Greer—somewhere in the neighborhood of a *million pages*" (p. vii). The "hunt" for Green clearly entailed keeping track of his wife and children.

24. Peggy Dennis, *Daily Worker*, October 2, 1956. In FBI file, Families of Smith Act Victims, SAC Philadelphia, document 100-384313-A, October 10, 1956.

25. Minutes, National Meeting, Families of Smith Act Victims, June 26–27, 1951, Gerson family personal files, Brooklyn, New York. Mimeographed.

26. Ibid., 2–6.

27. John T. McManus, printed letter, June 7, 1952, Helen Lima, personal files, Oakland, Calif.

28. Kryzak interview.

29. Ibid.

30. "Newsletter to and from the Families Committee of the Smith Act Victims," ca. Spring 1952, 2. Mimeographed. Gerson files.

31. In this new era of multicultural awareness I have begun to realize just how much a cultural vanguard these camps were. My education about labor struggles, civil rights, anticolonialist struggles, political repression was begun at summer camp, in an atmosphere free of the either the "political correctness" or humorlessness that current observers fear.

32. Jane Lazarre, "Growing Up Red: Remembering a Communist Childhood in New York," in *The Village Voice Anthology*, ed. Geoffrey Stokes (New York: Morrow, 1982), 249.

33. Jackson interview. Esther Jackson was working for "Freedomways," a black political and intellectual journal, at the time of the interview.

34. Sophie Gerson, Kryzak, and Weinstone interviews; Dennis, *Autobiography*, 215.

35. S. Gerson and Kryzack interviews.

36. Green, *Cold War Fugitive*, 59.

37. Dennis interview.

38. S. Gerson, Kryzak, and Weinstone interviews.

39. Leaflet, no date (ca. 1953), Gerson files.

40. Kryzak interview.

41. Dennis, *Autobiography*, 216.

42. Esther Jackson interview.

43. Dennis, *Autobiography*, 212.

44. For a fuller discussion of the origins, scope, and uses of the attorney general's list, see Caute, *The Great Fear*, 169–178.

45. Families of Smith Act Victims, *Is Family Devotion Now Subversive?* (New York City, n.d., ca. 1953), Gerson files.

46. Scales was the only communist actually to serve time after being convicted under a clause of the Smith Act that made individual CP membership punishable. In one of those great moments of historic irony—and tragedy—"he was convicted and served part of his term *after his departure from the Party.*" See Starobin, *American Communism*, 241 n. 2.

47. Elaine Tyler May, "Explosive Issues: Sex, Women, and the Bomb" in *Recasting America, Culture and Politics in the Age of the Cold War,* ed. Lary May (Chicago: University of Chicago Press, 1989), 155. See also E. T. May, *Homeward Bound,* for further examination of the links between domesticity and anticommunism.

48. This last one was a particular mystery to me as a child, having heard my mother describing strangers yelling out to her, "You want free love? Go back to Russia!"

49. Ellen Kay Trimberger, "Women in the Old and New Left," *Feminist Studies,* Fall 1979, 446.

50. Peggy Dennis comments, perhaps overstating her case, "We were all wives who had at one time been politically active in our own right." Dennis, *Autobiography*, 212.

51. Esther Cooper Jackson, *This Is My Husband, Fighter for His People, Political Refugee,* (Brooklyn: National Committee to Defend Negro Leadership, 1953). Gerson files.

52. Jackson interview.

53. In the aftermath of an exchange of fire between invading police officers and the union's armed guards at the strikers' tent colony on June 7, 1929, "about seventy-five of [the strikers] were arrested, and the Gaston County grand jury indicted sixteen of those for murder and seven for assault with a deadly weapon. Of the sixteen indicted for murder, three were women: Vera Buch Weisbord . . . Sophie Melvin, organizer of the children's section in the strikers' tent colony, and Amy Schechter." Philip Foner, *Women and the American Labor Movement, From World War I to the Present* (New York: Free Press, 1980), 235.

54. For a biographical sketch of Esther Cooper (Jackson) and history of the Southern Negro Youth Congress, see Robin D. G. Kelley, *Hammer and Hoe, Alabama Communists during the Great Depression,* (Chapel Hill: University of North Carolina Press, 1990), 204–207 on Cooper and 195–219 on the SNYC.

55. Paul Lyons, *Philadelphia Communists 1936–1956* (Philadelphia: Temple University Press, 1982), 87–108.

56. Jane Lazarre, "The Lessons of Radical Women," *Village Voice,* December 2–8, 1981.

57. Dennis, *Autobiography,* 215.

58. Lillian Green to Sophie Gerson, April 10, 1952, Gerson files. "Doris" was Doris Fine, wife of another Smith Act defendant. Both families, including children and other relatives, were under constant FBI surveillance and harassment.

59. Dennis, *Autobiography,* 217.

60. Ibid., 217–18.

61. S. Gerson interview.

62. Starobin, *American Communism,* 198–201, describes the campaign against "white chauvinism" as "an internal witchhunt . . . [which] . . . signified a contest for power within a dwindling movement."

63. S. Gerson interview.

64. Peggy Dennis, "A Response to Ellen Kay Trimberger's Essay, 'Women in the Old and New Left,' " *Feminist Studies,* Fall 1979, 453.

65. Weinstone interview.

66. Both E. T. May, *Homeward Bound,* and Marty Jezer, *The Dark Ages, Life in the United States 1945–1960* (Boston: South End Press, 1982) advance the notion that anticommunism and antifeminism were pieces of a cultural gestalt. Jezer quotes one postwar book as warning that "the political agents of the Kremlin abroad continue to beat the feminist drums in full awareness of its disruptive influence" (*The Dark Ages,* 227). See also L. May, ed., *Recasting America,* for a range of interpretations of the culture of the Cold War.

CHAPTER 9

Margaret Rose

GENDER AND CIVIC ACTIVISM IN MEXICAN AMERICAN BARRIOS IN CALIFORNIA

The Community Service Organization, 1947–1962

> *Queremos comida . . .*
> *Queremos camas . . .*
> *Queremos baños . . .*
> *Queremos comida . . .*
> Michael Wilson,
> *Salt of the Earth*

"We want food, we want beds, we want bathrooms." Esperanza Quintero, the wife of striking miner Ramón, was one of the many women denouncing jail conditions in this powerful scene from the now-classic film *Salt of the Earth*.[1] The labor struggle depicted in this motion picture, the 1950 zinc strike in Bayard, New Mexico, became one of the landmarks of Mexican American history in the immediate postwar years, although other confrontations took place before and after the war. Produced and released in the Cold War era, the movie about the fifteen-month walkout by members of Local 890 of the International Union of Mine, Mill and Smelter Workers, the great majority of whom were Mexican Americans or Mexican nationals, generated extraordinary controversy. A focus on the struggles of workers, of an ethnic minority, and of women filmed by blacklisted Hollywood activists (director, screenwriter, actors, and technicians) guaranteed a strong reaction and criticism during this politically charged period.

The film not only chronicled the successful outcome of the bitter strike but also conveyed a strong message about women's equality, rights, and concerns as it vividly portrayed the transformation of the heroine, Esperanza, from a passive to an active participant in the clash between workers and the company. She and other miners' wives insisted that better housing, hot water, and indoor plumbing be added to traditional demands of wages and safety. Moreover, the film illustrated the changes in the balance of power in her marriage. The startling personal and domestic issues raised in the movie offer tantalizing clues about gender, women's issues, family relations, and activism in the Mexican American community during the years after the war. Are the concerns developed in the film, in which union members played extras, found in other, less celebrated but equally important, struggles for economic and social justice in the late 1940s and 1950s?

In fact, the publicity accorded to the film eclipsed other instances of collective action on the part of the Mexican American community. Of equal importance, and perhaps more lasting, were the many organizations that sprang up after World War II. Groups such as the American G.I. Forum, founded in Texas by returning Mexican American veterans, or the Unity Leagues, organized by Mexican Americans in California, indicate heightened awareness of discrimination and the desire to combat it in expanding urban areas. The Community Service Organization (CSO) is still another example of postwar social activism. Mexican heritage women participated in all these groups.

Pioneering and creative scholarship has shown how an analysis of gender can enrich our understanding of Mexican American history and how an analysis of ethnicity, race, and class can expand our understanding of U.S. women's history.[2] Yet the postwar history of Mexican American women has received almost no attention. Traditional accounts of Mexican American history mask Latinas' postwar activism through narratives that recognize the leadership of men and only assume the support and cooperation of women.[3] And by focusing on domestic and apolitical women living in the suburbs, recent interpretations of U.S. women's history neglect the experiences of a great many women of color living in the barrios, black ghettos, and rural communities of the postwar era.[4]

This essay on the mixed-gender Community Service Organization (CSO) concentrates on the experiences of women and men primarily in the Los Angeles area but also in other chapters in California. Because much of the primary material on the group has not been systematically collected, only fragments survive. From this incomplete data no one model emerges to describe women's participation; still, patterns begin to take shape from comparisons of women's and men's personal backgrounds, their specific endeavors and responsibilities, their integration of social activism with work and family life, and the effects of their encounter with the CSO on their lives.

An analysis of the CSO suggests that the postwar cultural emphasis on home, family, and community had a less conservative meaning among Mexican American activist women and men. Women used their roles in the home, family, and community to organize for social change. In mixed-sex organizations they brought traditional female skills (cooking, neighborliness, clerical work, and teaching) and conventional women's issues (neighborhood improvements, education, and health) into the mainstream of the CSO reform agenda. Women and men did not establish a rigid division of labor but tended to participate in different ways in the CSO. Whatever the form of their participation, women's and men's civic activities in the late 1940s and 1950s laid the foundation for the better-known social activism of the 1960s.[5]

The heightened awareness of inequality raised by World War II and its aftermath stimulated civic and political activism in Mexican American communities across the Southwest. In southern California's Pomona Valley, Ignacio López, a local newspaper editor, formed the Civic Unity League, considered a precursor to the CSO, to mobilize for political representation for the barrio. Assisted by Anglo activist Fred Ross, the group succeeded in electing Andrew Morales to the City Council of Chino. Obtaining funding from the Industrial Areas Foundation, a Chicago group established by Saul Alinksy, who had organized such midwestern immigrant groups as Polish and Italian stockyard workers, Ross hoped to duplicate this success in the Southwest. At the same time, in East Los Angeles, a small coterie of civic-minded individuals, angered by postwar discrimination, inferior city services, and the narrow defeat in 1947 of Edward R. Roybal, who had run for a seat on the Los Angeles City Council, began to meet to discuss their grievances. Out of the keen disappointment over Roybal's loss, former campaign workers, other community activists, and Fred Ross cooperated to form the CSO.[6]

Despite the catalyst of the Roybal campaign and his installation as the first chair, the CSO defined itself as a nonpartisan group. In its literature it publicized itself as a "self-help, civic action agency, endeavoring to improve living conditions; to promote inter-community harmony; to work for more adequate education and youth-welfare programs; to protect group and individual interests; to protect, remedy and prevent violations of human and civil rights, and to provide a medium for social expression and 'on the spot' leadership development."[7] This broad conception of its role placed the CSO in the tradition of mutual benefit cooperatives established in the late nineteenth century in the Southwest. *Mutualistas,* as they were called, had begun locally and then had expanded regionally; they became important resources for recently arrived immigrants, as well as first- and second-generation families.[8]

CSO organizational accounts from the early 1950s provide insight into the participants' ethnicity, citizenship, occupation, age, and gender. A 1953 report calculated the CSO's membership at thirty-five hundred. Mexicans and Mexican Americans, three-fourths of whom were U.S. citizens, accounted for more than 85 percent of supporters. In its early years, meetings were conducted in both Spanish and English. Those not of Mexican origin were Jewish, black, or Anglos, like Fred Ross. A few supporters were professionals or small business people, but the majority of the membership was "white collar, factory and field workers in the low income bracket." The CSO was a youthful organization with the largest cohort ranging in age from twenty-five to thirty-five. Women were hardly token members. According to one report, "the branches are composed of men and women in about equal proportion." Although no breakdown was given on marital status, the CSO, like other Mexican American organizations of the time, was interested in involving the entire family. It would seem likely that the majority of female and male participants were married.[9]

Women's and men's participation in mixed-sex organizations is not easily separated, as clear division exists in some areas, but overlap and cooperation mark others. While men and women shared common ground, they also had different priorities. A comparative focus helps place these contrasts in greater relief. The presidency of local CSO chapters throughout the Southwest was generally the province of men, although there were exceptions. Los Angeles CSO presidents in the 1950s and early 1960s included Edward R. Roybal, Henry Nava, Anthony Rios, Gilbert Anaya, J. J. Rodríguez, Max García, and Arturo Martínez. When the CSO emerged as a national organization in the mid-1950s, this model of official male leadership continued in the selection of César Chávez, probably the most famous graduate of the CSO.[10]

These men generally matched the profile of a male CSO member regarding age, citizenship, background, and education. Edward Roybal was born in Albuquerque, New Mexico, in 1916 to a middle-class Mexican American family. His family moved to Los Angeles in the early 1920s. After graduating from Roosevelt High School, young Roybal briefly attended the University of California. In the early 1940s he secured a position as a public health educator with the California Tuberculosis Association. After the war, he became director of health education for the Los Angeles County Tuberculosis and Health Association, where he stayed until his historic election to the City Council in 1949.[11]

Roybal illustrates one end of the membership spectrum: Ralph C. Guzmán, a co-founder of the CSO, represents another. Born in Moroleón in Guanajuato, Mexico, in 1924, Guzmán moved with his family to the United States just before the Great Depression. They joined the migrant labor force traveling throughout Arizona and California. Although he would later achieve a career as a prominent Mexican American political scientist, the young Guzmán dropped out of high school as the United States entered World War II.[12]

Although they came from very different backgrounds, military service linked this generation of CSO men. Roybal served in the army in 1944 and 1945. Guzmán enlisted in the World War II merchant marine. Naturalized in 1944, he was inducted into the U.S. Navy, serving as a radio operator. Speaking of his military service, César Chávez noted, "I had little choice, either get drafted or sign up. Since I wanted even less to go into the army, I enlisted in the navy when I was still seventeen. . . . Those two years were the worst of my life. . . . And there was lots of discrimination. . . . The Mexican-Americans were mostly deck hands. That's what I was." [13] The military transformed men, and minority men in particular. In the Southwest, returning veterans began to challenge discrimination and second-class citizenship. Politicized *veteranos* began forming and joining organizations like the G.I. Forum in Texas and the CSO in California.[14]

The majority of these men were married and were able to pursue voluntary activities because of the support they received from their wives. Lucille Beserra Roybal shared an interest in political affairs with her spouse before he entered politics. She and her children passed out flyers on a Los Angeles street corner for Franklin Roosevelt's 1944 campaign. She was more active with her husband's contests for office in the late 1940s. When the CSO was formed after her spouse's initial electoral defeat, she attended meetings, socials, and conventions. A female admirer and colleague of Lucie Rios mused, "And she's [Lucie] the gal who was in there on issues, as articulate as I could possibly be, doing all the work that the rest of us were doing." Helen Chávez provided the critical link between her husband and the CSO. Fred Ross had received César Chávez's name as a prospective candidate for the first northern California chapter from a public health nurse at a well-baby clinic Helen Chávez visited. As a devoted wife, she followed her spouse, moving her growing family to the small towns of Madera, Bakersfield, Hanford, and Oxnard, and in 1960 to Los Angeles, where her husband assumed the national directorship of the CSO. She also helped in the office or at home after her domestic chores were done and the children were asleep. "If we were going to have a meeting," she recalled, "I would address all the envelopes or address postcards, whatever had to be done." [15] This pattern of wifely support appeared to be a consistent feature throughout the organization for male officers. While wives were often out of the public eye, many men in the organization enjoyed positions of visibility and recognition in their communities. If not presidents of their chapters, many served as chairs of various committees.

Several notable issues emerged in the Los Angeles CSO that drew the energy and commitment of male members. Police brutality was a particular concern. Police–community tensions had a long history in the East Los Angeles barrio. The wartime Zoot-Suit Riots and the Sleepy Lagoon incident were still fresh in residents' minds.[16] In the late 1940s, the CSO pressed for action in the Silva-Walker Castro incident in which several youths complained that they had been beaten in an East Los Angeles substation by sheriff's deputies. After a court defense supported by the CSO, the young men won a partial victory. In the Santo Niño 7 affair, seven Mexican American adolescents, members of a CYO (Catholic Youth Organization), were taken to the university police station and beaten after they were accused of stripping autos. Through the intervention of the CSO and the CYO, the charges were later dropped. The issue reignited in the 1950s when Anthony Rios—a CSO president, leader in a CIO union local, and delegate to the Los Angeles Central Committee of the Democratic party— and a friend, Alfred Ulloa, were arrested and charged with interfering with officers. The January 1952 event occurred when the two attempted to stop a fight behind an East Los Angeles restaurant. Also involved in the altercation were two plainclothes police officers. During the trial, Rios and Ulloa testified that they had been taken to the Hollenbeck police station, stripped, and beaten. A jury acquitted them, a victory for the two defendants as well as the CSO, which had committed itself to their defense.[17]

Other police brutality incidents kept the problem before CSO members and the public. Community activist Ralph Guzmán headed the CSO Civil Rights Committee and the Civil Rights Department of the Alianza Hispano-Americana and monitored and fought for the Rios–Ulloa complaint, among others. The notorious Bloody Christmas investigation during the same time involved the beating of seven Mexican American youths at the Lincoln Heights police station. Ultimately, several police officers were indicted, convicted, and sent to prison—a substantial and symbolic victory for the Mexican American community. Another success for the CSO and cooperating groups was the suit brought by a high school student, David Hidalgo, who received a settlement for his charges against the L.A. sheriff's department in the mid-1950s.[18] Although there were fewer sensational episodes in the late 1950s, the CSO continued to devote attention to this volatile community grievance, holding meetings to "air" police practices "good and bad" and to consider ways to improve police–community relations. In 1960 the group sponsored a police misconduct study.[19]

From time to time, women emerged in leadership positions in the CSO. Sara López served as president of the Madera CSO in central California in the mid-1950s. After the CSO matured as a national organization, women served on its Executive Board. Carmen García, from the Oakland CSO, was elected second vice-president in 1956, and Rosita Moreno, of the Harbor area CSO, won office as third national vice-president in 1956 and 1957.[20] Probably the best-known woman to emerge from the CSO was Dolores Huerta, who later became a prominent labor leader. Huerta, a third-generation New Mexican on her mother's side of the family and second-generation on her father's, benefited from her mother's relocation to Stockton, California, where she operated a hotel with her second husband. Huerta's comfortable lifestyle and family resources enabled her to graduate from high school and the local community college, a rare accomplishment for Mexican-heritage women in the years after World War II.[21] Her association with the CSO began in 1955, when a chapter was established in Stockton. Reflecting Cold War anxieties, Huerta requested an FBI check on Fred Ross through local authorities to certify that he was not connected with radical elements before she joined the group. At first, she performed a variety of traditionally "female" tasks, such as making arrangements for CSO meetings, but soon she moved into the more demanding and responsible position of paid legislative advocate for the CSO in Sacramento. An unusual undertaking for a woman in the 1950s, particularly so for an ethnic woman, this position broadened her exposure to political and labor issues as her involvement with the AFL-CIO–sponsored Agricultural Workers Organizing Committee (AWOC) demonstrates.[22] A divorced mother of two when the CSO was established, she moved up in the CSO while bearing and rearing five more children in an increasingly troubled second marriage. Family responsibilities were eased with the help of a supportive mother.

Dolores Huerta, however, was not typical of women in the CSO. In terms of class and educational background, Hope Schechter (formerly Mendoza) was more representative. Her personal history was not unlike many Mexican-heritage women at midcentury. "My parents came from Mexico. So I'm first generation," she noted in an interview. Further describing her mother's history, she added, "Her papers read 'walked'; they [her mother and her mother's brothers] walked across the border into Texas and then came into Arizona." Hope Mendoza was born in Arizona in 1921. When she was a year old, the family moved to Belvedere, part of the East Los Angeles barrio, and when she was a toddler her parents separated. Her mother worked as a domestic before remarrying and bearing six more children with her second husband.[23]

Mendoza's upbringing was fairly typical of the Mexican immigrant working-class family. But her stepfather's steady employment with Swift Packing Company and union membership provided unusual security during the 1930s when many unemployed families were thrust on public assistance and vulnerable to the repatriations and deportations of the era. "All through the Depression he [her stepfather] was one of the few who had a job, and while it was on the poverty level we never had to go on welfare. He was able to support us."[24]

Nevertheless, a large family, a paycheck stretched thin, and discouragement from schoolteachers placed limitations on education: "I went to the eleventh grade. It was rough going to school without proper clothes. I remember one winter I didn't have a coat. It was one of the coldest winters. . . . So that's when I decided that I would go to work." [25] Although she would return to school as an adult, her choice to seek employment expanded her world beyond the barrio.

In 1938 the teenager went to work in the garment industry. Enjoying a new independence, she worked there several years before finding a union position on the wartime assembly line at Lockheed. As the female defense job market contracted after the war, she returned to lesser-paid employment.[26] Disturbed by conditions at her new post, she soon became attracted to the International Ladies' Garment Workers Union: "I became interested in the union because I was working a non-union job. So I brought the girls to the union to talk about joining. The union, as usual, had a very difficult time finding women, who are on the militant side, who are articulate." [27] Afterward, Mendoza volunteered her time organizing her shop as well as other plants. She coaxed other young women to join, made signs, walked picket lines, and was arrested. Eventually ILGWU official Sigmund Arywitz "insisted" that the eager garment worker enroll in union-sponsored leadership-training classes. Identified as a determined and bright leader, she was hired as an organizer and business agent in the sportswear division.[28]

These activities gave Hope Mendoza valuable experience, confidence, and prominence in local labor circles and in the Mexican American community. When the idea for the CSO germinated, she was ready. Edward Roybal recalled that the twenty-six-year-old married and childless activist was a charter member.

> On the Tuesday following my defeat, members of my campaign met for a post mortem session to evaluate what we had done right and, more importantly, what had gone wrong. Interestingly, only men attended that first meeting. It was quickly decided that women should be a part of an evaluation session and another meeting was then called. One of the women present at that meeting was Hope Mendoza, a bright young woman who had gained both experience in labor relations and an understanding of human values in the picket lines of the International Ladies' Garment Workers Union. She and many other women became an integral part of CSO from its very beginning.[29]

Because of her union activism, Mendoza had a solid base from which to work for political and social change in the barrio. Although Mexican-heritage women were rank-and-file union members, it was unusual for them to emerge

Hope Mendoza (*far right*) on picket line, late 1940s. *Courtesy of the Regional Oral History Office, Bancroft Library, University of California, Berkeley*

as leaders in the white, male-dominated world of union organizing. In this regard, Hope Mendoza occupied a unique position. For many women in the CSO, however, exposure to unions, at whatever level, emerged as a significant factor in predisposing them to community activism—much as military service had done for men.[30]

Even as organized labor came under assault in the postwar years, the relationship between the CSO and labor was very clear. Albert T. Lunceford, secretary-treasurer of the Greater Los Angeles CIO council, noted labor's early endorsement of the CSO and pronounced, "It is performing a wonderful service for the community. . . . It is an outstanding service, which we wholeheartedly support and urge all members of the CIO support." The AFL Central Labor Council expressed similar enthusiastic approval. W. J. Bassett, a member of the group's advisory committee exclaimed, "CSO is a splendid example of a modern Town Hall, where people thrash out common problems, plan socially useful actions and carry them out."[31] CSO flyers also demonstrated the strong connection, noting in bold letters:

A PROVEN FORMULA

C.S.O. + LABOR = A BETTER COMMUNITY

Besides describing CSO programs and objectives, the flyer encouraged prospective members to join unions at their workplaces and to buy only union-made goods.[32]

As chair of the CSO labor relations committee, Mendoza was a vital link in this "formula." The labor committee engaged in a wide range of activities. It sponsored programs of union education and cooperation by distributing union newspapers and pamphlets to CSO members. The committee also provided moral support and aid for striking workers. In one instance, CSOers joined a packinghouse workers' picket line. In another, labor committee members gathered and donated canned goods and other nonperishables for striking CIO steelworkers. In still more cases, CSO activists prepared and distributed leaflets in other local labor disputes.

Besides demonstrations of solidarity, Mendoza called on the labor community for financial support for the CSO: "I remember one time we [the CSO] needed the money real fast, so I quickly, in one week, raised five hundred. How did I do it? I got fifty people to donate ten dollars each. Which wasn't a lot of money to ask him or her for, but it was enough to tide us over. . . . So what I would do is I would approach unions. They had a set amount of dollars that they set aside for community action."[33] She also solicited union members' support for CSO projects such as neighborhood improvement or youth programs.

> If the father was a meat packer, then you would call Rod Rodriguez, who was head of the Butchers Union, or if they were a waiter, you would call the Culinary Workers Union. I knew all the business reps there, too . . . so I got to know *every* Mexican American that worked for *every* union throughout the city, regardless of labor jurisdiction. . . . I got to know *all* the unions, because I was [also] on the Central Labor Council.[34]

As part of her responsibilities as labor chair, Mendoza interviewed political candidates who approached the CSO for its endorsement. The labor committee acted as advocate in other labor issues, such as educating the membership on the Fair Employment Practices Committee (FEPC). The labor committee also asked CSO chapters to send credentialed delegates to FEPC conferences, such as the one held in Sacramento in 1957.[35]

The antilabor, anticommunist, and antialien climate of the late 1940s and 1950s placed further demands on Hope Mendoza as she confronted the challenges of the Cold War era, "playing a dual role—as an activist in the Mexican-American community, and as part of the labor movement." [36] In the eyes of a rapidly expanding number of conservative politicians and the general public, unionism and subversion became increasingly linked. This combination put the Mexican American community at risk in a rising tide of nativism. The consequences were especially stressful on Mexican parents and their American-born children, who were intimidated by fears of deportation. The immediate causes of this new vulnerability were congressional laws and presidential programs that reflected the growing anticommunism. In particular, the McCarran-Walter Immigration Act of 1952, although not specifically directed at Mexican-heritage people, imposed stringent controls on all immigrants, aliens, and naturalized citizens and subjected them to harassment and deportations by the FBI and the Immigration and Naturalization Service (INS) for any "suspect" political views or activities. "Operation Wetback," initiated by the Eisenhower administration in 1953, did target Mexican immigrants and deported massive numbers of undocumented workers. Under the cumulative impact of these measures, one historian estimated that 3 million Mexicans were expelled from the United States between 1951 and 1954.[37] Although the vast majority of Mexican American activists were members of mainstream organizations, their protests and demands for collective bargaining and social justice were interpreted as "un-American" and exposed them to jeopardy.

The impact of these developments cannot be underestimated in the Southwest, California, and the Los Angeles barrio. A headline of an article appearing in the *Belvedere Citizen* noted: *More than 196,000 L.A. Aliens Begin Annual Registration.*[38] Civic organizations and political officials were besieged by requests for aid. The CSO announced meetings to discuss the "controversial [McCarran-Walter] act." It also responded by setting up an Immigration Committee in addition to its Civil Rights Committee. Sensitive to these concerns, Hope Mendoza served on the Immigration Committee. Congressman Chet Holifield, who represented much of the barrio, cooperated with local organizations to resolve problems. To coordinate and service his constituency better, in 1953 Holifield appointed Mendoza, who was well connected with the Democratic party, as his immigration liaison with the community. Most of her cases were routine; nevertheless, they inflicted great hardship and anxiety on individuals and families.

So we would have many people who needed help. Very often you find that you need expert help. . . . if they lived in this country for five years, then the Mexican consulate would give them the necessary documentation. So we had to document the fact that they had lived here five years in terms of receipts, et cetera. . . . I even had to help them fill out the papers. In some instances, you had to have special bills introduced where they were under pending deportations— in order to stay it.

She recalled the difficulties of one particular case: "There was one woman who was being deported, and she had five children and a husband who was going blind. She was a garment worker. Her remaining in this country with five children *born* in this country was crucial, and she was being deported. . . . Through Chet Holifield's office, we worked it out so we got all the paperwork done here." [39] The extent of the disruption of personal lives remains relatively undocumented. But the CSO, through Mendoza and others, exerted a critical impact on Mexicans and Mexican Americans throughout the turbulent 1950s not only in Los Angeles but elsewhere in the state. Without providing any specific details, the *CSO Reporter* commented on the activities of the Visalia CSO chapter in California's central valley: "Augie Serra is doing a wonderful job in the office. . . . One successful case had deportation proceedings stopped against a member and her three children." [40] Regardless of political views, average, hard-working, long-term residents became "security threats" and "undesirables" under the hysteria generated by McCarthyism.

Hope Mendoza's almost total immersion in the causes of the late 1940s and 1950s was in part a response to an unhappy first marriage to a husband who did not share her intense convictions: "I married a man who was very provincial, extremely so. . . . He wouldn't give me a divorce. So it took me a good two years before I could get a divorce. The way I finally did it was I'd stay out late; he never saw me. I just wore him down. Never, never saw me and I never got home before—at the earliest—ten o'clock. Sometimes two o'clock in the morning." Mendoza remained single until she met and married Harvey Schechter, a community activist and eventually regional director for the Anti-Defamation League of B'nai B'rith. This marriage, based on shared interests and commitments, proved an enduring success: "We're both so active in the community. We both understand the problems of two people who are activists. . . . It works out beautifully, because we both understand each other very well in that sense." [41]

Although Hope Mendoza achieved recognition in Mexican American, labor, political, and CSO circles, the contribution of many more CSO women has gone largely unnoted. Women in the CSO functioned in a wide range of positions from paid to unpaid office work, fund raising, voter registration, and community activism. Mostly we know these women through glimpses of the activities they engaged in. María Durán (later Lang) was "active in trade union work on the Eastside," a CSO founding member, and the first treasurer of the CSO; Bertha Villescas was a CSO assistant executive director and utilized her skills in behalf of the group's education and neighborhood projects; Pauline Holguin, formerly a secretary for the International Ladies' Garment Workers Union, became the executive secretary for the CSO; María Marichilar translated her interest in health issues into programs; and untold others exemplified Mexican American women's commitment and dedication to change during the 1950s.[42]

Mexican American women became the backbone of the CSO. They used traditional female skills—clerical work, hostessing, cooking, neighborliness, and teaching—in behalf of the groups. They contributed to the structural survival of the organization by assuming responsibility for the routine operation of the office. While men became chapter presidents, women occupied the positions of recording and corresponding secretaries. In the late 1940s and early 1950s Bertha Villescas, Carmen Medina, and Margarita Durán (daughter of María) staffed CSO headquarters, managing internal affairs, handling correspondence, running the mimeograph machine, and interacting with the public on a regular basis. Pauline Holguin shouldered this responsibility in mid-decade. Women were also essential in organizing CSO state and national conventions. A notice in the *CSO Reporter* recognized their efforts after a successful meeting in Fresno.

> Now that the Convention is over, MILDRED SERRANO, the hard-working Convention Chairman, must be heaving sighs of relief. She and all those who assisted her with the arrangements did a fine job in keeping everything running smoothly. . . . PAULINE SOLIS, Fresno County CSO's very capable Recording Secretary, spent many an hour down in the Work Room helping Gene Lowrey type stencils and OLGA HERNANDEZ, charming daughter of Sergeant-at-Arms Andres Hernandez . . . took over at the mimeograph machine. . . . Mildred Serrano's niece DONNA PALACIOS was also very much on hand to help. (Emphasis in original.)[43]

Women were a primary force in keeping the organization functioning and viable.

Women were also vital in providing operating funds for the CSO. In the first years of its existence the group survived with grants from Alinsky's Industrial Areas Foundation, a temporary arrangement until the group became firmly established. Nevertheless, the donated moneys never covered all the costs. CSO social committees were responsible for organizing the annual and semiannual meetings, banquets, and dances that not only brought the members together to celebrate accomplishments but were also an important source of funds. *Across the River,* a Los Angeles CSO brochure, recognized the committee's role: "Far from being what its name might imply, the group is one of the hardest working, most regular committees in the organization. The committee is a jack-of-all-trades, from its activities from cooking to cleaning at every social affair. In the last analysis the committee is the financial crutch on which the organization leans heavily for support"[44] Women often chaired such committees. Carmen Pujo, for instance, headed the Social Affairs Committee for the Imperial County CSO, as did Viola Cadena for the Santa Clara County branch. A variety of events helped raise money. María Durán Lang served a dinner "A la Mexicano" at a "Time of Your Life" get together at her home. Her enthusiasm and charm were well known. "When Maria walks into a room," the *Eastside Sun* reported, "it becomes charged with either atomic or cosmic energy. Only an atomic or cosmic energy battery could make a pint-size like her so dynamic." A fund-raising *menudo* breakfast was held at the home of loyal L.A. supporter Marian Graff. For a dollar, participants could enjoy the traditional Mexican stew and *pan dulce.* Energetic CSO member Pauline Holguin sponsored "a delicious tamale dinner" in her L.A. home while guests listened "to the melodies of the Mariachis." The next year she hosted a patio party that brought $91.50 to the CSO coffers. A Sunday *tardeada,* an early evening get-together, was also an occasion for fund raising in the L.A. barrio, as guests danced to the music provided by the Armenta Brothers. Apart from events for couples and families, specific female events were planned as well: "A series of Tupper Ware parties with a percentage of sales given to CSO are being conducted under the able leadership of Ursula Gutierrez." The *CSO Reporter* urged its members to attend these and other events "to increase the badly depleted L.A. CSO treasury." The CSO recognized its female membership in traditional terms. For example, it bestowed a "Mother of the Year" award on María Durán Lang for her years of service.[45]

Women also played a major role in perhaps the main program of the CSO in its early years—voter registration. Motivated by the defeat of Edward R. Roybal in his run for the City Council in 1947, the CSO launched its first voter registration drive. According to its literature the following year, "the group made its first large scale attempt to induce members to become Deputy Registrars and a contest was undertaken among them to see who could register the most people."[46] The drive began in Boyle Heights and spread to other areas in the barrio, first Belvedere, then Lincoln Heights, and finally the *colonias,* outlying areas such as San Fernando and San Gabriel. Concurrently, the effort stimulated the development of independent CSO chapters in these communities. In the 1950 campaign, "twenty men and women divided themselves into four teams of five each." The CSO volunteers and deputy registrars "painstakingly covered 2,242 blocks in 373 precincts, devoting 16,000 man-hours" to their effort. Although available records do not reveal the breakdown by gender, a photo in the *Los Angeles Daily News* in 1950, which published a series of stories on the CSO, demonstrates that nearly half the deputy registrars were women. Another photo and story in the series lauded Eliza Baker, "champ CSO registrar," for signing up a thousand new voters. Deputy registrar Hope Mendoza commented, "We just went out, door to door, literally door to door. . . . I think CSO is one that really had the greatest impact in terms of grass roots." Housewives, students, and other unemployed CSO members added 32,000 new voters to the rolls. The result of those early efforts was the election of Edward Roybal to the City Council representing the Ninth District and the selection of Ernesto Padilla to the San Fernando Council. CSO efforts were repeated throughout the 1950s, a particularly daunting task because failure to vote in a general election caused voters to be removed from the rolls.[47]

As CSO deputy registrars scoured their neighborhoods for potential voters, they were confronted with the fact that many long-time residents could not participate in the political system because they were not citizens. To overcome this obstacle, the CSO formed citizenship committees. Announcements of citizenship programs began appearing in the local press. In 1953 the *Eastside Sun* noted: "75 Spanish Speaking Aliens to Be Given Citizenship Classes by CSO in Three Eastside Locations," and praised the "untiring efforts" of Bertha Villescas. Five months later, the *Belvedere Citizen* announced: "200 Students Graduate from CSO Citizenship Classes Tonight."[48] The female membership was prominent in these campaigns. In the late 1950s more intensive activities were reported: "Los Angeles CSO's Citizenship Committee is going strong under the direction of Executive Secretary PAULINE HOLGUIN and Chairman PRISCILLA ENCINITAS. There are 14 classes now in progress and more could be started if additional teachers were available." As CSO chapters spread to other parts of California, more women became involved. The Visalia branch described its program: "Eighteen persons are ready for their citizenship examinations and many thanks are due to the two fine teachers, MRS. RUBY DE LA CRUZ and MRS. RAY LAUFFENBERGER. 45 persons are ready to start in Basic and Advanced English classes." Women predominated in this area, but men were also involved. Forty-four students were enrolled, for example, in a citizenship course taught by Leo Rojas of the Madera County CSO.[49]

Women also concentrated on municipal concerns, such as neighborhood improvements. Growing political awareness and power mobilized the Mexican American community to press local government to respond to barrio needs. As one CSO summary noted: "As lists of registered voters with Spanish surnames increased, authorities began to move." *The C.S.O. Story,* a brief pamphlet history of the organization, recorded that "a neighborhood improvement committee was one of the very first in CSO's organization. What can we do, they asked, about the problems of East Los Angeles' blighted areas, poor houses, unpaved streets and muddy walks?"[50] Bertha Villescas, chair of the CSO Neighborhood Improvement Committee, helped define the problems, publicize the issues, and focus community action. These concerns touched women directly as they moved throughout the barrio. Through petition drives, women organized to fight for their children's safety after injuries and deaths of youngsters occurred at dangerous intersections with no traffic lights. Women demanded improved street lighting. The lack of mobility and security were revealed by a concerned husband, who illustrated the dilemma plainly: "Suppose your neighborhood had so few street lights that your wife could not step out to the store after dark." Numerous announcements, such as "CSO to Launch Sidewalk, Curb Campaign Tonight," appeared in the barrio press. Participation in such campaigns to provide services "like those on the Westside" furnished women with important knowledge and insight into local economic relations and political obstacles to change.[51] CSO activist Hope Mendoza underwent such an awakening: "We were fighting to get sidewalks and that's when we found out about the tremendous number of absentee ownerships—the kind of situation that exists in these poor areas. . . . I found out about the word absentee landlord, and I never had heard about it before. You can't be effective if you don't know about the community, where the pressure points are."[52] Awareness of complex power relationships aided in confronting equally intransigent political forces arrayed against the interests of the Mexican American community. Bertha Villescas spearheaded the drive in opposition to county supervisors' plans to locate dumps in East Los Angeles. She arranged visits to proposed dump sites with other CSO officers and organized protests to the proposal.

These and other efforts resulted in measurable renovations in the area. A 1950 article in the *Los Angeles Daily News* described the changes initiated by the CSO since its inception.

> Three years ago, dirt roads and walkways stretched the length and breadth of Belvedere. In Boyle Heights were trash-strewn vacant lots, junk-jammed alleyways, cracked and rutted roads, broken curbings.
>
> Today pavements cover most of Belvedere's streets, and more than half of them are bordered by neat curbs and shining sidewalks.
>
> In Boyle Heights, street lights glow from 50 new installations, crosswalks protect youngsters in 35 places; stoplights at 20 corners and traffic signals at 25 other intersections safeguard lives; miles of roads have been repaved.[53]

Although these achievements seemed substantial, they were only the beginning of a sustained struggle judging from the repeated calls for meetings to press for more action throughout the 1950s. These improvements represented the persistent efforts of CSOers—and the female membership in particular. While the accomplishments may not have drawn headlines, they embodied tangible advances in the immediate surroundings as well as increased empowerment for barrio women and their families.

There were important victories, but the CSO also experienced crushing defeats in urban affairs. This was particularly evident in the painful destruction of parts of the barrio at the hands of highly organized and well-financed real estate interests and their political allies in the urban renewal and freeway projects in the late Eisenhower years. The battle over Chavez Ravine was one example of the disruption and displacement of barrio residents relocated from their homes in order to make way for Dodger Stadium despite the vigorous protests of the CSO and other local organizations. María Durán Lang, Henrietta Villaescusa, and Ralph Guzmán circulated petitions as part of an unsuccessful campaign to maintain the integrity and identity of the neighborhood.[54]

Voter registration and education and neighborhood concerns provide a general indicator of women's activism in the Mexican American community in the 1950s; however, these were not their only interests. They also turned their attentions to family health issues, a traditional preoccupation of women. Early in the decade, the CSO scheduled a "Health Hints Talk" and conducted first-aid classes for a largely female audience. Programs for children figured prominently in the group's calendar of events. In one project the organization sponsored hearing tests for children. María Marichilar, chair of the Los Angeles CSO's Health and Welfare Committee, addressed an important concern for mothers in her 1957 plans: "On March 30th of this year, 100 free shots of Salk polio vaccine were administered at the CSO office by the Health Department and other shots will be given later."[55] The Visalia CSO undertook a similar project to vaccinate children before the start of the polio season. Women in the Oakland CSO cooperated in an effort to offer free tuberculosis examinations in 1959.[56] These and other endeavors, such as recreational programs and scholarships for adolescents and aid to the elderly, further demonstrate the range of women's community activism in the postwar years.

Far from being a stagnant period for Mexican-heritage women, the late 1940s and 1950s were years of involvement and commitment. Despite the pall cast by the Cold War on political, social, and community activism, the CSO provided an important vehicle for women and men to attain a Mexican American version of the American dream—first-class citizenship, community services, and a decent standard of living.

To achieve their ideal of the Mexican American family, women in Mexican American communities in the Southwest joined organizations to protect themselves against deportation; through voter registration and education drives, they became active in campaigns to secure political rights taken for granted by others; and they engaged in efforts to correct substandard living and health conditions in their neighborhoods.

The CSO maintained this mainstream vision in the 1960s and after, continuing to work for local issues and to address neighborhood concerns not only in the Los Angeles barrio but also in Mexican American communities throughout the Southwest. One of its major Los Angeles programs during the decade was to establish credit unions and promote consumer education for its membership. The passage of state old-age assistance for elderly noncitizens in 1961 was a result of an eight-year struggle generated by CSO chapters across California.[57] In the 1970s, 1980s, and 1990s the CSO continued to sponsor dances and banquets, raise money for scholarships, hold queen and king contests, and deal with such pressing local concerns as drug use.

While the CSO was an organization on the leading edge of change in the Mexican American community, particularly in California in the 1950s, its preeminent role would come under challenge from new groups, more diverse constituencies, and different strategies for change in the 1960s. Instead of representing a clean break between the tactics and aspirations of the 1950s, however, the CSO can best be interpreted as an important bridge to the expanding options of the 1960s, whether exercised through new political associations, government programs, union organizing, or women's organizations.

The CSO provided an important training ground for both women and men. After serving twelve years as a member of the City Council, Edward Roybal was elected to the House of Representatives in 1962. The newly formed Mexican American Political Association (MAPA), departing from CSO's tradition of promoting a broad agenda, focused directly on politics and pursued a policy of electoral independence.[58] Serving as MAPA's first chair brought Roybal the prominence needed to secure national office.

Seasoned by their experience in the CSO, women rose to positions of visibility and power in government in the 1960s. Further developing her ties with the local Democratic party, Hope Mendoza Schechter initiated programs mandated by President Johnson's Great Society: "We were in charge of setting up all the Project Head Starts [*sic*] for the Mexican-Americans in Los Angeles County. And of course, it being a new program, we had to start from scratch finding the personnel, the sites, the food kitchens—everything from scratch."[59] In the expanding opportunities offered at the national level by an innovative Democratic administration, Schechter was tapped as a member of the National Advisory Council on the Peace Corps. In combining labor and community activism similar to Schechter, Eileen Hernández, also an organizer for the International Ladies' Garment Workers and a CSO member, was named to a position with the Fair Employment Practices Commission in the early 1960s. CSO member and community activist Henrietta Villaescusa received an appointment to the International Development Bureau for Latin America, a division of the Alliance for Progress, and later served at the department of Health, Education, and Welfare.[60]

Still other CSO members found options in labor organizing. César Chávez, Helen Chávez, Dolores Huerta, and other former CSO members founded the Farm Workers Association in Delano, California, in 1962. As vice-president, Huerta held a decision-making position as well as becoming the first contract negotiator and assuming such major responsibilities as the directorship of the New York boycott office. For over twenty years, Helen Chávez headed the organization's credit union. They applied organizing techniques learned at the CSO to this new endeavor. Combining the tactics of the CSO with new strategies of mass demonstrations, nonviolent resistance, civil disobedience, and boycotts, they demanded full membership in American society through collective bargaining for rural farm workers, a constituency overlooked in the more urban-oriented CSO. This group, later to become the United Farm Workers (UFW), emerged as a leading organization in California and later in the nation.[61]

Along with new opportunities for political action, government service, and union activism, options for Mexican American women multiplied with the revitalization and emergence of gender-specific groups. Encouraged by the civil rights, student, peace, and women's movements, as well as the emergence of cultural nationalism in the Chicano movement, Mexican American women began to press their grievances in women's groups. Organizations such as the League of Mexican American Women, the Chicana Welfare Rights Organization, and the Comisión Femenil Mexicana Nacional drew much publicity and new members. While their CSO mothers began to assert their rights in traditional mixed-gender groups, in the 1960s and 1970s some of their daughters, often referring to themselves as Chicanas, saw the need for separate women's groups to address their needs, particularly when confronted with traditional conceptions of women in male-dominated organizations.[62]

While it lost its preeminence as a leader for social change, the CSO retained a historic legacy as an important foundation for the emergence of the more militant activism of the Chicano generation. Its voter registration drives of the 1950s foreshadowed the emergence of the Southwest Voter Registration Education Project (SWVRP), founded by Willie Velásquez in 1974.[63] It thrived because of female participation in voter, citizenship, and other civic crusades and transformed a generation of Mexican American women.

Like the fictional heroine Esperanza Quintero in *Salt of the Earth*, CSO women combined family life with community activism. Like her, they brought living conditions and health concerns to their organization's agenda and applied their traditional female skills on behalf of their community. Like Esperanza, they learned organizing and leadership skills that they used effectively behind the scenes and sometimes in front. Both the film *Salt of the Earth,* with its powerful messages of organizing, solidarity, and women's rights, and the CSO laid the groundwork for activists of the 1960s and 1970s. As the once banned film reemerged to inspire the next stage of twentieth-century reform movements, the CSO provided practical training and experience to a generation of women who continued to push for social change.

NOTES

Acknowledgments: Special thanks go to Joanne Meyerowitz, Susan Lynn, and Vicki Ruiz for their thoughtful comments, suggestions, and recommendations. My gratitude also goes to Sara Timby at the University Archives at Stanford and Luis F. Pedroza at East Los Angeles Public Library for their generous assistance in locating several documents used in this paper.

1. From Michael Wilson, *Salt of the Earth,* with commentary by Deborah Silverton Rosenfelt (Old Westbury, N.Y.: Feminist Press, 1978), 70.

2. Alex Saragoza, "Recent Chicano Historiography: An Interpretive Essay," *Aztlán* 19, no. 1 (Spring 1988–1990): 1–77, esp. 42–44; Sarah Deutsch, "The Gendering of Chicano Historiography," paper presented at the Organization of American Historians meeting, Louisville, Kentucky, April 1991.

For examples of scholarship on Mexican and Mexican American women, see Vicki L. Ruiz, *Cannery Women, Cannery Lives: Mexican Women, Unionization, and the California Food Processing Industry, 1930–1950* (Albuquerque: University of New Mexico, 1987); Sarah Deutsch, *No Separate Refuge: Culture, Class, and Gender on an Anglo-Hispanic Frontier in the American Southwest, 1880–1940* (New York: Oxford University Press, 1987). See also Julia Kirk Blackwelder, *Women of the Depression: Caste and Culture in San Antonio, 1929–1939* (College Station: Texas A&M University Press, 1984); Rosalinda M. González, "Chicanas and Mexican Immigrant Families 1920–1940: Women's Subordination and Family Exploitation," in *Decades of Discontent, 1920–1940,* ed. Lois Scharf and Joan M. Jensen (Westport, Conn.: Greenwood Press, 1983), 59–84; Devra Weber, "Mexican Women on Strike: Memory, History and Oral Narratives," in *Between Borders: Essays on Mexicana/Chicana History,* ed. Adelaida R. Del Castillo (Encino, Calif.,; Floricanto Press, 1990): 175–200. Antonia I. Castañeda, "Women of Color and the Rewriting of Western History: The Discourse, Politics, and Decolonization of History." *Pacific Historical Review* 61, no. 4 (November 1992): 501–533.

See also Ellen Carol DuBois and Vicki L. Ruiz, eds. *Unequal Sisters: A Multi-Cultural Reader in U.S. Women's History* (New York: Routledge, 1990); Sara M. Evans, *Born for Liberty: A History of Women in America* (New York: The Free Press, 1989); Sarah Deutsch, "Coming Together, Coming Apart—Women's History and the West," *Montana: The Magazine of Western History* 41, no. 2 (Spring 1991): 58–61.

3. Christine Marín, "La Asociación Hispano-Americana de Madres y Esposas: Tucson's Mexican American Women in World War II," *Renato Rosaldo Lecture Series Monograph* 1 (Summer 1985): 5–18. Mario T. García, *Mexican Americans: Leadership, Ideology, and Identity, 1930–1960* (New Haven: Yale University Press, 1989); see, for example, chap. 6, "The Popular Front: Josephina Fierro de Bright and the Spanish-Speaking Congress," and chap. 8, "Mexican-American Radicals and the Cold War: The Asociación Nacional Mexico-Americana (ANMA)," esp. 218–219.

4. Elaine Tyler May, *Homeward Bound: American Families in the Cold War Era* (New York: Basic Books, 1988), passim. For a recent revision, see Joanne Meyerowitz, "Beyond the Feminine Mystique: A Reassessment of Postwar Mass Culture, 1946–1958," *Journal of American History* 79, no. 4 (March 1993): 1455–1482.

5. Amy Swerdlow, "Ladies' Day at the Capitol: Women Strike for Peace versus HUAC," *Feminist Studies* 8, no. 3 (Fall 1982): 493–520, describes women using "maternalist" strategies in advocating political change. Karen Brodkin Sacks contrasts the more public roles of black male hospital workers and unionists and the behind-the-scenes activism and networking of black "centerwomen" in organizational campaigns in the late 1960s and 1970s. See her *Caring by the Hour: Women, Work, and Organizing at Duke Medical Center* (Urbana: University of Illinois Press, 1988), esp. 119–142, 209–216. In her analysis of women's activism in the YWCA and the American Friends Service Committee, Susan Lynn argues that the 1940s and 1950s were also critical years for women's social reform activism. See her "Gender and Post World War II Progressive Politics: A Bridge to Social Activism in the 1960s USA," *Gender and History* 4, no. 2 (Summer 1992): 215–239, esp. 218.

6. Information on the CSO is sketchy and concentrates on the group's history in Los Angeles. Ralph Guzmán, *The Political Socialization of the Mexican American People* (New York: Arno Press, 1976), esp. 137–143; Rodolfo F. Acuña, *A Community under Siege: A Chronicle of Chicanos East of the Los Angeles River, 1945–1975* (Los Angeles: University of California, Chicano Studies Research Center, Publication 11, 1984). For mention of the CSO, see also Miguel D. Tirado, "Mexican American Community Political Organization," *Aztlán* 1, no. 1 (Spring 1970): 53–78; Richard Santillán, "El Partido La Raza Unida: Chicanos in Politics," in *Chicano Politics: Readings,* ed. F. Chris García (New York: MSS Information, 1973), esp. 136–137; Kaye Briegel, "The Development of Mexican-American Organizations," in *The Mexican-Americans: An Awakening Minority,* ed. Manuel P. Servín (Beverly Hills: Glencoe Press, 1970), 160–178. Maria Linda Apodaca is working on a dissertation at the University of California, Irvine, on women in the CSO that will include interviews with activists.

7. Quoted from Voter Registration Flyer, 1956, Edward R. Roybal Collection, Box 8, Community Service Folder, Department of Special Collection, University of California, Los Angeles. Hereafter cited as Roybal Collection, UCLA. Guzmán, *Political Socialization,* 141, notes Roybal's tenure.

8. José Amaro Hernández, *Mutual Aid for Survival: The Case of the Mexican American* (Malabar, Fla.: Robert E. Krieger, 1983).

9. See Anthony P. Rios, "Application for Funds to United Steelworkers of America," n.d. (ca. 1953), Roybal Collection, Box 9, Folder: CSO, UCLA. Guzmán, *Political Socialization,* 140, notes bilingual meetings.

10. Rodolfo F. Acuña, *Community,* 44, 563. *Belvedere Citizen,* July 4, 1957; *Eastside Sun,* July 30, 1959, and May 10, 1962.

11. Matt S. Meier and Feliciano Rivera, *Dictionary of Mexican American History*

(Westport, Conn.: Greenwood Press, 1981), 308. U.S. Congress, *Biographical Directory of the American Congress, 1774–1971* (Washington, D.C.: Government Printing Office, 1971), 1638.

12. Matt S. Meier, *Mexican American Biographies: A Historical Dictionary, 1836–1987* (New York: Greenwood Press, 1988), 99. *San Antonio News,* July 2, 1980, 9A. *Los Angeles Times,* October 13, 1985, pt. II, p. 14.

13. Quoted in Jacques Levy, *Cesar Chavez: Autobiography of La Causa* (New York: Norton, 1975), 84.

14. For Roybal, see Meier and Rivera, *Dictionary,* 308. For Guzmán, see Meier, *Mexican American Biographies,* 99.

15. For Lucille Roybal, see Steven Green, ed., *California Political Almanac, 1991–1992,* 2nd ed. (Sacramento, 1992), 269; *Who's Who in the California Legislature* (Sacramento, 1992), 227–228. Comment on Lucie Rios quoted in Hope Mendoza Schechter, "Activist in the Labor Movement, the Democratic Party, and the Mexican American Community," an oral history conducted 1977–1978 by Malca Chall, in "Women in Politics Oral History Project," Regional Oral History Office, University of California, Berkeley. Courtesy of The Bancroft Library, 68. (Hereafter cited as HMS.) For Helen Chávez, see Margaret Rose, "Traditional and Nontraditional Patterns of Female Activism in the United Farm Workers of America, 1962 to 1980," *Frontiers* 11, no. 1 (1990): 27; and Margaret Eleanor Rose, "Women in the United Farm Workers: A Study of Chicana and Mexicana Participation in a Labor Union, 1950–1980," Ph.D. dissertation, University of California, Los Angeles, 1988, 129–132.

16. Mauricio Mazón, *The Zoot-Suit Riots: The Psychology of Symbolic Annihilation* (Austin: University of Texas Press, 1984).

17. For the brutality cases against the youths, see *Across the River,* n.d. (ca. 1950), n.p., pamphlet on CSO in Ernesto Galarza Collection 13:7/8, Department of Special Collections, Stanford University. (Hereafter cited as Galarza, Stanford.) For Rios/Ulloa and later cases, see Kaye Briegel, "Alianza Hispano-Americana and Some Mexican-American Civil Rights Cases in the 1950s," in *An Awakened Minority: The Mexican-Americans,* ed. Manuel P. Servín, 2nd ed. (Beverly Hills: Glencoe Press, 1974), 184. *Eastside Sun,* February 7, 1952, March 6, 1952, and March 13, 1952.

18. Acuña, *Community,* 54; *Eastside Sun,* February 9, 1956.

19. *Eastside Sun,* October 31, 1957, and *Belvedere Citizen,* September 15, 1960.

20. *CSO Reporter,* April 1, 1957.

21. See Rose, "Women in the United Farm Workers," 17–28; *Who's Who in Labor* (New York: Arno Press, 1976), 283; *Stockton Record,* April 20, 1950. See also Jean Murphy, "Unsung Heroine of La Causa," *Regeneración* 1, no. 10 (1971): 20. See also Margaret Rose, "Delores Huerta: Labor Leader, Social Activist," in *Notable Hispanic American Women,* ed. Diane Telgen and Jim Kamp (Detroit: Gale Research, 1993), 210–214.

22. Having once worked in the sheriff's department, Huerta used her contacts there to investigate Ross. See "Dolores Huerta Talks About Republicans, César, Children, and Her Home Town," *Regeneración* 2, no. 4 (1975): esp. 20–21. Huerta is mentioned by name as a contact person in a newspaper article describing a regional CSO meeting in Stockton; see *Stockton Record,* July 25, 1958. Huerta's legislative activity is noted in *CSO Reporter,* n.d. (ca. 1959), 13:8, 2., Galarza, Stanford. For AWOC, see Rose, "Women in the United Farm Workers," 35–37.

23. HMS, 1–3, 26.

24. Quoted in HMS, 5. For father's union membership, see HMS, 29. For background on deportations and repatriations in the 1930s, see Abraham Hoffman, *Unwanted Mexican Americans in the Great Depression* (Tucson: University of Arizona Press, 1974).

25. Quoted in HMS, 6. For her discussion of her teacher's remarks, see 7.

26. For a recent perspective on the impact of work on union women in another wartime industry, see Nancy F. Gabin, *Feminism in the Labor Movement: Women and the United Auto Workers, 1935–1975* (Ithaca: Cornell University Press, 1990). Interviews with other Mexican American women are included in Sherna Berger Gluck, *Rosie the Riveter Revisited: Women, the War, and Social Change* (New York: New American Library, 1987), esp. 70–98, 198–219.

27. HMS, 6.

28. HMS, 6, 52–55. For a 1948–1949 photo of ILGWU Executive Board and Officers, including Mendoza, as well as a photo of her on a picket line in the late 1940s, see HMS, 71.

29. HMS, v.

30. CSO activists María Durán, Pauline Holguin, and Eileen Hernández all had connections to labor organizations.

31. Both cited in *Los Angeles Daily News*, December 28, 1950.

32. For flyer "C.S.O. + Labor," n.d. see Roybal Collection, Box 8, Community Service Folder, UCLA.

33. HMS, 77.

34. HMS, 71.

35. *Eastside Sun*, February 24, 1955, and May 5, 1955; *Belvedere Citizen*, February 24, 1955, and August 15, 1963. For conference announcement, see *CSO Reporter*, April 1, 1957.

36. HMS, 43.

37. Juan Ramón García, *Operation Wetback: The Mass Deportation of Mexican Undocumented Workers in 1954* (Westport, Conn.: Greenwood Press, 1980), esp. chart 236. Mario García, *Mexican Americans*, 53, 210, 212–213, 224.

38. *Belvedere Citizen*, December 18, 1952. For headline, see *Belvedere Citizen*, January 5, 1956.

39. Both quotes from HMS, 59–60. Mendoza's appointment by Holifield is noted in *Eastside Sun*, June 4, 1953.

40. *CSO Reporter*, n.d. (ca. June 1959), 8.

41. HMS, 50, 107.

42. *CSO Reporter*, n.d. (ca. November 1958); *Eastside Sun*, October 5, 1950, July 2, 1953, and July 14, 1955; Acuña, *Community*, 35.

43. For a photo of Margarita Durán and Carmen Medina in the CSO office, see *Los Angeles Daily News*, December 27, 1950. For Bertha Villescas, see *Eastside Sun*, March 25, 1954. Quoted material from *CSO Reporter*, April 1, 1957.

44. *Across the River*, n.d. [ca. 1950–1951], n.p., Box 13, Folder 7/8, Galarza, Stanford.

45. *Eastside Sun*, August 31, 1950, and October 5, 1950; *CSO Reporter*, April 1, 1957, October 1958, and n.d. [ca. June 1959]. For María Durán Lang's award, see *Eastside Sun*, May 10, 1962.

46. For quote, see CSO pamphlet, *Across the River*. See also *Belvedere Citizen*, August 27, 1948.

47. *Los Angeles Daily News*, December 25, 1950, and December 29, 1955; HMS, 33, 79, 86; Guzmán, *Political Socialization*, 141.

48. *Eastside Sun*, July 2, 1953. See also *Belvedere Citizen*, July 2, 1953. For graduations, see *Belvedere Citizen*, December 10, 1953.

49. For first quote, *CSO Reporter*, April 1, 1957; for second quote, *CSO Reporter*, October 1958. For Madera chapter, see *CSO Reporter*, April 1, 1957.

50. *The C.S.O. Story*, n.d. (ca. 1965), n.p., 13: 8, Galarza, Stanford.

51. For Villescas, see Acuña, *Community*, 35. For quote from John V. Carmona, see *Los Angeles Daily News*, December 27, 1950. For a sample announcement, see *Belvedere Citizen*, March 12, 1953. For reference to the differences between the Eastside and Westside, see *Across the River*.

52. HMS, 71.

53. *Los Angeles Daily News*, December 27, 1950.

54. Acuña, *Community*, 57–61, 65–72; *Eastside Sun*, October 31, 1957 and November 14, 1957.

55. For quoted material, see *CSO Reporter*, April 1, 1957. For announcements of health programs, see *Belvedere Citizen*, June 5, 1952; *Eastside Sun*, October 20, 1955 and March 14, 1957; *Belvedere Citizen*, February 23, 1956.

56. *CSO Reporter*, April 1, 1957, and *CSO Reporter*, n.d. (ca. June 1959).

57. Tirado, "Mexican American Community Political Organizations," 53–78; *The C.S.O. Story;* HMS, 72.

58. Juan Gómez-Quiñones, *Chicano Politics: Reality and Promise, 1940–1990* (Albuquerque, N.M.: University of New Mexico Press, 1990), 67–68, 92–93.

59. HMS, 14, 152.

60. For Hernández, see HMS, 40; Acuña, *Community*, 104; and *Belvedere Citizen*, November 15, 1962. For Villaescusa, see HMS, 115; Acuña, *Community;* and *Belvedere Citizen*, August 6, 1964.

61. Linda C. Majka and Theo J. Majka, *Farm Workers, Agribusiness, and the State* (Philadelphia: Temple University Press, 1982), 162, 169–170; Levy, *Cesar Chavez,* passim. Rose, "Women in the United Farm Workers," passim.

62. The next generation of women activists recast the activism of CSO women at the university. See Alma García, "The Development of Chicana Feminist Discourse, 1970–1980," in *Unequal Sisters: A Multicultural Reader in U.S. Women's History*, ed. Ellen Carol Dubois and Vicki L. Ruiz (New York: Routledge, 1990): 418–431. García discusses the formation of Mujeres Activas en Letras y Cambio Social (MALCS) for Chicana professors, graduate students, and undergraduates who found it difficult to have their concerns addressed in the mixed-sex National Association for Chicano Studies (NACS).

63. Gómez-Quiñones, *Chicano Politics*, 166.

CHAPTER 10

Dee Garrison

"OUR SKIRTS GAVE THEM COURAGE"

The Civil Defense Protest Movement in New York City, 1955–1961

On the morning of April 15, 1959, two young Manhattan mothers independently left home with their children to break the law. They expected to be arrested for refusing to take cover during the air-raid drill staged that day in sixty-one American cities. During the exercise, called Operation Alert, millions of Americans were required to take shelter for fifteen minutes. This civil defense drill seemed ridiculous to Janice Smith and Mary Sharmat, who felt that in the event of nuclear war most of New York City would be incinerated. The police decided to let Sharmat go, but Smith was placed in a police car. There she encountered the radical pacifist Dorothy Day, the sixty-two-year-old head of the Catholic Workers, whom Smith had never heard of. Day and a small number of radical pacifists had been arrested each year since 1955 for their refusal to take cover during Operation Alert. On their way to the police station in 1959, Day gave twenty-one-year-old Smith "a great hug and kiss" of approval, as Smith remembers.

The embrace is a powerful historical symbol. It represents the bridge between the tiny band of protesters who had kept radical pacifism alive in the 1950s and the thousands of civil defense protesters who would be energized by Sharmat's and Smith's organizing tactics. During the next year, the leadership of civil defense protest shifted from the older group of radical pacifists to young women who relied on the image of enraged motherhood to win public sympathy for their cause.

Historians have described the contribution of male radical pacifist leaders to the early civil rights movement in the late 1950s and the antiwar movement in the 1960s. Some scholars have noted the evolution of civil defense protest from a tiny effort led by radical pacifists into a real challenge to Cold War policy. The full story of why this shift occurred and the way the Smith–Sharmat team of young mothers defied and defeated Operation Alert has gone unreported, however. Tracing these events, I examine the state of the American peace movement when Operation Alert began in 1955, focusing on the postwar activity of radical pacifists. I discuss the changing nature of the resistance to civil defense in New York City from 1955 to 1962, to show how a group of young mothers restructured the civil defense protest into the largest mass peace action held in the United States since the 1930s. In the process, they transformed the American peace movement.

The mothers who reshaped the pacifist movement created a compelling counterritual that contrasted sharply with the ritual of Operation Alert. The air-raid drill was performed annually on a nationwide stage, with specially costumed officials, siren sound effects, and set scripts acted out by the powerful and poor alike. This drama repeatedly evoked traditional power and gender structures as the stay against extinction. The women protesters also emphasized the centrality of protective domesticity and the symbolic value of women to the reproduction of culture and hence to survival. But the political counterritual staged by Sharmat and Smith brought a new domestic model to public attention. Angry mothers, assisted by supportive fathers, defended their children's lives and refused what they perceived to be their victimization by civil defense officials and nuclear strategists. The mothers-with-children protest was the first large-scale public mobilization in the postwar era to make national security policy a widely contested issue. The counterritual devised by Smith and Sharmat worked to transform public consciousness through the provision of a competing set of political symbols that moved people to question the authority of the state.

In 1955, the American peace movement was demoralized and scattered. For a brief moment after Hiroshima, newly organized groups of atomic scientists and world federalists had called for international controls and the recognition of nuclear war as morally intolerable. But these liberal elements quickly succumbed to the growing power of Cold War ideology that followed Soviet development of the atomic bomb and the advent of war in Korea.[1] Only two groups of organized peace activists survived into the early 1950s.

One remaining peace camp, attracting mostly liberal pacifists, was composed of such older groups as the American Friends Service Committee (AFSC), organized in 1917, and the Women's International League of Peace and Freedom (WILPF), founded in 1919. While both organizations opposed Cold War militarism and attacks on civil liberties, they had little interest in building a mass movement. Their tactics generally favored polite dissent, chiefly in the form of letter writing, conference meetings, and publication of materials calling for disarmament, negotiation, and conciliation.[2]

Radical pacifists, including many World War II conscientious objectors, constituted the second peace camp in the 1950s. Radical pacifists favored nonviolent direct action and opposed both capitalist and communist forms of nationalism. Many held to a distinct pacifist lifestyle. In the demoralized mid-1950s organized pacifists of every stripe shared a common frustration as a tiny and ignored minority, dismissed by most as either comic or irrelevant idealists, foolishly resisting the power structure in America and the world. As one radical pacifist reported after an organizational cross-country field trip in 1950, "I've begun to feel at this point, simply to get people to know that the word pacifism exists is no mean accomplishment."[3]

The radical pacifist component within the surviving American peace movement in 1955 was much smaller than the liberal side of organized pacifism. Radical pacifists were centered in New York City, based in the Catholic Workers and War Resisters League (WRL). Male leaders included A. J. Muste, Jim Peck, and Bayard Rustin. Following Gandhian principles of nonviolent resistance, the small band of radical pacifists, with a strong component of women, supported democratic socialism, denounced communist dictatorship, and called for disarmament, civil rights, and democratization of the global order.

A tiny group of radical pacifists in the Catholic Workers in New York City began the civil defense protest, built a supportive pacifist alliance, and saw the movement through to eventual success. Founded in 1933 on New York's East Side by a tough-minded pilgrim of social justice, the remarkable Dorothy Day, the Catholic Workers ran "houses of hospitality" for the poor and hungry. They served as the leading voice of the religious wing of radical pacifism in the United States. In what she called "loving disagreement" with the church, Day criticized the failure of the Catholic hierarchy to live up to its teachings of peace, charity, and love. As one of the nation's leading advocacy journalists, Day preached absolute pacifism and nonviolent resistance in her influential monthly paper, the *Catholic Worker*. She espoused a libertarian socialism that fiercely opposed Soviet-style communism, even while she and the Catholic Workers defended the civil liberties of all, including American communists.[4]

Because radical pacifists in New York City were beleaguered, isolated, and fully committed to social change, they knew each other well and communicated frequently with one another. The Catholic Worker house in the Bowery functioned as far more than a base for radical pacifists; it served as a spiritual and intellectual mecca for creative young people drawn to New York City from across the country in the early 1950s. Dan Wakefield remembers the Workers' famous Friday night lectures: "There were old and young, men and women, graduate students and Bowery denizens, eager to talk about the night's speech, whether it was given by a priest or a politician, a migrant worker or a Yeats scholar, and no one was squelched or snubbed or shushed; anyone could have a say."[5] After the Friday night sessions, talk often continued at the White Horse Tavern. Here, soon-to-be-famous writers, artists, Beats, journalists, pacifists, civil rights activists, musicians, and assorted leftists discovered one another in perhaps the most significant intellectual and political community existent in the United States in the mid-1950s.

In this era of muffled but rising rebellion, radical pacifists felt increasing despair over their failure to raise a public alarm over the dangers posed by the Cold War nuclear build-up and McCarthyism. When Michael Harrington called for support of the socialist presidential candidate at a pacifist conference held in 1952, Ammon Hennacy, a long-time anarchic pacifist, reported wearily from the scene that Harrington "was practically alone among us. . . . Dorothy [Day] and I and others had gone through that parliamentary stage long ago."[6] Independently and together, a number of radical pacifist leaders had become convinced by the mid-1950s of the need for a stepped-up program of nonviolent civil disobedience.

It is not surprising that civil defense protest would become the focus for the first pacifist direct action of the 1950s. Unprotected by the "Top Secret" shield covering most activities associated with Cold War weapons and strategy, civil defense was uniquely exposed to public scrutiny. Civil defense was probably more dependent on public opinion than any other element of national security policy. Citizens had to be directly involved in civil defense, and the success of the effort depended on their understanding and cooperation. Civil defense was the only Cold War program in which the government had to make serious efforts to win public support; it was one of the few areas where citizens had a plausible opportunity to challenge state policy. By 1954, the American public had reawakened to the threat of nuclear weapons after the U.S. bomb test at Bikini Atoll. Radioactive fallout spread over seven thousand square miles of the

Pacific and led to the contamination of a group of Japanese fishermen. Public suspicion of the validity of civil defense was further aroused by too-optimistic reassurances from federal officials about the effect of radiation and by the indecision of political leaders who vacillated between strategies of providing fallout shelters or evacuating target areas.

Organized in 1950, the Federal Civil Defense Agency (FCDA) necessarily relied on thousands of volunteers and a massive advertising campaign to shape public consciousness and impart a sense of national order, legitimacy, and purpose. Cold War nuclear strategy required that the American public demonstrate a collective national will to assume the risk of containing Soviet aggression. Thus the public must be taught to see the role of nuclear deterrence in national security policy as a legitimate, rational choice. Yet policymakers worried that the American public might lack the necessary resolve.[7]

The civil defense establishment sought to convince the public that the gravest threat to national security was not the bomb itself, but the irrational terror of nuclear war. The failure of American will might create a breakdown in national discipline and threaten postwar survival. Val Peterson, President Eisenhower's first administrator of the FCDA, warned that mass panic could "produce a chain reaction more deeply destructive than any explosive known. . . . Mass panic—not the A bomb—may be the easiest way to win a battle, the cheapest way to win a war."[8] To Peterson, public acceptance of deterrence depended on the public belief that even if deterrence failed, the consequences would be tolerable. The essential purpose of civil defense was to create and reinforce this conclusion.

In the early months of its existence, the FCDA distributed 16 million copies of a booklet entitled *Survival under Atomic Attack,* sponsored and distributed nationally a movie with the same message, and sent a large civil defense exhibit around the country. Television, newspapers, and magazines cooperated in minimizing atomic danger. The FCDA also drew clerical, medical, and psychological experts into support of the civil defense campaign—all to convince Americans that any remaining public concern over the catastrophic effects of nuclear war was unjustified.[9]

This propaganda emphasized that traditional gender roles would be carefully maintained during and after nuclear attack. Federal civil defense material pictured happy families awaiting the all-clear signal to emerge from their shelter. It featured masculine fathers, often shown with shovels in their hands, alongside competent mother–homemakers with their alert children at their sides. "A mother must calm the fears of her child," one civil defense publication urged. "Make a game out of it: Playing Civil Defense." The FCDA told women that after the bomb blast, they should attend to child care, mass feedings, counseling, and medical care. The FCDA hired Jean Fuller, president of the California Federation of Republican Women, to direct its women's activities. In 1958 Fuller helped produce the most extensively publicized government brochure designed to domesticate the Bomb—*Grandma's Pantry*. The booklet gave women directions for providing a completely equipped bomb shelter. Women who stocked their shelter in accordance with instructions could be just as prepared for any social eventuality as Grandma had been. As studies of civil defense propaganda by historian Elaine Tyler May and others have shown, traditional family images such as these were intended to tame women's potentially subversive sexuality as well as to quiet public fears of atomic destruction.[10]

Air-raid drill procedures imposed in public schools were particularly abhorrent to women pacifists. School air-raid drills sent children to huddle in the halls or under their desks when the sirens wailed. "Duck-and-cover" drills were presented as mechanisms to give children and their parents a more mature approach to nuclear anxiety. FCDA officials described the purpose of school drills as a means to "alert, not alarm." In 1951, the New York City Board of Education approved a $250,000 budget for civil defense and took the lead in issuing army-style identification dog tags to all students in case they were lost, injured, or dead after a nuclear blast—a tactic later adopted by many other cities. Children were taught that nuclear war was just another hazard of modern life, and one that could be survived with little effort.[11] Millions of Americans still feel anger at those frightening exercises of their youth. As one student recalled those school-sponsored drills: "In many ways, the styles and explosions of the 1960s were born in those dank, subterranean high-school corridors near the boiler room where we decided that our elders were indeed unreliable." [12]

In 1954, the FCDA expanded its alert-not-alarm concept to new dimensions in the macabre exercise called Operation Alert, instituted as an air-raid drill to take place on the same day in over sixty major cities in the United States and Canada. During the simulated nuclear attack—annually observed for the next eight years—all citizens in selected cities were to take cover for fifteen minutes. At the same time, the highest federal government officials practiced their escape from destruction, while local civil defense officers tested preparations for nuclear war.

Like other radical pacifists of the mid-1950s, Dorothy Day was more than ready for a shift to direct action. Her receptivity was enhanced in 1954 when an FBI agent who visited the Catholic Worker office to query her about one of her friends brandished his gun in front of her. This event convinced Day that a new effort must be made to confront J. Edgar Hoover's political police.[13] When she learned that compliance with the Operation Alert air-raid drill would be made compulsory by New York State in 1955, with penalties of up to a $500 fine and one year in jail, she and Catholic Worker Ammon Hennacy organized a small group of radical pacifists who would refuse to take shelter—and notified the FBI, city authorities, and the media of their intent to defy the new law.

On June 15, the day of Operation Alert, headlines across the country described how President Eisenhower and fifteen thousand top executive officials successfully fled Washington to secret "control" centers, while members of the Supreme Court and Congress remained seated to carry on business as usual. In New York City the men and women who resolved to refuse cover ate their lunch at a local church. Seasoned dissenter Bayard Rustin advised them to hold their protest signs high above the crowd so as to give the press cameras a better shot. When the sirens sounded, they waited quietly in prayer and meditation on park benches in City Hall Park in lower Manhattan. Flanked by television and newspaper reporters, the protesters calmly restated their opposition to the government-manufactured illusion that the nation could devote major resources for preparation for nuclear war and at the same time shield people from its effects. A pamphlet distributed by Day read: "We will not obey this order to pretend, to evacuate, to hide. . . . We know this drill to be a military act in a cold war to instill fear, to prepare the collective mind for war." [14]

The police loaded twenty-seven pacifists ranging in age from twenty-two to seventy years into vans for booking. Most of the protesters were affiliated with the Catholic Workers, the Quakers, or the WRL. Seven of the eleven women arrested were Catholic Workers; two of the eleven described themselves as anarchists; another, Orlie Pell, also the president of New York Metropolitan ("Metro") chapter of WILPF, identified herself as a member of WRL. Members of Metro and the radical pacifist groups immediately formed a Provisional Defense Committee. They collected over $35,000 within a few days, and later obtained $150,000 for appealing the cases of those arrested to the U.S. Supreme Court. [15]

On the evening of the arrest, the protesters were brought before Judge Louis Kaplan. He called them murderers, presuming them responsible for the mock deaths of almost 3 million New Yorkers supposedly killed during the air-raid drill. He set bail at an exorbitant $1,500 each. After a heated exchange with one of the female protesters—the not-yet-renowned actress Judith Malina of Living Theater fame, then twenty-nine years old—Kaplan set off a small riot in the courtroom when he spitefully ordered her to Bellevue Hospital for psychiatric observation. Malina was held there for several days. [16] The trials of the accused took place in November. Judge Hyman Bushel displayed his hostility toward pacifists when he inquired if the defense attorney planned to call the Soviet official V. M. Molotov as a witness. Bushel dismissed the cases of two defendants, one because she was pregnant and another because a bootblack had been arrested by mistake. He pronounced the rest guilty and then suspended their sentences, claiming he had no wish to create martyrs.[17]

National press coverage of the protest was limited, although several progressive national magazines and *Harper's* were supportive. New York newspapers and CBS television gave accurate coverage, including the report that civil defense protesters in Boston, Chicago, and Philadelphia were ignored by the police, while citizens in Peoria, Illinois, chose to ignore the drill completely. Except for *Commonweal,* major Catholic publications blasted the Catholic Workers for disobedience to authority. The FBI hastily compiled many new pages for its files. J. Edgar Hoover made another unsuccessful attempt to persuade the Justice Department to prosecute the Catholic Worker movement for sedition.

In 1956 Dorothy Day spoke at a pacifist meeting held the evening before her next defiance of Operation Alert. Day told her audience that, like the Poles and Germans, who had recently revolted against their Soviet oppressors, she and the others who would refuse to take cover during Operation Alert had little chance of success. Yet they were bound by conscience to bear witness to the futility of defense against nuclear war. On July 20, six of those arrested in 1955 and twelve other Quakers, anarchists, and WRL members once again refused to take cover. Dozens of reporters and television cameramen recorded the drama. The following January, the protesters were sentenced to either five days in jail or a fine of $25. Day and three other Catholic Workers chose jail.[18]

In 1957 several other events strengthened the spirits of the small group of radical pacifists. Much of the energy came from Larry Scott, a forty-eight-year-old ordained Baptist minister and civil rights activist. Previously the peace education director of AFSC in Chicago, he had encountered a considerable amount of criticism from AFSC officials and supporters for his leadership of the civil defense protest held in Chicago during the 1955 Operation Alert. Scott left Chicago and the AFSC job in February 1957, announcing his disillusionment with "middle class pacifists . . . [who] have alienated themselves from any non-violent movement possibilities of a truly revolutionary character which would furnish the dynamic spark in [this] revolutionary era."[19]

In April 1957 Scott brought together leaders of the radical, liberal, and traditional pacifist camps for a historic meeting in Philadelphia. Because those present could not agree on strategy, a decision was made to split into three groups, all using different tactics, but all united to oppose preparation for nuclear war. One group consisted of liberal pacifists; this soon became the Committee for a Sane Nuclear Policy (SANE). The radical pacifists organized a direct-action group that would become the Committee for Non-Violent Action (CNVA). The more cautious third group, a coalition of older peace organizations, pledged to focus on opposition to nuclear bomb testing.[20] In May Scott went west to prepare for CNVA's first direct action—a civil disobedience demonstration at a Nevada bomb test site. With him were A. J. Muste and Bayard Rustin, both of whom had been arrested in previous civil defense protests in New York City. Rustin was also at that time deeply involved in the southern civil rights movement, having been the first Gandhian intellectual from the north to arrive in Montgomery, Alabama, during the bus boycott of 1955.

Because several veteran civil defense protesters were in Nevada, the July 12, 1957, demonstration in defiance of Operation Alert was sponsored solely by the Catholic Workers. This time the court handed down heavy sentences: thirty days for all twelve demonstrators. "You are a bunch of heartless individuals who breathe contempt of the law," the judge told the protesters.[21] For the third time, Day entered jail, where, despite her age, she was stripped, then bloodied by a rough vaginal search. The four imprisoned women, called the "air raid ladies" by the other female prisoners, included Day, actress Judith Malina, Deanne Mower, a shy, nearly blind, ex-teacher who had joined the Catholic Workers, and Joan Moses, whose husband was a conscientious objector. Daily picketing of the Women's House of Detention was conducted by the Catholic Workers and the WRL until the civil defense protesters were released in August.[22]

U.S. government policy continued to ignore pacifist concerns. Bent on developing a "clean" bomb, Eisenhower supported continued testing. The Russians launched the first *Sputnik* in the fall of 1957, creating new fears among American Cold Warriors. A few weeks later, leaks from the Gaither Committee, a high-level study group reporting to the president, revealed that the committee had recommended more money for arms and a greatly expanded civil defense program. Meanwhile, presidential hopeful New York Governor Nelson Rockefeller also called for an increase in weapons and an enlarged civil defense effort.

By early 1958, however, there were a few signs of growing public awareness of the threat to human survival posed by bomb testing, the arms race, and civil defense efforts. Congressional hearings sponsored by Congressman Chet Holifield provided more public information about the dangers of radiation and fallout from bomb tests than ever before.[23] Politicians and scientists began to speak up in opposition to testing. In November 1957 SANE had published its initial ad in the *New York Times* featuring appeals from prominent liberals for an end to above-ground testing. The response was so favorable that within a few months SANE had 130 local chapters and 25,000 members.

Yet 1958 seemed to be the nadir of the civil defense protest movement. Because CNVA members were engaged in an attempt to sail a vessel into the bomb test area in the Pacific, it was left to Day and only eleven other protesters, to defy Operation Alert. A black judge, Kenneth Phipps, gave most of the protesters suspended sentences. Five Catholic Workers, including Day, served ten days in jail. Again, Day suffered momentary discouragement, unaware that her years of lonely protest against civil defense drills would soon reap a massive return.[24]

Reflecting the coming revolt, the civil defense protest in New York City received welcome new publicity from the *Village Voice* in the spring of 1959. A picture of Dave McReynolds appeared on the front page a week before the Operation Alert drill with the notice that "This Man Will Commit A 'Crime' on Monday Morning." One of the first publicists of gay rights in the period, McReynolds worked for a while under civil rights activist Ella Baker, joined the staff of the new radical journal *Liberation* in 1957, and became field secretary of WRS in 1960. McReynolds called for volunteers to join him in defiance of the April 15, 1959, national air-raid drill. That year resistance also spread to Jamaica, Queens, and Haverstraw, New York, although the protesters there were not arrested. Dorothy Day and eighteen other protesters in New York City were taken to jail. First offenders received suspended sentences, and Day again served ten days.[25] But the most important development in the 1959 civil defense protest was the entry into the fray of the two young mothers, Mary Sharmat and Janice Smith.

On the morning of April 15, 1959, both young women left home with their small children to stage a personal demonstration against Operation Alert. Janice Smith's husband had told her he had heard of a group of Catholics who were to seek arrest in City Hall Park. When Smith arrived at the park, she heard the sirens wail and sat down with the children on one of the park benches. At the far end of the park, she saw a small group of protesters surrounded by police and television cameramen. Spotting Smith and her children, a group of newspapermen surged over to her park bench. "I refuse to act like a desert rat and run," Smith told the police. "All this drill does is frighten children and birds. I will not raise my children to go underground." After her hug from Dorothy Day, Smith was taken to the police station, where she sought to corral her gleeful four- and two-year-old children while listening to the police lecture her about disobeying the law. She was eventually released without charges.[26]

Meanwhile, a few miles away, Mary Sharmat, holding her six-month old baby, would also escape booking for her refusal to seek cover. The daughter of a Republican naval officer, twenty-four-year-old Sharmat had taken money from savings for possible bail before she set off to break the law. With her son Jimmy snug in his stroller, Sharmat sat down on a bench by the civil defense truck at the center island of Broadway and 86th Street:

I pushed Jimmy's stroller back and forth to keep him happy and gritted my teeth in determination not to become a coward and return home. . . . The sirens started blowing. I sat. . . . Then a man came to me and Jimmy. He demanded that I take shelter. I said "I cannot take shelter. I do not believe in this." . . . He said, "You are nuts." . . . Another Civil Defense man came over to argue sense to me and he screamed over the sirens and I just kept repeating "This is wrong. I refuse to take cover." He was terrified of me and I of him. . . . I gave Jimmy his bottle but nothing would stop his crying. Then a policeman got out of his car. He walked over and said, "Lady, we are going to give you a ticket." I said, "Give me a ticket." That was the least of my worries. He threw up his hands and got back into his car. Both he and the other policeman waved and smiled at me. The Civil Defense men were furious. By this time . . . there must have been several hundred people lining the streets all watching the incident. . . . The men from the local stock exchange office left the stock tapes and came out from Loew-Neuberger. This is most unusual. The Civil Defense men ran and took cover. Jimmy cried and I sat. The "all-clear" signal sounded. Commerce commenced and people continued their interrupted shopping. I picked up a pair of shoes at the repair shop and ran a few other errands and then went home. My husband was surprised to see us. He had anticipated a call from the jail. He went up to the bank and returned the bail money to our savings account. I unpacked the overnight case and put back the extra diapers and baby foods. Jimmy fell asleep in his crib.[27]

The next day, Sharmat read of Smith's arrest in the New York newspapers and set out to call all the Smiths in the city telephone book until she found her. Delighted to make contact, the women could hardly stop talking. If there were two women who had refused to take shelter, they reasoned, then there might be three; perhaps others "had stood with children in the playground, the local park, the neighborhood shopping area, and likewise disobeyed what they believed to be a bad law." Sharmat and Smith pledged to devote one hour a day on the telephone for the next year to finding eight mothers who would refuse as a group to take cover for the 1960 Operation Alert. Then they met Pat McMahon at the playground where Sharmat often took Jimmy. McMahon had four children, was a follower of Gandhi, and belonged to the WRL. Together, the three women located two other mothers in the Bronx who had refused to take shelter. One of them, Adrianne Winograd, took over recruitment efforts on the Central Park playgrounds. In six months they were fifty women. They began a vigorous public relations campaign, formed the Civil Defense Protest Committee and received permission to establish their headquarters at the office of the WRL.[28]

The women gathered by Smith and Sharmat brought an entirely new direction to the civil defense protest. Thinking of themselves as nonpolitical in comparison to the "old pros" whom they met at the WRL, the young women argued for a new publicity strategy that would appeal to a wide group of citizens unwilling to seek arrest but able to come to the park before the 1960 drill and participate in other ways. Some would merely pass out literature to the people who had taken shelter underground. Others would remain in the park until the police told them to take cover in the designated shelters. A third group, expected to be much smaller, would remain and suffer arrest. The appeal would thus be addressed to concerned but nonradical persons who were not politically active and especially to young mothers whose main concern was protecting their children from nuclear catastrophe.

The "old pros" were at first unenthusiastic about the wisdom of this new strategy. They feared that it might obscure their carefully devised radical political analysis or threaten their creation of a militant band of purists engaged in nonviolent confrontation with authority. A second group of experienced organizers interested in joining the civil defense protest, called the "politicos" by Sharmat and Smith, had recently left the Communist party after Khrushchev's revelation of Stalin's crimes. The "politicos" too had doubts about the validity of the Smith–Sharmat tactic of appealing to the political center. During two lengthy initial meetings of the new Civil Defense Protest Committee, Sharmat and Smith, with great difficulty, persuaded the "old pros" and "politicos" to give a place in the movement to all brands of political beliefs. In the beginning, only Day, Rustin, and Muste strongly supported the young women. But none of the radical pacifists or ex-members of the Old Left took a strong stand against the young mothers—especially since the women had already energetically assumed the major responsibility for organizing protest at the next annual drill, to be held on May 3, 1960.[29]

Almost all the newly united crew of activist women, many in their twenties, had full-time jobs as wives and mothers. But they gave all their spare time in preparation for the big day. They found eager recruits in the New York Metropolitan branch of WILPF and collected several thousand dollars in small contributions. The Metro WILPF chapter came alive. Probably unknown to the national office of WILPF, this sudden revival was partly the result of the entry into Metro of several energetic and organizationally talented women who had recently left the Communist Party. One member of WILPF, Bess Cameron, secretly visited the prominent ex-communist Lillian Gates, the wife of John

Civil defense protest, New York City, 1960. *Photo by Charley Solin. From the records of the Committee for Nonviolent Action, Swarthmore College Peace Collection*

Gates, once the editor of the *Daily Worker*. Lillian Gates quietly arranged for several experienced organizers to join the Metro chapter. As Cameron remembered, "We got a number of very, very, good people who were of tremendous help" who knew "how to plan publicity, write press releases, and do all kinds of activities." Within a few months, the Metro branch was turning out hundreds of leaflets and pamphlets, sponsoring well-attended workshops on the danger of nuclear war, and allying itself with other pacifist groups in the area. Two weeks before the 1960 Operation Alert drill, Sharmat and Smith's group, assisted by the Metro chapter, had collected pledges to join the protest from almost three hundred mother-with-children volunteers. Mary Sharmat was an aspiring actress with a sure sense of costume and dramatic effect. She in-

Civil defense protest, New York City, 1960. *Photo by Charley Solin. From the records of the Committee for Nonviolent Action, Swarthmore College Peace Collection*

structed the women volunteers to be polite to the police and to dress carefully for the protest in their best dress and hose; no one could suspect them of being "beatniks." [30]

In preparation for May 3, the women passed out thousands of leaflets at subway exits, recruited on playgrounds and at PTA meetings, and distributed material with supportive quotes from mainstream political leaders, famous scientists, notable writers and artists, and religious figures. Their most widely distributed flyer quoted Democratic Governor Robert Meyner of New Jersey, who called civil defense "a cruel deception on the American people," and President Eisenhower, who had said: "I think people want peace so much that one of these days governments had better get out of their way and let them have it." The leaflet stressed that the only purpose of civil defense was "to frighten children and to fool the public into thinking there is protection against an H-bomb." The literature reassured readers that the protesters were people without common religious or political opinions, representing only themselves, united by only one belief: "PEACE is the only defense against nuclear war." The material spelled out the three forms of protest that the reader might choose to participate in on the day of the drill. If prospective protesters did not want to come to the park, they could write supportive letters to government officials. Just in case anyone had missed the point, the leaflet reassured the hesitant that peaceful dissent was an "American tradition." [31]

Solicited by the civil defense protest committee, celebrities like Kay Boyle, Nat Hentoff, Dwight McDonald, and Norman Mailer promised to join the 1960 civil disobedience action. Kay Boyle explained that "war is not possible if we all say 'No'." Mailer promised to sign autographs in the park. Ever the masculinist, he vowed he would court arrest because he believed that "politics is like sex. You have to go all the way." [32]

The women's most brilliant innovation was their reliance on the image of protective motherhood to win public notice and support. They made detailed plans to surround themselves with children and toys during the Operation Alert protest, arranging for trucks to bring the heaviest items to the park before the drill began. Plans were made to pass out extra babies and toys to single male activists who would practice civil disobedience alongside the young mothers. All guessed correctly that police would not want to take parents, complete with children, playpens, trikes, and assorted childhood paraphernalia, into custody.

On May 3, 1960, President Eisenhower reviewed the troops in Georgia before he broadcast a warning that "civil defense is no joke." This year baseball players were forced to leave the field in Yankee Stadium during the drill; two thousand people from the bleachers huddled under the stands. The New York Stock Exchange floor was cleared; airplanes were grounded; bus traffic was halted; and hundreds of citizens were herded into Grand Central Station and other points downtown. Newspaper photographs showed eerie, deserted streets. All seemed quiet, except at City Hall Park.

The crowd began to gather around noon. Over a thousand people, about two-thirds women, including about five hundred well-groomed mothers with their many children around them, completely filled the small park when the sirens wailed at 2:15 P.M. Sharmat, wearing a large white hat trimmed in lace, described the scene:

> I was not alone, Janice was not alone, the two mothers from the Grand Concourse in the Bronx were not alone. Over five hundred friends gathered at City Hall Park. Many men came down. Our skirts gave them courage. We loaned out extra babies to bachelors who

had the misfortune to be childless. Dozens of children played in an
area designated "Stay Off the Grass." Some of the students brought
their musical instruments and softly played folk songs such as "We
Shall Overcome" and "We Shall Not be Moved." . . . The sirens
sounded. We stood. Mothers with children, fathers with mutual deep
concerns, bachelors who had hopes and a borrowed baby, maiden
aunts who had no children but were taking care of the rest of us. We
stood. There was dead silence through the park.[33]

When the sirens sounded, about five hundred people stood firm, refusing to
move. The other half of the crowd crossed Broadway when the police ordered
them to take cover and stood on the sidewalk but did not take shelter. They
were joined by hundreds of spectators who left the shelters to watch the arrests
of those in the park who had refused to take shelter. The civil defense officer
in charge stood on a park bench, waved his arms over the crowd, and pronounced them all under arrest. The crowd responded with cheers and applause.
The police made twenty-six token arrests, deliberately singling out men—and
women in slacks. The crowd surged up with more cheering and clapping for
the accused. Day and Hennacy, who had never missed a civil defense protest,
were not arrested because they were surrounded by protective admirers. Nor
were there arrests of any members of the Civil Defense Protest Committee, all
wearing special armbands, nor any of the celebrities, nor any of the jubilant
band of "old pros." Led by the women organizers, the audience sang "Gandhi
is our leader. We shall not be moved," as well as "America the Beautiful,"
"Battle Hymn of the Republic," and for a finale, "The Star Spangled Banner."
When the all-clear sounded, hundreds more moved back into the park, to shake
hands and to join Hennacy in the singing of "John Brown's Body" in joyful
celebration of what they had accomplished. As David McReynolds exulted in
the park that day: "This law is dead!"

After the arrests, there followed a preplanned march to the police station
to urge the freeing of the accused. Fifteen men and eleven women were sentenced to five days. The judge accused them of "disservice to their country"
because their arrests were used by communists to illustrate the restrictions on
free speech in the United States. He was met with laughter from the uproarious
crowd of supporters in the courtroom—some of whom one reporter judged to
look suspiciously like "Beatniks" with their beards, toreador pants, and flutes.
For the next five days, until the protesters were released, scores picketed the
Women's House of Detention. The newspapers featured pictures of the picket
line. Many finely dressed women wearing white gloves and hats marched with
baby carriages and strollers. One woman pushed her shopping cart around the
line before continuing on to the market.[34]

In 1960, hundreds of New York City college students joined the civil defense protest movement. Originally contacted by Smith, student leaders organized their peers. Three hundred City College students, as well as student groups at New York University, Barnard College, and Columbia University, refused to take cover. Fifty-nine students at Brooklyn College were suspended for four days for their action. About five hundred New York high school students protested, another sign of the revival of campus activism. A few arrests were made in New Jersey and in Rockland County. Mary Sharmat noted: "Civil defense at last became an issue. It was no longer ignored as an unimportant nothing to put up with because it's easier. . . . Voters back home at the polls began to care." New York columnist Murray Kempton summed it up: "We seem to be approaching a condition of sanity where within a year or so there'll be more people defying than complying with the Civil Defense drill."[35]

Any lingering doubts the "old pros" might have felt about the entry of non-pacifists into the peace movement disappeared. Jim Peck judged the April 1960 demonstration "the biggest civil disobedience peace action [ever] to take place in the United States . . . as phenomenal as the southern sit-ins." Another first was the large number of supportive pieces in the mainstream press, including a denunciation of civil defense in *Esquire,* the popular men's magazine. In a letter of reassurance to a concerned CNVA leader, A. J. Muste wrote that radical pacifists could not shape a mass peace movement if they were "arbitrary and schematic and imply that there can be no effective or justifiable activity except that which calls for immediate complete unilateral disarmament. . . . Undermining civil defense is no small part of understanding the deterrence mechanism. Listen to the brain trusters of the Rand Corporation and you will realize that *they* understand this." The organizational success of Sharmat and Smith also widened the options for David McReynolds of the WRL. Although he did not give the women public credit for their achievement, McReynolds now became a publicist for the tactic of "building a revolution by degrees." The April demonstration taught him that " 'discipline' often comes through action and not through long training sessions. . . . It is possible for the demonstrations to be truly a radical protest and yet also be a mass protest. . . . Let us find ways of involving people in our action projects *to whatever degree they are able,* rather than demanding that they come all the way with us or not take part at all."[36]

There was one more Operation Alert in New York City, held on April 28, 1961. Again the team of young mothers went to work. Their year-long effort brought twenty-five hundred protesters to City Hall Park, where the police made fifty-two random arrests. Significant demonstrations also occurred in New Jersey, Connecticut, Pennsylvania, Massachusetts, Illinois, and Minnesota. Hundreds of college students demonstrated at Princeton, Cornell, Drew,

Rutgers, Columbia University, and City College of New York.[37] The civil defense protest had assumed national dimensions, soon expanding to challenge observance of school air-raid drills.

By 1961, even President Kennedy's efforts and the largest-to-date congressional appropriation for the support of civil defense could not stem public disdain for the program. In November, at the urging of his advisers, Kennedy backed away from his original call for an enlarged civil defense effort and the building of family fallout shelters. An initial plan to distribute a Pentagon-produced civil defense booklet to every American household was dropped. According to Arthur Schlesinger, Kennedy "remarked ruefully that he wished he had never said the things which had stirred the matter up and wanted to diminish the excitement as expeditiously as possible." In 1962, federal officials quietly and permanently canceled Operation Alert.[38]

After the expenditure of millions of taxpayer dollars, the American civil defense program entered a long decline. In the 1980s, President Reagan attempted to revive the issue. Once more, an effort to strengthen civil defense against nuclear war met successful organized protest, this time led by the Physicians for Social Responsibility, sparked by Helen Caldicott.[39] Today, the civil defense program barely survives within the Federal Emergency Management Agency, the organization recently denounced in the press for its failure to respond effectively to disaster sites ravaged by severe weather.

The radical pacifists of the 1950s believed that peace required justice. They sought to transform America's core ideals and public consciousness through nonviolent acts of resistance that would challenge the violence of authority and open the way to spiritual growth for the nation.[40] In the late 1950s, radical pacifism prospered. Originating in nonviolent direct action against Cold War nuclear strategies, specifically against civil defense policy and the production and testing of nuclear weapons, radical pacifism was strengthened by its contact with the first stirrings of women's resolve to assume new roles. A revitalized radical pacifism, heightened by women's efforts to create a mass protest against nuclear war, converged with political liberalism, the New Left, and the civil rights movement, to produce by the early 1960s a significant challenge to the Cold War state.

The contribution of Mary Sharmat and Janice Smith and their gathering of young mothers to the restructuring of the American peace movement has gone unrecognized for too long. Through the tactics they devised, civil defense protest became a moral issue, rather than a political one. It served as a single cause thousands could support for a day, with no political tests required for participation. In his *Rules for Radicals,* the famed organizer Saul Alinsky taught that effective radical protest must go beyond the expectations of the opposed authority and encourage public laughter at that authority. The Smith–Sharmat team with their baby carriages and tricycles did just that. The confrontational tactics developed by Sharmat and Smith in 1959 would be used by the Women Strike for Peace (WSP) organized in 1961—with Mary Sharmat and Janice Smith among its earliest members. In 1962 WSP dealt a mortal blow to the House Un-American Activities Committee. When fifteen WSP leaders were called in December to testify before the feared committee, women affiliated with WSP brought their babies to the hearing, passed out bouquets to those subpoenaed, and applauded their leaders when they refused to denounce possible communists in their nonorganization. These tactics left the confused congressmen looking foolish and belittled by the press.[41] Sharmat, Smith, and the assembly of women they inspired helped to transform nonviolent direct action, once the province of a small band of radicals, into an effective weapon of ridicule used by angry mothers to discredit the nuclear policies of the militarist state.

Operation Alert presented a classic form of political ritual designed by the state to legitimize authority, assure mass solidarity, and calm public fears. It functioned to present a controllable, orderly pattern of action in an attempt to reorder the uncontrollable, ambiguous, and dangerous aspects of the situation and to make nuclear confrontation appear manageable. But reality defeated ritual. Operation Alert failed partly because its observance required that the public be given enough information to justify a civil defense program and assure widespread public cooperation with civil defense drills. Unlike other forms of government-held knowledge about nuclear strategies or nuclear weapon systems, the effect of nuclear war on the population could not be kept "Secret" or "Classified." Given some access to facts about the dangers of blast and fallout, especially after the development of the hydrogen bomb, the public soon realized that the rationale behind civil defense was ludicrous. As experts reacted to the federal denial of reality, political and scientific elites began to disagree in public. The federal pretense of an adequate defense against nuclear bombs could not endure.

Operation Alert also failed as political ritual because Sharmat and Smith shaped a powerful counterconstellation of symbols. Social movement theorist Antonio Gramsci describes the mode of cultural struggle between competing interests as a battle to determine the dominant symbolic paradigm—the fight for ideological hegemony. Gramsci noted that if consumer capitalism is to function smoothly, the state must obtain the cooperation and allegiance of the labor force through the construction of consent. Hegemonic control is established through educational and religious institutions, popular media, and other forms of cultural instruction. In the contest for power in the modern nuclear state, cultural symbolism becomes an important terrain of struggle; the transformation of consciousness becomes part of the revolutionary process. Such issues as community and the construction of identity become salient political forces. Inspired by the tenacity of Dorothy Day, the young mothers organized by Smith and Sharmat defeated Operation Alert because they reworked the cultural meanings of motherhood and protection of children. In so doing, they defined a new collectivity that not only provided protesters with an identity different from that urged by the nation-state but one that also served to attract others to their side.[42]

Today the concept of civil defense against nuclear war survives as a quaint cultural memory. Its visual artifacts are seen in the faded civil defense signs on the walls of public buildings. Its tales are related by elders, eliciting a kind of bemused wonder from younger Americans. The civil defense protest movement remains relatively unnoticed, partly because the national media did not pay it lavish attention, and partly because public interest turned to the fast-moving events of the Cuban crisis, test-ban treaty, presidential assassination, and civil rights movement. With the defeat of Operation Alert, Janice Smith and Mary Sharmat quickly returned to political anonymity. Although they continued their activism through the 1960s, they blended into the tens of thousands who marched in the antiwar, civil rights, and feminist movements of that decade.[43]

The spirit of the anti–civil defense movement they revitalized in 1959 greatly influenced the protest tactics of the early and mid-1960s, the process of "building the revolution by degrees" that David McReynolds noted. Organizers like McReynolds learned the value of bringing together people from a variety of political groups and with different levels of commitment into mass support of a moral issue judged to stand above traditional politics. The civil defense protest movement provides a rich case study for the analysis of such social movements; the clash of competitive symbols in the civil defense drama deepens our understanding of the construction of hegemony while expanding our knowledge of contemporary mass movements.

The relatively rapid success of the civil defense protest, largely secured through its reconstruction of female identity, is additional support for a revisionist view of the 1950s. This new perspective allows us to reconsider the old familiars of "McCarthyism" and "the Feminine Mystique," to see them not as triumphant features of presumed conservative retrenchment but as final, desperate—and ultimately failed—attempts to stave off a massive revolt against the Cold War state and the older gender roles that supported traditional authority. Indeed, it now seems evident that "The Sixties" actually began in the middle of the 1950s. A determined demand for significant social change appears in 1955 among civil rights activists and radical pacifists—in direct-action protests conceived and organized by women, from the Women's Political Council in Montgomery, Alabama, to the Catholic Workers in New York City.[44] The direct-action revolt spread by the late 1950s to other women who refused to play the part of obedient wives and mothers in the fallout shelters, the role assigned to them by the Cold Warriors.

Mary Sharmat summed up the female rebellion succinctly in 1960. Standing in City Hall Park, she viewed the field of battle where politely dressed women gathered with babies, toys, strollers, banners, and playpens. "Our skirts," she said—all shapes and sizes of skirts, with differing prices and quality, and their wearers believing in all kinds of rebellion, standing there outnumbering those in trousers and suits—drew the crowd into the park. "Our skirts," she realized, "gave them courage."

NOTES

Acknowledgments: I thank John Chambers, Sue Schrepfer, Sue Cobble, Barbara Tomlinson, Judith Zinsser, Scott Sandage, and John Leggett for helpful criticisms.

1. Paul Boyer, *By the Bomb's Early Light: American Thought and Culture at the Dawn of the Atomic Age* (New York: Pantheon, 1985).

2. In 1955, Orlie Pell, the fifty-year old president of the New York City Metropolitan branch, was representative of many older women in WILPF. With a 1930 Ph.D. in philosophy from Columbia University, Pell taught briefly, then worked as publications and research associate with the American Labor Educational Service in New York. A descendant of a wealthy New Jersey family, she was active in behalf of black civil rights. Pell served as U.S. President of WILPF from 1957 to 1962 and as an early officer of the New York branch of the National Committee for Sane Nuclear Policy (SANE). Orlie Pell Papers, Archives, Rutgers University Library, New Brunswick, New Jersey. See also Amy Swerdlow, "The Politics of Motherhood: The Case of Women Strike for Peace and the Test Ban Treaty," Ph.D. dissertation, Rutgers University, 1984; Harriet Hyman Alonso, *Peace as a Women's Issue: A History of the U.S. Movement for World Peace and Women's Rights* (Syracuse: Syracuse University Press, 1993), which describes how the "Metro" branch of WILPF, after several splits in the 1920s and near disbandment in the 1940s, emerged as the most ethnically and racially mixed national chapter.

3. Cited in Neil H. Katz, "Radical Pacifism and the Contemporary American Peace Movement: The Committee for Nonviolent Action, 1957–1967," Ph.D. dissertation, University of Maryland, 1974, 15. Also see Charles DeBenedetti and Charles Chatfield, assisting author, *An American Ordeal: The Antiwar Movement of the Vietnam Era* (Syracuse: Syracuse University Press, 1990); Maurice Isserman, *If I Had a Hammer . . . The Death of the Old Left and the Birth of the New Left* (New York: Basic Books, 1987); Lawrence S. Wittner, *Rebels against War: The American Peace Movement, 1933–1983* (Philadelphia: Temple University Press, 1984).

4. Nancy Roberts, *Dorothy Day and the Catholic Worker* (Albany: SUNY Press, 1984); Mel Piehl, *Breaking Bread: The Catholic Worker and the Origin of Catholic Radi-*

calism in America (Philadelphia: Temple University Press, 1982); William D. Miller, *A Harsh and Dreadful Love: Dorothy Day and the Catholic Worker Movement* (New York: Liveright, 1973); Patricia McNeal, "The American Catholic Peace Movement, 1928–1972," Ph.D. dissertation, Temple University, 1974; Patrick Coy, *A Revolution of the Heart: Essays on the Catholic Worker* (Philadelphia: Temple University Press, 1988); Ammon Hennacy Papers, Series W11.1, Dorothy Day Catholic Worker Collection, Marquette University Archives. Hereafter cited as DDCW.

    5. Dan Wakefield, *New York in the Fifties,* (New York: Houghton Mifflin/Seymour Lawrence, 1992), 80.

    6. Wittner, *Rebels Against War,* 227.

    7. Guy Oakes and Andrew Grossman, "Managing Nuclear Terror: The Genesis of American Civil Defense Strategy," *International Journal of Politics, Culture, and Society* 5, no. 3 (1992): 361–403; Guy Oakes, "The Cold War Conception of Nuclear Reality: Mobilizing the American Imagination for Nuclear War in the 1950's," and "The Cold War Ethic: National Security and National Morale," *International Journal of Politics, Culture, and Society,* Spring 1993, 339–363, 379–404.

    8. Oakes, "Managing Nuclear Terror," 371; also see Oakes, "The Cold War System of Emotion Mangement: Mobilizing the Home Front for World War III," in *The Age of Propaganda,* ed. Robert Jackall (New York: New York University Press), forthcoming.

    9. Boyer, *By the Bomb's Early Light;* Wittner, *Rebels Against War;* Thomas Kerr, *Civil Defense in the U.S.: Bandaid for a Holocaust* (Boulder: Westview Press, 1983); Allan Winkler, "A 40 Year History of Civil Defense," *Bulletin of the Atomic Scientists,* June–July 1984, 16–23; Spencer R. Weart, *Nuclear Fear: A History of Images* (Cambridge, Mass.: Harvard University Press, 1988); Wayne Blanchard, *American Civil Defense 1945–1975: The Evolution of Programs and Policy* (Washington, D. C.: Federal Emergency Management Agency, 1980); Lawrence J. Vale, *The Limits of Civil Defense in the USA, Switzerland, Britain and the Soviet Union* (New York: St. Martin's Press, 1987).

    10. Elaine Tyler May, *Homeward Bound: American Families in the Cold War Era* (New York: Basic Books, 1988); Weart, *Nuclear Fear;* Gillian Brown, "Nuclear Domesticity: Sequence and Survival," in *Arms and The Woman: War, Gender, and Literary Representation,* ed. Helen Cooper, Adrienne Munich, and Susan Squier (Chapel Hill: University of North Carolina Press, 1989); Jean Fuller Papers, box 1, Bancroft Library, University of California, Berkeley.

    11. JoAnne Brown, " 'A Is for Atom, B Is for Bomb': Civil Defense in American Public Education, 1948–1963," *Journal of American History,* 1989, 68–90, shows that school officials used civil defense as a political symbol to advance their drive for federal aid to education and to counter conservative attacks on "progressive" education. In Chicago's civil defense plan, citizens were to be tattooed with their blood types, underneath their armpits, in case their arms were blown off and "radiation sickness called for quick transfusion." Cited in Elizabeth and Jerry Mechling, "The Campaign for Civil Defense and the Struggle to Naturalize the Bomb," *Western Journal of Speech Communications,* Spring 1991, 105.

    12. Weart, *Nuclear Fear,* 340.

    13. Robert Ellsberg, "An Unusual History from the FBI," *Catholic Worker,* May–June 1979, presents a synopsis of FBI files on the Catholic Worker movement.

    14. For clippings and documents on the 1955 arrests, see W6.3, box 1, DDCW. Included is a letter from Eleanor Roosevelt to Dorothy Day, April 21, 1959, in which

Roosevelt chides Day for opposition to Operation Alert and concludes: "I cannot see why you go to such extremes to avoid complying with the law"; boxes 1 and 2, CDGA, Civil Defense Protest Committee, Swarthmore College Peace Collection (hereafter cited as SCPC); interview with Tom Cornell by Deane Mowrer, June, 5, 1968, W9, box 1, DDCW. For a general description of the civil defense protest movement, see John Leo LeBrun, "The Role of the Catholic Worker Movement in American Pacifism, 1933–1972," Ph.D. dissertation, Case Western Reserve University, 1973; Ammon Hennacy, "Civil Disobedience," *Catholic Worker*, July–August 1955, 3, 7; appeal for support of Orlie Pell in Bess Cameron to Dear WILPF Member, June 17, 1955, box 22, folder 2, WILPF Papers, Smith College, hereafter cited as SCWILPF.

15. Attorneys for the civil defense protesters argued that because the air-raid drill was not a real attack, there was no clear and present danger and thus the defendants' rights of free speech and religion had been violated. The attorneys also pointed out that substantial numbers of civilians other than those arrested had been exempted from participation in the air raid drill. *WRL News,* March–April 1960.

16. Judith Malina, *The Enormous Despair* (New York: Random House, 1972); *The Diaries of Judith Malina, 1947–1957* (New York: Grove Press, 1984), 367–72.

17. On the 1955 arrests, see also Jim Peck, "The Civil Defense Trial," *WRL News,* November–December, 1955, 1, 4; "The Rights of Non-conformity," *Commonweal,* July 15, 1955, 363–64; minutes, Fellowship of Reconciliation, box 31, SCPC; "On June 15, 1955," War Resisters League Papers, box 8, SCPC; file 97.3, FBI files on WRL, box 1, Marquette University Archives; box 1, CDG-A, Civil Defense Protest Committee, SCPC; DG13, box 31, SCPC. *WRL News,* September–October and July–August 1955, has descriptions and pictures of the arrests. The 1955 and 1956 cases were appealed on behalf of the civil defense protesters. In January 1961 the U.S. Supreme Court rejected the case without a hearing, although Justice William O. Douglass voted in favor of hearing the case.

18. July–August and September–October issues of *WRL News* has descriptions and pictures of the 1956 arrests.

19. Lawrence Scott Papers, box 1, SCPC.

20. Milton S. Katz, *Ban the Bomb: A History of SANE, The Committee for a Sane Nuclear Policy, 1957–1985* (Westport, Conn.: Greenwood Press, 1986); Milton Katz and Neil Katz, "Pragmatists and Visionaries in the Post–World War II American Peace Movement: SANE and CNVA," in *Doves and Diplomats: Foreign Offices and Peace Movements in Europe,* ed. Solomon Wank (Westport, Conn.: Greenwood Press, 1978), 265–288.

21. Malina, *The Diaries of Judith Malina,* 443.

22. Press coverage of the 1957 protest was limited. Day published letters from jail in the *Catholic Worker* and *Liberation,* the radical pacifist journal established in 1956. *The Nation* and *Commonweal* supported the protest action. For clippings about civil defense protest, see W6.3, box 1, DDCW. See also Eileen Fantino, "World Behind Bars," *Commonweal,* April 27, 1966, 93–94; Dorothy Day, "Thoughts after Prison," *Liberation* (September 1957); *WRL News,* September–October 1957.

23. In my interview with Congressman Holifield in 1989, he told me that prior to our conversation he had never told anyone but his wife that his real purpose in holding these hearings and calling for a nationwide system of federal fallout shelters was to make clear to the public that civil defense was an utterly unrealistic and futile preparation for nuclear war. If so, his motivation was not recognized then or later. Interview tape

in possession of author. Richard Wayne Dyke, *Mr. Atomic Energy: Congressman Chet Holifield and Atomic Energy Affairs, 1945–1974* (New York: Greenwood Press, 1989); interview with Chet Holifield, conducted by Enid Douglass, April 25 and May 7, 1975, in Graduate School Library, Claremont College, California.

24. The civil rights and peace struggles of the late 1950s built the framework for the emergence of the New Left. The Gandhian direct-action philosophy of radical pacifists set the intellectual basis for the new politics. The journal *Liberation,* founded in the winter of 1955–1956 by A. J. Muste, Bayard Rustin, Dave Dellinger, and others, provided an early forum to stimulate new thinking. *Liberation* encouraged mass participation in the struggle for civil rights and peace while rejecting both Soviet-style socialism and American Cold War policy. As peace historians Chatfield and DeBenedetti point out in *An American Ordeal, Liberation* "crystalized many of the differences between radical pacifists and other peace advocates, thereby defining the terrain on which the evolving antiwar movement would fragment between 1955 and 1975" (p. 25). The journal also inspired American radicals with news of the mass peace movement led by the Campaign for Nuclear Disarmament that began in England in the late 1950s. Moreover, *Liberation* was the first to reprint copies of the women's protest against sexism in the Student Non-Violent Coordinating Commitee—one of the crucial initial documents of Second Wave Feminism. Casey Hayden and Mary King, "Caste and Sex," *Liberation,* April 1966, 35–36.

25. Interviews with Janice Smith and Mary Sharmat, 1990, conducted by author; telephone interviews with Janice Smith, conducted by author, October, November, and December 1990; *WRL News,* May–June 1959; Larry Scott, "A Desperate Appeal to American Pacifists," Spring 1959, box 1, Scott Papers, SCPC; Correspondence, January–June 1959, series I, box 3, David McReynolds Papers, SCPC; telephone interview with Mary Sharmat, November 1990, conducted by author; *WRL News* January/February 1991, for special issue honoring McReynolds.

26. Interview with Janice Smith, conducted by the author, 1990. Sharmat is the granddaughter of Hilda Brungot, dubbed the "world's champion" woman legislator and an outspoken feminist, who was elected to the New Hampshire legislature in 1930 and served until 1960. Smith is the granddaughter of Samuel Aaron, the founder of the Bakers' Union. Also see report of Smith's 1959 arrest in *New York Post,* April 17, 1959.

27. Sharmat statement, in possession of author.

28. Interview, Sharmat and Smith, 1990.

29. Interviews, Sharmat and Smith, conducted by author, 1991; "Civil Defense Protest Day" and "Call to Sanity," box 22, Civil Defense Protest Commitee, SCPC; documents and clippings in box 6, SANE Papers, SCPC; box 22, series VI, Committee for Non-Violent Action, SCPC.

30. FBI files on WRL, boxes 8 and 14, and FBI files on WILPF, boxes 3 and 4, in Marquette University Archives; interview with Bess Cameron conducted by B. Parnes, December 30, 1987, in possession of author. The sudden revival of Metro is very evident in SCWILPF. On Sharmat, see Beverly Gary, "A Navy Officer's Daughter Leads Protest on Civil Defense," *New York Post,* December 11, 1961, 38; Gabriel Levenson, "Mary in Atomland," *Fire Island News,* August 4, 1962; "Women's Peace Campaign Gaining Support," *New York Times,* November 22, 1961.

31. Sharmat statement; box 22, Civil Defense Protest Committee, SCPC.

32. Descriptions of 1960 protest in boxes 6 and 33, SANE Papers, SCPC; documents and clippings in W6.3, box 1, DDCW; box 22, Civil Defense Protest Committee,

SCPC, includes names of those arrested and letter from Sharmat to Dear Friend; box 8, WRL Papers, SCPC.

33. Sharmat statement.

34. Box 6, SANE Papers, SCPC; Lincoln Adair, "Public Demonstration and Civil Disobedience," American Friends Service Committee, W6.3, box 1, DDCW.

35. Sharmat statement; Murray Kempton, "Laughter in the Park," *New York Post,* cited in Isserman; *If I Had a Hammer,* 147.

36. Jim Peck, "Biggest Civil Disobedience Action," *WRL News,* May–June 1960; Dan Wakefield, "Good-by New York: New York Prepares for Annihilation," *Esquire,* August 1960, 79–85; Muste to Bradford Lyttle, May 16, 1960, DG17, box 8, SCPC; McReynolds, "Revolution by Degrees," *Peace News,* June 24, 1960; McReynolds to Muste, DiGia, Peck, box 8, WRL Papers, SCPC. Scott seems less sure of the new tactic in Scott to Albert Bigelow, July 12, 1960, Scott Papers, SCPC.

37. Clippings and documents and lists of arrested persons on the 1961 protest are in CNVA, box 22, SCPC; W6.3, box 1, DDCW; box 22, folder 3, 7, SCWILPF. Also see SANE Papers, series I, boxes 6 and 13, SCPC; WRL Papers, box 8, SCPC. Jim Peck was brutally beaten in the civil rights Freedom Ride in Birmingham, Alabama, in May 1961. A key "proof" of Peck's association with communists offered by Alabama authorities was his membership on the Civil Defense Protest Committee, erroneously cited by the Alabama attorney general as the Civil Defense Protection Committee, *WRL News,* July–August 1961.

38. See JFK Folders, 1961 and 1962, Library, Federal Emergency Management Agency, Washington, D.C., for correspondence and discussion of the possible enlargement of the civil defense program and of the proposed civil defense booklet. John Kenneth Galbraith wrote the most withering critique of the booklet, noting, "I think it particularly injudicious, in fact incredible, to have a picture of a family with a cabin cruiser saving itself by going out to sea. Very few members of the UAW can go with them." Schlesinger, cited in Blanchard, *American Civil Defense,* 306. Janice Smith reports that even before the cancellation of the planned 1962 Operation Alert, the New York City police had made a special plea to city civil defense officials to end the exercise. Smith statement, in possession of author.

39. Robert Scheer, *With Enough Shovels: Reagan, Bush and Nuclear War,* (London: Secker and Warburg, 1982).

40. Radical pacifists Bayard Rustin, Jim Peck, and Dorothy Day served as the political link between the early civil rights and peace movements. Because Dorothy Day and other radical pacifists were vocal opponents of communist dictatorships, the American right and federal intelligence agencies found it difficult to discredit their ideas and actions. As opponents of the hysterical anticommunism embodied in McCarthyism, radical pacifists also refused to expel any communist supporters in their ranks. This was unlike the liberals in SANE, which suffered a damaging split after its McCarthy-like internal purge of suspected communist members in 1960.

41. Amy Swerdlow, "Ladies' Day at the Capitol: Women Strike for Peace Versus HUAC," *Feminist Studies,* Fall 1982, 493–519; Saul Alinsky, *Rules for Radicals: A Practical Primer for Realistic Radicals* (New York: Vintage Books, 1972).

42. Victor Turner, *The Ritual Process: Structure and Anti-Structure* (Ithaca, N.Y.: Cornell University Press, 1969); David Kertzer, *Ritual, Politics and Power* (New Haven: Yale University Press, 1988); Renate Holub, *Antonio Gramsci: Beyond Marxism and Postmodernism* (New York: Routledge, Chapman and Hall, 1992); Barbara Epstein,

Political Protest and Cultural Revolution: Nonviolent Direct Action in the 1970s and 1980s (Berkeley: University of California Press, 1991), esp. 21–58, 227–279.

43. After the defeat of Operation Alert, Sharmat and Smith were active supporters of the southern civil rights and antiwar movements. They were also active in organizing Women Strike for Peace in New York City. In the 1970s they jointly owned and operated the Ladies Hobby Shop in Manhattan. Aside from selling yarn and craft supplies, the Hobby Shop was a meeting place for women in the city. Mary Sharmat returned to the theater and performing arts in the late 1970s and has performed in plays in New York and around the country. She has appeared in dozens of TV commercials and was last seen as Frances on the Wisk commercials. Sharmat is very active with the Manhattan Plaza AIDS project. Janice Smith, now Janice Harrison, was a textile designer. She has written three craft books, sold real estate, and taught textile design. At present she is retired and serves with a volunteer fire department.

44. David J. Garrow, ed., *The Montgomery Bus Boycott and the Women Who Started It: The Memoir of Jo Ann Gibson Robinson* (Knoxville: University of Tennessee Press, 1987).

PART III

Constructions of
Womanhood

CHAPTER 11

Joanne Meyerowitz

BEYOND THE
FEMININE
MYSTIQUE

A Reassessment of

Postwar Mass Culture,

1946–1958

In 1963 Betty Friedan published *The Feminine Mystique,* an instant bestseller. Friedan argued, often brilliantly, that American women, especially suburban women, suffered from deep discontent. In the postwar era, she wrote, journalists, educators, advertisers, and social scientists had pulled women into the home with an ideological stranglehold, the "feminine mystique." This repressive "image" held that women could "find fulfillment only in sexual passivity, male domination, and nurturing maternal love." It denied "women careers or any commitment outside the home" and "narrowed woman's world down to the home, cut her role back to housewife." In Friedan's formulation, the writers and editors of mass-circulation magazines, especially women's magazines, were the "Frankensteins" who had created this "feminine monster." In defense of women, Friedan did not choose a typical liberal feminist language of rights, equality, or even justice. Influenced by the new human potential psychology, she argued instead that full-time domesticity stunted women and denied their "basic human need to grow." For Friedan, women and men found personal identity and fulfillment through individual achievement, most notably through careers. Without such growth, she claimed, women would remain unfulfilled and unhappy, and children would suffer at the hands of neurotic mothers.[1]

The Feminine Mystique had an indisputable impact. Hundreds of women have testified that the book changed their lives, and historical accounts often credit it with launching the recent feminist movement. But the book has also had other kinds of historical impact. For a journalistic exposé, Friedan's work has had a surprisingly strong influence on historiography. In fact, since Friedan published *The Feminine Mystique,* historians of American women have adopted wholesale her version of the postwar ideology. While many historians question Friedan's homogenized account of women's actual experience, virtually all accept her version of the dominant ideology, the conservative promotion of domesticity.[2]

According to this now-standard historical account, postwar authors urged women to return to the home, and only a handful of social scientists, trade unionists, and feminists protested. As one recent rendition states: "In the wake of World War II . . . the short-lived affirmation of women's independence gave way to a pervasive endorsement of female subordination and domesticity."[3] Much of this secondary literature relies on a handful of conservative postwar writings, the same writings cited liberally by Friedan. In particular, the work of Dr. Marynia Farnham, a viciously antifeminist psychiatrist, and her sidekick, sociologist Ferdinand Lundberg, is invoked repeatedly as typical of the postwar era.[4] In this standard account, the domestic ideology prevailed until such feminists as Friedan triumphed in the 1960s.

When I first began research on the postwar era, I accepted this version of history. But as I investigated the public culture, I encountered what I then considered exceptional evidence—books, articles, and films that contradicted the domestic ideology. I decided to conduct a systematic investigation. This essay reexamines the middle-class popular discourse on women by surveying mass-circulation monthly magazines of the postwar era (1946–1958). The systematic sample includes nonfiction articles on women in "middlebrow" magazines (*Reader's Digest* and *Coronet*), "highbrow" magazines (*Harper's* and *Atlantic Monthly*), magazines aimed at African Americans (*Ebony* and *Negro Digest*), and those aimed at women (*Ladies' Home Journal* and *Woman's Home Companion*). The sample includes 489 nonfiction articles, ranging from Hollywood gossip to serious considerations of gender. In 1955 these magazines had a combined circulation of over 22 million.[5] Taken together, the magazines reached readers from all classes, races, and genders, but the articles seem to represent the work of middle-class journalists, and articles written by women seem to outnumber ones by men.[6]

My goal in constructing this sample was not to replicate Friedan's magazine research, which focused primarily on short story fiction in four women's magazines. Instead, my goal was to test generalizations about postwar mass culture (that is, commodified forms of popular culture) by surveying another side of it. To this end, I chose nonfiction articles in a larger sample of popular magazines. Some of the magazines of smaller circulation, such as *Harper's* and *Negro Digest,* were perhaps outside the "mainstream." But including them in the sample enabled me to incorporate more of the diversity in American society, to investigate the contours of a broader bourgeois culture and some variations within it. Since my conclusions rest on a sample of nonfiction articles in eight popular magazines, they can provide only a tentative portrait of postwar culture. Future studies based on different magazines or on fiction, advertisements, films, television, or radio will no doubt suggest additional layers of complexity in mass culture and different readings of it.

My interpretation of the sample draws in part on recent theories in cultural studies. For Betty Friedan and for some historians, popular magazines represented a repressive force, imposing damaging images on vulnerable American women. Many historians today adopt a different approach in which mass culture is neither wholly monolithic nor unrelentingly repressive. In this view, mass culture is rife with contradictions, ambivalence, and competing voices. We no longer assume that any text has a single, fixed meaning for all readers, and we sometimes find within the mass media subversive, as well as repressive, potential.[7]

With a somewhat different sample and a somewhat different interpretive approach, I come to different conclusions about postwar mass culture than did Friedan and her followers. Friedan's widely accepted version of the "feminine mystique," I suggest, is only one piece of the postwar cultural puzzle. The popular literature I sampled did not simply glorify domesticity or demand that women return to or stay at home. All of the magazines sampled advocated both the domestic and the nondomestic, sometimes in the same sentence. In this literature, domestic ideals coexisted in ongoing tension with an ethos of individual achievement that celebrated nondomestic activity, individual striving, public service, and public success.

This essay first discusses nonfiction that focused on individual women. Despite frequent references to femininity and domesticity, most of these stories expressed overt admiration for women whose individual striving moved them beyond the home. In contrast to the "happy housewife heroine" whom Friedan found in magazine fiction, these "true stories" presented women as successful public figures.[8] Second, this essay examines nonfiction that directly addressed issues of gender. Such articles often applauded housewives, but they also supported women's wage work and urged greater participation in politics. Further, they often expressed ambivalence about domesticity and presented it as a problem. Here Dr. Farnham and her conservative fellow travelers voiced a distinctive minority position that in no way dominated the mass culture.

The postwar mass culture embraced the same central contradiction—the tension between domestic ideals and individual achievement—that Betty Friedan addressed in *The Feminine Mystique*. In this sense, I argue, Friedan drew on mass culture as much as she countered it. The success of her book stemmed in part from her compelling elaboration of familiar themes.

In popular magazines, the theme of individual achievement rang most clearly in the numerous articles on individual women. These articles appeared with frequency throughout the postwar era: they constituted more than 60 percent, or 300, of the 489 nonfiction articles sampled. These articles usually recounted a story of a woman's life or a particularly telling episode in her life. In formulaic accounts, they often constructed what one such article labeled "this Horatio Alger success story—feminine version." [9] Of these articles, 33 percent spotlighted women with unusual talents, jobs, or careers, and another 29 percent focused on prominent entertainers. Typically they related a rise to public success punctuated by a lucky break, a dramatic comeback, a selfless sacrifice, or a persistent struggle to overcome adversity. Such stories appeared in all the magazines sampled, but they appeared most frequently in the African American magazines, *Ebony* and *Negro Digest*, and the white "middlebrow" magazines, *Coronet* and *Reader's Digest*. Journalists reworked the formula for different readers: In *Negro Digest*, for example, articles returned repeatedly to black performers who defied racism; in *Reader's Digest*, they more often addressed white leaders in community service. [10] In general, though, the articles suggested that the noteworthy woman rose above and beyond ordinary domesticity. Or, as one story stated: "This is the real-life fairy tale of a girl who hurtled from drab obscurity to sudden, startling fame." [11]

At the heart of many such articles lay a bifocal vision of women both as feminine and domestic and as public achievers. In one article, "The Lady Who Licked Crime in Portland," the author, Richard L. Neuberger, juxtaposed domestic stereotypes and newsworthy nondomestic achievement. The woman in question, Dorothy McCullough Lee, was, the article stated, an "ethereally pale housewife" who tipped "the scales at 110 pounds." More to the point, she was also the mayor of Portland, Oregon, who had defeated, singlehandedly it seems, the heavyweights of organized crime. Before winning the mayoral election in 1948, this housewife had opened a law firm and served in the state legislature, both House and Senate, and as Portland's commissioner of public utilities. Despite her "frail, willowy" appearance, the fearless mayor had withstood ridicule, recall petitions, and threatening mail in her "relentless drive" against gambling and prostitution. She was, the article related without further critique, a "violent feminist" who had "intense concern with the status of women." And, according to all, she was "headed for national distinction." The article concluded with an admiring quotation describing Mayor Lee's fancy hats as the plumes of a crusading knight in armor. Here the feminine imagery blended with a metaphor of masculine public service.[12]

The joint endorsement of domestic and nondomestic roles appeared in numerous stories that offered a postwar version of today's "superwoman," the woman who successfully combines motherhood and career. As Jacqueline Jones has noted, *Ebony* magazine sometimes featured this type of article. One story, for example, presented Louise Williams, the mother of two and the only black mechanic at American Airlines. As *Ebony* reported: "She is a good cook, but an even better mechanic." She was also an inventor and an active member of her union. And, according to *Ebony,* she was "never a lazy house-wife." Such stories in African American magazines clearly provided lessons in surmounting racism. In *Ebony*'s female version of racial advancement, women often excelled both in the workplace and at home.[13]

Similar articles appeared regularly in magazines geared to white readers. *Coronet* magazine, for example, presented the "amazing" Dorothy Kilgallen, "star reporter," who wrote a syndicated column, ad-libbed a daily radio program, ran forty charity benefits a year, and had "a handsome and successful husband, a beautiful home, [and] two lovely children." The successful combination of home and career made her "Gotham's busiest glamour girl." Articles of this type resolved the tension between domesticity and public achievement superficially by ignoring the difficulties that women usually faced in pursuing both.[14]

While feminine stereotypes sometimes provided convenient foils that enhanced by contrast a woman's atypical public accomplishment, they also served as conservative reminders that all women, even publicly successful women, were to maintain traditional gender distinctions.[15] In their opening paragraphs, numerous authors described their successful subjects as pretty, motherly, shapely, happily married, petite, charming, or soft voiced. This emphasis on femininity and domesticity (and the two were often conflated) seems to have cloaked a submerged fear of lesbian, mannish, or man-hating women. This fear surfaced in an unusual article on the athlete Babe Didrikson Zaharias. In her early years, the article stated, the Babe's "boyish bob and freakish clothes . . . [her] dislike of femininity" had led observers to dismiss her as an "Amazon." But after her marriage, she "became a woman," a transformation signaled, according to the approving author, by lipstick, polished nails, and "loose, flowing" hair, as well as by an interest in the domestic arts of cooking, sewing, and entertaining. In this article, as in others, allusions to femininity and domesticity probably helped legitimate women's public achievements. Authors attempted to reassure readers that conventional gender distinctions and heterosexuality remained intact even as women competed successfully in work, politics, or sports. It is worth noting that in *The Feminine Mystique,* Friedan adopted this approach. She attempted to legitimate the early feminists by repeated insistence that most of them were feminine, married, and not man-hating.[16]

Nonetheless, the emphasis on the domestic and feminine should not be overstated; these articles on women's achievement did not serve solely or even primarily as lessons in traditional gender roles. The theme of nondomestic success was no hidden subtext in these stories. In most articles, the rise to public achievement was the first, and sometimes the only, narrative concern. When addressing both the domestic and the nondomestic, these articles placed public success at center stage: They tended to glorify frenetic activity, with domesticity at best a sideshow in a woman's three-ring circus.

The theme of domesticity and femininity was consistently less striking than the constant reiteration of a work ethic for women. Hard work, especially without complaint, figured most prominently in the recipe for success. Another article on Dorothy McCullough Lee stated: "The mayor lives, breathes, eats and sleeps her job." In other articles, an admirable woman had "tremendous energy," engaged in "ceaseless activity," got "along without sleep," or worked "a 12- or 14-hour . . . day, seven days a week." As author Anita Loos put it, "I am only alive when I work. . . . Just remember that if you don't work, you die." The flip side of this emphasis on hard work was a condemnation of idleness and frivolity. Articles opposed meaningful work to activities coded as the trivial pursuits of the woman of leisure: bridge playing, aimless shopping, and "summers on the Riviera." [17]

Marriage and domesticity were not prerequisites for star status in magazine stories. More than one-third of the articles on individual women featured unmarried women, divorced women, or women of unmentioned marital status. The African American magazines seemed least concerned with marital status, but all the magazines included articles that did not conjoin public success with connubial harmony. While a few such articles advocated marriage, others discounted it directly. Still other articles related the public achievements of divorced women, with consistent sympathy for the women involved.[18]

Only 15 percent of the articles on individual women focused primarily on women as mothers and wives. Most of these articles presented domestic success stories: tributes to devoted and brave wives and mothers or tales of the generally minor trials and major joys of wifehood and motherhood. Like the other articles on individual women, they tended to emphasize hard work and an uncomplaining attitude. As one such article stated (incorrectly): "You can't be busy and sorry for yourself at the same time." Many of these domestic articles appeared in the *Ladies' Home Journal*. The *Journal*'s editors seem to have made a conscious choice to publish populist stories that featured the average day of a white American housewife or the ordinary domestic doings of royalty or entertainers. But even the *Ladies' Home Journal* contradicted this domestic message with articles that praised public success, especially that of women politicians. Moreover, by the second half of the 1950s, the *Ladies' Home Journal* began to defy its own domestic formula. In 1958, for example, the *Journal* included a laudatory story about a housewife who, through "an act of sheer self-assertion," enrolled in medical school and became a physician.[19]

Throughout the era, the stories that defined success by nondomestic accomplishment overwhelmingly countered the few nonfiction stories that focused on individual wives and mothers. Despite the familism of the postwar era, it was public, not domestic, renown that placed such figures as Mary McLeod Bethune among "the world's greatest living women." Even Mamie Eisenhower joined in the celebration of public achievement when she sent "warm congratulations" to the "six most successful women" chosen by *Woman's Home Companion* in 1953. The six had won national recognition "in medical science, education, literature, the theater, and the field of human rights and social betterment." Eisenhower concluded, "We can all take pride in the forward steps women have taken during our own generation to a role of leadership in community and even national affairs." [20]

The focus on public achievement may have resulted in part from a journalistic imperative. Editors may have emphasized individual striving and its alleged rewards in order to sell their publications. Given the long-term American obsession with Horatio Alger stories, articles on Annie Oakley, Phillis Wheatley, a woman minister, or a roller derby star may well have attracted readers more than accounts of humdrum everyday existence. The twentieth-century cult of personality, which, in the words of Warren I. Susman, insists on the "importance of being different, special, unusual, of standing out in a crowd," probably further enhanced the marketability of stories of extraordinary individual success. Yet, other formulas might have sufficed. Melodramatic tales of endangerment and rescue, highly popular in the late nineteenth century, offered another possible formula for fast-selling, out-of-the-ordinary stories about women. By the postwar era, though, melodrama had virtually disappeared from nonfiction magazine narrative strategies.[21]

The success stories were more than journalistic devices; authors often explicitly stated that they intended to inspire readers. They suggested that effort, talent, persistence, courage, and just plain goodness brought women not only public honor but also personal fulfillment. In one article, for example, Mabel Powell, "a gallant teacher" who "lavished loyalty and affection on hundreds of humanity's waifs," was "the one completely happy person" the author had ever met. Other stories stated the point with homiletic pith: "Any woman will be all right if she learns to take care of herself"; "You can't lose if you never admit defeat"; "If you stumble today, pick yourself up tomorrow"; "You can do anything you want in life—*anything*—if you just try hard enough." [22]

The inspirational tone sounded most loudly in the articles on ill, disabled, and disfigured women. While not numerous, these articles in some ways epitomized the success-story genre. Helen Keller, a favored subject, was virtually sanctified in the mass culture, but other such stories carried much the same message: With "a remarkable mind and . . . remarkable will . . . pluck and courage, energy [and] tenacity" a woman could overcome adversity and achieve whatever she chose. In most of the stories, a woman persevered to live a "normal" life despite her disability. In a few cases, she also achieved striking public success, what the editors of *Reader's Digest* labeled a "triumph of will and courage." In these articles, one might read disease, disability, and disfigurement as metaphors for the handicaps faced by women generally. As such, the inspirational message applied to all women: Individual striving could overcome seemingly insurmountable barriers. [23]

Magazine articles, of course, do not reveal the responses of readers. Formulaic stories of success do not seem to have provoked controversy; magazines that published readers' responses rarely included letters regarding these stories. Some supplementary evidence, however, suggests that the language used in success stories also appeared in the language of at least some readers. The *Woman's Home Companion* conducted opinion polls in 1947 and 1949 in which readers named the women they most admired. In both years the top four women were Eleanor Roosevelt, Helen Keller, Sister Elizabeth Kenny (who worked with polio victims), and Clare Boothe Luce (author and congresswoman), all distinctly nondomestic women. Why did readers select these particular women? They seemed to offer the same answers as the success stories: "courage, spirit, and conviction," "devotion to the public good," and "success in overcoming obstacles." While a feminine version of selfless sacrifice seems to have won kudos, individual striving and public service superseded devotion to home and family. [24]

On the one hand, one might see these success stories as pernicious. They applied to women a traditionally male, middle-class discourse of individual achievement that glorified a version of success, honor, and fulfillment that was difficult enough for middle-class white men, highly unlikely for able-bodied women of any class and race, and nearly impossible for the ill, disabled, and disfigured. As fantasies of unlikely success, they offered false promises that hard work brought women public reward. They probably gave women readers vicarious pleasure or compensatory esteem, but they provided no real alternatives to most women's workaday lives. They usually downplayed the obstacles that women faced in the public arena, and they implicitly dismissed the need for collective protest. Further, they did not overtly challenge traditional gender roles. With frequent references to domesticity and femininity, narrowly defined, they reinforced rigid definitions of appropriate female behavior and sexual expression, and they neglected the conflicts between domestic and nondomestic demands that many women undoubtedly encountered.

On the other hand, these articles subverted the notion that women belonged at home. They presented a wide variety of options open to women and praised the women who had chosen to assert themselves as public figures. They helped readers, male and female, envision women in positions of public achievement. They tried openly to inspire women to pursue unusual goals, domestic or not, and they sometimes suggested that public service brought more obvious rewards than devotion to family. By applauding the public possibilities open to women, including married women, they may have validated some readers' nondomestic behavior and sharpened some readers' discontent with the constraints they experienced in their domestic lives. At least one contemporary observer noticed this subversive side to stories of individual success. Dr. Marynia Farnham, the antifeminist, railed not only against the "propaganda of the feminists" but also against "stories about famous career women," which, she claimed, undermined the prestige of motherhood.[25]

The postwar stories of women's achievement are not surprising. Famous women figured prominently in nineteenth-century inspirational biographies, and women appeared in popular magazine success stories at least as early as the 1920s and 1930s. The stories affirmed long-lived bourgeois platitudes about hard work, freedom, and upward mobility. In the postwar era, these platitudes gained new currency in the Cold War attempts to distinguish the autonomous individuals of the "free world" from the suppressed masses under communism. Applied to women, they reflect the superficial success of a diluted brand of early twentieth-century feminism that promoted "equality of opportunity" and "individual accomplishment." They may also reflect a desire to give utopian endings to the stories of middle-class women who increasingly entered the workforce in the postwar era.[26]

In any event, they offer a striking validation of nondomestic behavior for women, a significant counterpoint to the "feminine mystique." After a survey of fiction in postwar women's magazines, Friedan concluded: "The new feminine morality story is the exorcising of the forbidden career dream." But other, competing morality tales abounded in the public culture. In nonfiction articles in popular magazines, the most prevalent morality tale did not forbid careers;

it honored them. In that tale, heroic women of striving and worth won positions of public distinction. An ethos of individual achievement subtly subverted domestic ideals.[27]

The postwar popular discourse on women, then, did not simply exhort women to stay at home. Its complexity is also seen in the articles that addressed questions of gender directly. The topics of those articles ranged from women in India to premenstrual tension, but most of them fell into four broad categories: women's paid work, women's political activism, marriage and domesticity, and glamour and sexuality.[28] Most of these articles did not pose profound challenges to the variegated oppression of women. But they do differ significantly from most historical descriptions of a postwar domestic ideology. The articles in this sample reveal ambivalence and contradictions in postwar mass culture, which included a celebration of nondomestic as well as domestic pursuits and a tension between individual achievement and domestic ideals.

On the issue of paid employment, there was rough consensus. Despite concerns for the postwar economy, journalists in this sample consistently defended wage work for women. Articles insisted that women, including married women, worked for wages because they needed money. One early article, published in 1946, spelled this out in its opening lines: "Most American working women need their jobs. That's the stark and simple reason why hiring and firing policies arbitrarily based on sex discrimination don't make sense." [29] By the 1950s, arguments for wage work often included the personal "satisfaction" jobs offered as well as the economic benefits. These articles generally advocated part-time as well as full-time work, and they often stressed the opportunities available to older women. According to one such article, "a part-time job can bring a feeling of full-time usefulness and satisfaction." Foreshadowing more recent demands, another article recommended tax deductions for childcare expenses and flexible hours for working mothers. The articles endorsed wage work and represented it as positive for both women and society. Even the archconservative Farnham, who attacked feminism and promoted motherhood, insisted on more than one occasion that she supported paid work for married women. "I am *not* suggesting," she wrote in one article, "that all women remain in the home, especially on a full-time basis. There are many splendid careers for married women to pursue." [30]

Articles praised women workers in specific occupations, from secretaries to doctors. These articles related exciting, stimulating, or rewarding job possibilities or the "practically unlimited" opportunities allegedly available to women. Like the success stories, these articles sometimes encouraged individual striving. "Advancement," one such article claimed, "will be limited only by [a woman's] intelligence, application, and education." The African American magazines, *Ebony* and *Negro Digest,* alert to racism, showed more explicit awareness of institutional barriers to individual effort and sometimes noted discrimination based not only on race but also on gender. One article, for example, not only praised black women doctors but also denounced the "stubborn male prejudice" faced by "petticoat medics." In general, though, the articles on specific occupations did not attack sexism or the sexual division of labor directly; they simply encouraged women to pursue white-collar jobs in business and the professions.[31]

Beneath the consensus, though, a quiet debate exposed the tensions between the ideals of nondomestic achievement and domestic duty. Echoing earlier debates of the 1920s, some authors advised women to subordinate careers to home and motherhood, while others invited women to pursue public success. The question of careers was rarely discussed at any length, and the relative silence itself underscores how postwar popular magazines often avoided contended issues. But throwaway lines in various articles sometimes landed on one side of the debate or the other. In a single article in *Ebony,* for example, one unmarried career woman warned readers, "Don't sacrifice marriage for career," while another stated, "I like my life just as it is." Another article, "Profile of Success," published in the *Ladies' Home Journal* in 1946, captured the ambivalence in postwar discourse. The bulk of the article celebrated the achievements of career women, "the cream of the working-woman population," and analyzed the ingredients of their success. But toward the end of the article two paragraphs questioned whether a married career woman had time enough for her husband and children. The article concluded more positively: "In moments of weakness the woman at the top eyes with envy the occasional leisure of the housewife . . . the joys of total family life. The moment passes. . . . She knows what she wants, after all—and she wants what she has."[32]

By the 1950s, as more middle-class women entered the labor force, some journalists attempted to resolve the dilemma implicitly with an argument about the modern woman's life cycle: Accepting the difficulty of combining motherhood and career, they assumed that mothers with young children would work only part-time, that women, if they chose, would pursue careers when single or when their children had grown. Not all authors took this approach. One article in *Reader's Digest* insisted that women should work continuously, that older women had "a bleak time" trying to reenter the workforce. But many agreed that married women would pursue different interests in differents periods of their lives. This compromise position seems to have had broad appeal. In fact, Friedan herself appropriated it in *The Feminine Mystique.* In her "life plan" that could "encompass marriage and motherhood," she suggested that women pursuing careers might revert to "a period of study during pregnancy or early motherhood when a full-time job is not feasible."[33]

The postwar popular magazines were more unequivocally positive on increased participation of women in politics. The *Ladies' Home Journal*, not known for its feminist sympathies, led the way with numerous articles that supported women as political and community leaders. In 1947, lawyer and long-time activist Margaret Hickey, former president of the National Federation of Business and Professional Women's Clubs, launched the *Journal*'s monthly "Public Affairs Department," which encouraged women's participation in mainstream politics and reform. In one article, Hickey stated bluntly: "Make politics your business. Voting, office holding, raising your voice for new and better laws are just as important to your home and your family as the evening meal or spring house cleaning." Like earlier Progressive reformers, Hickey sometimes justified nondomestic political action by its benefits to home and family, but her overall message was clear: Women should participate outside the home, and not just by voting.[34]

For several years in the 1950s, Hickey's "Public Affairs Department" ran a series of articles under the rubric of "Political Pilgrim's Progress." In this version of the "pilgrim's progress," a woman rejected the temptations of full-time domesticity and found salvation through politics rather than religion. In a direct allusion to John Bunyan's *Pilgrim's Progress*, one housewife discovered that she could "become a political pilgrim, and come out of her slough of despond and find the straight road of progress." The articles encouraged women to become politically active, nationally as well as locally, not only in women's organizations but also through officeholding and political parties. They called for women to "enter actively into politics as a primary responsibility."[35]

Reports on women politicians stressed the series' recurring motif, "They Do It . . . You Can Too." This article presented women politicians as exemplars. With direct appeals to housewives, it praised women who ran for office, even mothers of "babies or small children" who could "find time and ways to campaign and to win elections." It presented political activism not only as a public service but also as a source of personal fulfillment. For women who held political office, it claimed, "there is great pride of accomplishment and the satisfaction of 'doing a job.' "[36]

In its promotion of women in politics, the *Journal* sometimes resorted to essentialist arguments about gender difference. Women had special, perhaps inherent, qualities needed in government. In the years just after World War II, the arguments seemed to reflect a peculiarly postwar international consciousness, reminiscent of the 1920s women pacifists' position. Women, especially mothers, some authors claimed, had a more civilizing, peace-loving influence than men. On the editorial page of *Ladies' Home Journal*, Dorothy Thompson elaborated this view and called for an international movement of mothers to push for disarmament and lasting peace. By the 1950s, when the pacifist emphasis had declined, journalists presented essentialist arguments more covertly. Authors still implied, though, that women had special affinity for moral and social housekeeping; that is, for cleaning up corruption and responding to threats to home and children. As one article stated, "cleaning house has always been a woman's job." As in the nineteenth-century woman's movement, alleged gender differences were used here, not to push women back into the home, but to encourage women to move beyond it.[37]

Historians sometimes contend that the Cold War mentality encouraged domesticity, that it envisioned family life and especially mothers as buffers against the alleged communist threat. But Cold War rhetoric had other possible meanings for women. In the *Ladies' Home Journal*, authors often used the Cold War to promote women's political participation. One such approach contrasted the "free society" of the United States with Soviet oppression, including oppression of women. Thompson condemned the Soviet Union not only because women there worked as "beasts of burden" in menial jobs but also because they held no positions of political leadership. Other articles stressed that Soviet citizens, male and female, did not participate in a democratic process. American women could prove the strength of democracy by avoiding "citizen apathy," by "giving the world a lively demonstration of how a free society can serve its citizens," by making "free government work well as an example for the undecided and unsatisfied millions elsewhere in the world." Senator Margaret Chase Smith made the case most strongly: "The way to reverse this socialistic, dictatorial trend and put more *home* in the Government is for you women, the traditional homemakers, to become more active in your Government." In this line of argument, the Cold War made women's political participation an international obligation.[38]

In general, then, popular magazines incorporated women's public participation as part of a positive image of the modern American woman in the postwar world. In an article on women in the Soviet Union, John Steinbeck defended the American woman: "[The Russians] had an idea that in America we have only overdressed, neurotic, kept women. . . . It had not occurred to them that we have farms and factories, and offices, too, and that our women also help to run our country."[39]

The popular literature generally gave facile support to women in a variety of activities. A celebratory photo essay in *Coronet* magazine in 1948, titled "The American Woman," presented a graphic depiction of the dominant view. The photographs ran from childhood to old age with laudatory comments at every stage of the life cycle. The photos of adulthood began with six pictures of women at work, including a young salesclerk, an elderly worker in light industry, and a middle-aged judge on her bench. A caption claimed that "the challenge of a career is irresistible." The essay proceeded with five pictures of brides and mothers. The captions here waxed more sentimental: "Proudest of all American women are those who know the joys of motherhood. . . . For in motherhood alone are all [their] girlhood dreams fulfilled." The section on adulthood continued with two more photos of middle-aged women involved in community activism. The captions said, "Her desire to be useful beyond the home keep[s] her active and vital . . . [in] the building of democracy in religious, political, and charitable movements."[40] Such stories do not imply that postwar popular magazines condemned or disparaged domesticity. To the contrary, marriage and motherhood stood strategically at the literal and emotional center, yet wage work and political activism also won resolute praise.

Despite the support for marriage and motherhood, the role of the housewife and mother was problematic in the postwar popular discourse. On the one hand, all the magazines assumed that women wanted to marry, that women found being wives and mothers rewarding, and that women would and should be the primary parents and housekeepers. In the midst of the baby boom, some articles glorified the housewife, sometimes in conscious attempts to bolster her self-esteem. On the other hand, throughout the postwar era, numerous articles portrayed domesticity itself as exhausting and isolating, and frustrated mothers as overdoting and smothering. Such articles hardly glorified domesticity. They provided their postwar readers with ample references to housewife's discontent.[41]

Women's magazines, targeted to the majority of American white women who were indeed housewives, showed special concern with domestic problems. Amid advertisements for household products and articles on food and home decor, the magazines investigated what one article labeled "The Plight of the Young Mother." That article presented an "informal forum" in which housewives, magazine editors, and "special consultants" explored "the rewarding and difficult role of the young mother in modern society." The experts defined the "plight" variously as confinement, isolation, loneliness, boredom, frustration, dissatisfaction, and nervous and physical fatigue. As one consultant said, "We have abolished . . . serfdom of women to men, but we have not yet emancipated women to the enjoyment of their full potentialities." While the experts assumed that the mother would always be "the principal person in the development of the human being," they offered palliatives to ease her burden: recreation, part-time jobs, volunteer work, "outside interests," more prestige for mothers, more help from fathers, cooperative babysitting, and nurseries.[42]

In the postwar magazines, marriage also presented problems. Although journalists expected most women to marry, they portrayed the search for a husband as a potentially troubling task. An article in *Ebony* stated: "Most women would rather be married than single but there are many who would rather remain single than be tied to the wrong man." The magazines gave readers contrasting advice on how to find a good husband. One article told women: "Don't fear being aggressive!" while another considered "aggressive traits" as "handicaps . . . in attracting a husband." Within marriage as well, journalists seemed to anticipate constant problems, including immaturity, incompatibility, and infidelity. They saw divorce as a difficult last resort and often advised both husbands and wives to communicate and adjust.[43]

The issue of "individualism" sometimes arose in the articles on marriage and domesticity. Some authors constructed the housewife problem as a conflict between gender roles and individuality. Often expressed in historical terms, the conflict pitted old-fashioned gender relations in which women were first and foremost doting mothers and submissive wives against modern relations in which women were individual human beings. Postwar authors did not, as Friedan's *Feminine Mystique* would have it, side automatically with "sexual passivity, male domination, and nurturing maternal love." They portrayed the ideal marriage as an equal partnership, with each partner intermingling traditional masculine and feminine roles. One article insisted: "The healthy, emotionally well-balanced male . . . isn't alarmed by the fact that women are human, too, and have an aggressive as well as a passive side. . . . He takes women seriously as individuals." This article and others condemned men who assumed an attitude of superiority. As another article stated: "The dominating husband and submissive wife are things of the past." Yet, to many it seemed that "individualism" could go too far and upset modern marriage. While husbands might do more housework and wives might pursue nondomestic activities, men remained the primary breadwinners and women the keepers of the home.[44]

Self-proclaimed feminist Sidonie M. Gruenberg wrestled overtly with the tension between domestic and individualist ideals. Gruenberg told wives not to "exploit" their breadwinning husbands by making them engage in too much housework. Even mothers who held "outside job[s]," she argued, were still "in charge" of the home. She insisted she was not a reactionary: "For as long as I can remember, I have fought the entire concept of 'woman's work' as confined to kitchen, hearth and child care. I wouldn't for the world go back to the days when all tasks were sharply divided into 'his' and 'hers.' " She acknowledged housewives' discontent, but she reminded mothers that they would have "half [their] life ahead" of them after their children had grown. "The point," she wrote, "is that primary responsibility for home and family engineering are your jobs and you know it." Still she waffled: "We are pioneering in recognizing the individual needs and rights of every member of the family. We must work out ways to meet these needs without being destructive or making a martyr of anyone." [45] As in this article, the postwar popular literature generally did not offer any serious challenge to marriage or to the sexual division of labor in the home. Some might argue that articles mentioned "individualism" only to dismiss or contain it. Nonetheless, as Gruenberg's ambivalence suggests, the can of worms opened was not so easily reshut.

The postwar magazines seemed least willing to entertain alternatives in the area of sexuality. As Friedan argued, popular magazines emphasized glamour and allure, at least for young women, and as Elaine Tyler May has elaborated, they tried to domesticate sexual intercourse by containing it within marriage. Magazines presented carefully framed articles with explicit directives about appropriate behavior. Young women were to make themselves attractive to men, and married women were to engage in mutually pleasing sexual intercourse with their mates. Articles presented "normal" sex through voyeuristic discussion of sexual problems, such as pregnancy before marriage and frigidity after. Other forms of sexual expression were rarely broached, although one article in *Ebony* did condemn "lesbians and nymphomaniacs" in the Women's Army Corps. [46]

While all the magazines endorsed a manicured version of heterosexual appeal, the African American magazines displayed it most heartily. This may have reflected African American vernacular traditions, such as the blues, that rejected white middle-class injunctions against public sexual expression. But it also reflected an editorial decision to construct glamour and beauty as political issues in the fight against racism. Articles admired black women's sex appeal in a self-conscious defiance of racist white standards of beauty. In this context, what some feminists today might read as sexual "objectification" presented itself as racial advancement, according black womanhood equal treatment with white. Thus *Ebony*, which in most respects resembled a white family magazine like *Life*, also included some of the mildly risqué cheesecake seen in white men's magazines like *Esquire*. One editorial explained: "Because we live in a society in which standards of physical beauty are most often circumscribed by a static concept of whiteness of skin and blondeness of hair, there is an aching need for someone to shout from the housetops that black women are beautiful." [47]

In a curious bow to individual striving, popular magazines, both black and white, often portrayed beauty and allure as achievements that any woman could attain if she tried hard enough. As the entertainer Dorothy Dandridge explained in *Ebony*, "Every woman can have some sex appeal." While a woman could achieve allure, she should attain it without "vulgarizing" sex or making an "open display" of it. Similarly, in the *Ladies' Home Journal*, an article proclaimed: "She Turned Herself into a Beauty." This woman's "achievements" included weight loss, better grooming, and medical help for acne, a deformed nose, and a bent back. Another article, in *Coronet,* stated bluntly: "If anything's lacking, she can take immediate steps to remedy it—go to a hairdresser, a psychiatrist, whatever is needed." With a middle-class faith in the individual's ability to rise, articles suggested that individual effort, careful consumerism, and reliance on experts could bring any woman success, even in the realm of beauty and appeal.[48]

Still, despite the magazines' endorsement of feminine beauty and heterosexual allure, Friedan's polemical claim that "American women have been successfully reduced to sex creatures" seems unabashedly hyperbolic. Try as they might, popular magazines could not entirely dictate the responses of readers. In most instances, we have little way of knowing how readers responded to magazine articles, but in the case of sex appeal we have explicit letters of dissent. In the African American magazines, some readers, women and men both, objected to the photos of semiclad women. One woman complained that the "so-called beauties" were "really a disgrace to all women." And another protested "those girl covers and the . . . so-called realism (just a cover up name for cheapness, coarseness, lewdness, profanity and irreverence)."[49]

In *Ladies' Home Journal,* too, readers responded with rare indignation to one article on sex appeal. In "How to Be Loved," movie star Marlene Dietrich lectured housewives on enhancing their allure. Dietrich linked appeal to unadorned self-subordination. "To be completely a woman," she wrote, "you need a master." She advised women to plan their clothes, their conversation, and their meals to please their husbands. After washing their dishes, "like Phoenix out of the ashes," women should emerge "utterly desirable." And they should not grumble. "Some women," Dietrich proclaimed, "could do with a bit of spanking to answer their complaining." The article evoked what the *Journal*'s editors called an "intense" response. Sarcastic letter writers objected to Dietrich's call for servile pampering of men and "utterly desirable" behavior. As one writer stated, "How *could* you hand the American woman such an article?" The letter writers portrayed themselves as down-home and unglamorous housewives, "all straight-haired and plain," who could not and would not emulate Dietrich's version of sexual allure. One woman wrote: "I resemble Eleanor Roosevelt more than I do La Dietrich, so that alters the visual effect." Another writer proclaimed: "Pish, tosh and hooey! Could be that Marlene could emerge from a stack of dirty dishes . . . and still be glamorous and desirable, but the housewife and mother I know gets dishpan hands and another twinge in the old back. . . . Marlene should talk about something she understands." For these women, marriage was a working partnership. Their husbands, they claimed, helped with the housework, accepted their scolding, and respected their "whims and fatigue." "Out here where I live," one woman wrote, "reasonably intelligent [married couples] . . . learn to live and work together." These readers used their domestic identities as hard-working house-wives, not to berate women of public achievement, but to reject a competing image of women as subservient sexual bait.[50]

A handful of letters, written by only a few readers, scarcely begins to sug-gest the range of responses that women probably had when reading the maga-zines. The frequent articles on work, politics, domesticity, and sexuality may have encouraged some women to take pride in, long for, or emulate maga-zine versions of public participation, home life, or glamour. At the same time, the flood of competing images—of housewives, workers, politicians, and sex bombs—may have inundated women who could not possibly identify with or remake themselves in all the proffered models.

The response to one article suggests that readers may have chosen among alternative versions of womanhood, appropriating the images that rang true or appealed to them and rejecting the others. In this set of letters, some house-wives accepted the "plight of the young mother" as a true description of their experience. They appreciated an article that validated their sense of domes-tic discontent. For these women, the article was a "morale lifter." "I have no words to tell what it means," one woman wrote, "to have all the facets of housewifery (that seemed to have sprung from my own deficiencies) held up as situations of national import." Other women rejected the article as a "very un-fair picture." They resented an article that depicted them as overworked victims who could not cope with their housework. "Oh, for pity's sake," one woman asked, "What old plight am I in that no one has told me about? . . . I have four children . . . and I don't put in a forty-hour week. . . . I think it's a great life." In short, both readers and articles were varied enough and ambivalent enough to enable more than one possible reading.[51]

In his ground-breaking 1972 book, *The American Woman,* William Henry Chafe offers what still stands as the best summary of the debates on woman-hood in the postwar era. In Chafe's reconstruction, a popular "antifeminist" position, promoted by such authors as Farnham and Lundberg, stood opposed to a more feminist "sociological" perspective, promoted primarily by social scientists such as Mirra Komarovsky and Margaret Mead. While the antifemi-nists insisted on marriage and domesticity, the social scientists called for new gender roles to match modern conditions.[52] In the popular magazines sampled for this essay, this debate rarely surfaced. Articles sometimes drew on one posi-tion or even both, but the vast majority did not fall clearly into either camp. Still, the antifeminist position did appear occasionally, as did an opposing "women's rights" stance. These positions emerged in various magazines, but they both appeared most unequivocally in the highbrow magazines, the *Atlan-*

tic Monthly and *Harper's,* which did not avoid controversy as assiduously as did others.[53]

The antifeminist authors promoted domesticity as a woman's only road to fulfillment. Women should not compete with men, they argued; instead, they should defer to, depend on, and even wait on men, especially their husbands. According to these conservatives, women and men differed fundamentally, and attempts to diminish sexual difference would lead only to unhappiness. Often invoking a version of Freudian thought, these authors sometimes engaged in psychological name-calling in which they labeled modern woman neurotic, narcissistic, unfeminine, domineering, nagging, lazy, materialistic, and spoiled.[54] These conservative arguments and the attendant name-calling were by no means typical of popular discourse. Of the 489 articles sampled, only 9, or less than 2 percent, even approached such starkly conservative claims.

This is where the oft-cited Dr. Marynia Farnham stood in the postwar discourse, at the conservative margin rather than at the center. For Farnham, modern women who attempted to compete with men or expressed discontent with their natural career as mothers suffered from mental instability, bitterness, and worse. Industrialization, Farnham claimed, had undermined women's productive functions in the home. Women, "frustrated at the inmost core of their beings," attempted tragically to emulate men in the world of work, led "aimlessly idle," "parasitic" lives as frigid housewives, or indulged in "overdoting, overstrict or rejecting" mothering, with a cumulative outcome of neurotic children, including future Adolf Hitlers.[55] Farnham called for a renewed commitment to motherhood, dependence on men, and "natural" sexual passivity. She spelled out these arguments in ceaseless detail in her 1947 book, *Modern Woman: The Lost Sex,* coauthored with Ferdinand Lundberg.

Although Farnham's position had some influence, especially among psychologists, it did not represent the mainstream in the mass culture; rather, it generated "a storm of controversy." Book reviews, some of them scathing, called *Modern Woman* "neither socially nor medically credible," "dogmatic and sensational," "intensely disturbing," "unfair," and "fundamentally untrue." And Farnham's articles in *Coronet* provoked enough letters that the editors promised to include opposing viewpoints in future issues, this in a magazine that generally avoided any inkling of debate. While bits and pieces of Farnham's arguments appeared in other popular magazines, the antifeminist position was rejected more often than embraced. In the era of positive thinking, magazines tended toward more upbeat and celebratory representations of women.[56]

Also at the boundaries of the discourse, a few "women's rights" articles counterbalanced the conservative extreme. They recognized some form of women's subordination and found that subordination could and should be challenged. While conservatives insisted on domestic ideals, women's rights advocates insisted on women's right to nondomestic pursuits. Like the antifeminists, the authors of these articles often argued that women's functions in the home had declined, and they, too, often found the modern housewife restless and discontented. These authors, however, condemned isolation in the home and subordination to men. They admired women who pursued positions of public responsibility and leadership, and they identified and opposed discrimination in the workplace and in politics. They insisted that women were individuals of infinite variety. In *Harper's,* Agnes Rogers wrote, "there would be a healthier distribution of civic energy if more attention were paid to individuals as such and if it were not assumed that men hold the executive jobs and women do what they are told." In contrast with antifeminist writings, these articles either downplayed sex differences or derogated men for their militaristic aggression or "masculine self-inflation." The women's rights articles were only slightly less common than the antifeminist attacks. (With a conservative count, there were five, about 1 percent of the sample.) Like the antifeminist articles, they sometimes generated controversy, especially when readers read them as frontal attacks on the full-time housewife.[57]

The antifeminists and the women's rights advocates competed for mainstream attention. Both tempered their arguments in seeming attempts to broaden appeal: Antifeminists sometimes disavowed reactionary intention and denied that married women had to stay in the home, and women's rights advocates sometimes disavowed feminist militance and denied that married women had to have careers. Through the 1950s, though, neither position in any way controlled or dominated the public discourse, at least as seen in nonfiction articles in popular magazines. Both antifeminists and women's rights advocates clearly represented controversial minority positions.

According to Friedan, the "feminine mystique" emerged full-blown in the mass culture of the late 1940s and 1950s. Friedan compared short story fiction in women's magazines of the late 1930s, late 1940s, and late 1950s, and she referred to fiction and nonfiction from various magazines of the postwar era. With this evidence, Friedan told a story of declension. In the 1930s, she claimed, women's magazines encouraged women to participate in the wider world outside the home. Short stories featured fictional career women "marching toward some goal or vision of their own." In Friedan's account, this "passionate search for individual identity" ended in the late 1940s.[58] The postwar magazines, she said, narrowed their scope to the housewife in the home and adopted Farnham and Lundberg's antifeminist stance.

My own research suggests a different history. To place my postwar sample in historical context, I supplemented it with comparable samples of nonfiction articles from popular magazines of the Great Depression and World War II. Most striking were the continuities, the themes that recurred throughout the mid-twentieth century. From the 1930s to the 1950s, magazine articles advocated both domestic ideals and nondomestic achievement for women. In the 1930s and 1940s as well as the 1950s, women's magazines presented housewives with romantic fiction, marriage advice, recipes, fashions, and ads for household products. And in all three decades, popular magazines, including women's magazines, spotlighted women of public achievement, addressed women as workers, and promoted women's participation in community activism and politics. Throughout the mid-twentieth century, conservatives called occasionally for women's subordination and women's rights advocates insisted occasionally on equality. More frequently, though, the magazines asserted both a long-held domestic ideal and a long-held ethos of achievement.[59]

Beyond the common themes, though, postwar magazines differed from earlier magazines in emphasis if not in kind. In my samples, the proportion of articles that focused on motherhood, marriage, and housewifery was actually smaller during the 1950s than during either the 1930s or the 1940s.[60] In the earlier decades, the articles on domesticity often expressed the special concerns of the Great Depression or World War II. During the 1930s, numerous articles praised, advised, and encouraged housewives, as families budgeted their money and adult children returned home. A few articles offered reasons why wives or daughters should not pursue jobs or careers, perhaps reflecting a veiled hostility to women in the depression-era workplace. And several articles presented marriage and domesticity as a "great opportunity" or "the best-paying and most soul-satisfying career that any woman can espouse."[61] During World War II, as expected, the magazines promoted women's participation in war industry, the military, and volunteer service. A couple of articles recommended ways of relieving working women's household burdens, and a few lauded women who combined motherhood and career. But the wartime magazines also lavished extensive praise on devoted mothers and loyal wives. Responding to a wartime fear of family breakdown, they stated explicitly that mothers had a primary duty to their children. The author of one such article called on the government to draft women who neglected their children and assign them "to duty in their own homes." Other articles warned women against taking husbands for granted or lowering housekeeping standards. Placed in this context, the postwar promotion of marriage and motherhood seems neither surprising nor anomalous.[62]

The presentation of women's public lives also shifted with the times. In the postwar era, Rosie the Riveter and her challenge to the sexual division of labor vanished from the mass culture. Magazines rarely presented women in heavy industry or in the armed services. In this sense, the postwar mass culture reverted to prewar assumptions about gender roles. But the sample from the 1950s did not represent domestic retreat. In fact, it included more laudatory stories on women who achieved public success than did the samples from either of the earlier decades. The postwar magazines devoted a greater proportion of space to individual women in business, professions, social service, politics, and entertainment.[63] The concept of public service also seems to have changed. The *Ladies Home Journal* is perhaps emblematic. In the 1930s, the *Journal* launched a campaign, "It's Up to the Women," inviting women to help end the depression. While the campaign acknowledged the work of local women's clubs, its central theme, repeated in several issues, urged housewives to bolster the economy simply by spending more money.[64] In the 1950s, when the *Journal* again asked housewives to join in public service, it invited them to enter mainstream politics as party workers and politicians. Public service had moved beyond the traditionally female sphere.

Why does my version of history differ from Betty Friedan's? The most obvious, and the most gracious, explanation is that we used different, though overlapping, sources. The nonfiction articles I read may well have included more contradictions and more ambivalence than the fiction on which Friedan focused. But there are, I think, additional differences in approach. Friedan did not read the popular magazines incorrectly, but she did, it seems, cite them reductively. For the prewar era, she seems to have chosen the stories that most embraced public achievement; for the postwar era, she seems to have chosen the stories that most embodied domestic ideals. A cursory review of some of Friedan's evidence suggests that her account of change over time may be somewhat skewed. For her prewar study, Friedan omitted the fiction that featured housewives and failed to mention that the "career women" heroines she cited relinquished or planned to relinquish their jobs for marriage and housewifery. In this way, she may have projected an imagined feminist past onto the mass culture of the 1930s. For the postwar era, she cited both fiction and nonfiction stories on domesticity. But she downplayed the articles on domestic problems (belittling one by saying "the bored editors . . . ran a little article"), ignored the articles on individual achievement, and dismissed the articles on political participation with a one-sentence caricature. Her forceful protest against a restrictive domestic ideal neglected the extent to which that ideal was already undermined.[65]

My reassessment of the "feminine mystique" is part of a larger revisionist project. For the past few years, historians have questioned the stereotype of postwar women as quiescent, docile, and domestic. Despite the baby boom and despite discrimination in employment, education, and public office, married women, black and white, joined the labor force in increasing numbers, and both married and unmarried women participated actively in politics and reform.[66] Just as women's activities were more varied and more complex than is often acknowledged, so, I argue, was the postwar popular ideology. Postwar magazines, like their prewar and wartime predecessors, rarely presented direct challenges to the conventions of marriage or motherhood, but they only rarely told women to return to or stay at home. They included stories that glorified domesticity, but they also expressed ambivalence about domesticity, endorsed women's nondomestic activity, and celebrated women's public success. They delivered multiple messages, which women could read as sometimes supporting and sometimes subverting the "feminine mystique." [67]

When *The Feminine Mystique* appeared in 1963, it won positive reviews. Reviewers appreciated Friedan's "passionate drive," "convincing" feminism, and "sensible" suggestions. They rarely dwelt on her analysis of popular magazines; they commented instead on her overall findings. They deplored the discontent of housewives and joined Friedan in welcoming reform. One reviewer stated: "Friedan has put her finger on the key problem of American women today: recognition as individuals." And another said: "The argument needed to be made; women, like Negroes, have too often been given equal rights in name only." [68]

Along with the general praise, though, negative comments abounded. Reviewers complained of Friedan's "sweeping generalities" and of her occasional tendency "to discover what she sets out to find." Several reviewers believed that the discontent Friedan uncovered had deeper roots. The women's magazines, Madison Avenue advertisers, Sigmund Freud, and individual psychology were not, various reviewers claimed, the source of the problem. The noted novelist and civil rights advocate Lillian Smith suggested that "a vast complex of world-size problems and ancient customs" created the attitudes and images that oppressed women, and other reviewers pointed to "social institutions" and women themselves. The most damning assessment came from the *Yale Review*. The anonymous reviewer claimed that Friedan's account was nothing new: "It would seem by now that it has been amply demonstrated that women are both human beings and women. . . . This is all very well—and we have heard it before." As to housewives' unhappiness, this reviewer claimed that Friedan had "discovered later than many of her readers how prevalent this discontent has been and for how long." [69]

Indeed, many readers had "heard it before." *The Feminine Mystique* was not only a visionary work, a harbinger of the new liberal feminism; it also remained remarkably rooted in postwar culture. A free-lance journalist herself, Friedan adopted the terms of the prevailing popular discourse and restated the postwar cultural contradiction between the ideals of domesticity and achievement. Like other postwar journalists, Friedan did not question women's responsibility for home and children. She encouraged marriage and femininity, disparaged homosexuality, and expressed fears that neurotic, overbearing mothers ruined their children. Also like other postwar journalists, Friedan embraced liberal individualism and validated women's public participation. She saw women's achievements outside the home as a source of both personal fulfillment and public service, and she presented domesticity as a problem.

This is not to say that Friedan's work was simply derivative. In the more liberal political climate of the early 1960s, Friedan reworked older themes in significant ways. While both achievement and domesticity were middle-class ideals, Friedan elevated nondomestic achievement to the higher status of a natural human need and demoted full-time domesticity to the lower status of a false consciousness foisted on women by mass culture and pseudo-scientific experts. She thus legitimated open protest against "the housewife trap." [70] She exposed the tension between public achievement and domesticity in ways that affirmed the undeniable anger many middle-class women felt as they increasingly tried to pursue both domestic and nondomestic ideals.

The continuities with the postwar discourse are nonetheless important because they may help explain Friedan's (and liberal feminism's) success. Friedan's account of the "feminine mystique" may have hit such a resonant chord among middle-class women in part because it reworked themes already rooted in the mass culture. The success of an oppositional discourse, like Friedan's, relies not only on how it counters the mainstream but also on how it draws on and reshapes familiar themes.

NOTES

Acknowledgments: Parts of this research were first presented at the Berkshire Conference on the History of Women, Douglass College, June 1990. For their helpful comments at various stages of this project, I thank Wini Breines, Mari Jo Buhle, William Chafe, Susan Hartmann, Susan Lynn, Ruth Milkman, Zane Miller, Leila Rupp, Judith Smith, David Thelen, and Winifred Wandersee. For expert research assistance, I thank Sarah Heath and Kriste Lindenmeyer.

1. Betty Friedan, *The Feminine Mystique* (1963; reprint, New York: Dell, 1975), 7, 37, 47, 58–59, 299. Human potential psychology entered the mainstream mass culture in the late 1950s and 1960s. Betty Friedan was especially influenced by the works of Abraham Maslow. Historians need to explore further the influence of human potential psychology on contemporary feminism. For insightful readings of Friedan's book, see Donald Meyer, "Betty Friedan," in *Portraits of American Women: From Settlement to*

the Present, ed. G. J. Barker-Benfield and Catherine Clinton (New York: St. Martin's Press, 1991), 599–615; Rachel Bowlby, " 'The Problem with No Name': Rereading Friedan's *The Feminine Mystique*," *Feminist Review*, September 1987, 61–75.

2. Testimony on the impact of the book is found in the many letters written to Friedan. See Elaine Tyler May, *Homeward Bound: American Families in the Cold War Era* (New York: Basic Books, 1988), 209–217. Friedan's discussion of American women implicitly excludes the experiences of many lesbians, women of color, and working-class, activist, employed, and unmarried women. For a different account of women's postwar experience, see Eugenia Kaledin, *Mothers and More: American Women in the 1950's* (Boston: Twayne, 1984); for an overview, see Sara M. Evans, *Born for Liberty: A History of Women in America* (New York: Free Press, 1989), 250–260.

3. May, *Homeward Bound*, 89. On the late 1940s, see especially Susan Hartmann, "Prescriptions for Penelope: Literature on Women's Obligations to Returning World War II Veterans," *Women's Studies*, no. 3 (1978): 223–239; on the 1950s, see especially May, *Homeward Bound*. This interpretation is also found in overviews of the era and in women's history textbooks: See, for example, Marty Jezer, *The Dark Ages: Life in the United States, 1945–1960* (Boston: South End Press, 1982), 226–231; John Patrick Diggins, *The Proud Decades: America in War and in Peace, 1941–1960* (New York: Norton, 1988), 211–225; Evans, *Born for Liberty*, 234–239, 246–250; Nancy Woloch, *Women and the American Experience* (New York: Knopf, 1984), 496, 499–501. For the most balanced extended account, which notes that social scientist dissenters from the domestic ideology had some impact on mass culture, see William Henry Chafe, *The American Woman: Her Changing Social, Political and Economic Roles, 1920–1970* (New York: Oxford University Press, 1972), 199–225.

4. Ferdinand Lundberg and Marynia F. Farnham, *Modern Woman: The Lost Sex* (New York: Harper & Brothers, 1947). For Friedan's view of their influence, see Friedan, *Feminine Mystique*, 37, 111. Historians who use Lundberg and Farnham to illustrate the postwar ideology include Diggins, *The Proud Decades*, 214; Jezer, *The Dark Ages*, 227; Evans, *Born for Liberty*, 238–239, 248; Woloch, *Women and the American Experience*, 499; Leila J. Rupp and Verta Taylor, *Survival in the Doldrums: The American Women's Rights Movement, 1945 to the 1960s* (New York: Oxford University Press, 1987), 19; Cynthia Harrison, *On Account of Sex: The Politics of Women's Issues, 1945–1968* (Berkeley: University of California Press, 1988), 24–25; Glenna Matthews, *"Just a Housewife": The Rise and Fall of Domesticity in America"* (New York: Oxford University Press, 1987), 209; Myra Dinnerstein, *Women Between Two Worlds: Midlife Reflections on Work and Family* (Philadelphia: Temple University Press, 1992), 4–5.

5. I read all nonfiction articles on women in these magazines for January through June of 1946, 1948, 1950, 1952, 1954, 1956, and 1958. (*Negro Digest* ceased publication in 1951, and *Woman's Home Companion* in 1957.) The 489 articles include 5 in *Atlantic Monthly*, 107 in *Coronet*, 106 in *Ebony*, 11 in *Harper's*, 117 in *Ladies' Home Journal*, 22 in *Negro Digest*, 62 in *Reader's Digest*, and 59 in *Woman's Home Companion*. The magazines with fewest articles on women (*Atlantic Monthly* and *Harper's*) had fewer articles (on all topics) per issue. On circulation, see N. W. Ayer and Son, *Directory of Newspapers and Periodicals: 1955* (Philadelphia: N. W. Ayer and Son, 1955). The figures range from *Reader's Digest* (estimated circulation 10 million) to *Harper's* (circulation 163,487). This figure excludes *Negro Digest*, which had ceased publication by 1955. *Negro Digest* had an estimated circulation of 100,000, according to N. W. Ayer

and Son, *Directory of Newspapers and Periodicals: 1950* (Philadelphia: N. W. Ayer and Son, 1950).

6. Some of the articles (virtually all in *Ebony*) do not list authors, and the author's name does not always indicate gender. Of articles in which the author's gender seems apparent, 168 were written by women, 127 by men. In the women's magazines, 70 percent of authors were women. In *Coronet, Negro Digest,* and *Reader's Digest,* male authors outnumbered female, with the female authors comprising 44 percent, 35 percent, and 42 percent, respectively. I did not find any significant differences between articles by women and those by men.

7. For influential theoretical formulations, see Stuart Hall, "Culture, Media, and the 'Ideological Effect,' " in *Mass Communication and Society,* ed. James Curran, Michael Gurevitch, and Janet Woollacott (Beverly Hills: Sage, 1979), 315–348; Fredric Jameson, "Reification and Utopia in Mass Culture," *Social Text,* Winter 1979, 130–148. For more recent accounts, see especially George Lipsitz, *Time Passages: Collective Memory and American Popular Culture* (Minneapolis: University of Minnesota Press, 1990); and Lawrence Grossberg, Cary Nelson, and Paula Treichler, eds., *Cultural Studies* (New York: Routledge, 1992). For a critique of this approach, see Jackson Lears, "Power, Culture, and Memory," *Journal of American History,* June 1988, 137–140.

8. "The Happy Housewife Heroine" is the title of Friedan's chapter on popular magazines. Friedan, *Feminine Mystique,* 28–61.

9. Alfred E. Smith, "Woman Realtor," *Negro Digest,* June 1950, 69.

10. The other articles on individual women covered a range of topics, including women royalty, women who overcame illnesses or disabilities, women who had telling experiences with racism (only in African American magazines), and women criminals. (The magazines were highly segregated. With only a few exceptions, the white magazines—*Coronet, Reader's Digest, Harper's, Atlantic Monthly, Ladies' Home Journal,* and *Woman's Home Companion*—presented stories about white women, and the African American magazines—*Ebony* and *Negro Digest*—presented stories about black women.) Stories about individual women were least prevalent in the highbrow magazines. The percentage of individual stories among all nonfiction stories on women was: *Negro Digest,* 95 percent; *Ebony,* 75 percent; *Coronet,* 69 percent; *Reader's Digest,* 61 percent; *Woman's Home Companion,* 57 percent; *Ladies' Home Journal,* 41 percent; *Harpers,* 36 percent; *Atlantic Monthly,* 20 percent.

11. "The Jane Russell Story," *Coronet,* March 1950, 107.

12. Richard L. Neuberger, "The Lady Who Licked Crime in Portland," *Coronet,* June 1952, 51–54.

13. Jacqueline Jones, *Labor of Love, Labor of Sorrow: Black Women, Work, and the Family from Slavery to the Present* (New York: Basic Books, 1985), 274; "Lady Plane Mechanic," *Ebony,* January 1948, 30. See also "Milwaukee's First Lady Councilman," ibid., June 1958, 40–45.

14. Carol Hughes, "Dorothy Kilgallen: Star Reporter," *Coronet,* June 1950, 53–57. For another example, see Jana Guerrier, "Wall Street Woman," ibid., January 1954, 26–29.

15. See, for example, Neuberger, "Lady Who Licked Crime."

16. Lawrence Lader, "The Unbeatable Babe," *Coronet,* January 1948, 158. For a similar, though more veiled, account of "maturing as a woman," see the article on pianist Dorothy Donegan: "Queen of the Keys," *Ebony,* March 1958, 86. For a strikingly

blatant account (outside this sample), see Gladys Bentley, "I Am a Woman Again," ibid., August 1952, 92–98. On postwar hostility to lesbians and gender transgression, see John D'Emilio, *Sexual Politics, Sexual Communities: The Making of a Homosexual Minority in the United States, 1940–1970* (Chicago: University of Chicago Press, 1983), 40–53; Donna Penn, "The Meanings of Lesbianism in Post-War America," *Gender and History*, Summer 1991, 190–203; and Lillian Faderman, *Odd Girls and Twilight Lovers: A History of Lesbian Life in Twentieth-Century America* (New York: Columbia University Press, 1991), 139–158. Friedan, *Feminine Mystique*, 73–94. For disparagement of male homosexuality, see ibid., 264–265.

17. "When a Woman Runs the Town," *Ladies' Home Journal*, January 1952, 49; Eleanor Harris, " 'I Gave Away 10,000 Babies,' " *Woman's Home Companion*, January 1954, 34; Eleanor Harris, "The Real Story of Lucille Ball," *Reader's Digest*, May 1954, 82; Mark Harris, "The Forty Years of Justina Ford," *Negro Digest*, March 1950, 43; Jhan and June Robbins, " 'Diamond Lil' of Madison Square," *Coronet*, February 1954, 68; Anita Loos, "This Brunette Prefers Work," *Woman's Home Companion*, March 1956, 6. For articles that opposed meaningful work to activities coded as trivial, see "Girl in the Back Room," *Ladies' Home Journal*, May 1952, 207; Elinor Goulding Smith, "The Undecided Ones," *Atlantic Monthly*, February 1946, 141; Blake Clark, "The Girl Who Does a Man's Job," *Reader's Digest*, January 1950, 94.

18. For example, in *Ebony*'s regular feature "Speaking of People," which presented six well employed African Americans monthly, the marital status of women was rarely discussed except through the use of "Mrs." or "Miss." For the period sampled, 56 of 180 workers presented in "Speaking of People" were women. Of the women, 21 appeared to be married, 16 single, and 19 of unknown status. (Monthly features on both men and women, including "Speaking of People," are not included in my quantitative analysis of nonfiction articles on women.) For articles that discounted marriage, see, for example, Elsa Maxwell, "Come to My Party," *Woman's Home Companion*, April 1954, 96; Cynthia Lowny, "A Talk with Mary Margaret McBride," *Woman's Home Companion*, May 1954, 68; Mary Braggiotti, "Haiti's First Woman Doctor," *Negro Digest*, January 1948, 61. On divorced women, see, for example, Grady Johnson, "Florence Chadwick: She Never Quits," *Coronet*, April 1954, 84–88; "Tamara Hayes," *Ebony*, February 1952, 37–41; "Carmen McRae," ibid., February 1956, 67–70. *Ebony* was the least apologetic in its approach to divorce; see "Gay Divorcees," ibid., February 1950, 72–76. But other magazines also discussed divorcees without condemnation; see "If You're Thinking of Divorce," *Coronet*, May 1956, 131–135.

19. Betty McDonald, "An Unforgettable Character," *Reader's Digest*, February 1954, 92. The sample included 44 domestic articles on individual women. (This category overlaps with categories mentioned above, as it includes 10 articles on the domestic roles of entertainers or royalty.) Of the 44 domestic articles, 20 were in the *Ladies' Home Journal*. Only a few of them openly contested nondomestic achievement. One author blamed her (and other women's) temporary sterility on "career and striving." Such calls for a retreat to domesticity were extremely rare. See "We Wanted a Baby," *Ladies' Home Journal*, March 1946, 29; Neal Gilkyson Stuart, "Mother Is a Doctor Now!" ibid., May 1958, 136. For a story in which domesticity is presented as a source of severe depression, see Betty Coe Spicer, " 'Mama Gets Too Tired,' " ibid., May 1956, 177–187. On women politicians, see "Girl in the Back Room," ibid., May 1952, 54, 204–207; "How Does She Do It?" ibid., June 1952, 46, 123–125.

20. Dorothy Walworth, "An Unforgettable Character: Mary Bethune," *Reader's*

Digest, February 1952, 146; "Honoring the *Companion*'s Most Successful Women," *Woman's Home Companion*, March 1954, 25. For the original announcement of the six, see "Six Most Successful Women," ibid., January 1954, 20. See also "The Most Successful Women of 1955," ibid., January 1956, 30–31.

21. Walter Havighurst, "Annie Oakley of the Wild West," *Reader's Digest*, June 1956, 125–29; Shirley Graham, "The Story of Phillis Wheatley," *Negro Digest*, January 1950, 85–97; Margaret Blair Johnstone, "I Walk with Faith," *Woman's Home Companion*, January 1954, 30, 95–97; "Roller Derby Star," *Ebony*, May 1954, 56–58; Warren I. Susman, *Culture as History: The Transformation of American Society in the Twentieth Century* (New York: Pantheon, 1984), 277. Melodramatic tales persisted in film and fiction. On melodrama in late nineteenth-century England, see Judith Walkowitz, Myra Jehlen, and Bell Chevigny, "Patrolling the Borders: Feminist Historiography and the New Historicism," *Radical History Review*, Winter 1989, 25–31; Judith R. Walkowitz, "Science and the Seance: Transgressions of Gender and Genre in Late Victorian London," *Representations*, Spring 1988, 3–29.

22. Carol Hughes, "Mabel Powell: Classroom Miracle-Worker," *Coronet*, June 1946, 140–144; Betty Furness, "I Had to Start Over," *Woman's Home Companion*, June 1954, 73; Norman Bradley, "Georgia's Great Lady," *Negro Digest*, February 1948, 78; "Janet Collins' Dance School," *Ebony*, January 1956, 30; Allen Rankin, "Sure, You Can Sing Grand Opera, Honey," *Reader's Digest*, May 1958, 36.

23. The sample included 19 articles on the ill, disabled, and disfigured. Van Wyck Brooks, "Helen Keller," *Harper's*, May 1954, 42; Helen Markel Herrmann, "Speediest Woman in the World," *Reader's Digest*, May 1952, 22. See also Alberta Williams, "She Blended Prayers with Her Paints," *Coronet*, June 1956, 102–106; "Scarf Designer," *Ebony*, May 1956, 80–85.

24. *Coronet* and *Reader's Digest* did not carry letters to the editor, and *Woman's Home Companion* did not carry letters that responded to particular articles. "The Women You Admire!" *Woman's Home Companion*, January 1947, 12; "The Women You Admire," ibid., January 1949, 8.

25. Marynia F. Farnham, "The Tragic Failure of America's Women," *Coronet*, September 1947, 4.

26. Martha Vicinus, "What Makes a Heroine? Nineteenth-Century Girls' Biographies," *Genre*, Summer 1987, 171–188; Susan Ware, "Amelia Earhart as Popular Heroine," paper presented at Berkshire Conference on the History of Women, Douglass College, June 1990 (in Joanne Meyerowitz's possession); Susan Ware, *Holding Their Own: American Women in the 1930's* (Boston: Twayne, 1982), 173. On the individualistic brand of feminism, see Nancy F. Cott, *The Grounding of Modern Feminism* (New Haven: Yale University Press, 1987), 275–283. On its representations in mass culture, see Ware, "Amelia Earhart." On the increase in women in the postwar labor force, see Alice Kessler-Harris, *Out to Work: A History of Wage-Earning Women in the United States* (New York: Oxford University Press, 1982), 301.

27. Friedan, *Feminine Mystique*, 40. These conflicting ideals are an example of "the internal contradictions between those different ideologies which constitute the dominant terrain." Hall, "Culture, the Media, and the 'Ideological Effect,' " 346.

28. The sample included 24 articles on women's paid work, including those on women in specific occupations; 51 on women's political and community activism; 51 on marriage and domesticity, including those on divorce and motherhood; and 19 on sexuality, including those on glamour and beauty.

29. Frances J. Myers, "Don't Take It Out on the Women," *Woman's Home Companion*, January 1946, 12. See also Nancy Barr Mavity, "The Two-Income Family," *Reader's Digest*, February 1952, 1–4; "What's Wrong with Negro Men?" *Ebony*, June 1958, 65. This argument also appeared repeatedly in the *American Federationist*, the official magazine of the American Federation of Labor, in the postwar era. Articles in the *American Federationist* often went further than those in popular magazines, sometimes arguing for equal pay and occasionally for what we now call comparable worth.

30. "When an Older Woman Wants a Job," *Ladies' Home Journal*, January 1954, 120; Elsie McCormick, "That Amazing Secretarial Shortage," *Reader's Digest*, February 1954, 55; Farnham, "Tragic Failure of America's Women," 8. See also Lundberg and Farnham, *Modern Woman*, 366. Farnham condoned part-time work only if it did not detract from a woman's central focus on motherhood.

31. Mary Van Rensselaer Thayer, "Uncle Sam's Nieces Are Nice," *Woman's Home Companion*, January 1948, 12–13; J. D. Ratcliff, "Careers in Saving Lives," *Woman's Home Companion*, April 1952, 109. See also "Career Girls in Europe," *Coronet*, April 1956, 69–78. "Petticoat Medics," *Ebony*, February 1948, 19. See also Harris, "Forty Years of Justina Ford," 42–45; Braggiotti, "Haiti's First Woman Doctor," 59–61. Comments on gender discrimination appeared most often in articles on women in the professions.

32. "Why They Don't Marry," *Ebony*, January 1958, 58–59; Evelyn Sager, "Profile of Success," *Ladies' Home Journal*, April 1946, 32, 109.

33. On mothers returning to work, see David R. Mace, "What Do You Want from Your Marriage Today?" *Woman's Home Companion*, April 1956, 109. Mavity, "Two-Income Family," 4; Friedan, *Feminine Mystique*, 336.

34. Of the 51 articles on women's political and community activism, 31 were in the *Ladies' Home Journal*. For examples from other magazines, see Carol Hughes, "A Women's Army 11,000,000 Strong," *Coronet*, January 1952, 108–111; Albert Q. Maisel, "How Good Is Your Woman's Club?" *Woman's Home Companion*, March 1954, 45, 79, 92. For a significant example (not in the sample) from a black magazine, see "Women Leaders," *Ebony*, July 1949, 19–22. Margaret Hickey, "What's the U.S. to You?" *Ladies' Home Journal*, April 1950, 23. Hickey had also served as chair of the Women's Advisory Committee of the War Manpower Commission. See "Meet Miss Hickey," ibid., March 1947, 56.

35. " 'We Can't Let the Children Down,' " *Ladies' Home Journal*, March 1952, 104; Millicent C. McIntosh, "Busy Women Have Time Enough," ibid., June 1952, 47. See also Erwin D. Canham, "It's Time Women Took Direct Action," ibid., January 1952, 48.

36. "They Do It . . . You Can Too," ibid., April 1956, 70. See also "Women Like You and Me in Politics," ibid., February 1952, 48–49, 122–124.

37. For women as peace loving, see Dorothy Thompson, "A Woman Says, 'You Must Come into the Room of Your Mother Unarmed,' " ibid., February 1946, 24–25. For other examples (outside my sample), see Dorothy Thompson, "If No One Else—We, the Mothers," ibid., July 1947, 11–12; Dorothy Thompson, "A Woman's Manifesto," ibid., November 1947, 11–12, 278–279, 281. See also James M. Wood, "Let the Women In!" *Woman's Home Companion*, November 1946, 8. For essentialist arguments in the 1950s, see "Women Like You and Me in Politics," 48. See also "They Do It . . . You Can Too," 70; McIntosh, "Busy Women Have Time Enough," 47.

38. On the Cold War and domesticity, see May, *Homeward Bound*, 16–36, 92–113.

Dorothy Thompson, "I Write of Russian Women," *Ladies' Home Journal*, March 1956, 11; Anna Lord Strauss, "You Can Ask Questions," ibid., March 1952, 62; Paul G. Hoffman, "Assignment for Women," ibid., April 1952, 112; Canham, "It's Time Women Took Direct Action," 108; Margaret Chase Smith, "No Place for a Woman?" *Ladies' Home Journal*, February 1952, 50, 83. For an example of women using Cold War rhetoric to support employment, see Kessler-Harris, *Out to Work*, 304. Many national women's organizations took Cold War political obligations seriously. See Dorothy G. Stackhouse, "Assembly of Women's Organizations for National Security," *General Federation Clubwoman*, January 1954, 10–11, 26–29.

39. John Steinbeck, "Women and Children in the U.S.S.R.," *Ladies' Home Journal*, February 1948, 45.

40. "The American Woman," *Coronet*, May 1948, 51–66.

41. For an attempt to bolster women's self-esteem, see, for example, "The American Housewife," ibid., March 1954, 45–60. For domesticity as a problem, see Anna A. M. Wolf, "Mothers Can Be Human Too," *Woman's Home Companion*, February 1948, 62–63; Herman N. Bundesen, "The Overprotective Mother," *Ladies' Home Journal*, March 1950, 243; Benjamin Spock, "Mothers Need a Break," ibid., February 1958, 20, 22, 132. On domestic problems presented in postwar magazines, see Matthews, *"Just a Housewife,"* 212. Friedan claims that the problem of housewife discontent captured public attention in 1960. Friedan, *Feminine Mystique*, 17.

42. "The Plight of the Young Mother," *Ladies' Home Journal*, February 1956), 61, 110–113. The other magazines were less likely to tackle domesticity directly. They sometimes portrayed women in domestic scenes and occasionally offered paeans to individual mothers. In one unusual editorial (outside my sample), *Ebony* endorsed domesticity, with qualifications: "Goodbye Mammy, Hello Mom," *Ebony*, March 1947, 36.

43. "Why They Don't Marry," 60; Leo Guild, "The 'How to Get Married' Chart," *Ladies' Home Journal*, June 1952, 93; "How to Be Marriageable," ibid., March 1954, 46; "If You're Thinking of Divorce"; "Our Own Young Married on Getting Along," *Ladies' Home Journal*, April 1952, 200–201, 220–222.

44. Friedan, *Feminine Mystique*, 37; John Kord Lagemann, "How to Pick a Mate," *Coronet*, February 1958, 116–117; Mace, "What Do You Want from Your Marriage Today?" 79. See also "What's Wrong With Negro Men?" *Ebony*, June 1958, 64. Gretta Palmer, " 'What Kind of Wife Has He?' " *Reader's Digest*, March 1948, 37–39.

45. Sidonie M. Gruenberg, "Test Yourself: Do You Exploit Your Husband?" *Woman's Home Companion*, February 1956, 36–37, 67–69.

46. May, *Homeward Bound*, 114–134; Marion Hilliard, "What Women Don't Know about Being Female," *Reader's Digest*, May 1956, 38–40; Goodrich C. Schauffler, "Today It Could Be *Your* Daughter," *Ladies' Home Journal*, January 1958, 43, 112–113; Mildred Gilman, "A Word to Troubled Wives," *Reader's Digest*, March 1950, 46–48; Abraham Stone, as told to Joan Younger, "What Wives Don't Know about Sex," *Ladies' Home Journal*, May 1956, 72–73, 126–127; "What WAC's Do about Love," *Ebony*, June 1954, 54.

47. "Hey, Good Looking!" *Ebony*, March 1956, 74. See also "African Beauties," ibid., April 1954, 32–36; "Jamaica's Rainbow Beauty Contest," ibid., February 1956, 30–34. Of the articles on glamour in white magazines, only one included nonwhite (Asian and African) women as beauties: James A. Skardon, "In Search of Beauty," *Coronet*, January 1958, 34–45.

48. "Don't Be Afraid of Sex Appeal . . . Says Dorothy Dandridge," *Ebony*, May

1952, 27, 30; Dawn Crowell Norman, "She Turned Herself into a Beauty," *Ladies' Home Journal*, March 1954, 59, 197–199; Patty De Roulf, "Must Bachelor Girls Be Immoral?" *Coronet*, February 1952, 58–59.

49. Friedan, *Feminine Mystique*, 250; Loretta Powell to editor, *Ebony*, December 1954, 10; Edith R. Beckham to editor, *Negro Digest*, January 1948, 98.

50. Marlene Dietrich, "How to Be Loved," *Ladies' Home Journal*, January 1954, 37, 85, 87; "Listen Marlene!" ibid., April 1954, 4, 6.

51. In April and June 1956 the *Ladies' Home Journal* published 21 letters in response to the article "The Plight of the Young Mother." Carol Evans to editor, ibid., April 1956, 4; Patricia L. Belanger to editor, ibid., June 1956, 7; Kathleen Tinguel to editor, ibid., April 1956, 4; Helen Kerwin to editor, ibid., 4.

52. My only quibble with Chafe is that he focuses on the dissenting minority voices of antifeminists and social scientists at the boundaries of the discourse and tends to omit the mainstream. Chafe, *American Woman*, 199–225. For a different view of postwar social science, see Wini Breines, "The 1950's: Gender and Some Social Science," *Sociological Inquiry*, Winter 1986, 69–92.

53. In this admittedly small sample, *Harper's* published articles supporting women's rights, while *Atlantic Monthly* presented both sides of the debate.

54. I use the term *conservative* here to indicate that these authors hoped to conserve or restore what they saw as traditional gender roles, not to suggest that they were necessarily politically conservative in other areas. For variants of this argument, see Marcelene Cox, "How to Prepare Your Daughter for a Divorce," *Ladies' Home Journal*, May 1946, 174–175, 216–217; Lynn White, Jr., "Educating Women in a Man's World," *Atlantic Monthly*, February 1950, 52–55; Betty South, "Why GI's Prefer Those German Girls," *Coronet*, April 1952, 51–55; Lee Graham, "Ten Secrets of Sex Appeal," ibid., March 1954, 28–35. The historical literature on the postwar era frequently cites another such article that falls outside this sample: Agnes E. Meyer, "Women Aren't Men," *Atlantic Monthly*, August 1950, 32–36. Also often cited is *Life's* special issue on women, December 24, 1956. This issue, however, is contradictory and includes "women's rights" articles as well as conservative and mainstream ones.

55. Lundberg and Farnham, *Modern Woman*, 123, 210.

56. The quotation is from her obituary: *New York Times*, May 30, 1979, 19. *Book Review Digest* cites nine reviews. Only three were positive, one written by the notorious misogynist Philip Wylie and another in the conservative *Catholic World*. Mertice M. James and Dorothy Brown, eds., *Book Review Digest 1947* (New York: H. W. Wilson, 1948), 573–574. Marynia F. Farnham, "Who Wears the Pants in Your Family?" *Coronet*, March 1948, 10–14. For editorial comment on the controversy, see ibid., 14. In keeping with its usual format, the magazine did not publish the letters sent to the editor. See also Farnham, "Tragic Failure." For direct rejection of Farnham and Lundberg (outside this sample), see Struthers Burt, "Women, Dog Dab 'Em," *Ladies' Home Journal*, November 1947, 11. This article appeared on the editorial page of the magazine.

57. The category that I call "women's rights" includes many of the works that Chafe places under the "sociological" perspective. It also includes articles by authors who would not call themselves feminists. I do not include the numerous articles in *Ladies' Home Journal* calling for greater political participation by women as women's rights articles. Agnes Rogers, "The Humble Female," *Harper's*, March 1950, 59; Dorothy Thompson, "Oh, Professor!" *Ladies' Home Journal*, June 1958, 16. In this refutation of a conservative antifeminist male academic, Thompson adopted, despite her ambiva-

lence on careers, a women's rights stance. See also Mary Patrick, "Revolution in Hats," *Woman's Home Companion*, June 1946, 20, 91; Dhanvanthi Rama Rau, "Women of India," *Atlantic Monthly*, January 1954, 61–64. For strong women's rights statements in a black magazine (outside this sample), see Pauli Murray, "Why Negro Girls Stay Single," *Negro Digest*, July 1947, 4–8; and Ann Petry, "What's Wrong with Negro Men?" ibid., March 1947, 4–7. In articles outside this sample, Della D. Cyrus provoked controversy because some readers read her work as an attack on the full-time housewife. The overwhelming response to her articles led *Atlantic Monthly* to publish a "reader's symposium" that included responses from conservative outrage to feminist support. See Della D. Cyrus, "What's Wrong with the Family?" *Atlantic Monthly*, November 1946, 68, 73; Della D. Cyrus, "Why Mothers Fail," ibid., March 1947, 57–60; "It's Up to the Women," ibid., June 1947, 42, 45.

58. Friedan, *Feminine Mystique*, 33–34.

59. For this longitudinal study, I read all nonfiction articles on women in *Readers' Digest, Ladies' Home Journal, Woman's Home Companion, Atlantic Monthly*, and *Harper's*, January to June 1932, 1934, 1942, 1944, 1952, and 1954. In this way, I constructed parallel samples of nonfiction articles on women for 1932 and 1934 ($N = 72$), 1942 and 1944 ($N = 96$), and 1952 and 1954 ($N = 104$). I did not include in this part of my research the magazines that did not begin publication until after 1932 (*Coronet, Negro Digest*, and *Ebony*). My sample corroborates findings that the domestic ideals described by Friedan were popular and influential before the postwar era. See Ruth Schwartz Cowan, "Two Washes in the Morning and a Bridge Party at Night: The American Housewife between the Wars," *Women's Studies*, no. 2 (1976): 147–171. On individual achievement, see Richard Weiss, *The American Myth of Success: From Horatio Alger to Norman Vincent Peale* (New York: Basic Books, 1969).

60. In the sample, the proportion that focused on mothers, wives, or housewives was 36 percent (26/72) in 1932–1934, 27 percent (26/96) in 1942–1944, and 21 percent (22/104) in 1952–1954.

61. Eudora Ramsay Richardson, "The Lady and the Peddler," *Reader's Digest*, January 1932, 26–28; Mary Heaton Vorse, "Children Come Home to Roost," *Woman's Home Companion*, February 1934, 14, 32; Marie Coudert Brennig, "Marry in Haste? Not by a Budget," *Ladies' Home Journal*, June 1934, 14–15, 115, 117; Jane Allen, "You May Have My Job," *Reader's Digest*, May 1932, 7–9; Philip Curtiss, "The Twilight of the Business Woman," *Atlantic Monthly*, February 1934, 167–171 (reprinted in *Reader's Digest*, March 1934, 37–39); Worth Tuttle, "A Feminist Marries," *Atlantic Monthly*, January 1934, 73–81; Mary Orme, "Fair Play in Marriage," *Woman's Home Companion*, January 1932, 20–21; Dorothy Dix, "And So You Are Married!" *Ladies' Home Journal*, February 1932, 45.

62. Bette Davis, "Could Your Husband Take It?" *Ladies' Home Journal*, April 1942, 18, 140–143; Priscilla Robertson and Hawley Jones, "Housekeeping after the War," *Harper's*, April 1944, 430–437; Kay Mulvey, "Hollywood Mothers," *Woman's Home Companion*, March 1944, 10; Aimee Buchanan, "The Lady Likes Business," *Atlantic Monthly*, April 1944, 76–79; Hilda Cole Espy, "Three's a Crowd in Seventeen Months," *Ladies' Home Journal*, February 1944, 40–41, 122, 124, 125, 127; Margaret H. Mackay, "My Baby's Nursery Was a Jap Concentration Camp," *Woman's Home Companion*, March 1944, 24–25, 44, 46; Louise Dickinson Rich, "Drama in Everyday Life," *Reader's Digest*, March 1944, 32–34; John Louis Bonn, "Women by the Sea," ibid., May 1944, 99–100; James Madison Wood, "Should We Draft

Mothers," *Woman's Home Companion,* January 1944, 21, 69; Leslie B. Hohman, "What Makes a Good Wife," *Ladies' Home Journal,* May 1944, 146–147; Helen Van Pelt Wilson, "Is Your Marriage Slipping a Little?" *Reader's Digest,* June 1944, 41–42.

63. In the sample, the proportion of articles on individual women increased from 35 percent (25/72) in 1932–1934 to 42 percent (40/96) in 1942–1944 to 56 percent (58/104) in 1952–1954. Among those articles, the proportion that focused on a woman's public achievement (excluding articles on mothers, wives, women royalty, women who conquered illnesses, etc.) ranged from 40 percent (10/25) in 1932–1934 to 40 percent (16/40) in 1942–1944 to 52 percent (30/58) in 1952–1954.

64. "It's Up to the Women: An Editorial," *Ladies' Home Journal,* January 1932, 3; "Pocketbook Patriotism: An Editorial," ibid., February 1932, 3; Samuel Crowther, "What You Can Do," ibid., March 1932, 3, 120; "It's Up to the Women," ibid., April 1932, 12, 67.

65. I chose one women's magazine, the *Ladies' Home Journal,* and read the three prewar issues that Friedan cited. My reading included all fiction in each issue, whether cited by Friedan or not. For stories on housewives, see Howard Fast, "A Man's Wife," *Ladies' Home Journal,* February 1939, 11, 12, 79; Gladys Taber, "Second Napoleon," ibid., May 1939, 18, 19, 49–52; Faith Ellen Smith, "Dinner for Mr. Hollis," ibid., June 1939, 22, 93–98. For career women heroines (cited by Friedan) who either relinquish their jobs for marriage or plan to do so, see Helen Everitt, "Between the Dark and the Daylight," ibid., February 1939, 21, 77, 78; Faith Baldwin, "Mother-in-Law," ibid., June 1939, 16–17, 67–73. Friedan, *Feminine Mystique,* 44.

66. See, for examples, Lynn Y. Weiner, *From Working Girl to Working Mother: The Female Labor Force in the United States, 1820–1980* (Chapel Hill: University of North Carolina Press, 1985), 89–96; Kessler-Harris, *Out to Work,* 300–311; Ruth Milkman, *Gender at Work: The Dynamic of Job Segregation by Sex during World War II* (Urbana: University of Illinois Press, 1987), 128–152; Nancy F. Gabin, *Feminism in the Labor Movement: Women and the United Auto Workers, 1935–1975* (Ithaca: Cornell University Press, 1990), 111–187; Jones, *Labor of Love, Labor of Sorrow,* 260–301; David Garrow, ed., *The Montgomery Bus Boycott and the Women Who Started It: The Memoir of JoAnn Gibson Robinson* (Knoxville: University of Tennessee Press, 1987); D'Emilio, *Sexual Politics, Sexual Communities,* 101–125; Susan Lynn, "Gender and Post World War II Progressive Politics: A Bridge to Social Activism in the 1960s U.S.A.," *Gender and History,* Summer 1992, 215–239; Rupp and Taylor, *Survival in the Doldrums;* Harrison, *On Account of Sex,* 3–65; Susan Ware, "American Women in the 1950s: Nonpartisan Politics and Women's Politicization," in *Women, Politics, and Change,* ed. Louise A. Tilly and Patricia Gurin (New York: Russell Sage Foundation, 1990), 281–299.

67. A few recent works of film, television, and literary criticism corroborate this view of a contradictory postwar mass culture. On film, see, for example, Brandon French, *On the Verge of Revolt: Women in American Films of the Fifties* (New York: Frederick Ungar, 1978); Janey Place, "Women in Film Noir," in *Women in Film Noir,* ed. E. Ann Kaplan (London: British Film Institute, 1980), 35–54; Andrea S. Walsh, *Women's Film and Female Experience, 1940–1950* (New York: Praeger, 1984); Janet Walker, "Hollywood, Freud and the Representation of Women: Regulation and Contradictions, 1945–Early 60s," in *Home Is Where the Heart Is: Studies in Melodrama and the Woman's Film,* ed. Christine Gledhill (London: British Film Institute, 1987), 197–214. On popular literature, see Paul Boyer, "Minister's Wife, Widow, Reluctant Feminist: Catherine Marshall in the 1950s," *American Quarterly,* Winter 1978, 703–721; Nancy

Walker, "Humor and Gender Roles: The 'Funny' Feminism of the Post-World War II Suburbs," ibid., Spring 1985, 98–113. On television, see James West Davidson and Mark Hamilton Lytle, *After the Fact: The Art of Historical Detection*, 2 vols. (New York: Knopf, 1986), II:364–392; and Lipsitz, *Time Passages*, 77–96.

68. Lillian Smith, "Too Tame the Shrew," *Saturday Review*, February 23, 1963, 44; Maurice Richardson, "Time for Eros," *New Statesman*, May 24, 1963, 798; Marya Mannes, "Don't Sweep the Ladies under the Rug," *New York Herald Tribune Books*, April 28, 1963, 1; Sylvia Fleis Fava, review of *Feminine Mystique* by Betty Friedan, *American Sociological Review*, December 1963, 1054; "The Segregated Sex," *Economist*, August 10, 1963, 519.

69. Lucy Freeman, review of *Feminine Mystique* by Friedan, *New York Times Book Review*, April 7, 1963, 46; review of *Feminine Mystique* by Friedan, *Virginia Quarterly Review*, Summer 1963, cviii; Smith, "Too Tame the Shrew," 44; Fava, review of *Feminine Mystique* by Friedan, 1054; Freeman, review of *Feminine Mystique* by Friedan, 46; review of *Feminine Mystique* by Friedan, *Yale Review*, March 1963, xii.

70. Friedan, *Feminine Mystique*, 325.

CHAPTER 12

Ruth Feldstein

"I WANTED THE WHOLE WORLD TO SEE"

Race, Gender, and Constructions of Motherhood in the Death of Emmett Till

The murder of the fourteen-year-old African American Emmett Till in the summer of 1955 was a grisly one. Late Saturday night on August 28, Roy Bryant, twenty-four years old, and his half-brother J. W. Milam, thirty-six, kidnapped Emmett Till, a native of Chicago, at gunpoint from his relatives' cabin in Money, Mississippi. Several days after the abduction, a white teenager found Till's body in the nearby Tallahatchie River. He had been brutally beaten, one eye was gouged out, and he was shot in the skull. In the hope of weighting the mutilated body in the water, Till's murderers had tied a 100-pound cotton gin fan to his neck with barbed wire.[1] Till allegedly had whistled at Carolyn Bryant, Roy Bryant's wife, and mother of two young sons. The two white men felt compelled to avenge what they perceived as a racial and sexual transgression.

The brutal murder transfixed the country. Thousands attended Till's funeral in Chicago and saw his mangled body. Bryant and Milam were arrested, indicted, and tried for murder. During the five-day trial in September, three television networks flew footage from Mississippi to New York daily for the nightly news.[2] "Will Mississippi Whitewash the Emmett Till Slaying?" asked *Jet* magazine in a photo essay depicting Till in life and death.[3] On Friday, September 23, the all-white, all-male jury deliberated for only sixty-seven minutes before returning a verdict of not guilty. Less than two months later, a grand jury chose not to indict Milam and Bryant on charges of kidnapping. They were free men. The acquittal fueled the horror and collective anger that the murder had evoked. In the weeks before and after the trial, dozens of protest rallies with thousands in attendance were held around the country. Till's relatives and others involved in the trial told of their experiences, raised funds for the NAACP, and urged voter registration. "Not since Pearl Harbor has the country been so outraged as by the . . . [Till] lynching . . . and the unconscionable verdict," commented one magazine.[4]

Till's murder occurred in 1955, a year of growing defensiveness and violence on the part of many white southerners. It marked the first year in the life of White Citizens' Councils, "respectable" and middle-class white supremacist organizations born in response to the Supreme Court's 1954 decision in *Brown* v. *Board of Education of Topeka*.[5] In Mississippi alone, two other black males were shot to death between May and August 1955; both had registered to vote. Yet 1955 was also a year of cautious optimism in some black communities and activism for civil rights workers. The African American newspaper, the *Chicago Defender*, for example, celebrated its fiftieth anniversary with an 80-page edition that "epitomizes the position of the American Negro today in relation to his native country. All of the elements that have gone into his development and progress in the United States are embodied in this issue . . . a hefty, tangible symbol of our democracy."[6] The year would end with the onset of the Montgomery bus boycott, a campaign that would break segregated public transportation in the Deep South city and bring an obscure black minister, Martin Luther King, Jr., to national attention.

Of course, the year of Till's murder was marked by many other, seemingly unrelated, events and attitudes. These included a sexually conservative message emphasizing that a "good" woman was concerned primarily with her home and family and, perhaps most important, was a nurturing mother. In a commencement address at Smith College in May 1955, liberal democrat Adlai Stevenson urged each graduate to become a mother and inspire "in her home a vision of the meaning of life and freedom . . . help her husband find values that will give purpose to his specialized daily chores."[7] Television moms projected images of fulfilled and fulfilling white motherhood onto recently acquired screens across the country, and these representations of motherhood frequently prevailed despite increases in women's labor force participation and alternative gender roles offered in popular culture. And although these were

prescriptions for white women, African American periodicals, too, often celebrated motherhood and domestic security.[8] "Goodby Mammy, Hello Mom,"
declared *Ebony,* heralding the alleged postwar retreat of black women to the
home and giving thanks that "Junior" has "been getting his bread and butter
sandwiches regularly after school and [now] finding that rip in his blue jeans
mended when he goes out to play." Indeed, columnist Roi Ottley praised black
mothers for disciplining their children successfully—more readily and effectively than did "modern" white mothers. "Perhaps the Negro mother's attitude
is old-fashioned," he wrote, "but in the final analysis it is more practical and
indeed involves a sense of personal responsibility."[9]

Mamie Till Bradley,[10] a thirty-three-year-old African American woman,
worker, and mother living in Chicago, was a part of these overlapping and
seemingly conflicting currents on race relations and gender roles. When Bryant
and Milam murdered her son, these currents forcefully collided and their interdependence crystallized. As this essay makes clear, a discourse on motherhood
was not incidental to the widely publicized murder of Emmett Till—an episode frequently cited as critical to the "birth" of the civil rights movement.[11]
Instead, constructions of gender were at the center of a case hailed solely as a
landmark in the history of the civil rights movement. An analysis of the southern born but Chicago-bred Mamie Bradley demonstrates that motherhood itself
was a battleground on which the meaning of Till's death was fought. Both
racists and antiracists, conservatives and liberals invoked, constructed, and relied on meanings of motherhood to formulate their views both on race relations
and on American citizenship.[12]

Scholars analyzing this murder have emphasized the racial, regional, and class
conflicts that Till's death brought to the fore. Initially, the majority of white
southerners condemned the murder and praised the speedy indictment of two
men now labeled "white trash" or "peckerwoods" by many southern whites
who, regardless of Bryant and Milam's financial positions, used class distinctions to distance themselves from such blatant and violent racism.[13] In the days
after their arrest, local lawyers intentionally demanded payment they knew
Bryant and Milam could not afford, and the men had no counsel.[14] But as white
southerners concluded that the South itself was under attack and on trial, and as
blacks around the country mobilized politically to protest the murder, a racially
specific alliance developed to defend Milam and Bryant—and to protect power
relations in the region. Within a week of the murder, all five of Sumner's attorneys agreed to collaborate in Bryant and Milam's defense; a "defense fund"
raised $10,000 for the two. The impact of the case, then, scholars have argued,
stemmed in part from the way in which one region of the country felt itself set
against another.[15]

Because Bryant and Milam murdered Till for alleged "advances" toward Carolyn Bryant, gender has not been wholly overlooked in discussions of the murder. But analyses situate gender onto a white woman exclusively, so Carolyn Bryant becomes "the woman" relevant to these events. Similarly, race is situated onto black men exclusively, so either Till or Moses Wright, Till's uncle and a prominent witness in the trial, are "the blacks" relevant to these events. As a result, the relationships among gender, race, and class and the ways in which together these fluid categories interact and structure power relations have not been considered. The power of Carolyn Bryant's gender as racially specific and class informed, for example, is obscured. Further, a central figure in understanding how the meaning of Till's death was constructed has been largely effaced: Mamie Till Bradley.[16]

Mamie Bradley—as an African American woman and an African American mother—was central to the politicization of her son's murder. She chose to open her son's casket to the world and thus helped make his death an international civil rights issue. Bradley actively involved herself in the events that followed the murder—the funeral, the trial, and the political mobilization the murder spurred—and in the process defined her own subjectivity as a black woman. She claimed the public role of grieving mother and thus reformulated conceptions of both white and African American motherhood.[17] Her actions enable a consideration of the political—even radical—potential of motherhood in the 1950s and a reconsideration of a women's history paradigm that renders mothers in the 1950s apolitical.[18] Bradley explicitly politicized motherhood on a number of levels—challenging black women's exclusion from the racially specific discourse of white motherhood and challenging women's exclusion from the gendered discourse of politics.[19] She thus exposed the ways in which citizenship relied on false distinctions between public and private and unquestioned assumptions about race and gender.[20]

As the story of Mamie Till Bradley suggests, an intervention into the dominant discourse on motherhood could have multiple meanings and consequences. In claiming her role as a grieving mother she helped inject motherhood more forcefully into the political landscape, but she could not control the terms of the debate or the ways in which she herself was a symbol. Till opponents consistently invoked assumptions about natural motherhood that privileged Carolyn Bryant and excluded Mamie Till Bradley in order to preserve citizenship as it was defined in the South. But more progressive claims to citizenship that included African Americans were also gendered, dependent on traditional divisions between a public and rational masculinity and a private and emotional femininity. As part of its political battle for black citizenship, the NAACP, too, would ultimately seek to contain Bradley and define the meaning of motherhood on these more "progressive" terms. Representations of Bradley underscored the fact that meanings of motherhood sat on the cusp between public and private—clearly relegated to the private sphere, yet infused with political meaning. The meaning of Till's death was structured around these tensions between public and private, between exposure and concealment. And precisely because Mamie Till Bradley existed and acted as she did—as mother, woman, and African American, in the public and private spheres—she became an object to be positioned, defined, and contained by those across the political spectrum.

"A Mother's World Came to an End":
The Meanings of Respectable Motherhood

The meanings of Till's death pointed to the contested meanings of motherhood and respectability. Who and what was a "natural" or a "good" mother? What sources of authority did this role confer, and who was excluded from this category? Who was and was not respectable? Could either the African American and northern Mamie Till Bradley or the white, southern, less financially stable Roy and Carolyn Bryant be cast as respectable?

Powerful as these categories were, their meanings were not fixed in 1955. Motherhood did not automatically confer on Mamie Bradley or Carolyn Bryant authority or sympathy. Indeed, despite the fact (or perhaps because of it) that motherhood was considered the ultimate form of womanhood, "experts" in psychology, sexology, sociology, and other "sex role" or "race relation" disciplines understood motherhood as the linchpin to a range of social and political problems—from communism and homosexuality to juvenile delinquency and poverty. In many instances, middle-class white mothers in particular were vilified in this period.[21] Nevertheless, white motherhood afforded potential power and demanded at least rhetorical loyalty. Since well before World War II, motherhood, for white women, had been explicitly prescribed and at least conditionally valorized.[22] In the same week that thousands waited in lines to view Till's body, reviewers praised Herman Wouk's novel *Marjorie Morningstar*—the tale of aspiring actress turned mother and homemaker. She "fulfilled her destiny," sang one voice in the chorus of praise, and was a model for women everywhere—"their lives at last disposed into the state which becomes them."[23] Even as mom bashing became something of a national pastime, then, critiques of "bad" white mothers were based on a basic belief in their potential power and importance as civilizers of men. Or, in the words of anthropologist Ashley Montagu, author of *The Natural Superiority of Women:* "It is the function of women to teach men how to be human . . . the true genius of women."[24]

The historian Elaine Tyler May has analyzed the emphasis on "early marriage, sexual containment and traditional gender roles" in the context of the

Cold War: "Domestic containment," she explains, was a way men and women could "bolster themselves against potential threats"—including atomic war and communism within America.[25] When the quest for civil rights is considered part of the 1950s, the political implications of domestic containment widens. For whites, and especially for financially insecure southern whites like Roy and Carolyn Bryant, adherence to traditional gender roles and the belief in motherhood's power were ways of containing "threats" to the racial caste system on which they depended for their socioeconomic security. Although both white families were notches above the sharecroppers and tenant farmers of both races who populated the rural South, the Bryants in particular lacked economic security.[26] Whiteness established the code in which "protecting" white womanhood enabled violence against African Americans. Relying on idealized images of white womanhood to strengthen white racial dominance was surely not new in 1955;[27] doing so, however, meant something different when it drew on a prevailing emphasis on motherhood to contest a burgeoning racial liberalism.

Although for Bryant and Milam definitions of masculine power and respectable womanhood were informed by both race and class, over the course of the trial their class status was curiously elided. Indeed, for racially conservative white southerners defending the two men, Milam and Bryant became symbols of all that was good about the middle-class white family—veritable commercials for *Father Knows Best:* clean-cut, seemingly pillars in their communities; quintessential family men; veterans of the Korean war; and "heroes."

Consequently, Carolyn Bryant had access to the image of motherhood as the ultimate state of womanhood despite her family's financial insecurities. The "feminine mystique" might envision women in middle-class suburbia and in fact rely on an economic expansion that depended on working women's labor outside the home; nevertheless, symbolically this ideology of womanhood accommodated *all* white women. *Mama,* for example, a popular television program on CBS, celebrated a working-class Norwegian immigrant family, especially the hard-working but domestic "mama" of the title. A 1956 *Look* magazine on American women lauded "this wondrous creature" who "married younger than ever, bears more babies and looks and acts far more feminine than the emancipated girl of the 1920s or even 1930s. *Steelworker's wife and Junior Leaguer alike* do their own housework." [28] Carolyn Bryant, twenty-one years old in 1955, was married and had two young sons; she worked in her home as well as in the small country store she and her husband struggled to maintain. She too, then, was a "wondrous creature."

African American motherhood was far more fraught with potential pitfalls and damaging effects, according to "race relations" authorities in sociology and psychology in this period. In part because of discriminatory hiring practices toward black men, a third of all black wives worked for wages in 1950, compared to a quarter of all married women in the population.[29] Nevertheless, as black women struggled to support and care for their families, twentieth-century race relations scholarship rendered them the cause of "Negro pathology" and as "not only damaged but also as *damaging* to black masculinity" and the black community generally.[30] According to an emerging consensus of liberal researchers led by E. Franklin Frazier in the 1940s, unmarried or otherwise overly dominating black mothers (the "matriarchy") transmitted "loose sexual behavior" and caused "moral degeneracy" in their children.[31]

By the 1950s, in part the result of the ascendancy of Frazier's theories, matriarchy and black pathology had become so interwoven, particularly for progressive intellectuals fighting discrimination, that "black departures from patriarchal gender relations and white-defined sexual norms became equated with the Negro's cultural inferiority and therefore inequality." [32] According to this analysis of race relations, to fight both racism and "Negro pathology" black men and women had to adhere to "traditional" (white-defined) gender roles. In this contradictory context Bradley's "credentials" as a mother, as a working single mother especially, were highly contested issues. Those who condemned the murder required confirmation that Bradley was a good mother and an appropriately feminine woman.

Thus, for Till defenders, constructing Mamie Bradley as a respectable mother was a means through which African Americans could assert their right to the American credo of equal rights to all.[33] The message was that if Till came from a family that loved him, that cried for him—a "good" family— then his murder, and racial discrimination generally, violated these American values. Indeed, the degree to which Till had been successfully mothered would corroborate his innocence and his "Americanism." His identity as an innocent victim depended on his position as a son in a stable family.

Mamie Till Bradley worked as a voucher examiner in Chicago's Air Force Procurement Office and earned $3,900 annually, well above the median income of black families in this period. Bradley could afford the $11.10 ticket for her son to take the segregated train for a vacation in Mississippi.[34] That the urban-bred Till was killed while vacationing in the country—a wholesome teenage experience gone awry—was not lost on observers, particularly sympathetic whites. "The boy's mother could not send him to the mountains, not to the seashore," editorialized *Commonweal*. "His uncle is poor and his home is a cabin, but to the boy from Chicago's streets, a vacation in Mississippi sounded fine." Race had intruded into the vacation, continued this editorial, and "tragically, a mother's world came to an end and thousands of Negroes stood in line to see what a vacation in Mississippi had done to one of their sons." [35] In 1955, a vacation was a desirable and potent symbol, signifying respectability, a healthy family life, and a strenuous work ethic that entitled one to leisure. Situating the teenager on vacation was a way of assigning a respectable and moral middle-class ethos to Till and his mother; indeed, garnering sympathy from progressive white audiences depended in part on erasing her race and foregrounding this middle-class lifestyle as a sign of respectability.

Within Chicago's black community, however, visiting southern kin had a long history and neither salary nor class position necessarily reflected a person's status or respectability. "What's a Middle Classer?" asked a *Chicago Defender* editorial unrelated to Till's murder. The answer, in a complex interweaving of class and race, indicted the African American "so-called middle class" for "adding to the racial separation" and indicted the poor who "strive to be middle class with a two car garage, a bath room and a powder room." Middle classers are "eagle-eyed against 'rosion' and 'intrusion,' they are America's most vigilant snobs."[36] For black women in particular, money or class position did not confer respectability. The Association of Mannequins' tenth annual "Ten Best-Dressed Women" awards, for example, honored "those women of the Race who have achieved an appearance that is fashionable and *appropriate. . . .* such women help to hold high the standard of good grooming . . . they deserve the accolade of best dressed, *regardless of financial status.*"[37] One columnist bemoaned the black working woman who "flaunts her independence and makes it clear that she can take care of herself. She resents and resists any inclinations to lean upon a man and to seek his help. She hardly ever cries."[38] A woman's competitive salary, then, was dangerous, even if it might enable a seemingly respectable middle-class lifestyle, because it endangered the equally important respectable femininity. These ideas would culminate in *The Black Bourgeoisie,* E. Franklin Frazier's scathing critique of an effeminate and frivolous black middle class. Women play a salient role in this analysis, appearing as selfish social climbers, dominating emasculators, and sexually frustrated self-haters—all qualities that Mamie Till Bradley would have to avoid in order to "earn" the politically necessary designation of respectable mother.[39]

As coverage of Till's funeral, trial, and protest rallies indicate, Bradley's "status" as a good mother and a respectable, feminine woman was as precarious as it was essential to a condemnation of the murder. Reestablishing the innocence and respectability of both Emmett Till and his mother was of particular importance to antiracists because of accusations that Till had violated racial and sexual boundaries. Bradley needed to confirm her role as a respectable mother in order for her son to be cast as an "innocent victim," but she needed to do so along multiple valences: to emerge as protective to Emmett, yet not emasculating; fashionable and well-groomed, yet not ostentatious and luxury laden; hardworking, yet not ambitious; and "universal" enough to attract the sympathy of whites without distancing herself from the black community.

"Mother Breaks Down": Constructing Mamie Till Bradley

Mamie Bradley learned on Wednesday, September 1, that her son's corpse had been discovered in the Tallahatchie River. Till's body then became the physical sign of what Mississippi wanted to forget and Bradley wanted remembered. The sheriff of Tallahatchie County and soon-to-be vocal defender of Bryant and Milam, Harold Strider, ordered that Till be buried in Mississippi—immediately. But Bradley insisted that her son's body be returned for burial in Chicago. "We [relatives] called the governor [William Stratton, Illinois governor], we called the sheriff. . . . We called everybody we thought would be able to stop the burial," she later explained. To the sympathetic white and black press in the North chronicling Till's murder, it was "the grieving mother of a Chicago boy" who "barely averted" this "hasty burial." [40]

When the casket arrived in Chicago, Bradley insisted that it be opened so that she could know for sure that it carried her son. And at that point, when she saw Till's beaten and bullet-ridden body, she decided he would have an open-casket funeral to "let the people see what they have done to my boy!" [41] Till's body lay first at Rayner Funeral Home and then at Roberts Temple of the Church of God in Christ until the burial on Tuesday, September 6. Thousands stood in long lines winding around the block outside the church to view the disfigured corpse dressed in a suit and the three enlarged photographs of Emmett Till in life. A public-address system broadcast the Saturday memorial service to crowds outside the church. Bradley postponed the burial for a day so that the many who wanted to could pay their respects. [42] Estimates regarding attendance vary, ranging from ten thousand to six hundred thousand, but there was little dispute that "the memorial service for young Till" had mobilized Chicago's "Negro community as it has not been over any similar act in recent history." [43]

Emmett Till's funeral blurred the boundaries between public and private; as a result of the open casket, his body and the individual pain he endured became the locus for a collective political mobilization of African Americans demanding citizenship for all blacks. [44] At the same time, this collective mobilization occurred on gender-specific terms. As thousands passed the bier, for example, one observer noted that "stern men gritted their teeth and turned tear-filled faces away from the ghastly sight, while women screamed and fainted." [45] Indeed, images of femininity were consistently central to the meaning of Till's death and funeral. And because the meanings of motherhood and respectability were so negotiable, crucial "American" categories—motherhood, femininity, citizenship, and respectability—were invoked and contested during the funeral, during the trial, and during the protest rallies before and after the trial.

The symbolic construction of Mamie Till Bradley during the funeral provided the basis on which Till's murder was challenged and at once afforded Bradley a degree of power even as it contained her. Sympathetic accounts of the funeral and protest rallies offered images of her that reconciled the various positive meanings of motherhood and respectability. She was represented not just as a mother but as *"Mrs.* Mamie Till Bradley," "a cautious, God-fearing, law-abiding mother." [46] In photographs, she was frequently flanked by ministers or pictured in familial domestic settings, "the elm-shaped stretch of St. Lawrence Avenue where Bobo [Emmett's nickname] lived. It is a family neighborhood where many own the buildings where they live." [47] Descriptions of Till as "polite and mild-mannered . . . with a near-perfect attendance at Sunday School" enhanced the image of Bradley as a good mother. A neighbor shared an anecdote when the dutiful son "was going to surprise his mother with a cake." One photograph even pictured Mamie Bradley holding a dog; according to the caption, "Mike [the dog] keeps nightly vigil in the boy's room, not knowing that his young master will never play with him any more." [48]

Mamie Bradley's patriotism was another component in her construction. *Newsweek* reported her "concern that the murder would be used by the Communists for anti-American propaganda." [49] (According to one account, Bradley "found it necessary to play sick . . . as a means of ducking 'Red' rallies"— a curious example of women's notoriety for dissemblance harnessed to patriotism.[50]) Patriotism was invoked most explicitly in ubiquitous accounts that the "bereaved mother" was the widow of a war hero. "Private Louis Till must have turned in his grave last week" began one account of the murder. Bradley had suffered "a double tragedy . . . for the boy's father had died abroad as a soldier in World War II." Indeed, Louis Till's allegedly heroic death was the cornerstone to a dramatic editorial in *Life,* saturated with religious imagery comparing Till to Jesus. Southerners who condoned the murder "are in far worse danger than Emmett Till ever was. He had only his life to lose, and many others have done that, including his soldier father who was killed in France fighting for the American proposition that all men are equal." [51] The condemnation of the murder in *Life* and elsewhere thus relied on Louis Till's heroism and patriotism.

But being religious, familial, and patriotic was not sufficient in the construction of Mamie Bradley as an appropriate symbol of exemplary motherhood and womanhood. References to Bradley as "the attractive Chicago woman" abound and serve multiple functions.[52] To some degree, the equation between "successful" womanhood and physical appeal suggests that certain types of sexism knew no racial boundaries. "At What Age Is a Woman Most Beautiful?" queried *Jet* (shortly after an issue with pages of bathing-suit-clad "1955 Calendar Girls").[53] But stories and advertisements that seemed simply to highlight black women's physical appeal "counter[ed] the image of black women as domestic drudges."[54] A repeated emphasis on Bradley's stylish appearance and physical appeal thus contested a racially specific standard of womanhood and beauty that had historically excluded black women. Photographs and physical descriptions of both Emmett Till and Mamie Bradley were integral to coverage of the case. Their bodies became icons and, in evoking horror and pleasure respectively, were agents in the politicization of the murder.

Simultaneously, images of Bradley as "well-dressed" or attractive reassured readers that she was "feminine," had not usurped any "male" prerogatives, and was ladylike—all without being overtly sexual.[55] Descriptions of her appearance and body, and references to her as "Till's Mom," tend to appear at precisely those moments when she was most public—during public speeches or her testimony at the trial, for example—and thus "prove" that while she might make her private grief a public and political issue, she was not questioning that feminine private role as her primary source of identity. In New York, "Mamie Bradley hardly had time to powder her nose from the time she stepped off a plane until after the rally."[56] Bradley had brought a long-denied racial violence and motherhood into the public and political sphere. These transgressions needed to be contained, even by her "supporters."

Bradley's emotionalism and her consequent dependence on men or male-dominated institutions were the crucial components in assuaging doubts regarding her respectability and motherhood. From the outset, her weakness, even hysteria, and her need to defer to men confirmed her femininity and her religiosity and were vehicles for asserting Bradley's "authenticity" as an American woman and mother. "Mother Breaks Down" announced the *Chicago Tribune*. "Mother's Tears Greet Son Who Died a Martyr" proclaimed the *Chicago Defender*. She was a woman "limp with grief"; an accompanying photograph showed her in a wheelchair, "sobbing" and "near collapse."[57] Bradley's physical weakness was politically valuable—an important resource in the mobilizations the trial generated—even as the emphasis on her body's limits suggested that, somehow, she was not a part of the active political community around her seeking power.

Contemporary depictions and subsequent analyses of the funeral are more readily understandable in this context. For although numerous accounts acknowledge that Mamie Bradley insisted on the open-casket funeral, representations of her as hysterical obscured her role in this political process.[58] Emotion, long coded as a feminine quality, precluded consideration of her as a political player, even as foregrounding emotionalism afforded Bradley some moral and maternal authority. Evidence indicates, however, that this emotionally infused decision was neither haphazard nor apolitical. "Lord, you gave your only son to remedy a condition, but who knows, but what the death of my only son might bring an end to lynching!" she said when she first saw the body at

This full-page photo spread reinforced the construction of Mamie Till Bradley as "grieving mother," dependent on clergy, other men, or her own mother. *Courtesy of the* Chicago Defender

Illinois Central Station. In the days before the burial Bradley explained that "she wanted people 'to realize the threat to Negroes in the Deep South and to what extent the fiendish mobs would go to display their hate.' "[59] Opening the casket, then, represented a challenge to false though enduring dichotomies between political, public (and masculine) subject and emotional, private (and feminine) nonsubject.

Segregationists and others drew on these same values—religion, family, patriotism, and femininity—to paint a very different picture of Mamie Bradley. The funeral was not a religious event but a fund-raising spectacle that attracted "curiosity seekers" because "against the advice of the undertakers" Bradley had insisted that the casket be opened—"macabre exhibitionism" according to a "moderate" southern newspaper. In these accounts, "Mamie Bradley of Chicago" was not a religious woman, but (at best) a pawn of NAACP "rabble rousers"; the funeral was not a religious ritual with political meaning but cheap "exploitation."[60] According to journalist William Bradford Huie, at the funeral "cash was collected at the bier in wastebaskets: Mamie Bradley received five thousand dollars the first week. . . . The explosion was a godsend to the NAACP. . . . It was a godsend to the Negro press."[61] Suggesting that the NAACP exploited Till's death also cast suspicion on Bradley's status as a mourning mother experiencing "authentic" grief in her church.

Milam and Bryant defenders also drew on a discourse of patriotism. Accusations ranged from the NAACP being "Red-inspired" to suggestions that a communist–NAACP plot had staged the murder to make the South—and the United States—look bad abroad. After Milam and Bryant had been acquitted, southern reporters learned that the army had hanged Louis Till in Italy for alleged murder and rape; Mississippi Senators James O. Eastland and John Stennis had obtained and released the information from the War Department. Although the details remained unclear, this news was the "most explosive of the developments" in the Till case, according to the *New York Times*. *Till's Dad Raped 2 Women, Murdered a Third in Italy,* shouted an oversized headline on the front page of one Mississippi paper.[62] To many, clearly, "like father like son"; given racist sterotypes of black men, if Louis Till had been hanged for rape, then his son must certainly have been guilty. Not only was Emmett's innocence imperiled, but so too were his family's claims to Americanism and Bradley's claims to respectable motherhood.

Images of Carolyn Bryant as a victim and as the wife of a hero provided the necessary antithesis to the rendering of Mamie Bradley as greedy, unfeeling, and unwomanly. One reporter, for example, located Mamie Till Bradley at Emmett's heavily publicized funeral where "a collection was *still* being taken up at his casket," in the same story that located Carolyn Bryant "in seclusion" (with her two sons of course). Carolyn, according to her mother-in-law, "went all to pieces after the incident. She has been unable to sleep and has to take sedatives." [63]

Indeed, opposing images of Mamie Till Bradley or Carolyn Bryant as *the* good or *the* bad woman were central to both indictments and defenses of the murder. The meaning of Till's death evolved out of these binary views of "good" versus "bad" women, which in turn suggested who was victim and who was perpetrator. In the *Chicago Defender,* for example, Mamie Bradley, the "grief-stricken mother" and innocent victim, was set against a photograph of Carolyn Bryant with the caption "The Cause of It All." [64] Similarly, according to at least one southern white woman, Till had died because his mother "permit[ted] her boy to visit here. . . . *She* should have had better sense than to let such a child come here." [65] Rendering either woman the "cause" of Till's murder deflected attention away from Roy Bryant and J. W. Milam and exemplified how women became sites for social anxieties regardless of whether or not they had access to power. [66]

The discourse in which Mamie Bradley appeared as greedy and unmaternal, on the one hand, and hysterical and unrefined on the other, and morally weak in any case, spun together racial and gender stereotypes that coded emotionalism as an inherently feminine and "negro" quality. This race/gender analogue conceptualizing African Americans as a weak and "feminine" race dated back to antebellum antislavery campaigns, and these links between African Americans and femininity pervade both racist and antiracist constructions of Mamie Bradley. [67] Huie, for example, sought "the truth" about the murder but also disapproved of the "emotional explosion" of the open-casket funeral, where "the corpse was displayed 'as is' to thousands of cursing, shrieking, fainting Negroes." [68] He and others scorned the primitive qualities—coded as feminine *and* black—they saw in the funeral.

Significantly, however, the antiracist construction of Bradley coded emotionalism as an inherently and exclusively feminine quality and thus rested on sexist stereotypes that undermined black women's strength and political agency. Only ostensible dependence and weakness enabled Bradley to transgress certain boundaries. It was permissible for her to go to Mississippi for the trial or attend protest rallies, since she had the support of her "advisers," was "accompanied by her father," and had deferred to the NAACP to prevent communist-front organizations from "trying to line her up for big meetings." She might recount events at the trial at a New York rally in a "calm intelligent voice," but she would be speaking from her "heart" and as "the victim's mother" exclusively. And she might even plan a civil suit against the Bryants and raise funds for the NAACP, but that was commended because she had abdicated control "and is placing her crusade in the hands of the NAACP." [69]

These contradictory configurations of race and sex, and the degree to which emotionalism was a sign for race or for gender would be even more pronounced during the trial of Roy Bryant and J. W. Milam—a trial in which far more was being judged than the actions of two men.

"Who Else Could Identify That Child?": Black Motherhood on Trial

The murder trial of Roy Bryant and J. W. Milam began on September 19, 1955, in Sumner, Mississippi. Above a Coca-Cola billboard, a sign welcomed some seventy reporters to a town with a population of 527: *Sumner, A Good Place to Raise a Boy.*[70] Here, for five brutally hot days, competing notions of womanhood, motherhood, and respectability—what it actually meant to raise a son successfully—occupied center stage and helped determine the outcome of the trial. Few had expected a conviction of two white men for the murder of a black teenager. Criteria for the defense and acquittal of the two men, however, revolved around a racially specific gender discourse that excluded Mamie Till Bradley. The defense refused to acknowledge that a black woman could be a worthy mother, and the prosecution countered by asserting a universal version of motherhood that crossed racial boundaries. Nevertheless, this assertion of universal motherhood, radical as it could be, further circumscribed Bradley and was, in any event, compromised by other constructions of her as a racialized mother, used by the prosecution as well as the defense. Meanings of motherhood, then, were central in the outcome of what has been hailed exclusively as a "race relations" battle.

The state presented its case first. Special prosecutor Robert Smith III and District Attorney Gerald Chatham offered six witnesses who confirmed the fact that Milam and Bryant had kidnapped Till and, with Bradley's testimony, confirmed the identity of the body found in the river three days later. Two "surprise witnesses" filled in some of the intervening time, testifying that they had seen Till with Milam and Bryant in a truck and had heard them beating the youth in a barn.[71] Moses Wright, a sixty-four-year-old preacher and sharecropper, "Uncle Mose" to defense attorneys and simply "Mose" to the prosecution, stood up in the witness chair and, with his "Dar he" and an outstretched arm, identified J. W. Milam and Bryant as Till's abductors.[72]

Four key witnesses for the defense raised questions regarding the identity of Till's body on the one hand and reminded the all-male, all-white jury of his alleged advances toward Carolyn Bryant on the other.[73] These strategies simultaneously cast doubts on the death and implied that in any case, it had been deserved. Sheriff Strider asserted that the body had been in the water for "at least ten days, if not fifteen," so it could not be Till's. "Experts"—physicians and morticians L. B. Otken and H. D. Malone—agreed and elaborated; the former testified that no one could identify this body because *even* the race of the body was a mystery.[74]

That motherhood and its power knew no lines of race—and challenges to this perspective—began during coverage of the funeral and continued in representations of Mamie Bradley during the trial. It "was her duty as a mother" to be in Mississippi, according to forty out of fifty blacks polled in the Washington, D.C., area; but, as her (male) "spokesperson" conveyed to the press and to District Attorney Gerald Chatham, she would not travel to Mississippi without official protection. As one headline proclaimed, *Mother Arrives with Her Pastor.* Her agreement to testify reinforced the image that Bradley was a mourning mother, committed to her dead son's memory. Speaking through a spokesperson, appearing most frequently with two male relatives "who stood like bodyguards," and demanding protection for herself further reinforced the image that she was a respectable woman, who adhered to "traditional" gender roles.[75]

This position was in fact highly untraditional. Mamie Bradley effectively drew attention to a long history of black women's physical vulnerability at the hands of white men. By insisting on physical protection, she challenged assumptions about black women's promiscuity; moreover, she bridged the chasm between women that had enabled the dichotomy between "chaste white woman" and "promiscuous black woman" to persist.[76] As well, in accommodating the two positions of mourning—emotional mother and public, respectable woman—in suggesting that emotional expressiveness and public decisiveness could co-exist, Mamie Till Bradley bridged the chasm between the public man and the private woman.

White supremacists repeatedly challenged this view of womanhood that crossed racial boundaries. Many southern newspapers suggested that Bradley's wariness about coming to Mississippi stemmed not from her physical vulnerability but from her indifference toward her son. According to the *Memphis Commercial Appeal*, District Attorney Chatham had to remind Bradley, repeatedly, of her duties as a mother: "It is important to the state's case that you appear," said one telegram. "Your failure to make yourself available as a witness for the state is not understandable." [77] Indeed, Till opponents would permit no rivals to their racially specific version of womanhood. According to one southern paper, Mamie Bradley, "the fashionably dressed Negro woman . . . caused a sensation [among the press] when she walked into the courtroom flanked by her father and advisers" and consequently "swept an expression of almost painful dislike across the faces of local spectators." [78]

The juxtaposition of Mamie Till Bradley to Carolyn Bryant escalated throughout the trial. Contrasting images of the two were central to competing views of who—and what—was on trial. Captions below adjacent head shots of "Mrs. Carolyn Bryant" and "Mrs. Mamie Bradley" in the *Pittsburgh Courier,* for example, were "doesn't like whistles" and "would avenge her son." While "Mrs. Bradley" was "plump and dimpled," the "coldly attractive" Carolyn Bryant appeared in "a family portrait which can be described in one word: unhappy." [79]

Similarly, those hoping to preserve the racial status quo relied on images of Carolyn Bryant to convey the message that the white nuclear family itself was on trial and must be preserved at all costs. Cooperative if embarrassed, Carolyn Bryant "wore a black dress with a white collar and red sash" on the stand and "demurely told a court" that "a Negro man" (the teenage Till) had grabbed her. One defense attorney positioned himself as Till to re-create the alleged scene between them. Judge Swango ruled that most of her testimony was inadmissible to the jury; *Woman's Story Barred,* explained one headline. Nevertheless, she was still regarded as the "key witness" for the defense, and jury members (who had heard these accusations previously) were reminded of the threats to "the pretty brunette" when they were briefly removed from the courtroom.[80] Carolyn Bryant's name rarely appears anywhere without the adjectives "attractive," "comely," or even more typically, as "Roy Bryant's wife, an attractive twenty-one-year-old mother." *Newsweek* successfully condensed the multiple attributes of respectable white motherhood into one sentence: "It was Bryant's wife, Carolyn, an attractive, dark-haired mother of two, whom Emmett was accused of insulting." [81]

Carolyn Bryant was thus central in the campaign to underscore her husband's innocence and to cast him, too, as a respectable and upstanding southern citizen. *Wives Serious, Children Romp as Trial Begins,* declared one headline, in a story with detailed attention to Milam and Bryant playing peek-a-boo with their "four handsome sons" as attorneys selected the jury. While guards frisked African Americans at the door of the jammed courtroom and had them sit at a segregated, crowded bridge table, Milam and Bryant came to the courtroom with "their wives and children" in a new "green 1955 Chevrolet" and sat "quietly and without handcuffs." The two men received daily shaves at the Sumner barber shop and lunched with the wealthy Sheriff Strider "at an air conditioned cafe." [82] In many respects, the trial deflected attention away from class differences in Mississippi and provided Bryant and Milam and their families access to middle-class standards and values—temporarily.[83] That segregationists managed to shape the trial into a tale about the white nuclear family tragically imperiled by Emmett Till and his family is evident in coverage of the acquittal: The not-guilty verdict marked a "happy ending" and was "a signal for Roy Bryant and his half brother J. W. Milam to kiss their wives." The sheer repetition of these accounts—of the two lighting cigars, of the women, both "the mother of two small sons," smiling radiantly—serve to celebrate the reconstituted white families.[84]

Mamie Bradley's testimony was the crucial space in which motherhood's meaning as universal or racially specific was negotiated. Because the defense challenged the identity of the body, her identification based on her authority as "the boy's mother" was pivotal; she was the "expert."[85] Bradley testified on Thursday, September 22, that she knew that the body was that of her son because she had "recognized Emmett's hair line, his hair, the general shape of his nose and his teeth. Especially his teeth, because I used to tell him daily to take care of his teeth." The jury could not discount Bradley's identification, according to Robert Smith in his closing statement, because "the last thing in God's creation a mother wants is to believe that her son is dead." Prosecutor Gerald Chatham concurred. "Who else could identify that child?" he asked dramatically. "Who else could say, 'That's my boy'?"[86] Black women "too," this argument went, loved and cared for their offspring and recognized their bodies almost viscerally.

But on closer inspection, "the grief-stricken mother's" authority was in fact predicated on racially specific behavior; further, assertions of universal womanhood were highly problematic and based on gendered distinctions between public and private.[87] Once again, Mamie Bradley's efforts to define herself as a subject were open to manipulation on all sides. First, as had been the case throughout the funeral and the rallies, Bradley had to "prove" that she had been a good mother to Till and had raised him "correctly." Concern about juvenile delinquency was widespread in 1955, and ineffective parenting was perceived as causing this new social ailment. "Discipline is a must, starting in infancy," stressed one advice column.[88] Mamie Bradley thus testified that she had warned Till "to be very careful" in Mississippi, cautioning him to "say 'yes sir' and 'no, ma'am'" and "to humble himself to the extent of getting down on his knees" to whites if necessary.[89] This portion of her testimony—widely quoted in the white press, North and South—indicates that Bradley had to prove herself a credible mother not in "universal" but in racialized and racist terms. Assigning guilt to Bryant and Milam required proof that Mamie Till Bradley had raised her son to "know his place"—specifically, to know his race—and that being polite and respectful was itself constructed by race.[90]

Second, Bradley's expressiveness during her testimony was highly contested, intersecting as it did with assumptions about respectability and motherhood, race, and gender. According to the *New York Times,* "young Till's mother . . . stoutly maintained that the dead body sent to her was that of her son. . . . Mrs. Bradley was a composed and well-spoken witness," who, when shown photographs of her son's body, "removed her glasses and wiped at her eyes." [91] In choosing to maintain her composure throughout these public proceedings, Bradley resisted gender and racial stereotypes that rendered women and African Americans emotional and lacking control.

Nevertheless, many Till defenders who condemned Milam and Bryant did not mention self-control; instead, Bradley was represented as a highly emotional "tragic figure" who "wept on the witness stand as she identified a police picture of the body of her son. . . . She ran her hand quickly across her eyes as tears trickled down her cheeks." [92] More "objective" accounts, too, foregrounded her inability to control her emotions as "proof" of her maternal authority. "The boy's mother, Mrs. Mamie Bradley, a $3,600 civil-service employee, weepingly told the jury that she was certain the body was that of her son," wrote *Newsweek*.[93] Images of the "naturally" emotionally distressed mother were resources in the condemnation of the verdict; those fighting racism *needed* Mamie Till Bradley to express her private emotions to corroborate her femininity and her maternalism. To Till defenders, private emotion was a sign for gender, "evidence" of her womanliness, which surpassed that of Carolyn Bryant, and of respectable gender difference among African Americans generally.[94]

The jury of white southern men "chose to believe" that the body was not Till's as a way to acquit Milam and Bryant and preserve power relations in Mississippi. "What could a black mother say that would be of any value?" asked *L'Aurore,* a French daily.[95] They thus rejected Bradley's identification of the body and rejected a definition of "natural" motherhood that included black women, privileging instead the rational, "scientific" testimony of the "experts." The jury's dismissal of her testimony derived from what they perceived as her *lack* of authentic expression of maternal grief. "If she had tried a little harder," said jury foreman J. A. Shaw, "she might have got out a tear." [96] In this interview with Shaw, in fact, Bradley emerges a manipulative, defeminized woman who did not cry "naturally" and had thus forfeited her moral and maternal authority to identify her son's body.[97] This depiction was consistent with racist representations of the funeral and the protest rallies: Bradley was not a "natural" mother because she did not express or experience true grief; she was, instead, a public performer of sorts, capitalizing on her son's death. This version of Mamie Bradley as morally undeveloped and unwomanly drew on race and gender-specific constructions of morality and motherhood.

In sum, during the trial, Bradley's potential power as a respectable African American mother was simultaneously subversive and reactionary. Her authority as a mother relied on racist assumptions that required Till to be "humble" and on an essentialist discourse that required mothers to be emotionally overwrought. And the all-male, all-white jury rejected even these conditional sources of power. "Where else," asked liberal critic I. F. Stone, "would a mother be treated with such elementary lack of respect and compassion?"[98] Racially specific constructions of both motherhood and respectability prevailed in Sumner, most powerfully evoked in photographs of the reconstituted Bryant and Milam families. But, significantly, Mamie Bradley chose not to be in the courtroom when the jury returned the verdict. "I was expecting an acquittal," she said, "and I didn't want to be there when it happened."[99] Her absence indicated her ongoing rejection of the values through which the verdict had been offered and her refusal to be contained—even in the walls of the courtroom. Even as Mamie Bradley absented herself, she further exposed the inequities of the southern judicial system; or in the words of one front-page editorial, the unpunished murder of blacks now lay "Naked Before the World!"[100]

"What Is True Story about Mrs. Bradley?": The Tide Turns

Protest rallies continued for six to eight weeks after the acquittal of Bryant and Milam, with their focus shifting from the case itself to the ongoing battle for African American citizenship and civil rights. It was time to "stop being emotional and start being smart," according to NAACP executive secretary Roy Wilkins. "Worry about those who are alive," said NAACP lawyer Thurgood Marshall at a New York protest rally and repeatedly urged the crowd to register to vote.[101] The NAACP placed a nearly full-page advertisement in the *New York Times* on October 3 entitled *Help End Racial Tyranny in Mississippi*. The ad detailed a "slaughter of personal rights" that included "Three Unpunished Murders—Open Defiance of Supreme Court School Decree" and "Over 900,000 Mississippi Negroes without an Effective Voice in Their Government" and concluded that Till's murder "climaxed a series of blows to American ideals that has horrified the country." Within a month, the ad generated $5,500 in donations and multiple requests for similar fund-raising appeals from newspapers across the country.[102] But the sympathetic construction of Mamie Bradley as the perfect mother—respectable, all-American, feminine, and deferential—did not persist alongside this bid for equal rights.

On November 8, the NAACP publicly severed its relationship with Mamie Bradley. The rupture—or divorce, as the marriage metaphors suggest—occurred as rumors regarding the propriety of Till-related fund-raising drives percolated, immediately after a grand jury refused to indict Milam and Bryant on kidnapping charges, and on the eve of Bradley's NAACP-sponsored West Coast speaking tour. Executive Secretary Roy Wilkins publicly condemned Bradley's request ·for remuneration, declaring that the "NAACP does not handle such matters on a commercial basis." Shortly thereafter, NAACP attorney William Henry Huff resigned as her legal representative. Reporters wondered, *Will Mamie, NAACP Kiss, Make Up?* but the organization quickly made the separation official when they arranged for Moses Wright to replace Bradley on the West Coast speaking tour.[103]

The conflict triggered a transformation in constructions of Mamie Till Bradley within the African American press that drew with remarkable consistency on entrenched images of motherhood and respectability. NAACP officials implied and others concurred that if Till's mother had asked for a $5,000 fee for public speaking engagements, she was neither a respectable woman nor a good mother, and in fact was little better than racist representations had suggested all along. Whereas those who defended Mamie Till Bradley did so by emphasizing her gullibility, vulnerability, and poor judgment—qualities implicit in earlier positive depictions of her.[104] No one changed the terms of this debate by suggesting that as a public figure working exclusively for the NAACP—she had been on an unpaid leave of absence from her job since Till's murder—Bradley might be entitled to a professional salary or might even be ambitious. Both sides in this conflict, then, reinscribed motherhood as a private, pure, and apolitical role—the very assumptions that Mamie Bradley had troubled.

As a result, the antiracist dichotomy that pit the good, respectable, and maternal Mamie Till Bradley against the bad, immoral, and cold Carolyn Bryant was reconfigured. Polarized views of good versus bad woman endured, but were now contained in opposing views of one woman—Mamie Bradley. Or in the words of one headline, *What Is True Story about Mrs. Bradley?*[105]

The backdrop to this "rift over money" was the ongoing negotiation of respectability and motherhood as each informed civil rights activism. From the moment that Mamie Bradley helped make her son's death a public issue, there were those who expressed concern about the money being raised. Fears of exploitation were allayed with guarantees that funds were for the collective cause rather than for personal gain. Immediately after the funeral, for example, the *Chicago Daily Tribune* reported that "the mother" authorized the NAACP to use donations made in her behalf for legal expenses the Till case incurred. Local NAACP branches asked churches to assume fund-raising responsibilities to ensure an air of virtue to these campaigns; the organization designated October 2 "NAACP Church Day."[106] By mid-October, however, hostility toward "the sycophants, moochers, jackals and charlatans who are always ready to ply their trade of capitalizing on human outrage" and who were "as busy as a pack of vultures on a freshly killed carcass in the Till case" would not be quelled—and were fueled by anger about the acquittal. "It is the opinion of myself and perhaps that of thousands of other Negroes throughout the country," wrote an Ohio woman, that "if the NAACP had worked as hard presenting evidence in the Till case as they did collecting money, more would have been done to convict the suspects. . . . The NAACP [should] make publicly known the amount of money they collected and the amount to which they have participated in gathering evidence in the Till case." [107] Proliferating rumors were evident in their denial: William Henry Huff, for example, issued a formal statement that he was not "clearing a lot of money in the unfortunate Till case"; in another instance, an editorial assured readers that Bradley "is taking her job very seriously of speaking out against the lynching of her son . . . in spite of reports to the contrary, she is not making any profits from her appearances." [108]

During the period after the trial, representations of Bradley continued to underscore her emotionalism and dependence on men and her relative unimportance to the larger political forces around her: "HEAR THE MISSISSIPPI STORY!! FROM THE LIPS AND HEARTS OF EMMETT TILL'S MOTHER and Mrs. Ruby Hurley," said one advertisement; the name "MRS. MAMIE BRADLEY" appears in parentheses, in small type and below "EMMETT TILL'S MOTHER." [109] According to a "verbal agreement" made in mid-October, the NAACP *exclusively* would coordinate Bradley's public appearances during her unpaid leave of absence from her job; the "mother of the slain boy" was to be at their disposal. [110]

Nevertheless, while her deference was highlighted and her authority emanated from these seemingly traditional sources, Bradley was increasingly a public figure with something to say. In late October, she went to Washington, D.C., in an (unsuccessful) effort to urge federal intervention into the case and to speak before the Senate Subcommittee on Constitutional Rights. [111] This extension of her public role was met by many with surprise, if not derision. "The demand for Mrs. Bradley at these mass meetings is astounding," wrote one black male columnist. Following her Washington, D.C., trip, a *Chicago Defender* editorial referred to "*Mamie,* who is really learning fast the ways of public officials." [112] The tension between two positions—grieving mother and public figure—was evident when Mamie Bradley asserted at a rally in New York that perhaps her sacrifice had not been in vain, if "a little nobody like me and a little nobody like my boy can arouse the nation." [113] It was this tension which could not be sustained indefinitely.

Doubts about Mamie Bradley's role, allegations about the propriety of Till fund raising, and frustrations regarding NAACP campaigns for African American citizenship, were resolved conjointly through the "break-up" between the NAACP and Bradley. She became a scapegoat of sorts, a receptacle for anger at the trial's outcome and overlapping anxieties about gender relations and the future of civil rights activism. Many reacted to reports that Bradley had requested a speaking fee by characterizing her as a "mercenary hard-hearted gold digger, seeking to capitalize on the lynching of her child" or a "greedy" woman who "had changed from a simple griefstricken mother to an arrogant celebrity full of her own importance." [114] "Don't Need to Worry About Ma'—

The NAACP promised that Mamie Till Bradley would speak from the "heart" as "Emmett Till's mother," as this announcement suggests. *Courtesy of the* New York Amsterdam News

She's Loaded!" was the title of a sardonic letter in the *New York Amsterdam News,* which described the less-than-positive transformation of one mother after Till's death: "Ordinarily, Ma is the quiet sort and legs it off to church every Sunday. . . . But ever since those two peckerwoods up and killed Mamie Bradley's boy, she's been riled up to the point of blaspheming." This fictional Ma had even "broke loose from her religion and . . . sent the rent money off to the NAACP Legal Fund." [115] With Bradley's credentials as a respectable mother jeopardized, the African American press referred to her simply as "Mamie" with far greater regularity.

But even more significantly, the defense of Bradley depended on her basic inability to conduct herself as a public, political, or professional player—an image that echoed representations of Carolyn Bryant by white supremacists. Reinterpreters of the "misunderstanding" argued that Bradley was "the victim of bad advice" or that the "plain, ordinary woman . . . has been misrepresented by those she trusted." Clearly, she was "ill-prepared for public life" and had been "catapulted from a humdrum existence . . . into a living martyrdom." [116] Defenders also drew attention to Bradley's emotional and physical frailty: Her "nervous condition prevented her handling the business end"; she was "worn to a frazzle," according to Anne B. Crockett, "special representative" to Bradley; and she had yet "to pay her own hospital bill when she suffered a nervous breakdown" (she was hospitalized for "nervous fatigue" in early October).[117] Indeed, Bradley's reaction to the public rebuke *proved* that she was "a sensitive woman": "Her almost complete withdrawal" into "semi-seclusion" followed the canceled speaking tour; the "announcement hit her hard and she hasn't recovered yet." [118]

NAACP leaders had behaved with an "obnoxious display of insensitivity (and) lack of loyalty" toward this "ordinary woman baffled and bewildered," according to Bradley's defenders.[119] A critique of the organization in the *Chicago Defender* titled "Indiscreet Rebuke," carefully reinforced progressive assumptions that more healthful race relations required healthful gender relations, as defined by a middle-class white norm. Although Bradley's "requests for money were seemingly greedy and conscienceless," the male-dominated organization "wield[ed] power in behalf of others" and, as such, had the responsibility to "accept certain disabilities and even tenuous loyalties" and to "renounce" emotional displays and "public demonstrations of petty irritations." By suggesting that the NAACP had erred in departing from traditional gender roles with its unmanly "public demonstration" of displeasure (Wilkins had "snarled," according to *Jet*), these critiques of the organization effectively bolstered the gendered and racialized split between public and private that Mamie Bradley had challenged.[120]

Finally, several of Bradley's defenders argued that she neither requested, demanded, nor perhaps deserved $5,000, and that Franklin Williams, West Coast regional director of the NAACP, made the offer after learning of her mounting expenses.[121] She was thus positioned once again as a passive and nonconfrontational figure being done to rather than actively doing, and as a woman who "wants to make it clear that she is not engaged in a fight with the NAACP" and "was anxious to straighten out the mess." [122] The need for Bradley's defenders to circumscribe her actions and feelings was most evident in coverage of a press conference she held in New York. Headlines such as *NAACP Criticized, Mamie Bradley Says NAACP Used Son,* and *Mother of Till Bitter!* suggested some anger toward the organization. But in the texts, only her father, John Carthan, is "vehement in his condemnation" and legitimizes any request for remuneration. It is he who suggests that Roy Wilkins "was attempting to punish his daughter," that the organization "is using Emmett Till and his mother," or that "as long as my daughter can be useful to them, everything's all right, but the minute she asks for something, it's a different story." With the anger and the demands displaced onto a male authority figure, Bradley emerges as hurt but remarkably conciliatory, "nonetheless hopeful" and "still interested in seeing justice done." [123]

At this press conference, Mamie Till Bradley released a letter she had written to Roy Wilkins after her dismissal from the NAACP. It reveals the contradictory ways in which she defied any one subject position and simultaneously relied on and transgressed gendered and racialized conceptualizations of motherhood, respectability and citizenship:

> The objective of the NAACP is of much greater concern to me than my pocketbook. I set out to trade the blood of my child for the betterment of my race; and I do not now wish to deviate from such course. I feel very bad that the opportunity to talk for the association would be taken from me. I know tht [sic] you have tried very hard and sincerely to see to my day-to-day financial needs. It is unfair and untrue for anyone to say otherwise. If the NAACP is willing to continue to do what it has to defray my travel and living expenses that should suffice. Please let me go forward for the NAACP. It is a duty. I would not want it said that I did anything to shirk it. [124]

Once again Bradley asserted, with some emotion, that the public cause was as important as her personal needs; that her private and maternal grief and her public and political service could and did reinforce each other and did not contradict NAACP claims for black citizenship. Implicit is a critique of political strategies "for the betterment of the race" that segregated these positions. Yet, in this letter, any rebuke is at most, implicit. Mamie Bradley, too, ultimately relied on her authority as a respectable woman and good mother to make her bid for credibility. Indeed, she emerged here as emotional, dutiful, respectful, and conciliatory to NAACP authorities. Ultimately, there may have been no other place from which she might hope to be heard or speak with any degree of authority. For racists, antiracists, and for Mamie Bradley herself, then, the "good mother" was a category potentially beyond criticism and, as such, was a viable if not potent position from which to shape politics.

Conclusion

Mamie Till Bradley's departure from the NAACP lecture and fund-raising circuit was permanent. She returned to school and became a public school teacher. Out of Till's death, she later explained, came a "burning . . . to push education to the limit." [125] But her actions following her son's murder reverberated beyond 1955. An analysis of constructions of her point to the interdependence of assumptions about sexual and racial difference and the interdependence of racial liberalism and sexual conservatism that seem at first to be at odds.

On the one hand, Bradley as symbol and person—the respectable woman, with an authority devolving from motherhood—posed a significant challenge to American power relations: to the racial caste system most prevalent in the South that valorized Carolyn Bryant, to dominant theories of sexual difference that often marginalized and depoliticized women, and to dominant theories of racial difference that held defeminized and emasculating black women responsible for racial inferiority. In laying claim to the overlapping values of the roles of "good mother" and respectable, moral woman, Bradley resisted definitions of womanhood that either excluded black women by virtue of their race or rendered black mothers as dominating and pathological. She politicized and publicized motherhood and racial violence with composure and emotion, dignity and grief.

That women could reach across lines of race, class, and even region to identify with Bradley confirms the subversive potential of explicitly politicizing motherhood in terms that challenged the split between public, masculine citizenship and private, emotional motherhood. "Womanhood without regard to color must be aroused," wrote one New Yorker. Another, a Canadian white woman, wrote to Milam and Bryant, condemning their violation of the "joys of parenthood that are so dear to us all. Young or old, black or white." And writing to Governor Hugh White of Mississippi, "As a white woman, a Texan, an American and the mother of a son," E. H. Johnson asked, "Since when did the testimony of strangers take priority over a mother's identification of a body—a mother who bore and raised the son? Do you think if someone took my boy and beat him to a pulp and threw him in the river, that I couldn't recognize him? . . . Think of his mother. Think of the Negro race. Think of the blot on Mississippi." She concluded by assuring White that she was not a "crackpot" but an "outraged American woman . . . taking action to see that the same justice is given for the death of a Negro boy as I would want for my own son. Do you have a son? How would you feel? Can we do less?" [126] For some, universal definitions of womanhood enabled a condemnation of Bryant and Milam and of American race relations generally.

Further, the political mobilization of blacks that the funeral and rallies helped generate was neither local nor short term. "It was the best advertised lynching that I had ever heard," recalled Amzie Moore, an NAACP Mississippi activist in 1955.[127] With a prescient accuracy, one reporter suggested that Bradley's desire to " 'let the people see' " could "easily become the opening gun in a war on Dixie which can reverberate around the world." [128] "Congratulations to your paper for putting the picture of the murdered Till boy on the front page," wrote one reader, "so the whole world can see what goes on in Mississippi." [129] And the world did see. As the famous and ordinary construct their own memories of that period, the case often figures as a pivotal moment. The teenage Cassius Clay (later Muhammed Ali) "couldn't get Emmett out of my mind." [130] Writing on the twenty-fifth anniversary of the *Brown* decision, sociologist Joyce Ladner recalled that "more than any other single atrocity, the *Jet* magazine photograph of Emmett Till's grotesque body left an indelible impression on many young Southern blacks who, like my sister and I, became the vanguard of the Southern student movement." [131] Bradley's decision to "let the whole world see" was instrumental in the impact the case had on the American body politic.

On the other hand, the symbolic construction of Bradley as a perfect and "natural mother" was fraught with contradictions. Frequent references to Bradley as "the mother" effaced her as a decision-making person even as it empowered her, as was evident during Till's funeral. A cross-racial definition of womanhood and motherhood relied on essentialist assumptions that women were emotional and that their identities were based on the biology of reproduction, as was evident during the trial. And the political impact she had as a speaker and fund raiser was predicated on her deference to the male-dominated NAACP, as was most evident during Mamie Bradley's conflict with the organization. The discourse on motherhood was consistently subject to conservative responses and symbolic manipulation—by both racial conservatives and racial liberals—and the radical potential of her position was thus undercut.

The reactionary responses to Mamie Till Bradley, despite the very different sources from which they sprang, illuminated how ostensibly universal notions of citizenship relied on race and gender. White southerners' efforts to contain her claims to motherhood enabled them to fight *against* racial integration; they claimed racially exclusive rights to respectable, rational, and masculine citizenship by propping up a discourse of white motherhood At the same time, the NAACP's efforts to contain her claims to motherhood enabled them to fight *for* racial integration; they claimed racially inclusive rights to respectable, rational, and masculine citizenship by adhering to traditional gender roles that constrained Mamie Bradley. In either case, notions of citizenship relied on meanings assigned to motherhood.

The ways in which ideas about motherhood and respectability infused and constructed the meaning of this event were not unique. In underscoring the radical potential and political meanings of women's "traditional" roles, Mamie Till Bradley offers an important lens through which to consider continuities in women's activism. This radical potential of traditional roles was realized, for example, by women in the civil rights movement in particular—the women who cooked for and fed civil rights activists, the "mamas" of many southern black communities who formed the "backbone" of the movement.[132] And in exposing how and why both racists and antiracists relied on a discourse of motherhood to contain Mamie Bradley, this incident offers an important lens through which to understand how many seemingly "universal" political categories are in fact gendered and racialized. Indeed, constructions of femininity would play a central though problematic role in civil rights and New Left activism. When Mamie Till Bradley opened her son's casket "to let the people see," she exposed more than her dead son's body. She had the courage and the determination to translate her personal pain and her family's tragedy into political terms. In negotiating her private role as a mother into the public and political sphere, she helped change the terms on which her son's death was understood and debated. Emmett Till was not just another statistic in the tragic history of American lynchings.

NOTES

Acknowledgments: I thank Mari Jo Buhle, Jacqueline Jones, Elaine Tyler May, Joanne Meyerowitz, and Jack Thomas for comments and questions on earlier versions of this essay. I particularly appreciate suggestions and support from Lucy Barber, Krista Comer, Dorothee Cox, Linda Grasso, Andrea Levine, Melani McAlister, Uta Poiger, Miriam Reuman, Jessica Shubow, and Lyde Sizer. Jane Gerhard read countless drafts; her insights and patience were invaluable.

1. Juan Williams, *Eyes on the Prize: America's Civil Rights Years, 1954–1965* (New York: Viking Penguin, 1987), 43; Henry Hampton and Steve Fayer, *Voices of Freedom: An Oral History of the Civil Rights Movement from the 1950s through the 1980s* (New York: Bantam Books, 1990), 1–16. Shortly after the trial, journalist William Bradford Huie paid Milam and Bryant $3,600 to tell "the real story," and they confessed to the murder. Huie's accounts were quite popular and, despite their many ambiguities, are frequently assumed to be the definitive texts on the murder. See William Bradford Huie, *Wolf Whistle* (New York: Signet, 1959); Huie, "The Shocking Story of Approved Killing in Mississippi," *Look*, January 24, 1956, 46–49, and in *Reader's Digest*, April 1956, 57–62; Huie, "What's Happened to the Emmett Till Killers?" *Look*, January 22, 1957, 63–68. Others who have tried to determine just what transpired include Hugh Stephen Whitaker, "A Case Study in Southern Justice: The Emmett Till Case," Master's thesis,

Florida State University, 1963, and Stephen Whitfield, *A Death in the Delta: The Story of Emmett Till* (New York: Free Press, 1988). Yet details regarding these events—the most controversial being whether or not Till actually whistled at Carolyn Bryant and who accompanied Bryant and Milam when they took Till—have never been clarified and are not my central concern. In particular, debates about Till's behavior often imply that what he did or did not do should determine his fate and/or our responses to it.

2. Whitfield, *A Death in the Delta*, 34.

3. "Will Mississippi Whitewash the Emmett Till Slaying?" *Jet*, September 22, 1955, 8.

4. Meeting of the NAACP Board of Directors, October 10, 1955, NAACP Papers, supp. to pt. I, 1951–55, reel 1, Widener Library, Harvard University; Report of the Secretary for the Month of September 1955, NAACP Papers, supp. to pt. I, 1951–55, reel 2; "Till Protest Meeting," *The Crisis*, November 1955, 546.

5. Southern whites formed the first White Citizens' Council in July 1954 in Indianola, Mississippi—barely two months after the landmark Supreme Court decision. By that November, there were 25,000 members in councils across the south. The Ku Klux Klan was also newly invigorated in this period. See Whitaker, "A Case Study in Southern Justice," 71.

6. *Chicago Defender*, August 13, 1955, 1; Harvard Sitkoff, *The Struggle for Black Equality, 1954–1980* (New York: Hill and Wang, 1981), 23; Hampton and Fayer, *Voices of Freedom*, 2.

7. Adlai Stevenson, quoted in Betty Friedan, *The Feminine Mystique* (New York: Dell, 1963), 53–54; and Sara Evans, *Born for Liberty: A History of Women in America* (New York: Free Press, 1989), 255. Historians have successfully revised the myth of the 1950s as a decade of monolithic conformity and passivity; women's historians in particular have shown that not all women in this period were ensnared in what Friedan would later label the "feminine mystique." See, for example, Sara Evans, *Personal Politics: The Roots of Women's Liberation in the Civil Rights Movement and the New Left* (New York: Knopf, 1979); Susan Lynn, "Gender and Post World War II Progressive Politics: A Bridge to Social Activism in the 1960s U.S.A.," *Gender and History*, Summer 1992, 215–239; Joanne Meyerowitz, "Beyond the Feminine Mystique: A Reassessment of Postwar Mass Culture, 1946–1958," *Journal of American History*, March 1993; Joan Nestle, *A Restricted Country* (New York: Firebrand Books, 1987); Susan Ware, "American Women in the 1950s: Nonpartisan Politics and Women's Politicization," in *Women, Politics and Change*, ed. Louise Tilly and Patricia Gurin (New York: Russell Sage Foundation, 1990), 281–299. Other scholarship that suggests continuities between the 1950s and the civil rights movement, the sexual revolution, or the 1960s counterculture includes Robert Korstad and Nelson Lichtenstein "Opportunities Found and Lost: Labor, Radicals and the Early Civil Rights Movement," *Journal of American History*, December 1988, 786–811; W. T. Lhamon, *Deliberate Speed: The Origins of a Cultural Style in the American 1950s* (Washington, D.C., and London: Smithsonian Institution Press, 1990); Uta Poiger, "Rock 'n' Roll, Female Sexuality and the Battle Over German Identities in the Cold War," paper presented at Brown University History Department Workshop, May 1992. All this scholarship is important in delineating the diversity of experiences in the 1950s; I am seeking to understand aspects of this diversity in relation to each other. In other words, I am exploring how and why sexually conservative prescriptive literature emphasizing motherhood and domesticity ran parallel to and informed other values and experiences in 1950s America.

8. For the preoccupation with security among white women, see Elaine Tyler May, *Homeward Bound: American Families in the Cold War Era* (New York: Basic Books, 1985), esp. 28–36. This emphasis on domesticity and security did not preclude constructions of femininity that emphasized glamour. For a discussion of these "utterly incompatible scenarios" for white women, see Wini Breines, *Young, White and Miserable: Growing Up Female in the Fifties* (Boston: Beacon Press, 1992), 37. For a discussion of conflicting images and roles for black women, see Paula Giddings, *When and Where I Enter: The Impact of Black Women on Race and Sex in America* (New York: Morrow, 1984), 238–258; Jacqueline Jones, *Labor of Love, Labor of Sorrow: Black Women, Work and the Family from Slavery to the Present* (New York: Basic Books, 1985), 268–274; and Jeanne Noble, *The Negro Women's College Education* (New York: Bureau of Publications, Teachers College, Columbia University Press, 1956).

9. "Goodby Mammy, Hello Mom," *Ebony,* March 1947, 36, quoted in Jones, *Labor of Love, Labor of Sorrow,* 271; *Chicago Defender,* October 15, 1955, 3. Clearly, this celebration of black motherhood is complicated, and I do not intend to suggest a parallel or equal "feminine mystique" for black women. As both these quotes suggest, an emphasis on black women as good mothers countered white-defined racial stereotypes. Nevertheless, this maternalist ethos, even if marshaled in part to resist racism, ultimately constrained women.

10. Mamie Till Bradley remarried and divorced after the death of Till's father, Louis Till. She used the name Mamie Bradley in 1955. I do the same throughout this article, unless I am specifically referring to her in the present, when I use the name she now uses, Mamie Till Bradley Mobley.

11. For peers' views that Till's death was a catalyst to the civil rights movement, see Ruby Hurley and Amzie Moore interviews in Howell Raines, *My Soul Is Rested: The Story of the Civil Rights Movement in the Deep South* (New York: Viking Penguin, 1983; orig. pub. 1977), 131–137, 233–237; Myrlie Evers and Charles Diggs interviews in Williams, *Eyes on the Prize,* 46–47, 49. For scholarly interpretations that link Till's death to the civil rights movement, see, among others, Sitkoff, *The Struggle for Black Equality,* 49; William Simpson, "Reflections on a Murder: The Emmett Till Case," in *Southern Miscellany: Essays in History in Honor of Glover Moore,* ed. Frank Allen Dennis (Jackson: University Press of Mississippi, 1981), 177–200; Whitfield, *A Death in the Delta,* 107. Indeed, Henry Hampton's critically acclaimed documentary on the civil right's movement, *Eyes on the Prize,* begins with a segment on the Till murder. These accounts underscore the psychological impact of Till's murder and, for the most part, do not pinpoint a direct cause–effect relationship.

12. This is a discursive analysis in two ways. For one, I am looking rather literally at how Till's funeral, the protest rallies, and the trial were talked and written about. (Because the transcript of the trial has either been lost or was never saved, there is no other point of entry into the "material reality" of the trial. See Simpson, "Reflections on a Murder," 187.) I also assume that the discourse about the case constitutes, rather than reflects, the "material reality" and that meanings of these events were constructed through and by discourse. With this in mind, discourse means more than simply "language" and instead refers to a system that produces material reality. Thus, throughout this analysis I do not delineate the boundaries between texts (most frequently, newspaper and periodical accounts) and social relations and events themselves; nor do I seek to pinpoint individual agency. For more on this theoretical framework, see Michel Foucault, *The*

History of Sexuality, vol. I, *An Introduction* (New York: Random House, 1978; orig. pub. 1976); Joan Scott, *Gender and the Politics of History* (New York: Columbia University Press, 1988); Carolyn Dean, "Discourse," in *Encyclopedia of Social History,* ed. Peter Stearns (New York: Garland Press, forthcoming).

13. Harold Strider's reference to the men as "peckerwoods" quoted in Whitaker, "A Case Study in Southern Justice," 127.

14. Simpson, "Reflections on a Murder," 181; Whitaker, "A Case Study in Southern Justice," 119–121.

15. In particular, many southerners reacted angrily to accounts labeling the murder a "lynching." See *Chicago Daily Tribune,* September 18, 1955, 1. For this line of analysis, see Simpson, "Reflections on a Murder"; Whitaker, "A Case Study in Southern Justice"; and Whitfield, *A Death in the Delta.*

16. In what is perhaps the the most notorious reading of gender and race in the Till case, Susan Brownmiller argues that Till's alleged whistle (which she assumes to be fact) proved what "Emmett Till and J. W. Milam shared"—a domination of women "just short of physical assault." See *Against Our Will: Men, Women and Rape* (New York: Simon & Schuster, 1975), 245–248. Angela Davis successfully changes the terms of this debate in her cogent analysis of white antirape feminists' reliance on racism. See *Women, Race and Class* (New York: Random House, 1981), 172–201. For the historical effacement of black women's sexuality in particular, see Darlene Clark Hine, "Rape and the Inner Lives of Black Women in the Middle West: Preliminary Thoughts on the Culture of Dissemblance," *Signs,* Summer 1989, 912–920. For the contemporary effacement of race in feminist theory and for formulations of black feminist thought, see, among others, Elsa Barkley Brown, " 'What Has Happened Here': The Politics of Difference in Women's History and Feminist Politics," *Feminist Studies,* Summer 1992, 295–312; Patricia Hill Collins, *Black Feminist Thought: Knowledge, Consciousness, and the Politics of Empowerment* (Boston: Unwin Hyman, 1990); Evelyn Brooks Higginbotham, "African-American Women's History and the Metalanguage of Race," *Signs,* Summer 1992, 251–274; bell hooks, *Yearning: Race, Gender and Cultural Politics* (Boston: South End Press, 1990). In *Reconstructing Womanhood: The Emergence of the Afro-American Woman Novelist* (New York: Oxford University Press, 1987), Hazel Carby provides a particularly helpful model for interrogating race in all women. See also Vron Ware, *Beyond the Pale: White Women, Racism and History* (London and New York: Verso, 1992).

17. For excellent analyses of how black women could alter and assign meaning to gender ideologies, see Carby, *Reconstructing Womanhood,* chap. 1; Jones, *Labor of Love, Labor of Sorrow.*

18. See note 7. For analyses of the political meanings and uses of "traditional" sex-role ideology for white women, see May, *Homeward Bound;* and Amy Swerdlow, "Ladies' Day at the Capitol: Women Strike for Peace versus HUAC," in *Unequal Sisters: A Multi-Cultural Reader in U.S. Women's History,* ed. Ellen DuBois and Vicki Ruiz (New York and London: Routledge, 1990), 400–417. Article originally published in 1982.

19. I emphasize "explicitly" here because it is clear, even from Adlai Stevenson's speech, for example, that motherhood was always infused with political meaning. What is new here is the reformulation of motherhood's political meaning.

20. Citizenship here refers not just to suffrage (a right that most southern African

Americans were denied in 1955), but in the words of Nancy Fraser, to "capacities for consent and speech, the ability to participate on a par with others in a [public] dialogue . . . capacities that are in myriad of ways deemed at odds" with femininity and blackness. See Nancy Fraser, *Unruly Practices: Power, Discourse and Gender in Contemporary Social Theory* (Minneapolis: University of Minnesota, 1989), quote on 126. See also Jean Bethke Elshtain, *Public Man, Private Woman* (Princeton: Princeton University Press, 1981). For historically specific analyses of gendered citizenship, see Lynn Hunt, *The Family Romance of the French Revolution,* (Berkeley: University of California Press, 1992). My thanks to Jane Gerhard for helping me clarify these ideas in this context.

21. See, for example, Philip Wylie, *Generation of Vipers* (New York: Holt, Rinehart and Winston, 1955; orig. pub. 1942). Wylie coined the phrase "momism" in this bestselling diatribe against the bad white mother, revised and republished in 1955. Other texts in "sex role" literature through which "momism" developed include Helene Deutsch, *The Psychology of Women,* vol. 2. (New York: Grune and Stratton, 1945); Ferdinand Lundberg and Marynia F. Farnham, *Modern Woman: The Lost Sex* (New York & London: Harper & Brothers, 1947); and Edward A. Strecker, *Their Mothers' Sons: The Psychiatrist Examines an American Problem* (Philadelphia: J. B. Lippincott, 1946, 1951).

22. May, *Homeward Bound,* 140–150; Susan M. Hartmann, *The Home Front and Beyond: American Women in the 1940s* (Boston: Twayne, 1982). See also Ruth Milkman, *Gender at Work: The Dynamics of Job Segregation by Sex During World War II* (Urbana and Chicago: University of Illinois Press, 1987), esp. chap. 7; Rickie Solinger, *Wake Up Little Susie: Single Pregnancy and Race Before Roe v. Wade* (New York and London: Routledge, 1992); Julie Weiss, "Womanhood and Psychoanalysis: A Study of Mutual Construction in Popular Culture," Ph.D. dissertation, Brown University, 1990.

23. *Chicago Tribune Magazine of Books,* September 4, 1955, 1.

24. Ashley Montagu, "The Natural Superiority of Women," *Ladies' Home Journal,* July 1952, 37.

25. May, *Homeward Bound,* 91,102. Nor was the domestic containment that May analyzes a racially specific phenomenon. See *Chicago Defender,* September 24, 1955, 9.

26. The Bryants owned a small country store, and J. W. Milam rented mechanical cotton pickers. The store could not support the family of four, and Roy Bryant engaged in a variety of other jobs to make ends meet. At the time of the alleged incident between Emmett Till and Carolyn Bryant, Roy Bryant was working in Texas. See Whitfield, *A Death in the Delta,* 16–23; U.S. Department of Commerce, *Statistical Abstract of the United States, 1955* (Washington, D.C.: Government Painting Office, 1956), 553; Huie, *Wolf Whistle,* 17–19. Huie also details their financial woes after the trial. For a discussion of how whiteness functioned as a compensatory wage of sorts for white workers in the nineteenth century, see David R. Roediger, *The Wages of Whiteness: Race and the Making of the American Working Class* (London: Verso, 1991).

27. See, for example, Gail Bederman, " 'Civilization,' the Decline of Middle-Class Manliness, and Ida B. Wells's Anti-Lynching Campaign (1892–1894)," *Radical History Review* 52 (1992): 5–30; Jacquelyn Dowd Hall, *Revolt against Chivalry: Jesse Daniel Ames and the Women's Campaign against Lynching* (New York: Columbia University Press, 1979).

28. George Lipsitz, *Time Passages: Collective Memory and American Popular Cul-*

ture (Minneapolis: University of Minnesota Press, 1990), 77; *Look,* October 16, 1956, 35, and quoted in Sara Evans, *Born for Liberty,* 249; emphasis added.

29. Jones, *Labor of Love, Labor of Sorrow,* 269.

30. Patricia Morton, *Disfigured Images: The Historical Assault on Afro-American Women* (New York: Praeger, 1991), 88; emphasis in original. Frazier first developed what would become the "matriarchy thesis" in *The Negro Family in the United States* (Chicago: University of Chicago Press, 1947; orig. pub. 1939). Other progressive "race relations" texts that elaborated on matriarchy as damaging include John Dollard, *Caste and Color in a Southern Town* (New York: Harper & Brothers, 1937); St. Clair Drake and Horace R. Cayton, *Black Metropolis: A Study of Negro Life in a Northern City* (New York: Harper & Row, 1962; orig. pub. 1945); Abram Kardiner and Lionel Ovesey, *The Mark of Oppression: Explorations in the Personality of the American Negro* (New York: Meridian Books, 1962; orig. pub. 1951). Despite similarities in discussions of black and white women and despite the similarities between "momism" and "matriarchy," debates about women remained segregated; within dominant white culture, black women were not part of the large literature on "sex roles" but remained the object of concern only within the parameters of "race relations."

31. Morton, *Disfigured Images,* 74–84; Frazier, *The Negro Family,* 299. See also Regina G. Kunzel, "White Neurosis, Black Pathology: Constructing Out-of-Wedlock Pregnancy in the Wartime and Postwar United States," Chapter 13 in this volume.

32. Morton, *Disfigured Images,* 76.

33. For an example of how and why respectability could be central to black women's political activism, see Jo Ann Gibson Robinson, *The Montgomery Bus Boycott and the Women Who Started It: The Memoir of Jo Ann Gibson Robinson* (Knoxville: University of Tennessee Press, 1987). See, too, Brown, " 'What Has Happened Here,' " esp. 304–306.

34. Whitfield, *A Death in the Delta,* 15; Williams, *Eyes on the Prize,* 41. Although black women's yearly pay was still less than half of white women's (itself less than two-thirds of white men's) the percentage of black women working as domestics declined from 60 percent in 1940 to 42 percent in 1950 and the percentage of black men and women in white-collar work doubled between 1940 and the mid-1950s. See Jones, *Labor of Love, Labor of Sorrow,* 261; Sitkoff, *The Struggle for Black Equality,* 18; Giddings, *When and Where I Enter,* 241.

35. *Commonweal,* September 23, 1955, 603–604. Sympathetic whites tended not to see the ways in which the lives of whites and blacks were structured by race; rather, race became a relevant issue only when Till was murdered.

36. *Chicago Defender,* October 22, 1955, 2.

37. *Chicago Defender,* November 5, 1955, 14; emphasis added.

38. *Pittsburgh Courier,* August 20, 1955, 9.

39. E. Franklin Frazier, *Black Bourgeoisie* (New York: Free Press, 1966; orig. pub. 1957).

40. Hampton and Fayer, *Voices of Freedom,* 5; *Chicago Daily Tribune,* September 2, 1955, 1.

41. Hampton and Fayer, *Voices of Freedom,* 5; *Pittsburgh Courier,* September 10, 1955, 1. The exact words Bradley used at this point vary slightly from one account to the next, but the message remains remarkably consistent in every report. The quote "I wanted the whole world to see what I had seen" appears in Hampton and Fayer, *Voices of Freedom,* 6.

42. *Chicago Defender,* September 17, 1955, 4; *Chicago Defender,* September 10, 1955, 1; *Chicago Daily Tribune,* September 4, 1955, 2.

43. Quote on impact of the service from "Chicago Boy," *The Nation,* September 17, 1955, 235. For estimates of 10,000, see "Mississippi: The Accused," *Newsweek,* September 19, 1955, 38; and *New York Times,* September 4, 1955, sec. VI, 9; for other figures, see *Chicago Daily Tribune,* September 4, 1955, 2 (40,000); *Chicago Defender,* September 10, 1955, 1 and *New York Amsterdam News,* September 10, 1955, 1 (50,000); *Pittsburgh Courier,* September 10, 1955 (100,000), 1; "Nation Horrified by Murder of Kidnapped Chicago Youth," *Jet,* September 15, 1955, 6–9 (600,000). Discrepancies could stem from daily versus cumulative estimates.

44. Jessica Shubow has helped me to see that black control of the body was in marked contrast to a long history of white-controlled displays of lynched African Americans in which published photographs of lynchings were designed to intimidate and disempower black communities. The near-unanimous outrage outside the South and the unprecedented media coverage of these events (the latter due in part to the advent of television) also distinguished the Till case from the heavily publicized, though always controversial, trial of the "Scottsboro boys."

45. *Chicago Defender,* September 17, 1955, 9.

46. Ibid.; emphasis added.

47. Ibid.; *Afro-American,* September 17, 1955, 1; *Chicago Defender,* October 1, 1955, 4; *Chicago Defender,* September 10, 1955, 5; *Afro-American,* September 10, 1955, 1.

48. "MISSISSIPPI: The Place, the Acquittal," *Newsweek,* October 3, 1955, 24; *Chicago Defender,* September 10, 1955, 1; *Pittsburgh Courier,* September 17, 1955, 1; *Chicago Defender,* October 1, 1955, 4; *New York Amsterdam News,* September 24, 1955, 1. Whether or not the teenage Till was a boy or a man and what black masculinity and sexuality should mean were also implicit in these and other images of both Till and Bradley. For example, Huie emphasized Till's size and tried to uncover his sexual history, while some critics of the murder specifically defended Till's "right"— as an American male—to whistle. According to the liberal *Commonweal,* for example, "coming from a 14-year-old white boy this [whistle] would have been dismissed as rudeness . . . and many would have laughed at the indication that the boy was on his way to becoming a man." See "Death in Mississippi," *Commonweal,* September 23, 1955, 603. Others constructed images of Till as young, innocent, and anything but masculine. In a fiery speech to an interracial crowd of twenty thousand, for example, Congressman Adam Clayton Powell declared that murdering Emmett Till was akin to "the lynching of the Statue of Liberty." See *New York Amsterdam News,* October 15, 1955, 1.

49. "Mississippi: The Accused," 38. Many in the liberal press feared that the negative publicity surrounding the murder and acquittal would be used by communists. According to the *New Republic,* for example, when Milam and Bryant were acquitted, "communists around the world got a new weapon against the United States." See "Notes," *New Republic,* October 3, 1955, 2. Others saw different international implications to the murder; a French reporter linked Till's death to "the eternal problem of colonialism . . . that numerous Americans are so quick to denounce in others." See "L'Affaire Till in the French Press," *The Crisis,* December 1955, 596–602.

50. *Pittsburgh Courier,* October 29, 1955, 9.

51. *Chicago Defender,* September 17, 1955, 9; *New York Amsterdam News,* October 1, 1955, 7; "IN MEMORIAM, EMMETT TILL," *Life,* October 10, 1955, 48. Bradley's

status as a "widow" deflected attention away from her second marriage and divorce. According to several sources, however, Bradley and Louis Till had divorced before he entered the army. See Whitaker, *A Death in the Delta*, 15.

52. *New York Amsterdam News,* October 1, 1955, 7.

53. "At What Age Is a Woman Most Beautiful?" *Jet,* March 3, 1955, 26–29 (the answer—"Experts Say All Women Beautiful at Least Twice in Life"); "Jet's Calendar Girls for 1955," *Jet,* January 6, 1955, 28–42.

54. Jones, *Labor of Love, Labor of Sorrow,* 272. In her analysis of *Ebony,* Jones also points out that an emphasis on attractive women accompanied an emphasis on prominent women—in politics, in the entertainment industry, and in other traditionally male-dominated professions. See note 8.

55. Black women are conspicuously absent in defenses of Till that do address sexuality. An editorial decrying the "mongrelization obsession" of southern whites, for example, argued that the "great majority of Negroes . . . do not aspire to wed the 'pure' womanhood of Dixie." See *Pittsburgh Courier,* October 1, 1955, 6. This absence countered long-standing stereotypes that rendered black women promiscuous and was part of a tradition in which, in the words of Elsa Barkley Brown, "black women, especially middle class women, have learned to present a public image that *never* reveals their sexuality." Brown, " 'What Has Happened Here,' " 306.

56. *Chicago Defender,* October 1, 1955, 2; ibid., 4; *Chicago Defender,* October 8, 1955, 2. This editorial discussed "petty jealousy" between the NAACP and the AFL/Brotherhood of Sleeping Car Porters regarding Bradley's attendance at an AFL-sponsored rally (which the NAACP suspected of "pinkish tendencies"), but in this account, Mamie Bradley had no role in the dispute.

57. *Chicago Tribune,* October 7, 1955, 5; *Chicago Defender,* September 10, 1955, 1; *Chicago Defender,* September 17, 1955, 4. In some accounts, Bradley's dependence extended to her relationship with her son. See *Afro-American,* September 10, 1955, 1.

58. The *Eyes on the Prize* documentary is an exception in that it draws attention to Bradley's role. Nevertheless, according to an accompanying text, "in vengeance" Bradley "declared" that the world would see her son's corpse. This language and other descriptions of her as overly emotional effectively depoliticize her actions. See Williams, *Eyes on the Prize,* 43–44. See also "30 Years Ago: How Emmett Till's Lynching Launched the Civil Rights Drive," *Jet,* June 17, 1985, 12–18. These more recent analyses duplicate accounts at the time. For example, her declaration, "Darling, you have not died in vain, your life has been sacrificed for something," is followed by "Mrs. Bradley hysterically shouted." See *Chicago Defender,* September 10, 1955, 2.

59. *Chicago Defender,* September 10, 1955, 1; *Pittsburgh Courier,* September 10, 1955, 3.

60. *Memphis Commercial Appeal,* September 4, 1955, sec. II, 4; ibid., 1, 2; *Memphis Commercial Appeal,* September 7, 1955, 6; *Greenville Delta-Democrat Times,* quoted in Whitfield, *A Death in the Delta,* 29.

61. Huie, *Wolf Whistle,* 26.

62. Whitaker, *A Death in the Delta,* 117–119; *Chicago Defender,* October 29, 1955, 2; *New York Times,* October 30, 1955, 87; *Jackson Daily News,* October 15, 1955, 1. The guilt or innocence of Louis Till and the details surrounding his court-martial and hanging remain in dispute, particularly in light of the fact that in Europe during World War II, eighty-seven of the ninety-five soldiers hanged for rape and murder of civilians were African American. At least one of Till's peers in the segregated unit suggested

that he had been "railroaded" by MPs enforcing "nonfraternization bans." At the time, Bradley asserted that the federal government had never told her how or why her husband had died; she has since noted that "Louis was never allowed to testify . . . the case was built on the testimony of what someone else said." See "GI Buddies Say Till's Dad Was 'Railroaded' in Italy," *Jet*, November 3, 1955, 4–5; *New York Amsterdam News*, October 1, 1955, 7; "Time Heals Few Wounds for Emmett Till's Mother," *Jet*, April 9, 1984, 55.

63. *Memphis Commercial Appeal*, September 6, 1955, 1, 8. *Memphis Commercial Appeal*, September 4, 1955, sec. II, p. 4; emphasis added.

64. *Chicago Defender*, September 17, 1955, 1. One black woman wrote that she would like to see a photograph of Carolyn Bryant, "the woman who started this 'shot heard around the world'— . . . this delicate example of female virtue, this outraged accuser of children and babies." See *Afro-American*, September 24, 1955, 4.

65. Mary Cain, quoted in Ira Harkey, *The Smell of Burning Crosses: An Autobiography of a Mississippi Newspaperman* (Jacksonville, Ill.: Harris-Wolfe, 1967), 106; emphasis added.

66. See Lynn Hunt, "The Many Bodies of Marie Antoinette: Political Pornography and the Problem of the Feminine in the French Revolution," in *Eroticism and the Body Politic* (Baltimore: Johns Hopkins University Press, 1991), 108–130; Solinger, *Wake Up Little Susie*. My thanks to Carolyn Dean for helping me to understand this dynamic.

67. Morton, *Disfigured Images*, 70–72. It is worth noting that links between African Americans and femininity were used toward progressive and reactionary ends at different points in American history. See Deborah Gray White, *Ar'n't I a Woman? Female Slaves in the Plantation South* (New York: Norton, 1985), esp. 13–61.

68. Huie, *Wolf Whistle*, 26. In contrast to accounts in the African American press, which seem intent on underscoring gender difference, he does not distinguish between male and female mourners.

69. *Chicago Defender*, September 17, 1955, 2; *New York Amsterdam News*, October 1, 1955, 12; ibid., 8; *Pittsburgh Courier*, October 29, 1955, 9; *Pittsburgh Courier*, October 22, 1955, 1. It is important to note that there were black women assuming increasingly prominent and political roles in this period, including civil rights activists Ruby Hurley, Daisy Bates, and Ella Baker, entertainment figures Lena Horne and Mahalia Jackson, and professional educators or public servants Mary McLeod Bethune and Edith Sampson, among others. While sexism and racism informed these women's lives as well, they were not subject to the same symbolic construction as was Mamie Till Bradley.

70. *Chicago Defender*, September 24, 1955, 1; Whitfield, *A Death in the Delta*, 33.

71. Ruby Hurley and Medgar Evers, NAACP staff workers in Mississippi, located Amanda Bradley and Willie Reed, the two "surprise witnesses," and encouraged them to testify. Report of the Secretary for the Month of September 1955, NAACP Papers, supp. to pt. 1, 1951–55, reel 2; David Shostak, "Crosby Smith: Forgotten Witness to a Mississippi Nightmare," *Negro History Bulletin*, December 1974, 320–325.

72. *New York Times*, September 22, 1955, 64; Hampton and Fayer, *Voices of Freedom*, 11; Whitfield, *A Death in the Delta*, 39.

73. Although 63 percent of the population in Tallahatchie County was African American, no blacks were eligible for jury service, dependent as it was on voter registration. In fact, jury duty in Tallahatchie County was so severely restricted through

age, gender, literacy, and residency requirements that, ultimately, only 5 percent of the county population was eligible. See Whitfield, *A Death in the Delta*, 35.

74. There were six other "character witnesses" for the defense. Sheriff Strider raised questions about the identity of the body shortly after Till's funeral, in direct contradiction to statements he had made earlier. Casting doubts on the identity of the body was an important part of the shift in southern whites' opinions generally, and in the condemnation of the NAACP in particular. See "MISSISSIPPI: The Place, the Acquittal," 25; Simpson, "Reflections on a Murder," 192.

75. *Afro-American*, September 24, 1955, 14; ibid., 1; *Memphis Commercial Appeal*, September 22, 1955, 8.

76. After the trial, Mamie Bradley reported that she had not been molested in Sumner but that men had pretended to shoot at her, yelling " 'Bang! Bang!' while others laughed." See *Memphis Commercial Appeal*, September 25, 1955, 1. Certainly, the physical dangers she faced were multiple. For more extensive analyses of polarized constructions of women, see, among others, Morton, *Disfigured Images*, esp. 1–27; White, *Ar'n't I a Woman?* esp. 27–61.

77. *Memphis Commercial Appeal*, September 8, 1955, 1; *Memphis Commercial Appeal*, September 20, 1955, 15. The texts of these telegrams suggest an adversarial attitude toward Mamie Bradley on the part of the district attorney and underscore just how difficult those days in Sumner were. Clearly, even the men prosecuting the case were not allies of Till's family. For more information on the legal team, see *Memphis Commercial Appeal*, September 18, 1955, sec. V, 10; Simpson, "Reflections on a Murder," 185–187; Whitfield, *A Death in the Delta*, 31, 41, 56; Whitaker, "A Case Study in Southern Justice," 131.

78. *Memphis Commercial Appeal*, September 21, 1955, 8.

79. *Pittsburgh Courier*, September 24, 1955, 1; ibid., 4; *Chicago Defender*, October 1, 1955, 4.

80. *Memphis Commercial Appeal*, September 21, 1955, 8; *New York Times*, September 23, 1955, 15; *Memphis Commercial Appeal*, September 22, 1955, 1; *Memphis Commercial Appeal*, September 23, 1955, 2; Whitfield, *A Death in the Delta*, 40–42. According to Judge Swango, the alleged incident between Bryant and Till had occurred "too long before the abduction" and hence was inadmissible.

81. *Memphis Commercial Appeal*, September 8, 1955, 1; *New York Times*, September 23, 1955, 15; "MISSISSIPPI: The Place, the Acquittal," 24.

82. *Memphis Commercial Appeal*, September 20, 1955, 1; *Chicago Defender*, September 24, 1955, 5; *Memphis Commercial Appeal*, September 7, 1955, 1; *Memphis Commercial Appeal*, September 22, 1955, 33; Whitfield, *A Death in the Delta*, 37. Congressman Charles C. Diggs (D-Mich.) was among those at this segregated table and was frequently referred to as "the nigger congressman."

83. After the trial (and after their paid confession to Huie), Milam and Bryant lost the support of the Mississippi establishment. Economic difficulties increased when Mississippi blacks refused to buy at the Bryant store and local banks refused to give either man loans; both ultimately left Mississippi. See Hampton and Fayer, *Voices of Freedom*, 14; Raines, *My Soul Is Rested*, 392; Huie, *Wolf Whistle*. For analyses of race and gender in relation to class tensions, see Dolores Janiewski, *Sisterhood Denied: Race, Gender, and Class in a New South Town* (Philadelphia: Temple University Press, 1985); Jones, *Labor of Love, Labor of Sorrow;* Jones, "The Political Implications of Black and

White Women's Work in the South, 1890–1965," in *Women, Politics, and Change,* ed. Louise Tilly and Patricia Gurin (New York: Russell Sage Foundation, 1990), 108–129. In "The Leo Frank Case Reconsidered: Gender and Sexual Politics in the Making of Reactionary Populism," *Journal of American History,* December 1991, 917–948, Nancy MacLean offers a particularly helpful analysis of how gender informed class conflicts, anti-Semitism, and racism during this notorious murder trial in 1913.

84. *Memphis Commercial Appeal,* September 24, 1955, 17; *Chicago Daily Tribune,* September 24, 1955, 1. See also *Memphis Commercial Appeal,* September 24, 1955, 1; ibid., 3; ibid., 4; *New York Times,* September 24, 1955, 1. Antiracist observers challenged this image of the happy family. A liberal Parisian weekly, *Aux Ecoutes,* labeled Carolyn Bryant a "cruel shrew"; in *Le Canard Enchaine* she was "a crossroads Marilyn Monroe." Others, nationally and internationally, drew attention to the irony of "Roy . . . looking like the model family man," to the " 'phony' sad faces of the wives," and to Milam and Bryant "playing with their children, seemingly callous of the charges against them, while their wives 'mugged' for the cameras." See "L'Affaire Till in the French Press," 596–601; *Pittsburgh Courier,* October 1, 1955, 1; *New York Amsterdam News,* October 15, 1955, 1; Roi Ottley both clung to and inverted notions of respectability in a biting column that characterized the trial as endorsing "vicious, lawless and barbarous" behavior and the southern whites as primitives. See *Chicago Defender,* October 8, 1955, 8.

85. Although the state called one funeral director who testified that he thought the body was Till's, prosecutors made no effort to confirm the identity of the body scientifically. See Simpson, "Reflections on a Murder," 189. In fact, as rumors about the identity of the body continued to circulate after the trial, Bradley expressed her willingness "to have my boy's body exhumed from the vault for a thorough examination if that would dispel these wild rumors." See *New York Times,* September 30, 1955, 18.

86. *New York Times,* September 24, 1955, 1.

87. *Chicago Defender,* October 1, 1955, 4.

88. *Chicago Daily Tribune,* September 1, 1955, 4; *Chicago Defender,* October 15, 1955, 3.

89. "Trial by Jury," *Time,* October 3, 1955, 18; *Memphis Commercial Appeal,* September 22, 1955, 1; I. F. Stone, "The Murder of Emmett Till," in *The Haunted Fifties* (New York: Random House, 1963), 107.

90. Many African Americans consequently objected to this emphasis on Till's willingness to humble himself. See, for example, NAACP Correspondence, Mississippi Pressures, 1955, NAACP Papers, Library of Congress, Washington, D.C.; *Chicago Defender,* September 17, 1955, 9.

91. *New York Times,* September 23, 1955, 15; *New York Times,* September 24, 1955, 1. Speaking at a Cleveland, Ohio, NAACP chapter meeting on her way to Sumner, Bradley "appeared quiet and composed, (and) urged the groups to write congressmen . . . and called on the audience to promote membership in the NAACP," according to the *Chicago Daily Tribune,* September 19, 1955, 2.

92. *Pittsburgh Courier,* October 1, 1955, 1; *Chicago Defender,* October 1, 1955, 1.

93. "MISSISSIPPI: The Place, the Acquittal," 25. (In one sentence *Newsweek* corroborated her respectability from a variety of perspectives—rendering Bradley a good mother, a hard worker, an emotional woman, and an ex-wife.) Gendered and racialized representations of Bradley did not always break down along regional lines. According

to the *Memphis Commercial Appeal*, September 22, 1955, 35, Bradley "wept silently," when shown the photograph of the body.

94. *Chicago Defender*, September 17, 1955, 2.

95. *Pittsburgh Courier*, October 1, 1955, 8; *L'Aurore*, quoted in "L'Affaire Till in the French Press," 600.

96. *New York Times*, September 24, 1955, 1; *Chicago Daily Tribune*, October 24, 1955, 1. The defense also tried to "prove" a relationship between Bradley and a public organization (particularly the NAACP), one that would discredit the "grieving mother" and make her motherhood itself suspect. This need for a woman to act exclusively as a "private" person has echoes in the Anita Hill–Clarence Thomas hearings; hostile senators repeatedly asked Hill if she was "acting alone." Any public or official affiliation would clearly have undercut her claims as a private woman who had experienced sexual harassment. For more on the Hill–Thomas hearings, see Brown, " 'What Has Happened Here,' " 302–307; Toni Morrison, ed., *Race-ing Justice, En-Gendering Power: Essays on Anita Hill, Clarence Thomas and the Construction of Social Reality*, (New York: Pantheon, 1992); Geneva Smitherman, ed., *Reflections on Anita Hill: Race, Gender and Power in the United States* (Detroit: Wayne State University Press, forthcoming).

97. This "damned if you do, damned if you don't" framework, which renders Mamie Bradley's words irrelevant both because of her composure *and* her irrationality, was replayed by the all-white, all-male "jury" of senators in the Hill–Thomas hearings. Anita Hill presented as a very rational, composed subject, and not as the stereotypically "hysterical woman." Arlen Specter used this composure and dignity against her when he argued that if she were in fact telling the truth, she would have either quit her job, kept notes after incidents of harassment, or reported her boss. Her rational behavior and demeanor was thus suspect; using those standards of rationality, he accused her of perjury and dismissed her charges. At the same time, Orin Hatch struggled to represent Anita Hill as the classically irrational, hysterical, and delusional woman by quoting *The Exorcist* and other sources. Using those standards, he too dismissed her charges.

98. Stone, "The Murder of Emmett Till," 108.

99. *New York Times*, September 24, 1955, 1, 38.

100. *Pittsburgh Courier*, October 1, 1955, 1. Mamie Mobley appeared on the Oprah Winfrey show in October 1992; at that time, she again emphasized that she had not wanted to be present when the verdict was offered.

101. *New York Amsterdam News*, October 1, 1955, 8; *New York Amsterdam News*, October 8, 1955, 21.

102. Board of Directors Meeting, October 10, 1955, NAACP Papers, supp. to pt. 1, 1951–55, reel 1; *New York Times*, October 3, 1955, 19. According to the Report of the Secretary to the Board of Directors for the Month of October 1955, as a result of the *New York Times* advertisement, letters and contributions "came from persons in all walks of life, a New England judge . . . business men . . . fraternities. A score of letters came from white Southerners." See NAACP Papers, supp. to pt. 1, 1951–55, reel 2.

103. *Pittsburgh Courier*, November 19, 1955, 2; *New York Amsterdam News*, November 19, 1955, 2; Board of Directors meeting, November 14, 1955, NAACP Papers, supp. to pt. 1, 1951–55, reel 1. Wright apparently agreed to NAACP terms for the tour: The organization would pay for travel expenses plus $100 per appearance, "which amount will be increased if the receipts from the meeting warrant it." Details of this conflict are unclear and again are not my central concern. More significant to me is how

the meaning of these events was constructed and how gender implicitly and explicitly informed the NAACP's political agenda. Further, I am less concerned with Bradley's intentions than with perceptions of them and the meaning derived from this "rift" with the NAACP.

104. *Chicago Defender,* November 19, 1955, 2; Board of Directors meeting, November 14, 1955, NAACP Papers, supp. to pt. I, 1951–55, reel 1.

105. *Chicago Defender,* November 26, 1955, 1.

106. *New York Amsterdam News,* November 19, 1955, 1, 2; Report of the Secretary for the Month of September 1955, NAACP Papers, supp. to pt. 1, 1951–55, reel 2.

107. *Pittsburgh Courier,* November 26, 1955, 12

108. *Chicago Defender,* October 15, 1955, 2; *Pittsburgh Courier,* October 29, 1955, 1; *Chicago Defender,* October 22, 1955, 2.

109. *New York Amsterdam News,* October 1, 1955, 9.

110. *Pittsburgh Courier,* December 24, 1955, 3; *Chicago Defender,* October 22, 1955, 2. For her leave being unpaid, see *Chicago Defender,* November 19, 1955, 2. According to statements by Wilkins in the NAACP papers, the organization also agreed to pay the travel expenses of her father.

111. *New York Times,* October 25, 1955, 27; *Chicago Defender,* October 29, 1955, 1. Bradley had also sent a telegram to President Eisenhower, then recovering from a heart attack; the president, who once told Chief Justice Earl Warren that white supremacists "were not bad people," did not respond. See Whitfield, *A Death in the Delta,* 72–74. Two rallies in Washington were held to coincide with her visit and "12,000 turned out to see her . . . the crowds were so great that Mrs. Mamie Bradley of Chicago, mother of the dead little Till boy, was almost prevented from entering the auditorium to address the throngs that awaited her." See *New York Amsterdam News,* October 29, 1955, 3.

112. *Pittsburgh Courier,* October 29, 1955, 9; *Chicago Defender,* October 29, 1955, 2; emphasis added. This editorial appears to be the first time Bradley is referred to simply as "Mamie" in the African American press; indeed, reporters and other observers had paid close attention to the titles—and lack thereof—whites had shown to black principals in the case.

113. *Pittsburgh Courier,* October 1, 1955, 1.

114. *Chicago Defender,* November 26, 1955, 1.

115. *New York Amsterdam News,* November 26, 1955, 8; "How the Till Case Changed 5 Lives," *Jet,* November 24, 1955, 10.

116. *Pittsburgh Courier,* November 19, 1955, 2; *Chicago Defender,* November 26, 1955, 1, 2; "How the Till Case Changed 5 Lives," 10. Chicago reporters seemed particularly intent on salvaging Mamie Bradley's reputation; perhaps to them, the city in general was potentially implicated in any scandal.

117. *Chicago Defender,* November 19, 1955, 2; *New York Amsterdam News,* November 19, 1955, 2; *Chicago Defender,* October 8, 1955, 1.

118. *Chicago Defender,* November 26, 1955, 1.

119. *Chicago Defender,* November 19, 1955, 2.

120. Ibid.; "How the Till Case Changed 5 Lives," 13.

121. *Chicago Defender,* November 19, 1955, 1, 2; *New York Amsterdam News,* November 19, 1955, 1, 2. The argument that the $5,000 fee was not her idea was made alongside descriptions of her financial problems (with quotes such as, "It is a strain to get food for my table"). Bradley, quoted in *New York Amsterdam News,* November 19, 1955, 1, 2. See also "How the Till Case Changed 5 Lives," 10–13.

122. *Chicago Defender,* November 19, 1955, 2; *Pittsburgh Courier,* December 24, 1955, 3.

123. *Pittsburgh Courier,* December 24, 1955, 3, 6; *Chicago Defender,* December 24, 1955, 1. Efforts to "rehabilitate" Bradley are also evident in the two-installment "Mamie Bradley's Untold Story, Told by Mamie Bradley, as Told to Ethel Payne," *Chicago Defender,* April 21, 1956, 8, and April 28, 1956, 10. In these autobiographical pieces, Bradley alludes to the controversy when she writes: "People wonder why I am so calm, and some even think I am cold," but then turns to a detailed description of her childhood , writing at length about her own mother's work ethic and religious commitment.

124. Quoted in *Pittsburgh Courier,* December 24, 1955, 3.

125. Studs Terkel, *Race: How Blacks and Whites Think and Feel about the American Obsession* (New York: Norton, 1992), 22; of her time with the NAACP in 1955, Mobley said only, "I was one of the best fundraisers they ever had." See also "30 Years Ago: How Emmett Till's Lynching Launched the Civil Rights Drive," *Jet,* June 17, 1985, 12–18.

126. *Afro-American,* September 24, 1955, 4; "Inside You and Me," *The Crisis,* December 1955, 592–595.

127. Moore, in Raines, *My Soul Is Rested,* 234–235.

128. *Pittsburgh Courier,* September 10, 1955, 1.

129. *New York Amsterdam News,* October 18, 1955, 8; *Afro-American,* September 24, 1955, 4.

130. Clay quoted in Whitfield, *A Death in the Delta,* 94; *New York Times,* May 17, 1979, A23 . For other memories of Till's death, see interviews in Hampton and Fayer, *Voices of Freedom;* Raines, *My Soul Is Rested;* and Williams, *Eyes on the Prize.* Endesha Ida Mae Holland, "Memories of the Mississippi Delta," *Michigan Quarterly Review* 26 (Winter 1987): 246–258; Anne Moody, *Coming of Age in Mississippi* (New York: Dell, 1968), 125–129; Cloyte Murdock Larsson, "Land of the Till Murder Revisited," *Ebony,* March 1986, 53–58; Shelby Steele, "On Being Black and Middle Class," *Commentary,* January 1988, 42–47. For fiction that draws on Till's murder, see, among others, Alice Walker, "Advancing Luna—and Ida B. Wells," in *You Can't Keep a Good Woman Down* (San Diego: Harcourt Brace Jovanovich, 1981); and Bebe Moore Campbell, *Your Blues Ain't Like Mine* (New York: Putnam's, 1992).

131. *New York Times,* May 17, 1979, A23.

132. Jones, *Labor of Love, Labor of Sorrow,* 279–280; Jones, "The Political Implications of Black and White Women's Work," 108–129. I am grateful to Jacqueline Jones for helping me think more carefully about women's "traditional" roles.

CHAPTER 13

Regina G. Kunzel

WHITE NEUROSIS, BLACK PATHOLOGY

Constructing Out-of-Wedlock Pregnancy in the Wartime and Postwar United States

"**W**hy does a girl become an unmarried mother?" Leontine Young asked in 1954.[1] It was a question that had plagued reformers and social workers since the late nineteenth century and had invited a series of responses that revealed the meaning of illegitimacy to be extraordinarily plastic. Shifting, competing, and contested over time, the scripts of out-of-wedlock pregnancy ultimately said more about their authors and the anxieties of their time and place than they did about the women they were describing.

Among the first to pose the question were evangelical reform women who founded national networks of maternity homes for unmarried mothers in the late nineteenth and early twentieth centuries under the auspices of the Salvation Army, the National Florence Crittenton Mission, and various religious denominations. These women called on the narrative conventions of melodrama—long used to explain prostitution—to comprehend single pregnancy.[2] The stories that filled maternity home publicity brochures cast unmarried mothers as seduced and abandoned heroines and criticized the double standard that forced women to pay the moral price for a "fall" surely initiated by a man. The unmarried mother who had been "lured into sin, robbed of her virtue, and left by the man who pretended he loved her, either to live or die whatever her lot chanced to be," formed the model for countless stories of male sexual irresponsibility and aggressiveness and female vulnerability and victimization.[3] Confronted by the changing sexual mores of the predominantly working-class women under their care, evangelical women used the script of seduction and abandonment to fix single women's sexuality firmly within the comprehensible lineaments of an old story that might explain women who had ruptured the conventional narrative of nineteenth-century femininity. In the language of melodrama, evangelicals found a way to transform an unsettling world into comprehensible patterns.

Not surprisingly, illegitimacy looked different when refracted through the lens of professional social work. Social workers had spent the first decades of the twentieth century in a strenuous, often anxious attempt to prove themselves professionals—a project that required them to distance themselves from nineteenth-century "ladies bountiful" as well as their clients. To those ends, social workers removed unmarried mothers from the melodramatic narratives authored by evangelical women reformers and cast them as a particularly serious and vexing part of a larger "girl problem." Calling on a discourse that enabled them to claim both professional legitimacy and jurisdiction over "problem girls," social workers placed single mothers alongside women diagnosed as "hypersexual," prostitutes, and bad girls of all persuasions in the long continuum of "sex delinquency." A diagnosis almost exclusively applied to working-class white women, "sex delinquency" encoded anxieties about working-class women's independence—in living arrangements, work, leisure, and sexuality—and offered a rationale for policing their behavior and curtailing their autonomy. By the 1930s, "sex delinquency" was a well-rehearsed script that recast the helpless victims of melodramatic tales into women who willfully violated moral sanctions. Instead of "fallen sisters" to be "saved," unmarried mothers became "problem girls" to be "treated." Once respectably passive, unmarried mothers were now dangerously sexual.[4]

But beginning in the 1940s, Leontine Young and her colleagues offered a new answer to the question posed by the unmarried mother. In their search for the cause of out-of-wedlock pregnancy, wartime and postwar social workers and psychiatrists looked not to male lust or female delinquency but to the psyches of young women. Drawing heavily on psychiatric theory, Young diagnosed out-of-wedlock pregnancy as a symptom of deeper emotional pathology and characterized the unmarried mother as "an unhappy and neurotic girl who seeks through the medium of an out-of-wedlock baby to find an answer to her own unconscious conflicts and needs." [5]

At the same time that the "neurotic" unmarried mother was attracting attention in social work circles, the many studies of illegitimacy in black communities that began to appear in the late 1930s revealed the race-specific nature of that diagnosis. Those who investigated out-of-wedlock pregnancy among African American women were little concerned with "underlying emotional patterns." Instead of focusing their attention inward, sociologists, anthropologists, and social workers turned their investigations outward, to scrutinize black communities and the family patterns allegedly nurtured and sustained there.

In the course of the 1940s and 1950s, the "problem" of the unmarried mother—once cast in the singular—fractured into several "problems" along the fault lines of race and class. While class had explicitly informed early twentieth-century discourses of illegitimacy, race had remained largely uninterrogated. Beginning in the 1940s, however, race combined with class to assume an increasingly visible, central, and defining place in constructions of single pregnancy. During and after the war, black and white unmarried mothers were cast as very different figures, pregnant for different reasons, and in need of the service of two different sets of experts.

Historian Rickie Solinger has documented the central importance of race in constructing the cultural meanings of out-of-wedlock pregnancy after World War II, in shaping public policies toward unmarried mothers, and in determining the ways in which women experienced single motherhood.[6] This essay seeks to locate some beginning points for the emergence of two very different stories about black and white unmarried mothers and considers the forces behind those changes—some of which had prewar roots—to argue that these ostensibly discrete discourses were deeply interconnected and interdependent. This effort to locate racialized narratives of illegitimacy historically is informed by the belief that the changes in the discourses of black and white out-of-wedlock pregnancy illuminate more elusive shifts in the ways in which gender, sexuality, class, and race were constructed in American wartime and postwar culture.

White Unmarried Mothers and Neurosis

In September 1941 Robert South Barrett, president of the National Florence Crittenton Mission, sent out a warning to Crittenton maternity home workers. "I think it necessary that I should raise the storm signal to our Homes in the same way the Weather Bureau raises one at the approach of a hurricane," he wrote. "We are facing a very serious time, and I beg you to make plans now to meet a situation that is fraught with many dangers."[7] These dangers—"the lure of uniforms, the emotional disturbances produced by men being taken away from their usual habitats, the assembling of large numbers of men in military camps"—were those of the homefront during wartime. Maternity home workers expected World War II to swell the illegitimacy rate and deluge the homes with applications.

Those working with unmarried mothers had reason to sound the alarm at the onset of World War II. Although in the early 1940s the illegitimacy rate rose in proportion to the general birthrate, instead of soaring dramatically as many had predicted, the relative increase in numbers of unmarried mothers created a heavy burden for maternity homes and social agencies. The year 1944 witnessed the first large wartime increase in the number of illegitimate births, and many maternity homes were so overcrowded they had to turn women away.[8] But to many observers, the changing demographic profile of unmarried mothers seeking aid was as striking as their numerical increase. In contrast to the predominantly working-class clientele that had filled maternity homes in the first decades of the twentieth century, maternity home staff and social workers all over the country reported a rise in the number of white middle-class women seeking the services of homes and social agencies. Social worker Helen Perlman attributed this demographic change to marriage postponements during wartime, the rising incidence of "illicit coition," and the more frequent use of social agencies by unmarried mothers.[9] Solinger has speculated that middle-class girls and women might have turned to maternity homes in greater numbers during and after the war because out-of-wedlock pregnancy threatened the aspirations of middle-class families in a new way. While the illegitimate pregnancy of a middle-class daughter was once a "private sorrow," to be attended with an appropriately private solution, the wartime and postwar family ideology rendered her a "public humiliation" that required a professional curative.[10]

Whatever the cause, the upsurge in the number of white middle-class women seeking aid drew considerable comment, and remarks on the class status of unmarried mothers marked every description of the clientele of homes and agencies in the 1940s. Cases cited by social workers in the professional literature, previously populated by the paradigmatic working-class sex delinquent characterized by a fondness for the dance hall, an excessive use of makeup, and an inclination toward slang, now pondered an altogether different unmarried mother. Social work theorist Leontine Young's description of a woman "in her mid twenties, quietly attractive, and well-dressed," who "spoke in a soft voice and with an educated accent," was filled with the signifiers of middle-class status.[11]

Social workers were initially baffled by the unmarried mothers they found "poised, calm and assured, quiet, unruffled, friendly and smiling"; the conventional causes of illegitimacy did not seem to apply to them.[12] "They are no longer limited to the tenement dwellers," Sara Edlin noted of the wartime and postwar residents of Staten Island's Lakeview home, whose history of "overcrowding, large families, and the deprivations and struggles of poverty" had explained their condition in the past.[13] Rose Bernstein was candid in her confusion when she noted that "the extension of unmarried motherhood into our upper and educated classes in sizeable numbers further confounds us by rendering our former stereotypes less tenable. Immigration, low mentality, and hypersexuality," she wrote, "can no longer be comfortably applied when the phenomenon has invaded our own social class—when the unwed mother must be classified to include the nice girl next door, the physician's or pastor's daughter."[14]

In their departures from the stereotypical unmarried mother, women seeking the aid of social agencies and maternity homes in the 1940s seemed to defy the explanations of out-of-wedlock pregnancy popularized first by evangelical women in the late nineteenth century and later revised by professional social workers. The increasing presence of middle-class girls and women in maternity homes and social agencies led social workers to reevaluate the causes behind out-of-wedlock pregnancy in an attempt to remove them from the larger category of "sex delinquency." In an effort to comprehend this new group of unmarried mothers, social workers turned from explanations of illegitimacy grounded in sociology, criminology, and sexology and called instead on psychiatry. Beginning in the 1940s, social workers viewed illegitimacy among white middle-class girls and women as a symptom of unconscious needs and desires. Rather than regard unmarried mothers as "delinquents, moral defectives, or prostitutes," social workers diagnosed them as neurotic.[15]

Social workers in the 1940s were not the first of their profession to turn to psychoanalytic explanations of behavior. The first wave of interest in psychiatry rose in the years immediately following World War I and crested in the 1920s, amounting to what historians of social work have since termed the "psychiatric deluge."[16] Especially influential in the mental hygiene movement, the child guidance movement, and the development of veterans' services, psychiatric social workers proposed an interior approach to the client's problems to replace the more sociological focus on external circumstances. As social work theory substituted personal maladjustment for environmental causes as the root of social problems, social workers proposed adjusting the individual to the environment, instead of reforming that environment.[17]

Psychiatric social work dominated the theoretical landscape of the profession after World War I. Yet psychoanalytic concepts seem rarely to have found their way from conference programs to casework practice.[18] Work with unmarried mothers, apparently like much of social work, was largely unaffected by psychiatric ideas through the 1920s and 1930s. Yet if the word "deluge" overstated the impact of psychiatry on social work in the early twentieth century, it can be used with little exaggeration to describe its dominance in the 1940s. Aided by the popularization of psychiatry during World War II, psychoanalytic ideas held undisputed sway over social work theory on illegitimacy, and social workers began calling on those ideas to comprehend out-of-wedlock pregnancy.[19] "We have learned from psychiatry and psychoanalysis that folks have inner selves that are inextricably bound up with the outer person whom we have thought we knew," wrote Doris Brooks in 1938 in an article predicting future trends in work with unmarried mothers. Brooks and her colleagues believed that psychiatric techniques offered a new way "to understand what these inner selves are saying to us, what needs are being expressed, and how to help."[20]

Some social workers, reluctant to dismiss so cavalierly the previous three decades of work on illegitimacy, proposed a bridge between psychiatric and sociological explanations. In 1938 Mandel Sherman argued that "a clear-cut differentiation cannot be made between the psychiatric and the social factors" and posited an "interrelationship" between the two.[21] But the psychological soon overwhelmed the sociological in psychiatrists' and social workers' assessments of unmarried mothers. Beginning in the 1940s, social workers joined psychiatrists and psychologists in viewing out-of-wedlock pregnancy as the unmarried mother's attempt to ease a larger, unresolved psychic conflict.

The psychiatric ideas that so saturated social workers' theoretical writing on illegitimacy in the 1940s also found their way into casework practice with unmarried mothers. Before 1940, psychiatry was, for the most part, irrelevant to the daily routine of maternity homes and social agencies. Historian Martha Field finds the case records of the Illinois Children's Home and Aid Society, a Chicago agency that served unmarried mothers, to have been "entirely unaffected" by psychodynamic conceptualizations of out-of-wedlock pregnancy before 1938.[22] Between that year and 1949, however, the agency's staff had grown familiar with psychoanalytic terminology and had begun using words like "neurotic" and "repressed" in their practice, "albeit imprecisely."[23] Other social workers incorporated the jargon and techniques of psychiatry into their treatment of unmarried mothers in this period as well. Dorothy Hutchinson, professor of casework at the New York School of Social Work, often used psychiatric concepts in her work with unmarried mothers in the 1940s. Judging one unmarried mother "a very neurotic girl," Hutchinson wrote that "unconsciously I feel that Marjorie was working out a love relationship with a man her father's age who represented her father to her but of all this she was totally unaware."[24] Of another client, Hutchinson proposed that "in the pregnancy situation, Jennie seems to be somehow acting out oedipus difficulties and oedipal attachment to father." [25]

Perhaps it is not surprising that a social work educator, abreast of the latest trends in her profession, would employ psychiatric terminology in her work with unmarried mothers. But even the Salvation Army–run Door of Hope in Jersey City embraced the new understanding of unmarried motherhood. Jane Wrieden, Salvation Army officer and trained social worker, was principally responsible for bringing psychiatric social work to the Door of Hope, where she served as superintendent in the 1940s. Asked to assess the cause of out-of-wedlock pregnancy, Wrieden stated that "I have come to think of these pregnancies as only symptoms of more deep-seated problems," adding that "here we try to treat the person, not the symptom." [26] To illustrate, Wrieden told the story of a Door of Hope resident, "Mary Roe," who had had an affair with a man she expected to marry. "But when she found she was pregnant, the man told her that he was not free to marry, and that he did not intend to divorce the wife of whom Mary never before had heard." [27] Although Mary's case contained the essential ingredients of the many tales of seduction and abandonment spun by Door of Hope workers in the past, Wrieden offered a different interpretation of the meaning of Mary's pregnancy. After receiving a psychological examination at the Door of Hope, "Mary finally gained real insight into her experience, and saw her love affair and her pregnancy as related to her conflict with her own mother." [28]

Although psychiatrists and social workers agreed that illegitimacy was a neurotic symptom, they varied in their more specific analyses of the deeper pathology that produced it. Explanations of out-of-wedlock pregnancy ran the gamut of psychoanalytic diagnoses, covering a range of deep-seated problems including self-punishment for forbidden sex fantasies, unresolved "oedipal" relationships with either or both parents, and fantasies of rape, prostitution, or immaculate conception. Many social workers believed that either a dependency on or rejection by the mother or a seductive attachment to the father could precipitate illegitimacy.[29] Others described out-of-wedlock pregnancy as a masochistic act. Helene Deutsch transformed the traditional story of seduction and abandonment—"being left 'on the street' with the illegitimate child of a seducer"—into the "masochistic fantasy" of an unmarried mother.[30]

However they diagnosed its underlying cause, psychiatrists and social workers believed out-of-wedlock pregnancy to be a purposeful, albeit unconscious, act on the part of a neurotic woman. Although she sought pregnancy, in the minds of wartime and postwar experts, she did so for reasons lodged deep in her unconscious. Leontine Young likened the unmarried mother to a "sleepwalker," who "acts out what she must do without awareness or understanding of what it means or of the fact that she plans and initiates the action," and claimed that "there is nothing haphazard or accidental in the causation that brought about this specific situation with these specific girls." [31]

The psychiatric reconceptualization of single pregnancy was accomplished in less than a decade, so by the mid-1940s, neurotic unmarried mothers were entirely predictable. Psychiatrist Helene Deutsch described Ida, whose pregnancy she diagnosed as the result of "the rebellious struggle against her mother," as "a fundamentally banal story of illegitimacy." [32] In 1944, Viola Bernard remarked on the redundancy of the case of the neurotic unmarried mother: "With repetitious regularity the background histories of all the cases . . . show conspicuous maternal and paternal failure to meet the essential life-long emotional needs of these girls." [33] By the 1940s, social workers were as little surprised to find an unmarried mother with seductive designs on her father as they had been just ten years earlier to find her the promiscuous patron of dance halls, or, as evangelical women before them, the victim of an unscrupulous man.

Like these earlier narratives of out-of-wedlock pregnancy, the new psychiatric understanding of the unmarried mother was heavily weighted with meaning for its authors. Even as late as the 1940s, social workers continued to fret over the insecurity of their professional status. Because psychiatry was invested with such cultural authority in the postwar period, it boosted social workers' claim to expertise. Even more than the earlier conceptualization of sex delinquency, the new psychiatric explanation promised to place the study of illegitimacy on the lofty level of science. Robert Fleiss, in his foreword to *Out of Wedlock,* congratulated Leontine Young for transporting single pregnancy "from the nineteenth century where it had to be judged, into the twentieth where it has to be understood." [34] Young agreed that psychiatry took illegitimacy out of the emotional, moralistic world of old-fashioned benevolence and grounded it in science: "Not until the discoveries of Freud," she boasted, were social workers able to consider the unmarried mother "from a scientific rather than a moral point of view." [35]

The psychiatric understanding of single pregnancy offered social workers a discourse of illegitimacy cast in an esoteric language appropriate to the professional, filled with medical terms and cloaked in the legitimizing mantle of science. Resonating with scientific reliability, the psychiatric understanding of the unmarried mother afforded unprecedented opportunities to label and categorize, to assign unmarried mothers to "types," the resulting classification scheme signaling the culmination of rigorous research and testing. Psychiatrists and social workers created new typologies of unmarried mothers based on psychiatric categories that recalled earlier attempts to delineate various levels of sex delinquency and rivaled those classifications in their scientific pretensions. In 1938 Mandel Sherman arranged unmarried mothers into three categories: "the emotionally inadequate, the emotionally disorganized, and the neurotic." [36] By 1949, social workers had ventured more sophisticated diagnoses. In that year, Miriam Powell classified thirty unmarried mothers according to the following categories: "Primary behavior disorder, 17; psychoneurosis, 3; schizophrenia, with excessive sexuality, 2; schizoid personality, with homosexual tendencies, 1; psychopathic personality, 3; neurotic character of the hysterical type, 1; adult maladjustment, 1; childish personality with a non-existent ego, 1." [37] In an act of surprising humility, Powell listed one unmarried mother as "undiagnosed."

More broadly, the recasting of illegitimacy as a psychological rather than a sociological problem—the causes of which were to be sought not in environmental conditions but in individual psyches—must be understood in the context of the World War II and postwar period, when a family-centered culture and rigidly differentiated and prescriptive gender roles took shape and a therapeutic approach to social problems gained immense popularity.[38] At a time when "health" was measured in terms of how well an individual adjusted to his or her appropriate place in the nuclear family, it should come as no surprise that out-of-wedlock pregnancy was stigmatized as an "abnormal" departure from "normal" gender roles. Out-of-wedlock pregnancy thus became an index of abnormality that was defined in opposition to normal femininity. According to Marynia Farnham and Ferdinand Lundberg in their 1947 antifeminist classic, *Modern Woman: The Lost Sex,* not only was the unmarried mother "a psychological mess," she was also "a complete failure as a woman." [39] In large part, the core of the unmarried mother's failure lay in her refusal of married heterosexuality—newly sexualized, privileged, and compulsory in postwar America. "Certainly, the girl's wish to have a baby without a husband is neither an adult nor a normal desire," Young wrote, invoking two damning postwar epithets— immaturity and abnormality—in a single sentence.[40]

Professional aspirations of social workers and their participation in a culture that stigmatized all departures from conventional gender roles as neurotic go some distance toward explaining the rise of the neurotic unmarried mother. The fact that not all unmarried mothers were so diagnosed, however, suggests that class and race informed this new conceptualization in powerful ways. In large part, social workers' reframing of illegitimacy as neurotic seems to have been linked to their attempt to explain the changing demographic profile of unmarried mothers seeking aid during World War II. Helen Perlman was careful to specify race when she wrote that "prevailing social work theory about the illegitimately pregnant white girl or woman is heavily dependent on psychoanalytic theory." [41] Exploring the reasons behind the new concern for "the psychological well-being of the unmarried mother" in the 1940s, Perlman argued that "there arose some wish to protect the 'good girl' of 'good family' who was considered to have 'made a mistake.' "[42] Diagnosing the unmarried mother as neurotic rather than as a sex delinquent offered that protection. Psychiatric explanations gave social workers a way to comprehend the illicit sexual behavior of young white women of the middle class as something other than willful promiscuity.

Accordingly, psychiatric explanations desexualized out-of-wedlock pregnancy. Branding single mothers as sex delinquents had defined them as hypersexual; diagnosing white middle-class unmarried mothers as neurotic defined them as sexually passive, even asexual. In fact, "contrary to the layman's notion," Viola Bernard reported, not one of the ten unmarried mothers in her study experienced "full sexual enjoyment," and for most of them "intercourse proved chiefly unpleasant." [43] Young also found that unmarried mothers "show much less concern and initiative in attracting men than the average girl." [44] Helene Deutsch asserted that "conception takes place under specific conditions that have nothing to do with love or sexual excitement." [45] Of seventeen-year-old Louise, Deutsch wrote that when a man propositioned her, "she became a passive object and could not say 'No.' "[46] "The idea that all the girls are boy-crazy, oversexed, or downright bad is idiotic," Hildegarde Dolson claimed in 1942. To support this claim, Dolson noted that the unmarried mothers she observed at the Youth Consultation Service included "a nurse, a debutante, a waitress, a highschool junior, two college graduates, a young schoolteacher, and the nineteen-year-old daughter of a well-to-do businessman." [47] Dolson's assumption, shared by many of her colleagues, was that class exempted these women from the label of sex delinquency.

It is interesting to note that despite this desexualization of out-of-wedlock pregnancy, the behavior of unmarried mothers as described by social workers and psychologists was objectively no less sexual. For example, nineteen-year-old Virginia, a client of Helene Deutsch's whose "love life had its locale in restaurants and dance halls," reported having had sex with a man she met at a restaurant.[48] Just a decade earlier, Virginia's manner of meeting men would have easily earned her the title of sex delinquent. Her occupation of domestic servant, which had long connoted both sexual impropriety and sexual vulnerability, would only have confirmed the label.[49] Deutsch was more interested in what she understood to be the underlying psychic causes of out-of-wedlock pregnancy than its superficial symptoms, however, and diagnosed the cause of Virginia's pregnancy as psychological, rooted in her loss of her mother at an early age.

One social worker surely spoke for many of her colleagues when she identified the sexual behavior of the unmarried mother as "one of the most difficult problems for the worker." [50] And indeed, it must have been difficult for social workers to transform behavior that had been understood as unambigu-

ously promiscuous into behavior consistent with the sexual passivity that social
workers and psychiatrists insisted was characteristic of the white middle-class
unmarried mother of the 1940s. They accomplished this feat, in large part,
by focusing attention on pregnancy, rather than the precipitating sexual act;
the new psychiatric understanding of illegitimacy deemphasized sex and foregrounded maternity. Whereas sex with a casual acquaintance would have once
marked a woman as sexually aggressive, it was now understood as a deliberate and neurotic attempt to become pregnant outside marriage, the man in
question simply a "tool" by which to achieve the pregnancy and the steps a
woman took to accomplish that end only incidentally sexual. "All the evidence
points to the fact that most of the girls in this group are truly disinterested in
the actual fathers of the babies," Young wrote; "for such a girl, the man is
apparently a necessary biological accessory who serves only one purpose—to
make her pregnant—and then is of no further interest or concern." [51] By transforming illegitimacy from a discourse of illicit sexuality into a discourse of
motherhood, psychoanalytic diagnoses deemphasized the sexuality of overtly
sexual women, maternalized women who flouted so many postwar family imperatives, and repositioned unmarried mothers within a structure of family
relations rather than opposed to it.[52] If their sexuality could not be contained
within a nuclear family of their own formation, the understanding of illegitimacy as springing from obsession with one's mother or a desire for one's father
contained unmarried mothers' sexuality within their family of origin.[53]

Finally, by subjecting unmarried mothers to individual treatment, the psychiatric approach worked to shrink the problem of the unmarried mother down
to manageable proportions. In her new incarnation as neurotic, the unmarried
mother appeared considerably tamer than in her older role of sex delinquent.
Once an issue of national concern, illegitimacy might now be understood as
the psychological problem of the individual. Leontine Young was particularly
insistent that unmarried motherhood carried no grave moral consequences,
criticizing the earlier tendency to view illegitimacy as posing substantial danger to the security of the family and society as "fallacious." [54] Once devoted to
assessing the damage wrought by the unmarried mother to the moral fiber of
the nation and the sanctity of the family, social workers, Young wrote, now en-
deavored "to define the special problems which trouble them as individuals." [55]

Black Unmarried Mothers and "Cultural Pathology"

While illegitimacy among white middle-class women appeared less menacing
when cast as a problem of individual pathology, illegitimacy among other
groups began to take on a more threatening hue. "Bad girls" had not disap-

peared in the 1940s; on the contrary, they loomed large on the national land-scape. The psychiatric narrative of out-of-wedlock pregnancy that essentially desexualized white middle-class unmarried mothers is all the more striking when viewed in the larger context of the national preoccupation with female promiscuity and delinquency that accompanied World War II, when observers noted with alarm "the increase in the number of footloose, unprotected girls roaming Main Street, loitering in parks, hanging around juke joints, and often getting themselves into serious trouble." [56] Much of this fear focused on the threat of venereal disease to men in the armed services and precipitated a massive drive against prostitution. [57] Many came to believe, however, that prostitution was less a problem than "promiscuity," although contemporaries were disconcerted to find the line dividing the two "difficult, if not impossible to draw." [58] Of the girls and women who came to Hartford, Connecticut, to be near soldiers and defense workers, Helen Pigeon wrote: "They do not belong to the rank of professional prostitutes but it is evident from case histories that many are promiscuous." [59] "Sex delinquency" had been a working-class diagnosis since the 1910s, and class assumptions continued to inflect understandings of wartime and postwar "promiscuity." [60] Laura Waggoner of the Community Welfare Council of San Antonio, Texas, identified these girls and women as "almost entirely from farming and working-class homes of low economic level" and characterized them as "casual fun-seeking girls wanting male companionship, immature in judgment, sometimes lonely, unstable, and easily influenced." [61] These women who drew so much attention, condemnation, and fear from public officials and wartime media—those dubbed "Victory Girls," "khaki-wackies," and "patriotic prostitutes," who socialized with soldiers on the streets, in restaurants, and in dance halls—were not given psychiatric examinations but were rounded up by local law enforcement officials. [62] Race, then, did not completely eclipse class in the postwar understanding of out-of-wedlock pregnancy. The discourse of sex delinquency retained its explanatory appeal to social workers who attempted to understand the behavior of girls and women whose pregnancies still seemed to spring from familiar causes long assumed to have a working-class etiology: broken homes, bad companions, a disdain for authority, and an addiction to urban pleasures. The psychiatric understanding of out-of-wedlock pregnancy simply ensured that white middle-class unmarried mothers would no longer be cast among their ranks.

Even more than working-class white women, black unmarried mothers attracted increasingly intense concern beginning in the late 1930s and accelerating during and after the war. Social workers who went to great lengths to defuse the "problem" of the white unmarried mother drew attention to that posed by her black counterpart. While the psychiatric discourse of illegitimacy attempted to remove white middle-class unmarried mothers from the roster of problems facing postwar America, a reconceptualization of black illegitimacy catapulted African American women to the top of that list.

Observers had commented on a disproportionately high black illegitimacy rate since the early twentieth century, but black unmarried mothers had not attracted a great deal of attention or interest before the late 1930s.[63] Indeed, in the early twentieth century, when illegitimacy among working-class white women came under such intense scrutiny, their African American counterparts seemed hardly worthy of notice. Most of those who did investigate black illegitimacy wrote in the racist tradition that viewed out-of-wedlock pregnancy as the natural and unsurprising result of the constitutional hypersexuality and immorality believed to be characteristic of the race. Beginning in the 1920s and 1930s, however, historians, sociologists, anthropologists, and social workers moved from arguments based on racial degeneracy to new explanations that emphasized the "cultural acceptance" of illegitimacy in some black communities. Rather than provide an index of immorality, illegitimacy, these investigators argued, was better understood as an adaptation to environmental and social conditions. Some, most notably anthropologist Melville Herskovits, argued that African American attitudes toward illegitimacy were rooted in preslavery African traditions.[64] E. Franklin Frazier, in his path-breaking 1939 study, *The Negro Family in the United States,* argued instead that black family patterns were born of the conditions of enslavement in the United States.

Social workers were quick to incorporate sociological and anthropological arguments into their own investigations of black illegitimacy. Frazier, in particular, exerted enormous influence among social workers, perhaps because of his background in the profession.[65] Patricia Knapp, in a 1945 study of black unmarried mothers, assumed that "for culturally determined reasons, the morality codes of many Negroes do not include a prohibition against illegitimacy."[66] Leontine Young echoed Frazier when she wrote that "the matriarchal system and the difficulty of maintaining a strong, enduring family structure, both conditions bred and fostered in slavery, in general promoted an attitude of acceptance of the unmarried mother and her child."[67]

Before the 1940s, the argument that illegitimacy was culturally accepted in black communities led most social workers to dismiss it as a problem deserving serious concern and provided them with a convenient rationalization for devoting so few resources to black unmarried mothers. Although hundreds of maternity homes across the country offered services to unmarried mothers, the vast majority of those homes either restricted applications to white women or accepted only a very few black residents. In explanation, Ruth Reed wrote in 1926, "there is a belief held by many social workers that illegitimacy among Negroes creates few social problems which are comparable in importance with those produced among white people by unconventional birth." [68] Social workers drew support for this rationale from social scientists, some of whom concluded that the supposed acceptance of illegitimacy among blacks rendered it virtually meaningless as a concept. In his 1934 study of Macon County, Georgia, Charles Johnson suggested that because out-of-wedlock pregnancy was so much a matter of course, "there is, in a sense, no such thing as illegitimacy in this community." [69]

Beginning in the late 1930s, however, black illegitimacy came under closer scrutiny and began to appear less benign. Frazier was perhaps the first to question the casual acceptance of black out-of-wedlock pregnancy and to complicate its causes. By Frazier's own account, the necessary survival strategies adopted by black families during slavery—including a "matriarchal" family structure, "disorganized" kinship ties, and illegitimacy—took on new meaning in twentieth-century urban life. Before that time, Frazier argued, illegitimacy in rural black communities reflected "the simple and naive behavior of peasant folks"—behavior that was "not licentious and could scarcely be called immoral." [70] The new subjects that captured Frazier's attention, however, were no longer rural blacks, but those who had migrated from the rural South to southern, northern, and western cities. The migration of illegitimacy from rural areas into newly visible urban venues accompanied the geographical migration of blacks that began in the 1910s and accelerated during World War II. Historian Hazel Carby argues that African American migration "generated a series of moral panics" about urban immorality, in which black women were targeted as "sexually dangerous and therefore socially dangerous." [71] Frazier was among the first to assert that the migration of blacks to cities rendered illegitimacy, once harmless, newly problematic: "During the course of their migration to the city, family ties are broken, and the restraints which once held in check immoral sex conduct lose their force." [72] Declaring black illegitimacy in Chicago to be "the result of family and community disorganization," Frazier argued that out-of-wedlock pregnancy was "the result of casual and impersonal contacts through which random and undisciplined impulses found expression." [73] In its new urban incarnation, illegitimacy no longer ensued from an adaptive black family structure but from "an awakened imagination fed by the cheap romance of the movies and the popular magazines" that Frazier argued "led some to licentiousness and debauchery in the sex relation." [74]

The migration of African Americans to cities seemed to Frazier to reconfigure rural folkways into urban problems, and disproportionate black illegitimacy rates that had once seemed expressive of naive peasant customs now signaled a dangerously dysfunctional black family. To Frazier, illegitimacy was not only a product of unstable family relations but, more dangerously, the catalyst for "matriarchal" families, which, he claimed, "originate through illegitimacy."

Illegitimacy, then, was simultaneously cause and effect of the disorganized black family. In a passage that illuminates the anxiety about black women's autonomy that underlay this characterization of the black family, Frazier wrote that "the man's or father's function generally ceases with impregnation. . . . He has no authority in the household or over his children." [75]

The manifestation of this new matriarchal autonomy most disturbing to Frazier was his belief that single black women were more inclined to give up their children, to him an important indicator of the new and dangerous character of black illegitimacy. This charge was altogether new and reflected a complete reversal in representations. For decades, social commentators had invested black unmarried mothers with instinctive maternal warmth and praised their tendency to keep their children. But by the 1940s, many observers were noting with great anxiety the desire on the part of some black unmarried mothers in urban areas to give up their children. Frazier found that "on the whole, the unmarried mothers in the city exhibit less of the elemental maternal sympathy toward their children which one finds in rural communities in the South." [76] Frazier went so far as to accuse black single mothers of infanticide: "In the alleys of southern cities as well as in the tenements in northern cities, the unmarried mother sometimes kills her unwanted child by throwing it in the garbage can." [77]

In attempting to understand the forces generating his reconceptualization of black single pregnancy, it is important to note that many scholars and social workers, Frazier foremost among them, initially invoked the argument of cultural acceptance to repudiate the racist assumptions of biological theories of black family life and morality that underlay earlier prevailing explanations of black illegitimacy.[78] Frazier's analysis, for example, gave Leontine Young the ammunition to criticize those who looked for racial explanations for illegitimacy as "stupid and clearly fallacious." [79] Replacing the natural immorality argument with one that stressed cultural acceptance allowed investigators to posit black family patterns as social, rather than biological, products. As Maurine LaBarre wrote in 1940, "many social workers attribute the problems of Negro clients to racial characteristics, as if they were physically inherited, rather than to social and cultural factors. We shall not find the solution to the Negro problem in physical differences but in a study of his cultural history and situation." [80]

As eager as many sociologists and social workers were to present black illegitimacy as culturally constructed rather than biologically ordained, they were also concerned that distinctive African American family patterns presented obstacles to racial integration. Thus they found some relief in their "discovery" that not all black Americans regarded illegitimacy with the same apparent nonchalance. Studies of urban black communities that proliferated in the 1930s and

1940s sought to show how the family patterns of the most "advanced" black families resembled those of the white middle class, a resemblance most often measured according to morality and sexuality. In her 1944 study of illegitimacy in Durham, North Carolina, Hilda Hertz noted that middle- and upper-class blacks "accept the same values in regard to sex behavior and family life accepted in white society." [81] Investigators of black urban communities turned to moral and sexual measures as often as economic indicators to map the geography of class. Believing out-of-wedlock pregnancy to be the most accessible index of moral values and sexual behavior, those investigators used illegitimacy to chart the emergence of a class-stratified black urban community. Hertz, for example, distinguished the "Negro upper and middle class" from the "lower class" by their respective "sex codes," and psychologist Margaret Brenman cited the difference in sexual standards and behavior between middle- and "lower-class" black teenage girls as "probably the most reliable single criterion in establishing class membership." [82] Some residents of black communities joined investigators in describing illegitimacy in class and spatial terms. Many of the black college students that Hilda Hertz interviewed marked illegitimacy geographically: "The girls who are most likely to become unmarried mothers are those who stay in the bad sections of town," one told her. Another reported that "in some parts of the city it is the usual thing to be pregnant and not be married." [83]

This sexual cartography of class enabled both investigators of black communities and middle-class residents of those communities to combat the popular notion of a homogeneous and pathological black family and to distinguish a new black bourgeoisie from its "lower-class" neighbors. Representing this new middle class required contrasting its assimilated manners with those of a new black proletariat. [84] At least as important, this formulation also allowed sociologists to posit a hopeful trajectory: If black illegitimacy was most prevalent among recent migrants who had brought their rural ways to the city— if, as St. Clair Drake and Horace Cayton argued, illegitimacy among blacks was a reflection not of immorality but "of the incomplete urbanization of the rural southern migrants"—then perhaps the black family was moving on an evolutionary path toward the standard set by the middle-class white family. [85] The argument that illegitimacy was "culturally accepted" among blacks served the intellectual and political interests of sociologists and social workers of the 1930s and 1940s—some of whom were themselves African American—and the class interests of a new black bourgeoisie, each of whom used this conceptualization of out-of-wedlock pregnancy to plot a liberal path toward racial integration and assimilation.

Frazier's work had a tremendous impact on social workers; it also captured the interest of a new group of "experts" in social policy. In 1935, the Carnegie Corporation commissioned a massive study of American race relations and invited Swedish economist Gunnar Myrdal to synthesize and popularize scholarly work and statistical data on African American life. Published in 1944, *An American Dilemma* was a monument to 1940s racial liberalism. As historian David Southern explains, Myrdal understood the "American Dilemma" as "the conflict between verbally honored American ideals" of freedom and equality and "the pervasive practice of white racism." [86] Myrdal devoted an important section of his 1,400-page volume to the black family. Strongly influenced by Frazier, Myrdal credited him with offering "such an excellent description and analysis of the American Negro family that it is practically necessary only to relate its conclusions to our context and to refer the reader to it for details." [87] In arguing that "the uniqueness of the Negro family is a product of slavery," Myrdal joined Frazier in characterizing the black family as pathological and in placing ultimate blame for "deviant" black family patterns on white racism. [88]

Postwar social policymakers and politicians were as impressed as Myrdal with Frazier's research on the African American family and were as inclined to appropriate his arguments. They were less inclined, however, to focus on the aspects of his analysis that indicted racism and more likely to name the black family itself as the dilemma that demanded national attention. As the specter of black illegitimacy that would dominate public policy debates about the black family in the 1950s and 1960s began to take shape under the weight of wartime and postwar pressures, what was once seen as "cultural acceptance" became "cultural pathology."

The principal architect of this new construction, Daniel Patrick Moynihan positioned illegitimacy at the heart of the "tangle of pathology" of the black family. [89] Whereas Frazier had blamed white racial oppression for "pathology" and "disorganization," Moynihan suggested that the causes were intrinsic to African American culture. Moynihan's strategy of locating the causes of problems faced by black Americans in the structure of their families served to deflect blame from broader structural problems and institutionalized racism at a time when a militant civil rights movement was demanding their attention. Invoking both Frazier and Myrdal, sometimes virtually verbatim, Moynihan's *The Negro Family: The Case for National Action,* published in 1965, articulated a view of the black family that has proved to have remarkable staying power. [90] Investigations of the "culture of poverty" nurtured by a pathological "underclass" in the 1960s and 1970s further collapsed cultural "difference" and cultural pathology and moved closer to attributing illegitimacy to innate immorality. In the 1980s and 1990s, the discourse of "family values" even more aggressively racialized the "decent" American family and pathologized black single mothers.

It was in a way ironic that policymakers and politicians would use an argument that sociologists and social workers posed to integrate blacks into the urban social order to marginalize and pathologize them further. As grimly as Frazier depicted black illegitimacy, he went to great lengths to locate its roots in a history of enslavement and oppression. But in many ways, Frazier lent himself to appropriations of his work that would indict the black family and black women in particular. In 1939 Frazier predicted that illegitimacy would result in "disease and in children who are unwanted and uncared for"—a double-edged warning that resonated portentously in wartime and postwar America.[91] The first reference invoked long-held racist associations between African Americans and venereal disease and was particularly threatening in the 1940s, when fears about the health of men in the armed services ran high.[92] The second half of this warning—the specter of unwanted black children—reinforced a growing fear that black illegitimacy would drain welfare coffers. This fear was fueled in the 1940s, when, for the first time, unmarried mothers and their children became eligible for public assistance under the Aid to Dependent Children (ADC) program. While many more white single mothers than black obtained public assistance, black women bore the brunt of white anger at increasing public welfare costs and became the targets of efforts to deny public assistance to illegitimate children.[93]

As with the psychiatric discourse of white illegitimacy, new fears surrounding black illegitimacy took shape in the larger context of the powerful familial ideology that crystallized during and after the war. It was no accident that the black family should alarm policymakers at a time when family values were being so rigidly prescribed and the "normal family" was portrayed as white, middle-class, male-headed, and suburban-dwelling. This hegemonic postwar family both implicitly and explicitly excluded black Americans. Mass media celebrations of the American family rendered blacks all but invisible, while suburban developments restricted housing to whites. A crucial site for fighting Cold War battles, the family was charged with nothing less than providing refuge from nuclear weapons, halting communist subversion, ensuring economic progress by operating as a consuming unit, and reviving conventional gender roles from the beating they had taken during the Great Depression and World War II. The stakes invested in the postwar family rendered any deviation from its norms tantamount to treason.

Conclusion

In the first decades of the twentieth century, class had resided at the heart of discourses about illegitimacy. By the 1940s, race had taken center stage. In 1927, social worker Henry Schumacher declared illegitimacy a "socio-psychiatric" problem.[94] In the years that followed World War II, the hyphen in that label came to separate rigidly dichotomized constructions of black and white illegitimacy. The wartime and postwar years witnessed the construction of white illegitimacy as a symptom of individual pathology and the simultaneous reconceptualization of black illegitimacy as a symptom of cultural pathology. While psychiatric explanations for single pregnancy were almost exclusively applied to white women, black unmarried mothers were burdened with the heavy weight of explanations "sociological" in nature.

Both constructions enlisted new groups of experts in the study of illegitimacy, and the ways in which single pregnancy was cast and recast reveal the extent to which those discourses were shaped by concern for professional legitimacy. But the fracturing of discourses on illegitimacy in the 1940s illuminates a contest over issues of sexuality and the family that transcended the struggle for professional status. Illegitimacy had long been a lightning rod that attracted anxieties about gender, race, class, and sexuality. In the wartime and postwar years, out-of-wedlock pregnancy functioned as a language through which people might contain, contest, and resolve issues of social change and sexual and racial conflict far broader than the issue of illegitimacy. The psychiatric explanation for white middle-class out-of-wedlock pregnancy promised to forestall the "woman question," which resurfaced in the 1940s when women's sexual and economic autonomy collided with efforts to reinvigorate traditional gender roles. Mounting fears over black illegitimacy expressed larger anxieties about race relations that crystallized and intensified during and after the war. The new militancy and assertiveness on the part of blacks expressed both in an incipient civil rights movement and in the wartime race riots of the summer of 1943 brought new urgency to the politics of race and posed the "Negro question" in new and unsettling terms that raised doubts as to its resolution.[95] The wartime and postwar discourse on illegitimacy illuminates the way in which anxieties about gender and race were mapped onto sexuality and maternity in the larger culture.

The new constructions of illegitimacy were fraught with meaning for their authors. More difficult to gauge is the meaning of these new discourses to their subjects. On the rare occasions that the voices of unmarried mothers came through in the literature that defined them as "problems," they made clear that they were not passive recipients of others' constructions but struggled to author their own meanings of out-of-wedlock pregnancy. One white woman suggested that the "experts'" understanding of illegitimacy as purposeful and neurotic bore little resemblance to her understanding of her own pregnancy: "I've been reading a book on the psychology of the unwed mother," Jean Thompson wrote in 1967. "The book says such a pregnancy is rarely accidental. It says the girl nearly always wants it—as a crutch, an excuse to fail, a way to rebel or demonstrate against her parents. . . . Phew, that sounds like a mouthful, as if the author is really looking for symptoms where there aren't any." [96] One black single mother of five told Chicago investigators that her boyfriend "wants to marry, but I don't want to be bothered. I've been my boss too long now. I go and come and do what I want to do. I can't see where I can have anyone bossing me around now." [97] Although her forthright defense might have reinforced assumptions of black matriarchal power, she made it clear that she understood out-of-wedlock pregnancy as something other than cultural pathology. Perhaps more significantly, she transformed pathology into autonomy, insisting on her own independence in the face of a construction that denied individuality to African American women.[98]

Yet women struggling to construct their own identities as single mothers had to contend with the terms of the dominant postwar discourses that defined them as either mentally ill or culturally deviant. While out-of-wedlock pregnancy relegated postwar women and girls to outcast status regardless of race, "neurosis" was, in a relative sense, a privileged category. As Solinger argues, since psychiatric diagnoses made illegitimacy "contingent upon the mutable mind, rather than upon fixed, physical entities," they offered the hope of rehabilitation.[99] In short, the (white) girl could change. At the same time, the diagnosis subjected white middle-class girls and women to ever more intrusive scrutiny and aggressive intervention. While the mostly white, predominantly working-class unmarried mothers who had sought the services of social workers and maternity homes before World War II had been subjected to the intrusions of casework for decades—interrogated by social workers about how many times they had had sex, with whom, and under what circumstances—the new psychiatric diagnoses, which located the cause of out-of-wedlock pregnancy not in the environment but in the mind, legitimized a widening of the scope of intrusion from women's behavior to their psyches. On the other hand, the argument that the pathological black family produced illegitimate children was used to justify public policies directed against African American single mothers and their children, to subject them to harassment by welfare officials, to deny them public funds and services, and in some cases, to license their sterilization.[100]

Racialized discourses of out-of-wedlock pregnancy had material consequences for single mothers. For historians, they underline a phenomenon we have only begun to explore in any detail: the mutual constitution of ideologies of gender and race. Though the worlds of black and white unmarried mothers rarely intersected, constructions of black and white single pregnancy were constantly in dialogue. Each a reference point for the other, race-specific etiologies of illegitimacy illuminate the ways in which gender and sexuality were enlisted in constructing racial hierarchies in the wartime and postwar period. While recent studies have revealed the ways in which postwar politics were profoundly gendered, these representations of unmarried mothers suggest that race, as powerfully and pervasively as gender, determined the form and shape of the ideology of the family that stood at the heart of the postwar political agenda.

NOTES

Acknowledgments: I thank Stuart Clarke, Nancy Cott, Jacqueline Dirks, Susan Johnson, Mark Naison, Kathryn Oberdeck, and Catherine Stock. I am especially grateful to Joanne Meyerowitz for her helpful suggestions on several versions of this essay, and to Siobhan Somerville. Research for this essay was supported by a National Endowment for the Humanities Summer Stipend.

1. Leontine R. Young, *Out of Wedlock* (New York: McGraw-Hill, 1954), 21.

2. I use the term "evangelical" to refer to the group of women who founded maternity homes in the late nineteenth century and staffed them into the early 1940s. These women shared a common belief in religious conversion, followed by a changed life, and felt their commitment to work with unmarried mothers to be religiously inspired and motivated. They expressed a kinship with the larger community of predominantly white, Protestant, middle-class women engaged in temperance and social purity reform and home and foreign missionary activity, with whom they shared a common sensibility. See Regina G. Kunzel, *Fallen Women, Problem Girls: Unmarried Mothers and the Professionalization of Social Work, 1890–1945* (New Haven: Yale University Press, 1993), chap. 1.

3. "Brief Sketches Taken from the Record of Thirty-One Years in Redemption House," Springfield, Ill., Redemption House, *Annual Report* (1934), Box 8, File 94, National Florence Crittenton Mission papers, Social Welfare History Archives, University of Minnesota. (Hereafter cited as NFCM.)

4. For a fuller discussion of the ways in which constructions of illegitimacy changed in relation to professionalization, see Kunzel, *Fallen Women, Problem Girls,* chaps. 1, 2.

5. Leontine Young, "The Unmarried Mother's Decision about Her Baby," *Journal of Social Casework* 28 (January 1947): 27.

6. Rickie Solinger, *Wake Up Little Susie: Single Pregnancy and Race Before Roe v. Wade* (New York: Routledge, 1992). In this thoughtful and thorough analysis, Solinger traces the relationship of postwar racialized constructions of out-of-wedlock pregnancy to social policy regarding black and white single mothers. In this essay, I am more concerned with the ways in which those constructions became legitimizing vehicles for social workers and policymakers in their struggles for cultural authority during and after the war. I also intend in this study to begin the complicated and crucial project of exploring the interdependence of ideologies of gender and race; to that end, I hope to show that these constructions of out-of-wedlock pregnancy depended on and were in dialogue with each other.

7. "Annual Report of the National Officers," *Florence Crittenton Bulletin* 16 (September 1941): 10.

8. The Bureau of the Census reported a decrease in illegitimate births in 1942, from 40.8 per 1,000 in 1941 to 37.2 in 1942. This represented a decrease of 8.8 percent

from that of 1941 and was the lowest reported proportion since 1931. U.S. Bureau of the Census, Vital Statistics—Special Report, *Illegitimate Births by Race, United States, 1942* (April 27, 1942), 19:142. Later in the decade the illegitimacy rate rose markedly. Illegitimate births rose from 82,586 in 1943 to 87,001 in 1944. U.S. Bureau of the Census, Vital Statistics—Special Report, *Illegitimate Births by Race: United States and Each State, 1944* (October 31, 1946), 25:255.

   9. Helen Harris Perlman, "Unmarried Mothers," in *Social Work and Social Problems*, ed. Nathan E. Cohen (New York: National Association of Social Workers, 1964), 301.

   10. Solinger, *Wake Up Little Susie*, 93.

   11. Young, *Out of Wedlock*, 1.

   12. J. Kasanin and Sieglinde Handschin, "Psychodynamic Factors in Illegitimacy," *American Journal of Orthopsychiatry* 11 (January 1941): 71.

   13. Sara B. Edlin, *The Unmarried Mother in Our Society* (New York: Farrar, Strauss, and Young, 1954), 85. See also Kasanin and Handschin, "Psychodynamic Factors in Illegitimacy," 68; *Florence Crittenton Bulletin* 22 (July 1947): 36; Edith Balmford to Maud Morlock, February 21, 1944, box 173, folder 7-4-0, Children's Bureau papers, National Archives, Washington, D.C. (Hereafter cited as CB.)

   14. Rose Bernstein, "Are We Still Stereotyping the Unmarried Mother?" *Social Work* 5 (1960): 24.

   15. Young, *Out of Wedlock*, 241. Rickie Solinger provides an excellent analysis of psychiatric diagnoses of white unmarried mothers in *Wake Up Little Susie*, chap. 3.

   16. Grace Marcus used this phrase in "The Status of Social Case Work Today," *Compass* 16 (1935): 8. Historians since have adopted it to describe the influence of psychiatry on social work in the 1920s. See, for example, Kathleen Woodroofe, *From Charity to Social Work in England and the United States* (Toronto: University of Toronto Press, 1962), chap. 6.

   17. Many historians argue that psychiatry served to deflect social work from its former concern with social reform. See Clarke A. Chambers, "Creative Effort in an Age of Normalcy, 1918–33," in *Social Welfare Forum* (New York: Columbia University Press, 1961), 257–258; John H. Ehrenreich, *The Altruistic Imagination: A History of Social Work and Social Policy in the United States* (Ithaca: Cornell University Press, 1985); Roy Lubove, *The Professional Altruist: The Emergence of Social Work as a Career, 1880–1930* (Cambridge: Harvard University Press, 1965); Herman Borenzweig, "Social Work and Psychoanalytic Theory: A Historical Analysis," *Social Work* 16 (January 1971): 7–16. Not all social workers embraced psychiatric social work. Florence Day remembered a colleague's remark that "the depression would have at least one good result if it whacked 'this psychiatry business' out of case work." Florence Day, "Changing Practices in Case Work Treatment," in *Readings in Social Case Work*, ed. Fern Lowry (New York: Columbia University Press, 1939), 333.

   18. However important to some social work educators and theorists, psychoanalysis bore little relation to what social workers actually did. From a review of social work theoretical literature and case records from the 1920s, historian Leslie Alexander argues that "psychoanalytic theory influenced an elite minority fringe rather than the main body of theory and practice during the 1920s" and concludes that psychiatry was much less influential for both theory and practice than historians have contended. Leslie B. Alexander, "Social Work's Freudian Deluge: Myth or Reality?" *Social Service Review* 46 (December 1972): 517–518. See also Ehrenreich, *Altruistic Imagination*, 123.

19. On the expansion and popularization of psychiatry during World War II, see John Burnham, "The Influence of Psychoanalysis upon American Culture," in *American Psychoanalysis: Origins and Development,* ed. Jacque M. Quen and Eric T. Carlson (New York: Brunner/Mazel, 1978); William C. Menninger, *Psychiatry in a Troubled World* (New York: Macmillan, 1948); Walter Bromberg, *Psychiatry between the Wars, 1918–1945: A Recollection* (Westport, Conn.: Greenwood Press, 1982), 102–122.

20. Doris P. Brooks, "Future Trends in Work with the Unmarried Mother," Child Welfare League of America, *Bulletin* 17 (January 1938): 1.

21. Mandel Sherman, "The Unmarried Mother," 1938, 2, box 52, folder 3, United Charities of Chicago collection, Chicago Historical Society. See also Florence Clothier, "Psychological Implications of Unmarried Parenthood," *American Journal of Orthopsychiatry* 13 (July 1943): 548.

22. Martha Heineman Field, "Social Casework Practice during the 'Psychiatric Deluge,' " *Social Service Review* 54 (December 1980): 494.

23. Ibid., 496.

24. Case of Marjorie, July 26, 1946, 6, box 1, folder 3, Dorothy Hutchinson papers, Columbia University Archives, Columbia University.

25. Case of Jennie, May 13, 1942, 13, box 2, folder 18, Dorothy Hutchinson papers, Columbia University Archives.

26. Beulah Amidon, "Front Line Officer," *Survey Graphic* 37 (October 1948): 439.

27. Ibid., 439–440.

28. Ibid.

29. See Babette Block, "The Unmarried Mother: Is She Different?" National Conference of Social Work, *Proceedings,* 1945, 283; Frances H. Scherz, " 'Taking Sides' in the Unmarried Mother's Conflict," *Journal of Social Casework* 28 (February 1947): 57–58; Viola W. Bernard, "Psychodynamics of Unmarried Motherhood in Early Adolescence," *The Nervous Child* 4 (October 1944): 40; Young devoted chapter 3 of *Out of Wedlock* to "The Mother Ridden," and chapter 4 to "The Father Ridden."

30. Helene Deutsch, *The Psychology of Women: A Psychoanalytic Interpretation* (New York: Grune and Stratton, 1945), 2:369.

31. Young, *Out of Wedlock,* 36; Young, "Personality Patterns in Unmarried Mothers," *Family* 26 (December 1945): 82.

32. Deutsch, *Psychology of Women,* 349.

33. Bernard, "Psychodynamics," 40. See also Young, *Out of Wedlock,* 40.

34. Robert Fleiss, "Foreword," in Young, *Out of Wedlock,* v.

35. Young, *Out of Wedlock,* 21.

36. Sherman, "The Unmarried Mother," 17.

37. Miriam Powell, "Illegitimate Pregnancy in Emotionally Disturbed Girls," *Smith College Studies in Social Work* 19 (June 1949): 173.

38. Elaine Tyler May documents the "widespread endorsement of this familial consensus in the cold war era," in *Homeward Bound: American Families in the Cold War Era* (New York: Basic Books, 1988), 20.

39. Ferdinand Lundberg and Marynia Farnham, *Modern Woman: The Lost Sex* (New York: Harper & Brothers, 1947), 280.

40. Young, *Out of Wedlock,* p. 37.

41. Perlman, "Unmarried Mothers," 288.

42. Ibid., 301.

43. Bernard, "Psychodynamics," 39.

44. Young, *Out of Wedlock*, 22.

45. Deutsch, *Psychology of Women*, 374.

46. Ibid., 338.

47. Hildegarde Dolson, "My Parents Mustn't Know," *Good Housekeeping*, May 1942, 159.

48. Deutsch, *Psychology of Women*, 355.

49. In 1915 George Mangold noted the disproportionate representation of domestic servants among unmarried mothers he studied and asked, "Is domestic service a morally extra-hazardous occupation? Is the class of women employed in this branch of industry mentally and morally inferior?" Mangold, "Unlawful Motherhood," *Forum* 53 (February 1915): 342. Most social workers believed in some combination of the two, and closely linked domestic service and sex delinquency. See, for example, U.S. Senate, *Report on the Condition of Women and Child Wage Earners in the United States*, vol. 15, *Relation between Occupation and Criminality of Women*, Doc. 645 (Washington, D.C.: Government Printing Office, 1911), 86–87; Ida R. Parker, "A Follow-up Study of Five Hundred and Fifty Illegitimacy Applications," Research Bureau on Social Casework, Boston 1924, 30–31; Carol Aronovici, *Unmarried Girls with Sex Experience* (Philadelphia: Bureau for Social Research of the Seybert Institution, 1922), 27; Ruth Reed, *The Social and Health Care of the Illegitimate Family in New York City* (New York: Research Bureau Welfare Council of New York City, 1932), 38–39.

50. Sherman, "The Unmarried Mother," 13.

51. Young, *Out of Wedlock*, 50. See also Scherz, "Taking Sides," 59.

52. Interestingly, this new emphasis on unmarried mothers as mothers, rather than as sex delinquents, did not garner any more respect for their right to make their own decision regarding the disposition of their children. Social workers had argued that sex delinquents were unfit to be mothers, and neurotic unmarried mothers were considered no more competent. In the 1940s, social workers took a more active role in encouraging unmarried mothers to put their children up for adoption. See Young, "The Unmarried Mother's Decision about Her Baby," 33; Young, *Out of Wedlock*, 39; Deutsch, *Psychology of Women*, 376; Scherz, "Taking Sides," 61; Bernard, "Psychodynamics," 43; Ruth F. Brenner, "Case Work Services for Unmarried Mothers," *Family* 22 (November 1941): 218. Rickie Solinger discusses what she terms the "postwar adoption mandate" in *Wake Up Little Susie*, chap. 5.

53. The metaphor of "containment" is developed by Elaine Tyler May in her analysis of the "containment" of sexuality within the family during the Cold War. May, *Homeward Bound*, chap. 5.

54. Young, *Out of Wedlock*, 7.

55. Ibid., viii.

56. American Social Health Association, "The Social Challenge of Prostitution: An Outline for Communities Fighting Prostitution and Venereal Disease," 1945, 14, box 129, folder 3, American Social Health Association papers, Social Welfare History Archives, University of Minnesota. Elaine Tyler May discusses this fear of premarital female sexuality that resurfaced during World War II and the postwar period in *Homeward Bound*, chap. 4. See also Estelle B. Freedman and John D'Emilio, *Intimate Matters: A History of Sexuality in America* (New York: Harper and Row, 1988), chap. 11; Karen Anderson, *Wartime Women: Sex Roles, Family Relations, and the Status of Women During World War II* (Westport, Conn.: Greenwood Press, 1981). May points out that the wartime fear of promiscuity extended to include all forms of nonmarital sexual be-

havior, including prostitution and homosexuality. See also John D'Emilio, *Sexual Politics, Sexual Communities: The Making of a Homosexual Minority in the United States, 1940–1970* (Chicago: University of Chicago Press, 1983), chaps. 2, 3; Estelle B. Freedman, " 'Uncontrolled Desires': The Response to the Sexual Psychopath, 1920–1960," *Journal of American History* 74 (June 1987): 83–106.

57. See Allan M. Brandt, *No Magic Bullet: A Social History of Venereal Disease in the U.S. Since 1880* (New York: Oxford University Press, 1985), esp. 165–169.

58. Francis E. Merrill, *Social Problems on the Home Front: A Study of War-Time Influences* (New York: Harper & Brothers, 1948), 99. The American Social Hygiene Association proposed a redefinition of prostitution to include "all sex relations which are indiscriminate or without sincere emotional content." American Social Health Association, "The Social Challenge of Prostitution," 2–3.

59. Helen D. Pigeon, "Effect of War Conditions on Children and Adolescents in the City of Hartford, Connecticut," Connecticut Child Welfare Association, New Haven, 24. See also Venereal Disease Control Conference, March 5, 1945, San Antonio, Texas, 23–24, box 129, folder 1, American Social Hygiene Association papers, SWHA.

60. James Gilbert observes that "social class had become, by the end of the fifties, a major element in both structural and cultural interpretations of delinquency." Gilbert, *A Cycle of Outrage: America's Reaction to the Juvenile Delinquent in the 1950s* (New York: Oxford University Press, 1986), 18.

61. Venereal Disease Control Conference, 24, 25.

62. Many discussions of the unwholesome influence of war on girls focused on illegitimacy. See, for example, U.S. Children's Bureau, *Services for Unmarried Mothers and Their Children* (Washington, D.C.: Government Printing Office, 1945), 1; Dorothy Ellsworth, "Precocious Adolescence in Wartime," *Family* 25 (March 1944): 3–13; Merrill, *Social Problems on the Home Front,* 89–124; Elsa Castendyck, "Helping to Prevent Sex Delinquency," National Conference of Social Work, *Proceedings,* 1943, 140–48; Morlock, "Unmarried Mothers in Wartime."

63. See Ruth Reed, *The Social and Health Care of the Illegitimate Family in New York City* (New York: Research Bureau Welfare Council of New York City, 1932), 17; Helen S. Trounstine, "Illegitimacy in Cincinnati," *Studies from the Helen S. Trounstine Foundation* 1 (September 1919): 221; Reed, "Illegitimacy among Negroes," *Journal of Social Hygiene* 11 (February 1925): 73–91; Hilda Hertz and Sue Warren Little, "Unmarried Negro Mothers in a Southern Urban Community," *Social Forces* 23 (October 1944): 73–79; E. Franklin Frazier, "An Analysis of Statistics on Negro Illegitimacy," *Social Forces* 11 (December 1932): 249–257; Olive Davis Streater, "Some Aspects of Illegitimacy among Negroes, Inter-City Conference on Illegitimacy," in Child Welfare League of America, *Bulletin* 10 (May 1931): 8; Hertz, "Negro Illegitimacy in Durham, North Carolina," Master's thesis, Duke University, 1944, 14–15, 101.

64. Melville J. Herskovits, *The Myth of the Negro Past* (New York: Harper & Brothers, 1941), 167.

65. Frazier won a research fellowship in 1920 at the New York School of Social Work, where he took several courses. From 1922 to 1927, Frazier served as acting director of the Atlanta University School of Social Work. For a discussion of Frazier's career in social work, see Anthony M. Platt, *E. Franklin Frazier Reconsidered* (New Brunswick: Rutgers University Press, 1991), chap. 7.

66. Patricia Knapp, "The Attitudes of Negro Unmarried Mothers toward Illegitimacy," *Smith College Studies in Social Work* 17 (December 1946): 153.

67. Young, *Out of Wedlock*, 121. See also Hertz, "Negro Illegitimacy"; Maurine Boie LaBarre, "Cultural and Racial Problems in Social Case Work with Special Reference to Negroes," in *Cultural Problems in Social Case Work* (New York: Family Welfare Association of America, 1940), 1–20; Knapp, "The Attitudes of Negro Unmarried Mothers toward Illegitimacy," 153.

68. Reed, *Negro Illegitimacy in New York City* (New York: Columbia University Press, 1926), 7. The relative silence in social work on black illegitimacy before the late 1930s was part of a larger silence on the lives of African Americans. Anthony Platt finds that "between 1920 and 1928, *The Family* carried only three articles that addressed the specific problems of Afro-American families. The National Conference of Social Work regularly devoted a whole section to the problems of European immigrants but rarely included panels on African Americans." Platt, *Frazier Reconsidered*, 70.

69. Charles S. Johnson, *Shadow of the Plantation* (Chicago: University of Chicago Press, 1934), 49. See also Hertz and Little, "Unmarried Negro Mothers in a Southern Urban Community," 78. For examples of maternity home workers using the "cultural acceptance" of illegitimacy to justify denying their services to black unmarried mothers, see *Florence Crittenton Bulletin* 4 (January 1929): 5; Charlotte Abbey, "Illegitimacy and Sex Perversion," in *A Child Welfare Symposium*, ed. William H. Slingerland (New York: Russell Sage Foundation, 1915), 29.

70. Frazier, "An Analysis of Statistics on Negro Illegitimacy in the United States," 255. On the rural–urban transmission of black illegitimacy, see also St. Clair Drake and Horace R. Cayton, *Black Metropolis: A Study of Negro Life in a Northern City* (New York: Harcourt, Brace, 1945), 590; Hertz, "Negro Illegitimacy," 35.

71. Carby discusses the ways in which this characterization legitimized the "policing" and disciplining of black women by both black and white institutions and intellectuals, in "Policing the Black Woman's Body in an Urban Context," *Critical Inquiry* 4 (Summer 1992): 739.

72. Frazier, *The Negro Family in the United States* (Chicago: University of Chicago Press, 1939), 267.

73. Frazier, "Analysis of Statistics on Negro Illegitimacy," 256.

74. Ibid.

75. Frazier, "Traditions and Patterns of Negro Family Life in the United States," in *Race and Culture Contacts*, ed. Edward Byron Reuter (New York: McGraw-Hill, 1934), 194–195.

76. Frazier, *Negro Family in the United States*, 265. See also Reed, *Social and Health Care*, 17; Trounstine, "Illegitimacy in Cincinnati," 198; Hertz, "Negro Illegitimacy," 87.

77. Frazier, *Negro Family in the United States*, 265. This condemnation of the black unmarried mother who did not want to keep her baby coincided with the diagnosis of the white woman who wanted to keep her child as "neurotic."

78. See Platt, *Frazier Reconsidered*.

79. Young, *Out of Wedlock*, 120.

80. LaBarre, "Cultural and Racial Problems in Social Case Work," 3. See Platt, *Frazier Reconsidered*, 139.

81. Hertz, "Negro Illegitimacy," 75. See also Margaret Brenman, "Urban Lower-Class Negro Girls," *Psychiatry* 6 (August 1943): 308.

82. Hertz, "Negro Illegitimacy," 77; Brenman, "Urban Lower-Class Negro Girls," 316. See also Drake and Cayton, *Black Metropolis*, 593. Many social historians have

also been interested in the dynamics of class divisions within black urban communities. See Joe William Trotter, Jr., *Black Milwaukee: The Making of an Industrial Proletariat, 1915–1945* (Urbana: University of Illinois Press, 1985); Gilbert Osofsky, *Harlem: The Making of a Ghetto, 1890 to 1930* (New York: Harper & Row, 1966); Allan Spear, *Black Chicago: The Making of a Negro Ghetto, 1890 to 1920* (Chicago: University of Chicago Press, 1967); Kenneth Kusmer, *A Ghetto Takes Shape: Black Cleveland, 1870 to 1930* (Urbana: University of Illinois Press, 1976); Thomas Philpott, *The Slum and the Ghetto* (New York: Oxford University Press, 1978).

83. Hertz, "Negro Illegitimacy," 76–77.

84. Hazel Carby characterizes this period as one of "ideological, political, and cultural contestation between an emergent black bourgeoisie and an emerging black working class." Carby, "Policing the Black Woman's Body," 754.

85. Drake and Cayton, *Black Metropolis,* 593. G. Franklin Edwards points out that "the concepts of social disorganization and social reorganization as related aspects of a process were first used by W.I. Thomas and Florian Znanieski in *The Polish Peasant* to analyze the problems encountered by peasant communities as their contacts with the wider community increased in number, variety, and intensity. A period of social disorganization . . . is followed by a period of social reorganization or social reconstruction, in which new rules and institutions, better adapted to the needs of the group, are fashioned from preexisting elements of the peasant culture." Edwards, "E. Franklin Frazier," 101.

86. David W. Southern, *Gunnar Myrdal and Black-White Relations: The Use and Abuse of 'An American Dilemma,' 1944–1969* (Baton Rouge: Louisiana State University Press, 1987), 55. See also Walter A. Jackson, *Gunnar Myrdal and America's Conscience: Social Engineering and Racial Liberalism, 1938–1987* (Chapel Hill: University of North Carolina Press, 1990).

87. Gunnar Myrdal, *An American Dilemma: The Negro Problem and Modern Democracy* (New York: Harper & Brothers, 1944), 930–931.

88. Ibid., 931. On the influence of Frazier on Myrdal, see Jackson, *Gunnar Myrdal and America's Conscience,* esp. 245–270.

89. Daniel P. Moynihan, *The Negro Family: The Case for National Action* (Washington, D.C.: U.S. Department of Labor, 1965).

90. Anthony Platt argues that Moynihan actually misused Frazier's scholarship. Platt, *Frazier Reconsidered,* 115–120. See also Jackson, *Gunnar Myrdal and America's Conscience,* 303.

91. Frazier, *Negro Family in the United States,* 100.

92. On the association of African Americans and venereal disease, see Brandt, *No Magic Bullet,* 116, 157–158, 169–170; Elizabeth Fee, "Venereal Disease: The Wages of Sin?" in *Passion and Power,* ed. Kathy Peiss and Christina Simmons (Philadelphia: Temple University Press, 1989), 181–183.

93. Rickie Solinger traces the turning point in public attitudes toward black single pregnancy in the 1940s to the uneasiness of whites toward ADC and other forms of public assistance. Solinger, *Wake Up Little Susie,* 29–34, 56–76. See also Winifred Bell, *Aid to Dependent Children* (New York: Columbia University Press, 1965).

94. Henry C. Schumacher, "The Unmarried Mother: A Socio-Psychiatric Viewpoint," *Journal of Mental Hygiene* 11 (October 1927): 780.

95. Although disproportionately high black illegitimacy rates drew anxious attention, especially in the 1940s, the 1944 increase in the ratio of illegitimate births was

especially apparent among white females aged 20–29. While out-of-wedlock pregnancy among whites rose from 16.3 per 1,000 live births in 1943 to 19.6 in 1944, comparatively little change was noted among nonwhite women during the same period. See Merrill, *Social Problems on the Home Front*, 114.

96. Jean Thompson, *House of Tomorrow* (New York: Harper & Row, 1967), 7–8.

97. Drake and Cayton, *Black Metropolis*, 592–593.

98. I discuss the efforts of unmarried mothers to represent out-of-wedlock pregnancy in their own terms more fully in Kunzel, *Fallen Women, Problem Girls*, chap. 4.

99. Solinger, *Wake Up Little Susie*, 16.

100. Rickie Solinger describes in detail "a two-tiered service system, coercive and humiliating to white and black women, but particularly threatening to blacks" in *Wake Up Little Susie*, 34. While some black unmarried mothers were sterilized, Solinger explains that efforts to pass sterilization legislation on the state level were largely unsuccessful. Solinger, *Wake Up Little Susie*, 53–57.

PART IV

Sexual Outlaws and Cultural Rebels

CHAPTER 14

Rickie Solinger

EXTREME DANGER

Women Abortionists and Their Clients before Roe v. Wade

Nobody knows how many illegal abortions were perfomed in the years before *Roe* v. *Wade*. Like other crimes, abortions occurred in secret places. Public health officials, police, or criminologists who wanted to describe the magnitude of the problem generally sized up the tip of the iceberg—the number of women who landed in hospitals with "botched" abortions—and guessed. Whatever the actual number, the experts agreed that it was very large. In 1960 the American Medical Association (AMA) determined that there were approximately a million illegal abortions in the United States annually and argued that the laws against abortion were unenforceable.

Indeed, unhappily pregnant women looked for, and found, criminal abortionists in every city and many towns in the United States in the decades before *Roe*. But even as antiabortion laws were flouted, they were nevertheless powerfully effective. The laws created the niche for and structured arenas of extreme personal danger for women seeking abortions and for their abortionists. When abortionists and their clients met each other, together they occupied "immoral terrain," a place where human beings are very likely to encounter danger.

The contemporary struggle to preserve legal abortion draws often and icono-graphically on the physical dangers associated with abortion before *Roe:* the back-alley butcher, the coat hanger, the knitting needle, the perforated uterus, the filth, the raging infection, death. It is important to remember that these images were woven into the full fabric of peril that clothed females in the postwar decades.

In fact, after World War II, women in the United States occupied numer-ous, overlapping arenas of danger, arenas constructed and controlled by their alleged protectors. For example, many employed women met race and gen-der discrimination and frequently sexual harassment on the job, as well as social opprobrium in the community. Thousands of married women—often fully financially dependent on their mates—had husbands who had insecure or insufficiently remunerative jobs, husbands who might stop loving them, or leave them, or husbands who were violent. Many unmarried women, impor-tuned more urgently than ever before to "go all the way," were labeled and ostracized if they did, especially if they "got themselves pregnant." For most women, the chivalric promise that a woman could buy masculine protection with the coin of female submission was radically at odds with real life. It is fair to say that most fertile women in the United States after World War II lived in the neighborhood of danger, the promise and patina of safety notwithstanding.

Nothing, in fact, reveals the thinness, even the lie, of this promise of safety more starkly than the experience of unhappily pregnant girls and women seek-ing to control their own bodies, lives, and fertility by seeking abortions in the years after World War II. The experiences of these girls and women reveal a widespread interest in protecting society, not women, by vitalizing a nostal-gic fantasy of the status quo ante: life before the Great Depression, before the war, life on Elm Street, when all the women were young and pretty, chaste or faithful, fertile and obedient and dependent.

In practice, unhappily pregnant girls and women seeking abortions stepped, with that intention, into a dangerous arena and often met there other "un-protected" women—abortionists—who promised to help them when no one else would.[1] Along with other women who defied the law or flouted conven-tion, such as black women who forged the civil rights movement, lesbians, divorcees, and career women, women seeking abortions, and the women abor-tionists, were postwar deviants, vilified but useful benchmarks in a culture desperate to define normalcy.

This essay considers only encounters between women seeking abortions and lay women abortionists. Certainly in the illegal era, many doctors—mostly male, but some female—performed criminal abortions, as did male lay prac-titioners, trained and untrained. The essay focuses on this particular dyad for a number of reasons, including the fact that not all abortionists were equally vulnerable to arrest. Not all, therefore, worked under equally constrained and dangerous conditions. District attorneys often determined that abortion prosecutions against female lay practitioners were fairly likely to be successful because women abortionists were presumed to be untrained, unskilled, and unprotected. Doctors, in contrast, were presumed to have skills and resources and could be assumed to have respectable colleagues who would stand up in court and claim that a given abortion was not criminal, but medically necessary. Such testimony would, of course, undermine a conviction. Beyond this, the woman abortionist and her client in the headlines and in the courtroom provided then and provide now a rich source for exploring some of the fundamental cultural and political purposes of abortion prosecutions in the postwar decades.

Back-Alley Encounters

This essay describes the separate, interlocked, and overlapping arenas of extreme danger in which women abortionists lived and worked and in which unhappily pregnant girls and women sought help. To begin with, we can recapture the poisonous flavor of some of these encounters. Following the contemporary commitment to evoke the difficult circumstances of unhappily pregnant girls and women before *Roe*, I recall their circumstances first.

Despite the reputation of illegal abortionists as crude practitioners before *Roe*, some women were able to choose their abortionists carefully. Many women in Southern California, for example, chose the practice of Laura Miner, a chiropractor who had perfected her abortion technique in the 1930s when she worked under infamous abortion entrepreneur, Reg Rankin. Miner, her associate, Josephine Page, and her assistant, Nedra Cordon, ran a highly professional abortion business in San Diego in the 1940s, until the crackdown after the war.

Women who chose this practice did not have to worry about a botched procedure, but they were still far from safe. In mid-September 1948, after nine years of undisturbed business, Miner and her partners became suspicious that their offices were being watched and might be wired. The women were correct. Investigators from the San Diego D.A.'s office had been observing the office for 106 days, taking meticulous note of "the large number of women . . . coming to and going from these premises." When Miner, Page, and Cordon realized their situation, they closed the office and hung a sign on the door saying, *Office closed indefinitely. Hours by appointment.*

That afternoon, a number of women arrived at the office, expecting to terminate their pregnancies, read the sign, and left. One can imagine their confusion and fear as they turned to leave, still pregnant, their best chance down the drain. One woman showed up the next day and found the door open. When she walked into the waiting room, Nedra Cordon motioned for her to enter a small inner office. The two women sat together, and Cordon explained apologetically that they would not be able to help the woman that day because they were in the midst of a "slight investigation," and the doctors had to be very careful. Cordon said that the woman should come back in a week, the following Monday, if she still wanted the abortion.

A week later, the woman was still pregnant. The end of the safe period for abortion was closing in on her. She still wanted to end her pregnancy but had not been able to find any other safe provider. So that Monday morning she returned to Miner's clinic as Cordon said she could. This time, she found a note on the door reading, *Office closed indefinitely. Gone to the East Coast.* Again, one can imagine this woman's disappointment and fear as she turned around and faced another day and another night still pregnant, inexorably moving toward having a baby she felt she should not have.[2]

A woman in Missouri, like many others all over the country in these pre-*Roe* years, did not know where she was going, even after she was well on her way to the "office" of the abortionist, in this case, Fraulein Scown, a St. Louis practitioner her doctor had recommended. All she knew was that she was supposed to stand in a certain doorway at eight on Saturday evening, April 28, 1956. She was a married woman with three children and had to make lots of arrangements to get to the doorway on time, but Mrs. Black (a pseudonym) did everything to make it. When she got to the place, a few minutes before eight, she found three other women already there, anxious, waiting, and pregnant. Each clutched a brown paper bag holding a nightgown and some sanitary pads.

A little after eight, a red-haired woman walked up to the huddle of waiting women, counted noses, and escorted them to a nearby parking lot. She told them to get into a blue and white Cadillac parked there. The redhead got into the driver's seat. Before she pulled out of the lot, she leaned over and took four pairs of sunglasses out of the glove compartment. Each pair had dark paper pasted over the lenses. She handed a pair to each of the women and told them to wear the glasses so that they would never know where they had been. Then the driver told her passengers to squat on the floor of the car. As she drove, she described what was going to happen to them. According to Mrs. Black, she said that "she would open our wombs, it wouldn't hurt, and we would be given sleeping pills . . . that Sunday our wombs would be scraped and we would be given gas."

When the women arrived at the house where the abortions were to be performed, they were put into bedrooms, two to a room. Late that night, when

Mrs. Black told Fraulein Scown that she had only $60 toward the $125 required for the abortion, Scown got very angry. Mrs. Black had come this far, and now she was about to be put out on the street. Talking very quickly, Black convinced the abortionist that she was good for the money, but it would just take a bit more time for her to come up with the full amount. In fact, she convinced Fraulein Scown that she would be able to take the balance to her doctor very soon, and the doctor would, in turn, pass the money on to the abortionist.

On both Saturday night when she was dilated with a catheter and Sunday morning when her uterus was scraped, Mrs. Black was blindfolded after she had been put on a padded kitchen table and her feet placed in stirrups. Scown wanted to make sure that her clients would not be able to identify the others involved in the procedure. When the abortion was over, Mrs. Black slept a bit. Then she woke and dressed. All four of the women who had arrived together the night before were taken down to the basement and resupplied with dark glasses. The red-haired woman told them to crouch again on the floor of the car where they stayed until, all together, they were left at a bus stop at the city limits.[3]

Today the most frequently invoked abortion seekers from the pre-*Roe* era are the ones, like Estelle Bach in San Francisco, who lost their lives at the hands of abortionists far less skilled or scrupulous than Scown or Miner and her associates. Bach had the extreme misfortune to have gotten pregnant in 1955 by a man who knew Stanley Odmann. Odmann had recently decided that he was not making enough money as a salesman for the Suit Club in San Franciso where his job was to find men who wanted to rent suits for $2 a month. So he made up his mind to go into the abortion business with his wife, Vera, a former nurse with some experience in anesthesiology. Odmann began to roam the city, looking for unhappily pregnant women. He had little trouble finding clients desperate enough to pay this dubious couple $450 for an abortion.

When Estelle Bach's boy friend put her in Odmann's hands, she was crying and very upset. She told him she was pregnant and needed help badly because she had two children and no husband. She said that if she could not get help, she would kill herself. On February 2 and again on February 18, 1955, Vera Odmann attempted to abort Estelle Bach, using catheters and curettes. After the second attempt, Bach was still pregnant, and in very bad shape, according to an old friend of Bach's who went to fetch her at the hotel where the Odmanns had taken her. This man described her as looking "awful, half-dead." He said, "I tried to [make her comfortable], she was hanging out around the doorway— I tried to put a coat on her, tried to wrap her up. I couldn't dress her, she was so helpless. . . ." Once again, in the middle of March, Vera Odmann operated on Estelle Bach. Somehow, by March 18, Bach made her way to the San Francisco

Hospital where she was examined by Dr. Joseph Wedell. The doctor noted that she was "a woman who was in a very acute and critical illness, she was in a state of shock, her blood pressure was 15 over zero, she had a fever of 102, there were signs of peritonitis and inflammation within the abdomen, there was muscule guarding and tenderness and . . . evidence of puncture marks [at the cervix]." Three days later, Bach was operated on in an effort to save her life. At that time, doctors found "considerable fluid within the abdominal cavity, and when the pelvic area was explored, a loop of intentines was found to be severed; also on the top portion of the uterus there was . . . a perforation." Estelle Bach lingered near death for nearly a month and then died. The autopsy indicated that she died of "a renal shutdown, acute peritonitis secondary to traumatic perforation of the uterus, multiple abcesses throughout the abdominal cavity." It also showed that her "bowel was very degenerated and necrotic, and covered with pus and fibrous tissue."[4]

Evocations of the pre-*Roe* era today usually cast the pregnant woman as a double victim, first of the restrictive laws that denied her reproductive autonomy, and second the victim of unskilled, dirty, and predatory abortionists. The fact is, when desperate girls and women knocked on those notorious back-alley doors, the doors were often opened by women who were, in their own ways, as desperate or endangered as the ones seeking abortions.

Consider, for example, the dangerous life of Eva Muszynska. Muszynska had been a midwife for thirty-three years and had been convicted for performing abortions three times, when a half-crazed man in Passaic, New Jersey, William Sudol, began to hound her in 1955 about performing an abortion on his wife, Elizabeth, who was severely depressed and had recently received shock therapy. She was also what we call today a battered wife. The Sudols had three children and had farmed each one out to a relative or an orphanage. Sudol told Muszynska they did not want any more babies. As the midwife remembered it, Sudol said, "I ask you be so kind and help my wife. She lost her menstruation; then we don't want to have any children. We got four. That is enough for us. I have to pay for one month for four children one hundred and sixty dollars. Then I absolutely don't want any more."

But Muszynska refused to get involved. Twice Sudol returned to the midwife's house, and twice more she refused. But the fourth time, Sudol arrived with what Muszynska thought was a concealed weapon, and he threatened to kill her if she did not do the abortion. This time, she agreed and asked for a fee of $175. Elizabeth Sudol was brought to Muszynska's house. She told the midwife that they had come to her because they could not afford a doctor. Eva Muszynska performed the abortion, and as she finished scraping the woman's uterus, she said, "Now is clean. Nothing there except blood." Just at that moment, as the midwife took the speculum out of Elizabeth Sudol's vagina, William Sudol appeared in the doorway of the bedroom and snapped a "flashlight" picture of the midwife and the lower portion of his wife's body.

Eva Muszynska recounted later that she looked at Sudol and demanded to know why he took the picture. He said, "That means you did [an] abortion for my wife; that I got evidence." He took her instruments and demanded $4,000 including the return of the $175. When Muszynska pleaded with Mrs. Sudol to intercede, "[Elizabeth] started crying saying, 'he wouldn't listen to me.' Sudol . . . turned upon his wife (this is in Eva's rather broken English), 'I don't want you anymore; I don't need you anymore; if I want woman I am going to get anyone and anytime. I am going to take divorce from you.' Mrs. Sudol cried so loudly that Eva thought she was going to be terribly sick. Later he said to Eva, 'I have no pity for nobody. I want to make easy money if I get a chance.' " Eva Muszynska endured weeks of Sudol's threats and unexpected visits and harassment by Sudol and his relatives, who were in on the project. She tried very hard to raise the money he demanded, but never came close. At last, she went to the police.[5]

Consider, as well, the risk that Florence Stallworth took in 1959 when she agreed to perform an abortion on a pregnant woman who didn't have enough money to pay a willing doctor she had consulted first. Stallworth was a fifty-two-year-old black public health nurse who had trained at the Freeman's Hospital in Washington, D.C., graduating in 1932. From then through the 1950s, Stallworth held a series of very responsible positions in hospitals in North and South Carolina. Doctors and other colleagues, her neighbors and minister, all of whom had known Florence Stallworth for years, lined up to testify at her trial. They spoke of her excellent character and her high level of professional competence. Her medical colleagues took pains to cast considerable doubt on the charge of abortion. But Florence Stallworth was convicted anyway, and sent to prison "for not less than one year," leaving her nearly thirty-year career as an effective and respected health-care provider in shambles.[6]

Finally, alongside the circumstances of women who experienced serious postoperative hemorrhaging or life-threatening infections from abortions, and even alongside those who tragically died, we must place the experiences of Ilsa, a midwife for thirty-one years, who described her life as an abortionist from her jail cell. It was not the money, she said, that inspired her to do abortions. It was her desire to help girls who came to her house and threatened to kill themselves if she would not help them. She did help, but achieved no peace. In fact, her life was a nightmare: "Racketeers would come to her house and request money. She felt she was in danger and actually welcomed arrest. She claimed that racketeers frequently approached abortionists, posing as law enforcement officers, in order to extort money from them. She told the prison psychiatrists that she was held up at least fifteen times in this manner." Indeed,

Ilsa had good reason to believe that racketeers and police played interchangeable roles. She was once forced to pay law enforcement officers $500 to settle her case without an arrest or trial.[7]

The life circumstances of Muszynska, Stallworth, Ilsa, and the more than fifty other women abortionists whose prosecutions form the basis of this study begin to furnish the grisly back alley with some new complexity. It is not my point to shine up the back alley so that it looks as good as a contemporary abortion clinic. But there is historical worthiness in capturing the fullest possible picture of the dangers caused by antiabortion laws, including the danger experienced by practitioners. Also, it is useful to separate many of these women abortionists from the stereotypical "back alley butchers" invoked so often today, in warning.

Carole Joffe has recently written very effectively against the "back alley butcher" symbol, demonstrating that numerous "physicians of conscience" resisted the law by performing thousands of safe and illegal abortions successfully in the decades before *Roe*.[8] Joffe's isolation and renaming of these good doctors, while very helpful, inadvertently reinforces the power of the symbol for the others, especially those who were not doctors and the many who were women. The butcher symbol has been so useful, of course, because it suggests a crude vulgarity, literally a person who slaughters and dresses meat. Symbolically, he is cruel, brutal, and ruthless, a barbarian. The midwives, nurses and other women whose prosecutions I have studied do not fit this bill.

The point is that we are rarely dealing here with greedy, ignorant, knife-wielding women in filthy kitchens, women who deserved to be arrested for preying on helpless, pregnant females often convinced that their pregnancies were a fate worse than death. It is true that some of the so-called back-alley abortionists, women and men, were untrained and unsanitary and mercenary.[9] And some pregnant women were desperate and resourceless enough to take whatever they got. But it is not helpful to remember only the desperate, pregnant women. We must also remember that the long and terrifying arm of the law created the niche for and structured the extreme personal vulnerability of the abortion provider, whether or not she should have been performing abortions.

Beyond this, it seems crucial to recognize that when we invoke the dangers women would face in a post-*Roe* v. *Wade* society, we must consider that lay abortionists operating in their kitchens and bedrooms were, strangely, a minor problem, an unfortunate inconvenience almost, in comparison to the danger that lay, before *Roe,* at the heart of the matter. The experiences of Stallworth and the others reveal, first, a world in which men conducted conversations with other men, across the heads of the formerly pregnant women and their abortionists. In fact, these cases became first-rate occasions for men—doctors, lawyers, judges, jury members, police—to gather together in a public place, the courtroom, and reaffirm their gendered right to govern women's bodies and abrogate women's rights. And that was not all. More men, journalists and editors, doggedly (and salaciously) pursued these stories of prime-time crime. They prodded police to bust women abortionists with long-established practices and plastered their front pages with lurid prose and sensationalized photos depicting gruesome raids. Finally, the raids, the yellow journalism, and the trials justified and strengthened legislators' commitment to nineteenth-century antiabortion laws. In these ways, every woman who might want to decide whether and when to become a mother, and all those who wanted to help such women, were placed in extreme danger.

As the lawyers and policemen spoke to each other across the heads of the women whose bodies and livelihoods were at issue in these trials, the judge, the manager and arbiter of the proceedings, often assessed the woman on trial. At the close of Florita Gomez's 1963 Illinois trial, for example, the judge explained his disinclination to be lenient with this woman because she had not entered the courtroom humbly. He said:

> The Court has to take into consideration not only the protection of society and the rehabilitation of the defendant, but the Court must also take into consideration the example to society, the example to others, the deterrent to crime, and I just don't think that I could in good conscience allow anyone, unless that is some very, very unusual circumstances, anyone guilty of an abortion to go on probation. . . . I don't want the court to have a reputation of giving probation to abortionists. . . . I have never up to now . . . but I never grant probation to someone unless you come in and plead guilty and throw themselves upon the mercy of the Court and start out with a penitent spirit. Now, this defendant stood trial.[10]

The moral of these stories is that danger in the abortion arena was pervasive and spread quite thickly among all the women involved. By extension and by example, any woman who considered having an abortion, if she had her wits about her, had to recognize that if she went ahead with the operation, she would be in danger. In fact, it was probably the case that the twenty-year period just before some states legalized abortion in the late 1960s and early 1970s was the worst time in the history of the United States to be a woman abortionist and quite possibly the worst time to be a woman seeking an abortion.

New Postwar Danger

Certainly the postwar experiences of the women described here were a far cry from the prewar experiences Ruth Barnett, a prominent naturopath and abortionist in Portland, Oregon, from 1918 to 1968, has described. Barnett called her life as an abortionist between the wars as "those happy prosperous years." She wrote: "There was nothing secret about the operations of the Stewart Clinic in the Broadway Building [her place of business in Portland]. We had no locks on any of the doors except the one leading to the hall, which we locked at night. The majority of our cases were referrals from licensed physicians and surgeons. A great many cases even came to me from a prominent Catholic gynecologist who would tell women who insisted on an abortion to 'go to the Broadway Building and ask for Dr. Ruth.' "

Ruth Barnett described how one woman who came to her office "was amazed by its cleanliness and tasteful furnishings. Most of all she was surprised by the way we conducted business. We had no secrecy in those days." Barnett went on, "Women came and went in my clinic with scarcely anymore fuss than there would be in keeping an appointment at a beauty salon. Many girls came to me during their lunch hour and returned to work the same afternoon with no distress." [11] Other practitioners have described the conditions of their work before World War II similarly. [12]

But beginning in the mid 1940s, the situation changed. Ruth Barnett herself, after practicing openly and even with the protection of "the duly elected officers of the law, members of the medical profession, and state medical board" for thirty-three years, was arrested for the first time in 1951 and thereafter many times throughout the postwar years. [13]

In three areas particularly, professional and cultural attitudes emerged that were devastatingly threatening to women abortionists and their clients. First, misogynistic strains of American culture were allowed full expression in the postwar period, a development that had major implications for the treatment of all women involved in the abortion arena. Second, the attitudes of many doctors toward pregnancy, pregnant women, and fetuses shifted considerably at this time in a direction that certainly caused an increasing number of women to search back alleys for abortionists, but also intensified the danger they risked. Third, in the context of uninhibited misogyny, politicians and police and newspapermen found crime involving women's bodies and their sexuality particularly profitable.

Misogyny

Many historians and commentators of the postwar era have noted that this period was especially hard on women. [14] Many have noted that in the wake of nearly a generation of economic depression and war, image makers, politicians, and many wornout Americans drew on nostalgic notions of normalcy. They summoned up dreams of docile wives making homes for their men, who, for the first time in a generation, were encouraged to realize their masculinity and fulfill their potential out from under the shadow of the breadline or the un-employment line, far from the infantry lines. Freed from depression and war, men were urged to express their individualism and especially their masculinity by holding American women hostage to these ends. Elaine Tyler May has ar-gued persuasively that postwar cultural imperatives for women were peculiar and aberrant, not traditional. But even without the imprimatur of tradition, these imperatives were powerful, and they were enforced. As men began to reconstruct their civilian lives under a quasi-peacetime economy, the media, clergy, educators, psychiatrists, and others insisted, implicitly and explicitly, that real women in this country were dependent women. Independence in a woman—economically, sexually, intellectually—was often cast as deviance and as illness.

In this context, a rash of women were accused and tried for the crime of abortion after the war. An important function of these trials was to expose such females as multiple deviants. Simply as illegal abortionists, the women were deviants because they had broken the law. But beyond the misdemeanor or the felony (depending on the state and sometimes on the consequences of the abortion), they stood charged, as it were, with a number of other "crimes." They suffered opprobrium, for example, for acting as "economic women," for plying a trade for cash, instead of being supported by a man.[15]

Louise Roper Furley went on trial in 1956 for performing an abortion on a young woman in Fayetteville, North Carolina, and found that part of the im-plicit indictment against her involved her alleged earnings. Furley was a forty-two-year-old junk dealer and day care provider who was pressed, repeatedly, during her trial to explain her economic status. Toward the end of her testi-mony, Furley, who had been accused by the prosecution of numerous violations of femininity, including publicly fighting with her husband and violating the state Prohibition law, fought back with astonishing dignity to establish herself as an unimpeachable woman, and not incidentally, as a black who did not need to be told her place. She said: "As to how I make my living, I has a husband; his work is a telephone man. I do some work; I work on the junk yard. As to how much I make a week . . . sometimes I gets about 38 dollars or 40 dollars a load. I don't rent no houses over there of my own; I rent Mr. Byrd's houses. I do not own my own house; I rent. I do not have a new automobile; my husband has got an automobile. Quite naturally, I use it to ride in at my pleasure, your wife or husband rides in your car." [16] Most emphatically, Lousie Furley Roper denied receiving any money for performing abortions, an important element in the defense of many women accused, most of whom, unlike Furley, did not have a husband.

In Sacramento, California, another abortionist, Geraldine Rhoades, was fundamentally charged with perverse economic interests in 1948. She was accused of making money to spend on "diamond rings and perhaps Buick automobiles and things which might mean her comfort and might make it possible for her to live in comparative luxury." The prosecutor accused Rhoades of wantonly enjoying her ill-gotten money; he asked the jury to convict her because she was greedy; "she wasn't considerate, and she didn't care," presumably as a real woman would. At length he described the plight of unhappily pregnant women who "submitted to that operation by reason of social condition, the fear of a lifetime of shame and a lifetime of embarrassment and because of economic conditions which made it impossible, in their minds, to carry that pregnancy. Their minds were full of horror and fear and they did not think reasonably, but Geraldine Rhoades," he argued, "was not activated by fear and horror and shame, and her mind was clear as crystal. Geraldine Rhoades operate[d] for those forty thousand pennies, ladies and gentlemen, that jar full of pennies." [17]

Prosecutors and judges across the country singled out the economic motive as particularly disgusting, especially in a woman abortionist cast as a crass entrepreneur, benefiting from another woman's sexual misadventure and stunted maternal urge. In Cincinnati in 1953, a judge who was more conflicted than many about the evils of abortion, described the defendant before him, Mary Paige, in this way: "Mrs. Paige in every way outside of [her abortion activities] has led an exemplary life and she sits here this morning as a woman, one of God's creatures. My heart goes out to her and yet is there anything to be said in her favor from a penological viewpoint? She has . . . [performed abortions] for the purpose of greed, for the purpose of lining her pocket with money." This judge, like others, pointed his finger at the accused abortionist's alleged lack of womanly feeling: "So far as I know there is little evidence of performing an act that may be inspired by sympathy." [18]

According to the court, perhaps the most fundamental violation committed by the women accused was the crime of getting mixed up in the mess of other women's sexual lives. Whether the unhappily pregnant women were married or not, they *were* guilty of having had sex without procreative intentions. The women abortionists, it was said, cashed in on the wages of sexual misadventure and in the process were smeared with the stain of sex. The presiding judge in the case of Faye Wasserman, a New Jersey woman who ran an abortion and adoption racket in the late 1950s, was certain of this. His oral opinion, delivered at the close of Wasserman's probation hearing, referred to Wasserman's client as a "woman of admittedly easy virtue." He ruled that counsel "had a right to attack her character because this is the type of person this court would not pin any medals on." The judge made his position clear: "I am not here to speak about morality. I *would* say that if we didn't have the people of easy virtue, we wouldn't have [the Faye Wasserman's]. It is only people of this kind who are subjective [*sic*] to be preyed upon." Having established Wasserman as a predator, the judge provided the court with his vision of her strategy, and his opinion of it:

> How does she know all these people who get into trouble; these people that are pregnant for three months, four months and five months? She meets them on the street, she meets them in the meat-shop, they meet her there, and she meets them here. Respectable people do not meet that type of person in those type of places. . . . Mrs. Wasserman has an uncanny habit of dining in these places where there are people that are [pregnant]. Of all the restaurants, she winds up in the places where there are people in trouble. . . . It's an amazing coincidence. You have to be naive in order to swallow that sort of thing, not this Court. I don't intend to.[19]

Unhappily pregnant women who had sought abortions were not, of course, technically on trial. But in the court of public opinion, a girl or woman who had undergone an abortion, and had to admit to it publicly in court, was cast, like Faye Wasserman's client, as a female of easy virtue and as a sexualized, but de-feminized, not-mother. One doctor defined women seeking abortions in such a way as to cast the ultimate aspersion on a female deviant. He said an abortion seeker is "the independent, frustrated woman who has been conditioned to and yearns for the male world and feels that maternity, the greatest reward of the female world, is much less satisfying—in fact, highly unsatisfying." [20] Another doctor classified females seeking legal, "therapeutic" abortions as "clever, scheming women, simply trying to hoodwink the psychiatrist and obstetrician" in their appeals for permission to undergo the procedure.[21] Simply the desire to have an abortion, according to another doctor, was "proof [of the petitioner's] inability and failure to live through the destiny of being a woman." [22] A woman who went ahead with the operation could be diagnosed as doomed. She "will become an unpleasant person to live with and possibly lose her glamour as a wife. She will gradually lose conviction in playing a female role." [23]

According to one male abortionist with an extraordinarily large and long-lived practice in Baltimore, the treatment of girls and women who chose abortion was sadistic and misogynistic. He said: "Society's present attitude toward abortion stems from hatred, a hatred of women. Why else would it force them to submit to such terror and degradation in the seeking of an abortion, to endure in most cases the agony of an operation without even a pill to sustain them through shock and pain? Why else would it cause the maiming and death of thousands of women each year? This is love?" [24] Dr. Timanus, the writer here, was eventually arrested and jailed for acting counter to these cultural beliefs.[25]

Many observers of the postwar abortion scene must have found Dr. Timanus's fate surprising, since doctors who performed abortions were rarely arrested unless a death was involved. And among those few who were arrested, convictions were extremely rare, largely because of medical, and medical–legal, solidarity and the high status of doctors in the eyes of the public at large. Edwin Schur, the sociologist who studied these matters and was himself an early champion of liberalized abortion laws, wrote of this period: "Although most abortion laws do not specifically distinguish between operations by physicians and by laymen, in practice the courts do tend to make such a distinction: a presumption of good faith may be extended to a physician defendant. Juries are loath to convict doctors and judges do not like to impose harsh sentences on them." [26] In fact, in Chicago in these years, approximately fifty to seventy-five abortionists were prosecuted a year; maybe five or six of these were doctors. Dr. Kinsey noted that his research showed that in Indiana and California, "nearly all the persons who come into prison . . . convicted on abortion charges are not physicians." Kinsey asked his colleagues to consider this fact and challenged them to answer this question: "Why is it that the persons who are not physicians are the ones most often prosecuted?" [27]

Ruth Barnett and Hazel King and the many other women on trial, all of whom were sent to jail, might well have cocked their ears to catch the doctors' responses to this question. After all, many of them were midwives or had other credentials that, at other moments in the history of the United States, would have well suited them for their work as abortionists. By the mid-1940s, however, midwifery as a profession had all but disappeared in most regions of the United States because mostly male gynecologists had taken over its two traditional functions, abortion and birthing. Soon after the war, a doctor could earn up to $500 for an illegal abortion. A midwife operating outside the law and underground could often command no more than one-tenth of that amount.

Many state antiabortion laws were written so that it did not matter *who* performed the operation—a doctor or a layperson. If it was not necessary to save the life of the pregnant woman, it was illegal. Many prosecutors ignored this and hammered away at the accused woman's lack of medical credentials and her violation of medical authority and medical prerogative. This tactic emphasized that the defendant was not only an abortionist but an abortionist who possessed merely *female* credentials. At the New Jersey trial of Hazel King in the late 1940s, for example, the prosecutor was unrelenting, demanding over and over of one witness: "You knew Mrs. King was not a doctor, didn't you?" "You didn't call a doctor?" "You know she was not a doctor?" and in apparent frustration, "Do you know whether or not Mrs. King is a doctor?" When the witness stated firmly that Mrs. King was a nurse, the prosecutor whooped in triumph, "So you never did have a doctor!" [28]

Midwives and other female practitioners were not only "deskilled." They sustained an even worse kind of damage during this time when it became a status symbol among males to degrade women: They were demonized. It became fashionable and evocative to describe a midwife abortionist as tied to ancient, antiquated, even animistic traditions, as in the portrait of Rachel as

> a wrinkled, tottering Negro woman who was just a few months short of her ninetieth birthday. Rachel had lived in Fairfax County [Virginia] for more years than she knew. Her mother, once a slave, had been a midwife. Rachel had learned the art from her mother and had worked as a midwife all of her active life. By the time she had grown too old to keep up the work, she found that there was no longer much demand for midwives anyway [except for] an occasional request for her services as an abortionist. Rachel lived in a smoke-blackened grimy log cabin back in the woods . . . a surprisingly primitive little voodoo refuge.[29]

It also became fashionable to cast midwife abortionists as know-it-all harridans, isolated in crazy covens. An extraordinary, really breathtaking novel about the abortion scene in New York after the war includes a characteristic treatment of woman abortionist as witch. "The only ones you could go to were the clannish group of midwives who earned extra money for their families by doing abortions. The midwives sometimes met to discuss their methods, babbling their systems to each other like witchdoctors in passionate search of the miracle solution. Over coffee or tea, they speculated about tissue-tearing mixtures or how to shape kitchen utensils so there was only a little pain." [30]

Probably most fresh and convincing to a public becoming deeply steeped in the misogynistic strains of psychiatry in this era, midwife abortionists were described as emotionally distorted females. A court psychiatrist described one such woman as "without psychosis [but] . . . as an unethical type with a strong need to be punishing, domineering, and even sadistic toward members of her own sex. She feels inadequate as a woman and has some masculine traits both psychological and physical. Her most compulsive need to amass cash causes her to deprecate her very real financial holdings and she has an irrational fear of poverty which is deeply rooted on a neurotic basis." The psychiatrist determined that this unfortunate specimen was virtually a sideshow freak as well. Her emotional distortions were mirrored by her repulsive physical anomalies: "There is an unusually large clitoris present which extends beyond the prepuce and the labia. The mammae are seen to be flat with undersized involuted nipples. Hirsutic growth is remarkable and somewhat masculine in distribution." All this almost fully explained the woman's profession, but required, to be complete, one further observation. That is, women abortionists, as a class, were "reacting in large part, to an unconscious need to reject children or to deny them to others of [their] sex by reason of certain emotional deprivations in [their] own background." [31]

Here was the unkindest cut of all: Women abortionists were not-women, not-mothers, and were compelled by their own disabilities to destroy other women's potential as women and mothers. Psychiatrists had license to cast these aspersions as part of their general appraisals of "independent" women. Other doctors, the media, lawyers, and judges could pick up on the diagnoses, trade them back and forth, and perforce, woven through the culture, they became true. Of course, not all women abortionists were midwives. Many were naturopaths or chiropractors or nurses. Many had no sort of medical credentials whatever. But the court of public opinion, like the courts of law in which women abortionists were tried, was populated by skilled syllogists. Women abortionists were perceived, by definition, as midwives, as out-of-date, unskilled charlatans, sadistic and sick.

Doctors Redefine Pregnancy

As obstetricians appropriated birthing and abortion, and as psychiatrists diagnosed the motives and behavior of women who remained in these arenas, male medical practitioners went even further to consolidate their control over women's fertility.[32] By the mid-1940s, many doctors had come to feel that there were no longer many, if any, medical contraindications to pregnancy. Many argued that recent medical and technological advances diminished the incompatibility of pregnancy and disease. But the law still required that doctors decide whether and when a woman could have an abortion. So, having been pushed into a defensive posture by the combination of medical advances, the specter of legal liability, and the presence of large numbers of women in their offices asking for abortions, doctors acted strategically. They transformed their uncomfortable defensiveness into an offensive posture toward women. In most non-Catholic hospitals in the decade after the war, doctors set up hospital abortion committees that required any woman seeking a hospital abortion to appeal to a (male) panel of the director of obstetrics/gynecology and the chiefs of medicine, surgery, neuropsychiatry, and pediatrics. In Mount Sinai in New York City, for example, which set up an abortion committee in 1952, the panel of doctors met once a week and considered cases of women who could bring letters from two specialists diagnosing them as impaired and unfit to be mothers, usually on psychiatric grounds. As a consequence of establishing these committees, legal, therapeutic abortion rates plummeted in hospitals across the country in the postwar decades.

At this time, doctors also drastically redefined pregnancy in a direction pro-choice advocates still confront today. In the postwar decades, medical and psychiatric discourse uncoupled the pregnant woman and the fetus and at the same time bound women in ever-tighter traces to their pregnancies. It was not only that medical–technological advances removed most physical impediments to pregnancy. Even more profoundly important, some of these same advances—for instance, imaging techniques—could reveal the fetus-as-homunculus. With this innovation, pregnant females in turn became carriers and agents of protective custody. One prominent doctor expressed his sense of this development in the strongest possible terms. A pregnant woman, he said, "is a uterus surrounded by a supporting organism and a directing personality." [33]

Many medical commentators, and others, came to cast pregnancy first as a process of fulfillment and realization for the fetus. As the fetus was constructed as a little person, the woman, along with her doctor, acquired the *moral* duty to sustain the container (her body) as fit. The embryo with a human face demanded a *morally* nourishing environment. Providing that had become the pregnant woman's job and the meaning of pregnancy.

Forestalling a loss of authority over pregnant women, then, doctors banded together to arbitrate decisions regarding abortion and infused those decisions with a new dimension of moral authority. These innovative strategies successfully disqualified many women from being served by doctors in hospitals and probably kept many other, embarrassed women from seeking help from hospital-affiliated doctors. So many, surely, had to look elsewhere for a way to solve their problems. They had to look in the so-called back alleys.

In an important sense, girls and women searching for such assistance had determined not to sustain themselves as moral and fit containers for fetuses. And by making this decision, girls and women were refusing to buy into the prevailing terms of medical judgment and control. This was a brave stance, since, increasingly, resistance had become a moral issue and, in effect, an immoral act.

"Prime-Time" Crime

Grace Schauner, an abortionist in Wichita, and Louise Malanowski in Phenix City, Alabama, and their clients, encountered extreme danger in part because of the high taste for crime busting in both these cities, and in most towns and cities after the war.[34] Newspapermen and municipal officials were especially interested in the most sensational and sleaziest kind of crime, the kind that involved women's bodies and their sexuality.

In Wichita after the war, federal and local investigators were swarming across the city, turning up gambling rings, grain price-gouging rackets, and liquor scandals. But the crime-busting efforts that screamed across the front

page day after day in the early 1950s carried such headlines as: "ABOR-
TION RING SMASHED HERE: LOCAL POLICE SWEEP DOWN ON VICE HOME,
ELEVEN WOMEN TAKEN IN RAID UPON WICHITA ABORTION MILL."[35] In
Wichita; Portland; Baltimore; Los Angeles; St. Louis; Chicago; Dallas; San
Diego; Cincinnati; Norman, Oklahoma; Pittsburgh; and hundreds of other
cities and towns in these postwar years, newspapermen and politicians invested
substantial and high-yielding resources to produce such headlines.

In the Cold War, witch-hunting climate of the postwar era, so much of the
practice of law enforcement in the United States was probably as complex an
expression of American culture as it ever has been. In addition to its traditional
"protective" function, law enforcement served as highly politically profitable,
explicitly titillating, and morally bracing, at once. When law enforcement officers went after women abortionists, usually at the behest of politicians, in
league with journalists, all these conditions were satisfied to a tee.

As the famous New York ethicist Algernon Black observed, in relation to
the motivations for abortion prosecutions in these years, "We know what politicians are. They wet their fingers and put them up to find out which way the wind
is blowing—not which way is the right way or the best way for the people."[36]
Kinsey, an ethicist in his own way, noticed a similar phenomenon. "The chief
thing that the laws [against abortion] do is provide a basis for yellow journalism
to put on a campaign once in a while."[37] Ruth Barnett, the Portland, Oregon,
abortionist, was an acutely intelligent observer of her culture. Regarding the
relationship between politicians and abortionists in the postwar years, she remarked, "It is the young, politically ambitious district attorney who hounds
the abortionist." Barnett was convinced that these men arrested abortionists in
order to mount politically remunerative "moralistic juggernauts . . . crusades
that would yield a harvest of headlines."[38]

During the abortion trial of Roberta Jarquin in Wichita Falls, Texas, in
1950, Jarquin's lawyer was not reluctant to express an opinion about the political value of his client's predicament. He said, "William N. Hensley [the district
attorney, is] the Sir Gallahad of the legal profession, an ambitious young man,
and a diligent prosecutor, who, to obtain the first abortion conviction in the
history of Bexar County, will do anything."[39] Presumably, the trial paid off for
Hensley when Roberta Jarquin was sentenced to five years in prison, the stiffest
allowable sentence.

Perhaps the most interesting behavior of law enforcement officials engaged
in busting "abortion mills" in these years occurred on the front lines. Police
officers sent to stake out office buildings and houses where abortions took
place tended to linger indecently, like insatiable voyeurs. The police in San
Diego observed the Miner–Page offices for 106 days. In Baltimore, between
May 1, 1950, and August 11 of that year, police reported scores of different

women going in and out of Dr. Timanus's office. Police observed and photo-graphed women for weeks, getting on and off a yacht where abortions were performed in San Francisco Bay.[40] In 1949 two police inspectors characterized their observation of Alta Anderson's place of work in Colma, California, as a "vigil."[41]

The police, the prosecutors, the politicians, the journalists, even the jury— Sir Galahads all—involved in these cases rarely dwelt publicly on issues re-garding the inception of life or the abortionist's crime against the sanctity of the unborn child. The abortionist as sex criminal, as a violator of womanhood, was a far more prominent subject. The men who peeped, and the men who aimed to govern women's bodies, were transfixed, and then mobilized, by the spectacle of women thus engaged.

Ernie Warden, a crusading Wichita newspaperman and the indefatigable engine behind the persecution and prosecution of Grace Schauner from 1952 to 1954, was typically articulate about the wages of the abortionist's crime. He described the typical carload of women coming back from their abortions performed on Thursday mornings in a house just outside of town. "The same evening the sickening load of *aborted women* is returned to Wichita where in shame each no longer expectant mother may go to her own residence and pon-der upon the vicissitudes of life." According to Warden, and to many of the men who structured the abortion arena by their efforts at law enforcement, both women abortionists and their clients had fatally compromised their femininity and "transformed [themselves] into hardened and disillusioned women."[42]

Conclusion

The most profound irony and the most cautionary aspect of the abortion arena in the immediate pre-*Roe* decades was that the surge of cultural, medical, and legal efforts to control women's bodies created the niche in which women abortionists and their clients needed and found each other. At the same time, this surge filled the niche with terrible danger.

One journalist sympathetically described the plight of girls and women roaming the back alleys at this time:

> The choices open to a pregnant high school girl are abortion, dis-grace or reluctant and often disastrous marriage. The choices seem equally cruel to many housewives with unwanted pregnancies. A policeman who knows the dangers of abortion says, "You won-der why they take the chance, but you have to consider the mental outlook of a desperate girl. Whether she's a high school girl or a housewife who doesn't want another kid, when somebody says, 'I

can get you an abortion,' that's all they want to hear—they don't give a damn about the abortionist's credentials. Some women pawn their television sets and furniture to pay for an abortion. Some even steal." [43]

As for the women abortionists, many had been rendered equally desperate, by the loss of their profession, by husbands who abandoned them, by poverty, by age. Many of the women on trial *were* desperate women. Many were also deeply compassionate and compelled, in part by their own desperation, to identify with other women *in extremis*. In Wichita, Grace Schauner, forty-seven, hounded for months by Ernie Warden's exposes, finally decided to meet the reporter and, through him, tell the public her version of the life she led. She told Warden, "I know that you can ruin me. . . . You already have hurt me very much." But now, she insisted Warden had to listen to her. "I feel," Schauner explained,

> that every person was put on this earth for some purpose and that for that person to fail to fulfill that purpose would be a sin. In my own case, I think God put me on earth to care for unfortunate girls. There is no girl in the world who cannot be seduced if there is the right room and the right boy. Many of these girls who get into difficulty beat a path to my door for help. . . . I felt it was my duty to help these girls. . . . I have talked to my minister. I told him I was doing the right thing. In every community there must be someone to do the work that I have done. [44]

According to Grace Schauner, by destiny she was a sanctified abortionist. But Ernie Warden was not impressed or convinced. He continued to hound Schauner until she was arrested, convicted, and finally imprisoned. As he pursued her, Warden was in league with a number of other men, including Floyd Hanon and Charles Prowse, the police detectives who staked out Schauner's place and carried out the arrest; including also the D.A. and the judge who sent her to the State Industrial Farm for Women in Lansing, Kansas.

For girls and women seeking abortions in Wichita, life got tougher. For Grace Schauner and Ruth Barnett and Hazel King and Florence Stallworth, life got much tougher. But the men who had gathered together in the courtrooms where these women were tried had their say, and they got their way. The trials of each of these women gave large numbers of men a prominent public stage to mount, a stage from which to enact a full-dress drama about male power and male prerogatives. A reading of these trial records today suggests, above all, the extreme vulnerability of all women in that era because the lives of *all* women were shaped by those proceedings.

NOTES

1. A retired male abortionist in Portland, Oregon, described his sense of the resurgence of women abortionists in the postwar era: "For a good many years," he said, "abortion operations have been largely a male doctor's profession. But that is changing. . . . In time of stress [these days] a woman turns to a woman." Dr. Ruth Barnett, as told to Doug Baker, *They Weep on My Doorstep* (Beaverton, Ore.: HALO, 1969), 39.

2. *People of the State of California* v. *Laura Miner et al*, 214 P2d 557 (California, 1950). Also see 74 P2d 71 (California, 1937) for material on the abortion practice and the arrest and trial of Reg Rankin.

3. *State of Missouri* v. *Fraulein Scown* (1955), Circuit Court of the City of St. Louis, Missouri, transcripts in Missouri Superior Court Law Library, Jefferson City, Missouri. Among the women who testified against Fraulein Scown, none experienced hemorrhaging or an infection; none became mortally ill. It is interesting that during this trial there was no mention of fetuses or babies or unborn children. Nevertheless, Fraulein Scown was sentenced to three years in prison. The trial judge was clear about one criterion he used to calculate the appropriate punishment: Scown had exercised her right to a trial, a trial he called "difficult for all." Thus, he determined, she was entitled to no leniency. I call the woman seeking an abortion in this case "*Mrs.* Black" to convey the fact that her marital status was central to the way she presented herself in the courtroom and to the way she was perceived by others there.

4. *The People of the State of California* v. *Vera Odmann and Stanley Odmann* (1958), Superior Court, City and Country of San Francisco, California, transcripts in California State Archives, Sacramento, California.

5. *State of New Jersey* v. *Eva Musyznska, Irene Musconsey, Walter Musconsky and William Sudol* (1956), Passaic County Court, New Jersey, transcripts in New Jersey State Library, Trenton, New Jersey.

6. *State of North Carolina* v. *Geneva Phifer Hoover and Florence Stallworth* (1960), Superior Court, Mecklenburg County, North Carolina, transcripts in North Carolina State Supreme Court Law Library, Raleigh, North Carolina.

7. Walter Reckless, *The Crime Problem* (New York: Appleton-Century-Crofts, 1961), 88–89.

8. Carole Joffee, "Portraits of Three Physicians of Conscience: Abortion Before Legalization in the United States," *Journal of the History of Sexuality*, July 1991, 46–67.

9. See, for example, *People of the State of California* v. *John L. Flynn*, 217 Cal. Reptr. 2d 289 (1961), for a case involving a male abortionist who charged women $250 for services performed in his trailer. But this man actually exacted a much higher price: "As security . . . the defendant insisted that [his clients] allow him to take several photos of them in the nude" just before he operated. When this man was arrested in a trailer park in Redwood City, California in 1961, police found, among other things, a flash camera, a folder of pictures of nude women, and the negatives of twenty-five photographs of nude women.

10. *The People* v. *Florita Gomez*, 194 NE 2d 299 (Illinois, 1963).

11. Barnett, *They Weep*, 39, 43.

12. See Dr. X, as told to Lucy Freeman, *The Abortionist* (Garden City, N.Y.: Doubleday, 1962).

13. Barnett, *They Weep*, 55.

14. See, for example, Elaine Tyler May, *Homeward Bound: American Families in the Cold War Era* (New York: Basic Books, 1988); Wini Breines, *Young, White and Female: Growing Up in the Fifties* (Boston: Beacon Press, 1992); Rickie Solinger, *Wake Up Little Susie: Single Pregnancy and Race Before Roe v. Wade* (New York: Routledge, 1992).

15. Claude Chabrol's film "L'Histoire Des Femmes" unambiguously portrays the female abortionist as economic woman.

16. *State of North Carolina* v. *Lucille Roper Furley* (1956), Superior Court, Cumberland County, North Carolina, transcripts in North Carolina State Supreme Court Law Library, Raleigh, North Carolina.

17. *State of California* v. *Geraldine Rhoades* (1948), Superior Court, Sacramento County, California, transcripts in California State Archives, Sacramento, California.

18. *State of Ohio* v. *Mary Paige* , 120 NE 2d 504 (1954).

19. Faye Wasserman, Probation Hearing, March 27, 1962, Hudson County Criminal Court, New Jersey, transcripts in New Jersey State Library, Trenton, New Jersey.

20. Flanders Dunbar, *Psychiatry in the Medical Specialities* (New York: McGraw-Hill, 1959), 279–281.

21. Nicholas J. Eastman, "Obstetrical Forward," in *Therapeutic Abortion*, ed. Harold Rosen (New York: Julian Press, 1954), xx.

22. Theodore Linz, "Reflections of a Psychiatrist," in Rosen, *Therapeutic Abortion,* 279.

23. Flanders Dunbar, "Abortion and the Abortion Habit," in Rosen, *Therapeutic Abortion,* 27.

24. Dr. X, as told to Freeman, *The Abortionist,* 197.

25. *Adams et al.* v. *State of Maryland,* 88 A2d 566 (1952). In many ways, this man's fate was unusual. But what stands out especially is that when the law collided with the medical profession in this case, doctors closed ranks but left their colleague abortionist out in the cold. Dr. Timanus claimed that 353 doctors who had referred clients to him for abortions over a period of decades all abandoned him after his arrest. Not one would testify in his behalf at his trial.

26. Edwin Schur, *Crimes without Victims* (Englewood Cliffs, N.J.: Prentice Hall, 1965), 38.

27. Mary S.Calderone, ed., *Therapeutic Abortion in the United States* (New York: Harper & Brothers, 1858), 39.

28. *State of New Jersey* v. *Hazel King* (1945), Supreme Court of New Jersey, transcripts in New Jersey State Library, Trenton, New Jersey.

29. Paul W. Keve, *Prison, Probation or Parole? A Probation Officer Reports* (Minneapolis: University of Minnesota Press, 1954), 226–227.

30. Leonard Bishop, *Creep into Thy Narrow Bed* (New York: Dial Press, 1954), 154.

31. Jerome E. Bates and Edward S. Zawadzki, *Criminal Abortion: A Study in Medical Sociology* (Springfield, Ill.: Charles Thomas, 1964), 126.

32. This paragraph and the two following are drawn from Rickie Solinger, "Abortion and the Politics of Hospital Abortion Committees, 1950–1970," *Feminist Studies* 18, no. 2 (Summer 1993).

33. Calderone, *Abortion,* 118.

34. The U.S. Senate's "Kefauver Committee" sharply focused public attention on federal and local crime-busting efforts all over the country in the early 1950s, a phe-

nomenon that Robert Lacey has recently called "the national epidemic of Kefauverism."
Lacey has also noted that the committee "helped generate a nationwide hysteria [about
crime, which it] did little to discourage." *Little Man: Meyer Lansky and the Gangster
Life* (Boston: Little, Brown, 1991), 197–200. Also see U.S. Senate, Organized Crime
in Interstate Commerce, *Hearings Before the Special Committee to Investigate Organized Crime in Interstate Commerce,* 81st Cong., 2nd sess., and 82nd Cong., 1st sess.
(Washington, D.C.: Government Printing Office, 1950–1951).

35. *Wichita Beacon,* October 8, 1954.

36. Algernon Black, "Social, Moral and Economic Causes and Control of Abortion," in *The Abortion Problem* (Baltimore: Williams and Wilkins, 1944), 102.

37. Calderone, ed., *Therapeutic Abortion,* 39.

38. Barnett, *They Weep,* 29, 97.

39. *Roberta Jarquin v. The State of Texas,* 232 SW2d 736 (1950).

40. *People of the State of California v. Ruth Bawden* (1962), Superior Court of San
Francisco, California, transcripts in California State Archives, Sacramento, California.

41. *People of the State of California v. Alta Anderson* (1949), Superior Court of San
Francisco, transcripts in California State Archives, Sacramento, California.

42. *Wichita Beacon,* April 9, 1952, and April 11, 1952.

43. John Bartlow Martin, "Abortion," *Saturday Evening Post,* May 20, 1969, 21.

44. *Wichita Beacon,* April 16, 1952.

CHAPTER 15

Donna Penn

THE SEXUALIZED WOMAN

The Lesbian, the Prostitute, and the Containment of Female Sexuality in Postwar America

The 1962 production of *Walk on the Wild Side* centers on Jo [Barbara Stanwyck], Dove [Laurence Harvey], and Hallie [Capucine], characters in a love triangle in depression-era New Orleans. Dove Linkhorn finds Hallie Gerard, the woman who left him three years earlier, living with Jo Courtney in the building that houses Jo's business establishment—a brothel and bar where the women in Jo's employ wait for their customers. What emerges is the story of Jo's possessive obsession for Hallie—her mean-spirited, overbearing, domineering, authoritarian expressions of jealous rage. Jo, who seems to live twenty-four hours a day in a highly tailored suit, the uniform of the "masculine" woman, carries on a "maternal" relationship with the young sculptress, who might otherwise be a "normal" woman. Instead, Hallie's potential is dwarfed by the power of Jo's possessiveness, leaving "hooking" as her only form of sexual expression. In the end, this story of lesbian love, right down to the quintessential lesbian nickname "Jo," employs the plot formula used in many stories of the fallen woman. Jo, while attempting to shoot Dove, accidentally kills Hallie. Tried for murder and for her illicit business activities, she is imprisoned, while Dove may finally secure peace.

This film must be understood as part of a national crusade to make lesbianism visible to an otherwise unsuspecting public. Partly in response to fears of sexual chaos and partly in response to the increasing public visibility of lesbian subcultures, by the second half of the twentieth century, "experts" and disseminators of expert opinion demonized the lesbian in order to position her, along with the prostitute, as the essence of female sexual degeneracy. Cultural critics and various professionals intensified an assault on those with "lesbian tendencies or inclinations" as sexually deviant and depraved women. Lurid and sensationalistic accounts of those who strayed from monogamous, heterosexual bliss filled the cultural landscape. In their efforts to make absolutely clear to an otherwise ignorant public what dangers lurked in the shadows, the purveyors of the dominant discourse painted a sinister association between the lesbian and the prostitute as sisters of the sexual underworld. In this way, they linked two haunting images of fallen womanhood.

Earlier in the century, the most prevalent culturally constructed image of lesbianism was rarely linked to prostitution. Instead, expert observers often associated lesbians and "mannish women" with unmarried career women, social reformers, and feminists. By the 1920s, all these women were vilified for their gender transgression. In this earlier version of the "lesbian threat," white middle-class lesbians, and unmarried women generally, threatened "race suicide" by rejecting or otherwise compromising their proper and "natural" social role to bear and rear children. These prewar New Women were castigated primarily as asexual gender traitors.[1]

In the postwar era, the "lesbian threat" took on more ominous meanings. Lesbians were portrayed not only as gender transgressors but also as sexual demons. The rather tame cultural response to Katherine B. Davis's study of 1929, which found a significant proportion of homosexual experiences among the 2,200 women surveyed, contrasts sharply with the uproar that accompanied the publication of Alfred Kinsey's studies two decades later.[2] These differing cultural responses bespeak the very different cultural climates into which these two studies were received and thereby underscore the sometimes subtle but nevertheless significant shift in thinking about the lesbian from the prewar asexual career woman to, like the prostitute generally, a postwar sexual devil.

Walk on the Wild Side therefore gave expression, through the medium of film, to an increasingly prevalent view that fused the lesbian with the prostitute as symbols of female sexual desire, female sexual excess, uncontained female sexuality, and therefore female sexual deviance and danger. The subject of this essay is the degree to which and purpose for which these two powerful images of fallen womanhood came to be associated during the postwar years. I examine the ways in which public discussions and portrayals of deviant female sexuality captured in this association served to establish the boundaries of culturally sanctioned female heterosexuality. These two examples of deviant female sexual behavior were constructed to define, bind, and contain the so-called norm. Prescriptions for the "normal" were defined in strict inverse relationship to that which was deviant. Whereas the prostitute had historically served as the symbol of female wantonness and degeneracy, during the postwar years the lesbian, in the popular culture, joined her in filling that role. As such, this association helped make publicly visible those who formerly went undetected and thereby helped define the parameters of the normal and acceptable.

The Sexualized Lesbian

Sociological studies of deviance provide models for analyzing the social role of the deviant and deviant behavior. Instead of psychologizing deviance as the aberrant behaviors of individuals against the group norms, Kai Erikson understands deviance to be, in fact, the definer of norms. Deviants and deviant behaviors mark the boundaries within which are contained culturally approved persons, values, and expressions. The deviant, her condition, and the social response to her stand as object lessons for what will become of those who fail to stay within the boundaries that define social propriety. Deviance stands at the line that divides culturally sanctioned rules from all else. The deviant is "the other" against which the norm is measured and determined. Erikson contends:

> The "visible deviant" is a reminder of the forces that threaten a group's security. As a trespasser against the group norms, he represents those forces which lie outside the group's boundaries: he informs us, as it were, what evil looks like, what shapes the devil can assume. . . . Thus deviance cannot be dismissed simply as behavior which *disrupts* stability in society, but may itself be, in controlled quantities, an important condition for *preserving* stability.[3]

While this description is useful, it fails to detail adequately the *shape* of the relationship between deviance and norm. That is, Erikson's discussion suggests a kind of duality or polarity with deviant and normal bolstering up either side of the line that divides them from one another. Instead, I want to suggest that with female sexuality during the postwar period, a circular metaphor more accurately reflects the model employed. Proper female sexuality, heterosexual in orientation and reserved for the home and within marriage, was, in the postwar framework, surrounded by uncontained, rather public expressions of illicit sexual behaviors. These behaviors were constituted in the form of the prostitute, the lesbian, and the prostitute as lesbian.

The broader cultural context within which to place the specific experience of those defined by the postwar culture as sexual deviants is provided by Elaine Tyler May in her study documenting the fears of sexual chaos that preoccupied the American imagination during the Cold War years. May suggests that "it was not just nuclear energy that had to be contained, but the social and sexual fallout of the atomic age itself . . . the nation had to be on moral alert." [4] As May has shown, this anxiety informed not only prescriptions for private behavior but preoccupations about the destiny of the nation. The program for moral readiness focused on a domestic ideology that sought to contain female sexuality in the home, within marriage, and attended by motherhood. This formula, according to May's reading of the experts, promised to save the nation and the American family from foreign and domestic threats. In its most blatant form, it made the future of the American way of life dependent on the containment of female sexuality within certain culturally determined bounds. In so doing, deviant female sexuality achieved an unprecedented place and face in the American imagination, for it served to define not only the parameters of prescribed gender and sexual behavior but also the fate of the nation. In this context, we can make meaning of the cultural preoccuption with the lesbian and the prostitute as the symbols of moral decay associated with uncontained female sexuality.

My focus on sexual deviance challenges a dominant approach in lesbian historiography. Much of the scholarship in this emerging field has dissociated lesbians from deviant sexual styles and emphasized, instead, the romantic love shared by some women. This analytical approach has been most successful as a strategy for resurrecting lesbians (and those claimed as such by historians) from the dustbins of history.[5] Nevertheless, this strategy suffers on two counts. First, it utilizes a definition of "lesbian" so broad that it potentially includes many who did not experience their lives from a deviant subject position during historical moments when it was nearly impossible to construct a life including same-sex desire and escape this taint. Consequently, historians claim as "lesbian" women who did not necessarily, during their lifetimes, suffer the specific cruelties and marginalization reserved for sexually deviant women. Furthermore, an essentialist view of women as nurturant and romantic, rather than fueled by "lust and desire, seduction and fulfillment," [6] combined with the methodological difficulty in documenting genital contact in the historical source material, has led some historians to employ a definition of lesbian that, in effect, desexualizes these subjects. As a result, the centrality of lesbian sexual desire in our working understanding of the lesbian is at best obfuscated and at worst rendered invisible.

It is in the context of these concerns that I restore sexual agency, sexual desire, sexual adventure, sexual fulfillment, and sexual deviance to my examination of the dominant cultural understanding and subcultural experience of lesbianism during the postwar era. This "sexualized" approach is particularly relevant when exploring the postwar decades because expert observers and popular culture attempted to link the lesbian with the prostitute as the essence of female sexual degeneracy in the period. Yet, although we may be tempted to credit or fault the authorities with responsibility for creating this new sexualized image of the lesbian, they did so in the context of a flourishing lesbian subculture that was, in fact, fueled by subversive models of lesbian/female sexual desire. Therefore, I am suggesting that the experts *discovered* the centrality of lesbian sexuality and lesbian desire prevailing in the lesbian world, rather than created it. What they did do, however, was to draw together these two symbols of the sexualized female, publicize their deviance, and thereby develop the boundaries and terms for proper female heterosexuality. Certainly, both lesbians and prostitutes have been assigned to the category of deviance since the late nineteenth century. What was new in the postwar era was the extent to which experts exposed and publicized this connection and the uses to which it was put.

Therefore, as sexual outlaws and symbols of fallen womanhood, lesbians and prostitutes share a history. The history of lesbianism must therefore be explored in the context of deviant sexual behavior. As sexually defined women, Joan Nestle suggests, "both dykes and whores . . . have an historical heritage of redefining the concept of womanhood." [7] Furthermore, both the lesbian and the prostitute have found themselves subject to the control of the state and other authorities. Gayle Rubin stresses that although it may disturb many lesbians who come out of a lesbian-feminist or radical lesbian tradition, as far as the state, the public, and legal and medical experts are concerned, the lesbian has "shared many of the sociological features and suffered from many of the same social penalties as have gay men, sadomasochists, transvestites, and prostitutes." [8]

Both these analyses urge and require that we recognize the powerful discursive and experiential, constructed and actual, links between the lesbian and the prostitute as symbols and examples of lost womanhood. Rather than sanitize the history of lesbianism we develop, I suggest that we acknowledge and claim deviant sexual desire as the cornerstone of lesbian identity, of the dominant cultural construction of lesbianism, as well as its role in setting the terms for proper female heterosexuality. What follows, then, is a discussion of the development of this connection between the lesbian and the prostitute that was specific to post–World War II America, and of the particular constellation of factors that fueled it.

Early Examples of the Lesbian–Prostitute Connection

In the nineteenth century, some European observers associated both the lesbian and the prostitute with physical degeneracy. According to the historian Sander Gilman, a standard gynecological text published in 1877 associated the "over-development of the clitoris" with those "excesses" that "are called 'lesbian love.' " [9] A Russian physician, Pauline Tarnowsky, in a work published in 1893, also claimed that one could read deviance on the body. Her work examined the physical changes in appearance from which the prostitute allegedly suffered as she aged. Tarnowsky concluded that as she aged, the prostitute appeared more and more mannish, characterized by "strong jaws and cheek-bones, and their masculine aspect . . . hidden by adipose tissue, emerge, salient angles stand out, and the face grows virile, uglier than a man's; wrinkles deepen into the likeness of scars, and the countenance, once attractive, exhibits the full degenerate type which early grace had concealed." [10] Thus, according to Gilman, "the link is between two . . . models of sexual deviancy, the prostitute and the lesbian. Both are seen as possessing physical signs that set them apart from the normal." [11]

American social scientists, adapting this work to less rigidly hereditarian models of degeneracy, conducted extensive studies at the turn of the century that linked the lesbian, the prostitute, and female criminal offenders generally. Their chief area of concern was to establish the environmental and social influences contributing to the formation of the "criminal type," rather than strictly biological explanations for deviant behaviors. These issues and debates formed the heart of American criminological inquiry from its inception, but they did not extend widely in the popular imagination until after World War II. [12]

Although various early references testify to or at least suggest a connection between the prostitute and the lesbian, in the American context the full power of this linkage was reserved for the post–World War II decades. During the war, psychiatric authority on the homosexual question expanded by virtue of wartime opportunities for these professionals to advise the military on procedures for diagnosis, hospitalization, surveillance, interrogation, and discharge. [13] After the war, the psychiatric world was in a position to consolidate its power as an agent of cultural authority. At the same time, the criminal justice system marshaled its powers to respond to the believed menace of the "sexual psychopath" who roamed American streets threatening innocents and time-honored sexual morality, and law enforcement agencies were mandated to cleanse the streets of vice and immorality. [14] Various experts attacked a deviant sexual underworld, including an emerging lesbian subculture that promised to challenge and perhaps disrupt the efforts of those who sought to contain female libidinous excess. Whereas earlier efforts, particularly those of American social scientists, sought to explain with compassion the social circumstances that might lead *individuals* down the wrong path, some postwar authorities saw in these deviant populations quasi-organized *communities* whose existence threatened the social order. In a Cold War atmosphere infused with fears of external threats to national security, psychiatric personnel, with the full backing of institutional and professional authority only recently acquired during the war, as well as legal authorities and their popular supporters, mobilized their ranks in order to deploy their collective forces in the name of containing a moral menace that no longer threatened as individuals but now constituted a social group.

The Postwar Era: The Sexual Demonization of the Lesbian

This belief that homosexuals, like prostitutes, now constituted an expanding, quasi-organized sexual underworld was not merely a homophobic phantasmagoria but was a reflection of real social and cultural shifts taking place as a consequence of the war. The scholarship in the field of gay and lesbian history singles out World War II as something of a "national coming out" experience: Many gay men and lesbians took advantage of wartime social dislocation and employment opportunities to leave their families of origin and pursue the ever-increasing possibilities for establishing a gay way of life in many of the nation's urban centers. For women, fashioning a lesbian way of life generally required economic independence from men, a situation increasingly possible in the wartime and postwar cities. This reality did not go unnoticed by lesbians themselves. "Lisa Ben," whose pseudonym is an anagram for lesbian, singlehandedly produced and distributed the first known lesbian newsletter in America beginning in 1947, in which she declared the following:

> In days gone by, when woman's domain was restricted to the fireside, marriage and a family was her only prospect. The home was the little world around which life revolved and in which, unless wives were fortunate enough to have help, they had to perform innumerable household chores besides assuming the responsibility of bearing children. But in these days of frozen foods, motion picture palaces, compact apartments, modern innovations and female independence, there is no reason why a woman should have to look to a man for food and shelter in return for raising his children and keeping his house in order, unless she really wants to. Today, a woman may live independently from man if she so chooses, and carve out her

own career. Never before have circumstances and conditions been so suitable for those of lesbian tendencies.[15]

Social commentators, equally aware of the expanding possibilities for those with "lesbian tendencies," now vigorously lamented the deplorable lack of information on the lesbian. They commented often on the wealth of material available on the male homosexual, the cumulative effect of which, they believed, was the achievement of real understanding of that "problem." But there were few studies and therefore little expert knowledge about the lesbian, thereby leaving that problem culturally invisible. Those who speculated on the reason for this difference generally concurred that fewer lesbians sought psychiatric or related therapeutic intervention than male homosexuals, thereby limiting the pool of available cases for investigation. They agreed that lesbians less often faced criminal or civil prosecution, the sentences for which generally included some sessions on the couch. As for those who might voluntarily seek therapy to remedy their condition, many fewer lesbians than male homosexuals availed themselves of the opportunity, indicating, at best, a better adjustment to their neurotic and pathological condition. At worst, the fewer numbers of female homosexuals seeking cure indicated and reflected the rather large cultural space available for them to go undetected. A leading psychoanalyst, Clara Thompson, wrote in 1949:

> Until recent times there was a much stronger taboo on obvious non-marital heterosexual situations. Two overt homosexual women may live together in complete intimacy in many communities without social disapproval if they do not flaunt their inversion by, for example, the assumption of masculine dress or mannerisms on the part of one. Sometimes even if they go to this extreme they are thought peculiar rather than taboo. On the other hand, two men attempting the same thing are likely to encounter marked hostility.[16]

Experts grew increasingly dissatisfied with the broad range of affectional expressions permitted two women that enabled many inverted and deviant women to live together unsuspected—a luxury rarely afforded two men. These purveyors of the dominant discourse now took it upon themselves to make the lesbian visible and narrow the cultural space previously available that allowed them to go unnoticed, thereby delimiting if not establishing the boundaries of deviant female sexuality.[17]

In their efforts to make the lesbian visible to the unsuspecting public, an image emerged that characterized the lesbian as a promiscuous, over-sexed, conquering, aggressive dyke who exercised masculine prerogatives in the sexual arena. Whereas earlier images, especially those of the middle class,

Lurid paperback covers were common features of the pulp lesbian fiction of the postwar era. This cover, from 1960, reflects the cultural attitudes that cast lesbians as sexual deviants.

centered on companionable relationships between two "ladies" who controlled their sexual appetites and lived quiet lives together, this new image sexualized the lesbian and saw the jealous rage as the cornerstone of the lesbian relationship. Particularly when describing those of the working classes, the image of the lesbian took on a dark and sinister quality. The very essence of the lesbian, like the prostitute, was an expression of uncontained female sexuality—in this case, a sexuality that in no way required the participation of men or held the promise of marriage.

Therefore, a somewhat repressed deviant sexuality, as seen in the film character Jo, was rivaled in the popular imagination by another expression of lesbian love prevalent at the time, namely, the aggressive, promiscuous dyke who, according to one touted as knowledgable on the subject, "will bust a gut for a toss in the hay." [18] Another claimed that she came "to know homosexual women, but they exhibited such elemental passion, brutality, sensuality, that, notwithstanding all my yearning for 'homosexual' love, I remained unresponsive." [19] In these cases, a sexualized and necessarily demonized image of lesbians was broadcast and disseminated into the popular culture of the postwar era. Lesbians were increasingly described and publicized as a predatory lot whose lives were based on sexual conquest and the determined pursuit of sexual gratification, which, ultimately, they could not achieve anyway, since, according to the experts, lesbians engaged primarily in mere mutual masturbation, which in itself was an indication of immature if not deviant female sexuality. Frank Caprio, a psychoanalyst whose area of expertise during these years was female homosexuality and sexual variance generally, went so far as to suggest that female promiscuity, masturbation in marriage, and "unconventional sex practices" such as cunnilingus, fellatio, and anal penetration were themselves indicative of latent homosexuality. [20]

Yet active, rather than latent, female homosexuality was the area of chief concern in the immediate postwar years. Estelle Freedman describes the national hysteria concerning the perceived epidemic of sexual psychopathology during this period. Medical experts, social hygiene reformers, and law enforcement officials sought to squelch the new moral menace to youth and women. [21] Lesbians, although less often the subject of widespread public concern, did achieve a place on the rostrum of sexual deviants who threatened public decency. In 1947, Dr. Carleton Simon, criminologist for the International Association of Chiefs of Police, addressed members of the association at its annual convention on the subject of "Homosexualists and Sex Crimes" in which he asserted:

> Psychopathic women homosexualists—commonly called Lesbians,
> also Sapphists . . . are fickle minded and always eager to add

to their list of conquests. They seek new acquaintances, not solely as passive victims but also as active participants. . . . They
are . . . extremely jealous of the object of their lust. . . . Usually
large cities attract them, where the selective field is more expanded
and where, if necessary, they can cover up their predilections. . . .
Though the victim of acquired sexual obsession, they may have
lofty ideals and many marry and find eventually a normal sex adjustment.[22]

   Simon's depiction of sexual wantonness, reflecting the achievement of
popular dissemination of expert ideas, helped expose the "truth" about lesbians to an otherwise ignorant public. Literature on prison conditions similarly
painted a portrait of the aggressive predatory lesbian who, in this instance,
had a captive audience in the inmate population. A 1958 report of the Special
Legislative Committee on the Women's Massachusetts Correctional Institution
at Framingham was a response, in part, to charges of widespread homosexuality among the inmates. The report charged that the "aggressive homosexuals
and trouble makers" had taken advantage of access to the receiving annex
and thereby "indoctrinated the new admissions." Their recommendations
included relocating the receiving annex away from ready exposure to the
"hard-core" homosexual element as well as proposed isolation units for the
aggressive homosexuals and for those who were termed "belligerent nonconformists."[23] In all these cases, the "true" lesbian was identified by her insatiable need for sexual conquest, which made her a threat to the social order
as well as to the containment of female sexuality within the home and marriage.
   Despite, or perhaps because of, a rhetoric in which deviant women might
disguise themselves under the cloak of asexuality, many postwar experts and
their popularizers sought to give these women a face and a name that the public could recognize for the neurotic, pathological, faulty adjustment that the
experts believed it to be, thereby further narrowing the terms of and space
for appropriate female sexuality. Thus the lesbian, now sexualized, joined the
prostitute to form the boundaries of a circular model of deviance that contained culturally sanctioned female sexuality. As fallen women by virtue of
their demonized sexuality, the association between the lesbian and the prostitute further elaborated the contours of female sexual deviance and served as
a warning of what might befall those who would dare to stray from the
increasingly restricted "straight and narrow" sexual ideology of these years.
As Erikson would say, together they revealed "what shapes the devil can assume."

The Lesbian—Prostitute Connection: Evidence of the Link

In Polly Adler's 1953 autobiographical memoirs of life as a New York madam, she recounts that "inevitably I had a few Lesbians, some of them troublemakers, some very peaceful souls. It has often been said that a prostitute becomes so tired of being mauled by men that she turns to a woman for tenderness. Maybe so. I have no figures on the incidence of female homosexuality, but it's my observation that it occurs in every walk of life." [24] The tone of nonchalance with which she reports this phenomenon bespeaks an increasingly accepted view in which the lesbian and the prostitute, whether distinct individuals or one and the same, shared a cultural space as sexually defined women, thereby placing them at the margins of respectability. Whereas the prevailing image of the lesbian for the prewar generation was generally one of lifelong companions of the middle class or mannish upper-class women like Radclyffe Hall's protagonist in *The Well of Loneliness*,[25] this image of genteel unmarried women altered during the postwar years. The lesbian was now, like the prostitute, a sexual demon. If she repressed her inverted desires, she was likely to suffer frigidity in sexual relations with her husband, which, in this Kinseyan era of devotion to sexual satisfaction, spelled certain disaster. Consequently, heterosexual marriage was generally not recommended as appropriate treatment for curing homosexuality. It would likely fail the individual and make a mockery of the heterosexual union.

As suggested earlier, a primary strategy employed for exposing the lesbian was to identify her as a sexual degenerate and to link her with the prostitute as the essence of female sexual deviance and danger. The image of these two sexual demons and efforts to portray the degree to which they supposedly overlapped is most sensationally summed up in a 1965 *Life* magazine photoessay, titled "Lesbians Try to Peddle Each Other." The author suggested that "telling the players without a program can be all but impossible in Times Square. The four people in the three pictures at left all are women. Two are drug addicts, and one is a pusher. Two are prostitutes, the other two are pimps. All are Lesbians. They are among hundreds of perverts, prostitutes, and addicts drawn to the Times Square area by each other and by the easy marks they can prey on." The text that accompanied the photos told a sordid tale of perverted sexuality, drug addiction, and crime that served to reenforce the public's view of the sexual psychopathology that afflicted those who strayed from rigid prescriptions for female sexuality.

> Five minutes after giving her a shot of heroin, a Lesbian dressed as a man leads her pony-tailed girlfriend around the corner to meet two other Lesbians. Both "fems" (Lesbians dressed as girls) sit in a

movie theater entrance, nodding from heroin shots. Their "butches" (Lesbians dressed as men) stay with them waiting for a John. One encourages her fem with a kiss. In a few minutes a John arrives in a taxi driven by a "hawk" (a taxi driver who prefers a few illicit but high-paying fares to a night of conventional hacking). After talking things over, the John agrees to pay the butches for a few hours with their two addicted fems.[26]

Popular efforts to develop and disseminate this image of the "butch-as-pimp-for-her-fem-junkie-whore" served to dispel further the previously prevailing image of the lesbian as a middle-class social activist and, instead, call attention to the lives of true depravity that those of her ilk fashioned for themselves.

The connection increasingly disseminated into the popular culture between these two examples of female sexual degeneracy was also explored by experts, among whom Frank Caprio is perhaps the most notable. His work during this period commented extensively on his many adventures in Europe and elsewhere where he encountered many lesbians among brothel workers. He asserted that

> while it would seem paradoxical to think of prostitutes as having strong homosexual tendencies, psychoanalysts have demonstrated that prostitution in many instances represents a form of pseudo-heterosexuality—a flight from homosexual repressions. In short, many prostitutes are latent homosexuals insofar as they resort to sexual excesses with many men to convince themselves that they are heterosexual. A large percentage of them eventually become participants in lesbian activities.[27]

Caprio decided that this topic of the relationship between lesbianism and prostitution required further study. Consequently, he conducted his own investigation in major U.S. and Canadian cities followed by a world tour in 1953 during which he "interviewed prostitutes in the following cities: Havana, Cuba; Panama City, Panama; London, England; Paris, France; Venice, Genoa, Naples, Rome, Isle of Capri, Italy; Vienna, Austria; Honolulu, Hawaii; Tokyo, Japan; Manila, Philippine Islands; Singapore, Penang, Malay; Hong Kong; Bombay, India; Cairo, Egypt." He found that "the prevalence of lesbianism in brothels throughout the world has convinced me that prostitution, as a behavior deviation, attracts to a large extent women who have a very strong latent homosexual component. Through prostitution, these women eventually overcome their homosexual repressions."[28] Thus, what Caprio offered was a pseudo-psychoanalytic explanation for the lesbian as prostitute and the prostitute as lesbian—the repressed lesbian fled from her fears of homosexuality into a life of heterosexual excess in which, because of her true homosexual desires, she failed to find sexual satisfaction, which in turn led her to find fulfillment in the arms of another of her sex. The prevailing image in this and other accounts of its kind is of sexual activity run amok.

For many psychologists and their popularizers, these two examples of sexually deviant females not only represented two sorts of maladjusted women but often were one and the same. When speaking of lesbians, Carleton Simon reminded his audience that "a great many are predatory prostitutes to obtain their living and to enable them to carry on their licentious practices without financial worry." [29] Whether true or not, accurate or contrived, the significance of these portrayals lies in their power to fuse the lesbian and the prostitute as individuals and social categories that represented uncontained and therefore deviant female sexuality.

Portrayals that fused the lesbian and the prostitute also served a larger purpose: to ensure national security through domestic tranquility and sexual containment. A major strategy in this effort was the national campaign to squelch what was perceived to be an epidemic of sexual offenders. Although largely concerned with the perpetrators of violent crimes motivated by a sexual "abnormality," public attention extended to the nuisance offender as well. Members of the sexual underworld became prime targets of state-sanctioned harassment. Homosexuals and prostitutes represented moral decay associated with sexual excess that had to be eradicated or, at the least, driven further underground. Legislative committees rewrote statutes dealing with the disposition and treatment of sex offenders that now made efforts to view these criminals as psychologically impaired individuals in need of treatment, rather than mere criminals deserving incarceration. And psychiatrists jockeyed for position as this new approach promised them a central role in rehabilitative treatment centers as well as in advising members of the criminal justice community on the proper adjudication of such cases. [30]

Vice-control units of local police departments, in association with liquor licensing boards, private reform groups like the American Society for Social Hygiene, and public health officials routinely executed round-ups of those involved in "immoral" social and sexual activities. Law enforcement officials made efforts to clean lesbians and prostitutes, whose public presence disturbed moral decency, off the city's streets. Sex deviants and sex workers of various shades found themselves the targets of a law enforcement crusade during the 1950s and 1960s that was conducting a kind of urban renewal of the social landscape to clean the cities of "degenerates" and "deviants." The hooker, the whore, the B-girl, [31] the call girl, the expense-account girl, and the homosexual all became victims of police raids, harassment, and arrests. [32] In Boston,

for example, a spate of newspaper articles during this period document police
activities designed to harass and arrest individuals associated with sexual deviance and shut down establishments that catered to them. Stories abound of
"girls" picked up on morals charges and of bars and clubs under investigation
by the Alcohol and Beverage Control Commission for alleged illicit activities.
Names of individuals held by the police for idle and disorderly conduct were
routinely printed in the newspapers.[33]

The relationship between the lesbian and the prostitute, whether discovered
or created, conceptual or actual, was by this period real. Although members
of both groups worked, played, and lived in all parts of the metropolitan area,
at least one spatially defined area was generally designated as the locus of the
sexual underworld. In many cities, the very same territory identified as the
red-light district, in which prostitutes conducted their business, also contained
or was adjacent to neighborhoods that housed many of the city's sites of gay
nightlife. For example, during much of this postwar, pre–gay liberation period,
many of Boston's lesbian bars, gay male bars, and those that served both segments of the "twilight world" were to be found in and around the streets of
the city's red-light and porn district, locally referred to as the "Combat Zone."
The clusters of streets today known as Bay Village and the downtown shopping district were once the home of the majority of lesbian bars, which shared
the territory with sex workers and other institutions of the sex industry. These
sexually marginalized and stigmatized populations not only shared a sinful
pathology in the expert and popular imagination but shared an urban geography as well. The very real spatial proximity of these two segments of the sexual
underworld underscores the degree to which they shared the role of sexual and
social blight on the urban landscape.

The Centrality of Sexuality in the Lesbian World

Lesbians themselves struggled with the newly publicized strictures of the culture in an effort to make sense of their lives. In 1947 Jane MacKinnon, a
self-proclaimed lesbian, published a piece in the *American Journal of Psychiatry.* Despite her plea for understanding, MacKinnon seemed to accept the
prevailing cultural views, and her article fanned the flames that portrayed the
lesbian as one guided by an insatiable hunger. In her taxonomy of lesbianism,
Types I and II were the aggressive sorts whose relationships with their partners
could "be likened to that of a mother with a helpless child. . . . They cannot
be satisfied unless they dominate. . . . Education, breeding, all those things
do not prevent the homosexual from drawing . . . a woman into her orbit of
dominance if she possibly can. Her need for relief from sexual tension . . . is
too great."[34]

To varying degrees, other lesbians also absorbed dominant cultural messages concerning them. In few cases did they escape unscathed during these postwar and pre-Stonewall years. At one extreme there were those who did not survive, like Bobby, who described herself repeatedly and with self-loathing to Dusty as a "dirty dyke, nothing but a dirty dyke." Bobby committed suicide at the age of twenty-eight in 1968.[35] Yet many did survive, despite failing to renegotiate the terms of the dominant culture. Edie, after living forty-two years with another woman, still does not identify herself as a lesbian. She explains: "I saw very predatory people . . . and incredibly fickle. They run from person to person. They have lots of relationships. . . . I do not have a very flattering picture of them." For Edie, who just happened to share her entire adult life with another woman, lesbians were "the other," sexually fickle, predatory women. Edie's direct contact with the lesbian subculture was so limited that it appears she derived much of her impressions from the dominant discourse. Consequently, what she absorbed never reflected back to her what she herself felt, leaving her without a label or identity with which to define her experience.[36]

Her partner, Mary Jane, never did much associating with the lesbian subculture either. Instead, the postwar years for her were those of the "perfect suburban husband." For these two, life approximated the postwar ideal of a home in the suburbs with children, albeit with one significant difference— the husband was a woman. Mary Jane drove Edie's kids to the dentist and doctor and dance class, and she mowed the lawn, yet she understood that despite Edie's commitment to seeing the lesbian as "the other," Edie's perfect suburban husband was a woman. As Mary Jane suggests:

> I had much more of an awareness that there was a gay life out there, there was a gay world out there, that there were gay people out there living whatever kind of lives they were living. But I think living in a small suburban town surrounded by heterosexuals it never occurred to her (Edie) that she was anything other than a suburban housewife. She had all the recruitments [*sic*] of it. She had the house. She had the grass. The lawnmower. She had the husband mowing the lawn. It never occurred to her to take an honest look at me and say, "This is not a male husband. This is a woman husband." It never occurred to her.[37]

Other lesbians engaged to varying extents in the transformation of dominant cultural messages concerning them. While Edie and Mary Jane, among countless others, lived discreetly in the suburbs and elsewhere, many were constructing a more aggressive challenge to the dominant discourse. By and large, lesbians who participated in the vibrant bar culture of the pre-Stonewall years, who found community in that setting, interpreted their lives in ways that bore resemblance to the dictates of normal female sexuality but fundamentally challenged it in that they were, by all accounts, deviant and homosexual. Aware of some of the basic recipes for deviance being articulated by the experts, they made efforts to employ and apply those "scientific facts" to themselves before eventually abandoning them as false. As Mary explains:

> To realize . . . you were . . . sick. . . . We used to think that. Well, we were told that. You know, the guys would say, "Gee, I wasn't a mama's boy. I wonder how I ever became gay because I had a good relationship with my father? Maybe there's something wrong with me. I'm not the right kind of a queer like I'm supposed to be. I'm supposed to be a mama's boy and I wasn't." Or maybe, "She was attacked by men when she was young and that's why she's gay." [We heard] all these kinds of things and [we'd] think, "Gee, that never happened to me. How did I ever become gay?" You tr[ied] to figure out how you became gay because according to all the information out there something awful should have happened to you to make you that way. So you kept saying, "So what is it? What happened? Why am I gay?" [38]

Yet these individual struggles with the terms of the dominant discourse were eventually altered in the context of community. Among the aspects of lesbian life and sexuality that captured this renegotiation and transformation most elegantly were the dynamics of butch and femme. The failure of most experts and their popularizers to break outside the heterosexual paradigm led many to assert "truths," such as the following by A. M. Krich: "We tend to forget that the homosexual affair is never between a man and a man or a woman and a woman. The assumption behind the homosexual relationship is always that one of the partners belongs to the other sex. Though all human beings share a common mammalian background, only a few, it seems, have this capacity for self-deception." [39]

Lesbians themselves subverted the dominant discourse to make meanings more consistent with their own feelings and experiences. It is in this context that the social organization of the butch and femme becomes an important area for analysis. The butch–femme experience both resembled dominant cultural prescriptions for culturally sanctioned sexuality and fundamentally challenged and altered those terms. That the butch was supposed to be the aggressor in sexual contacts and the femme was the "passive" one appears, on the surface, to resemble the format for postwar heterosexual relations. And yet, as Elizabeth Lapovsky Kennedy and Madeline Davis's work on Buffalo indicates, butches and femmes quite radically renegotiated the terms of the dominant discourse while retaining a model that superficially approximated it. They assert:

> Butch-fem roles did indeed parallel the male/female roles in hetero-sexuality. Yet unlike the dynamics of many heterosexual relation-ships, the butch's foremost objective was to give sexual pleasure to a fem; it was in satisfying her fem that the butch received fulfill-ment. . . . As for the fem, she not only knew what would give her physical pleasure, but she also knew that she was neither object of nor receptacle for someone else's gratification. . . . Thus, although these women did draw on models in heterosexual society, they trans-formed those models into an authentically lesbian interaction.[40]

And yet butch–femme did not merely describe and govern a set of *private* sexual relations or rituals but, perhaps most significantly, represented a defiant *public* challenge to the dominant code. As Nestle suggests, by appear-ing together in public, butch and femme couples achieved a "style of self-presentation that made erotic competence a political statement in the 1950s."[41] She explains:

> Does the longevity of butch-femme self-expression reflect the per-nicious strength of heterosexual gender polarization—or is it, as I would argue, a lesbian-specific way of deconstructing gender that radically reclaims women's *erotic* energy? . . . [L]esbian life in America . . . was organized around a highly developed sense of sexual ceremony and dialogue. Indeed, because of the surrounding oppression, ritual and code were often all we had to make public erotic connections. Dress, stance, gestures, even jewelry and hair-styles had to carry the weight of sexual communications. The pinky ring flashing in a subway car, the DA haircut combed more severely in front of a mirror always made me catch my breath, symbolizing as they did a butch woman announcing her erotic competence. A language of courtship and seduction was carefully crafted to allow for expression of both lust and love in the face of severe social repression.[42]

During a historical moment when women's fulfillment was to be accom-plished within marriage, home, and motherhood, these women, both by choos-ing other women as sexual partners and by daring to explore their sexual desires and longings, aggressively and publicly carved out an alternative meaning from the dominant code. They demonstrated that uncontained female sexuality and female sexual autonomy were their right and privilege.

This defiantly public sexual presence was largely organized around the lesbian bar, which was the site of community formation during a period in which few other social or political organizations catered to the sexual deviant. As such, lesbian bars served various purposes. They were where lesbians found others like themselves with whom to interrupt the sense of isolation that frequently accompanied gay life in this period. Perhaps more important, they were where lesbians found sexual adventure. Lesbians who went to the bars uniformly admit that possible arrest was a risk they were willing to take for the opportunity to participate in a social life rich with sexual possibilities. Stories lesbians tell about their evening adventures at lesbian and gay bars are filled with a tone of anticipation that clearly betrays lesbian sexual desire. The thrill of going to a bar was fueled by desire. Joan recalls her evenings out thirty-five years ago with a note of excitement one might mistake for last night's activities:

> Remember the old days? They (butches) used to light our (femme) cigarettes. As soon as you put your cigarette in your mouth, you'd sit there with your butt, and the lighters would come out. They used to walk us to the toilet. They'd open the door for us and let us walk in. . . . I liked the old days. I still like it. You never paid your way. I liked that. You never bought your own drinks. . . . I loved those days. It was a nicer environment. . . . You'd get all spiffed up and you didn't know what was going to happen. I loved the way H and I would get all dressed up and go down and they'd all be sitting there—all the butches would be there with their Lucky's rolled up in their T-shirts—and they'd be sitting there looking so tough and we'd go bopping in in our heels and we'd sit and they'd be checking us out. If you wore a dress in those days and you were a lesbian it was like "wow" and you'd dance all night long. Everybody would ask you to dance and you'd have flowers all over the place. All the femmes would be sitting there with their flowers. I just loved it.[43]

Similarly, lesbian pulp fiction of the era provided messages about the gay life and lesbian desire that were an alternative to the prescriptions proliferating in the dominant culture. For those fortunate enough to pluck the novels of Ann Bannon, Claire Morgan, Valerie Taylor, and Paula Christian off the dime-store racks, tales of lesbian struggle and fulfillment entered their consciousness and validated their experience, thereby challenging the expert and popular diagnoses of sexual deviancy and perverted desire. The first paragraph of Valerie Taylor's *Return to Lesbos* suggests the excitement and anxiety connected to sexual longing that the lesbian found in the bar:

Karla's place was jumping. Frances Ollenfield stood at the edge of the sidewalk and watched the blue door swinging open and shut behind the couples: two girls in bermudas and knee socks, two slim boys moving gracefully in unison, more girls. Smoke and voices and juke music drifted out. Frances shivered a little, although it was a June evening in Chicago.

She hadn't been in a gay bar for a year. She had promised never to visit one again. But her need was too strong. She took a deep breath and walked down the three stone steps, feeling her mouth go dry and her heart begin to hammer with excitement. The blue paint was flaking off the door and the gold scroll letters had faded. It's been a while, Frances thought.[44]

This passage, which opens the final volume in the Erika Frohmann series, is describing a sexual adventure as much as a visit to a gay bar. Frances "shivered" despite the summer heat because "her need was too strong." This "need" that made her "mouth go dry" was to be engaging in lesbian sexual activity, not merely having a cocktail. When Taylor writes that for Frances, "it's been a while," the reader would have to go to great lengths to miss the point. We all know, truly, what "it's been a while" since.

During a period in which a national crusade was on to contain female sexuality within the home and marriage, women daring to desire was a bold act. That the form this desire took was same sex was a dangerous act. That they actively, passionately, and relatively publicly pursued their desire was a revolutionary act.

Conclusion

During the war and after, lesbian sexual subjectivity was seen publicly in the subcultures of the gay underworld and sexual demimonde. In the postwar era, these subcultures were discovered and publicized by the "experts." Medical, psychiatric, and legal authorities marshaled their collective powers to establish and exploit a connection between the lesbian and the prostitute as representatives of female sexual deviance in order to proscribe the behaviors at odds with proper female heterosexuality. As sexually defined women, the lesbian and the prostitute did share a relationship to the state, to urban territory, and therefore, to one another. On the one hand, the experts succeeded in bolstering this association in the popular culture and in demonizing both lesbians and prostitutes. On the other hand, they did not succeed in containing the lesbian (or, for that matter, the prostitute). Women in the sexual underworld established their own communities and renegotiated the terms and codes of the dominant culture. In an era of sexual containment, they asserted public identities based on sexual expression and sexual desire.

NOTES

1. For a discussion of this earlier meaning and application of the "lesbian threat," see Christina Simmons, "Companionate Marriage and the Lesbian Threat," *Frontiers,* Fall 1979, 54–59.

2. Katharine B. Davis, *Factors in the Sex Life of 2200 Women* (New York: Harper & Row, 1929); Alfred Kinsey et al., *Sexual Behavior in the Human Female* (Philadelphia: W.B. Saunders, 1953). For responses, see, for example, M. J. Exner, "The Sex Side of Life," *Survey,* April 15, 1930, 74–75; Edmund Bergler, *Homosexuality: Disease or Way of Life?* (New York: Hill and Wang, 1956); Edmund Bergler, "The Myth of a New National Disease: Homosexuality and the Kinsey Report," *Psychiatric Quarterly,* 1948, reprinted in *The Homosexuals: As Seen by Themselves and Thirty Authorities,* ed. A.M. Krich (New York: Citadel, 1954), 226–250.

3. Kai Erikson, "Notes on the Sociology of Deviance," in *The Other Side: Perspectives on Deviance,* ed. Howard S. Becker (New York: Free Press, 1964), 15. Originally appeared in *Social Problems,* 1962.

4. Elaine Tyler May, *Homeward Bound: American Families in the Cold War Era* (New York: Basic Books, 1988), 93–94.

5. See, especially, Blanche W. Cook, "Historical Denial of Lesbianism," *Radical History Review,* Spring/Summer 1979, 60–65.

6. Joan Nestle, *A Restricted Country* (Ithaca, N.Y.: Firebrand Books, 1987), 10.

7. Ibid., 161.

8. Gayle Rubin, "Thinking Sex: Notes for a Radical Theory of the Politics of Sexuality," in *Pleasure and Danger: Exploring Female Sexuality,* ed. Carole Vance (Boston: Routledge and Kegan Paul, 1984), 308. For another example of the current efforts to examine the history of the lesbian as sexual outlaw, see Theo Van Der Meer, "Tribades on Trial: Female Same-Sex Offenders in Late Eighteenth-Century Amsterdam," *Journal of the History of Sexuality,* January 1991, 424–445.

9. Sander Gilman, *Difference and Pathology: Stereotypes of Sexuality, Race and Madness* (Ithaca: Cornell University Press, 1985), 89.

10. Ibid., 96. This concern with reading deviance on the body is strikingly like the studies conducted by the Committee for the Study of Sex Variants in New York during the 1930s. See George Henry, *Sex Variants: A Study of Homosexual Patterns* (New York: Paul B. Hoeber, 1941).

11. Gilman, *Difference and Pathology,* 98. It is significant that Tarnowsky's data figured prominently in the work on female deviance by Cesare Lombroso, called the founder of modern criminology, which was extremely influential in the United States.

12. I am indebted to Jessica Shubow for calling my attention to these developments. See also Rosalind Rosenberg, *Beyond Separate Spheres: The Intellectual Roots of Modern Feminism,* (New Haven: Yale University Press, 1982), for a discussion of the work of Frances Kellor on female offenders. See also Arthur Fink, *Causes of Crime: Biological Theories in the United States 1800–1915* (Philadelphia: University of Pennsylva-

nia Press, 1938); Estelle Freedman, *Their Sisters' Keepers: Women's Prison Reform in America, 1830–1930* (Ann Arbor: University of Michigan Press, 1981); Frances Kellor, "Psychological and Environmental Study of Women Criminals," *American Journal of Sociology,* July 1899–May 1900, 527–543, 671–682; Dorie Klein, "The Etiology of Female Crime: A Review of the Literature," *Issues in Criminology,* Fall 1973, 3–30.

13. Allan Berube, "Marching to a Different Drummer: Lesbian and Gay GIs in World War II," in *Powers of Desire: The Politics of Sexuality,* ed. Ann Snitow, Christine Stansell, and Sharon Thompson (New York: Monthly Review Press, 1983), 88–99; see also Allan Berube, *Coming Out Under Fire: The History of Gay Men and Women in World War Two* (New York: Free Press, 1990).

14. Estelle B. Freedman, " 'Uncontrolled Desires': The Response to the Sexual Psychopath, 1920–1960," *Journal of American History,* June 1987, 83–106.

15. "Lisa Ben," "Here to Stay," *Vice Versa,* September 1947, 5.

16. Clara Thompson, "Changing Concepts of Homosexuality in Psychoanalysis," in *A Study of Interpersonal Relations,* ed. Patrick Mullahy (New York: Hermitage Press, 1949), reprinted in Krich, *The Homosexuals,* 255.

17. For examples of this, see William Simon and John Gagnon, "The Lesbians: A Preliminary Overview," in *Sexual Deviance,* ed. J. Gagnon and Wm. Simon (New York: Harper & Row, 1967); Clara Thompson, "Changing Concepts in Psychoanalysis," in Krich, *The Homosexuals;* William Simon and John Gagnon, "Sexual Deviance in Contemporary America," *Annals of the American Academy of Political and Social Science,* March 1968, 118; Harvey Kaye et al., "Homosexuality in Women," *Archives of General Psychiatry,* 1967, 627; Ernest Havemann, "Scientists Search for the Answers to a Touchy and Puzzling Question: Why?" *Life,* June 26, 1964, 79; Robert Laidlaw, "Clinical Approach to Homosexuality," *Marriage and Family Living,* February 1952, 43; Lawrence Hatterer and Nancy Mayer, "What Every Parent Should Know about Homosexuality," *Parents Magazine,* March 1968, 56; George Silver, "The Homosexual: Challenge to Science," *The Nation,* May 25, 1957, 451; William Simon and John Gagnon, "Femininity in the Lesbian Community," *Social Problems,* 1967, 218.

18. As quoted in George Henry, *All the Sexes* (New York: Rinehart, 1955), 293.

19. Anonymous, "To What Sex Do I Really Belong?" in Iwan Bloch, *Sexual Life of Our Time* (1900) reprinted in Krich, *The Homosexuals,* 12. Although the original publication date of this case study dates to 1900, what is significant for this discussion is that it was excerpted and anthologized in a 1954 collection on the homosexual, indicating the further circulation and dissemination of these images of the predatory lesbian for a postwar audience.

20. Frank Caprio, *Female Homosexuality: A Psychodynamic Study of Lesbianism* (New York: Citadel, 1954), 303–307.

21. See Freedman, " 'Uncontrolled Desires.' "

22. Carleton Simon, "Homosexualists and Sex Crimes," speech to International Association of Chiefs of Police, September 1947, Massachusetts Society for Social Hygiene Papers 6, 57, Radcliffe College Schlesinger Library.

23. Special Legislative Committee, "Correctional System of Massachusetts: Report of Special Legislative Committee," May 12, 1958, Massachusetts Society for Social Hygiene Papers 8, 70, Radcliffe College Schlesinger Library.

24. Polly Adler, *A House Is Not a Home* (New York: Rinehart, 1953), 110.

25. For more discussion of prewar images of lesbians and New Women that distinguish them from postwar portraits, see, for example, Esther Newton, "The Mythic

Mannish Lesbian: Radclyffe Hall and the New Woman," in *Hidden from History: Reclaiming the Gay and Lesbian Past,* ed. Martin Bauml Duberman et al. (New York: New American Library, 1989), 281–293.

26. J. Mills, "Lesbians Try to Peddle Each Other," *Life,* December 3, 1965, 98–99.

27. Frank Caprio, *Variations in Sexual Behavior* (New York: Citadel, 1955), 183.

28. Ibid., 183–184.

29. Simon, "Homosexualists and Sex Crimes," 57.

30. On the consolidation of psychiatric authority, see Seymour Halleck, "American Psychiatry and the Criminal: A Historical Review," *American Journal of Psychiatry,* March 1965, i–xxi.

31. "B-girls" were members of the sex industry along with prostitutes, strippers, call girls, etc. Their particular job involved "enticing" men in bars, especially "strip joints," to purchase more and more drinks, for which they received a percentage, or commission of sorts.

32. For an example of the association of vice campaigns with urban renewal, see "Hub Vice Raids Trap 10 Girls," *Boston Record American,* December 4, 1965, in which Judge Francis X. Morrissey of the Boston Municipal Court is quoted as saying, "Keeping our streets clean goes hand in hand with the renaissance in Boston."

33. For some examples of newspaper coverage of Boston area police and Alcohol and Beverage Control Commission vice campaigns, investigations, shutdowns, and arrests affecting bars and their owners, patrons and employëes suspected of immoral and illicit activities, and related violations, allegedly conducted in these establishments of the sexual underworld, see "35 Arrested in Raid at Revere Club," *Boston Daily Globe,* November 29, 1955, 3; "Revere Show Group Held," *Boston Traveler,* November 29, 1955, 1, 14; "Jail Terms and Fines for 13 in Revere Raid," *Boston Traveler,* December 12, 1955, 9; "Board to Get Morals Report from 25 Liquor Places Here," *Boston Herald,* May 3, 1957, 7; "District Attorney Orders Probe of Night Spots," *Boston Herald,* September 12, 1961, 24; "Trial September 26 for Five Women," *Boston Sunday Herald,* September 10, 1961, 31; "Legislators Hear a Story of Vice," *Boston Herald,* February 7, 1962, 5.

34. Jane MacKinnon, "I am a Homosexual Woman," in Krich, *The Homosexuals,* 5.

35. Interview with "Dusty," conducted by author, January 18, 1990.

36. Interview with "Edie," conducted by author, October 24, 1989.

37. Interview with "Mary Jane," conducted by author, February 13, 1990.

38. Interview with "Mary," conducted by author, January 7, 1990.

39. Krich, *The Homosexuals,* ix.

40. Elizabeth Lapovsky Kennedy and Madeline Davis, "Oral History and the Study of Sexuality in the Lesbian Community: Buffalo, New York, 1940–1960," *Feminist Studies,* Spring 1986, 14. For Kennedy and Davis, the very essence of the butch–femme sexual dynamic fundamentally altered the prescriptions of female sexual passivity. Butches, both in courtship rituals and sexual relations, absolutely devoted themselves to making their femmes feel special and satisfied. Their commitment to the pleasure of the "other," rather than, or through which they received, their own pleasure, was perhaps a uniquely lesbian experience. Similarly, femmes have indicated that it was with butches that they came to know and understand their bodies. One femme who had been married and given birth to four children explained how she felt like an adolescent in terms of her knowledge of her sexual desires until she began to be with women. Her sexual self-discovery completely depended on her experience as a femme in lesbian relationships

where she acquired the space to explore and exploit her own desires. From interview with "Joan," conducted by author, January 7, 1990.

41. Nestle, *A Restricted Country,* 104.

42. Joan Nestle, *The Persistent Desire: A Femme-Butch Reader* (Boston: Alyson, 1992), 14–15; italics added.

43. Interview with "Joan."

44. Valerie Taylor, *Return to Lesbos* (Tallahassee: Naiad Press, 1982), 7. Originally published in 1963.

CHAPTER 16

Wini Breines

THE "OTHER" FIFTIES

Beats and Bad Girls

In 1956 Paul Goodman published *Growing Up Absurd: The Problems of Youth in the Organized Society.* Early in the book, he describes a growing problem: "We see groups of boys and young men disaffected from the dominant society. The young men are Angry and Beat. The boys are Juvenile Delinquents." Angry, Beat, and Juvenile Delinquents are capitalized; they were major social categories in the 1950s. Thus the "youth" in the subtitle refers to the problems of boys and young men, the usual concern of postwar social science. Work devoted to analyzing youth reproduced the male bias of work devoted to studying adults. Goodman defended his focus saying that the problems he wanted to discuss "belong primarily, in our society, to the boys: how to be useful and make something of oneself. A girl does not *have* to, she is not expected to 'make something' of herself. Her career does not have to be self-justifying, for she will have children, which is absolutely self-justifying, like any other natural or creative act . . . our 'youth troubles' are boys' troubles." [1] The adolescent heroine in Caryl Rivers's novel about growing up in the 1950s, *Virgins,* echoes Goodman,

I have a memory of myself at eleven or twelve, trying to imagine my future. There would be a house with grass around it. There would be a white picket fence around the house. And there would be a married woman standing in the backyard, staring over the fence. I knew I would be unhappy. I knew I would not want to be there, but I imagined this future nonetheless.

Laurie Stone, "Memoirs Are Made of This," *Voice Literary Supplement,* April 1983

"I want to do things I dream about. I want to be a journalist. But I won't be. I'll just dream about it. It's different for boys. Boys *have* to do something. Girls don't." [2]

Goodman was far from alone in worrying about the boys and the men; indeed he was joined by many male observers of the postwar American scene. Whether considering family, gender, or youth, commentators often excluded, ignored, misinterpeted, or blamed females. "Deviants" such as Beats, hipsters, juvenile delinquents, homosexuals, even communists, were almost always males (psychologically damaged by "bad" mothers) in the scholarly and public mind. Social commentators took for granted Goodman's perspective: A girl did not have to make something of herself, her biology was reason enough for her existence, she would be wife and mother. If she wished to achieve outside the family, she was often discouraged, even punished.

There was, however, a barely visible cultural rebellion of some white middle-class girls and young women in the 1950s, a number of whom flirted with or lived a bohemian life. Despite the pitfalls and constraints, some young women did find inspiration in defying sexual rules, in Beat and bohemian subcultures, and in rock 'n' roll. Thus I want to revise the view that girls and young women were full participants in postwar America, conformists where many boys were not. Furthermore, their restlessness was significant; they were laying the groundwork for rebellion in the years ahead. In many cases, early nonconformists pioneered the social movements of the 1960s—civil rights workers, campus activists, and youthful founders of the women's liberation movement of the late 1960s.

This story of the attraction of the Beats and Greenwich Village is based on retrospective autobiographical accounts of growing up in the postwar period and on interviews, letters, fiction, and cultural histories and analyses. [3] The sources I utilize and the perspective I bring to the work of interpretation and reconstruction are provided by women who share a sense that our earlier lives were marked off from our later lives by a deep fracture. Our understanding of the postwar period is shaped by our experiences in the 1960s and 1970s, especially the women's movement, which changed much about us and the way we see the world, including our own pasts. Our memories are imbued with the sense that the 1950s were not good years for women because we learned to understand our own lives as a flight from that time. I employ, then, as primary sources writings of women who, like me, have looked back on that time from vantage points in the 1970s and 1980s; thus this is an interpretation about how I and a distinct group of women from my generation view our gendered pasts. Perhaps the material is best described as a sociological memoir, sociologically inspired yet informed by subjective and personal interpretations, partial and incomplete, but not necessarily untrue. [4]

It is East Coast–skewed data, even New York City focused, both because being a real Beat required living in Greenwich Village (or, to a lesser extent, North Beach in San Francisco) and because many of the written accounts are by women who were born, grew up in, or migrated to New York City. The women I interviewed had some past or present connection with New York City because as middle-class Beats, bohemians, or rebels, New York City beckoned. New York City also had the largest Jewish population, among whom were a disproportionate number of people with left-wing politics; it is likely that their children, red-diaper babies, were also disproportionately represented among teenage dissenters.[5]

That being said, I believe that Beat women provide parameters for understanding young white middle-class feminine dissidence in the 1950s. The dissatisfactions articulated by the most rebellious reflected the frustrations and tensions of the less politicized. Evaluations by those who dissented openly are crucial for understanding issues facing the others. The appeal of the Beats and of rock 'n' roll suggests that young women were drawn to difference. Interest in outsiders and others, values and people excluded or occluded in postwar America, is a thread that connects the Beats and rock 'n' roll and links both to black culture in the lives of young white women.

In addition to the voices of those who were teenagers in the 1950s and early 1960s, I include experiences of a slightly older group of women, born in the early to mid-1930s, who were the real postwar pioneers in that they lived a Beat life.[6] The older group was the immediate predecessor, real and fictional, of the teenage cohort, women who participated in the Beat or bohemian subculture in Greenwich Village in the 1950s. The slightly older cohort provides evidence of the existence of rebellious women in the 1950s and their experiences offer clues to the motivations and attractions for such a life. Adolescents, women born during or near the war years, in contrast, were more likely to imitate and fantasize from afar about such a life, unless they lived in or near New York City. They were discontent with the life set out for them but, for the most part, still only incipient rebels. Some were or wanted to be nonconformists; frequently that inclination was a prelude to the independence for which the women's movement later fought. Both groups of women prepared the foundations for young women's rebellion in the 1960s.

Middle-class white girls' disaffection was barely discernible because few thought to consider it and because its expression was often oblique. When girls were considered problems, "promiscuity" and premarital pregnancy were its sites, understood in individual psychological terms.[7] In contrast to boys, stricter gender rules for girls dictated covert dissidence. Girls' "deviance" was more circumspect and less dramatic than was that of boys, especially working-class boys, the subject of much concern in the 1950s with its alarm about juvenile delinquency. When that decade's defiance was and is portrayed, however, young white women are invisible. They dissembled; they appeared to conform. Sexism in mainstream and alternative cultures constrained and shaped their defiance into forms not easily recognizable, especially by analysts not predisposed to discover gender rebellion. But it was gender rebellion. These stirrings prefigured its full-scale articulation a decade or so later.

Because Beat and delinquent subcultures were predominantly male, and often working class, and were masculine in conventional and chauvinist ways, girls' processes of identification were complex. Middle-class white girls who rejected dominant values had little choice but to utilize and adapt male versions of rebellion and disaffection.[8] For these girls, the attraction of outsiders, of hoods and greasers, of movie stars James Dean and Marlon Brando in roles of alienation and working-class defiance, and of black and black-inspired music, was profound. Males who were inappropriate as boy friends and potential mates and who represented an alternative to their bland teenage world played a significant role in girls' psychic lives. Ethnic, class, and racial differences had meaning in the lives and minds of heterosexual, middle-class white girls. Difference was ignored and denied in both adult and teenage mainstream culture, but it was alive, even thriving, for many young women.

There were few female models. Analysts such as Paul Goodman, Kenneth Keniston, and Edgar Friedenberg, who studied youth and American culture, defined male disaffection and nonconformity as a genuine social problem. Girls were conspicuously absent in their accounts.[9] Evidence from memoirs, novels, and cultural studies written later and from interviews suggest, however, that they were there. Even more suggestively, Goodman's critique of American society in *Growing Up Absurd,* with its exclusive focus on boys, inspired girls. Contrary to what might be expected, a recurrent theme surfaces in which males were the inspiration for these girls, whether as movie cowboys, delinquents, oddballs, or rebels.[10]

Teen Culture

One of the peculiar characteristics of the 1950s, an expression of a peculiar postwar link between optimism and anxiety, was that fun-loving conformist teens existed side by side with disaffected teens—the delinquents, hoods, and Beatniks who loomed much larger in the cultural and psychic life of America than their numbers might suggest. The "right kind of teen" was "liberal, clean-cut, concerned about reputation, rarely kissed on a first date, never went too far sexually, avoided delinquency, studied and planned for the future, and hung around the malt shop." [11] In hindsight, these ponytailed and crew-cutted, virginal, neat (and white) teenagers provoke some derision but more than a little nostalgia as well, perhaps for a youthful innocence long past, undoubtedly made especially compelling by its absence today. Novels such as *Vic Holyfield and the Class of 1957* by William Heyen, *Blooming* by Susan Toth, and *Virgins* by Caryl Rivers, and autobiographies like *An American Childhood* by Annie Dillard and *Aphrodite at Mid-Century* by Caryl Rivers, paint middle-class white adolescent lives of simplicity and love. Vic Holyfield, unlike Holden Caulfield, whose namesake he is, wants only to return to his high school days and high school classmates and does so thirty years later by buying Smithtown High School and paying all his classmates to live there together for a year. It is an idyllic re-creation of the best years of their lives; the class of 1957 goes back to the golden age of teenagerdom and wants it never to end. They have sock hops in the gym, assemblies, basketball games to their favorite rock 'n' roll songs (especially Elvis), rooms for slow and fast dancing, and concerts by entertainers popular then. Vic Holyfield has a dream: "It was the end of the world, a nuclear cloud moving across the country like a curtain, and he was back in Smithtown, huddled in the gym with all of us, and he was happy he would be dying this way, here, with us." [12] This is a picture of innocence but, characteristically, innocence menaced by impending doom, like the science-fiction movies so popular at the time. Even rock 'n' roll in this context is experienced as sweet and asexual.

Another novel about teen life, very different from *Vic Holyfield*, reveals the "other," less wholesome 1950s, the attraction of which I explore here. *The Red Menace* by Michael Anania is the story of a boy growing up in the Midwest. Although he is white, his life is far from the middle-class suburbs. He lives in a racially mixed housing project, many of whose inhabitants are on welfare. The story unfolds in the shadow of the bomb—hence the anticommunism suggested by the title—and intimates the importance of the black experience for white teenagers, of working-class boys for middle-class girls, of cars, sex, social class, delinquency, air-raid drills, and *machismo* in the cultural matrix of teenage life. Here the rhythm and blues is not romanticized. Anania is more explicit about the appeal of its sexual content, more crude about sex. For his teenagers, the atom bomb is linked to male sexuality (and to their nightmares), and communism to the polio epidemic, "which bred the same fear of contact and association that Communism created." [13] Unlike Vic Holyfield, the narrator of *The Red Menace* was an outsider, so alienated from America he wants to become a communist. That he is working class is central to his story.

It is significant that large numbers of adolescents did not feel happily engaged in typical teenage life in the historical period most remembered for its discovery and celebration of the teenager. In an analysis of teenage culture, the sociologist Jessie Bernard reported that a sizable proportion of high school students felt like outsiders. Citing the findings from one huge survey that indicated, according to Bernard, the extent of alienation among teenagers, she states, "There are the clods, the outs. And they constitute a sizeable proportion of the high school population"; 22 percent felt out of things, 11 percent felt different, 44 percent seldom had dates, 13 percent felt they were not wanted, 20 percent felt lonesome, and 25 percent felt ill at ease at social affairs.[14] These figures run counter to nostalgic reconstructions of the 1950s that leave little room for feelings of teenage marginality and exclusion. They are not surprising, however, in view of many young women's memories.

Social analysts in the 1960s and 1970s have explored the roots in the postwar period of student and youth rebellions. Richard Flacks has been one of the more perceptive among many who concur that the sources of middle-class youth discontent lay in a nexus of postwar American economic and social transformations. Like others, he has suggested that the postwar period experienced a socioeconomic crisis as technological potentialities, the shift from entrepreneurial to bureaucratic organizations, and consumerism based on abundance rather than scarcity had outstripped the society's social and cultural arrangements and values.

Middle-class families were confused about how and what to teach their children when faced with new levels of consumerism and the decline in relevance of the Protestant Ethic. According to Flacks, the childrearing of many college-educated parents fostered in their children a critical stance toward society. Flacks suggests that in this period of political and economic transition and cultural incoherence, the institutions of socialization, especially middle-class parents, contributed to the creation of an alternative youth subculture. "In the schools, the media and the churches, such contradictory values as self-denial and self-expression, discipline and indulgence, and striving and being are preached, dramatized, fostered, and practiced all at once." In a study by Kenneth Keniston, young middle-class men were depicted as alienated and uncommitted; in Flacks's terms, they were intellectual and critical, a small subculture that looked "at first like a deviant group but turned out to be a vanguard" of the youth rebellion. A new generational cohort was in the making, and by the end of the decade, according to Flacks, a critical mass of alienated, intellectual youth existed.

Many of these young people felt "excluded from and repelled by the prevailing youth culture" in the 1950s. They were disgusted by the "frivolity, antiintellectualism, and social indifference of the middle class peer culture and by its stereotyped sex role definitions and superficial conventionalism." According to Flacks, they were uneasy in the dating, grooming, and peer culture. Consequently their status was low and their anxiety and self-doubt high.[15] These were some of the young people who showed up in surveys as unhappy or outsiders. Other hints of this unhappiness were the large numbers of teenage advice books and columns and educational films that simply assumed confusion on the part of teenagers; like childrearing manuals, they multiplied in the postwar period. Teenagers shared with their parents the experience of new and unclear rules of behavior.[16] Insecurity was heightened by the media celebration of the frivolous, happy-go-lucky, confident teenager; it was almost impossible not to define oneself in relation to popularity. Not all white middle-class adolescents participated with ease, then, in teen culture.

Replicating other social science, most studies of youth did not utilize gender as a category of analysis. Keniston's *The Uncommitted,* for example, is about male Harvard students. Flacks makes no mention of gender in his discussion of the postwar origins of middle-class discontent. We have seen that Goodman, in concert with social commentators and sociologists of deviance, did not consider feminine rebelliousness an issue. Although many of these analyses are helpful for understanding the class and generational aspects of white youth discontent, they are not enlightening as to its gendered sources; they miss identifying girls' dissatisfaction as a phenomenon distinct from boys'. As we see below, much of this dissatisfaction had its sources in the narrowness of the expectations for girls and of the latitude permitted them.

Ironically, girls growing up in the postwar period shared in the high expectations of the postwar generation. Over and over again, white middle-class girls recall their sense of the new options open to them. Despite their sex, limitless possibilities seemed to stretch before them. In a collection of essays by British women who grew up in the 1950s, Liz Heron writes: "Along with the orange juice and the cod-liver oil, the malt supplement and the free school milk, we may also have absorbed a certain sense of our own worth and the sense of a future that would get better and better, as if history were on our side." She continues: "It seems also that as little girls we had a stronger sense of our possibilities than the myths of the fifties allow. There was a general confidence in the air, and the wartime image of women's independence and competence at work lingered on well into the decade." [17] An American girl says, "I do not remember any deprivation during the war—or at any time in my life—or any inconvenience. . . . What I do remember clearly is the burst of consumption at the war's end. It seems to me that at the very moment we were banging pots and pans . . . there was an explosion of fresh cream and strawberries." [18] Constricted feminine goals learned in the family and wider culture generated specifically feminine discontent, but for some girls, postwar expansiveness, the comfortable homes and consumer goods, media glamour, and the anticipation of happy futures counteracted and even transformed that discontent into the urge to explore and the expectation of achievement.

Girls and "Real" Life

It is the "other" 1950s, the subterranean culture that percolated beneath and around the dominant harmonious image, particularly as it relates to girls, that we want to consider. Some white middle-class girls grew up anticipating what was expected of them—a life in the suburbs as a wife and mother—with great ambivalence, often expressed as ambivalence about their mothers. One recalls the suburbs where she grew up and "knew no white, middle-class woman with children who had a job or any major activities beyond the family. . . . During the day, it was safe, carefully limited, and female. The idea that this was all made me frantic." [19] In Caryl Rivers's novel *Virgins,* the teenage heroine tells her girl friend that they have minds like men, which makes them, happily, different from most girls: "That was worst of all, I thought, a life where nothing ever happened. I looked around me and saw women ironing dresses and hanging out clothes and shopping for food and playing mah-jong on hot summer afternoons, and I knew I couldn't bear to spend my life that way, day after drab day, with nothing ever happening. The world of women seemed to me like a huge, airless prison where things didn't change. Inside it, I thought, I'd turn gray and small and shrivel up to nothing." [20]

The life plan set out for these girls was unacceptable to them. Their society's expectations and, closer to home, those of their parents, did not coincide with their own yearnings. "I couldn't stand girls who wanted to get married and have engagement rings. I knew I was different, and I was glad," recalls one young woman, who became a Beatnik.[21] Janis Joplin, in Port Arthur, Texas, during the 1950s, expressed a more earthy version of these sentiments. She described herself as "just a plain overweight chick. I wanted something more than bowling alleys and drive-ins. I'd've fucked anything, taken anything. I did." [22] Letters to Betty Friedan from this generation provide evidence of girls who felt trapped in the grip of the feminine mystique. They rebelled against the bourgeois respectability and timidity of middle-class conventions that included narrow domestic gender expectations. The banality of middle-class values was an important Beat theme that found female adherents despite the sexism of its vision. Girls imagined themselves as free as Beat men, domesticity (and the women they were supposed to become) left behind. In this period of family celebration, even popular culture contained critiques of middle-class family life. The movie *Rebel Without a Cause,* for example, did find a cause: pathetic parents. Nora Sayre comments about films of the 1950s: "Rarely has family life looked so repulsive as it did in movies of the decade that also tried to uphold the family as an institution, while the parents who didn't 'understand' or cherish their children were as guilty as the gangsters of the previous era." [23]

Domestic life provided these teenagers with little inspiration. For them, its values were materialistic, constricting, and boring, and for girls there were additional gender issues: They were ambivalent about the only future anticipated for them, becoming wives and mothers. Another recalls feeling confined in her family, aware that their lives could not satisfy her. "That's what it is like for me, I think. Everything I want is outside." [24] Marge Piercy remembers: "All that could be imagined was wriggling through the cracks, surviving in the unguarded interstices. There was no support for opting out of the rat race or domesticity. . . . Marry or die!" [25]

Disaffected teenage girls longed for something significant in their lives. "Authentic," "genuine," and "real" were words used repeatedly. The 1950s did not provide them with a sense of being real. They felt that being sheltered, virginal, and female (the first two adjectives equivalent to the third for middleclass white girls) precluded the experience of meaningfulness. The sense that the culture was rife with hypocrisy, everyone keeping up appearances in one form or another, generated a yearning for genuine feeling. So did the smallness of their futures. Alienation and its inverse, a search for authenticity and intensity, ran through bestselling postwar fiction, tapping not only a youth but an American nerve.[26] Beats, bohemians, and sectors of middle-class youth shared disdain for making money at an unfulfilling job, working as a full-time housewife, conforming in the suburbs, and searching for security. "What unforeseen catastrophe would send me up the river to decorate a home in Westchester?" asks a young woman settled in Greenwich Village, referring to the prosperous New York suburb where Herman Wouk's Marjorie Morningstar ends up a housewife after flirting with the Village and an artistic life.[27] Although the development of a separate teen culture created a generational schism by setting adolescents off from adults in this period, for the most part they were more separate than dissident. In considering Beats and bohemians, it is the dissidents in whom we are interested, however, girls who did not participate wholeheartedly in the dominant culture.

Briefly, the Beat generation refers to a group of predominantly male, young, white writers and artists who spurned the establishment—literary, art, and government, indeed all middle-class conventions. In the midst of upbeat, suburban, prosperous, white, nuclear-family America, they developed a perspective and lifestyle that stood for everything mainstream America apparently rejected. They reveled in exposing their psyches and sexual fantasies, were expressive and self-revelatory, felt and declared themselves outcasts and rebels. Above all, they devoted themselves to experience: sexual, spiritual, artistic. The Beats rejected materialism, careers, monogamy, and conventional marriage. Allen Ginsberg and Jack Kerouac are the best-known Beats, "Howl" and *On the Road* their best-known writing. They reacted against the conformity and rigidity of postwar politics and culture, rejecting norms of normality and respectability. The Beats were committed to freedom of movement, back and forth across America, in their writing and in their relationships. They were deeply influenced by their version of black culture, and many embraced Zen Buddhism. In the midst of the great American material and family celebration of the postwar years, and despite their small numbers, the Beats loomed large as beacons and icons of dissent and rebellion. Thousands of young people, dubbed Beatniks, imitated them, or wanted to, in their efforts to explore spaces outside the dominant culture's narrow boundaries.

In *Minor Characters,* the chronicle of her infatuation with Jack Kerouac and the Beats, Joyce Johnson, who grew up in Manhattan and was a student at Barnard in the 1950s, writes: "Moving back and forth between antithetical worlds separated by subway rides, I never fully was what I seemed or tried to be. I had the feeling I was playing hooky all the time, not from school, but from the person represented by my bland outward appearance." [28]

She was not what she appeared to be; appearance disguised her real self. Appearance (in all its meanings) and facade run through many teenagers' and young women's stories; they struggled to conform, often through approximating acceptable beauty standards, dissimulating and curious at the same time. These themes surface repeatedly in memoirs and literature of the period. Girls' discontent was articulated, as it was for others in the society, as a hidden longing for meaning, for something more real than the middle-class lives set out for them. Jan Clausen grew up in Southern California. In 1957, when she was sixteen, she read Kerouac's *On the Road.* In it she discovers the "moral and intellectual intensity" she has been looking for: "Emerging from a childhood of many advantages, I was bitter, suddenly, against my parents, on account of certain experiences withheld from me: Smith Act trials overhanging my formative years; alcoholic binges; steamy dramas of marital infidelity; the benny-popping, reefer puffing role models they might have been, tearing back and forth across the continent with infant me asleep in the back seat . . . my background had been deficient." [29] Bonnie Raitt, who also grew up in Southern California, went to a summer camp in Massachusetts run by Quakers, where most of the people were Jewish or Progressives: "It counteracted the whole beach boy scene in California, which I couldn't stand. I started wearing peace symbols around my neck and listening to Odetta records." Joyce Johnson writes of herself, Jack Kerouac, and his book: "The 'looking for something' Jack had seen in me was the psychic hunger of my generation. Thousands were waiting for a prophet to liberate them from the cautious middle class lives they had been reared to inherit." [30] For Johnson, Greenwich Village and the Beats "seemed to promise . . . something I'd never tasted in my life as a child—something I told myself was Real Life. This was not the life my parents lived but one that was dramatic, unpredictable, possibly dangerous. Therefore *real,* infinitely more worth having." Johnson's central impulse was a rejection of bourgeois respectability. "Real life was not to be found in the streets around my house, or anywhere on the Upper West Side." A younger girl echoes Johnson's impatience: "Do you understand? We were hungry for experience, for some kind of real life, for some way to tap our energy." [31] And another woman: "The basic awareness grew that truth, whatever it was, was something we had all our lives been protected from. Reality had been kept in quarantine so we could not become contaminated." [32]

Zane, the eighteen-year-old heroine of Alix Kates Shulman's novel *Burning Questions*, flees the Midwest to find a more exciting life. She finds it in Greenwich Village, a place in which experimentation is permissible, where expressing oneself creatively or sexually is the highest achievement. She leaves Indiana Babbittry behind in order to find her true self. Shulman's is an ecstatic description of the mecca Greenwich Village represented for a generation of young people. Thus Diane Di Prima, one of the few female Beats in her own right, a poet who had sexual relationships with both men and women, writes in her *Memoirs of a Beatnik* about what a good friend will miss by not living with her and a third friend in a "pad" in the Village. The opportunity for the three of them to live together means "light and freedom, air and laughter, the outside world." It means "one's blood running strong and red in one's own veins, not drawn to feed the ineradicable grief of the preceding generations." [33]

To find themselves, girls had to leave their families behind. Janis Joplin says of her adolescence, "I was raised in Texas, man, and I was an artist and I had all these ideas and feelings that I'd pick up in books and my father would talk to me about it, and I'd make up poems and things. And, man, I was the only one I'd ever met. There weren't any others. There just wasn't *anybody,* man, in Port Arthur. . . . I mean, in other words, in the Midwest you got no one to learn from because there's not a reader down the street you can sneak off and talk to. There's nobody. Nobody. I remember when I read that in *Time* magazine about Jack Kerouac, otherwise I'd've never known. I said 'Wow!' and split." [34] Like Janis Joplin, Zane, Shulman's middle-class Indiana girl rebel, says she knew from her sixteenth birthday on what she wanted and pursued it with enthusiastic singlemindedness: "To get out." [35] Dean Moriarity, the hero of *On the Road,* conveys the appeal of leaving, of finding life: "The only possible people for me are the mad ones, the ones who are mad to live, mad to talk, mad to be saved, desirous of everything at the same time, the ones who never yawn or say a commonplace thing, but burn, burn, burn like fabulous roman candles." [36] Annie Dillard found in books what she lacked in life as a teenager. "I myself was getting wild; I wanted wildness, originality, genius, rapture, hope. I wanted strength, not tea parties." [37] Growing up in England as part of the generation in which we are interested, Sheila Rowbotham echoes her American sisters. She

describes how her image of the ultimate man was based on a mixture of James
Dean, Marlon Brando, and the Beats, a man of few words but intense emotions, expressed through a grunt or a flick of the eye, always on the run. (Again,
On the Road figures significantly in a young woman's vision of herself and
the men to whom she was attracted.) Such a friendly psychopath, she hoped,
would notice that under her "healthy exterior" she was "in fact suitably intense and fraught for the most extended and crazed imagination." Rowbotham
describes herself: "I picked up an insistence on direct experience and feeling.
I was inordinately suspicious of reason and analysis. Only moments of intense
subjectivity seemed to have any honesty or authenticity." Above all she wanted
"intense experiences where everyone spoke of intense subjects and *never* said
'pass the bread and butter.' " [38]

Talking was important for these women. For one Beat woman, moving to
Greenwich Village after college meant moving "home." Her apartment in the
Village was filled day and night with people talking, eating, and drinking; many
of them painters, writers, and musicians—all part of a vibrant community for
which she had longed. She felt she had found "life." In all accounts of the
Village in this period, of bohemian life in general, talking figures prominently.
For these women, who felt starved for serious talk, it was paramount.[39]

Shulman's heroine experiences her first Village meal in a tiny apartment
filled with artists and talk. She is amazed at the pots filled with spaghetti sauce
set directly on the kitchen table, the long loaves of garlic bread, the wine and
salad to which everyone helps themselves, and the unending stream of words.
Zane marvels at how much and how excitedly they can talk about one Swedish
director and his movies and says, " 'It's a lot better than what they talk about in
Indiana.' 'What do they talk about there?' 'Cars and clothes. And communists
in the government.' " [40]

Diane Di Prima describes her life in the Village in the early 1950s before
the arrival of masses of young people. A coffee shop for the bohemian crowd
had opened on MacDougal Street. "We all sat there in the long afternoons,
reading and making each other's acquaintance, nursing twenty-five cent cups
of espresso for hours, and drawing pictures on paper napkins." [41] Joyce Johnson loved the slums, "my slums, the sweet slums of Bohemia and beatnikdom,
where sunflowers and morning glories would bloom on fire escapes in the
summer." [42] These women found in the Village scene what Ronald Sukenick
describes as a "grungy purity . . . in its deliberate isolation from the world of
Uptown." He suggests that such rebels were "confronted with the promised
land of previously repressed impulses, a risky new underground landscape to
explore consisting of everything deemed unreal by the dominant culture, which
amounts to almost everything." [43] Di Prima captures the isolation and clarity of
the early days. There were only a handful "who raced about in Levi's and work

shirts, made art, smoked dope, dug the new jazz, and spoke a bastardization of the black argot. . . . Our isolation was total and impenetrable." Their chief concern was keeping their integrity and their cool; they "looked to each other for comfort, for praise, for love, and shut out the rest of the world." [44] They sought and found for a time real life, authenticity. "I think of us trying to laugh off the fifties. . . . I think we were trying to shake the time. Shake it off, shake it up, shake it down. A shakedown," writes Hettie Jones.[45]

The Artistic Underground

Although it deserves more attention than it receives here, the American cultural ferment of the 1940s and 1950s is critical to this story. The underground artistic renaissance under way in Greenwich Village (and San Francisco) came as a surprise in the light of representations of postwar American culture as consumerist and anti-intellectual.[46] Al Young refers to a "sort of ferment in American culture that eventually rose from subterranean level" to shape contemporary art and music. Jazz, poetry, and abstract expressionist painting flourished during the decades after the war. A wildly innovative bohemian lifestyle thrived. Jazz was the central art form for white artists. The story of jazz in these years is of enormous vitality and creativity. Abstract impressionist painting and writing, particularly Beat writing, tried to create jazz on canvas and on the printed page and to imitate the lives of jazz artists. Jazz music and jazz musicians were inspirations for white artists. Young suggests that "jazz mythology has always affected American intellectuals and artists when they were looking for a way out of what Artaud once called the 'the bourgeoisification' of everything in life." [47]

Central to the story of the 1950s is the powerful influence of black culture, seen most clearly in the influence of jazz and rhythm and blues, but in other art as well. White rebels and artists were particularly drawn to black people and black culture, often in racist and exploitative ways. Interracial couples were prominent in Greenwich Village, as were a "bastardization of black argot" in the Beats' language and jazz-inspired art and lives. But even in the rest of America, the denial of the black contribution to white culture—especially clear in the effort to whiten rhythm and blues for a white teen audience and in the general project of creating a homogenized white popular culture—was accompanied by its opposite, curiosity and enthusiasm on the part of young whites.

The flavor of Greenwich Village at this time is revealed in Beat women's accounts. Diane Di Prima writes: "Jazz was for us the most important, happening art; Bird in Louis' Tavern on West Fourth Street on weekday nights handed out posters for his incredible weekends at the Open Door on West Broadway, weekends when he would take us all with him, teach us all to fly. And later, Miles at the Cafe Bohemia, slick and smart as they come, exchanging sets with Charlie Mingus, cool then and cool now. . . . Later the jazzmen were followed by the painters, a big, hulking breed of hard-drinking men who spoke in oils and came on very paternal and sexy." [48]

For Joyce Johnson, who did not know what she was supposed to see when she looked at abstract expressionist canvases or how to decide whether they were good or bad, "goodness or badness didn't even seem important." What she had wandered into "wasn't the beginning of something, but the coming into light of what had been stirring for years among all these artists. . . . Major or minor, they all seemed possessed by the same impulse—to break out into forms that were unrestricted and new." Johnson recounts the invasion of artists and would-be artists, the galleries and illegal loft living, the excitement of being where life felt intense and real.[49] The painters, writers, and musicians of the 1940s and 1950s strained against the boundaries of academic or acceptable art. Young writes: "I think that one of the things that the Beat Generation did was to take art out from under glass . . . to restore poetry and literature to the people."[50] Hettie Jones remembers that "the Beats *looked* okay to me, and I applauded their efforts, successful or not, to burst wide open—like the abstract expressionist painters had—the image of what could be (rightly) said."[51] The horrified reaction of the Columbia University literary establishment to the Beats—writing in *Partisan Review* Norman Podhoretz referred to them as a "revolt of all the forces hostile to civilization itself" and as "know-nothing bohemians"—was proof enough that the younger writers were attempting to crash the gates.[52] Johnson's insight into the artists' impulse to "break out into forms that were restricted and new" and Jones's sense that the artists were "bursting wide open" described the women as well. The dramatic inclinations to which they and younger women responded flourished in them too. As women, they wanted to be out from under glass.

Sexism

In the midst of the Beat scene in 1958, Joyce Johnson describes herself as she would have been seen by someone else: "With her seat at the table in the exact center of the universe, that midnight place where so much is converging, the only place in America that's alive. . . . As a female, she's not quite part of this convergence. A fact she ignores, sitting by in her excitement as the voices of the men, always the men, passionately rise and fall and their beer glasses collect and the smoke of their cigarettes rises toward the ceiling and the dead culture is surely being wakened. Merely being here, she tells herself, is enough."[53]

Joyce Johnson, Shulman's Zane, and other female bohemians became Beats by becoming the girl friends of the "real" Beats; ironically, in so doing, they discovered themselves. Disaffected girls often became the girl friends of male dissidents and delinquents, like Natalie Wood to James Dean's hero in *Rebel Without a Cause*. Restless teenage girls in 1950s movies were not themselves rebels but joined boys who were because they were in love. In life, as in the delinquent subculture portrayed in film, girls' identities were inextricably bound up with boys, their acceptance determined by whether they belonged to a male.[54] Nonconformity was articulated within traditional gender forms; these were the last to fall, even in "deviant" subcultures. Shulman's *Burning Questions* explores the secondary status and exploitation of women by male Beats. In their search for liberation, Joyce Johnson and fictional Zane, like so many other women, discovered virulent sexism.[55] But they were thrilled, nonetheless, in Johnson's words, to be near the convergence of all that was alive in America in the 1950s. Like women in the New Left, who initially often did not recognize the sexism of male radicals, the excitement of participating in an oppositional movement overrode all else. "We lived outside, as if. As if we were men? As if we were newer, freer versions of ourselves?"[56] The rupture with the dominant culture was enthralling. Even if one were ignored or treated shabbily, the break was initially more significant than the male chauvinism.[57]

The Beats were *macho* and sexist. Not intending a gendered point, but making it all the same, thirty years ago Norman Podhoretz complained that "what juvenile delinquency is to life, the San Francisco writers [Beats] are to literature," adding that the Beat generation was a "conspiracy" to replace civilization with the "world of the adolescent street gangs."[58] Confirming this model of male delinquent gangs, the Beat poet Allen Ginsberg dreamed that "the social organization most true of itself to the artist is the boy gang."[59] One of the most sexist and racist eulogies to the Beats was Norman Mailer's "The White Negro," published in 1957. A romantic celebration of the outsider— a mixture of the juvenile delinquent, hipster, and black male he dubbed the "white negro"—Mailer's depiction of revolt was of the male urban outlaw who lived on the edge, searching out sex, using marijuana, appreciating jazz, finding momentary truth through his body. Mailer portrayed a nighttime adventurer who lived according to Mailer's black man's code of drugs, sex, and jazz, a sexual fugitive in love with violence, a man whose interest in women began and ended with sex. The hipster used women's bodies; emotional or material claims were taboo. According to Nelson George, Mailer and other white artists and intellectuals turned their "romance with blackness," their fascination with the alternative world of black America, into "a strange, often unintentional rape of black ideas and styles. Ironically, this was committed by some of the very people who loved (or at least claimed to love) black creativity."[60] The dehumanizing exoticization of the other, the construction of the meaning of whiteness through the romanticization of blackness, is nowhere more obvious than in Mailer's "white negro."

Women existed in Beat culture for sexual satisfaction. No responsibilities, commitments, or roots marred the marginal heterosexual man's effort to liberate himself from the superego of society (and from women, particularly their domestication of men). The Beats were about male adventure and irresponsibility. For many, the goal was to get women to support them so they would not have to work, so they would be free from routine and able to experience life to the fullest. Barbara Ehrenreich argues that the Beats were inspired by the underclass and underworld, by a fantasy of lower-class masculinity in a period in which the white-collar, middle-class male was seen as emasculated. This fear and disdain for the loss of traditional masculinity were widespread. In a culture ideologically devoted to eviscerating social class through the assimilation of everyone into middle-class whiteness, "the "lower" class, denied a name or image, lived on in the middle-class male mind as a repressed self, primitive, dissatisfied, and potentially disruptive." [61]

Joyce Johnson articulated what was attractive to her in these men, sardonically noting their sexism: "Some pursuit of the heightened moment, intensity for its own sake, something they apparently find only when they're with each other." [62] The Beats attempted to reconstitute male bonds, exalting in a brotherhood of male friendship and love, the "Beat Brotherhood." [63] They were fearful of women, dichotomizing them into madonnas and whores, mothers and lovers, the latter conceptualized in terms of carnality and sexual submission. The masculinity they enacted was in conscious contrast to the postwar image of feminized, middle-class men; it provided drama and danger and a critique of the converging sex roles noted by sociologists. In a critical analysis of the sexual politics of the Beats, Catherine Stimpson points out that they exaggerated traditional gender definitions even in their homosexual relations, suggesting "how much harder it is to be free and to extend freedom than to be sexual, and homosexual." [64] Shulman's Zane, exploited and discarded by Beat men, discovers this, as do other female Beats.

Despite her recognition that the Beat men seemed to find intensity, which she also sought, only with each other, Joyce Johnson, like other women who lived among or were inspired by them, felt more real and alive than in her middle-class environment. In deciphering the different experiences of women slightly older than those who were adolescents in the 1950s, it becomes apparent that women who actually lived among Beat men had more complicated experiences than those who fantasized about or imitated the Beats from afar. Shulman has written a devastating portrait of what happened to Beat women at the hands of their misogynist and sexist men. But she also suggests that it should not surprise us that the dream was more inspiring than the reality.[65] A perceptive reviewer of *Minor Characters* remarks, "In retrospect we see that the young Joyce Glassman loved Kerouac's expansive male privilege to move about, see things, and write about them as much as she loved the mobile guy himself." [66] The expansiveness and male privilege of the Beats, their intensity, adventures, frenetic activity, interest in black culture, and rejection of conventional middle-class life attracted young women. But they were interested not simply as girl friends (and fans of rock 'n' roll stars), which was the simplest form their attraction could take; they were interested in them as models. They wanted to *be* them. Girls identified with the male adventurers in *On the Road*, and there is evidence suggesting a profound rejection of gender mores, that many identified with male literary and movie heroes in order to achieve agency in the world.[67]

A rejection of middle-class masculinity was operating for both Beat and younger women, as well as for men. This was perhaps an indirect way of exploring new versions of femininity. Although female subordination was not yet collectively in question, an interest in sexual ambiguity or a rejection of mainstream heterosexuality may have been. James Dean, as Jon Savage observes, represented an androgynous sexuality. Widespread interest in Dean, Elvis, the Beats, and young men from the "other side of the tracks" suggests an attraction to what Joyce Johnson referred to as a life that was "dramatic, unpredictable, possibly dangerous," the antithesis of white middle-class life in postwar America. Popular teenage movies featured troublemakers like the delinquents in *Blackboard Jungle*, with its rock 'n' roll score; Marlon Brando in *The Wild One*, disrupting girls' lives; and James Dean, whose identity is so fragmented in *Rebel Without a Cause* "that he appears as more than an outsider, as a sleepwalker vainly trying to learn the language of an alien landscape." [68] Girls were involved with, even created, these media heroes, as they did with Elvis Presley, another sexually and racially ambiguous male heartthrob. Put simply, girls were attracted to males who were different from themselves, usually meaning not middle class. Annie Dillard's idyllic and privileged childhood was characterized by odd romances. "I would give my heart to one oddball after another— to older boys, to prep-school boys no one knew, to him who refused to go to college, to him who was a hood, and all of them wonderfully skinny." [69] We have seen that Sheila Rowbotham's image of the ultimate man was "a mixture of James Dean and Marlon Brando," definitely not the man in the gray flannel suit.[70] Alice McDermott's novel *That Night* is about the doomed romance between a middle-class girl who gets pregnant and is sent away and her hood boy friend and his friends who invade and menace her quiet suburban street. Tragic stories filled true romance and confession magazines about young women attracted to the wrong type of man, someone from the wrong side of the tracks.

This was a middle-class fantasy, Barbara Ehrenreich argues, because it spoke to an "unassimiliated corner of the middle-class psyche."[71] Some girls escaped middle-class material and sexual expectations but still were only accomplices to the major actors in these narratives.

The possibility of a break with domesticity was critical to this appeal. Despite the Beats' chauvinism, for young women their rejection of bourgeois respectability and the family was explosive. As from other parts of sexist culture, girls took what they could where they could get it, and as Ehrenreich suggests, it *was* threatening. Some girls' longing for adventure, for a life undefined by suburban domesticity, was fulfilled, in fantasy or fact, by sexist male bohemians. The Beats provided them with alternative images of living, even if as boy friends they did not. For girls, they served as an early stop in the journey away from mainstream teenage culture and domesticity. Paradoxically, just as Paul Goodman did not worry about alienated young females, neither did their countercultural male heroes take them seriously, assuming, like Goodman, that their biology was all that counted.

Darkness and Difference

It is far from irrelevant that hoods and "bad girls" wore black—black leather jackets, boots, and belts—and in comparison were represented as darker than innocent suburban teens. Reproducing the adult culture's dualism of light and dark—with its profound and unacknowledged racial meanings—obvious in fair movie stars, models, and beauty standards, dissident white teens chose darkness. Sometimes they *were* dark because of their immigrant backgrounds. The "good" approved teen culture was light and white, the threat black. Jazz and rhythm and blues were the subtext for the 1950s drama of "good" versus "bad" teens, only whitened versions of black rhythm and blues acceptable for white teenagers. It was a white time in America; success was represented in the burgeoning postwar media, on television, in advertising, and other forms of popular culture in white terms, assimilation only the most obvious example. Thus it is not surprising that dissenters were, felt, or were imagined to be dark. Hoods were not the only ones in black; the Beats wore black. Black clothes signified you were Beat or bohemian: black turtleneck shirts, black stockings, black sunglasses. "I dumped out my inheritance of pastel colours and princes and collected a new bag of black sweaters, jeans, psychopaths and beat fantasy," recalls Sheila Rowbotham.[72] Another adolescent says, "I just wanted to be a beatnik. I quit wearing pink and orange and always wore darker colors. I was one of the first people in Charleston to get dark stockings. I was in a shop once and a girl goes, "Look, Mommy, that lady has white arms with black legs." [73]

The fictional heroine Zane recounts a tale of her town, Babylon, Indiana, when the white middle-class girls in her school sponsor a rummage sale in a poor black section of town: "In Babylon certain color combinations were forbidden. Such combinations as green with blue, orange with red (or red with pink or pink with orange), brown with black, or purple with anything were considered quite untenable. Such breaches of taste, variously called loud, gauche, stupid, Italian, Jew, were simply prohibited." The room filled with people who "so consistently violated these simple, basic rules that one could only conclude they were unaware of them. . . . Their very skin and hair violated Babylon minimal rules of decorum." Zane points to a fact of American cultural life in the 1950s. "Different was wrong. The wrong attitude, the wrong amount of hair . . . the wrong color skin . . . the wrong clothes from the wrong stores, made you unfit for Babylon."[74] A central incident in Dan Wakefield's novel *Going All the Way* involves a beard. A friend of Sonny's grows a beard and is refused service in bars and restaurants, is not permitted to swim in a pool (because he will contaminate it: "It's plain common sense you can't go into a swimming pool with a beard. You'll get the water dirty"), and is generally ostracized. Sonny says, "Having a beard in the summer of 1954 was like running around without any clothes on or passing out copies of the *Communist Manifesto* or reading a dirty book in a crowded bus. It was asking for trouble."[75] A fixation on grooming, cleanliness, and controlling the body thrived. Pastels and fair and light hair were linked to being a "good" girl. Hair was short for males, contained and curled for women. Unruly hair, too much hair, hair in the wrong places, "was asking for trouble." Controlling the body was about controlling sex, and it is not surprising that in the student, counterculture, and women's movements of the next decades hair symbolized freedom of all kinds. (The musical *Hair*, made into a movie, enshrined it.) In the 1950s, hair, too, had to stay in its place.

There are at least two things going on here. First, there is the issue of difference, specifically the intolerance and repression of race and class difference, and second, its active life in the imaginations and behavior of white middle-class youth. Difference was supposed to be invisible in postwar America. In this version, America was a welcoming melting pot into which everyone could and would be incorporated. Erasing one's difference, assimilating, was a sign of Americanness. And assimilation meant passing for white. Beauty standards were white. So were pluralist theories of democracy and models of the family and gender. Deviants and doubters, often dark or swarthy in representation, were outcasts. The America presented in mainstream movies, television, magazines, and advertising was white. Black people were practically invisible in the mass media, and when they were not, their portrayals were racist, as in the "Amos and Andy" and "Beulah" television shows. Michelle Wallace writes: "I . . . grew up watching a television on which I rarely saw a black face, reading Archie and Veronica comics, Oz and Nancy Drew stories and *Seventeen* magazine, in which 'race' was unmentionable."[76]

White girls expressed their dissatisfactions with domesticity and suburbanism through their infatuations with boys, including Beats and rock 'n' roll and movie stars, who could not fit into their lives. These were males they could not possibly marry. The attraction to danger was more complex than that, however. The awareness of difference was complicated by the issue of darkness. Wearing dark or clashing colors or being dark signified difference in even more explosive ways. It meant being unable to attain, or rejecting, prevailing values and standards of attractiveness, being an outsider. The good taste and decorum of Babylon, the pastels and middle-classness, excluded those who did not or could not conform. As Zane says of the black people who filled the rummage sale, not only did their color combinations shock respectable people, their skin and hair were indecent. People who violated these rules were unassimilated into white America. They threatened middle-class orderliness. In Philip Roth's *Goodbye Columbus,* the following dialogue takes place. When Neil telephones college student Brenda for a date, she asks, " 'What do you look like?' 'I'm . . . dark.' 'Are you a Negro?' 'No.' " Brenda is middle class and Neil is working class; both are Jews. The mixture of working class and masculine darkness reappears, amalgamating different and dark. For WASPS, Jews were dark, exercising a fascination for Christian girls. Even in this story, Jewish Brenda is effectively a WASP, so successfully has she assimilated. In postwar America, assimilation entailed becoming white; Brenda has succeeded and Neil is trying, his difference undoubtedly one of his attractions. But darkness was less attractive in girls, and so they worked to disguise it as they simultaneously listened to rock 'n' roll and dreamed of dark and different young men.[77]

"As an outsider Jew I could have tried for white, aspired to the liberal intellectual, potentially conservative Western tradition. But I never was drawn to that history, and with so little specific to call my own I felt free to choose," says Hettie Jones, who married Leroi Jones, a black man, in the 1950s. She tells how black and white were slippery divisions for her because Jews were different. She didn't "*feel* American." Her outsider status and her love of music, especially jazz, created for her more commonalities with black people than with mainstream Americans.[78] It may be, too, that her working-class background compounded her outsider status and that various combinations of working- or lower-middle-class and immigrant backgrounds, as well as lesbianism, predisposed some women toward the margins and bohemia. But it is also true that young middle- and upper-middle-class women were drawn outside their cultures; what they all rejected and what they all sought, however, undoubtedly differed depending on the specificity of their family, class, and immigrant backgrounds. Stultification within their own environments made rebellious white girls more responsive to and interested in people outside them. Jones was able to act on the interest in difference that other young women only dreamed of. Blackness, darkness—symbolized for many girls by Beatnik or hood clothes, in fantasies of romance with nonconformist or outsider boys, in the love of rock 'n' roll and interest in black culture—exerted the pull it did because the denial of difference was so central to conceptions of whiteness. From this perspective, whiteness was a color defined by blackness or, rather, its denial. In a way, these young women sensed the deprivations that segregation of all kinds imposed, recognizing that they suffered from a whiteness so hegemonic that most white people with whom they came in contact never even noticed it.

A subterranean life, acted out or dreamed about, was generated by a culture that penalized girls and young women who were unable or unwilling to fit the model of the perky, popular teenager eagerly anticipating marriage and motherhood. The rigidity of what was acceptable in that culture made some young women feel discontented and unreal, as if their lives had not yet begun. The parameters of feminine beauty, personality, intelligence, and ambition were narrow enough that a minor deviation meant exclusion and discomfort and, often unintentionally, became a wedge that grew into insurgence. Some young women looked to the Beats with an interest that betrayed their dismay at the thought of a life of suburban domesticity. Their at times articulated and at other times mute rebelliousness led them to men who broke the rules. It also led them to break the rules themselves. Young white middle-class women who were curious about what lay outside the family and their towns and suburbs became Beats and Beatniks—or wished they could. They latched on to signs of otherness in music and subcultures, in effect rehearsing lives they hoped would be different from their mothers'. Practically invisible then, we see now that their explorations were the opening salvos in what came to be known as the women's movement.

NOTES

1. Paul Goodman, *Growing Up Absurd* (New York: Vintage Books, 1960), 11, 13.
2. Caryl Rivers, *Virgins* (New York: Pocket Books, 1984), 65.
3. The formal interviews for this essay were with Nancy Dannenberg, Cambridge, Massachusetts, March 3, 1990; and in New York City: Rosalyn Baxandall, December 26, 1988, October 7, 1989, May 6, 1989; Hettie Jones, May 5, 1989; Ann Lauterback, May 6, 1989; Evan Morley, October 9, 1989; Carolee Schneeman, October 6,

1989; Alix Kates Shulman, December 26, 1988; Ellen Willis, May 4, 1989. In addition, informal interviews with women of this generation contributed to my interpretation.

4. See James Clifford, "Introduction: Partial Truths," *Writing Culture: The Poetics and Politics of Ethnography* (Berkeley: University of California Press, 1986).

5. See Sara Evans, *Personal Politics: The Roots of Women's Liberation in the Civil Rights Movement and the New Left* (New York: Knopf, 1979), 60–61; and Doug McAdam, *Freedom Summer* (New York, Oxford University Press, 1988), 20–21.

6. While the focus of my study is primarily middle-class heterosexual white women, bohemian subcultures included working- and lower-middle-class, lesbian, and black women. For the most part, this account does not reproduce that diversity other than in the few white working-class women whose voices are heard and in the larger issues of the attraction black and working-class cultures had for middle-class white women. See my *Young, White, and Miserable: Growing Up Female in the Fifties* (Boston: Beacon Press, 1992), esp. Introduction.

7. See Rickie Solinger, *Wake Up Little Susie: Single Pregnancy and Race before Roe v. Wade* (New York: Routledge, 1992).

8. David Matza and Gresham Sykes, "Juvenile Delinquency and Subterranean Values," *American Sociological Review* 26 (October 1961): 712–719, argue that the values of juvenile delinquents were not different from the larger society's values (e.g., leisure, aggression, conspicuous consumption). They suggest that juvenile delinquents acted out these values differently but that they were an extension of the adult world, not a rejection of it. Also see Bennett Berger, "Adolescence and Beyond," *Social Problems* 10, no. 4 (1963): 394–408; and F. Elkin and W. Westley, "The Myth of Adolescent Culture," *American Sociological Review* 20, nos. 1–6 (February–December 1955): 680–684, for similar points.

9. This was explicitly so in the study of juvenile delinquency. In a major study from the 1950s, *Delinquent Boys* (New York: Free Press, 1955), 44, Albert K. Cohen says, "The subcultural delinquency we have been talking about is overwhelmingly male delinquency. In the first place, delinquency *in general* is mostly male delinquency." See Mike Brake, *The Sociology of Youth Culture and Youth Subcultures* (London: Routledge and Kegan Paul, 1980), for a discussion of the masculine basis of the study of youth culture, esp. chap. 5.

10. A study of the popularity and reception of cowboy movies among young people would yield interesting insights. There is evidence that girls watched and liked cowboy movies and identified with the cowboys (the good guys). This is interesting because they identified with men and with the racist project of wiping out the Indians. In *In Search of Our Mothers' Gardens* (New York: Harcourt Brace Jovanovich, 1984), 386, Alice Walker tells of being a tomboy and of playing cowboys, "rustling cattle, being outlaws, delivering damsels in distress," but of becoming an Indian when her brothers got BB guns and she did not because she was a girl. She then became the hunted (and her eye is shot by one of her brothers). Stokely Carmichael, a black man, recalls that he loved Westerns and cheered wildly for the cowboys until one day he realized *he* was an Indian and had been rooting for the wrong side. In Marion Meade, "The Degradation of Women," in *The Sounds of Social Change,* ed. Serge Denisoff and Richard Peterson (Skokie, Ill.: Rand McNally, 1972), 174. Also see "What We Want," in *The Sixties Papers,* ed. Judith Albert and Stewart Albert (New York: Praeger, 1984), 142, where Carmichael describes rooting for Tarzan as he attacked black natives until Carmichael realized that by yelling, " 'Kill the beasts, kill the savages, kill 'em.' I was saying: Kill

me. " In "It's in My Blood, My Face—My Mother's Voice, The Way I Sweat," in *This Bridge Called My Back,* ed. Cherrie Moraga and Gloria Anzaldua (New York, Kitchen Table Press, 1981), 42, Anita Valerio, a Native American, writes: "Being an Indian . . . I didn't even realize that's what I was—an Indian—in fact I jumped up and down in protest 'I'm not an Indian—I'm not an Indian!' when my relatives would tell me I was. After all, Indians were the bad guys on T.V. and though we didn't have running water that year or even telephones—yes—we did have television." The social movements of the next decade, especially the civil rights movement, suggest that young people in the 1950s did not digest in intended ways the stories of the forces of good (white, male) triumphing over the forces of evil (people of color) in Western movies, stories that reproduced similar struggles between white people and people of color within the United States and internationally.

11. Douglas Miller and Marion Nowak, *The Fifties: The Way We Really Were* (Garden City, N.Y.: Doubleday, 1975), 277.

12. William Heyen, *Vic Holyfield and the Class of '57* (New York: Ballantine, 1986), 20; Annie Dillard, *An American Childhood* (New York: Harper & Row, 1987); Caryl Rivers, *Aphrodite at Mid-Century: Growing Up Catholic and Female in Post-War America* (Garden City, N.Y.: Doubleday, 1973); and idem, *Virgins* (New York: Pocket Books, 1984); Susan Toth, *Blooming: A Small Town Girlhood* (Boston: Little, Brown, 1978).

13. Michael Anania, *The Red Menace* (New York: Thunder's Mouth Press, 1984), 29.

14. Jessie Bernard, "Teen-Age Culture: An Overview," *The Annals* 338 (November 1961): 10. Data from Remmers and Radler, *The American Teenager* (1957), 80–85, the first public opinion report on a fifteen-year youth survey called Purdue Opinion Poll, which polled 10,000–18,000 teenagers. For other references to Radler and Remmer polls, see William Graebner, "Coming of Age in Buffalo: The Ideology of Maturity in Postwar America," *Radical History Review* 34 (January 1986): 59; and Charles H. Brown, "Self-Portrait: The Teen-Type Magazine," *The Annals,* November 1961, 18.

15. Richard Flacks, *Youth and Social Change* (Chicago: Markham, 1971), quotations from 56, 33, 51, 52.

16. Referring to teenagers' confusion about what was permissible sexually, John Modell, *Into One's Own* (Berkeley: University of California Press, 1989), 236, says, "Young people in the baby boom era often felt as uncertain about this as did their parents."

17. Liz Heron, ed., "Introduction," in *Truth, Dare, or Promise: Girls Growing Up in the Fifties* (London: Virago, 1985), 6.

18. Elinor Langer, "Notes for Next Time," *Working Papers,* Fall 1973, 48–83, 51.

19. Ann Snitow, "Pages from a Gender Diary: Basic Divisions in Feminism," *Dissent,* Spring 1989, 219.

20. Rivers, *Virgins,* 23.

21. David Wallechinsky, "The Beatnik," *Class Reunion '65* (New York: Penguin, 1986), 398.

22. David Dalton, *Piece of My Heart: The Life, Times and Legend of Janis Joplin* (New York: St. Martin's Press, 1985), 147.

23. Nora Sayre, *Running Time: Films of the Cold War* (New York: Dial, 1982), 102.

24. Hettie Jones, *How I Became Hettie Jones* (New York: Dutton, 1990), 62.

25. Marge Piercy, "Through the Cracks: Growing Up in the Fifties," in *Particolored Blocks for a Quilt* (Ann Arbor: University of Michigan Press, 1982), 115–116.

26. See Elizabeth Long, *The American Dream and the Popular Novel* (Boston: Routledge, and Kegan Paul, 1985); and Miller and Nowak, *The Fifties*, chap. 14.

27. Jones, *How I Became Hettie Jones*, 26. See Herman Wouk, *Marjorie Morningstar* (New York: Pocket Books, 1955), for a bestselling novel about a curious, single, young woman who ends up a safe, Westchester housewife.

28. Joyce Johnson, *Minor Characters* (Boston: Houghton Mifflin, 1983), 41.

29. Jan Clausen, *Sinking Stealing* (Trumansburg, N.Y.: Crossing Press, 1985), 146. A male recalls his adolescence in the 1950s: "It was, of course, this very safety—read isolation, read blandness, read blindness—that made our lives so horrifically dreary, so basically lonely. Most of my friends, like me, spent most of our time waiting for whatever this was to end and life, whatever *that* was, to begin." Tom Engelhardt, "Kid Stuff," *In These Times*, November 1–7, 1989, 13. He, too, was waiting for real life to begin, as was the hero of Dan Wakefield's novel, *Going All the Way* (New York: Dutton, 1970, 1989).

30. For Bonnie Raitt, *Boston Globe*, February 23, 1990, 53. Johnson, *Minor Characters*, 137. Piercy, "Through the Cracks," 119, wonders where she found the strength to "cling to my own flimsy reality" against official reality. See Tom Hayden's autobiography and memoir, *Reunion* (New York: Random House, 1988), about the 1960s for a New Leftist who found inspiration in the Beats and other marginal characters. "There were several alternative cultural models beckoning to those of us who in a few years were to become activists: the fictional character Holden Caulfield, the actor James Dean, and the writer Jack Kerouac. The life crises they personified spawned not only political activism, but also the cultural revolution of rock and roll. Elvis Presley, it is said, watched James Dean in 'Rebel Without a Cause' a dozen times. These characters, in their different ways, were responding to the human absurdity and emptiness of the secure material life parents of the fifties had built" (p. 17). Hayden says of Kerouac's inspiration in 1957, the year he graduated from high school and *On the Road* was published: "In the coming three years, I too hitchhiked to every corner of America, sleeping in fields here, doorways there, cheap hotels everywhere, embracing a spirit of the open road without knowing where I wanted to go" (p. 18). The maleness of the models and options is hard to miss.

31. Johnson, *Minor Characters*, 29, 30; Kathy Mulherin, "Memories of a Latter-Day Catholic Girlhood," in *The Movement toward a New America*, ed. Mitchell Goodman (Philadelphia: Pilgrim Press; New York: Knopf, 1970), 637; reprinted from *Commonweal*, March 6, 1970.

32. Ellen Maslow, "Storybook Lives: Growing Up Middle Class," in *Liberation Now! Writings from the Women's Liberation Movement*, ed. Deborah Babcox and Madeline Belkin (New York: Dell, 1971), 174. Describing Kate Millett, a member of the older group, a former student says, "Kate, like Joyce Glassman [Johnson], fell in love with the beat rebellion against orderliness, straightness, and ties based on friendship instead of blood." See Laurie Stone, "Memoirs Are Made of This," *Voice Literary Supplement*, no. 16 (April 1983): 10.

33. Diane Di Prima, *Memoirs of a Beatnik* (San Francisco: Last Gasp of San Francisco, 1988; originally 1969), 51.

34. Dalton, *Piece of My Heart*, 162.

35. Shulman, *Burning Questions* (New York: Knopf, 1978), 39.

36. Jack Kerouac, *On the Road* (New York: New American Library, 1957), 9.

37. Annie Dillard, *An American Childhood* (New York: Harper & Row, 1987), 183.

38. Sheila Rowbotham, *Womens' Consciousness, Man's World* (Baltimore: Penguin, 1973), 14, 16; Heron, *Truth, Dare, or Promise,* 208.

39. Points from Jones, *How I Became Hettie Jones,* 71. See Di Prima, *Memoirs of a Beatnik,* and Johnson, *Minor Characters,* for similar experiences. Also see Wini Breines, *Community and Organization in the New Left: The Great Refusal* (New Brunswick, N.J.: Rutgers University Press, 1989), for the importance of talk in the New Left.

40. Shulman, *Burning Questions,* 64.

41. Di Prima, *Memoirs of a Beatnik,* 65.

42. Johnson, *Minor Characters,* 208.

43. Ronald Sukenick, *Down and In: Life in the Underground* (New York: Macmillan, 1987), 34, 27.

44. Di Prima, *Memoirs of a Beatnik,* 126.

45. Jones, *How I Became Hettie Jones,* 34.

46. See Andrew Ross, "Containing Culture in the Cold War," in *No Respect: Intellectuals and Popular Culture* (New York: Routledge, 1989), 42–64, for a discussion of postwar and Cold War intellectuals and their relationship to popular culture.

47. Al Young, *Things Ain't What They Used to Be* (Berkeley: Creative Arts Books, 1987), 190, 194.

48. Di Prima, *Memoirs of a Beatnik,* 94.

49. Johnson, *Minor Characters,* 162. See also Jones, *How I Became Hettie Jones,* for a description of Greenwich Village in the 1950s.

50. Young, *Things Ain't What They Used to Be,* 192.

51. Jones, *How I Became Hettie Jones,* 46.

52. For the Norman Podhoretz remark, see Todd Gitlin, *The Sixties; Years of Hope, Days of Rage* (New York: Bantam, 1987), 49. Also see Miller and Nowak, *The Fifties,* 384–386; and Paul S. George and Jerold M. Starr, "Beat Politics: New Left and Hippie Beginnings in the Postwar Counterculture," in *Cultural Politics: Radical Movements in History,* ed. Jerold M. Starr (New York: Praeger, 1985), 205–206. For material about postwar artistic ferment, Young, *Things Ain't What They Used to Be,* "Jazz and Letters," 189–233; Lewis A. Ehrenberg, "Things to Come: Swing Bands, Bebop, and the Rise of a Postwar Jazz Scene," in *Recasting America: Culture and Politics in the Age of the Cold War,* ed. Lary May (Chicago: University of Chicago Press, 1989); Charles Mingus, *Beneath the Underdog* (New York: Penguin, 1971); Serge Guilbaut, *How New York Stole the Idea of Modern Art: Abstract Expressionism, Freedom and the Cold War* (Chicago: University of Chicago Press, 1983); Sukenick, *Down and In.*

53. Johnson, *Minor Characters,* 261–262.

54. See Marjorie Rosen, *Popcorn Venus: Women, Movies and the American Dream* (New York: Coward, McCann and Geoghegan, 1979), 286–289. In Simon Frith, *Sound Effects: Youth, Leisure and the Politics of Rock and Roll* (New York: Pantheon, 1981), 238–239, Frith argues that music and dancing both expressed and released the sexual tensions implicit in girls' preparation for their domestic role. He suggests that the most important function of 1950s teenage culture was to articulate sexuality "in a setting of love and marriage" where it reinforced peer-group sex conventions that emphasized marriage.

55. In a review of Joyce Johnson's *Minor Characters* in *Voice Literary Supplement,*

April 1983, 8–11, Laurie Stone says that the feminist Kate Millett, Stone's teacher, was inspired by the Beats but understood they would never really see or hear her, that she would never be real to them.

56. Jones, *How I Became Hettie Jones*, 81.

57. For this point about New Left women, see Wini Breines, "A Review Essay: Sara Evans's *Personal Politics,*" *Feminist Studies* 5, no. 3 (Fall 1979): 495–506.

58. Miller and Nowak, *The Fifties*, 386.

59. Johnson, *Minor Characters*, 79.

60. Nelson George, *The Death of Rhythm and Blues* (New York: Pantheon, 1988), 61–62; also see Michael S. Harper's remarks in Young, *Things Ain't What They Used to Be*, "Jazz and Letters," esp. 208 about Kerouac's racism; and Ross, "Hip, and the Long Front of Color," in *No Respect*, where he discusses the white hipster, 79ff.

61. Barbara Ehrenreich, *The Hearts of Men: American Dreams and the Flight from Commitment* (Garden City, N.Y.: Doubleday, 1983), 58.

62. Johnson, *Minor Characters*, 171.

63. John Tytell, "Foreword" to Arthur and Kit Knight, eds., *Kerouac and the Beats* (New York: Paragon House, 1988), ix.

64. Catherine Stimpson, "The Beat Generation and the Trials of Homosexual Liberation," in *Salmagundi*, no. 58–59 (1982–1983): 373–392, esp. 375. Stimpson argues that a sexist model of heterosexuality infected the Beats' homosexual relations. Thus they mistreated the male identified as a fag, the submissive, passive, and degraded feminine partner, and in this way lessened the distinction between heterosexuality and homosexuality.

65. "The Beat Queens," *Voice Literary Supplement*, June 1989, 18–23. See also interview and personal correspondence with Shulman, March 9, 1989. See Michael Davidson, *The San Francisco Renaissance: Poetics and Community at Mid-century* (New York: Cambridge University Press, 1989), chap. 6. See also less critical treatments of Beat and bohemian men in Johnson, *Minor Characters*, and Jones, *How I Became Hettie Jones*.

66. Frederika Randall, "Fifties Forever," *Working Papers*, May–June, 1983, 48–51.

67. See Caryl Rivers, *Aphrodite at Mid-Century* (Garden City, N.Y.: Doubleday, 1973), 224–225; Rowbotham, *Women's Consciousness, Man's World*, 14–15; Ellen Willis, "A Feminist Journal," *Conversations with the New Reality* (San Francisco: Canfield Press, 1971), 157.

68. Jon Savage, "The Enemy Within: Sex, Rock, and Identity," in *Facing the Music,* ed. Simon Frith (New York: Pantheon, 1989), 143–144. It is undoubtedly true that for some white middle-class girls a rejection of middle-class masculinity was also a rejection of heterosexuality. The role of lesbianism in some girls' rebelliousness is research waiting to be pursued.

69. Dillard, *An American Childhood*, 93.

70. Rowbotham, *Women's Consciousness, Man's World*, 15–16.

71. Ehrenreich, *The Hearts of Men*, 58. Roland Marchand, "Visions of Classlessness, Quests for Dominion: American Popular Culture, 1945–1960," in *Reshaping America: Society and Institutions, 1945–1960,* ed. R. Bremmer and G. Richard (Columbus: Ohio State University Press, 1982), 163–182. "A mystique emerged that fused the elements of Marlon Brando's role in *The Wild One*, James Dean's portrayal in *Rebel Without a Cause*, J. D. Salinger's Holden Caulfield in *Catcher in the Rye,* and the rebels

of *Blackboard Jungle,* and the driving energy and aggressive sexuality of the new heroes of rock 'n' roll into a single image. The mystique emphasized a hunger for authenticity and sensitivity . . . with nuances of sexuality, pain, and violence. Raucous, exhibitionist rock 'n' roll singers disdained the 'cool' of James Dean, but both expressed a contempt for hypocrisy and conventionality and used body language to convey emotion" (p. 179).

72. Rowbotham, *Women's Consciousness, Man's World,* 16.

73. See "The Beatnik" in David Wallechinsky, *Class Reunion '65* (New York: Penguin, 1986), 397. She continues that she didn't participate in high school activities and never went to the cafeteria: "I used to spend that time each day writing poems on toilet paper in the stalls for privacy and inspiration, or else go to the library and read."

74. Shulman, *Burning Questions,* 29, 15.

75. Wakefield, *Going All the Way,* 219–220, 209.

76. "Modernism, Postmodernism, and the Problem of the Visual in Afro-American Culture," in *Out There: Marginalization and Contemporary Cultures,* ed. Russell Ferguson et al. (Cambridge, Mass.: MIT Press, 1990), 41.

77. Philip Roth, *Goodbye Columbus* (New York: Bantam, 1959), 5. See Langer, "Notes for Next Time," for a discussion of suburban Jews' painful efforts to assimilate in the postwar period.

78. Jones, *How I Became Hettie Jones,* 35.

About the Contributors

HARRIET HYMAN ALONSO is associate professor of history at Fitchburg State College in Massachusetts. She is the author of *The Women's Peace Union and the Outlawry of War, 1921–1942* (Knoxville: University of Tennessee Press, 1990), and *Peace as a Women's Issue: A History of the U.S. Movement for World Peace and Women's Rights* (Syracuse: Syracuse University Press, 1993). She is a co-editor of the series Syracuse Studies on Peace and Conflict Resolution.

XIAOLAN BAO is assistant professor of history at California State University, Long Beach, where she teaches Chinese and women's history. She is revising her dissertation, entitled "Holding Up More Than Half the Sky: A History of Women Garment Workers in New York's Chinatown, 1948–1991."

WINI BREINES teaches in the Department of Sociology and Anthropology and in the Women's Studies Program at Northeastern University in Boston. She is the author of *Young, White, and Miserable: Growing Up Female in the Fifties* (Boston: Beacon, 1992). Her book *The Great Refusal: Community and Organization in the New Left* (New Brunswick, N.J. Rutgers University Press, 1989), and a book of original documents from the 1960s (New York: Oxford University Press, forthcoming), in conjunction with further work on the 1950s, represent her continuing interest in issues related to and raised by the social movements of the 1960s.

DOROTHY SUE COBBLE is associate professor at Rutgers University, where she teaches history, women's studies, and labor studies. Her book *Dishing It Out: Waitresses and Their Unions in the Twentieth Century* (Urbana: University of Illinois Press, 1991) won the 1992 Herbert A. Gutman Award. She is currently writing a book with Ruth Milkman on the American labor movement.

RUTH FELDSTEIN is completing her doctorate in history at Brown University. Her dissertation analyzes constructions of black and white mothers from the 1940s to the 1960s. Her research addresses connections among sexual conservatism, racial liberalism, and changes in the liberal welfare state.

DEE GARRISON is professor of history at Rutgers University. Her most recent book is *Mary Heaton Vorse: An American Insurgent* (Philadelphia: Temple University Press, 1989). She is currently writing a history of American Cold War culture in the 1950s, including studies of Philip Wylie and Herman Kahn.

DEBORAH A. GERSON is a graduate student in the Department of Sociology at the University of California, Berkeley. She is writing a dissertation, "Consciousness as Politics: Building a Women's Movement through Consciousness Raising," on the early women's liberation movement. A long-time political activist, she serves on the executive board of the Association of Graduate Student Employees (AGSE/UAW).

SUSAN M. HARTMANN is professor of history and women's studies at Ohio State University. She is the author of *The Home Front and Beyond: American Women in the 1940s* (New York: Twayne, 1982) and *From Margin to Mainstream: American Women and Politics Since 1960* (New York: Knopf, 1989). Her current book-in-progress, *Allies of the Women's Movement,* is a study of the development of feminism in male-dominated organizations.

REGINA G. KUNZEL is assistant professor of history at Williams College, where she teaches U.S. history and women's studies. She is the author of *Fallen Women, Problem Girls: Unmarried Mothers and the Professionalization of Social Work, 1890–1945* (New Haven: Yale University Press, 1993).

SUSAN RIMBY LEIGHOW received her Ph.D. from the University of Pittsburgh in 1992. She is currently assistant professor of history at Shippensburg University. The article in this volume is excerpted from her dissertation, " 'Nurses' Questions/Women's Questions': The Impact of the Demographic Revolution and Feminism on United States Working Women, 1946–1986."

SUSAN LYNN teaches at Portland Community College, Portland, Oregon. She is the author of *Progressive Women in Conservative Times: Racial Justice, Peace, and Feminism, 1945 to the 1960s* (New Brunswick, N.J.: Rutgers University Press, 1992).

JOANNE MEYEROWITZ teaches U.S. history and women's studies at the University of Cincinnati. She is the author of *Women Adrift: Independent Wage Earners in Chicago, 1880–1930* (Chicago: University of Chicago Press, 1988).

DONNA PENN is a doctoral candidate in the Department of American Civilization at Brown University. She is currently working on a dissertation on competing discourses on lesbianism in twentieth-century America.

MARGARET ROSE teaches history at California State University, Bakersfield. She received her Ph.D. from UCLA in 1988. Her dissertation deals with Chicanas and Mexicanas in the United Farm Workers, 1950–1980. She has published articles on women in the United Farm Workers in *Frontiers* and *Labor History*.

RICKIE SOLINGER is a Visiting Scholar in Women's Studies at the University of Colorado, Boulder. Her recent publications include "A Complete Disaster: Abortion and the Politics of Hospital Abortion Committees, 1950–1970," *Feminist Studies,* Summer 1993; and *Wake Up Little Susie: Single Pregnancy and Race before Roe* v. *Wade* (New York: Routledge, 1992). She is currently writing a book entitled *The Abortionist* about pre-*Roe* female practitioners.